This book studies later medieval culture (c. 1150–1500) through its central symbol: the eucharist. From the twelfth century onwards the eucharist was designed by the Church as the foremost sacrament. The claim that this ritual brought into presence Christ's own body, and offered it to believers, underpinned the sacramental system and the clerical mediation upon which it depended.

The book explores the context in which the sacramental world was created and the cultural processes through which it was disseminated, interpreted and used. With attention to the variety of eucharistic meanings and practices – in procession on the feast of Corpus Christi, devotions, prayers, drama, in dissent, abuse and doubt – the author reveals and considers ways in which a religious culture is used as a language for the articulation of order and power, as well as for the most private explorations. The book moves from the 'design' of the eucharist in the twelfth century to its re-design in the sixteenth – a story of the emergence of a symbol, its use and interpretation and final transformation.

# CORPUS CHRISTI

# CORPUS CHRISTI

## The Eucharist in Late Medieval Culture

### MIRI RUBIN

*Pembroke College, Oxford*

The right of the
University of Cambridge
to print and sell
all manner of books
was granted by
Henry VIII in 1534.
The University has printed
and published continuously
since 1584.

## CAMBRIDGE UNIVERSITY PRESS

*Cambridge*
*New York   Port Chester*
*Melbourne   Sydney*

Published by the Press Syndicate of the University of Cambridge
The Pitt Building, Trumpington Street, Cambridge CB2 1RP
40 West 20th Street, New York, NY 10011, USA
10 Stamford Road, Oakleigh, Melbourne 3166, Australia

First published 1991

Printed in Great Britain by the Bath Press, Avon

*British Library cataloguing in publication data*
Rubin, Miri *1956–*
Corpus Christi.
1. Christian church. Eucharist, history
1. Title
264′.36′09

*Library of Congress cataloguing in publication data*
Rubin, Miri, 1956–
Corpus Christi: the Eucharist in late medieval culture / Miri
Rubin
p.   cm.
Includes bibliographical references.
ISBN 0–521–35605–9
1. Lord's Supper – Catholic Church – History.   2. Lord's Supper –
History – Middle Ages, 600–1500.   3. Mass – History.   4. Corpus
Christi festival – Europe – History.   5. Catholic Church – Doctrines –
History.   6. Catholic Church – Liturgy – History.   7. Lord's Supper
(Liturgy) – History.   8. Europe – Church history – Middle Ages,
600–1500.   1. Title.
BV823.R78   1991
264′.02036′0940902 – dc20   89–77241 CIP

ISBN 0 521 35605 9 hardback
BS

# CONTENTS

vii

# ILLUSTRATIONS

ix

# Acknowledgements

An historian embarked on the study of medieval culture is bound to travel far and wide when following the trails of words and images. My debts of gratitude have been collected in libraries, archives, offices, restaurants, halls, churches, during walks and talks with colleagues and friends all over Europe and across the Atlantic. Their contributions will sometimes be apparent in the text, but some I would like to mention by name: Michael Heyd of Jerusalem, Jean-Claude Schmitt of Paris, Anne Hudson and Keith Thomas of Oxford, Henri Platelle of Lille, Peter Johanek of Münster, Richard Beadle and Peter Burke of Cambridge, and Gary Macy of San Diego.

One of the lines pursued in this book is the study of the eucharistic feast, Corpus Christi, which was founded in Liège in 1246, and spread all over Europe in the next century. This necessarily brought me in touch with Belgium and its scholars. I was fortunate to have Professor Raul Van Caenegem's advice at the outset, and on a trip to Belgium in the summer of 1985, funded by a British Academy Research Grant, benefited from the hospitality and attention of Professor Dirk van den Auweele and Jan Goossens in Louvain, from conversations with Professor Ludo Milis in Ghent and Drs Jean-Louis Kupper and Christine Renardy in Liège. While I worked in Ghent Dr Walter Simmons was a constant friend and guide, who literally led me through the sources and helped me to acquaint myself with the Low Countries in the Middle Ages.

Tracing the spread of eucharistic practices through liturgical manuscripts took me of necessity to the Vatican, to the vast collection which includes books from all over the medieval Christian world. The British School at Rome Grant in Aid of Research provided a home in Rome for months at a time in 1986 and 1987, while I studied these manuscripts. At the Vatican Library I enjoyed the erudition of its Prefect, Father Leonard Boyle, who welcomes medievalists with special warmth. A generous research grant from the Gladys Krieble Delmas Foundation supported my stay in Venice in 1987, where I explored the rich manuscript collection at the Biblioteca Marciana. Hundreds of precious liturgical manuscripts were studied in the Bibliothèque Nationale in

Paris, thanks to a Research Grant from the British Academy, and closer to home at the Bodleian Library, the British Library, and the Fitzwilliam Museum. I continued the search in smaller collections, those of colleges (Emmanuel, Gonville and Caius, Jesus, Magdalene, and Trinity in Cambridge, Corpus Christi and Keble in Oxford), cathedral libraries and in the University Libraries of Birmingham, Glasgow and London. In these libraries and archives I, like all scholars, enjoyed the quiet help of many librarians and assistants, the staff which one rarely gets to know by name but whose efforts are, none the less, appreciated and remembered.

A British Academy Research Fellow since 1986, I was able to work on this book as a member of the History Faculty in Cambridge in the friendliest of colleges, Girton, where I was a Research Fellow in 1984–6, and in the most amenable and pleasant of libraries – the Cambridge University Library. To those of us who work in Cambridge and to many who visit it regularly this is more than a house of books. Scholarship and friendship blossom in its corridors, advice and references are exchanged, much-needed encouragement and criticism are offered by friends and colleagues. Many friends who also worked there are part of my life, of this book and of the effort to make history in new ways, to think afresh and yet together.

Finally, I had the great fortune and honour to complete the book during a period as Visiting Member at the School of Historical Studies of the Institute for Advanced Study at Princeton in 1988/89. The exciting atmosphere in which historians and social scientists lived and worked together with faith in a collective intellectual project and in the value of shared interests and differing opinions, was enjoyable and enriching. Such colleagues at the Institute and at Princeton University as Susan Amussen, Giles Constable, Bill Courtenay, Natalie Davis, Jim Fernandez, Harold James, Bill Jordan, Chantal Mouffe, Debra Pincus, Lawrence Stone, David Underdown, and particularly Peter Brown, Stuart Clark and Robert Lerner offered criticisms and inspiration, some chiding me for excessive enthusiasm, others pressing for further adventure. The weekly sessions at the Davis Center for Historical Studies at Princeton University sharpened the sense of accountability owed by a medievalist to historians who study other periods and places. The period at Princeton also enhanced my belief that the study of human activities in the past – the battles fought, those lost and those won, the variety of human experience which is not easily classifiable or reducible to simple propositions but which rather demands from us, its students, great efforts of mind and spirit in the unravelling – that this project is not only worthy but absolutely necessary, and only achievable through collective critical efforts. Attempts to turn universities and intellectual life into just another form of enterprise, a business to be run like a corner shop, must be resisted through mutual help and with an awareness of the gravity of our work.

In acknowledgements, those who have helped one most and most consistently are customarily left to the end. Marjorie Chibnall, Barrie Dobson, David Luscombe have been supportive allies and friends. Christopher Brooke has generously given me his support and unfailing criticism since the first time I met him in 1981. He read this book with dedication and helped me turn it into a far better thing, offering his wide-ranging erudition in helpful suggestions. Life would have been far less enjoyable without friends such as Ian Archer, Jon Parry and Jayati Rao; without the wisdom and support of Richard and Peggy Smith; without the periodic visits of Zvi Razi and Shula Shahar. Bob Scribner, who has changed our understanding of religious culture, has encouraged me in this study since we met in 1985. His methodological rigour and theoretical sophistication are given freshness and immediacy by his scholarly commitment. I would like to think that I have followed his lead, even in a different period and with a very different temperament.

And last, how does one offer thanks for inspiration? Perhaps just by mentioning that it and so much more were given by Gareth Stedman Jones.

# Abbreviations

| | |
|---|---|
| 1200×15 | Some time between these years |
| AASS | Acta sanctorum . . . editio novissima |
| AFH | Archivum franciscanum historicum |
| AFP | Archivum fratrum praedicatorum |
| AH | Analecta hymnica |
| AHP | Archivum historiae pontificiae |
| AHR | American historical review |
| ALK | Archiv für Literatur- und Kirchengeschichte |
| BL | London British Library |
| BN | Paris Bibliothèque nationale |
| CCCM | Corpus christianorum: continuatio medievalis |
| COD | Conciliorum oecumenicorum decreta |
| CPL | Calendar of entries in the papal registers relating to Great Britain and Ireland |
| CUL | Cambridge University Library |
| DM | Dialogus miraculorum |
| EETS | Early English Text Society |
| EETS.ES | Early English Text Society. Extra Series |
| EETS.SS | Early English Text Society. Supplementary Series |
| EL | Ephemerides liturgicae |
| HBS | Henry Bradshaw Society |
| JEGP | Journal of English and Germanic philology |
| JEH | Journal of ecclesiastical history |
| JWCI | Journal of the Warburg and Courtauld Institutes |
| Mansi | Sacrorum conciliorum nova et amplissima collectio |
| MGH | Monumenta germaniae historica |
| MGH.SS | Monumenta germaniae historica: scriptores, Berlin, 1826– |
| MLN | Modern language notes |
| MOPH | Monumenta ordinis praedicatorum historiae |
| MS | Mediaeval studies |
| PL | Patrologiae cursus completus: series latina, ed. J.-P. Migne, 221 vols., Paris, 1841–64. |
| PMLA | Publications of the modern language association |

| | |
|---|---|
| PP | *Past and present* |
| PRO | London Public Record Office |
| RB | *Revue bénédictine* |
| REED | *Records of early English drama* |
| RHE | *Revue d'histoire ecclésiastique* |
| RHGF | *Recueil des historiens des Gaules et de la France* |
| RIS | *Rerum italicarum scriptores* |
| RS | *Rolls series* |
| RSPT | *Revue des sciences philosophiques et théologiques* |
| SCH | *Studies in church history* |
| ST | *Summa theologiae* |
| *Studia eucharistica* | *Studia eucharistica DCC¹ anni a condito festo sanctissimi Corporis Christi, 1246–1946*, Antwerp, 1946 |

# INTRODUCTION

At the centre of the whole religious system of the later Middle Ages lay a ritual which turned bread into flesh – a fragile, small, wheaten disc into God.[1] This was the eucharist: host, ritual, God among mortals. In the name of the eucharist some of the most humbling, and the most audacious, claims have been made: that God and humans could meet and unite, mix and merge, that a disc of baked wheaten dough could embody the saving body of Christ, that the lives of men and women, of cities and nations, could be encompassed, redeemed, transformed or forsaken through it. The eucharistic wafer was constructed as a symbol for which over hundreds of years, and all over Europe, people lived and died, armies marched, bodies were tormented or controlled by a self-imposed asceticism. Lives of scholarship were dedicated to fathoming its mysteries, or censored when their findings threatened to denude the eucharist of its essential secrets.[2] The drama of the eucharist is the drama of human creativity and of human frailty: its force deriving from the tension inherent in human action, between the capacity to construct meaning-laden symbols, and the consequent imperatives of living by them, adhering to them and maintaining their meanings when they become susceptible to the vagaries and vicissitudes of human interpretation. The eucharist provided an idiom through which life-worlds, interests, experiences and needs came to be articulated, in positions taken, and the claims made, for and against and about it.[3] In the Middle Ages the language of religion provided a language of social relations, and of a cosmic order; it described and explained the interweaving of natural and supernatural with human action, in a paradigm which from about 1100 was one of sacramentality, with the eucharist at its heart. An ethical world was constructed through this language, with the final sanction that reception of the eucharist could be experienced beneficially only by those who lived in a certain type of virtue, or who made amends for trespasses through the penitential system of the church.

[1] This paraphrases Geertz (1960), p. 11.
[2] For the case of Galileo, see Redondi (1987).
[3] On the eucharist as symbol, see Firth (1973), pp. 415–26.

In his now classic article, 'The mass as a social institution', John Bossy interpreted the medieval mass as a catalyst which helped to create social fusion among its participants. In the mutual prayers for the dead and the living, the kissing of the *pax,* the sharing of Christ's body, he sees experiences of *communitas*,[4] a state of pre-political, undifferentiated human affinity, which dissolved tensions and bound people together despite the differences between them in the non-ritual space and time. The notion of community which underpins this interpretation is a problematical one,[5] but Bossy evades it by assigning to the ritual the efficacy which liturgical texts designed and ascribed to it. In expositions on the mass, which provide much of the material for Bossy's study, medieval liturgists and theologians interpreted every word and gesture in the ritual as part of an edifice of meaning about sacramentality and sacerdotal efficacy. Every gesture, vestment, vessel of the ritual was explained to reinforce a harmonious image of the central Christian story, a story which was thus conveyed for the guidance of the ritual practitioner, the priest.[6] The normative texts tell us about the ideal-types which were taught from the centres of power as representations of principles of hierarchy and authority. But the masses which they described, such perfect rituals, were never celebrated. Nor do people ever experience ritual from a unitary position, in a homogeneous way, and whatever its effect, *communitas* is dissolved as soon as the sweat evaporates off the brow of the ritual performer.

A wide range of material relating to the eucharist has been used in this book: the theology of the eucharist formulated in the schools, the ritual and liturgy designed for it, legislation on access to it, teaching and preaching of its meanings, legislation and correction of its liturgical practices at the provincial, diocesan, parochial levels, the imagery which surrounded it in paintings, and eucharistic artifacts. What was taught and what was done are both examined and compared: how the mass was celebrated in reality not only in the recommendations of manuals for the clergy. The mass will also be seen through *exempla*, the didactic tales aimed at correction and edification, which conjure up aspects of a world of practice, and convey utterances about the eucharist reported in order to be corrected through miraculous intervention.[7] This material was produced by churchmen, often disapprovingly, and

---

[4] On the term *communitas* in the analysis of ritual, see Turner (1969), chapters 3 and 4, pp. 94–165. See also Turner (1974).

[5] On the use of 'community' by historians, see Calhoun (1980), and on the medieval community, see Rosser (1988) and Rubin (1991b).

[6] For a critique of Bossy, see Reinburg (1985), pp. 201–90.

[7] On the miraculous mood of medieval culture, see Platelle (1979), pp. 475–7.

with corrective aims in mind. Yet they none the less leave traces of the eucharistic symbolic world in action. On careful reading, an ethnography of practices which were sometimes deemed by the clergy to be aberrant and in need of correction can be teased out of these sources, which were discursively constructed within a nexus of power relations. In their self-conscious, even self-parodic, attempts to curb and correct manifestations of the symbolic creativity which the eucharist engendered, the friar, the itinerant preacher, and the parish priest offer an entry into the ethnography which is local and personal. They allow us to play the role of ethnographer, of an informed interpreter attempting to validate the continuous and the changing, one who is always mindful of the power relations in the midst of which these texts were created.

Such an approach forces us to identify, understand and organise diversity into meaningful patterns, not to seek the replication of uniformity.[8] It examines the struggle for consensus at work, a picture of ritual as variously used and understood. It is the scrutiny of religious practices which construct as well as question hierarchies like processions,[9] or an iconoclastic orgy,[10] or the mass,[11] emphasising the interplay of the spoken and the unspoken. Because we never encounter an utterance in isolation, be it picture, ritual, or word; the range of uses is inscribed before the use actually takes place. It is therefore necessary in critical practice to capture and differentiate the meanings of uses within the range of possibilities, to make sense of action within the sphere of possibilities, rather than to ascribe preordained meanings to them.

To one working with such an approach a practical joke of the past is not a neutral record of an event, but one which must be seen from the victim's point of view, and which challenges us to ask why we do not share the mirth.[12] Taking religion seriously in this way can dignify our subjects and yet differentiate them, so that the emaciated bodies of female saints who lived on nothing but the host will raise problems rather than pieties. The medieval language of religion posited so many of its claims on, invested so much power in, and was able to silence so many views about the eucharist, that those utterances which we do encounter must disturb and be made to account for those absent.

Thinking, thus, of the abundance rather than of the scarcity we can explore the rhetoric, the idioms of the language of religion developed

[8] Wilson (1970), chapter 1; Fernandez (1988), pp. 117–18
[9] James (1983); Phythian-Adams (1972); Davis (1983); Darnton (1984), pp. 106–41.
[10] Scribner (1987).
[11] Bossy (1983).
[12] La Capra (1988), pp. 95–6, 103–5.

by the subjects of our study. This will not, therefore, be an exhaustive study of every type of eucharistic practice or attitude, but rather an unravelling of many such uses in their interrelationships, and of the rules which they followed. This approach will particularly seek to interpret the richness of practice, through 'thick description' of such expressions. Through appreciation of the eucharistic symbolic world one can make sense of the heroine of Chaucer's Prioress' Tale, that genteel lady who proceeds to tell a chilling tale of ritual murder after protestations of worthlessness;[13] within the eucharistic world we can make sense of the tropes of sanctity used by those women who pinned desire onto the eucharistic flesh of the crucified Christ.

Discussions of the eucharist have usually taken place within studies of theology and canon law, in works of ecclesiastical history.[14] In recent years, as social historians have turned to the study of popular religion, pageantry and ritual practice, a number of attempts have been made to integrate eucharistic processions, and even the mass, into a broader and more complex picture of medieval culture. John Bossy has analysed the works of liturgists and theologians on the mass in the late medieval and early modern period and tried to derive from them a sense of the changing ritual experience;[15] Mervyn James has studied Corpus Christi processions and their contribution to civic life in late medieval English towns;[16] and Charles Zika has looked at eucharistic processions in fifteenth-century Germany and demonstrated their importance as a ground for stuggle between secular and ecclesiastical authority, between normative and popular culture.[17] In these studies the eucharist, the mass, or the eucharistic processions were treated as symptoms which reflect some more basic and on-going political or social process. Their insights are bound, therefore, to highlight a single strand of the socio-political world, and to impute a determining power to it in the realm of religious culture. For Bossy this strand is the tension between the institutional church and the church of believers, within the social miracle of the mass; for James, the variety of interests of the urban craft-gilds, and the political unity demanded by patriciates and civic prerogative; for Zika, the drama of clerical–secular struggles for control of pilgrimage sites and processional ritual. These are fruitful studies of single expressions within a wider language of religion. Claims, hopes, dissent and strife are articulated in all these cases through a eucharistic

---

[13] Hahn (1988).
[14] See, for example, de Lubac (1949); Magivern (1963); Jungmann (1951–5); Macy (1984).
[15] Bossy (1983).
[16] James (1983).
[17] Zika (1988).

symbol of mass, procession, eucharistic miracles and Corpus Christi drama. But they are utterances which alone cannot fix the meaning, nor unfold the nature of the language which endowed them with meaning, of the cultural system which made the eucharist a potent symbol in collective and individual life endeavours. Inspired by the diversity of such utterances and the ubiquity of eucharistic symbols within the medieval culture, we must attempt to expound the language of religion in order to understand the variety of its expression. This book aims to penetrate that language, the system of meanings within which the eucharist possessed so central a position.[18]

This book began as another kind of enterprise. I conceived it as a study of the feast of Corpus Christi, a new eucharistic feast founded in the mid thirteenth century and disseminated from the early years of the next century. It was meant to be an examination of ritual practice, of how a feast is founded and celebrated – an exercise in social history following the inspiration of Bakhtin, Le Roy Ladurie, Carlo Ginzburg and Robert Scribner. But as the work developed more fundamental questions suggested themselves. Why a new *eucharistic* feast, and why just then?[19] And when founded, why did the eucharistic feast prompt so lively a response, so much activity and creativity? I was moving from the study of the *utterance* to the study of the *language* which gave that utterance meaning; from a particular text – procession, liturgy – to a framework of meaning within which it was constructed. This approach will seek a higher order of structure in the culture, and yet trace the lines of association which produce its unique features. Corpus Christi is still the theme of this book, but treated as part of a system of meaning, of a chain of associations, in which the eucharist possessed a central signifying power.[20]

A concept of language has informed my approach to the religious culture of the Middle Ages.[21] Inasmuch as we communicate through

---

[18] On the need of any religion to possess the attributes of a language and, by consequence, to be seen as such, see Rhees (1969), esp. p. 121.

[19] Glynn Wickham has commented that before drama scholars argue about the impact of Corpus Christi on vernacular drama, they ought to ask why Corpus Christi was founded, Wickham (1959), I, p. 9. This has never really been done; Devlin (1976) brings together some of the liturgical and theological material related to the foundation of the feast, and a number of Belgian scholars have explored the immediate context of its foundation in Liège. For bibliographies of studies related to the feast see Gallet (1946); Hässling (1986).

[20] On 'key symbols' and formulations about them, see first Ortner (1975), p. 134. On contingency in associations induced by symbols, see Fernandez (1977), p. 130.

[21] I suggest the following as a working definition of culture: 'an historically transmitted pattern of meanings embodied in symbols, a system of inherited concepts expressed in symbolic forms by means of which men [and women] communicate, perpetuate, and develop their knowledge about attitudes towards life', Geertz (1973b), p. 89 (my brackets).

language, we apprehend the world through linguistic categories; thus, all culture, all meaning can be usefully studied as a language and through its salient symbols.[22] It is through the symbolic that our own lives come to have meaning to ourselves, and the lives of those, present or past, with whom we interact, become comprehensible. And this realm of the symbolic, the signifying system within which meaning is constructed, can be encountered in two compatible ways: by seeking its structure and by unravelling difference and the variety of voices within it. Only by studying both, the unity and the diversity, can we develop a critical interpretive approach to language/culture. The linguistic paradigm cannot capture the totality of mental and creative processes which constitute the human experience,[23] but insofar as so much of our social behaviour is acquired through language, it is apt and turns our minds helpfully to interpretation,[24] to hermeneutic rather than limited causal understanding. Only thus can we hope to encompass the variety of expression which invariably exists around us, and within which we none the less manage, albeit partially, to communicate with others.[25] When a child is born it encounters symbols in the words and expressions, gestures and noises surrounding it, and in its local culture: stories about the world, about God, good and evil, virtue, the reasons for suffering, reward and punishment. These life-worlds are expressed and lived through local knowledge – that combination of common-sense and experience – in metaphors embodied in rituals and tales and in the universalising narratives of law, religion and kinship.[26] Knowledge is continually culled from ritual moments packed and rich with symbols, which convey meanings embedded in the particular structure of the local idiom, and knowledge is used to mediate order and disorder. Any symbols learned through experience and participation in turn are continually articulated through personal growth and action, through imagination, in the play of fantasy upon symbols and their referents, in the on-going process of self-understanding. So symbols convey knowledge,[27] they are emotionally packed,[28] they communicate infor-

---

[22] Symbols can be artifacts or acts, they are 'historically created vehicles of reasoning, perception, feeling and understanding', Geertz (1968), p. 95.
[23] Luhrmann (1989), pp. 91–5 on use of visualisation rather than language.
[24] Clifford (1983), pp. 130–1.
[25] Geertz (1979–80), pp. 175–7.
[26] Geertz (1973b), p. 94; on the work of metaphors in culture, see Fernandez (1974) and Fernandez (1977) esp. p. 105, and at p. 126: 'Religious metaphors recast the inchoate (and ineffable) whole of primary experience into various manageable perspectives . . . by taking experience from more manageable domains, into which some aspects of the experience can be extended, to represent it.'
[27] Sperber (1975), (1982).
[28] Turner (1967), pp. 28–9.

mation,[29] and induce moods which cannot always be expressed in words.[30] Inasmuch as people communicate and interact, they reckon to understand each other, through the use of shared symbols, through the metaphors whose use is recognised even if their meanings are diametrically opposed.

This book is written in the conviction that religion can be best understood if it is not set apart from the social, not seen as an entity *sui generis* but rather as a culture, a system of meaning which represents and constructs experience and imagination. And in treating it as such we will also find that approaches which fix culture as a neat expression of other determinants – economic, environmental, gender-linked – fail to interpret and explain the ways in which culture not only communicates difference but also negotiates it. The model of elite/popular culture which has informed so many of the fruitful studies of religion in the last two decades,[31] fails to account for sufficient phenomena, since it vouchsafed the primacy of determining power to extremely undifferentiated and static social categories. Neither have attempts to replace that primacy with one of gender,[32] or environment,[33] provided an overarching framework for analysis, even when they highlighted a certain cultural context. We should try to turn our optic on its head, starting with the culture and its many voices as the privileged entity – it is, after all, always with us. We will then be able to look at a religious culture as a language, not as something fixed but as a variety of coexisting idioms, whose configurations and evolution produce cultural change.

Let us, then, give language privilege but not determination. At the end of the exercise of analysis and decoding, after teasing out the rules and locating the ambiguous gaps within a symbolic system, we should be better equipped to examine them in motion, in context. Roger Chartier has developed some useful historical approaches to the symbolic in the social by drawing our attention to variety in access to symbols within any society, showing that the books of the *Bibliothèque bleue*, once thought to have been read by artisans and servants and thus taken as a useful source for the study of popular culture, were read in seventeenth-century France by a variety of classes, notably by the bourgeoisie.[34] The question thus raised shifts the emphasis in the understanding of culture from the cultural product to the user, with the

---

[29] Leach (1976), chapter 1.
[30] Fernandez (1982), p. 554.
[31] Clark (1983), p. 63.
[32] Bynum (1987); see also the collection *Gender and religion* and in it Bynum (1986b).
[33] Underdown (1985).
[34] Mandrou (1975).

implication that a single artifact can be used, read, understood very differently by different types of users.[35] Chartier thus brings us back to the importance of *context*:[36] any symbol of artifact – a book, a procession, a prayer – will have 'receptions' amongst different groups and individuals which may be vastly different, or surprisingly similar. This difference will be the product of the context into which the symbol is inserted, the pre-existing ideas against which its use will take place. The experience of the mass will, thus, differ according to cultural milieu, local history and personal experience, through its incorporation into horizons of ideas and attitudes about the sacred, about the world, about physics, about clerical efficacy. Once we have made sense of the inscriptions on the text, we will be better positioned to appreciate the specific historical meaning of the use of the symbol in a given context. The users of the language will become more comprehensible, no longer muttering in a quaint dialect but speaking in meaningful and rich sentences. And we will find that in the language of sacramental religion the most disparate experiences were articulated: experiences of religious women in hermitages, powerful patricians in their towns, kings at coronations, defiant factions of villagers rising against others, Christians against Jews, all acting and enacted through its use.

Looking at medieval religion as a cultural system does not mean, then, that we need go no further. It does not induce neglect of the study of relations of power, oppression, coercion, and the experiences they entailed. On the contrary, equipped with an understanding of it we can go on to trace its operation in localities, in context. So acknowledging the essential indeterminacy of symbols is a concomitant of an investigation of the working, and the unmaking, of power, since it is through power that attempts to fix meaning are made. Power, invested in institutions, operates to supply, suggest and reinforce certain narratives and they symbolic make-up, to allow access to certain rituals and artifacts rather than others, to suggest as strongly as possible the aptness of certain metaphors.[37] Those who sought divergent modes of expression, those who questioned the aptness of dominant metaphors, could pay with their lives, or their freedom. Evidently, those who could influence representation could influence the construction of legitimacy, or the order of things material, social and spiritual. The whole structure of the church, the approval of secular authorities, the very naturalness of the only place of worship and of a comprehensive world-

---

[35]  Chartier (1984).
[36]  Chartier (1988).
[37]  Fernandez (1974).

view preached and taught frequently, was empowered in the claim of sacramentality and in the practice of an exclusive right of mediation. A Christian narrative of sacramentality was the dominant tale which embraced man, the supernatural, order and hierarchy, sin and forgiveness; it punctuated life, marriage, birth and death.[38] Yet although power at a variety of levels – local, provincial, national, urban and rural – raised some views over others, the story was always vulnerable to criticism. In the making of a unitary sacramental system, the language of religion was also made to possess gaps, inconsistencies and contradictions; its unmaking and questioning were dialectically inscribed in the very assertions which it made. So sacerdotal religion suggested anticlericalism, and transubstantiation – its ridicule in claims against the material nature of the host. Even so, power defined the centre of discussion: the sacrament was a central symbol or test of orthodoxy and dissent throughout the later Middle Ages. Christ's presence in the sacrament, the need for sacerdotal mediation, the practice of gazing at the sacrament, the notion of certain inherent magical properties of the host, the body of Christ: all these could be crucial tests. And we find them conducted by people across the social spectrum, just as we now know that Lollard criticism and dissent were alive not only among the poor.[39] And although a gendered understanding of religious experience has proven fruitful, it is only one of the numerous analytical categories which we must apply. The eucharistic language belonged to everyone – Christocentric devotions did not attract women exclusively, and women were attracted to it in a variety of ways.[40] The ethnography of eucharistic understanding and practices will reveal many surprising voices.

But can an ethnography of sufficient density, variety and precision be produced from our sources, to match the aim of thick interpretation, of a contextualised reading? Doubts about the feasibility of any historical ethnography have recently been voiced by James Fernandez, a master ethnographer.[41] It is the absence of an interactive element of personal contact between ethnographer and informant which allows the former to ask pointed questions – to 'interrogate' as some would have it[42] – to smell and hear and touch and capture a moment, which challenges the historian's attempt to penetrate her subject.[43] This is

---

[38] But this is of course not the only narrative, Chartier (1985), p. 690.
[39] As shown for the late Middle Ages in Plumb (1987) and Hudson (1988b).
[40] Bynum (1987) would tend to essentialise the female religious experience.
[41] Fernandez (1988).
[42] Rosaldo (1986).
[43] On these problems in ethnographic practice, see Clifford (1983); Clifford and Marcus (1986); and for a critique, see Sangren (1988).

undoubtedly true, and just as ethnographers are currently questioning their own ethnographic authority,[44] historians have traditionally possessed an awareness of the distance between them and their subjects. This consciousness has been turned by the best historians into an intuitive 'dialogic' engagement,[45] which appreciates the opaque nature of the sources and the alterity of the past, but which also creates an intimacy of inquiry through a critical awareness of the rhetoric and discursive formulation of actions and pronouncements, as well as the traces they have left in the sources. For a medievalist there is a particular problem of the fragmentary nature of evidence, and that much of it is in the alien construction of the written word.[46] The fruitfulness of this investigation of the language of religion will hinge largely on the nature of available evidence, and on the ability to match a broad concept of culture with a diverse body of material to be contrasted and compared.[47]

This book will follow the eucharistic world as it was designed and constructed in new ways by theologians, canonists and ecclesiastical administrators in the schools of Christendom, in monasteries and episcopal palaces from the eleventh, but mainly in the twelfth and thirteenth centuries. We will observe how the claim that God could be brought into the presence of men and women through repeated sacramental action, and that Christ could be received into their bodies, was planted in the eucharist and the mass (chapter 1). We will look at this symbolic system as it was disseminated through ecclesiastical institutions, taught in vernaculars, and elaborated in images which interpreted and applied it to existing knowledge and to evolving questions and understanding of it (chapter 2). Where the potent symbol entered a context of heightened religious activity, as in the thirteenth-century diocese of Liège, with its religious lay women, the beguines, with Dominicans, and ecclesiastics intent on reform, it emerged in the form of a new eucharistic feast, Corpus Christi. The new ritual spread in the area around Liège, to Rome, and ultimately became a universal observance by dissemination from Avignon in the early fourteenth century (chapter 3). The eucharistic feast became an occasion for concentrated creative use of the symbol and provided new contexts of meaning for the eucharist in the feast's evolving iconography, sermons, processions, liturgy, and ritual drama. We will see the eucharist used, tested and

---

[44] Clifford and Marcus (1986).
[45] LaCapra (1988), pp. 135–42.
[46] On the awkwardness of text as ethnographic vehicle, see Chartier (1985), p. 685.
[47] On the importance of variety of types of sources in the study of 'popular religion', see Lauwers (1987), p. 224.

applied by institutions, groups and individuals, in town and country-side in private and in public (chapter 4). The reinforced eucharistic currency will also be traced as new symbolic connections were created for it within the culture, in the language of religion which expressed practices and ideas, in utterances which were personal or sectional, and which were often deemed aberrant and dangerous. By the fifteenth century we encounter a variety of idioms in the eucharistic language of religion: some which traversed the normative code – like mysticism; some which opposed it – as in heresy; some which occasionally trans-cended it – fantasies into the inchoate which none the less hinged somewhat on the eucharistic symbol (chapter 5). The implications of this late medieval picture for the understanding of the thorough re-thinking of the eucharist at the two Reformations of the sixteenth century bring the book to a close.

This study will unfold along two axes, a synchronic one which keeps in view the system of symbolic meanings surrounding the eucharist, and a diachronic one, which delineates some aspects of change over time, the outcome of the transformation of language as it evolves and interacts with events, needs and experiences. At the beginning of the period, the eleventh century, the eucharist was emerging as a refigur-ation in the language of religion which placed at its heart the ritual of mediation rich with new meanings together with a powerful ritual – the mass. Looking at the ensuing medieval centuries I will set forth the formal pronouncements, the uses, objections and applications within which the eucharist was experienced, understood and discussed. The institutions of the church, its thinkers, administrators and teachers were well-positioned to influence ideas and images, to suggest and often to impose particular practices and ideas about the eucharist, and by extension about virtue, authority and hierarchy. But I will show that these powerful institutional privileges could determine and fix only some of its meanings. Dissent, powerlessness, eccentricity, adherence to and rejection of normative values, the variety of personal and collective positions inhabited in societies, must all find an expression in the language. Once said, they exist, and a historian must try to tease out such utterances, to unravel the scopes of meaning, the range of experi-ence, the vast field of action which a single symbol could ground and sustain.

# CHAPTER I

# Designing the eucharist: new ideas and procedures in the mass from c. 1000

And whilst they were at supper, Jesus took bread and blessed and broke and gave to his disciples and said: 'Take ye and eat. This is my body'. And taking the chalice, he gave the thanks and gave to them, saying: 'Drink ye all of this. For this is my blood of the new testaments, which shall be shed for many unto remission of sins'.[1]                                    Matthew 26,26–8.

Emerging from disparate, separate, only loosely connected economic and political entities, the culture of the high Middle Ages created a symbol of the utmost uniformity to accommodate a complex world – the eucharist. The intensification of exchange, of enterprise in learning, government, trade and architecture, the diversification of a social body whose parts were all the more interdependent, created identities which came to be articulated in a unifying symbol of mediation and in a ritual of overarching universality – the eucharist.

The eucharist was designed and articulated most forcefully in the variety of forums of debate on ecclesiastical and religious matters – monasteries, episcopal schools, papal curia. And it was discussed particularly vigorously from the eleventh century, a time when popes were attempting tooo enforce claims of primacy and universality, against regional political powers and local liturgical customs. This transformation demanded from feudal kings and ecclesiastical magnates alike the subjection of local political and religious dialects, the vernacular liturgies and law-codes, to a greater conformity to a universal language of religion. Out of a wide range of religious practices and diverse understandings of the place of priests in communities a new blueprint was carefully drawn, one which could bring together disparate regions and peoples through adherence to a single ritual practice and a shared ethical and mythical framework. The acceptance of a Church with the pope at its head, as a shared arbiter in ethics and in politics, and the

---

[1] Coenantibus autem eis, accepit Jesus panem, et benedixit ac fregit, deditque discipulis suis, et ait: Accipite, et comedite: hoc est corpus meum. Et accipiens calicem, gratias agit: et dedit illis, dicens: Bibite ex hoc omnes. Hic est enim sanguis meus novi testamenti, qui pro multis effundetur in remissionem peccatorum', Matthew 26,26–8.

acceptance of the clergy as prime cultural producers and as exclusive performers of the rituals, were being formulated as criteria for membership in the *societas christiana*.[2] An administrative network of parishes was cast over Europe, replacing in most places the territorial churches which pursued local traditions in liturgy and cult and which had served a world which was as yet less integrated than it would later become.[3] Within the cultural system of this world and the language of sacramental religion which communicated so many of its meanings, the eucharist offered access to the supernatural, grace, hope for salvation, and a framework for meaning in human relations.

The Church through its administrators and intellectuals was forging a language of religion which enhanced embryonic claims to clerical privilege and which systematised practices and cults that had developed in the world of the early Middle Ages.[4] Whereas early Christianity looked to holy men and early medieval society turned to saints to effect the connection between God and humankind through prayers of intercession, a different order was now emerging.[5] It was embedded in procedures and mediating practices, in a neatly defined mystery, rather than in the inspiration of charismatic and exemplary figures. Now the unifying grace was being claimed and disposed of through sacerdotal mediation, not without exception, but definitely through strong sacramental routines which orientated Christian life on earth. In a complex world brought together through its language of religion, the eucharist was becoming a focus for claims to universality and efficacy which had to be made stronger, more uniform and applicable everywhere and at every time. This meant that the particular function of mediation had to be pronounced in much clearer and more emphatic terms. The priest was endowed with the power to effect a singular transformation in the world, one which was vital and necessary, so the claim of mediation was developed in the twelfth century into a robust theology of sacramentality.[6] Within this symbolic order the claim was made that through sacerdotal ritual action matter could be transformed into something quite different, a repository of supernatural power, and that only such sacerdotal action could effect this change.

---

[2] Southern (1986), pp. 237–8.
[3] On the type of cure of souls and priestly presence developed in the pre-parochial stage in Brittany, see Davies (1983).
[4] On the parochial system, see Gaudemet (1973); Reynolds (1984), pp. 79–100; and Violante (1982). On the local churches, see Kempf (1973) and Schieffer (1960).
[5] Straw (1988), pp. 70, 74, 94.
[6] See William Durandus' exposition on the functions of instruction and intercession: 'Mediatores enim sunt sacerdotes inter Deum et homines, dum et percepta Dei populo deferunt predicando, et vota Deo porrigunt supplicando', *Rationale* lib. 2, c. 11, no. 14, p. 97.

This was an outrageous claim, but one which was potentially universal and exclusive without parallel. It emerged from an intellectual tradition of exegesis which had a strong symbolic element, but it also possessed an inherent problem. That ideas about nature, matter and the sacred would come into contest more sharply as the sacramental claims became clearer was inevitable. This tension inherent in them persisted, even in the most wide-ranging edifice of eucharistic theology; in Thomas Aquinas' *Summa* the present Christ was not really eaten by believers:

Whatever is eaten as under its natural form, is broken and chewed as under its natural form. But the body of Christ is not eaten as under its natural form, but under the sacramental species.[7]

So sacramentality was the unique *trope* of the eucharistic language.

The eucharist placed Christians within a symbolic system operating within a history of salvation, and it was lived as a drama re-enacted at every altar during every mass.[8] The God who was everywhere in every facet of nature, had to be domesticated, located, and his supernatural power had to be apportioned and routinised.[9] It is this economy of the sacred, commuted into sacramental currency, that was being explored, and its most precious coin, the eucharist, evaluated and defined.[10] And above all, the eucharist, the most powerful transaction, was being designed.

## THE THEOLOGICAL DISCUSSION ON THE NATURE OF THE EUCHARIST

It is interesting to note how many rather basic eucharistic issues had remained only loosely formulated until the eleventh century. The nature of sacramental change, the nature of Christ's presence, the moment of transformation, the symbolic link between matter and God. An early discussion of the eucharist took place in the first half of the ninth century in the monastery of Corbie. In response to pastoral queries sent by young churches founded during the Saxon conversion,

---

[7] '. . . illud quod manducatur in propria specie, ipsum et frangitur et masticatur in sua specie. Corpus autem Christi non manducatur in sua specie, sed in specie sacramentali', *ST* III q. 77 a. 7 ad. 3, p. 153.

[8] For earlier views of the mass, see Straw (1988), pp. 103, 104–5.

[9] Funkenstein (1986), pp. 55–6, on Aquinas.

[10] On eucharistic theology, see Geiselmann (1926); Megivern (1963); Macy (1984); Burr (1984).

and with the heightened liturgical awareness which followed Carolingian reforms and the romanisation of the Gallican rite,[11] Paschasius Radbert (*c.*785–*c.*860) responded in his *De corpore et sanguine domini* of *c.*831×3 with the assertion that the very body of Christ was present in the eucharist through the operation of the priest's words:

Imagine, then, whether indeed any corporeal thing could be worthier than the substance of the bread and wine for the purpose of changing internally and in fact into Christ's flesh and blood, so that following the consecration Christ's real flesh and blood is truly created.[12]

Bread and wine were more suitable for reception, and they were easily transformed into flesh by God who had created Christ's flesh in a virgin:

But since it is not proper that Christ be eaten by the teeth, He wished to make truly in this mystery bread and wine into His flesh and blood by the power of the consecration of the Holy Spirit . . . so that just as real flesh was created from a virgin by the Spirit, without coition, thus from the substance of bread and wine, that same body and blood of Christ is miraculously consecrated.[13]

Whatever his immediate reason for writing, Paschasius was a fine biblical commentator, who had long wrestled with questions of meaning. He was mindful of the metaphoric breadth in even the most literal statement. Yet to him, acknowledging the signifying power did not diminish the hard 'reality of things', be it in the words of the prophet of *Lamentations,* the book for which he had written a commentary,[14] or in the words of the consecration. Paschasius was probably the most literal of contemporary exegetes, and it was thus that he approached scriptural statements such as 'Hoc est corpus meum'.[15] This statement engendered a response from a younger fellow-monk at Corbie, Ratramnus (d.868), in a polemical interpretation of Christ as a 'figure' in the

---

[11] Reynolds (1983), pp. 59–61.

[12] 'Cogita igitur si quippiam corporeum potest esse sublimius, cum substantia panis et uini in Christi carnem et sanguinem efficaciter interius commutatur, ita ut deinceps post consecrationem iam uera Christi caro et sanguis ueraciter creatur', *De corpore et sanguine domini* lib. 8, pp. 42–3; Macy (1984), pp. 21, 27–31.

[13] 'Sed quia Christum uorari fas dentibus non est, uoluit in misterio hunc panem et uinum uere carnem suam et sanguinem consecratione Spiritus Sancti potenitaliter creari . . . ut sicut de uirgine per Spiritum uera caro sine coitu creatur, ita per eundem ex substantia panis ac uini mystice idem Christi corpus et sanguis consecretur', *De corpore et sanguine domini* lib. 3, pp. 27–8.

[14] Smalley (1952), pp. 38–9; Colish (1983), p. 65.

[15] Smalley (1952), pp. 90–2.

eucharist, as an image of a spiritual truth which resided elsewhere. In their exchange both used the authority of the Fathers in texts related to the sacraments, and reproduced some of the main patristic positions. Ratramnus took a view closer to Augustine's view of the sacraments as 'visible' words, quite distinct from the *res* which they signified, although correlated to them. Paschasius stressed the identity of sacrament and matter, perhaps in a mode associated with the sacramental theology of Ambrose,[16] and the relation between the two as simple *being* through a change in essence.[17] As can be seen, problems of signified and signifier long predated modern linguistics.[18] But in the context of monastic routine the issue was not so burning as to demand quick and authoritative resolution.[19]

The debate continued throughout the tenth century in the sustained interest of a number of substantial scholars, mainly in the diocese of Liège, and they tended to the realist view. Although never very public, nor sharply polemical, the discussion systematised the opposing positions which followed from Paschasius and Ratramnus, and examined them with the tools of dialectic.[20] A good example is Heriger of Lobbes (*c*.940–1007), who in his *De corpore et sanguine Domini* (or the *Dicta Herigeri*), attempted to reconcile the positions on the eucharist with patristic authorities and into a harmonious resolution.[21] The monks' interest in the eucharist was a product of their patristic learning, and related to their liturgical routines, sharpened by the pastoral need which had originally inspired the search for definition. In the monasteries work on the subject continued in studies such as Gezo of Tortona's *Liber de corpore et sanguine Christi* of *c*.981, which he wrote for the edification of the monks of his abbey in Lombardy.[22] The eucharistic material was being considered in the monastic milieu and the episcopal school of Liège where interesting applications of biblical exegesis and even mathematical and biological knowledge were applied to bolster an all but dominant *realist* view of the eucharist.[23] When Berengar of Tours refused to adhere to these positions early in the next century, the debate reopened. On the realist side Paschasius's writings formed a core, together with miracle tales and recent writings; on the

---

[16] Straw (1988), p. 180.
[17] Gibson (1978), pp. 74–6; Macy (1984), pp. 24, 27–31.
[18] See Shoaf (1989) on medieval preoccupations with the theory of language.
[19] On monastic attitudes as opposed to clerical ones in this context, see Chadwick (1989), p. 436.
[20] Shrader (1973), pp. 181–3.
[21] *Ibid*, esp. p. 181.
[22] Shrader (1973), p. 185.
[23] On Gezo and other tenth-century writers see Shrader (1973), pp. 183–5.

other side, there emerged Berengar with Augustine, logic and grammar.[24]

This happened in the centres of eleventh-century learning, the schools of northern France, and it elicited immediate responses from papal circles.[25] Discussion followed the lead of Berengar of Tours (*c.*999–1088), who was a student of Fulbert of Chartres (d.1028),[26] and who was teaching at Tours from the mid-1030s. Berengar had a reputation for excellence at biblical exegesis, even before his views on the eucharist became known in the 1040s.[27] Berengar was applying the tools of dialectic and grammar to the eucharist. He was using grammar and particularly the Aristotelian grammar of Boethius which was being increasingly integrated into the study of the arts from the tenth century on.[28] Through grammatical analogies to biblical texts and through the application of logic to the words of consecration he demonstrated the concordance of scripture with this view.[29] Berengar reproduced the combination of Platonism and Aristotelianism so startling in Boethius's thought: dialectic and logic in the ordering of knowledge of the universe, and a leaning towards pure essence in metaphysics.[30] Berengar was intensely interested in the rules of nature, of language, which he felt that the eucharist consistently broke.[31] The idea of sacramentality developed by Berengar assigned to the eucharist a 'figurative' relation to Christ's body, in an attempt to avoid the separation between accidents, the appearances of natural objects, from the essence/substance to which they belonged.[32] Berengar was unwilling simply to accept an imputed miraculous operation in the all-important sacrament, but rather sought to find a symbolic link between that which stood to reason and that which scripture taught and faith accepted.[33] Holding a view similar to Ratramnus, Berengar's utterances were articulated in the newest terms of the scholarly endeavour. This was, however, no longer the ninth-century debate; the eucharist was discussed in this

---

[24] Cristiani (1986), pp. 187–8.

[25] Macy (1984), pp. 33–4; Gibson (1978), p. 83; Radding (1985), pp. 166–7. On this debate, MacDonald (1930) is still fundamental.

[26] Gibson (1978), pp. 19, 64–5.

[27] Smalley (1952), pp. 47, 65–6; MacDonald (1930), p. 32; Gibson (1978), pp. 19, 64–5, 78–9.

[28] Lewry (1981), pp. 95–108; Chadwick (1989), p. 427.

[29] On the Berengarian debate, see Montclos (1971).

[30] Chenu (1968), pp. 72–9.

[31] As put in a letter to Ascelinus, a monk of Bec, after 1050: 'Sapis enim contra omnis naturae rationes, contra evangelicam et apostolicam sententiam, si cum Paschasio sapis, in eo quod solus sibi confingit sacramento Dominici corporis decedere panis omnino substantiam', *PL* 150, col. 66. Colish (1983), p. 72.

[32] In his time the term used most often was *subiectus essentia*, and *substantia* was being introduced, but was only to be fully developed in the next century, Southern (1948), p. 40.

[33] Sheedy (1947), pp. 40–1.

debate within the space created between the breakdown of Augustinian symbolism and the emergence of Aristotelian realism.[34]

Even the nascent theory of sacraments of the eleventh century was coming round to an insistence that what the church had to offer was something *real (verum)*.[35] Or so it came to claim in its response to Berengar's challenge. Lanfranc of Bec (1005–1089), Berengar's oppo-nent, was also a grammarian, and he too used grammar in analysing the eucharistic words, Christ's words repeated at the consecration, in his *Liber de corpore et sanguine Domini* of c.1063–8.[36] Lanfranc opposed the view which took the eucharist to be a sign of Christ's body, albeit a very material sign in bread and wine, and argued against the type of reality which similitude imputed.[37] He argued against the claim that accidents and substance could not exist separately, and although he could not fully specify the nature of their relation in separation, he marked the claim which was to be explored by future theologians. The argument which Lanfranc constructed was faithful as to the text, closely argued in dialectical rhythm.[38] He claimed that in the phrase 'Hoc est corpus meum' the subject and predicate must be fully equal, and used a Platonist grammarian as support to employ equipollent propositions to prove the enduring signifying power of the noun.[39] Berengar insisted that this would be a contradiction, if the 'hoc' was totally destroyed.[40] So in his reply to Lanfranc's criticism, *De sacra coena*, written by 1070, Berengar argued point by point against Lanfranc, requiring that Christ's body be treated as incorruptible, and as residing on the right of God in heaven, not dwelling on the altar.[41] Here he also restated that what the senses perceive must be related to their subject; thus the appearance of bread and wine must relate to the substance of the eucharist.[42]

Berengar's case was also an exercise in Aristotelian grammar, applying the terms substance and accidents to grammatical constructs. Grammar taught the different signifying positions of noun and pro-

[34] Becker (1981), pp. 57, 67–8; Russell (1965), p. 63. Berengar protested against the betrayal of the Fathers just as Gregory VII canonised Paschasius in 1073.

[35] Häring (1948).

[36] *Ibid*, p. 65; Montclos (1971), pp. 195–8, 249–325.

[37] Lanfranc, 'De corpore et sanguine domini', *PL* 150, cs. 6, 7, cols. 415–18, esp. c. 6, col. 416: 'Sicut enim qui dicit: "Christus est lapis angularis" non revera Christum lapidem esse constituit, sed propter aliquam similitudinem'.

[38] Southern (1948), p. 43.

[39] Colish (1983), pp. 73–5.

[40] Southern (1948), pp. 44–5; Radding (1985), p. 169.

[41] Berengar, *De sacra coena*, p. 177; Montclos (1971), pp. 503–15; on Berengar and current grammar see Southern (1948), pp. 35, 46.

[42] Berengar, *De sacra coena*, p. 53.

noun and allowed Berengar to argue that in 'Hoc est corpus meum', 'Hoc', the pronoun, signified the bread on the altar. If this was so, could a predicate, destroy its own subject? This was obviously impossible.[43] Restating the argument in eucharistic terms, the dilemma which scholars were faced with allowed for no compromise; in the words of an anti-Berengarian tract by Hugh of Langres (d.1050/51):

It is therefore necessary that you either remove the bread from its nature totally, or do not dare to claim that it is Christ's body.[44]

Berengar came to be seen as the heresiarch; he represented the spirit and the views which were most threatening to the sacramental-sacerdotal world-view.[45] Lanfranc's view, however, led directly to the formulation 'accidents without subject', which so utterly offended Berengar's outlook.[46] Lanfranc's position was the one which twelfth and thirteenth century theologians would further explore, separating the colour, taste, smell and texture of the sacrament from their original substance of bread and wine, through a miraculous transformation, after the words of consecration were uttered. The first sustained debate on the eucharist took place in the eleventh century and, significantly, around the views of a secular scholar, a product of the foremost school, of Chartres.[47] The debate was animated by a new intellectual contribution – Aristotelian logic – and a new political one – a Church which was making new universal claims about its authority and about the powers of its clergy.[48]

But unlike the argument of the monks of Corbie, this debate at the heart of the Christian intellectual world became heated and involved feudal lords, scholars, abbots, bishops and popes. Berengar was repeatedly criticised by councils and in 1059 he was forced to take the following oath dictated by Rome, and probably formulated by Cardinal Humbert of Silva Candida (d.1061), the foremost theorist of papal reform:

I believe that the bread and wine which are laid on the altar are after the consecration not only a sacrament but also the true body and blood of our Lord Jesus

---

[43] Berengar, *De sacra coena*, pp. 130–1; Colish (1983), pp. 72–3.

[44] 'Quapropter necesse est ut aut panem omnino a sua natura dejicias, aut ipsum Christi corpus dicere non praesumas', Hugh of Langres, 'Tractatus de corpore et sanguine Christi contra Berengarium', *PL* 142, col. 1327.

[45] See Macy (1988); and on Berengar's views among later scholars Russell (1965), pp. 163–5.

[46] On applicability of the terms 'Platonist' and 'Aristotelian' to the protagonists of this debate see Montclos (1971), pp. 445–60.

[47] Gibson (1978), p. 19; Mitchell (1982), pp. 139–40.

[48] On the link between sacramental action and simony, see Humbert of Candida's views in Chadwick (1989), pp. 422, 432.

Christ, and they are physically taken up and broken in the hands of the priest and crushed by the teeth of the faithful, not only sacramentally, but in truth.[49]

For a while a position most opposed to Berengar's triumphed,[50] but it soon became clear that even Lanfranc could not live with it. Its terms were revised in the theological debate that followed almost immediately upon the oath's circulation.[51]

Very soon it became clear that for most scholars the formulation of 1059, which was destined to enter the *Decretum*, was too crude and too constricted for fruitful thinking about the eucharist.[52] Berengar's view of nature was the one to triumph in the twelfth century. But before it did, and before the rise of Paris to predominance, another chapter was written. In northern schools, and particularly in Liège, a Platonist-Augustinian interpretation of the eucharist, grounded in the tradition of scriptural exegesis, continued and offered a critique of the grossly realist view, but still within a Paschasian framework[53] – the eucharist as manna, as lamb, as sacrifice, without consideration of substance or accidents. Sympathy of scriptural images rather than logical analysis was here the primary aim.[54] The discussion in the early twelfth century introduced no new terms into the eucharistic debate.

But the implications of the eleventh-century debate were followed through by some. Rupert of Deutz (1076–1129), while monk of St Laurence, Liège, confronted the eucharistic problems in his work on the liturgy of the church, the *De divinis officiis* of 1111.[55] Rupert

---

[49] 'profiteor . . . eam fidem tenere . . . scilicet panem et vinum quae in altari ponuntur, post consecrationem non solum sacramentum, sed etiam verum corpus et sanguinem domini nostri Iesu Christi esse, et sensualiter non solum sacramento sed in veritate manibus sacerdotum tractari frangi et fidelium dentibus atteri', Lanfranc, 'Liber de corpore et sanguine domini', c. 2, cols. 410–1; Gibson (1978), p. 81, n. 1. Another oath was enforced by Gregory VII in 1079; 'Ego Berengarius corde credo et ore confiteor panem et vinum, que ponuntur in altari, per mysterium sacre orationis et verba nostri Redemptoris substantialiter converti in veram et propriam vivificatricem carnem et sanguinem Iesu Christi domini nostri et post consecrationem esse verum Christi corpus quod natum est de Virgine et quod pro salute mundi oblatum in cruce pependit et quod sedet ad dexteram Patris, et verum sanguinem Christi, qui de latere eius effusus est, non tamen per signum et virtutem sacramenti, sed in proprietate nature et virtutem sacramenti', Lanfranc, 'Liber de corpore et sanguine domini', c. 2, col. 411; *Reg. Gregory VII*, VI, 17a, II, pp. 426–7; on this oath see Gibson (1979), pp. 94–6 and Chadwick (1989), esp. pp. 421–3.

[50] On Berengar's defeat, see Somerville (1972); Radding (1985), pp. 107–9. Berengar became the symbol of eucharistic heterodoxy in the Middle Ages and later. Wyclif was alleged to have been his disciple by Thomas Netter in his anti-Lollard tract *Defensor fidei II*, col. 236.

[51] Gy (1983), pp. 82–3; Chadwick (1989), pp. 423–6.

[52] Macy (1984), pp. 28–35; and (1983). On the reception of this oath and later commentaries, see Hödl (1962).

[53] Russell (1965), pp. 163–5; Macy (1984), pp. 49–51.

[54] Macy (1984), pp. 60–5.

[55] Arduini (1987), pp. 102–11.

rejected Berengar's errors which stressed the difference between the sign and the *res* in the sacrament, and wriggling between the positions of Berengar and Lanfranc he attempted to link Christ's divine and historic nature with his sacramental and carnal presence. To Rupert Christ became bread, and this seemed very much like a theory of *impanation* which was quite different from the claims that Christ remained in his substance even in the accidents of bread and wine. His contemporary and colleague Alger, canon of Liège (1050–c.1132), was worried by the meanings of impanation and turned another way. Although he conceded full substantial change in the sacrament, he went further than most in exploring the spiritual meaning of such a change. To Alger the eucharist was not the actual immolation of Christ, which had occurred hundreds of years earlier, but the sacrament which could bring forth an image of it:

In a figure and imitation of His passion, which Christ did not really suffer twice, but the memory of which is reiterated to us every day.[56]

Alger's understanding was a subtle one; he recognised the problems of location and space posed by the eucharist, but was still able to live with a formulation that Christ's body was agile and free.[57] By suggesting moral connections between accidents and substance which do not inhere, he was free to develop the idea of the sacrament, as a mode of existence different from either the material or the figurative; an ambivalent mode which allowed for two simultaneous eatings – spiritual and carnal.[58] Thus, one of the most imaginative late attempts to rethink the eucharist in pre-scholastic terms was made in Liège, where eucharistic interests were acute and were to remain so for a long while. By concentrating on sacramentality, a mode of existence which retained both the physical bread and Christ in heaven, Alger contributed an important direction for consideration in the century to come.

The symbolic order which was being drastically refigured was that which had accommodated early Christian culture well into the eleventh century. It saw in the eucharist a ritual of great importance, a sacrament, which was celebrated in a variety of local usages. It was a central Christian ritual, but a mystery, and in that lay its virtue; the virtue of a practice which persisted unexamined, unexplored, but which remained

---

[56] 'Hic in figura et imitatione passionis ipsius, qua Christus non iterum vere patitur, sed ipsius vere memoriae quotidie nobis iteratur', Alger of Liège, 'De sacramento altaris', *PL* 180, cols. 786–7.
[57] Sheedy (1947), p. 89.
[58] Macy (1984), p. 38; Häring (1958), pp. 57–64; de Lubac (1949), pp. 166–7, 173–5.

attractive and pregnant in meaning, offering a presence of God among men and women. This mode was explained by Augustine:

If you ask how this can be so, I shall briefly tell you. A mystery of faith can be profitably believed; it cannot be profitably examined.[59]

It was considered more closely under the pressure of political or intellectual context: like Paschasius who was preoccupied with exegesis, but even more so, who had to explain the liturgy to new Christians, to spell out what could otherwise be left more vague and undefined and sustained by tradition. And as the eucharist was explored by him it became more mysterious still, not the mystery of the unfathomable, but mystery as the very way God operated in the sacrament. As we have seen, Paschasius triumphantly claimed that he who has created Christ's flesh in Mary's womb without a seed could also form him from the bread and the wine,[60] and Peter Damian (d.1072) stressed this too, that one incarnation created the precedent for another, the very body which was once in Mary's womb was the one placed on the altar:

That same body of Christ which the blessed Virgin bore, which she cherished at her bosom, girded in swaddling clothes, nurtured with maternal care, it is that, I say . . . which we now receive from the sacred altar, and we drink its wine in the sacrament of our redemption.[61]

The discussion was opening up, but it did not rest with one type of argument. Power and aesthetics turned the eucharist into the battle-ground where the new vision of Christian society would be won or lost.

The vision which posited a moral relationship between material object and the truths represented by them and which lay beyond them, had animated Ratramnus in the ninth century, as it did Berengar and Hugh of St Victor (c.1096–1141) after him. It was based in an Augustinian epistemology which privileged the order of the signified over the order of things material which served as tokens carrying meaning.[62] Master Simon in a cathedral school in Flanders or in the Lower Rhineland around 1145, still tackled the question of the nature of the eucharist in traditional terms:

[59] 'Si quaeris modum quo id fieri possit, breviter dico. Mysterium fidei salubriter credi potest, investigari salubriter non potest', as quoted in Peter Lombard, *Sententiae* IV D. 11, col. 1,096.
[60] *De corpore et sanguine domini* lib. 4, pp. 27–8.
[61] 'Illud siquidem corpus Christi quod beatissima Virgo genuit, quod in gremio fouit, quod fasciis cinxit, quod materna cura nutriuit, illud, inquam . . . nunc de sacro altari precipimus, et eius sanguinem in sacramentum nostrae redemptionis haurimus', Peter Damian, *Sermons*, p. 267.
[62] Boyle (1986), p. 51; Häring (1948), p. 126.

What is consumed in this form? Just as one bread is made of many grains which are first sprinkled with water, ground, baked so as to become bread, just so Christ's mystical body, that is the Church, is assembled of many persons, or grains, is cleansed by the water of baptism, ground between the two mill-stones of the two testaments, that is the new and the old, or between the two mill-stones, of hope and of fear.[63]

Master Simon was grasping the question through an image, and then treating it like a biblical text, fitting image with transcendent truth, meaning and form. He recoiled from the gross physicality of some formulations, but was as yet lacking a system which was inherently coherent in its attempt to relate appearances of the world with causal and dynamic powers. Hugh of St Victor was struck by the tension of signification and, unable to resolve it, understood it as bearing meaning and as fruitful. His approach was that of decoding a system of signs from a universe wholly grounded in biblical revelation: the incarnation was a sign, as was Christ's death and resurrection. The sacrament was a sign, at once a similitude and a truth.[64]

But the growing interest in the unifying theme of eucharistic sacramentology came at the moment when new terms turned minds towards explanations of the world which ruptured its philosophical basis. By introducing a natural 'realist' relation between matter and its attributes, represented in the working terms of substance and accidents, the world became a system of predictable and fathomable relations which adequate grammar and logic could explain and thus control.[65] In the latter half of the twelfth century new ideas were being considered in the university of Paris, still seeking its institutional form, before the formation of an organised *magisterium*.[66] This freshness has led one modern scholar to claim 'it seemed to the new European intelligentsia as if all ideas might be tried on for size', which is probably an exaggeration of the real flexibility of any concept.[67] But it is true that there was a commitment to intellectual work which was *disputandi more, non asserendi more* (by the way of disputation, not of assertion), a mood which was precipitated by the intoxicating effect of new philosophical

[63] 'Cur autem in tali specie sumatur? Sicut vero unus panis ex multis granis fit, quod prius aqua aspergitur, molitur, coquitur, ut panis efficiatur, sic misticum Christi corpus, id est Ecclesia, ex multis personis velut granis collecta, aqua baptismi abluitur, inter duas molas duorum testamentorum, id est novi et veteris, vel inter duas molas, spei et timoris', Master Simon, *De sacramentis*, pp. 27–8.

[64] 'Ergo mors Christi vera fuit; et tamen exemplum fuit . . . Quare ergo altaris sacramentum similitudo esse non potest, et veritas? In alio quidem similitudo, in alio veritas', Hugh of St Victor, 'De sacramentis libri duo' II, c. 6, *PL* 176, col. 466.

[65] Southern (1948), esp. pp. 33–7.

[66] Ferruolo (1985), pp. 279–300.

[67] Funkenstein (1986), pp. 45–6.

horizons and the need to test them and apply them not only to grammatical problems, but to the very metaphysics of faith.[68] As long as a consensus about the wish to formulate a living ideology for Christian society prevailed, a large degree of latitude was allowed within it. The search for a unity within diversity pointed towards a sacrament of mediation, one which, once closely examined, appeared ill-defined, ambiguous and only loosely formulated. Basic questions like concomitance and transubstantiation were still open; similarly, the nature of communion and frequency of celebration were issues which were regulated by local customs and which, by and large, were not at the centre of pastoral interest. In fact the organising pastoral experience which was stressed by most twelfth-century scholars and bishops was that of penance, creating a unified disciplinary and jurisdictional basis for social and religious organisation. But to be effective, it had to be private; whereas the symbol which created the framework of meaning was the emerging eucharist, publicly containing the man/God, the visible and the invisible, reconciling the most acutely felt differences.[69] This symbol was now being discussed, rethought and ultimately, redesigned.

In this discussion the eucharist was being scrutinised in terms of substance and accidents. Transubstantiation was a neologism which arose from the eleventh-century debate, and developed in the twelfth century within a realist philosophy of the universe.[70] The term described the process of conversion, once the resulting substance, Christ's body, was being upheld. Robert Pullen (d. 1146) and Peter Lombard (c. 1095–1160) claimed that only the accidents were broken at the altar, and Christ's body remained whole. The traditional view, such as that put forward by Gilbert de la Porée (1076–1154), would have been described/explained through allegory: the breaking of the bread is like that of a stick which seems broken in water, but which remains, in fact, whole.[71] Peter of Poitiers (d. 1216) suggested that Christ's body was covered by accidents like a hand under a coat,[72] while others concentrated on the ecclesiological meaning of the unbroken body in the host.[73] This was by no means an unproblematic metaphor; it was

---

[68] Chenu (1968), pp. 280–1.

[69] On this strain in Gregory the Great's 'prematurely' medieval thought, see Straw (1988), p. 105.

[70] Already in the pronouncement of the pre-Lent synod of 1079 which reformulated Berengar's eucharistic oath, the term which described the change after consecration, the bread into vivifying flesh and the wine into Christ's own blood was 'according to their true substance', (*substantialiter*), Gibson (1978), p. 95.

[71] Macy (1984), pp. 30–31.

[72] Dumoutet (1943–45), pp. 217–18.

[73] Macy (1984), pp. 122–6.

later used by Bonaventure, but rejected by Aquinas who saw it as detracting from the accidents.[74] Thus, Bonaventure (1221–1274) in his sermon on Christ's body is reminded of the meat cooked on ashes which sustained Elijah on his way to Mount Horeb; the meat was covered with ashes, enveloped in their accidents, like Christ's flesh in the eucharist.[75] In the twelfth century and even in the thirteenth there were those who would not relinquish allegory, those who did not argue purely in philosophical terms. Allegory was an important rhetorical device, one which often played on the tension between substance and accidents; transubstantiation was a total conversion of substance, but any type of corruption or ill that might befall the eucharist was deemed to influence the accidents only. When the eucharist was consumed at communion, the union was created through the incorporation with Christ's substance, but the undignified digestion affected the accidents only.

The realism which had been formulated in reaction against Berengar and which was necessarily inscribed in the allegorical mode of arguing, and definitely in the formulations designed for pastoral utility, created a counter-response in such thinkers as Albert the Great (c. 1200–1274), Thomas Aquinas (c. 1225–1274) and even Bonaventure. Albert simply derided the sort of formulations of the mass which were being created and disseminated to the celebrating clergy through genres such as expositions on the mass;[76] while Thomas felt that the realist views constrained God in time and space. The formulation which satisfied Thomas, that the species realised Christ's physical presence, but only in an invisible spiritual, and non-materialist way, was not easily teachable, nor did it purport to be so.[77] Side by side with the formulation of neat explanatory didactic lines, the author of the words:

> That which you do not understand,
> That which you do not see,
> Faith will strengthen,
> According to the order of things.[78]

[74] Thomas had some objections to the acceptance of accidents without subject, and four of the articles of his work which were condemned in 1277 were related to this problem, Hissette (1977), pp. 287–91.

[75] Gy (1983), p. 77; see Bonaventure, 'Sermones selecti de rebus theologicis', sermon 3: 'De sanctissimo corporis Christi', *Opera omnia* v, p. 556.

[76] White (1974), p. 46.

[77] *ST* III q. 75 a. 1, ad. 3.

[78] 'Quod non capis,
Quod non vides,
Animosa firmat fides,
Praeter rerum ordinem'.

In the sequence for Corpus Christi *Lauda, syon*, see below, pp. 191–3.

also held that up to a point there was some latitude, a space within which people could achieve their understandings and reason, and finally support their belief:

For a man cannot assent by believing what is proposed without understanding it in some way.[79]

This was not the sort of eucharistic formulation which was easily translatable into a pastoral programme. Bonaventure settled for the terms 'speciebus sanctissimorum symbolorum' to describe the state of the eucharistic consecrated species.[80] In their reaction against the limiting, and intellectually constraining formulations of the first eucharistic debates and of the physics of their day, some of the refinements of eucharistic understanding achieved by these thinkers were only empowered when combined with an admission of their limitations and the invocation of mystery as the crowning explanatory device.[81]

In the eucharist there was a powerful assimilation of eating, the most common of human functions, into the economy of the supernatural. The offer of oneness with God through physical assimilation was combined with the promise of all that was beneficial in this life and the next, and gave the eucharist enormous potential appeal. The promise of being one with God in a bodily sense could hardly be surpassed. More symbolically elaborate readings presented the eucharist as refreshing food to the hungry, in images of feeding and nurturing.[82] Matthew of Rievaulx's poem on the eucharist of 1208 × 18 is an example:

> This food, which no hunger can expel,
> This is the bread which the Spirit has cooked in a holy fire.
> This is a liquid which no thirst can destroy,
> This is the wine which the grape of a virgin's womb has brought forth.[83]

William of St Thierry described the eucharist as a sequence of eating

---

[79] 'Non enim posset homo assentire credendo aliquibus propositis, nisi ea aliqualiter intelligeret . . .', *ST* II–II q. 8, a. 8, ad. 2.

[80] Bonaventure, IV *Sent.* d. 8, a. 2, q. 1, *Opera omnia*, p. 208.

[81] In the fifteenth century Gerson spoke of a God in the eucharist who was so free, so unbound by rules, that there was no wonder that He could not be understood by man, Brown (1985), pp. 87, 161.

[82] All of which are explored at length by Bynum (1986) and (1987), *passim*, esp. pp. 67–8, 114, 117–19, 270–5, 285, 411–12.

[83] Hic cibus quem nulla fames exterminat; hic est
Panis quem sacro spiritus igne coquit.
Hic liquor est cui nulla sitis preiudicat; hoc est
Vinum quod sacre virginis uva parit.
Wilmart (1940), no. 26, p. 58.

and love whose end and prize would come in the future.[84] Humbert of Romans described the progression through sacramental rites in life-giving images: one is regenerated by baptism, strengthened by confession and fed by the eucharist 'Just as physical food succeeds in restoring the hungry . . . thus, this food protects the spiritual life'.[85] In the pastoral this aspect was emphasised in no ambiguous terms by those of the Paschasian persuasion; physical contact informed the immediacy of the experience and the unambiguous nature of the union which the eucharist brought about.[86] Through the mouth which had eaten the apple, by the sense through which Adam had sinned, man was to be saved:

Just as by Adam's tasting we all died, thus by tasting Christ we all recover life.[87]

The union was one of substances, it was stressed, and nowhere better than in Bonaventure's sermon for a Lent Sunday, on the Song of Songs 8,6:

Since in the other two types there is a certain separation and distinction between the giver and the given, but this type is a wondrous and unending union between the eaten and the food, and there is a conversion of one into the other. And because of this union Christ said to the soul of the eater of the sweetness of sacrament and of love: *place me as a sign* of charity and mercy, *upon thy heart . . . as a seal upon thy arm . . . for love is strong as death.*[88]

Bonaventure delighted in the union which the eucharist promised,[89] a quality which the pastoral generally tended to emphasise. Offering such a compelling vision of fusion and incorporation in a sacrament-Christ was also bound to raise doubts about the iterability of such eating of Christ's body, again and again, at every mass, at every altar, in every mouth.

Eating and food, vessels and nourishment, were essential parts of

---

[84] 'Hunc autem cibus plus manducat qui plus amat; et plus amando rursum, plus et plus manducat, et plus et plus amat, licet huius amoris in hac vita nonnisi pignus quoddam accipimus, plenitudinem ejus in praemium ejus in futuro saeculo exspectantes', 'De sacramento altaris', c. 5, col. 353.

[85] 'Sicut autem cibus corporalis, valet ad reparationem deperditorum . . . ita et iste cibus ad vitam spiritualem conservandam', Humbert of Romans, *Sermones*, fols. 59^vb–60^ra.

[86] Cristiani (1968), pp. 177–8.

[87] 'Et sicut per gustum in Adam omnes mortui sumus, ita per gustum in Christo omnes vitam recuperamus', James of Vitry, 'De sacramentis', p. 208.

[88] 'Nam in aliis duobus modis est quaedam separatio et divisio inter dantem et datum, sed isto modo est mirabilis et interminabilis unio inter cibatum et cibum et conversio unius in alterum. Et ratione istius unionis dicit Christus animae gustanti dulcedinem sacramenti eucharistiae et amoris. *Pone me ut signaculum*, caritatis et benevolentiae, *super cor tuum . . . ut signaculum super brachium tuum . . . quia fortis est ut mors dilectio*', Bonaventure, *Opera omnia* v, p. 265, whole sermon pp. 258–66.

[89] Gy (1983), p. 94.

eucharistic symbolism. The eucharist developed into something good to eat, it could be experienced directly and assimilated into one's own body. The gift of food was the most satisfying of offerings, directly experienced and lovingly given, as put by the German preacher Berthold of Regensburg (*c.*1210–1272):

aber der minne, daʒ er unser spise ist worden, der moht im elliv div werlt niht gedanchen.[90]

The fine grape-wine, gently diluted with water, and the wheaten bread quenched thirst and satiated hunger, and no form of assimilation was more direct than that through eating. Other important 'eatings' built on this sense, like that of Jeremiah or St John the Evangelist's eating a book, which Hugh of St Cher (*c.*1195–1263) explained through the book being the image of Christ, the sacraments and the church.[91] In *Piers Plowman* the whole moral allegory is constructed around images of ploughing and food production, a merging of the images of physical food and spiritual food which is particularly powerful:

> 'Comeþ, quod Conscience, 'ʒe Cristene and dyneþ,
> That han laboured lelly al this lenten tyme.
> Here is breed yblessed, and goddes body þerunder.[92]

The host conveys truths that some can read in books, but even they need it, and cannot do without it as a medicine, a remedy, in John Lydgate's words in the fifteenth century, 'a restoratyf'. Eating is a primordial function, the need for food motivates human action; labour is rewarded by food, and spiritual labour, by spiritual food, the eucharist.[93] The urgency of hunger and the satisfaction of eating forcefully combine in the reception of the image of eucharistic food.

So similar to other activities, it was essentially different, too. And the nascent eucharistic symbol had to be carefully fashioned, its attendant ritual closely designed. So theologians questioned and answered, discarded some and invented other terms and ideas, and created in their deliberations a wholesome, health-bringing, clear, implausible yet teachable and desirable symbol, to convey a sacramental world-view, a language of religion. On the one hand, the eucharist was removed from other practices, sacraments, rituals, and on the other, it was built up and imbued with meanings and uses. The intellectual project was main-

---

[90] Berthold of Regensburg, *Deutsche Predigten*, no. 6, pp. 63–7, at p. 63.
[91] Gellrich (1985), p. 22. On the theme of Christ's body as a parchment, a charter, see below, pp. 306–8.
[92] *Piers Plowman* B Text, Passus XIX, lines 383–5, p. 653.
[93] Mann (1979), p. 43; *passim.*

tained by theologians, canonists, monks, preachers, bishops, engaged in this formidable task; to teach that a thin wheaten disk could become God through the words of the clergy. What Gary Macy has called 'the legacy of diversity' in eucharistic thinking of the thirteenth century entertained the acceptance of the eucharist, celebrated daily, as providing grace, hope and redemption. Within the project there were those more and those less committed to the pastoral aims, and thus more or less willing to provide the intellectual underpinning which it required.[94] There were those like James of Vitry (*c.*1160/70–1240) who operated with a strong sense of the pastoral imperative; he could not write his treatise on the sacraments without frequent reference to those dissenting views which challenged and even endangered the very truths he was expounding.[95] But then, James was a canon and a master of the liberal arts, but not a schoolman; his realm of activity was in the pastoral and administrative ecclesiastical sphere.

It is customary to present the development of the intellectual project of medieval Christendom as a story of rise, climax and decline. This is a familiar narrative in which the twelfth century bravely but still only partially masters new philosophy and opens to discussion and reformulation a vast Christian world-view, to be followed by the giants of the thirteenth century who achieved in their vast *Summae* a degree of synthesis which was the finest edifice for Christian life, only to be thwarted by those fourteenth-century nominalists who shattered the very necessary consensus on the degree of God's intervention in the natural world, on the one hand, or by the ultra-realists on the other. It is claimed that this led to a relativising and anti-nomian character in the elephantine commentaries of the later Middle Ages, from which a governing pastoral responsibility was absent.[96] This cannot fully be accepted, since intellectual inquiry never really does stand still; and the myth was created more by Thomists in the last one hundred years than by contemporaries.[97] Fourteenth-century discussions scrutinised those gaps and inconsistencies which the synthesising effort necessarily created. They also examined such edifices in the light of new social and political problems, of which the fourteenth century certainly had an overwhelming share. The implications of Aristotelian philosophy were being explored by Duns Scotus (*c.*1264–1308), by William Ockham (*c.*1300–1347), even by John Wyclif (1335–1384) in an ongoing project

[94] Schillebeeckx (1968), pp. 11–12.
[95] James of Vitry, 'De sacramentis', pp. 230–31.
[96] See, for example, Southern (1987), pp. 140–1.
[97] On this matter I have benefited from discussion with William Courtenay; see Burr (1984), p. 99.

which was inherently open to more or less 'realist' or 'nominalist' explanations.

The development of eucharistic theology turned between 1150 and 1350 to an espousal of Aristotelian philosophy of matter, tentatively first by Peter Comestor and Peter the Chanter, moderately by Thomas Aquinas, and totally by Duns Scotus. In this view bodies were constituted by two metaphysical principles: matter and form. A body was extended from matter, in a form which governed its particular appearance, in quantity and shape. The substance exists within these two principles, which are none the less separate. So the substance of Christ's body in the eucharist could exist in the appearance of bread, as an extension of the substance of Christ's body in heaven. Thomas Aquinas was thus able to claim that

All the substance of the bread is transmuted into the body of Christ . . . therefore, this is not a formal conversion but a substantial one. Nor does it belong to the species of natural mutations; but, with its own definition, it is called transubstantiation.[98]

and mean that the whole substance was changed, and yet could be apprehended by the senses through properties or accidents, separate from that substance. Aquinas' formulation of transubstantiation posited a wholly articulated *conversion* in order to explain the change of Aristotelian predicates.[99] But ultimately this relied on a greater claim, that of God's intervention in the miracle of transubstantiation. This approach, to which Bonaventure and a number of other theologians subscribed in the second half of the thirteenth century,[100] was countered by the critique of Franciscan theologians who wished to avoid arguments which seemed to coerce God into eucharistic operation in one single mode.[101] It was also rejected by Duns Scotus, who went further still in the 'realist' inquiry by ceasing the attempt to construct a metaphysics which possessed a built-in and necessary place for sacramental mysteries.[102] For Scotus God's will was exercised to work a specific change, that of *annihilation* of the bread at consecration; substitution took place and not change, one enacted by God's unlimited powers. From the generation following Thomas, and in the next century within the study of logic in Paris and within the study of mathematics and physics in Oxford, nature was explored through rules

[98] *ST* III q. 75 a. 4.
[99] Burr (1984), pp. 8–24.
[100] *Ibid*, pp. 32–59.
[101] *Ibid*, pp. 60–75, 99–107.
[102] On his views see Burr (1972).

of natural observation, with an internal test of logic. Here quality, appearance and quantity, and their external manifestations, were privileged over signification links between nature and spiritual truths.

Even a student of Thomas Aquinas, the Dominican John Quidort (or John of Paris) (d.1306), recognised this in an intellectual exercise contained in a *Determinatio* which he argued and wrote in 1304×5.[103] This is a tract dealing with the way in which Christ's real presence comes to be in the consecrated host through a process other than transubstantiation. Quidort accepted Christ's real presence in the eucharist *de fide,* but claimed that he was not bound to accept this explanation of the transformation (which was being taught by Bonaventure and Aquinas) since this was merely a plausible one, but not one sanctioned either by council or by pope.[104] He proceeds to propose a theory of impanation,[105] by which the bread is not annihilated at consecration, but rather drawn into, assumed, by the Word to coexist with Christ's body within the person, the *supposit,* of the Word in the eucharist:

I say that the bread in the sacrament of the altar is not immediately drawn into the *esse,* or the *supposit,* of the Word; rather, through the mediation of corporality, and not only by the mediation of corporality but manifestly: in the nature of bread assumed into the Word.[106]

Thus, no annihilation, no accidents without subjects, the thorny issues which both Thomas and Bonaventure had wisely left alone, or ambiguously worded,[107] so much so that the Dominican John Quidort, member of the Dominican *studium* of Paris, could consider them as worthy of investigation.[108] Many of the terms which he uses, and especially those related to God's power to assume and discard non-human form, anticipated some of the nominalist positions which would surface twenty years later. Quidort's aim was a pastoral one, to find a convincing way of explaining something that he wished to maintain due

---

[103] Martin (1973).
[104] *Ibid,* pp. 201–2.
[105] For earlier formulations of alternatives to substantial change in the eucharist, see the example of Heriger of Lobbes, Shrader (1973), pp. 181–2.
[106] 'Dico igitur quod panis in sacramento altaris trahitur ad esse, vel suppositum Verbi non immediate, sed mediante corporeitate, et non mediante corporeitate quae est totum; quod patet sic: natura enim panis assumpta a Verbo . . .', Martin (1973), p. 215. The *syppositum* is 'that which is capable of existing', a concrete individual with all necessary accidents and qualities, as the *hypostasis* in Greek.
[107] Thomas did, after all, use the term *conversio* to describe the change at transubstantiation, Bueschner (1950), p. 29.
[108] But this was definitely not the *curia*'s view, since he was suspended from teaching in 1305, following the publication of this text, Martin (1973), p. 201. On papal attention to intellectual work in this period see Southern (1987), esp. pp. 137–41.

to faith, the sacramental view of the eucharist. And he clearly states this at the beginning of the tract:

And if someone finds another way, I am willing to help him and sustain him so that our faith in the real existence of Christ's body in the sacrament of the altar be saved and defended in many ways.[109]

John Quidort was not troubled by the pull of philosophy, drawing conclusions from physics into theology, as were such later thinkers as William Ockham or Peter d'Ailly (1351–1420);[110] rather he was pre-occupied by the need to explicate and argue a truth which had always been and was increasingly difficult to teach and sustain.[111]

Ockham strove to pursue the study of nature unfettered by theologi-cal prerogatives, quite outside the theological project, which he acknowledge as extraneous and as autonomous, and whose doctrine of transubstantiation he was willing to accept.[112] He treated the eucharist as a *quantum* with quality and form, like other bodies, which was subject to the rules of nature, rather than as a numinous floater with substance that could not be apprehended, and in which matter and qualities were not totally linked.[113] Yet Ockham did not really dwell on the nature of transubstantiation,[114] but rather, like Scotus before him, accepted it as it was doctrinally formulated, as the total replacement of the host by Christ's body: 'it is truly contained in the whole host and in every one of its parts at once'.[115] He introduced the term *successio* to describe the rhythm by which the substances replace each other under the same accidents,[116] and probably in order to avoid consideration of remanence, a stage in which both the bread and Christ's sacramental body coexisted under the accidents of bread. Although the papacy sensed the danger of this type of reasoning, these nominalists could claim faithfulness to Aristotelian physics, Aristotle himself having

---

[109] 'Et si quis aliam [*sic*] modum inveniat, paratus sum iuvare ipsum ad sustinendum eum ut sic fides nostra de vera existentia corporis Christi in sacramento altaris possit pluribus modis salvari et defendi', Martin (1973), p. 215.

[110] *Ibid*, p. 214; Sylla (1973), pp. 363, 373–5.

[111] On Quidort's views, see the version in the Chronicle of St Denis: 'dicens . . . commuta-tione substantiae panis . . . per assumptionem substantiae panis vel paneitatis in Christo', William of Nangis, 'Chronique de St Denis', p. 592.

[112] See for example his views on the sacrament as reported in Avignon in 1326, Pelzer (1922), articles 19–23, pp. 260–2.

[113] See for example on the issue of accidents, and especially of location, *ibid*, a. 23, p. 263; Catto (1985), p. 272.

[114] William Ockham, *De sacramento altaris*, pp. 29–64.

[115] 'Sub tota hostia et qualibet parte simul vere et realiter continetur', 'De sacramento altaris', p. 7; quote from p. 9, n. 22. On Scotus' view of transubstantiation, see Burr (1984), pp. 90–1.

[116] William Ockham, *De sacramento altaris*, pp. 29, 36–7.

recognised the enormous difficulty of separating quantity substance.

So while the questions asked in the fourteenth century were n necessarily irresponsible they came increasingly to be seen as menacing and were evaded by some thinkers – for example, to a large extent by Scotus and by Ockham, who were troubled by the problems of fitting the concepts of quantity and location to the eucharistic species.[117] Ockham stated the problem as:

It is argued that things which occupy the same place are equal . . . But Christ's body and the species of bread occupy the same place . . . because where one is the other is, and one does not contain the other.[118]

But he decided not to argue on this issue, and acknowledged that some truths are made known by God, and others he chooses not to reveal to man.[119]

The later fourteenth century saw the nominalist project pursuing the critique of Thomism, pressing against the boundaries of discipline and the test of pastoral utility. Eucharistic presence was being discussed in increasingly technical language, with far less of the mystery which had revealed itself in some of Aquinas' eucharistic explanations.[120] Rather than discuss the doctrine, another point was brought home again and again, that a *quantity* must be identical with a material substance to which it is attributed.[121] In Oxford the Dominican Robert Holcot (c.1290–1349), and Ockham's disciple the Franciscan Adam Wodeham (d.1358) pursued these questions. In his lectures Adam asked questions which had not been unfamiliar to Berengar in his day:

About the sacrament of the eucharist I ask whether Christ's body is really contained under the species which were the accidents of bread and wine.[122]

From a realist direction, one which attempted to penetrate the ultimate and abstract realities of things in the world, thus attaining knowledge of God's pre-ordained truth, Wyclif broke the disciplinary link by offering a theory of remanence, not of transubstantiation, which was in fact

---

[117] See his questions 6, 7 and 8 in *IV Sent.*, pp. 62–151. Sylla (1983), pp. 354, 357–8.
[118] 'Arguitur, quia quae occupant locum aequalem sunt aequalia . . . sed corpus Christi et species panis occupant aequalem locum, igitur etc. Cum igitur ubi unum est, reliquum est, unum non continet reliquum', *IV Sent.* q. 6; and *ad oppositum* 'Hoc est corpus meum', p. 62.
[119] Bueschner (1950), p. 11.
[120] Gy (1983), pp. 86, 94.
[121] Catto (1985), p. 272.
[122] In the *Reportatio Oxoniensis*, notes of his lectures, IV q. 4: 'Circa sacramentum eucharistiae quaero: utrum corpus Christi realiter sub speciebus quae fuerunt accidentia panis et vini contineatur', Courtenay (1948), p. 185.

quite close to Ockham's consubstantiation. As the realist and nominalist challenges mounted, so did the adhesion to accidents of bread
without their substance, in words which were fiercely stated at the
Council of Constance in 1415,[123] and later at the Council of Trent.[124]
Rather than open the doctrine to fundamental inquiry in their own
terms, critics returned and repeated one basic objection, that a quantity
must be identical with the substance to which it is attributed.[125] Even
when accepting the accidents without substance, its implications were
unacceptable to Scotus and Ockham: the nominalists questioned
whether a thing without substance was worthy of receiving the sacramental body of Christ[126] and conversely whether the union with a
figure of Christ, a reflection in a mirror was not a more appropriate way
of designating the union of mortals with God. This strong line of
criticism was also echoed in the world outside the schools, and it is
against its romantic and symbolic postulation that most pastoral energy
and teaching expertise surrounding the sacraments was directed in the
later Middle Ages.

In tracing the design of the eucharist and the mass, one reaches a
point in the late thirteenth century when all was said and done – not
intellectually but in terms of the construction of a pastoral edifice, one
which was conveyed through the guide-books, the synodal legislation,
the sermons, and *exempla,* collected in the thirteenth century as never
before. Although theologians continued to disagree about the eucharist
throughout the late Middle Ages, they were suspicious of any change in
its pastoral design. This cautious tread lasted until the fourteenth
century, but the critique of thinkers such as Wyclif and reformers such
as Hus, forced theologians and ecclesiastical administrators to pronounce ever more starkly on the pre-eminence of the pastoral end, and
the clerical link which established and supported it. Thus Gerson in the
early fifteenth century insisted, like Hugh of St Victor 300 years earlier,
that the eucharist was granted as a sign of God, to demonstrate His
omnipotence, His lack of limitation, His freedom from the laws of
nature.[127] Similarly, at the close of the fifteenth century theologians
such as Gabriel Biel (*c.*1412–1495), who adhered to a very large extent
to Thomas Aquinas' formulations, still found sacramental theology,
and especially the eucharist, difficult to accept. As it stood, with
transubstantiation at its heart, it seemed to constrain God's free will

---

[123] *COD* session 15–6 July 1415, c. 2, p. 422 (see also cs. 47–48, p. 426).
[124] *COD* session 13–11 October 1551, esp. cs. 2–4, pp. 694–5.
[125] Catto (1985), p. 272.
[126] Catto (1985), p. 274.
[127] Brown (1987), p. 87.

through sacraments which were effective *ex opere operato* and which were resented in an intellectual mood of reform.[128] It is for this reason that the Hussite challenge, encompassed symbolically in the practice of Utraquism, communion to the laity in both bread and wine, provoked so strong a reaction, culminating in Jan Hus' condemnation at the council of Constance in 1415, in the words of the same Gerson. By the late Middle Ages offering the chalice could also imply that the clergy possessed no inherent powers denied to the laity. It was also a breach of obedience to one of the practices that had evolved as a practical response to the clearer formulations of transubstantiation in the twelfth century. Utraquism expressed a trenchant critique of the clergy, and the valorisation of personal, more frequent and direct access to the holy for the laity.[129] And Hus was right in this assessment because the fears of anti-Hussites like Andrew of Brod (d.1427) who claimed that utraquism would lead to the diminution of priestly office, and even to women's claim to administer, were fulfilled in the ideas which arose in another dissenting milieu, amongst Lollards in England. Sacramental power, and particularly performance of the eucharist were the basis for sacerdotal power, built up over four centuries. It was an edifice which was all too vulnerable to misinterpretation and criticism, and thus its external manifestations, and symbolic representations were jealously guarded.

## MATTER AND PERFORMANCE: BREAD, WINE AND CELEBRANT

The eucharist was being removed from other practices with which it had traditionally been assimilated, like the worship of relics. It found its place among the rituals which by the mid twelfth century were being discussed as the seven sacraments, including procedures which were undergone once in a lifetime, like baptism, ordination, confirmation and extreme unction, and those which were iterable: eucharist, marriage and penance.[130] These formulations went against the grain of more legalistic formulations by Ivo of Chartres in the eleventh century, which insisted that sacraments should have apostolic origins, and that they could not be repeated.[131] But what came to prevail was a more Augustinian view of the sacraments, one which distinguished between the visible sign (*sacramentum*), the bread or the water, and the sacramental reality behind it (*res*), and wished to retain this distinction rather

[128] Farthing (1983), pp. 87–91, 96–109, 112–31 and conclusion, pp. 191–6.
[129] Catto (1985); Kaminsky (1967), esp. chapter 3, pp. 96–104.
[130] Häring (1976), pp. 488–91.
[131] *Ibid*, pp. 483–4, 493.

than to see it collapse.[132] In this sense some of Berengar's formulations on sacramentology did persist,[133] and in the 1140s Peter Lombard reformulated the link between matter and sacramental effect as a causality.[134] William of St Thierry represented the sacramental economy as the working of spirit through visible signs of divine reality.[135] These signs require intelligence in the unravelling, and their effect is more than physical; it is elevating. The sacramental sign is thus both insufficient and totally necessary; it cannot be missed.[136] Thus the sacraments came to be seen as efficacious signs which were integrated into and punctuated the life-cycle, or in Bonaventure's words: 'Since it is a greater thing to restore than to create . . . only God is both the physician and the medicine'.[137] But as claims about the nature of the eucharist became more ambitious and clearer in the very same years, the eucharist was also distinguished within the group of sacraments.[138] It was stressed that the eucharist was a special type of sacrament, an arch-sacrament. Unlike baptism, marriage and extreme unction, it could not be administered by a lay person, even *in extremis*. This special nature was expressed by Humbert of Romans in the thirteenth century:

That in all other sacraments Christ's power is spiritual, but in this one – Christ exists corporeally; and this is a greater thing; just as it is greater thing to be king in person, than only potentially. It is also true that in other sacraments there is a single marvel, and in this one there are many. In this there is a physical entity in many places, a large thing in a small one, accidents without subject, and many other such marvels.[139]

It was also distinguished from relics. It was no longer to be used for the consecration of altars, as it was God's very body, not a sign of holiness.[140] Yet Durandus, bishop of Mende (1230–1296), still described

[132]  Häring (1948), pp. 19–12; Chenu (1968), pp. 117–18. But this distinction collapsed in early medieval theology, Straw (1988), p. 190.
[133]  As in *De sacra coena*, c. 26, pp. 55–6; Häring (1948), p. 113.
[134]  Häring (1948), pp. 129–30, 146.
[135]  Verdeyen (1987), pp. 221–2, 223.
[136]  *Ibid*, p. 225.
[137]  'Quoniam magis est recreare quam creare . . . solus Deus sit medicus et medicina', Bonaventure, *IV Sent*. d. 1, a. 1, q. 1, *Opera omnia* IV, p. 11.
[138]  For a survey of thirteenth-century views on the pre-eminence of the eucharist, see Kinn (1960).
[139]  'Quod in omnibus aliis sacramentis est virtus Christi spiritualis, sed in hoc Christus corporaliter, et hoc est maius, sicut maius est regem esse presentialiter alicui, quam per virtutem. Item licet in aliis sacramentis sint quedam mirabilia, tamen in hoc sunt plura. In hoc, enim est una res corporalis in pluribus locis, et res magna in re parva, et accidentia sine subiecto, et similia multa', in a sermon on communion, Humbert of Romans, *Sermones*, fol. 59^rb.
[140]  Herrmann-Mascard (1975), p. 167; Geary (1978), pp. 39–40.

the older custom in his *Rationale* of c.1289,[141] while John Andrea (c. 1270–1348) early in the next century explained the difference in that the eucharist is strictly food for the soul, which should not be used for any other purpose; any such use would be improper and unreasonable (*indecens et irrationabile*).

The effect of sacraments is in the ritual transformation of matter into a *locus* of supernatural power, and the material transformed bore some symbolic relation to the force emerging from it. In the eucharist the bread and wine were designed to appear compatible with their inherent essence, based on Christ's words of ritual transformation. Robert Grosseteste's *Templum dei* of 1220×35 required the following features for eucharistic efficacy: wheaten bread, incorrupt wine, pure water, well-pronounced words of consecration, a male priest and good intention in celebration.[142] The external features of the materials, which were seen and tasted, although their appearance never changed, were a subject of close attention in the design of the eucharist.

First, the nature of the change, and the conversion was indeed a full transformation, as put in Hugh of St Cher's commentary on the *Sentences*:

But when the bread becomes Christ's body nothing at all remains of the bread, that is, nothing is shared in common.[143]

It was clearly transubstantiation and not consubstantiation. The body of Christ alone was present in every bit of what still appeared as bread and wine, no ordinary food, since the accidents were not there to nourish the body of Christ, only to save.[144] The question of digestion was related to the function of eating through which the eucharist was consumed; the degradations of eating, breaking, digestion, and excretion could not be allowed to work on the holy substance, not even in appearance, and this question was often raised in criticism of the eucharist. In Roland Bandinelli's section 'De sacramento altaris', a tale was told of a person who attempted to live on nothing but the host. The author explains that such a person was, in fact, consuming his own body from inside, digesting himself, and after fourteen days, died. So it was not the eucharist which was being digested and excreted by him.[145]

[141] 'Sane sine sanctorum reliquiis, aut ubi illi haberi non possunt, sine corpore Christi non fit consecratio altaris fixi, sed viatici sed portatilis', *Rationale* lib. 1, c. 7, no. 23, p. 54.

[142] *Templum dei* xviii. 1, p. 63.

[143] 'Sed quando de pane fit Corpus Christi, nihil penitus manet de pane, ergo nihil est ibi commune', Jorissen (1965), pp. 39–40.

[144] *Ibid*, p. 146.

[145] Roland Bandinelli, 'Sentences', p. 232. See below about such testing of the eucharist, pp. 337–8.

The eucharist was food like no other, in James of Vitry's words: 'This food is not bodily food but food of the soul; not of the flesh but of the heart'.[146]

This special food, Christ's very body, was a small and fragile object which needed protection from abuse and ridicule, from loss, breakage and decay, and a whole set of regulations developed to contol its making, keeping, disposal and reservation. Traditionally, theologians had described the symbolic nature of the host in tracts of the genre *De sacramentis* and *De sacramento altaris*, and such analysis still appears in a twelfth-century eucharistic tract containing questions based on I Cor. 11,20, like the following question about the host:

Why is the bread made only of wheat?
. . . Thirdly, the reason that bread is put in this sacrament, rather than any other food. This bread is made of nothing but wheat, patently because Christ compared himself to a grain of wheat; as he said: 'A grain of wheat remains a solitary grain unless it falls into the ground and dies'.[147]

Another answer to a similar question was given by Master Simon writing in 1145×60 at a cathedral or monastic school in the Low Countries, and it reflects a more up-to-date scholastic terminology:

The bread which is placed on the altar must be made of wheaten grain, to which the Lord wished to compare his body when he said: 'A grain of wheat' etc. If it is made of another grain it cannot be offered; what we have said makes sense by the change whereby in substance it is transformed into God's body.[148]

And slightly later Peter Comestor explained the meaning of the fraction of the host after consecration:

Christ's body is indeed the universal church, that is, the head and members are Christ and the believers. The two parts which remain distinct outside the chalice on the altar signify Christ and the saints who have already left this world and who live outside its sufferings, and together with its head, that is Christ, will be in glory . . .

---

[146] 'Hic enim cibus, non corporis sed anime, non carnis sed cordis', James of Vitry, 'De sacramentis', p. 214.

[147] 'Quare panis non est nisi de frumento? . . . [Tercio] importat, quare magis panis apponitur in hoc sacramento quam alius cibus. Quod autem panis iste non est nisi de frumento, patens est ratio, quoniam Christus comparavit se grano frumenti, ut ait: "Nisi granum frumenti cadens in terram mortuum fuerit", ipsum solum manet', 'Tractatus de sacramento Eucharistie' (on John 12,24), II, q. 3 in Boeren (1978), p. 198.

[148] 'Panis qui in altari ponitur ex grano triticeo debet fieri, cui Dominus corpus suum voluit comparare cum ait: 'Nisi granum frumenti cadens' etc. . . . . De alio grano si fuerit, non est offerendus; hec illa quam diximus, nobis incomprehensibili commutatione substantie eius corpus dominicum commutatur', *Master Simon*, pp. 37–8.

And the third part, which is put in the chalice, signifies those who so far live in this suffering, until they pass from this life . . .[149]

These requirements were laid down in diocesan legislation.[150] The synodal of Western France of 1216×19 required that the host be whole and form a full circle (see figures 1 and 2).[151] Every aspect of the host's appearance was important. In 1350 William Russell, bishop of Sodor in the Isle of Man, explained the symbolism of the host's features:

The wheaten host should be round and whole and without blemish, like the lamb without a blemish who has not had a bone removed from it. Hence the verse: Christ's host should be clean, wheaten, thin, not large, round, unleavened. It is inscribed, not cooked in water but baked in fire.[152]

And the manual for parish priests *Manipulus curatorum* of 1333 stressed that no corn but wheat would do for the preparation of the host:

I say, therefore, of wheat, because the mass cannot be celebrated in any other type of bread such as rye-bread or barley-bread or bread of any other grain but wheat.[153]

The theologian Hildegard of Bingen (1098–1179) connects Mary's purity with the nature of corn, wheat being the strongest and finest of all crops, having no sap or pith in its stalks.[154] In the next century James of Vitry put it more simply, 'Only that which is of grain will be transubstantiated'.[155] So the host was to be white, round, thin and was usually inscribed with a cross, the letters IHS, and from the twelfth century, a crucifixion scene or the lamb of God.[156] Graffiti in Chippen-

---

[149] 'Corpus enim Christi universa est ecclesia, scilicet caput cum membris, id est Christus et fideles. Due igitur partes que sunt extra calicem seorsum in altari significant Christum et sanctos qui de hac vita iam egressi sunt et extra passiones huius seculi cum capite suo, id est Christo, gloriantur . . . Tercia vero pars qui in calice ponitur, significat eos qui adhuc vivunt in passione hac, donec et ipsi ab hac vita transeat . . .', in appendix to Master Simon's, *De sacramentis*, p. 57*.

[150] See for example the French synodal statutes like those of Nîmes, Arles and Béziers of 1252: 'Hostias autem de alio quam de puro et mundo et electo grano frumenti fieri prohibemus', *Statuts synodaux* II, c. 73, p. 326.

[151] 'Quod hostia sit integra et integrum habeat circulum', *Statuts synodaux* I, c. 6, p. 142.

[152] 'Hostia de frumento sit rotunda et integra et sine macula, quia agnus extitit sine macula, et os non fuit comminutum ex eo. Unde versus: candida, triticea, tenuis, non magna, rotunda, expers fermenti non mista, sit hostia Christi. Inscribatur aqua, non cocta sed igne sit assa', *Concilia* III, c. 2, p. 11.

[153] 'Dico etiam de tritico, quia in alio pane sicut in pane de siligine vel ordeo de quocumque alio grano nisi de tritico non posset celebrari missa', *Manipulus curatorum*, fol. xx.r.

[154] Newman (1987), pp. 192–4.

[155] 'Id solum quod de frumento est transubstantiatur', James of Vitry, 'De sacramentis', p. 219.

[156] Jungmann (1955), II, pp. 381–2.

1  Elevation of the host; initial of the Corpus Christi mass

2 Communion to the laity; decoration of the Corpus Christi mass

ham Church (Cambridgeshire) show seven simple circles with a cross – seven hosts.[157]

The baking of hosts was a ritualised procedure in religious houses, accompanied by recitations of psalms throughout the process of collection, washing and drying of the grains, the milling, mixing with water, and baking of the host. Lanfranc's *Constitutions*, which record the rituals of Cluniac daily life, describe it in the section about the sacrist's duties.[158] They stress the utmost care required, the choice of reliable and properly vested servants, of a clean table, total silence but for the recitation of psalms. The fire for baking was to be quiet and controlled; in his large and varied donation to Daventry Priory (Northamptonshire) of 1190×1200 Walter FitzHerbert also granted twenty-four burdens of firewood for the use of the sacrist in baking hosts.[159] Details of the baking were considered by William of Blois, bishop of Worcester in 1229:

The most diligent care must be taken over the materials used in the sacrament, so that the hosts [*oblate*] be made of pure wheaten grain. The ministers of the church should be dressed in surplices and sit in a proper place while they make the hosts. The instrument in which the hosts are roasted should be coated with wax, not with oil or any other fat. Those hosts of the appropriate colour and roundness are to be offered to the table of the altar.[160]

They were thus to be baked in a vessel coated with wax, rather than oil or fat which might fry them. The provision of hosts in parishes was regulated through diverse agreements between rector, vicar and parishioners. The confirmation of the vicarage at Tetlebury in the diocese of Worcester in 1374 obliged the vicar Nicholas Alyn to provide the celebrants and servers, a lamp, oil and candles for the mass, while the parishioners provided the corn for making Easter hosts.[161] In 1403 Bishop Clifford of Worcester ordered the vicar of Kidderminster to provide for a deacon, a chaplain, and the bread and wine for Easter

---

[157] Pritchard (1967), p. 26, fig. 36.

[158] Lanfranc, *Constitutions*, pp. 83–5; Hirn (1958), p. 90.

[159] Baker (1822), I, p. 310.

[160] 'Circa species itaque que ad idem sacramentum exiguntur, cura diligentior adhibenda est ut scilicet oblate de puro grano frumenti fiant. Ministri ecclesie induti suppelliciis in loco honesto sedeant quando oblatas faciunt. Instrumentum in quo oblate coquende sunt cera tantum lineatur, non oleo vel alio sagimine; oblate honestum candorem et decentem rotunditatem habentes supra mensam altaris offerantur', *CS* II, I, c. I, p. 170. See also James of Vitry, 'De sacramentis', p. 219.

[161] *Reg. Worc. Vac.* p. 326. For a bequest providing Easter wafers from four bushels of wheat see the Chantry Certificate of Heston church, *London and Middlesex chantry certificates*, no. 187, p. 76.

communion, as well as for the use of priests.[162] A parish priest's work-book of the fifteenth century included a recipe for the baking of hosts.[163] Recesses in the walls of some parish churches may have been baking areas; some have flutes from which smoke would have escaped.[164] The recess could be in the chancel wall or, as in Snettisham (Norfolk), in the south-west corner of the church, and these blackened areas would have also served for other liturgical functions such as the burning of old vestments.

Even crumbs of the host were precious and were saved from falling out of the mouths of communicants by the introduction of the hous-ling-cloth which was held under the chins of recipients (see figure 2). This seems to have been a particularly English custom; an illustration showing a row of boys at communion in Queen Mary's psalter of *c*.1310–20 has a long housling-cloth held under their chins,[165] and the fifteenth century octagonal fonts at All Saints', Great Glenham, and St Mary's, Woodford, both in Suffolk, include communion scenes where a man and a woman hold a cloth under their chins while kneeling for communion.[166] The inventory of St Mary's, Scarborough, lists six 'howselyng towell longis',[167] and the inventory of Rotherfield (Sussex) had in 1509 '2 houslyng towells'.[168]

Consecrated hosts were to be kept in a manner which emphasised their fundamental difference from any other artifact in or outside theee church. They were to be consumed only by priests, servers, and on special occasions, like Easter, by the communicating laity, and were occasionally taken out on visitations of the sick, for some healing and blessing *functiones sacrae*, and for use in the Easter sepulchre.[169] Bishop Walpole of Ely ordained the form and explained the reason for careful reservation clearly in 1300:

We ordain that henceforth the pyx with Christ's body and the chrismatory containing the oil for the sick be placed in the new chapel situated near the old bell-tower, and there it should be kept respectfully under the safe custody of keys, so that day and night the secular priests who will be in charge of administration of

---

[162] *Reg. Clifford*, no. 231, p. 134. These stipulations were, of course, not always observed, and Bishop Nykke's visitation of Wymondham abbey found bread and wine of poor quality, *Wymondham*, p. 14.

[163] In a document discovered by Dr D. M. Owen on the fly-leaves of CUL Ll 2.2, and showed to me by her.

[164] Crowley and Bloxham (1967).

[165] BL Royal B vii 2, fol. 207v.

[166] Fryer (1902), p. 51.

[167] *Scarborough, St Mary*, p. 66.

[168] *Rotherfield*, p. 30.

[169] These will be discussed below, pp. 294–7, 340–1.

sacraments at the time, will be able to lay hands on them easily, and to fulfil their duties without any danger.[170]

Tracts on the mass and synodal legislation limited the period of reservation of a consecrated host to seven days, and on the eighth it was to be replaced by fresh hosts.[171] The Westminster council of 1200 stipulated that the host taken to the sick 'be renewed every Sunday',[172] and similarly other English synods like Canterbury council of 1213×14 which explains how the old hosts are to be disposed:

That the eucharist be reserved in a clean pyx, and consecrated hosts be kept for seven days, and be renewed every week on Sunday, so that after the reception of the newly consecrated host and before the reception of the Lord's blood, the reserved hosts be consumed by the celebrant.[173]

Similarly, in the diocese of Bordeaux in 1234:

And care should be taken that the sacrament of the Lord's body should be reserved for no longer than eight days.[174]

At the Lambeth Council of 1281 Archbishop Pecham reminded the gathering of the respect due to the eucharist and of the need for renewal of the hosts every Sunday lest the species contained be corrupted.[175] Neglected hosts might reach the state of those described by the archbishop of Geneva in his visitation of 1443–5: 'Christ's body . . . is kept in great disgrace, scattered uselessly in the pyx among dust and worms and without a corporal.'[176] Those hosts awaiting consecration were also to be carefully kept. The bishop of Bordeaux warned against neglect of

---

[170] '. . . precipimus ut pixis cum corpore Christi et chrismatorium cum oleo infirmorum in capella nova, iuxta vetus campanile situata, de cetero reponantur, et ibidem sub clavium tuta custodia honorifice conserventur, ut sic tam de die quam de nocte presbiteri seculares qui pro tempore curam gerent de sacramentis huiusmodi ministrandis facilius manus suas apponere ad eamdem [possint] et omnia facere que incumbent absque omni periculo', *Ely chapter ordinances*, c. 37, p. 22.

[171] For other examples see Braun (1924), II, p. 574.

[172] 'Renovetur quoque hostia ipsa singulis dominicis diebus', *CS* I, 2, p. 1061.

[173] 'Quod eucharistia in munda pixide conservatur, nec ultra vii dies serventur hostie consecrate, post solutum scilicet interdictum, set septimana qualibet in die dominicis innoventur, ita quod post perceptionem consecrate recenter hostie ante sumptionem sanguinis dominici, reservate hostie a missam celebrante sumantur', *CS* II, 1, c. 14, p. 27; also the Worcester statutes of 1240, *CS* II, 1, c. 3, p. 299. For similar Italian legislation see the synod of Cingoli, of the Forentine province in 1327, *Synodal law in Florence*, pp. 57–8.

[174] 'Sacramentum corporis domini reservetur nec ultra octo dies aliquatenus observetur', *Statuts synodaux* II, c. 38, p. 62.

[175] 'Corrumpantur species continentes', *CS* II, 2, c. 1, p. 894; Peckham (1934), pp. 29–30, 41.

[176] 'Corpus Christi . . . in frustra dispersum in pisside, macilentum, inter pulveres et inter vermes et sine corporali cum omni ignominia teneri', in the description of St Sixtus' church, Vitelley, Binz (1973), p. 210.

these hosts in 1234 'lest they be eaten by wood-worm', and they were to be renewed every month.[177]

Early medieval custom was to keep the hosts on a paten in the vestry. A gift to Abingdon Abbey of 1100×1135 was described as 'a vessel in the shape of a paten in which the host is carried to the refectory for holy communion'.[178] From the late twelfth and by the thirteenth century it is clear that the appropriate mode of keeping was in lockable vessels, both before and after consecration. Following the recommendations of the Fourth Lateran Council of 1215 Bishop William of Blois ordered in the statutes of Worcester Council II of 1229 that churches should have:

Two pyxes, one of silver or ivory or enamel (Limoges work) or some other suitable pyx, in which the hosts are to be kept, and are reserved in due safety in locked-custody.[179]

They were contained in a pyx, a vessel made of precious metal which often had an inner chamber made of ivory or copper and in which such holy substances as oil and chrism were reserved.[180] Pyxes were meant to be closed and with a lock; the requirements of Bishop Quivil of Exeter in 1287 were: 'The eucharist pyx should be of silver or at least of ivory with a lock'.[181] The provision of such costly vessels was made the responsibility of parishioners. In 1240 Archbishop Walter Gray of York defined the parishioners duty to provide: 'Chalice, missal . . . corporal . . . decent pyx for Christ's body'.[182] This was reiterated in synodal legislation and it was finally established in the so-called Statutes of Archbishop Pecham of 1279×92 that the parishioners' duty was to provide the chalice, the missal and vessels.[183] It was ordained at Exeter II in 1287, with recommendations as to the number and selection of the churchwardens.[184] When a daughter church was situated in an existing parish the parishioners were obliged to provide all the new vessels, as in Thiollaz near Geneva where the archbishop's visitation of

---

[177] *Statuts synodaux* III, c. 26, p. 56.
[178] 'Vasculum unum in modum patenae in quo hostiae deferuntur in refectorio pro communione sancta', *Chronicon monasterii de Abingdon* II, p. 151.
[179] 'Due pixides, una argentea vel eburnea vel de opere Lemovitico vel alia ydonea in qua hostie reserventur et sub fideli custodia clavi adhibita conserventur', *CS* II, 1, c. 2, p. 171.
[180] See some in *Age of chivalry*, nos. 118, 119, and in Collins (1972), p. 50, no. 7; p. 51, no. 8.
[181] 'Sit pixis argentea vel saltim eburnea ad eukaristiam cum serura', *CS* II, 2, c. 12, p. 1,006.
[182] 'Calix, missale . . . corporalis . . . pyxis pro corpore Christi honesta', *Reg. Bainbridge* I, pp. 371–2.
[183] 'Ut autem existant parochiana in singulis subsequentibus certiores, sciant et intelligant, et observent universi quod calix, missale, vestimentum ipsius ecclesie principale . . . osculatorium . . . ad ipsos parochianos pertinere', *CS* II, 2, c. 7, pp. 1122–3; *Reg. Peckham* III, pp. cxl–cxlii; Peckham (1934), p. 60.
[184] *CS* II, 2, c. 12, p. 1008.

1443 ordered them to produce a tabernacle for the host, two portable pyxes, one with a lantern and a bell for carrying the eucharist to the sick.[185]

So parishioners raised the funds for these collective and costly purchases, and selected churchwardens to manage the funds.[186] St Nicholas', Bristol, had a silver gilt box 'for godys body' in 1432,[187] and Bridgewater's inventory of 1447 recorded two cups of silver for the sacrament.[188] In the mid thirteenth century Highbridge Church had a pewter pyx, but a silver gilt chalice,[189] Tillingham had a gilt pyx and a silver chalice,[190] and St Pancras Church had a white silver chalice weighing 20s and a pewter vase without a lock (for the eucharist).[191] These expensive vessels were sometimes granted as a gift, like that made by William Briwere to Salisbury Cathedral in 1220 of 'a well-gilt silver cup with a silver crown . . . in which the eucharist is placed'.[192] The vessels were often decorated with a cross on top, like the one in Bassingbourn (Cambridgeshire) in the late fifteenth century,[193] but also with purely ornamental patterns like the silver gilt pyx decorated with trefoils and dragons' tongues in an early sixteenth century inventory from St Peter Mancroft, Norwich.[194] But the visitation of churches appropriated to St Paul's, London, of 1249×52, reveals some of the common faults found in the vessels: at Twyford and Westlea the pyxes lacked a lock,[195] Nostock parish had a chalice with no inner chamber,[196] and Pelham Fornell had an ivory pyx and inside it a small pewter chamber 'an altogether useless and cheap object',[197] while at Chiswick there was no pyx at all and the silver chalice was of low quality and tottered on one side.[198] Improper keeping could be seen as a serious offence to the consecrated species which were Christ's body. A story current within the Franciscan order told of St Francis' desire to have

---

[185] Binz (1973), p. 253. On visitation of the sick, see below, pp. 77–82.
[186] Mason (1976).
[187] Nichols (1881–2) II, p. 160.
[188] *Bridgewater* IV, pp. 38–40.
[189] *St Paul's churches*, p. 11.
[190] *Ibid*, p. 14.
[191] *Ibid*, p. 6.
[192] 'Cuppa argentea bene deaurata cum corona argentea . . . in qua reponitur eucharistia', in an entry in the list of ornaments kept by the treasurer in 1222, *Vetus registrum* II, p. 137; the record of the gift is on p. 13.
[193] *Bassingbourn*, p. 14. Bridgewater spent 2d in 1452/3 on a silver cross to be mounted on the pyx, *Bridgewater*, p. 65.
[194] *Norwich, St Peter Mancroft*, p. 164.
[195] *St Paul's churches*, pp. 5, 9.
[196] *Ibid*, pp. 22–3.
[197] 'Res nihil et vilis', *ibid*, p. 19.
[198] *Ibid*, p. 7. The synodal statutes of Cambrai of 1231×60 required the chalice be stable: 'et calix sit cum firmo pede non titubans', *Cambrai, Statuts synodaux*, p. 140.

friars distribute to all the order's provinces good metal boxes for their hosts, since these were all too often left scattered and neglected.[199]

By the late Middle Ages in England the pyx was often kept hanging over the altar, and sometimes was controlled by a set of pulleys,[200] and a fringed cloth such as was usually hung over it, known as 'a kerchief', survives from Hessett (Suffolk).[201] Churchwardens' accounts contain entries related to this manner of reservation: at Bridgewater 1½d were spent in 1386–7 'For a line for the hanging of the pyx with Christ's body'.[202] At Launceston (Cornwall) in 1461–2 the parish expenses incorporated in the stewards' accounts recorded 1d for a cord for hanging the body of Christ.[203] At All Saints', Derby, in 1465, there were two pyxes of silver gilt, one of which was to hang over the altar, the gift of Hugh Willoughby.[204] In St Edmund's and St Thomas' parish, Salisbury, 3d were spent in 1491–2 on a cord to fasten the sacrament,[205] and at St Andrew Hubbard, London, 10d were paid in 1494–5 for the making of a 'clothe for the pyx and a ryband thereto'.[206] Another cloth hanging over the pyx is recorded in 1508 at St Laurence, Reading, where 1d was paid for a 'carpyntors lyne to draw the black sarsenet before the canopy over the High Altar'.[207] In his will, which was proved in 1517, Thomas Awsten of London, bequeathed to his parish church 'a tache of silver and gilt for to make a howke for the pyx over the hygh alter ther'.[208]

Hanging the draped pyx above the altar was not the only arrangement for the reservation of hosts within the church, though it was the most common in England. The north walls of chancels often contain recesses, cupboards or aumbries, for keeping the sacrament and other sacred objects. The earliest surviving eucharistic cupboard-shrine is that of St Martin of Lennick, in Flanders. This late-thirteenth-century shrine has a trefoil arch at the top of the recess.[209] A fifteenth-century *armarium sacramenti* from the region is decorated with the scene of the

[199] *Scripta Leonis*, c. 80, pp. 227–9.
[200] Cox (1923), pp. 39–41.
[201] *Ibid*, pp. 41–2. For a later French example see the illumination at the beginning of the canon of the mass in the missal of the abbey of the Holy Trinity, Vendôme, of 1457, Municipal library Vendôme 16, fol. 161r.
[202] 'Pro j. funiculo ad pendendum pixidem cum corpore Christi', *Bridgewater* II, p. 191.
[203] *Launceston*, p. 141; see also 1466/7, p. 149.
[204] *Derby, All Saints*, pp. 157–8.
[205] *Salisbury, St Edmund and St Thomas*, p. 40.
[206] *London, St Andrew Hubbard*, p. 399. At Tintinhull (Somerset) in 1507 a 'frenge with bottyns and tassels to a kerchew to hang over the sakerment' cost 2s 8d, *Tintinhull*, p. 198.
[207] Cox (1923), p. 91 also another mention in 1511. At Rotherfield (Sussex) the inventory boasted in 1511 'a canopy with a peace of grene silk aboute the pix', *Rotherfield*, p. 27.
[208] *London consistory court wills*, no. 65, p. 38.
[209] Destrée (1930), p. 119.

washing of the feet and the Last Supper, appropriate in the eucharistic context, and these scenes were also shown in relief on a cupboard from Cortenaken in Brabant.[210] Another example, unusual in England, is in Rothersthorpe (Northamptonshire) where a door has survived; and Sutterton parish (Lincolnshire) recorded in 1517 12d as payment 'for making of an ambre or cupboard'.[211] Elaborate cupboards housing the eucharist developed particularly in the Low Countries, northern France and parts of Germany, while in southern Germany elaborate gothic towers were built in the later Middle Ages, filling at once the roles of pyx, ostensory and tabernacle.

The other eucharistic element, the wine, drew far less attention despite the fact that it was far more vulnerable to accidents of handling. This is related to the fact that by the twelfth century communicants received the eucharist in one element only. Wine was reserved for clerical communion and in religious houses, although there was some local variation. As consecrated wine was withdrawn it was replaced in many places by a sip of unconsecrated wine, for symbolic symmetry and easier swallowing of the host.

In treatment of the wine attention was paid to its colour and appearance, as in the case of the host. The Winchester council of 1070 stipulated that neither beer (*cervisia*) nor water should be used but instead a mixture of wine and water.[212] John Beleth's treatise on the mass explained its preparation:

On that day Christ's bood will be made of new wine, if it can be found, or at least a little be squeezed into a chalice from some ripe grapes, and the wine be blessed, and thus people shall communicate.[213]

The wine had to be fresh, otherwise vinegar would be consecrated in the chalice. It was important to retain the colour, flavour and general appearance of wine, and Honorius III described in a letter which became part of the decretal 'De materia eucharistie' the error of using wine which was too diluted:

A baleful abuse has developed in your parts, that a larger part of water than of wine

---

[210] *Ibid*, pp. 120–1.
[211] Anderson (1955), p. 48; *Sutterton*, p. 61.
[212] CS I, 2, p. 575: 'Quod sacrificium de cervisia vel sola aqua non fiat, sed solummodo de vino aqua mixto'.
[213] 'Ea die conficitur sanguis Christi de nouo uino, si inueniri possit, aut aliquantulum de matura uua in calice eliquatur saltem, et benedicuntur racemi et communicant inde homines', John Beleth, *Summa de ecclesiasticis officiis*, p. 280(c).

is placed in the sacrifice: while according to the Church's general and reasonable custom more wine than water should be put.[214]

The *Templum dei* of Robert Grosseteste noted the important aspects of the sacramental liquid which was to be mixed with water, but not too diluted: 'Wine that has not been spoilt, which has not turned sour', and 'pure water mixed with wine in which the wine none the less retains its character'.[215] In 1350 William Russell, bishop of Sodor (Isle of Man), stressed the preference for red wine over white wine and referred to the danger of corruption of the species:

And above all to seek and prevent that the wine which is used for celebration should be spoilt, or turned into wine-vinegar; and it is preferable to use red wine than white wine. The sacrament is well made in white wine, but not in wine-vinegar, because in it all the powers of the substance have been transformed, and the wine's power is lost. And a moderate quantity of water should be placed so that the wine be not absorbed into the water.[216]

The sacramental potential was located in the wine, and its transformation in any way would render a consecration over it useless, since transubstantiation would not take place.

### THE RITUAL: ELEVATION AND PARTICIPATION

A sacrament was designed out of the fruits of wheat and wine, carefully prepared, combined, and cared for, but it depended on the handling and words of a celebrant – the priest.[217] The priesthood and its life were designed as closely as the eucharist, since like it they supported the church's claim to exclusive and universal mediation of grace, of supernatural power. As the church came to be the articulator of hegemonic culture, of the symbolic order of the world, the place and role, edu-

---

[214] 'Perniciosus in tuis partibus inolevit abusus, videlicet, quod in majori quantitate de aqua ponitur in sacrificio quam de vino: cum secundum rationabilem consuetudinem Ecclesiae generalis plus in ipso sit de vino quam de aqua ponendum', Decretals of Gregory IX, Lib. 3, tit. 41, c. 13, *CIC* II, col 643.

[215] 'Vinum non corruptum, non acetosum, and 'aqua pura mixta uino in qua nichilominus uinum remaneat in sua specie', *Templum dei*, XVIII.1, p. 63. See also James of Vitry's section 'De materia eucharistie' in 'De sacramentis', pp. 221–4. Alexander of Hales on the need for water and wine for the sacramental blood. *IV Sent*. D. 11, c. 13, pp. 178–9. On the case of wine freezing in the chalice see *Rationale* lib. 4, c. 42, no. 11, p. 269.

[216] 'Et summopere praecaventes ne vinum cum quo celebratur, fit corruptum, vel in acetum commutatum, et quod potius fit rubrum quam album. In albo tamen bene conficitur sacramentum, et non de aceto, cum in aceto mutantur omnes substantiales vires et vinum vim amisit. Et aqua in tam modica quantitate apponatur, ut non vinum ab aqua sed aqua a vino absorbeatur', *Concilia* III, c. 2, p. 11.

[217] For some views of the priesthood as eucharistic celebrants in early Christianity see Brown (1988b), p. 144.

cation and privilege of the clergy, were reconceived. The clergy was
rethought as the carrier of the church's newly claimed and acquired
privileges and duties. *Libertas ecclesiae* could only be justified through
the visible fitting and effective nature of the clergy, which was to
embody an already fully fledged ideal of celibacy formulated in the
reformed monastic orders. Priests were seen as teachers but above all as
ritual performers of sacramental acts, those acts which tie the Christian
world to God through repeated, and reiterated procedures that only the
priests could perform.[218]

Mass could be celebrated and the eucharist could be carried to the
sick only by a priest.[219] Increasingly, limitation of celebration to one
mass a day, except on Christmas, was developing:

It is enough for a priest to celebrate mass once a day, since Christ suffered once, and
redeemed the whole world.[220]

And it was also increasingly necessary to claim that the mass had effect
*ex opere operato,* as a ritual which was effective independently from the
priest's character and virtue. Throughout the next centuries this regular
priestly celebration was used as an argument for infrequent communion by the laity, inasmuch as the priest communicated daily for all
Christians. Thus, the priest was separated from lay custom, creating a
link of dependence, as he was increasingly presented as Christ's mouth-
piece for the laity. Conversely, there was an assimilation of Christ the
priest into the officiating priest.[221]

Another issue which divided scholars was the value of masses for the
dead, which had such immediate pastoral ramifications. Early medieval
notions about the effects of the mass for the dead were further developed in the eleventh century.[222] Its importance was stressed by the
allegorical commentators on the mass such as Alger of Liège (c.1132),
and Renier of St Laurent (d.1182), later in the century.[223] Peter Lombard denied that the fruits of a mass could accrue to one person in
particular,[224] as did Huguccio (d.1210) in the next century.[225] But from

---

[218] Tellenbach (1959), pp. 126–37.
[219] An *exemplum* tells the story of a deacon who was punished for celebrating mass, *La
tabula exemplorum,* no. 177, pp. 48–9 and notes on p. 120.
[220] 'Sufficit sacerdoti unam in die una celebrare missam, quia Christus semel passus est, et
totum mundum redemit', *Decretum* part III, 'De consecratione' c. 53, *CIC* I, col. 1308.
[221] Morrison (1982), p. 134. See below, pp. 205–6.
[222] On early medieval attitudes, see Straw (1988), pp. 104–5.
[223] Le Goff (1984), pp. 165–73, 212.
[224] Peter Lombard, *De consecratione* c. 24, d. 5; Iserloh (1961), pp. 46–7; Le Goff (1984), pp.
148–9.
[225] Iserloh (1961), p. 48.

the late twelfth century the developing concept of purgatory provided a neat framework for integration of masses into penitential practice, promoted in pastoral care.[226] The mass itself offered moments for commemoration of the dead. Thirteenth-century rubrics directed the priest to say, while holding the host over the chalice, 'gracias agimus tibi', offering thanks for the beatified, for those in purgatory, as for the living. An early-sixteenth-century guide to the mass directed the priest to hold two memories in his mind: 'In the furst he prayeid for the qwyke, In the secund for the deide.'[227] But these were not controversial aspects; more difficult were the masses directed at particular souls.[228] Lollard criticism rejected the idea of purgatory, and of the prayers and masses which were supposed to alleviate suffering there: 'the mass profiteth not the souls that are in purgatory'.[229] Rather, they were seen as a product of clerical corruption, a means of extracting payments from the laity.

By the twelfth century, with the propagation of the Church's new claims which attained a measure of consensus (not without contest) in every European kingdom, a process of normalisation and application of the Church's privileges and duties was at work. If clerical appointments were to be more independent of secular involvement, then a system of supervision and punishment was necessary in the form of a parochial network embedded within diocesan administration; if the clergy were granted legal autonomy then ecclesiastical courts needed to be developed to enforce the law; if priests were to be loyal to the church alone, then their livelihood should be provided sufficiently and regulated; and if claims were to be made about their sacramental efficacy, then they must possess some knowledge which set them apart. So attempts began to try and turn the clergy into an international bureaucracy, a body which would transcend national, regional, local connections, and relate to a supra-local centre, Rome. The clergy was increasingly set apart in life-style, duties, clothing, training, language, from its 'community', and drew its authority from a central source.[230] *Vita clericorum* was much discussed in canon law with clearer ideas about duties, rights, expectations, and their enforcement. The transformation was spectacular, if neither complete nor free from difficulties.

The drive towards uniformity in ritual action was part of this re-

---

[226] Le Goff (1984), pp. 213–20, 289–95.
[227] The attribution to Langforde is a mistake, this is William Bonde's *Pilgrimage to perfection*, in *Tracts on the mass*, p. 24.
[228] Iserloh (1961), pp. 55–8, 60; Bossy (1973), pp. 136–8.
[229] Hudson (1988b), p. 310.
[230] Goering (1982), pp. 328–9.

thinking. The priest was an essential link in the sacramental world-view; he was, therefore, the subject of guidance, teaching and grooming. What was desired and necessary was that every priest, in every parish, at every altar, during every mass, should encapsulate the church's message of mediation, in a way that was recognisable, uniform, and supportive of sacramental claims. This meant that the mass was designed as a ritual in which the words of consecration, said at every altar, by every priest, conjured the same very body of God, without fail.

This was an ambitious programme. Treatises were written to help and teach the new design of the ritual. Treatises on the mass were not a new genre – from Carolingian times the *Expositio missae* was the framework in which exegesis on the text and its symbolic interpretation were conducted.[231] These works aimed to decipher and read meaning into the mass, particularly for monastic use. They were complemented by the *Ordo missae* which was a running commentary on the rubrics, which became very popular in the eleventh and especially in the twelfth century.[232] It is within this genre that systematic interpretation of the mass was expounded and related to the ritual performance, in the twelfth-century works of Rupert of Deutz (d.1135) who stressed the narrative of Christ's life, of William of St Thierry (d.1148) who emphasised spiritual reception in the mass, and in John Beleth's *Summa* which imbued the mass with a neo-platonic allegorical reading.[233] Eucharistic tracts were often sections of a larger work on all seven sacraments, of the type *Summa de sacramentis* written by almost every Parisian master, like those of Hugh of St Victor, Peter Comestor and Peter the Chanter, and in them the eucharist was accorded special attention.[234] Some works treated the sacrament separately, like William of Auvergne's *De sacramento altaris*. New formulations could be contained within them as they were created within the most advanced theological milieu: thus Peter the Chanter could claim, for the first time, that eucharistic substance had nothing at all to do with the accidents.[235] They also reflected current interests such as the refutation

---

[231] Reynolds (1983), esp. pp. 59–61.
[232] White (1974), pp. 4–32.
[233] *Ibid*, pp. 32–5, 43.
[234] On *summae*, see Teetaert (1930) and Macy (1984), pp. 159, 172, 201, 229, and listing of their works in the bibliography.
[235] 'Quinimmo, cum panis naturaliter sit confortatiuus et uinum exhilaratiuum, hec uidentur etiam post transsubstantiationem remansisse . . . et sicut accidentia exteriora . . . dicuntur a mutlis in nullo esse subiecto', Peter the Chanter, *Summa de sacramentis* I, c. 55, p. 134, see Boeren (1978), p. 186. See also Grosseteste's formulation which was later taken up by Wyclif, Southern (1986), pp. 302, 326.

of objection made against the eucharist by heretics and others, incorporated into James of Vitry's tract.[236]

The classic in this genre, and the treatise with the most enduring
influence was undoubtedly the *De mysteriis missae* written by Lothar
of Segni, the future Innocent III, *c*.1195. The treatise set out to reveal
the encoded meanings of the mass since 'all these divine matters are full
of mysteries', and it is an original interpretation of the four elements of
the mass which we have already encountered: the persons, the things,
the words, and the works (acts), which provide the work's structure.[237]
Lothar gave fresh meaning to an old genre and in scholastic method
analysed the mass by its constituent parts: the types of prayers, the
readings, and the flow of sacramental action, and this structure was
amenable to pastoral use. By incorporating contemporary thinking on
the mass within the traditional allegorical framework, it provided the
basis for future manuals, and this was used as the basis for many other
summaries, simplifications and translations destined to reach the lower
clergy. It was a major influence on the late-thirteenth-century classic of
the genre, the *Rationale divinorum officiorum* which was written by
William Durandus (1230–96), bishop of Mende *c*.1289.[238] Still, other
approaches to the mass coexisted with it; Albert the Great's rarefied
taste is revealed in his *De sacrificio missae* of 1270 which was speculative, moral and almost mystical in tone.[239]

Having shaped a ritual in which Christ's body was sacramentally
made present through the words of a priest, theologians continued to
weigh the new design and its implications, and to convey the new ideas
of transubstantiation and of ritual conformity in the genre of mass
commentaries. The presence of pastoral considerations in theological
formulations is evident in a fundamental eucharistic issue hotly discussed and settled only at the very end of the twelfth century: the
decision on the moment of consecration. Now bread, now God, the
host showed little change; when did it happen, and how was this
knowledge to be conveyed?[240] Again we witness early and vaguer
formulations giving way to scrutinised and closely considered ones: the
mid-twelfth-century version 'Transubstantiation occurs by the power

---

[236] James of Vitry, 'De sacramentis', pp. 230–1.
[237] Wright (1977), pp. 295–6.
[238] White (1974), pp. 42, 48–9. Urban IV quoted from Innocent III's work in the bull
*Transiturus* of 1264 which instituted the feast of Corpus Christi, Franceschini (1965),
lines 49–61, p. 236, from *PL* 217, col. 885.
[239] White (1974), pp. 43–4.
[240] See solutions in cases when consecrated hosts could not be distinguished from consecrated ones, offered in the 1252 statutes of the dioceses of Nîmes, Arles and Béziers,
*Statuts synodaux* II, c. 76, p. 330.

of the words' (*ex virtute verborum fit transsubstantiatio*) accepted by
Peter the Chanter, could no longer do in the face of meticulous
eucharistic design. Christ's words which had become the priest's words
of consecration were uttered in two separate parts, a blessing of the
bread and then a blessing of the wine, and each was accompanied by a
gesture. The moment was all-important; before it, gazing and adoring
matter was tantamount to idolatry,[241] after it, spiritual gazing could
convey great benefits. In their heightened awareness of the pastoral
implications of their decisions, theologians shifted in their consensus
from the view of Peter the Chanter that only after all was said and done
was Christ's body present, to one which held that already after the first
consecration, over the bread, Christ was fully present.[242] The former
view, based on Peter Comestor's words earlier in the century, 'He said
that when all is said, all is done',[243] was more in keeping with the
biblical spirit and was accepted by Lothar of Segni in his *De mysteriis
missae*: 'At the utterance of the words *Hic est sanguis meus,* the wine
changes into blood.[244] But by the end of the century the great practical
difficulties with such a position became evident: was Christ ever
present as body without blood? – a cadaver? – and what was the nature
of the consecrated bread if a priest fell ill or died between the two
consecrations? Peter of Poitiers clearly expressed the new view, that
even after one consecration all was done, and the body was full in flesh
and blood, the historic body which suffered on the cross.[245] Thus the
synod of Paris of 1204×5 resolved the ambiguities by recommending
clearly that if a priest fell ill after the first consecration another priest
could continue at *Simili modo*, the consecration of the wine, and not say
a redundant consecration over the transformed bread.[246]

This formulation on the moment of the consecration gained support
from another idea which developed some decades earlier, that of
concomitance, which, when applied to the eucharist, meant that
Christ's flesh and blood, were together present in every bit of sacramental matter.[247] The custom of communion in one species depended
on this idea, without which communion would have been robbed of its

---

[241] See on this Alexander of Hales, *IV Sent* lib. III d. 9, q. 6, a. 7, p. 107.
[242] Kennedy (1944). On the continuing support for Peter the Chanter's view see Gerald of
Wales, *Gemma ecclesiastica* II, p. 124.
[243] 'Dicebat manducator quod quando totum dictum est, totum factum est', Gy (1980b), pp.
224–5.
[244] 'Ad prolationem istorum verborum *Hic est sanguis meus*, vinum mutatur in sanguinem',
Lothar of Segni (Innocent III), 'De sacro altaris mysterio', *PL* 217, col. 868.
[245] In his *Sentences*, Kennedy (1944), pp. 126–8.
[246] *Statuts synodaux* I, c. 72, p. 78. But this was not uniform, in the customs of the West of
France the priest is directed to start at the beginning, at *Te igitur, ibid*, c. 48, p. 142.
[247] See below, pp. 70–2.

meaning. So having settled the question of place – in every piece – and of time – after the first consecration – a high point of the ritual was created, marking the point at which God came into presence, to be addressed, gazed upon, supplicated, experienced.

A gesture of elevation came to mark the moment of consecration, and to offer its meaning to the audience (figures 1, 7, 9, 19). A number of explanations for the development of an emphatic gesture in the late twelfth century have been proposed; that it was a response to popular demands to see God,[248] that it was a didactic gesture against heretical claims,[249] or that it was the necessary concomitant of the theological decision on the moment of transubstantiation being after the first consecration.[250] What is beyond doubt is that every aspect of the eucharist in its pastoral setting was of great importance to the thinkers who discussed, designed, and celebrated the eucharist. Those who debated in the schools, were later to promulgate their views in diocese or province, like Maurice of Sully (d.1196), or to fight heresy, like James of Vitry. By the late twelfth century a gesture was introduced for the specific showing of Christ's body. The earliest explicit text about it is one of the statutes of the synod of Paris of 1198×1203 under Bishop Odo of Sully:

It is ordained to priests that, when they begin the canon of the mass, at *Qui pridie*, holding the host, they should not immediately raise it too high so that it can be seen by the people; rather, only keep it in front of their chests while they say *hoc est corpus meum* and then they should elevate it so that it can be seen by all.[251]

Then followed a small elevation after the consecration of the chalice.

The elevation of the chalice did create some disagreement. The teaching on concomitance really meant that by gazing at one species one was in fact viewing the whole body, veiled under the accidents of the host. Yet the impulse towards ritual symmetry meant that at least those designing the mass insisted on the parity of elevations, even if the parity of consecrations had been relinquished. The chalice was to be elevated though its contents could not be seen, and despite the fact that this was dangerous and open to spilling and accidental loss. After discussing and accepting the reasons for consecration over both the bread and the wine, Durandus goes on to conclude, in line with the

---

[248] Dumoutet (1940) and for different trends see in Brooke (1971), pp. 180–1.
[249] Grant (1940).
[250] Kennedy (1944).
[251] 'Praecipitur presbyteris ut, cum in canone misse inceperint "Qui pridie", tenentes hostiam, ne elevent eam statim nimis alte, ita quod videri possit a populo, sed quasi ante pectus detineant donec dixerint "Hoc est corpus meum" et tunc elevent eam ita quod possit ab omnibus videri', *Statuts synodaux* I, c. 80, p. 82.

drive for symmetry of design and respect for scripture, that 'For these reasons, although the blood cannot be seen, the elevation of the chalice is not superfluous,[252] and liturgists insisted on this in missal rubrics.[253] But some orders totally discarded anything but a slight raising of the chalice, and the Cistercian order reintroduced it in 1444 for those who 'clare valeant respicere et eorum devotionem augere'.[254] The danger posed by elevating a chalice full of Christ's blood was mentioned by Durandus, and was discussed in the chapter of St Albans' abbey in 1429:

It has been decided in this solemn chapter, that the chalice should be raised at the mass by all [monks], except for those weighed down by age or infirmity, who cannot elevate the chalice as is the custom of priests.[255]

Those who might trip or swoon would not practice the elevation of the chalice, just as the secular clergy did not. So the type of danger inherent in protecting a precious liquid which gradually removed the wine from lay communion, also limited its integration into the ritual of the mass. And the elevation of the chalice never captured the imagination as a symbol of the sacrament in the iconography of the mass, as the elevation of the host did.

Although the full discussion of the elevation took place in Paris,[256] some movement towards raising the consecrated host is evident even earlier in the century and elsewhere.[257] Its discussion continued in the thirteenth century,[258] and by mid-century it was a feature of missal rubrics. Its entry into the Roman missal was mediated through the liturgical books of the new orders, the Franciscan missal of 1243, and the Dominican missal of 1256.[259] The former reads, for example:

*Hoc est corpus meum* and as the Lord's body is adored, he raises it reverently with a moderate inclination so that all those surrounding can see it. Then he puts it back in its place.[260]

---

[252] 'Propter easdem quoque causas, calicis elevatio, licet sanguis videri non possit, superflua non est', *Rationale* lib. 5, c. 41, nos. 47–51, pp. 264–5, and no. 52, p. 265.

[253] *Le Cérémonial papal I: du* XIIIe *siècle*, pp. 122–3; see Vatican SMM 52, fol. 142r.

[254] *Statuta* IV, 351.

[255] 'In hoc vero capitulo solemni diffinitum est, quod ad missas ab omnibus potentibus calix elevetur, nisi hii qui senio vel debilitate depressi non calicem, more saecularium, elevare poterunt', *St Albans chronicle* I, p. 40.

[256] On the predominance of Paris as an intellectual centre see Furruolo (1985), pp. 11–26.

[257] Dumoutet (1926), pp. 46–8.

[258] See for example William of Middleton, *Opus super missam*, p. 50.

[259] Van Dijk (1963), II, p. 11.

[260] '*Hoc est corpus meum* Et adorato corpore domini cum mediocri inclinatione elevat illud reverenter ita quod circumstantibus possit videri. Postea ponit in loco suo', *Le Cérémonial papal I: du* XIIIe *siècle*, p. 120.

The elevation was disseminated through the usual channels of legislation and instruction. The statutes of an English diocese of 1222×5 demanded that parishioners kneel and join hands at that moment; they were to venerate by looking and bowing:

And this should particularly be done at the time of the consecration at the elevation of the host, when bread is transubstantiated into the real body of Christ.[261]

The statutes of Coventry of 1224×37 stress the importance of the moment as an encounter with God:

And now we can say that this is our God, and no other can compare with him, he is seen here on earth everyday when he is elevated by the hands of the priest, and comes into the company of men.[262]

In 1287 Bishop Quivil of Exeter mentions the question of visibility emphasised by the Parisian statute, and the fulfilment of transubstantiation after the first consecration:

Since it is by the words *Hoc est corpus meum* and not by others that the bread is transubstantiated into the body, the priest should not elevate the host beforehand . . . And the host is thus raised high so that it can be contemplated by all surrounding believers. And by this the devotion of believers is excited, and an increase in their faith is effected.

And the laity were to be exhorted that during the elevation:

Not only should they bow with respect but kneel and adore their creator with all devotion and reverence.[263]

The canons of Lincoln Cathedral were expected to stay in their seats throughout the canon of the mass and until the *Pater noster,* except 'When they halt at the altar at the elevation of the host they should bow with respect.[264]

A centre of eucharistic ritual action, and a core for the expression, testing and participation in eucharistic meaning was thus created. In the

---

[261] 'Et hoc maxime fiat tempore consecrationis in elevatione ostie, quando panis in verum corpus Christi transsubstantiatur . . .', *CS* II, 1, c. 19, p. 143.

[262] 'Nunc autem possumus dicere quod hic est deus noster, et non estimabitur alius adversus eum, hic in terris cotidie videtur dum per manus sacerdotum elevatur, cum hominibus conversatur . . .', *CS* II, 1, c. 3, p. 210.

[263] 'Quia vero per hec verba: "Hoc est enim corpus meum", et non per alia, panis transsubstantiatur in corpus, prius hostiam non levet sacredos . . . Hostia autem ita levetur in altum ut a fidelibus circumstantibus valeat intueri. Per hoc etenim fidelium devotio excitatur et fidei meritum suscipit incrementum', 'nedum reverenter se inclinent sed genua flectant et creatorem suum adorent omni devotione et reverentia . . .', *CS* II, 2, c. 4, p. 990.

[264] 'Dum tamen erigant se in elevatione hostiae ad altare se reverenter inclinent', *Statutes of Lincoln* III, p. 152.

words of Durandus' *Rationale* the elevation was an efficacious moment
for supplication:

*Hoc est corpus meum* the priest raises Christ's body first, so that all those standing
there will see and petition for all that is necessary for salvation.[265]

The elevation's emblematic value was also potent in relation to clerical
office, and it was expressed in the myriad representations of the mass at
that very moment, with the priest standing at the altar, in profile or
from the rear, wearing a crossed chasuble, and raising the white round
object that was the host-God. From the rear we capture the lay person's
view from the chancel, as in Rogier van der Weyden's famous 'Altarpiece of the Seven Sacraments' of the 1450s, with the elevation at the
centre of the composition, and a ribbon inscribed with the words 'Hoc
est corpus meum' signalling the moment of the elevation.[266]

At the elevation all senses were called into play. Bells pealed, incense
was burnt, candles were lit, hands were clasped, supplications were
mouthed. The regulation of these audio-visual effects operated through
the system of diocesan legislation.[267] William of Seignelay, bishop of
Paris (1219–24), repeating earlier statutes, explained the importance of
the peal of bells in announcing the consecration throughout a parish:

At that elevation, or just before it, a bell should be rung, as has been previously
decreed and thus the minds of believers will be turned towards prayer.[268]

The statutes of Coventry of 1224×37 describe the ringing of bells as
heralding the moment:

And we therefore ordain that at the elevation, when it is finally raised up high, the
bell will first sound, to be like a gentle trumpet announcing the arrival of a judge,
indeed of the saviour.[269]

Similar judgements were made by the bishop of Bordeaux in 1234,[270]
and by William Cantilupe, Bishop of Worcester in 1240:

---

[265] 'Sane dictis verbis illis: *Hoc est corpus meum* sacerdos elevat corpus Christi. Primo ut
cunctis adstantes videant, et petant quod proficit ad salutem . . . Secundo, ad notandum
quod non est aliud dignum sacramentum . . . Tertio, . . . signat Christum verum panem',
*Rationale* lib. 4, c. 41, no. 51, p. 265.

[266] Antwerp, Royal Museum. Lane (1984), pp. 82–4.

[267] On corporals and other clothes around the eucharist and the altar see Franz (1963), pp.
87–92.

[268] 'In ipsa elevatione vel paulo ante, campana pulsetur, sicut alias fuit statutum, et sic mentes
fidelium ab oratione excitentur', *Statuts synodaux* I, c. 15, p. 101.

[269] 'Unde precipimus quod in elevatione eucharistie quando ultimo elevatur et magis in
altum, tunc primo sonet campanella, que sit modica tuba denuntians adventum judicis,
immo salvatoris . . .', *CS* II, 1, c. 3, p. 210.

[270] 'Campana vero specialis habeatur que in elevatione corporis Christi pulcetur [sic] vel
[pulsant] ipsam campanam ecclesie', *Statuts synodaux* II, c. 35, p. 62.

When during the celebration of mass the Lord's body is raised high by the hands of priests, a bell should be rung and thus arouse devotion in the sluggish.[271]

A small sacring-bell marked the moment within the church. In 1287 Bishop Quivil of Exeter ordered the ringing of a small bell immediately before, and three peals of a great bell during the elevation:

They will be initially excited by the sound of the small bell, and then in the elevation the [large] bell should ring thrice.[272]

At the close of the century Durandus describes the importance of bells not only in cheering believers, but in increasing devotion.[273] Synodal legislation was codified in the Lambeth council of 1281, and became part of the common stock of knowledge in the fifteenth century in Lyndwood's *Provinciale*.[274] The *Lay folks' mass book* of c.1378, a catechetical vernacular tract about the mass, instructed people to take their cue from the 'sacring-bell':

> þen tyme is nere of sakring,
> A litel belle men oyse to ring.[275]

Parish inventories and accounts record expenditure on bells and their maintenance.[276] In 1447 the parish of Thame had:

> a little bell at the High altar to ring sacring with
> a little bell hanging in the chancel by the choir door to
> ring sacring and another sacring bell.[277]

In 1457/8 Yeovil parish spent 1d on a bell-clapper 'serving for corpus Christi'.[278] Visual representations of the mass often include the bell as a requisite of the mass. The panels of octagonal fonts which often show a scene of the elevation depict it, like the font at Brooke (Norfolk) where an acolyte pulls the bell-rope, and at Badingham (Suffolk) and Marsham (Norfolk) where an acolyte holds the bell in his hands.[279]

Bell-ringing could inform and edify, but it could also cause distraction as people rushed towards the altar. Bishop Grandisson's ordinances for the collegiate church of St Mary Ottery in 1339 attempted to

---

[271] 'Cum autem in celebratione misse corpus domini per manus sacerdotum in altum erigitur, campanella pulsetur ut per hoc devotio torpentium excitetur', *CS* II, 1, c. 14, p. 299.
[272] 'Per campanelle pulsationem primitus excitentur, et in levatione ter tangatur campana maior', *CS* II, 2, c. 4, p. 990.
[273] *Rationale* lib. 4, c. 41, no. 53, p. 265; Duteuil (1961), p. 35.
[274] 'De celebracione missarum', *Provinciale* lib. III, cols. 226–41.
[275] *LFMB* Text B, lines 400–1, pp. 36–8. On the *LFMB*, see Hudson (1985); Hudson (1988a).
[276] See drawing of a sacring-bell in BL Royal 10 E IV, fol. 167[ra].
[277] *Thame*, p. 33.
[278] *Yeovil*, p. 139.
[279] Fryer (1902), *passim*, esp. pp. 22, 25–6.

control this behaviour by prohibiting the ringing of bells at private masses while the choir offices were taking place:

For which reason we prohibit that bells be rung at the elevation of the sacrament, so that those singing in the choir will not leave and turn themselves to see the sacrament, but attend properly to their office.[280]

When ringing sounded at the wrong moment, it could even be harmful. Bishop Nicholas Gellent of Angers reported after his visitation of 1272 that in many churches bells were rung *after* rather than *before* the elevation, thus failing to warn people of the impending moment of transformation.[281]

But the essence of the rite lay in seeing the host, and so candles were part of any scheme of veneration; bearing warmth and illumination into the dark chancels of medieval European churches, they were essential at the moment when the holiest appeared. Lighting was provided for illumination as long as consecrated hosts were kept in the church,[282] as well as for the duration of the mass, and additional lights were required during the elevation. In the late twelfth century Lothar of Segni recommended two candlesticks at the corners of the altar with a taper and a cross between them, and two additional lights to be lit before the altar during the elevation.[283] The statutes of an English diocese of 1222×5 required at least two lights during the mass: 'When the mass is celebrated two candels will be lit, or at least one with a torch.'[284] And the council of Exeter of 1287 ordered that at least one should be of beeswax:

And they will have at least two lights both for the honour of the sacrament and against the chance of accidental extinction, and one should always be of wax.[285]

[280] 'Quo casu prohibemus ne campanelle ad eleuacionem sacramenti pulsentur, quodque canentes in choro non exeant nec se diuertant ad uidendum sacramentum, sed deuote officio suo intendant', *The collegiate church of Ottery St Mary*, c. 6, p. 153.

[281] 'Vidimus post elevacionem dominici Corporis cum campana pulsari, cum hoc ante elevacionem predictam fieri debeat, ut corda fidelium ad veneracionem dominici Corporis excitentur', *Statuts synodaux* III, c. 1, pp. 112–14, at p. 112.

[282] See in the 1339 statutes of *The collegiate church of Ottery St Mary*, c. 2, p. 231; also in the synodal statutes of Bordeaux of 1234: '(corpus domini) et semper lucerna ad minus de nocte ardet coram ipso', *Statuts synodaux* II, c. 38, p. 62.

[283] Lothar of Segni, 'De mysteriis misae', *PL* 217, c. 811.

[284] 'Tempore quo missarum sollempnia peraguntur accendantur due candele vel una ad minus cum lampade', *CS* II, 1, c. 25, p. 144.

[285] 'Duo saltim luminaria habeantur tam ob reverentiam sacramenti quam extinctionis casum fortuitum, quorum semper alterum sit de cera', *CS* II, 2, c. 4, p. 990. A settlement of a dispute over a tenement in St Clement's, Candlewick St, London, in 1368, resolved that the mayor and aldermen should provide the church with wax torches on a number of occasions, including the elevation of Christ's body, *London assize of nuisance*, no. 544, pp. 136–7.

An ordinance of the Carthusians of Certosini of 1222×60 refers specifically to the need for lights at the elevation:

When the body of Christ cannot be seen because it is celebrated early in the day, the priest should have a well lit wax-taper behind him so that Christ's body will be visible in this area.[286]

By the end of the thirteenth century Durandus considered a lit altar to be an established custom.[287] But more importantly additional lighting enhanced and brightened the most important moment of the ritual.[288] So Bishop Quivil of Exeter and Bishop Woodlock of Winchester granted ten days' indulgence to those who held torches during the canon of the mass.[289]

A variety of arrangements were created for the provision of lighting, from provision by the laity, to incomes towards the expenditure, to the provision of torches and lights for the elevation. Around 1250 Hugh of Westwood granted the canons of Bushmead 12d *per annum* in rents from land for a variety of common lights and elevation lights, for the benefit of his wife's soul.[290] In 1325 a grant was made to the parish church of Rapallo near Genoa for 'ceriolum seu brandonum de cera quando corpus Christi levabitur'.[291] In an agreement of 1393 the stewards of the gild merchant of Bridgewater and their chantry priest stipulated that the latter should provide

Two torches which are to burn and illuminate every day during the elevation of Christ's body in the mass said for the Blessed Virgin in the said choir, weighing 16 lb.[292]

John Weston, a citizen and merchant of London, left in his will of 1407 a yearly income of 8s for the sustenance of two wax torches on Sundays and feast days: 'in the masse tyme at the levacion of the blessed sacrament and after as is the use'.[293] The five candles which were to burn around her bier at her funeral were granted to the priory church of

---

[286] 'Quando non potest videri corpus Christi, eo quod mane celebretur, potest sacerdos tenere cereum bene ardentem in retro sacerdotis ut corpus Christi in hoc parte possit videri', Righetti (1956), p. 355, n. 266.
[287] *Rationale* lib. 4, c. 6, no. 5; lib. 6, c. 85, no. 5, pp. 567–8.
[288] Priests were also reminded to ventilate, since smoke could thicken and obstruct the view of the elevation, Dumoutet (1926), pp. 38–41, 50–3.
[289] Dendy (1959), p. 89.
[290] 'Ad duos tortos qui ad consecracionem et elevacionem corporis domini accenduntur 6d, et ad commune lumen 6d', *Bushmead cartulary*, p. 154.
[291] Cambiaso (1917), p. 64.
[292] 'Duos tortices singulis diebus ad elevationem corporis Christi in missa Beate Marie in prefato choro dicenda illuminandos et arsuros ponderis sexdecim librarum', *Bridgewater* II, p. 218.
[293] *London, St Mary at Hill*, p. 11.

St Clement's at York by Margaret, widow of John Stapelton of York, in her will of 1466, for later use as elevation lights.[294] In 1521 an anonymous donor 'man that will not be named' gave 16d to the parish of Thame to find a candle which was to burn before the rood every Sunday at the sacring.[295] The moment was also enhanced by the operation of special effects, sometimes a grandiose gift to a church. Like that of Thomas Goisman, an alderman of Hull, who left in his will of 1502 £10 to the Holy Trinity chapel, for the construction of a machine by which angels would descend from the roof at the elevation, and ascend after the end of the *Pater noster*:

I bequeath . . . in honour of the sacrament, to make [a machine] which will rise and descend at the high altar, as angels go up and down, between the elevation of Christ's body and blood, and the end of the chant, *Ne nos inducas in temptacionem* [the *Pater Noster*].[296]

The parish of St Peter Cheap, London, had an altar cloth with the picture of the crucifixion for display during the elevation.[297]

Poorer parishes must have gone without proper illumination, and visitations reveal failures in provision, which prompted reiteration of lighting instructions in synodal legislation and pastoral guides. Around 1320 the *Pupilla oculi* reminded the parish priests that 'without fire, that is without light, celebration should not take place'.[298] John Mirk observes in his *Instructions to parish priests* of the early fifteenth century:

> Loke þat þy candel of wax hyt be,
> And set hyre so, þat þow hyre se,
> On þe lyfte half of þyn autere,
> And loke algate ho brenne clere,
> Wayte þat ho brenne in alle wyse
> Tyl thou haue do þat servyse.[299]

So by the early thirteenth century a focus for eucharistic awareness, a moment designed to encompass and communicate every aspect of the

---

[294] Vale (1976), p. 16 and note 66.
[295] *Thame*, p. 51. As we shall see below, when Corpus Christi fraternities were founded they often undertook to improve and provide lighting for the elevation, below pp. 235–6, and Rubin (1986), pp. 104–6.
[296] 'Lego . . . in honore sacramenti, ad faciendum ad summun altare descendent et ascendent [sic] ad tectum capellae inter levationem corporis Christi et sanguinis Domini, si . . . scilicet angelis ascendetur et descendetur usque ad finem cantationis, et *Ne nos inducas in temptacionem*', *Testamenta Eboracensia* IV, p. 209, he had seen such a machine in King's Lynn.
[297] *London, St Peter Cheap*, p. 259.
[298] 'Sine igne, id est sine lumine, celebrare non licet', Dendy (1959), p. 38.
[299] *Instructions (a)*, p. 58, lines 1,875–80.

message which the church wished to convey, one which provided space for participation and for submergence in a ritual-communal moment, was in place. Taught, illuminated, heralded by the peal of bells, striking in its special lights and effects, it was attractive as a moment of encounter with the very Christ, from which some very real physical and spiritual benefits flowed. In a sermon for a Sunday after Epiphany 1375 Bishop Brinton of Exeter taught that after seeing God's body no need for food would be felt, oaths would be forgiven, eye-sight would not fade, sudden death would not strike one, nor would one age, and one would be protected at every step by angels.[300] This is just one version of the ubiquitous list of *Merita missae*, the Merits of the Mass, which proliferated in the pastoral from the thirteenth century on.[301]

### ELEVATION, COMMUNION AND SUBSTITUTES

As the elevation was built up in practice and in meaning it came to be seen as possessing some sacramental efficacy. The enhancement of the power of the eucharist, as it was formulated to be the very body of Christ, had made access to it more problematical, and communion less easy and simple. Elevation offered a sort of substitute 'sacramental viewing', which like communion was taught to affect one markedly. As the significance of the elevation was stressed, and the benefits of the elevation seemed so great that questions were posed as to how different it was from spiritual communion. Already in the late twelfth century Peter the Chanter wondered whether priests in a state of sin:

who are present with celebrating priest in a state of devotion and concord should concelebrate, and receive Christ's body, even merely spiritually, and not sacramentally, would further sin mortally.[302]

Similarly William of Auxerre (d. 1232) believed that viewing in a state of sin was not detrimental, as reception of communion in such a state would be; viewing could move towards the love of God:

---

[300] *The sermons of Thomas Brinton*, no. 48, pp. 212–17, at pp. 215–16.
[301] See below, pp. 108, 341.
[302] 'Utrum vero mortaliter peccent qui . . . tamen cum ministris altaris per devotionem et consensum debent corpus Christi conficere, et spiritualiter et si non sacramentaliter sumere', Peter the Chanter, 'Verbum abbreviatum', col. 108 d.

We say that seeing Christ's body is not . . . a crime . . . [S]eeing Christ's body provokes towards the love of God.[303]

The solution was made by Alexander of Hales in his *Sentences* of *c.*1222, through the distinction between eating by taste, and eating by sight (*manducatio per gustum* and *manducatio per visum*), the former, sacramental, the latter, not. Inspiring as it was, according to Bonaventure, seeing could not generate grace, which is what the sacraments were all about. Additionally complex was the growing notion of 'spiritual communion' which could be experienced through a fervent viewing, even without tasting, of Christ.[304] The tension between the two rituals informs much of the writing, teaching, criticism, and confusion which we will encounter on the trails of eucharistic symbolisation.

Thus, communion was protected as the highlight of sacramental experience, the tasting, 'smackyng', of the host-God. The question of the rise or fall of frequency of reception by the laity cannot be neatly resolved. John Beleth explained that originally communion was taken daily, then only on Sundays, and ultimately thrice a year.[305] Durandus explained that due to sinfulness the laity communicated only once a year since 1215, but that the priest communicated daily for them.[306] But a combination of greater regulation and examination before reception, of the stronger meaning attached to it, and the evidence of writers who complained about the decline in frequency, all topped by the requirement of annual communion as both sufficient and obligatory made at the Lateran Council of 1215, creates a picture of infrequent but fairly consequential communion in this period.[307] Peter Comestor lamented the general decline in frequency of reception which may be related to fears of unworthy reception which he describes elsewhere.[308] Requirements for minimal age at communion appear in thirteenth-century synodal legislation: Aquinas recommended that children should not receive communion before the age of ten. In the synodal statutes of the diocese of Sisteron of 1225 × 35, boys of seven or more were required to

---

[303] 'dicimus quod aspicere corpus Christi non est . . . peccatum . . . aspicere corpus Christi provocativum est ad dilectionem dei', William of Auxerre, *Summa aurea* lib. 4, tract 7, c. 7, q. 3, p. 170.

[304] On spiritual communion in the thought of Bonaventure, Albert the Great and Thomas Aquinas, see Schlette (1959).

[305] John Beleth, *Summa de ecclesiasticis officiis*, c. 48, p. 85.

[306] 'Postmodum autem, quia nec digne hoc potuit observare; tertia secuta est institutio, ut ter saltem in anno quilibet christianus acciperet Eucharistiam, vel hodie ad minus in Pascha . . .', *Rationale* lib. 4, c. 53, no. 3, pp. 309–10, at p. 310.

[307] *COD* c. 21, p. 245.

[308] 'Sermones', *PL* 198, cols. 1765a–b.

learn their Pater Noster and Creed in preparation for confession and communion,[309] and the statutes of the diocese of Liège of 1287 reiterated the age of ten, taken to be the age of reason.[310] The synod of Paris of 1204×5 decreed under Odo of Sully that for the sake of appearance and safety children should not be given hosts, even if these were not consecrated ones, and that blessed bread, which was quite different in form, should be distributed. 'And we also ordain priests strictly that hosts, even consecrated ones, should not be given to boys by any means.'[311]

3 Communion to the laity; initial of the Corpus Christi mass

The unambiguous definitions of Christ's real bodily presence in the eucharist had turned communion into an enormous event. The canon *Omni utriusque sexus* of Lateran IV required annual communion after due confession and penance (figures 2 and 3).[312] Theologians discussed the criteria for reception and the consequences of their infringement. The questions of merit were compounded by the issue of conscience and intent, which had come to inform all moral theology from the mid

---

[309] 'Pueros a septennio et supra "Pater noster" et "Credo" doceant . . . et in die sancto Pasche, ut corpus Christi, prius tamen confessi, recipiant', *Statuts synodaux* II, c. 19, p. 192.
[310] *Statuts synodaux de Liège*, p. 20.
[311] 'Item districte precipimus presbyteris ne hostias, licet non sacratas dent pueris ullo modo', *Statuts synodaux* I, c. 91, p. 86; and in the Synodal de l'Ouest, *ibid*, c. 15, p. 150.
[312] *COD*, p. 221.

twelfth century and which made the definitions of absolute categories of merit all the more difficult. Peter Comestor (*c.* 1100–1178) addressed questions such as 'Quibus danda est eukaristia?', and answered:

It is given both to the good and to the bad, and is received both by the good and the bad. But the good receive it unto their salvation, and the evil to their damnation.[313]

The definition of good or bad recipients given here is:

Evil is the person who sins against God . . . who remains in a criminal state and revels in it . . . The good or the deserving is not only the perfect, of whom there is no doubt that s/he should receive, but also the person who has repeatedly committed sins, and has no longer the wish to sin; and after confession of sin has been made, s/he can receive the eucharist.[314]

Thus, the eucharist was available even to those who had sinned, so long as they were no longer attracted to sin, and had undergone sacramental penance and absolution. Corporal union with Christ was offered even to those who had sinned, not only to the perfect. And as all people are sinners this was the only possible formulation since windows could not be torn into people's souls. Still the question of conscience meant that there would be those who would receive unworthily, but also those who would abstain out of fear, and these too were considered. Thus, Peter Comestor reminded that abstention was dangerous to the soul:

It is grave and very dangerous for a Christian to abstain from reception of that sacrament, and not to communicate at least once a year, at Easter.[315]

And this is the spirit which animated the canon of the Lateran Council.

The divergence of Franciscan and Dominican approaches to the interdependence of philosophy and theology which we have encountered in other aspects of the eucharistic discussion are also evident in formulations regarding communion. As the eucharist was accepted as Christ's body on the altar, and moreover was taught to be that unequivocally, from the thirteenth century greater distinction in the discussion of the nature of the eucharistic reception is evident. In his commentary on the *Sentences* Alexander of Hales, who was to join the Franciscan order in the next decade, distinguished between recep-

---

[313] 'Datur tamen et bonis et malis, et sumitur et a bono et a malo. Sed boni sumunt ad salutem, mali vero ad sui dampnationem', Peter Comestor, *Sententiae de sacramentis*, c. 20, p. 50*.

[314] 'Malus dicitur qui peccat contra Deum . . . qui manet in criminali et delectatur in hoc . . . Bonus autem vel dignus dicitur non solum perfectus, de quo non est dubium quin recipere debet, sed etiam qui convertitur de comissis, nec est ei de cetero voluntas peccandi; et hic facta confessione suscipiat eukaristiam', *Ibid.*

[315] 'Grave namque et valde periculosum est christiano ut abstinere a percepcione huius sacramenti ut saltem semel in anno, in Pascha scilicet, non communicet', Peter Comestor, *De sacramentis*, p. 51*.

tion of the species, and reception which appreciated the significance of the species as Christ's real body:

Because he did not say that Christ's body in the sacrament is a sense experience, but rather one of reason; that which is sensible can be received by animals, that is, the species of bread; but that which is in the order of reason they do not receive, that is, Christ's body.[316]

This really returned to the vexing question which was already discussed by Augustine, and then by Berengar: in what sense was Christ's body *received* when sacramental bread was consumed by an infidel, or eaten by an animal? Alexander argues that the reception could happen in three modes: in thought, in love, and in nature; adults with good intention could consume in all three ways, animals, only in nature.[317] After him, in the middle of the century, the Franciscan William of Middleton (d. 1260) claimed that irrational animals swallowing the host consumed only the accidents.[318] Thus a moment of cognitive participation, an understanding and a faith in what was signified in the appearance of bread distinguished the reception of a believing Christian, from the 'reception' of a mouse. The greatest Franciscan theologian, Bonaventure, continued this line in his commentary on the *Sentences* of *c.* 1240–50, stressing that the ability to appreciate the sign was paramount in experiencing Christ's body in the sacrament; thus mice and angels could not truly experience reception.[319] And this led to the claim that nothing that could happen within a person's body could demean or detract from Christ. Christ's body was present in the host only so long as the accidents of bread existed, and only in the body of a person who truly appreciated and purely intended to be part of the union. Animals, infidels, and the irrational or unthinking could not, by definition, experience such a fusion.

We see how much strain this Franciscan theology, intent on the dignity of the sacrament and on the affective nature of sacramental bonding, exerted on the realist approach to the eucharist. Dominican scholars took a somewhat different view. Albert the Great stressed the importance of appreciation of the sign, but was loath to separate Christ's body from the accidents within which it resided; he was

---

[316] 'Quia ergo corpus Christi sub sacramento non dicit tantum quod ad sensum pertinet, sed quod ad rationem, quod sensum est a brutis sumitur, scilicet species panis; quod in ordine ad rationem est non sumitur, scilicet corpus Christi', Alexander of Hales, *iv Sent.*, d. 13, q. 8, pp. 204–5.

[317] For a pioneering discussion of these issues see Macy (1989).

[318] William of Middleton, *Quaestiones de sacramentis* II, p. 696.

[319] Bonaventure, *iv Sent.*, d. 9, a. 1, q. 3, *Opera omnia* IV, p. 204; and on spiritual reception, d. 9, a. 1, q. 2, pp. 201–2.

forced, therefore, to concede that Christ's body must be said to exist in
the body of a man or beast which had swallowed the consecrated host.
Thomas developed these disturbing aspects in his commentary on the
*Sentences* in 1252–6, reiterating the irreversible nature of transubstantiation: so long as a species exists in the form of bread and wine its
substance, that of Christ's body, cannot be said to have ceased to
exist.[320] This adherence to the rule of his metaphysics was a minority
approach. It could breed extreme views such as that of the Dominican
Peter de La Palu (*c.*1277–1342) who argued that the mouse who had
swallowed the consecrated host must be caught and burned and his
ashes washed down a *piscina*, the treatment accorded to old vestments,
crumbs of the host and other sacred materials. John Quidort following
Thomas explained that the unbelieving received only the sacrament,
not the *res* which was elicited through its significatory power. Duns
Scotus further distinguished four types of reception, but stressed the
importance of intention in effecting the spiritual union. So the very
thinkers who were most systematic in their insistence on the enduring
reality of the sacramental bread were those forced to privilege the moral
link between sign and recipient in order to realise the sacramental-
spiritual potential of the enduring matter. And thus from very different
philosophical positions we find Franciscan and Dominican scholars
elaborating the subtle distinctions between types of communion, based
on predisposition, understanding and aptness at decoding of sacramental signs. Echoing the exact terms of this debate, the *Manipulus
curatorum* of 1333 instructed the priest under the heading *Cui debet
dari eucharistia*, that giving communion to an unbeliever was like
casting pearls before the swine, and that those who received without
faith, merely received corporally, just as infidels did:

those who consume the sacrament corporally do so like an infidel who does not
believe that Christ's body is really in the sacrament.[321]

And the more faith and intention were stressed in communion, the
more elevated and awesome it became.[322]

Similar in spirit are the admonitions towards repeated reception
when necessary, presenting the sacrament of the altar as an iterable
sacrament, as opposed to baptism or marriage. The synod of Paris

---

[320] Thomas Aquinas, *IV Sent.*, pp. 370–1; Macy (1989), p. 10. Following Thomas, at the very
end of the fifteenth century Gabriel Biel insisted that the sacrament's validity was
independent of the recipient, Farthing (1988), p. 146.

[321] 'Quidam enim sumunt istud sacramentum corporaliter tamen sicut aliquis infidelis qui
non credit in isto sacramento esse veraciter corpus Xristi', *Manipulus curatorum*, fol. 32[r].

[322] For a Middle English sermon (of 1389×1404) on unworthy reception see *Three Middle
English sermons*, no. 3, pp. 71–2.

encouraged people to seek communion when on their death-bed; and priests were reminded to teach that sexual intercourse was permissible after communion, contrary to what must have been a popular belief that this was unfitting while God still dwelt in one's body.[323] Besides such attractions there were controls; communion was always to be taken in public, as decreed by the council of Westminster in 1200:

And we decree that it be added that [the] communion of the eucharist should not be given secretly to the impenitent, but that it should be given publicly and immediately to the asker, unless the crime is a public one.[324]

Under the eyes of friends and relatives unworthy reception was probably less likely. But the personal accountability was fundamental, and it was not to be denied even in the case of suspicion of sin. Alan of Lille (c. 1120–1202 × 3) taught that it was not to be denied even to those who were out of peace:

And he should not dissuade him in such a case from receiving the Lord's body, nor enjoin him to abstain. Rather he should instruct him that if he receives while being in that state, he would be eating at his own peril.[325]

The priest was to explain the gravity of undeserving reception, but not to deny communion. But obstinate and malevolent, overt and unequivocal breaking with charity, called for penance of forty days.[326] When a question of Alan of Lille recalls that some people were denied communion, like those about to be executed, three days before their hanging, the explanation is not that this is due to their sinfulness (since they might always repent and make satisfaction before their last communion, and since equally they might be totally innocent) but rather due to the sacrament's dignity:

The eucharist is denied not because of the nature of the crime, but due to the sacrament's dignity; ... but if he is taken to hanging within three days, we deny the eucharist because it would be an enormity if Christ, who was still believed to be in the stomach, should be handed over to hanging. So he should believe, and this would suffice.[327]

---

[323] *Statuts synodaux* I, c. 48, p. 70.

[324] 'Hic adiciendum decrevimus ut secreto non detur communio eucharistie impenitenti, set publice et instanter petenti danda est, nisi publicum sit eius delictum', *CS* I, 2, c. 2, p. 1061.

[325] 'Nec moneat eum in tali proposito corpus Domini sumere, nec iniungat eum abstinere; sed in hoc eum instruat quod si in hoc statu manens sumpserit, judicium sibi manudcabit', Alan of Lille, *Lib. poen.* lib. 3, c. 4, p. 47.

[326] *Ibid*, lib. 2, c. 82, p. 90.

[327] 'Id est eucharistia solet denegari non propter reatum peccati, set propter dignitatem sacramenti quia post ea ante tres dies non deberent suspendi, sed si tradantur suspendio, eucharistiam denegamus, quia scandalum esset si Christus qui adhuc creditur esse in ysofago, tradetur suspendio; ergo credat et sufficit', Alan of Lille, *Lib. poen.* lib. 3, c. 24, p. 141.

The degradation which would follow if the eucharist was still in the stomach was too great, but the criminal would live in his faith.

The Lateran decree required annual communion at Easter, but most synodal legislation recommended three communions.[328] In an Advent sermon Maurice of Sully, bishop of Paris (d.1196), exhorted:

This you must know, that just like at Easter, so at Pentecost and at Christmas, all Christians must communicate in the Lord's flesh.[329]

The Florentine sumptuary legislation of 1310 similarly recommended communion on these three feasts, and made that at Easter obligatory.[330] But critics such as John Wyclif and Jan Hus saw the purpose and climax of the mass in communion, and elevation gazing as mere idolatry.[331] Gazing and veneration were offered as substitutes, and were seen by them as clerical attempts to distance the laity from the sources of grace. Wyclif's theology of the eucharist and view on images combined to liberate the mass from its sacramental trappings, and to dismiss exposition and gazing as forms of image-worship. Conversely, communion was a channel of grace which elevated a Christian's life daily, and frequent communion was an important aspect of the life of mystics and saints, and of reforming groups such as the *Devotio moderna*.[332] But these were exceptions to the rule of infrequent communion, accompanied by almost unlimited opportunity for sacramental gazing.

Even a single Easter communion by the laity exposed the sacramental species, Christ's body and blood, to great dangers.[333] The fragile host might drop and break, the wine might spill to the ground.[334] And as these dangers of the new-style mass emerged pastoral guidebooks and manuals for the mass attempted to address and guide the clergy through them. One of the consequences of the enhancement of eucharistic significance was that it became more clearly the preserve of the clergy, which protected and officiated it, and that consequently some of its aspects were withdrawn. Throughout the twelfth century the chalice was removed from lay communion. This was facilitated by the cur-

---

[328] Confession was recommended more frequently: before journeys, before childbirth, at marriage, on major feasts, Tentler (1977), pp. 79–80.

[329] 'Hoc enim scitote quod sicut in Pascha iam in Pentecosten, et in Natale Domini omnes christiani debent communicare carni et sanguini Domini', in the sermon 'Ecce nomen Domini venitur longinquo', Longère (1975), II, n. 35, p. 142.

[330] *Synodal law*, p. 166.

[331] Catto (1985), p. 282.

[332] Browe (1938a), pp. 109–10.

[333] See an image of communion administered by a priest in the Gorleston Psalter, produced in East Anglia c.1310–25, BL Add. 49622, fol. 13ʳ.

[334] On accidents, see James of Vitry, 'De sacramentis', pp. 245–6. See also the synodal statutes of the diocese of Nîmes, Arles and Béziers, of 1252, *Statuts synodaux* II, c. 74, pp. 326–8.

rency of the notion of concomitance, an Aristotelian term introduced through the works of Avicenna: concomitance was a link between a reality and something which is outside its essence, but inseparable from it. This provided a philosophical framework within which the claim that Christ's body was present after the consecration in the bread and in the wine, and thus supporting communion in one kind.[335] So Robert Pullen (d.c.1146) recommended that the bread alone be given to the laity:

He does not show himself to believe well who show to every one when he gives the flesh and dips it in the blood; because [this means] either that the flesh lacks the blood, or that the blood exists outside the flesh.[336]

Peter the Chanter explained that consecrated wine was not reserved like hosts to be taken to the sick, 'propter aciditatis incommodum'.[337] In the section on the eucharist in his 'De sacramentis' James of Vitry stated 'Because of possible danger the eucharist is not given to the laity under the species of wine'.[338] But he explained that this involved no loss since in each species there is flesh and flesh is received, as well as blood, and blood is received.[339] Thomas Aquinas explained that the priest should receive both, for the sake of the laity.[340] Durandus' *Rationale* follows this line of reasoning, presenting the priest as a mediator at communion.[341] Teaching and enforcing this practice required some effort. It seems that in some places there was a custom of dipping the host in the wine, which the Westminster council of 1175 prohibited.[342] Bishop Richard Poore's decrees for Salisbury diocese of 1217×19 addressed the need to explain to recipients that they were receiving the body and blood, but mentioned the reception in both kinds:

And you must instruct as often as they communicate that they should not doubt in any way the reality of the body and the blood. Because that which they receive under the species of bread, is without doubt that which hung on the cross for us, and what they receive in the chalice, that which flowed from Christ's side.[343]

---

[335] Gy (1983), pp. 82–3; James of Vitry, 'De sacramento altaris', pp. 234–6; and see Magivern (1963).
[336] 'Non tamen se bene credere ostendit quisquis dum carnem tribuit, sanguine intingit, quasi aut caro sanguine careat, aut sanguis extra carnem existat', Robert Pullen, 'Sententiae', *PL* 186, co. 964.
[337] Peter the Chanter, *Summa de sacramentis*, p. 143.
[338] 'Laicis autem propter periculum non est danda eucharistia sub specie sanguinis', James of Vitry, 'De sacramentis', pp. 244–5.
[339] Peter the Chanter, *Summa de sacramentis*, c. 57, pp. 142–5, esp. p. 143.
[340] *ST* III q. 80, a. 12, ad. 3.
[341] *Rationale* lib. 4, c. 54, nos. 10 and 14, p. 313.
[342] *CS* I, 2, c. 16, p. 990; from *De consecratione* D. 2, c. 7 pr. and 1, *CIC* I, col. 1315–17.
[343] 'Debetis instruere quotiens communicant quod de veritate corporis et sanguinis nullo modo dubitent. Nam hoc accipiunt proculdubio sub panis specie quod pro nobis pependit in cruce, hoc accipiunt in calice quod effusum est de Christi latere', *CS* II, 1, c. 55, p. 77.

In the Lambeth constitutions of 1281 Archbishop Pecham directed the clergy to instruct the laity that in receiving in one kind they were given the whole body:

And they will carefully . . . teach that under the species of bread is at once given to them the body and blood of the Lord, Christ indeed whole and real . . . It is only granted . . . to the celebrants to receive the blood under the species of consecrated wine.[344]

This was obviously already an established custom, but one which required explanation; and Bishop Quivil of Exeter repeated it in 1287.[345] The laity was given a drink of diluted and unconsecrated wine for symmetry's sake and, more practically, to wash away the dry crumbs of the host; but to avoid confusion it was important to stress that this was not Christ's body. A fourteenth-century manual for the parochial clergy demonstrates how this should be clarified:

Also ye shal understonde that the drynke that ye receyve in the chalyce after your howsyl is no sacrament but wyne or water to bryng the lightlokyr the sacrament in to thy body.[346]

But the removal of the chalice was not universal. In fact, only at the Council of Constance of 1415 was reception of the chalice by the laity forbidden, and those priests who offered it to the laity were to be excommunicated.[347] There is inconographic evidence to support the lingering communion of the wine, such as the miniature in a four-teenth-century Venetian missal where six people kneel with hands crossed on their chests to the host out of a bowl held by the priest, behind whom a cleric is shown offering a drink of wine through a straw to a lay person.[348] Were it not the precious blood why should it be served through a straw?

In addition to these possible lingering customs of reception in both kinds, in some regions there was Utraquism, an emphatic and directed practice which was a purposive reintroduction of the practice which the church had withdrawn.[349] The practice by Hussites in the late four-teenth century of offering communion in both kinds and frequent communion to the laity was a statement of their criticism of the church,

---

[344] 'Sollicite . . . instruant sub panis specie simul eis dari corpus et sanguinem domini, immo Christum integrum et verum . . . Solis enim celebrantibus sanguinem sub specie vini consecrati sumere . . . est concessum', CS II 2, c. 1, p. 895.
[345] *Ibid*, c. 4, p. 991.
[346] *Manuale curatorum*, p. 21.
[347] Cutts (1914), p. 235n; *COD*, pp. 418–19.
[348] Venice Marciana III (111) 2116, fol. 176ʳ.
[349] Kaminsky (1967), pp. 110–21.

and of the clerical privilege enshrined in its rituals.[350] It was against the idolatry of lay gazing – that private contemplation of the eucharist at elevation – which was the most common eucharistic encounter of most layfolk, and in favour of frequent and spiritually regenerating communion, rescued from clerical mystification, that Matthew of Janov and Jan Hus directed their practices.[351] This was the unmaking of the very design which had emerged in the twelfth and thirteenth centuries.

Most people received communion once a year, at Easter, in their parish church, following confession and penance, and in one kind, but encounters with the eucharist or with symbolically linked rituals and kindred images were more frequent. The importance of the elevation, and the quasi-sacramental, even the sacramental value which was posited in it, have been discussed above. Another type of substitution was the ritual distribution of blessed bread at the end of the mass.[352] By the twelfth century this was an established custom and with the growth in the magnitude of communion it was acknowledged to have its benefits, even if these were not sacramental. John Beleth recommended those who missed communion to take the kiss of peace, the *eulogia* (blessed bread), or to receive the priest's blessing:

A threefold remedy has been found: that on each and every Sunday the kiss of peace be given, the *eulogia,* that is holy bread . . . and that a prayer [*collecta*] be said over the people at the end of the mass.[353]

Durandus similarly recommended the kiss, the blessed bread and the *oratio* over the people.[354] Parishes regularly spent money on observance of the custom, using leavened bread which was quite distinct in shape from eucharistic wafers. The constitutions of Giles of Bridport, bishop of Salisbury, of 1256, ordered that households should provide in rotation the loaf which was to be blessed and distributed:

And they must provide blessed bread, with candles, every Sunday of the year, in each church of the Christian world.[355]

[350] Catto (1985), p. 283.
[351] *Ibid,* pp. 283–4.
[352] Franz (1965), pp. 247–56. For the blessing over the bread see the Westminster custom, *Manuale ad usum Ecclesie Westmonasteriensis* II, col. 524. On substitutes, see Macy (1984), pp. 93–5.
[353] 'Invento tamen triplici remedio, ut singulis diebus osculum pacis daretur in dominicis diebus, eulogia etiam, id est panis benedictus, . . . ut collecta diceretur super populum in fine missae', John Beleth, *Summa de ecclesiasticis officiis,* c. 48(g), p. 85.
[354] *Rationale* lib. 4, c. 53, no. 3, pp. 309–10, at p. 310: 'et pro communione, quae signulis diebus dominicis fieri solebat, daretur in diebus dominicis panis benedictus sanctae communionis vicarius, qui et eulogia [ευλογια] dicitur. Sed et loco quotidanae communionis, in quadragesima dicitur in fine Missae oratio super populum . . .', no. 4, p. 310: 'sane populus sese in Missa osculatur'.
[355] 'Et debent invenire panem benedictum cum candelis qualibet dominica per annum, in omni ecclesia de mundo christiano', *CS* II, I, c. 8, p. 513.

The churchwardens of Bridgewater spent in 1463/4 10d on 'la basket ad ponendum panem benedictum',[356] and the parish of St Edmund and St Thomas, Salisbury, spent 5d in 1511 to purchase a 'coffane' for the bread.[357] The vicar sometimes shared in the loaf as in Andover in 1470–3 where ½d was paid to redeem 'his part of ye holy loffe'.[358] In some parishes collections were made at the end of festive masses just as parishioners received their portion of the blessed bread. The churchwardens of St Peter in the East, Oxford, collected 2s 2d 'de pane benedicto per annum', probably at Easter and Christmas,[359] and in Tintinhull in Somerset in 1473–6 2s were reported as collections for blessed bread over two years.[360] The existence of this ritual at the end of the mass proved to be an important inducement for keeping people in church even after the high-point of 'seeing God'. It is for such benefit that a Cathar woman kept a piece of bread which had been blessed by a prefect, to use in case there would be no one to give her the *consolamentum* on her death-bed. Blessed bread had the same value, she claimed.[361]

Another ritual which allowed participation and which conveyed eucharistic meanings besides elevation and communion was the circulation and kissing of the pax. The pax entered Roman liturgies around the year 1000 and particularly in the monastic milieu,[362] but entered parish usage increasingly in the later centuries, as substitute for reception of communion. This was usually an object as round and smooth as the host, made of wood or precious metal, and inscribed with a crucifixion scene or the Lamb of God. This was passed down from the celebrant to his attendant clergy, and to the congregation, to be touched and kissed as a token of charity, before all attention returned to the altar to view the priest's sacrifice.[363] It sometimes appears in the inventories of plate and in churchwardens' accounts. The church of St Mary, Scarborough, possessed a precious pax in 1434 'unum osculatorium de argento et deaurato';[364] the churchwardens of St Katherine's, Launceston, paid for 'painting a pax'.[365] The churchwardens of Bridgewater similarly spent 2d 'pro pictura de la pax' in 1463/4,[366] and in the same year the

[356] *Bridgewater* IV, no. 839, p. 131.
[357] Cox (1913), p. 96; *Salisbury, St. Edmund's*, p. 57.
[358] *Andover*, p. 16.
[359] *Oxford, St Peter in the East*, p. 28.
[360] *Tintinhull*, p. 192.
[361] *Reg. Fournier* III, p. 216. For a discussion of an interesting system of blessed bread sharing in a modern Basque village see Ott (1980).
[362] Bossy (1973), p. 141.
[363] James (1961), p. 144.
[364] *Scarborough, St Mary*, p. 66.
[365] *Launceston, St Katherine*, p. 136.
[366] *Bridgewater* IV, no 839, p. 131.

4 Crucifixion, at the opening of the canon of the mass, and cross mark for the
priest's kiss

parish of (Saffron) Walden bought a pax for 3d for its altar of St Mary.[367] In 1509 the parish of Rotherfield (Sussex) possessed three 'paxbreads',[368] and St Peter Mancroft's church, Norwich, recorded in its early-sixteenth-century inventory, a silver pax with blue enamel work.[369]

Much has been said of the pax or the *osculatorium* as a symbol of communal unity amongst the attendant congregation.[370] The circulation of a costly object within a community be it a familiar group of villagers, or the congregation assembled in a big urban church, would have created a ritual moment when people concentrated their minds on the nature of the links between them; but one should not ascribe too much efficacy to such an exercise. The pax was taught as a symbol of the communal quest for redemption in the mass. The *Lay folks' mass book* encouraged people to pray for peace as it approached them:

> So þat ilke man lyf wel other
> Als he ware his awen brother
> And amung us, be þat sacramente
> Þat now is presente
> And be vertue of this messe . . .
> Þat wee may come unto thy blysse.[371]

But by pointing at the nature of relations between its members, the pax could bring out and emphasise existing tensions and divisions. In his *Livre des seyntez medicines* of 1354 Henry of Lancaster confesses to having given many false kisses of peace at the mass.[372] With the increasing popularity of pews and family boxes in churches, and of oratories even in gentry households, the pax would have reinforced relations of kinship, patronage, deference, within an already close-knit group.[373] And the frustration raised as the trail of the pax delineated hierarchy is also apparent: in 1494 the churchwardens of the parish of All Saints, Stanyng, presented Joanna Dyaca because

It is noted that she threw the pax-bread to the ground in the church because another woman of the parish had kissed it before her.[374]

She submitted to correction, and was made to buy the parish a new pax.

[367] *Walden*, p. 224.
[368] *Rotherfield*, p. 27.
[369] *Norwich, St Peter Mancroft*, p. 165.
[370] Bossy (1973), p. 141; Bossy (1983), pp. 52–60; Jungmann (1955) II, p. 325.
[371] *LFMB* lines 335–9, 342, p. 54.
[372] *Livre des seyntez medicines*, p. 75.
[373] Richmond (1984), p. 199; Mertes (1987).
[374] 'Notatur quod projecit le paxbrede ad terram, in ecclesia, ea occasione quod alia mulier ejusdem parochie osculavit ante eam', *A series of precedents*, no. 191, pp. 53–4.

It is particularly here that the limited nature of that which can be learnt about practice from normative material such as expositions of the mass which has provided the basis for Bossy's study becomes apparent.[375] In this chapter we have dealt with the design of the mass, which was disseminated and enforced through a whole system of teaching and legislation. But the mass was more than the application of a blue-print and one must look at the variety of sources in order to discern the ways in which it was apprehended, experienced and used. Texts which designed the mass take us only a short way in this direction.

A sacrament administered by priests was established within the ritual of the mass and within a narrative of sacrifice and of redemption through grace.[376] A symbol which was simple and all powerful was placed in the midst of the culture, promising salvation through physical incorporation into Christ, or doom through the undeserving and the sinful proximity or reception of the sacrament. Throughout we have seen that appearances, the visual encounters which people had with the sacrament and its environment, were carefully thought out and designed to enhance the claim that a wheaten disc over which a priest uttered the words of consecration, turned into Christ's crucified body, the source of hope and well-being through grace. Within the sphere of protection and design of encounters with the sacrament occurred an interesting development concerning the bringing of the sacrament to the sick. The dilemma which it posed and the solutions found encapsulate the sort of problems in design which theologians and canonists, the designers of religious practice, had in mind.

In communion to the sick we encounter a death-bed ritual, inasmuch as the arrival of the priest allowed confession and penance to be enacted before reception of the sacrament, and other less formal services to be given by the priest, such as the writing of wills, support to the dying in their last moments,[377] and the comforting of relatives. But as the sacrament's significance became clearer and more awesome, and as a cordon of reservation and careful handling was set up, the bringing of the eucharist to the sick became increasingly ritualised, displaying those aspects of in-door veneration and protection befitting Christ's body which had been developing. So the taking of the eucharist to the sick became a veritable procession, with lights and incense and atten-

---

[375] Bossy (1983).
[376] On the meaning of the offertory stage in the mass see Clark (1980).
[377] See the description of this moment in romance:

'The kyngez confessour come, with Criste in his handes,
For to comforthe the knyghte kende hym þe wordes',

*The alliterative Morte Arthure*, lines 2193–4, p. 100.

dant acolytes – a ritual which required suitable responses from those witnessing it.

During the last third of the twelfth century French and English synods regularly instructed on the modes of handling the *viaticum*, the sick or dying person's fare on the last journey.[378] In 1200 the council of Westminster ordered:

The eucharist will be put . . . and carried to the sick in a clean and decent pyx . . . with a clean cloth over it, and a lamp and cross preceding it, except when the sick person lives very far away.[379]

The Synod of Paris of 1204×5 insisted that only priests could carry the eucharist to the sick, not even a deacon, except in cases of greatest necessity,[380] and that it should never be carried by a lay person; and penitential psalms and litanies were to be recited *en route*.[381] The statutes of Coventry of 1224×37 stipulated that

When the eucharist is carried through town to the sick it should be carried solemnly with lit candles and ringing bells. And it should not be carried only by a priest, but with the presence of a cleric or at least a lay person of good repute, dressed in a surplice.[382]

In Albi diocese in 1230 Bishop Durand of Beaucaire ordered that the priest carry the eucharist with a bell and a light in front, chanting the seven penitential psalms, and if it was a long way, with gradual psalms and a litany.[383] The ordinances of the diocese of Liège of 1288 instructed the priest to have a decent pyx and lay the host in it on a napkin, to ring a bell and draw a crowd to the procession.[384]

In some places this became a veritable procession with followers and an audience. Scholars annexed to churches and poor folk were included in the procession, like the two bedesmen of Sherbourne almshouse who

---

[378] Avril (1983), pp. 89–90. For an image of communion to the sick on a French seal, see Demay (1880), fig. 447, p. 358.

[379] 'Reponatur eucharistia . . . et in pixide munda et honesta deferatur ad egrum, lintheo mundo superposito et lucerna precedente ac cruce, nisi eger valde remotus fuerit', *CS* I, 2, c. 2, p 1061; see also the Synod of Paris which required that the chalice be beautiful and clean, *Statuts synodaux* I, c. 17, p. 58.

[380] Never to be administered by a deacon, according to Gratian, 'De consecratione', c. 29, *CIC* I, col. 1,156. See the statutes of Angers, *Statuts synodaux* III, c. 1, p. 116: a deacon should not carry the host to the sick, but this often happened.

[381] *Statuts synodaux* I, c. 19, pp. 58–60, and in the 'Synodal de l'Ouest', *ibid*, c. 70, p. 186.

[382] 'Cum eucharistia portetur ad infirmum per villam, portetur cum sollempnitate accense lucerne et sonantis campanelle. Et hoc non portetur a solo sacerdote, immo cum testimonio alicuius clerici vel saltem laici boni testimonii, et in superpellicio', *CS* II, 1, c. 4, p. 211.

[383] *Statuts synodaux* II, c. 37, p. 22; see also c. 68, pp. 322–4, and in the synod of Paris *Statuts synodaux* I, c. 19, p. 59.

[384] *Statuts synodaux de Liège*, c. 15, pp. 18–19.

participated in parish processions to the sick.[385] Four scholars of the parish of Dinkelsbühl (mid-Franconia) accompanied the *viaticum* singing songs, ringing bells and carrying lanterns,[386] as did the young scholars of the college of *Ave Maria* in Paris according to the requirements of their founder's statutes of 1346.[387] The audience beholding the procession was directed towards behaviour similar to that at elevation. Gregory IX's decretals record Pope Honorius III's recommendation of 1219:

Every priest should frequently teach his flock that when during the celebration of the mass the host is elevated, every person should bow with respect, doing as is done when the priest carries it to the sick.[388]

People were taught to fall to their knees and recite prayers when they heard the ringing of the bells announcing the passage of the *viaticum*. An early-fourteenth-century pastoral manual provided the following teaching on due behaviour:

As ofte as any cristenman yt blessude body seyy at
messe or y-bore in preste hondys to any syke he schal
devotly knele a don & worschepe hys god bydde hys
pater noster or what praȝer yt he can.[389]

Or a century later, in Mirk's instruction for veneration:

Teche hem also, I the pray
That whenne þey walken in þe way
And sene þe preste a-gayn hem comynge,
Goddes body wyth hym berynge,
Thenne wyth grete deuocyone,
Teche them þere to knele a-downe;
Fayre ne fowle, spare þey noghte
To worschype hym þat alle hathe wroghte.[390]

To encourage this aspect of veneration indulgences were given for those following the procession, and this was particularly common on the Continent, where indulgences were generally more current. An addition made *c.*1260 to the synodal statutes of Cambrai increased the indulgences for kneeling and venerated the *viaticum* from ten to twenty

[385] Bettey (1979), p. 27.
[386] Rücklin-Teuscher (1933), pp. 113–14; see also Pfleger (1933), p. 460.
[387] Gabriel (1955), no. 117, p. 104, p. 365, plate XVIII, 13.
[388] 'Sacerdos vero quilibet frequenter doceat plebem suam, ut, cum in celebratione missarum elevatur hostia salutaris quilibet se reverenter inclinet, idem faciens, cum eam defert presbyter ad infirmum', Gregory IX's Decretals, Lib. 3, tit. 41, c. 10, *CIC* II, col. 642.
[389] CUL Dd.12.69, fol. 31ʳ as below p. 104.
[390] *Instructions (a)*, p. 10, lines 304–11.

days.[391] The bishop of Angers, Nicholas Gellent, granted twenty days' penance to those who followed the procession to the sick, after his visitation of 1270 revealed that 'when Christ's body was carried to the sick by the priests, it had no or only a small accompaniment'.[392] Archbishop John of Strasbourg granted in 1310 ten days' indulgence to those who accompanied the eucharist as it was brought to the sick or to women before child-birth with their *Pater nosters* and *Ave Marias*,[393] and Francis, bishop of Metz, promised twenty days' indulgence in his synodal statutes of 1431.[394]

The removal of the eucharist from the safety of the church into the public outdoor, where it was exposed to the elements, to accidents, to irreverent gestures, was accompanied by attempts to protect and enhance its symbolic impact. The vessel containing the eucharist was to be closed and made of precious metal, and some churches had special pyxes for the procession to the sick. As ordered by the Exeter statutes of 1287, a parish was to have a 'bell to be carried to the sick and for the elevation of Christ's body'.[395] The parish of Willesden (Middlesex) had an ivory pyx with a good pewter lock for carrying the *viaticum* in 1249×57,[396] and in 1251 Kirkby parish (Yorkshire) had a silver chalice (albeit with a rickety foot) in a pewter vase for the sick.[397] Expensive vessels were sometimes given as gifts: in 1303 Roger Girdler granted the parish of All Saints, Bristol, a silver gilt cup, gilt within and without, studded with precious stones, with a crucifix on its head, and a gilt inner cup – a valuable object worth 67s, which was to be used for the *viaticum*

So that Christ's precious body be put and always be kept in it, and that the same cup with the said bowl within it, always be carried with Christ's body to the sick of the parish, in order to administer and serve them.[398]

John Redness of Holderness left in his will of 1451 a monstrance for the visitation of the parish sick;[399] and Agnes Brightwell's gift to the parish of Thame of a little bell of latten for the visitation of the sick was recorded in an inventory of 1447.[400] Parishes provided lighting on these

[391] Avril (1983), p. 98.
[392] *Statuts synodaux* III, c. 1, p. 104.
[393] Pfleger (1933), p. 459.
[394] Binz (1973), p. 175.
[395] 'Campanella deferenda ad infirmos et ad levationem corporis Christi', CS II, 2, p. 1006.
[396] *St Paul's churches*, p. 3.
[397] *Ibid*, p. 31.
[398] 'Ita quod preciosum Corpus christi infra apponetur et semper custodietur, et quod illa cuppa cum predicto cypho infra existente ad infirmos eiusdem parochie, semper portetur cum corpore christi, ad eisdem infirmis ministrandis et serviendis', *Bristol, All Saints (a)*, pp. 167–8; 151–2; *Bristol, All Saints (b)*, pp. 234–5.
[399] Vale (1976), p. 26.
[400] *Thame*, p. 33.

occasions, as in the case of St Edmund and St Thomas's, Salisbury, where 13d were spent in 1482/3 and 12d in 1483/4 on wax 'for the use of the sacrament of the altar during the visitation of the sick',[401] or that of All Hallows, Sherborne, which acquired a lantern 'to go with the sacrament valued 7d'.[402]

But as in the case of provision for vessels and lights within the church, the processions to the sick required time and resources which were often not available. The mandate of Bishop Giffard of Worcester of 1270 ordered the parish of Westbury to purchase vessels and vestments by the next Easter, among which a lamp for carrying before the *viaticum* to the sick was mentioned.[403] Bishop Grandisson's ordinance of 1335 for the diocese of Exeter dealt with irreverent administration of the eucharist to the sick:

They do not show due respect, nor do they minister to those languishing on the sick-bed with due decency, and, as is proven by daily offences, they negligently fail to carry the venerable sacrament to the sick wearing surplice and stole, with light and bell before them, as it is appropriate to do . . . and they thus damnably transgress both provincial and synodal statutes which have been circulated in these parts.[404]

The danger of disrespect which followed from human handling of the body of Christ, encountered above in the discussion of eucharistic design, emerged urgently in the context of communion to the sick. In his *Liber poenitentialis* Alan of Lille recommended appropriate behaviour in cases when the host was vomited up by a sick person.[405] The Synodal de l'Quest, which was compiled in Angers *c*.1225 and applied in many dioceses, ordered that the vomited host be crumbled into a chalice with wine and be consumed by the priest, or given in communion to a person with a pure conscience.[406] A sick person who was too

[401] 'Ad usum sacramenti altaris in tempore visitationis infirmorum', *Salisbury, St Edmund and St Thomas*, pp. 30, 32. But we also find the monks of the parish of St Hippolyte in Vivoin to whom the local parish church was appropriated, wrangling with the parish vicars over respective responsibilities in providing lights 'in honorem Eucharistie in visitacionibus infirmorum', Binz (1973), p. 13.

[402] Bettey (1977), p. 27.

[403] *Reg. Giffard*, pp. 42–3; for similar demands on routine visitations of the archdiocese of Geneva see Binz (1973), p. 205.

[404] 'Reverenciam debitam non exhibent, nec id cum decencia qua convenit in extremis languendibus ministrant, et, quod cotidianis scandalis experimur, ad infirmos idem deferentes venerabile sacramentum, superpellicium ad stolam induere, lumen et tintinabulum ante se, prout convenit facere deportari, negligenter omittunt . . . constitutiones provinciales et eciam synodales in hac parte editas damnabiliter transgrediendo', *Concilia* III, pp. 786–7.

[405] Alan of Lille, *Lib. poen.*, III.14; see also Burchard of Worms on this earlier *PL* 140, col. 939.

[406] *Statuts synodaux* I, c. 71, p. 186.

ill to swallow was allowed to consume the host from a chalice. John Beleth expressed doubt about the propriety of leaving the host in the mouth of a sick person who died before properly swallowing it, and wondered whether it should be removed from the mouth before burial.[407] A tale attributed to Bonaventure reflects the dilemma faced by priest who had to deny communion to those who could not handle the species. It describes the eucharist entering the side of the sick person miraculously: 'Christ's body entered his chest and reached his heart and then he died in great comfort'.[408]

This sacramental moment was taken by the laity to be as much its right as communion. A priest who denied the *viaticum* was likened to a murderer by the synodal statutes of St Malo in the mid fourteenth century.[409] When parishioners believed that their rights were not being respected they complained. In 1510/11 Archbishop Warham's visitation of Kent heard the complaint that the rector of Charleton had neglected his duties and that one Stephenson had died without 'shrift or hosylle', to which the rector accused answered that the deceased had communicated only a fortnight earlier and, therefore, was in no urgent need of communion when he died.[410]

Both the parishioners' complaint and the rector's reasoning were expressed in the language of sacramental religion. And they reflect a symbolic system which was designed throughout the twelfth century, disseminated through procedures which developed in the next century and which was thereafter constantly interpreted and reproduced. At its centre was Christ's body and the grace which offered a place in the narrative of redemption. The ways of access to Christ's body and its uses and abuses were constant sources of tension and conflict as the body was packaged, used, experienced, touched, carried, smelt and contemplated. Multiple and on-going appropriations make up the tale of the reception of the eucharistic symbol, and the modes of its teaching and subsequent imaging and understanding will be discussed in the next chapter.

---

[407] John Beleth, *Summa de ecclesiasticis officiis* II c. 159(t), p. 157: 'Si forte contigat quod aliquis sumens corpus Domini antequam transgluciat, moriatur, utrum corpus Domini debeat extrahi ab ore eius vel cum eo sepelliri'.

[408] 'Corpus Christi penetravit ejus pectus et pervenit ad cor et tum magna cum consolatione decessit', *Anecdotes*, p. 135. For an expression of the desire to receive communion before death in contemporary romance see *The alliterative Morte Arthure*, lines 4,307–15, pp. 156–7.

[409] Avril (1983), p. 100.

[410] *Warham visitation*, no. 65, p. 119. This was a debatable point, since canon law recommended that the eucharist be taken to the sick every 8–15 days, and according to the sick person's relapses, Peter Lombard, *Sententiae* IV D.23, *PL* 192, cols. 899–900; Gerald of Wales, *Gemma ecclesiastica* D. 1, c. 3, pp. 14–15.

# CHAPTER 2

# Beyond design: teaching and reception of the eucharist

## DISSEMINATION OF EUCHARISTIC KNOWLEDGE TO THE CLERGY

An intellectual edifice which was presented as sanctioned by sacred authority, as being harmonious and coherent, and as serving the general weal was effective only inasmuch as it was able to provide a language which could service experience. The central symbol of this language was the eucharist. The making of this language was accomplished through emphatic teaching, the symbolic contents and ritual procedures of which provided the basis of instruction, and to which was added the suggestion of associated images, acting like trains of associated thoughts. For us the intended teaching is the easier part to study: the contents of sermons, the frequency of preaching, the form of parochial instruction. What we must try to examine in new ways are the uncharted areas of *reception*[1]; what we lack is a picture of the horizon against which eucharistic teaching was received, understood, interpreted, and then put to work in the world.

Religious instruction was based on local teaching through preaching on the one hand, and personal examination and instruction, on the other. Ecclesiastical administrators and thinkers were convinced that deficient teaching led to error and was all too common. The weak link in the dissemination of a dominant world-view was an indifferent system of instruction. When encountering a knight who did not go to mass since he thought that this was merely an occasion for bringing offerings to priests, James of Vitry explained the reason for his error in that 'he had never heard the truth in preaching, nor had he been well instructed in the faith'.[2] Here the parish was the basic framework for examination and teaching, in which instruction could be given and

---

[1] On the concept of *Rezeption*, see the classic Iser (1974).
[2] 'Nunquam veritatem audiebat in predicatione, nec bene instructus erat in fide', James of Vitry, *The exempla*, no. 140, p. 62. On the enormities which followed from clerical ignorance of scripture see Gerald of Wales, *Gemma ecclesiastica* II, cs. 35–36, pp. 259–65.

sanctions brought to bear against those who did not adhere.[3] It was widely held that the better the teaching aids at the disposal of the clergy, the better the teaching they produced, and the more thorough and correct their parishioners' views and practices were bound to be. This understanding induced widespread activity of simplification, collection, categorisation and translation of doctrine, especially in those areas of knowledg most frequently encountered and used by the laity.

It was to ensure easy access to and unerring grasp of these doctrines and practices, that leading theologians, legislators and administrators of the Church applied their efforts. The twelfth century had seen the rise in importance of the personal encounter at confession,[4] and the thirteenth century added a test and site of adhesion in the reception of the eucharist. Thus, beside the genre of *Libri penitentiales* (the guidebooks for the clergy in the confessional exchange), new works of the type *De sacramento altaris* and the *Summae de sacramentis* from Paris, Bologna and Rome, were being created.

Communion and confession were bound together in the attempt to create an effective focus for examination of conscience and for the imparting of new knowledge. These were occasions for the integration of doctrines and practices which were finally reinforced through the eucharist which followed.[5] The continual supervision and teaching which were so essential to the system were maintained between confession and communion. The growing emphasis on the confessional in the twelfth century had established sacerdotal control over membership in the sacramental community, and once this was achieved, the event was further enhanced into an occasion for exchange of orthodox views from the mouth of the priest, for incomplete and often erroneous ones, from the confessed. But the initiative which boosted confession, as both dependent upon and confirming sacerdotal mediation, was matched and ultimately surpassed by another, which designed the eucharist and communion so that eventually confession became essentially a form of preparation for communion.[6] Confession dignified people and prepared them for eucharistic reception: 'it makes wo/man worthy like a tree with whose fruit eternal life can be bought'.[7] In fact,

---

[3] When in 1314 the bishop of Angers refused licences to celebrate mass in private chapels he explained it by the detrimental effect of missing instruction at the parochial mass: 'quia morum informacio non metitur, cum sermo divinus populo seminatur in ecclesiis parochialibus, qui absentibus et non audientibus fructuosus esse not potest', *Statuts synodaux* III, c. 4, p. 250.

[4] On the confessional see Murray (1981), pp. 275–86 and Boyle (1986), pp. 51–2.

[5] Browe (1940), pp. 23–5.

[6] Browe (1932).

[7] 'Hominem dignificat ut sit arbor tam digna ut fructibus ejus ematur vita eterna', quoted from Stephen of Bourbon in Berlioz (1981), p. 137.

the merging of the two in the programme of instruction, so clearly displayed in the formulations of Lateran IV has recently been summarised: 'L'histoire de la pénitence au moyen-âge, est associée à celle de l'eucharistie'.[8] The interaction between learning and confessing was complex, and in the rhythm of instruction one was meant to be led through edifying and effective preaching, towards confession and penance, as 'dire', in Berlioz's words, led to an ultimate 'faire dire'.[9] The confessional, then the penitential and finally the sacramental moods conceptualised and sealed a cognitive and sensory whole. The requirements of Lateran IV were that this should be an annual event properly done, as conveyed by John Mirk:

> And ben y-schryue alle and some,
> And be I-hoseled with-owte bere
> On Aster day alle I-fere.[10]

Penance was essentially private, and its private, personal, corrective, exhortative nature encompassed and enacted demands for conformity. The eucharist which followed it, however, introduced the universal, cosmic, timeless, supernatural intervention in the world which legitimated and explored the very grace to which access was made through the sacrament of confession and penance. Although internally bound these two sacraments were not interchangeable. Nor was the rapidly growing use of indulgences – packets of ready absolution for transgression – ever a meaningful alternative to participation in the eucharist. The public ritual of the mass, in which God was exposed and with him a multitude of benefits, was bound to private penance, but was a different type of ritual and symbol altogether.[11]

In some ways university masters of the thirteenth century were especially well placed for dissemination of the hegemonic Christian world-view. Open relations between the student body of priests and aspiring priests and their teachers provided channels for discussion of pastoral problems. An example of such an exchange is the institution of quodlibetal discussion, questions raised from the student floor at annual or bi-annual meetings which were answered by a regent master. *Quodlibeta* usually raised questions which were not covered by the curriculum and were to be answered on the morrow. They were often urgent and practical questions, reflecting the application of theological

---

[8] Payen (1977), p. 44.
[9] Berlioz (1981), pp. 300–301. On the many questions to be considered when studying sermons, see Bataillon (1980).
[10] *Instructions (a)*, lines 239–41, p. 8.
[11] On penance in the twelfth century, see Anciaux (1949), and Payen (1977).

maxims, and were collected and used as series of precedents and even inserted in some cases into pastoral guidebooks.[12] Such masters as Peter the Chanter were committed to examination of practical theological problems; in his *Summa de sacramentis* he discussed questions arising from pastoral experience.[13] This type of activity falls in with Robert of Courson's image, conveyed in his *Summa* of 1207, of the priest as knocking at the doors of theology like a child hungry for solid food.[14] But there was a pastoral awareness in such circles, expressed in James of Vitry's criticism of those scholars who condescended to parish priests.[15] The process was not a simple one, and the theological Latin writings were useful primarily to the upper clergy. However, the radiation from the intellectual heart of the culture, which is evident from the twelfth century, created sources for future transmission, translation and simplification, getting ever closer, and to a significant extent by the end of the thirteenth century, to vernacular pastoral parochial application.

A handbook such as the *Manuale de mysteriis ecclesiae* by Master Peter of Roissy, Chancellor of Chartres (*fl.* 1208–13) reflects a keen awareness that such a work was ultimately a source for parochial pastoral care.[16] In his tract on the sacraments, which is the last section of the manual, Peter quotes twelfth-century authorities and follows the order of discussion laid down by Peter the Chanter in his *Sententiae*.[17] In the section 'De sacramento corporis Christi' he discusses the eucharist's foundation, its nature, the priest, conditions of worthy reception, in a succession of short chapters which resemble a series of practical questions and answers. Such a work was the product of a new theological trend and of reformulated pastoral objectives: the sacraments had never been so speculatively discussed, and yet their implications so neatly packaged for dissemination.[18] This reorientation in Latin pastoral writing is most evident from the later twelfth century, in the period between Lateran III and Lateran IV 1179–1215.[19] For the first time the fruits of sacramental theory were to come within reach of parochial application.[20]

---

[12] Boyle (1974), esp. pp. 252–3.
[13] Baldwin (1970) I, pp. 53–4.
[14] Boyle (1986), p. 47.
[15] Ferruolo (1985), pp. 202–3, 215.
[16] Kennedy (1943). On the use of *summa* material in manuals for the clergy, see Gillespie (1980), p. 37.
[17] *Ibid*, pp. 29–38.
[18] *Ibid*, p. 34.
[19] Boyle (1986).
[20] Robertson (1947), p. 172.

In this process of dissemination of pastoral knowledge, Englishmen played an important role as scholars, bishops and friars.[21] Years of training in the continental schools and the highly developed English diocesan system to which they ultimately returned provided a suitable combination for the production of some of the most interesting pastoral writings. William de Montibus (*c.*1140–1213), Chancellor of Lincoln, was one of the earliest conveyers of the new learning from the schools to parish priests, in his *Carmen de septem sacramentis* of *c.*1250–60.[22] English mendicant scholars contributed to the *Summa* genre such as Simon of Hinton in his *De septem sacramentis*,[23] and the Franciscan lector at Oxford, Henry of Wodestone, in his *Summa de sacramentis* of 1261.[24] Other contemporary works, though less widespread, were part of the same project, such as Richard of Wetheringsette's (*fl.*1220) *Summa* 'Qui bene presunt' of *c.*1216×22[25] and John of Wales' (*d.c.*1300) *Monoloquium.*[26] Robert Grosseteste, who was bishop of Lincoln from 1235, had been to Paris and had spent a number of years as the Franciscan lector in Oxford before writing his great pastoral work, the *Templum dei* of 1220×30.[27] This is a penetrating allegorically constructed guidebook for parish priests who possessed some Latin, offering a summary of pastoral theology constructed through the simile of Christian faith as a Temple. The discussion of the foundations, walls and roof of the edifice of belief was accompanied by diagrams and cross references.[28] In a traditional vein, it laid great emphasis on the confessional. It was a very popular work in England and on the Continent, and was translated into English by the late fourteenth century as *The clensyng of man's soule.*[29] Grosseteste's interest in instruction was also demonstrated in his more popular work in Anglo-French, the *Château d'amour*, for the edification of a select lay readership.[30]

Throughout the thirteenth century synodal decrees provided the framework for, if not the contents of, the transmission of the necessary

[21] Goering in introduction to *Templum dei*, pp. 6–7; Gillespie (1980).
[22] MacKinnon (1969).
[23] CUL. Mm. 4.15.
[24] Bodleian Laud. lat. misc. 2, fols. 132ʳ–64ᵛ. On the friars' contribution to *pastoralia*, see Boyle (1956), pp. 210–29.
[25] Kemmler (1984), pp. 46–59.
[26] Pfander (1938), pp. 245–6. On thirteenth-century manual see Boyle (1955), pp. 81–2 and Boyle (1956), pp. 210–61.
[27] *Templum dei*, pp. 2–3; on Grosseteste and pastoral care see Boyle (1979); on Grosseteste's career, see Southern (1986), pp. 3–5.
[28] For diagrammes, see also the *Compilatio brevis* of the Dominican friar Thomas of Brackley, CUL Ff.1.18.
[29] Bodleian Bodley 923.
[30] Southern (1986), pp. 225–30. On these writings, see the basic survey in Boyle (1956) II, pp. 3–52.

instruction to the clergy.[31] In France, as in England, it was often the
ecclesiastical administrators who also compiled the guide-books and
manuals. Embryonic directives can be found in those comprehensive
synodal statutes, copied and circulated as separate pamphlets, such as
those of Lambeth of 1281. Bishop Quivil's *summula* of 1287,[32] and the
similar statutes of Cambrai of the mid thirteenth century which were
eventually incorporated into the synodal statutes of Liège of 1287.[33] In
England Archbishop John Pecham's formulations of a basic curriculum
for parochial instruction in 1281 provided the basis for all future
parochial guidebooks. It included teaching of the fourteen articles of
faith, the decalogue, the seven works of mercy, the seven vices, seven
virtues and the seven sacraments.[34] Future writings provided at least the
contents of the programme and, in addition, often gave a more elaborate explanation.[35] Pecham's programme was reiterated by later English
synods, by Bishop Quivil in Exeter in 1287, Archbishop Winchelsey of
Canterbury in 1301, Henry Woodlock, Bishop of Winchester, in 1308,
and Richard Kellaw, Bishop of Durham, in 1312, as well as twice by
Archbishop Simon Langham in 1359 and 1364.[36] The programme,
which came to be known by its *incipit* as the *Ignorantia sacerdotum*,
was so pervasive a didactic model that in the anti-heretical drive of the
fifteenth century it was defined as the framework out of which no
preachers or teachers should venture.[37]

The thirteenth century saw the elaboration of the syllabus in Latin in
*summae* and *specula* with cycles of manageable and easily usable knowledge later to be translated into the vernacular.[38] Tracts considered and
explained items in the syllabus in the vernacular, in manuscripts that
were unadorned, working books of parish priests.[39] Such was an
anonymous and useful pastoral poem of the fourteenth century, 'Of the
sacrament of the altar', which explained the doctrine of transubstantia-

---

[31] For an analysis of the speed at which thirteenth-century synodal statutes spread in
Germany, see Pixton (1985).

[32] *CS* II, 2. c. 9, pp. 900–5; *CS* II, 2, pp. 1060–77.

[33] Boeren (1953) and Boeren (1954).

[34] *CS* II, 2, c. 9, pp. 900–5.

[35] See Friar Thomas of Brackley's *Compilatio brevis*, CUL Ff.1.18, which is constructed in
this way: the eucharist is discussed as a subsection (fols. 28ʳ–32ʳ) to the section on the
sacraments.

[36] Peckham (1934), pp. 83–8.

[37] See the Arundel injunctions of 1409, *Register Hallum*, p. 141. On the influence of
*Ignorantia sacerdotum*, see also Cawley (1975), pp. 130–1.

[38] Wimsatt (1970), pp. 137–62.

[39] Like CUL Dd.12.69, fols. 24–31; see also the *Manuale credencium*, BL Harley 2398,
(which may have been written by Richard Rolle), with an exposition in English on the ten
commandments, the *Pater noster* and the eucharist ('Nota de sacramento altaris' on fols.
48ʳ–50ʳ).

tion, the scriptural basis for the eucharist discussed concomitance, unworthy reception and the meaning of the feast of Corpus Christi.[40] *Ignorantia sacerdotum* recalled in its very words that the syllabus was for parochial teaching and its needs 'in the vernacular without any subtlety in fanciful structure'.[41] Yet the most successful and inspired of the catechetical compositions seem to have combined the two: law and tale, influenced by the techniques and achievements of the friars. Thus the *Manuel des pechez* of William of Wadington, of the late thirteenth century, summarised in Anglo-French the articles of the faith, the decalogue, the cardinal sins, and the ways of confession, and accompanied these with lively illustrative tales – an early attempt at vernacular exposition on the Pecham syllabus.[42] *Handlyng synne* is an example of brilliant adaptation. Written by Robert Mannyng of Brunne in 1303 it was based on the Anglo-French model but gave a broader more popular English treatment with many useful *exempla*.[43] *Ayenbite of Inwyt* of *c.*1340 and the *Book of vices and virtues* of *c.*1375 were translations and adaptations of the thirteenth century *Somme le Roi* of the Dominican Laurence of Orléans.[44] The English writings of the fourteenth century were usually constructed in sermon form, ready-made for Sunday or feast day preaching for those priests whose Latin was poor.

Such expanded versions of the basic formulations of knowledge did not, however, suffice in providing the sort of training in depth which was needed in order to make the priest into an effective agent of cultural mediation. Thirteenth-century theologians and legislators had more in mind: provision wider access to the discussions in the schools, not merely to the final formulaic conclusions, was necessary. Synods legislated whole sections about the eucharist, dealing with rules and procedures, like the seventeen clauses on 'De eucharistia et extrema unctione' in the synodal statutes of Nîmes in 1252.[45] The *Oculus sacerdotis*, a book which was deep yet all-encompassing – indeed, quite encyclopaedic – was finally produced *c.*1320–30 by William of Pagula.[46] The *Oculus* proved to be an effective and popular handbook and was unique in discussing English custom as it had evolved over 200 years of steady diocesan legislation. The *Oculus* was divided into three

---

[40] *Twenty-six political poems*, pp. 103–7; the poem is contained in a manuscript of *c.*1400, Bodleian Digby 102.
[41] 'Vulgariter absque cujuslibet subtilitatis textura fantastica', CS II, 2, c. 9, p. 901. On vernacular instruction, see also Russell (1962).
[42] Arnould (1940); Robertson (1945).
[43] Boitani (1982), pp. 23–5; Pfander (1936), p. 250.
[44] *The book of vices and virtues*, pp. xxxii–xxxvi.
[45] *Statuts synodaux* II, pp. 322–32.
[46] Boyle (1955); Boyle (1956), pp. 348–401; Ball (1976), pp. 55–6.

parts: the *Pars oculi* which summarised canon law and particularly local English variations; the *Pars dextera* which considered practical moral precepts related with the confessional, the sacraments and pastoral guidance in general; and the *Pars sinistra* of speculative theology for more abstract edification. It encompassed all that was needed for reflection, reference and preaching, was up-to-date including some material from the *Clementines* published in 1317, and was all-inclusive. The *Oculus* combined a number of pastoral genres: the mass commentary, the penitential *summa*, exposition on the sacraments, as they had developed since the twelfth century. It was criticised on some issues of structure and was updated by John de Burgh in 1358 in the *Pupilla oculi*;[47] it also circulated in separate sections, the *Dextera pars* being a popular pastoral handbook of the later Middle Ages. It is noteworthy that the *Pupilla* paid even greater attention to the eucharist than the *Oculus* had done earlier in the century.[48] An equally important manual was the *Manipulus curatorum* of the Aragonese priest Guy of Montrocher, written in Teruel in 1333.[49] This was a handbook on the sacraments, penitential practice, the *Pater noster,* and the ten commandments, and about a half of its volume is devoted to the eucharist. It was useful and widely used, and was often recommended by Continental synods as the classic pastoral manual.[50]

Two main trends in intellectual production are discernible from the thirteenth century: ambitious compilations which summarised theology, law and practice which only a minority of priests could afford, or use, on the one hand, and shorter and often thematic tracts providing sermons or formulae for teaching with little background knowledge.[51] It is probably the latter genre which reveals most about what was the more frequently heard in parochial teaching, and the large space devoted to the eucharist within the genre reflects the appreciation of its importance and of the many errors which might arise in its teaching.[52] Even with the great compilations like the *Oculus* and the *Pupilla*, it is clear from the evidence of annotation and extraction, that the eucharist drew more attention than other sacraments, that its sections were thumbed through more frequently.[53] The tracts on the mass extracted

---

[47] Pfander (1937), pp. 99–103.
[48] Ball (1976), pp. 261–2.
[49] Michaud-Quantin (1970b), p. 81.
[50] See Binz (1973), pp. 348–50.
[51] Payen (1977), pp. 417–18.
[52] In eucharistric manuals it is also possible to distinguish between those meant to induce a mood, and those more oriented towards practice, see Michaud-Quantin (1970b), pp. 82–3.
[53] Ball (1976), pp. 265–72.

from such inclusive compilations were working books for the parochial clergy, who seem to have shifted from annotation of penitential sections, to that of eucharistic sections in the fourteenth and fifteenth centuries.[54] Thus, a Latin tract 'De eukaristia' of the fourteenth century is a summary of theological discussions of the preceding two centuries, which combined ideas from the schools, and presented resolutions and formulations perfected by some of the best minds of Christendom.[55] The tract-sermon taught that there were four important matters in the sacrament: the priest, the bread and wine, the intention to consecrate, and the proper utterance of the words of consecration. It emphasised Christ's presence in the sacrament, explained the meaning of the wine and water as the blood and water which flowed from Christ's side, and stressed the concomitance of flesh and blood in every bit of the host. The sermon also reminded the hearer that the eucharist had been established under the form of wine and bread so as to test faith, to avoid abhorrence of raw flesh, and to save the body of Christ from the ridicule of heretics.[56] It also taught that fasting must precede reception and that when well received the eucharist saved from sin and enhanced grace. One can almost hear in the answers the questions and issues which vexed people on the nature of the sacrament, of God's body, of their communion. A vernacular version of such an exposition can be found in the anonymous tract on the sacraments in the *Manuale sacerdotum parochialium* of 1380×1400.[57] The treatment of the eucharist here is more devotional, with directions about appropriate thoughts and images during the mass:

The ferthe sacrament is godies bodi in forme of brede þat ye prest sacrith atte masse yat eche cristene man schal bileve yat it is veralyche godis bodi yat was ibore of ye maide marie & hend of on ye rode. (fol. 170ᵛ)

People were directed that every time God's body was seen at mass or borne to the sick: 'worschep hys god bi byddyng hys pater noster or wat he best can . . .'.[58] This sort of writing assisted the clergy by providing a text to be followed almost verbatim, yet its essential link to more scholarly texts was never lost.

---

[54] *Ibid.*

[55] BL Add. 24660.

[56] See similar arguments in Peter the Venerable, *Contra Petrobrusianos*, p. 122; James of Vitry, 'De sacramentis', p. 209; and in Berthold of Regensburg's sermons, Trachtenberg (1943), p. 110.

[57] Oxford Bodleian Bodley 110, fols. 155ᵛ–66ᵛ; also in Oxford Trinity College 7, fol. 70ᵛ; Ball (1976), pp. 43–6. For a Spanish vernacular tract on the mass issued by the Council of Segovia in 1325, see Conde (1986).

[58] Pfander (1936), p. 252.

The English tradition was particularly lively through the workings of a developed administrative system. Pecham's syllabus was the basis for parochial instruction and yet it was constantly reworked at different levels of scholarly accomplishment, Latin and English, producing tens of works in hundreds of surviving manuscripts. The most impressive official attempt to provide the basic needs of the parish priest was the *Lay folk's catechism* of 1357. An entry in the register of Archbishop Thoresby of York, who had commissioned the composition of this text, complained that better instruction was needed on *pastoralia* and a brief exposition followed first in a Latin and then in an English version.[59] Of similarly practical nature was the highly popular *Speculum christiani* of c.1360–70 which treated the ten commandments and incorporated long quotes from the *Ignorantia sacerdotum*,[60] and the extremely popular work, Mirk's *Festial*. This was a series of sermons of c.1405 collected by John Mirk, canon of Lilleshall (Shropshire), which comprised seventy-four sermons for Sundays and feasts, together with tales and useful refutations of contemporary Lollard errors. In his *Instructions to parish priests* Mirk provided neat formulae for the examination of faith and a summary of the traditional Pecham's syllabus on the articles of faith, the ten commandments and the seven sacraments, under the heading 'quod sufficit scire in lingua materna' and in the guidelines for examination of confession.[61]

And many less well-known writers were part of the same project. An anonymous fifteenth century author of *A discourse upon the constitution* announced his aim in writing such a work:

I entende after suche auctours as I have seen to distribute forth to symple curates, curales or upplandisshe, hou thei shal have hem aftere God man in their demenyng . . . and also hou thei shal declare unto theire parisshens the matieres conteyned in the seid constitucion, in fulfillyng of the charge leide upon hem.[62]

So he dipped into Lyndwood's *Provinciale* and into thirteenth-century works on vices and virtues, used tales from James of Vitry and of Caesarius of Heisterbach, exploiting the stock prepared for this very end, and adding to these an individual touch in the choice of devotional themes. The process was inventive, if not quite creative, and the translation and adaptation of material was made with an eye to utility

---

[59] On the dating, see *Lay folk's catechism*, p. xvii; Gillespie (1980), pp. 43–6; Hudson (1985) and Hudson (1988a).

[60] Cawley (1975), p. 131; Gillespie (1980), p. 38.

[61] *Instructions (a)*, pp. 25–30, 30–43. See another example using the variety of schemes: commandments, petitions, sacraments, virtues, vices, gifts and beautitudes, in Thomas of Brackley's *Compilatio brevis* CUL Ff.1.18.

[62] Oxford Bodleian Eng.Th.C. 57, fol. 3r. Hodgson (1948), pp. 2–3.

and ease of reference.[63] The utility of such works is demonstrated in their wide use well into the fifteenth century; a large part of Caxton's output was in the form of such handbooks as Mirk's *Festial* and Clement Maydston's *Directorium sacerdotum.*[64]

From the embryonic *ordines* of the eighth century a different type of manual was developing on the celebration of the mass; the new manuals were practical in tone and addressed questions on such matters as the frequency of celebration, the preparation of the altar, and the bread and wine.[65] Above all they considered the meanings of the ritual, and were often appended to synodal statutes.[66] This type proliferated in the thirteenth century: one such is a tract which provided more in the way of a symbolic commentary on the ritual of the mass, as in this passage on the symbolism of vestments:[67]

AMICE   chastity, because it girds all round as the saviour said take this yoke of God . . .
STOLE   the stole signifies the band with which he was bound to the column

This is an interesting example of dissemination of allegories from mass commentaries which were a common traditional genre for discussion of the mass in the twelfth and thirteenth centuries. The genre applied techniques from symbolic biblical exegesis which explained why features of the mass had developed, and induced greater awareness on the part of the celebrant. Such was the imaging offered by a thirteenth century work by a Praemonstratensian canon 'De canone missae', which reminded its reader, the priest, that:

The Lord Jesus Christ in His Passion was a pure host/victim; in His resurrection – a holy host/victim; in His Ascension – an immaculate host/victim, the bread of eternal life.[68]

Meanwhile the mass was augmented and decorated by lights, bells, incense, and by a priest in fine array. The genre *De sacramento altaris* from which this exposition developed was now giving greater sub-

---

[63] Hodgson (1948), pp. 5–8.
[64] Bennett (1952), p. 184.
[65] See instructions in the section 'Ordinarium missae' of the *Sarum missal*, pp. 216–29.
[66] *Liège, Statuts synodaux*; Boeren (1953) and Boeren (1954).
[67] 'Amictus   Castitatem quia precingitur circalculos unde ait salvator hic jugum domini suscipite
    Stola   stola signat legaturam qua legatus fuit ad columpnam',
Bodleian Rawlinson C241, fol. 141ʳ. For a Spanish example of symbolic interpretation of the vestments, see the diocesan handbook of Segovia of 1325, Conde (1986), pp. 132–3.
[68] This tract is in a collection of exegetical and theological writings, CUL Gg.4.16, fols. 94ʳᵃ–98ᵛᵇ. Quote from fol. 96ᵛᵃ: 'Dominus ihesu xristus in passione sua fuit hostia pura, in resurreccione hostia sancta, in ascencione hostia immaculata, panis vite eterne'.

stance to the priestly office, and guiding the performers themselves in the significance of their tasks.[69]

In addition to clerical instruction which was aimed to facilitate the teaching of the laity, the necessary prerequisite of a mission of teaching, works were also being written to help priests *perform* better. Such awareness of the rituals and their meanings could contribute to the sense of Christian purpose and helped release previously exclusive knowledge into the new bureaucracy of the Christian world. Furthermore, ritual could teach more effectively than great numbers of words. Tracts on the mass attempted to go through every rubric and explain its meanings, and shorter versions were entered into pastoral guidebooks such as the *Oculus sacerdotis* and the *Pupilla oculi*.[70] Religious houses and orders codified their customs and traditions in manuals such as the thirteenth-century Dominican directions on the conventual mass,[71] the customaries of St Augustine's, Canterbury, of *c.*1330-20,[72] and the Carthusian mass commentary.[73] These texts differed in detail but they all attempted to impart uniformity and unity between words and gestures through the explication of their symbolic meanings. The *Alphabetum seu instructio sacerdotum* surveys the priest's preparation, the confession and penance, the preparation of vestments, vesting and celebration, with details on posture and gestures, in a mechanical tone which, if somewhat dry, was probably useful.[74] Lydgate's *Exortacion to prestys when they shall sey theyr masse*, written *c.*1430-40, is quite unique as it is not related to rubric order in the mass.[75] More like the exhortative literature to layfolk, it is freer in discussing the state of mind and the comportment appropriate to priestly status, not through mechanical instructions but through suggestion of a mood. In English verse, it guides the priest on such matters as the approach to ritual and the preparation for it by contrition and prayer, above all calling for meditation on the blood, the wounds, and the love of Christ:

> Ye shall also most louyngly remembre
> Uppon hys most peynfull passyoun.[76]

In itself the ritual was meant to be instructive. But not only did the

[69] See also Goering (1982), pp. 323, 328.
[70] For thirteenth-century tracts, see *Tracts on the mass*, pp. 219-29, 255-69; and for the fourteenth century, pp. 3-15, 23-5.
[71] *Tracts on the mass*, pp. 73-96.
[72] *The customary of the Benedictine monasteries* I, pp. 283-90.
[73] BL Nero A III; *Tracts on the mass*, pp. 99-104, see pp. 104-10 on votive and festive masses.
[74] *Tracts on the mass*, pp. 32-51, printed from its Paris, 1499 edition.
[75] *Lydgate's minor poems*, pp. 84-6; Pearsall (1970), pp. 258-9.
[76] *Lydgate's minor poems*, p. 86, lines 33-4; Pearsall (1970), p. 258. Lydgate also wrote a poem for the instruction of the Countess of Suffolk during the mass, see below, pp. 158-9.

liturgical actions convey meaning, the mass was an occasion for preaching in a highly charged setting.[77] If ritual was to convey clear messages it had to support an edifice of clear interpretations, ready explanations of its various parts. Thus, as the mass became more elaborate, the points at which it could go wrong – its typical accidents – unfolded, and synods attempted to provide suitable remedies. For example, the synodal statutes of Bordeaux of 1234 reminded priests not to elevate the host before 'hoc est corpus meum' since it was not yet Christ's body!78 The earliest synodal statutes of the diocese of Cambrai, of 1231×60, recommended the practice of sheltering the altar from falling impurities by hanging curtains.[79] Corrective as well as normative works were written, addressing the difficulties and potential abuses of ritual practice as these unfolded. The customal of St Peter's, Westminster, of c. 1266 dealt with remedies for accidents, as when a host fell into the wine, or when a host was vomited.[80] The *Manipulus curatorum* of 1333 contained a large tract on the eucharist and within it a section which discussed and advised on 'The defects which may occur in the mass', such as spilling of wine, vomiting, and sudden death of the priest.[81] The *Secreta sacerdotum* of Henry of Hesse (d.1397) is a pamphlet aimed at the discussion and correction of aberrations which had developed in the form of the mass. Like the writers of mass commentaries he followed the rubrics, and after a general exhortation about the behaviour due during the mass, he condemns the custom of elevating the chalice before consecration. At the rubric 'Suscipe sancta Trinitatis' he comments:

In these parts some elevate the chalice high above their heads, a practice which is avoided by wiser people lest they commit idolatry.[82]

He abhors the exaggerated gestures which had developed in some places; there were priests who insisted on all but touching their head to the altar at 'Te igitur' when a gentle inclination would have done nicely:

Where some are in the habit of placing their head on the altar when bowing, which I

---

[77] On preaching from the rood-screen in Italian churches, see Hall (1974), pp. 339–40, fig. 17.
[78] *Statuts synodaux* II, c. 29, p. 58.
[79] *Cambrai, Statuts synodaux*, p. 140: 'Cortina conveniens sursum super altare entendatur quae protegat et defendat altare ab incommodis immunditiarum descendentium'.
[80] *The customary of the Benedictine monasteries* II, pp. vi–ix, 217, 221–2.
[81] Guy of Montrocher, *Manipulus curatorum*, c. 11, fols. 42ᵛ–45ʳ.
[82] 'In hac parte quidam alte ultra caput solent calicem elevare quod a magis sapientibus ideo vitatur ne idolatoriam committant', *Secreta sacerdotum*, fol. a. iiiʳᵇ.

consider to be superfluous and indeed careless. The bowing should be in moderation of limbs and with the utmost humility of mind.[83]

The words of the canon, the most solemn part of the mass, were to be uttered neither too slowly nor too fast, and only in a measured tone.[84] The sign of the cross was to be made with two fingers, the index signifying prudence and the middle finger symbolising justice, thus signifying the double nature of the sacrament, deity and humanity. When hands were extended in the form of the cross just before the consecration, too flamboyant a movement could end by toppling the chalice altogether:

And those things whose effect is evidently good, are not always safe, because at the extension of arms the hanging of the alb-sleeve might easily cause the chalice to be overturned.[85]

Not only measure, but prudence in bodily gestures was required by Henry. This moment of extension of arms was an important one; the priest turned into a symbolic crucifix, the cross on the back of his chasuble was a golden image of a cross from which the arms and hands extended sidewise, a living cross.[86] But its effect would be lost if the chalice and its contents, allegedly blood to be, were spilt.[87] The moment of the consecration itself was laden with deep meaning and required dignified performance:

It is sufficient for the sake of devotion and consecration to enunciate the words simply and clearly as it is said during the consecration of the Lord's body.[88]

Another danger was the possible marking of the wrong moment for adoration as Nicholas Gellent, bishop of Angers, found in the visitation of his diocese in 1272:

We saw in many churches that the bell is rung after the elevation of the Lord's body rather than before the elevation as it ought to be.[89]

---

[83] 'Ubi quidam solent caput quasi super altare ponere inclinando quod non solum reputo superfluum immo dico quod est incautum. Sit illis modestia membrorum inclinatio et maxima mentis humiliatio', *ibid,* fol. a. iii$^{\text{vb}}$.

[84] *Ibid,* fol. a. iiii$^{\text{rb}}$.

[85] 'Quidam etiam longa signa faciunt, hec quamuis sint bona, quia manifesta, non tamen sunt secura, quia per brachii extensionem dependens albe manica faciliter pararet calicis eversionem', *ibid,* fol. a. iiii$^{\text{vb}}$.

[86] On cross symbolism in other features of the mass, like the fraction of the host see the Dominican mass tract, *Tracts on the mass,* p. 82, and Heitz (1974).

[87] On remedies for spilt wine, see the statutes of the diocese of Nîmes of 1252, *Statuts synodaux* II, c. 74, pp. 326–8.

[88] 'Satis est ad devotionis et consecrationis effectum ut verbis simpliciter et discrete prolatis sicut dictum est dum corpus dominicum consecratur', *Secreta sacerdotum,* fol. a. v$^{\text{rb}}$_v$^{\text{a}}$.

[89] *Statuts synodaux* III, c. 1, p. 112.

The words of the consecration required only gentle enunciation. In *Piers plowman* a wish is expressed for proper enunciation, reflecting the fact that the laity depended on the priest for the adequate treatment of the Latin text:

> Lord lete þat this prestes lelly seien here masse
> That they ouerhippe nat hastile as y hope they do not.[90]

The English *Fasciculus morum,* a fifteenth-century treatise on the vices and virtues, similarly decried those priests who failed in pronunciation of the words through sin:

> Longe-slepers and over-lepers
> For-skyppers and over-hyppers
> For Thay shulen to hell pyne.[91]

Henry of Hesse discusses the elevation, the focus of the mass and a moment particularly fraught with abuse. Some priests elevated the host a number of times,[92] some raised it and bent their heads backwards to look at the host and were overtaken by dizziness which endangered the host:

When during the elevation he gazes at the host in the usual manner turning his face to it, he feels a dizziness of the head and begins to vacillate as if he is about to fall.[93]

Equally dangerous were movements and gyrations while elevating the host:

I believe that such turns and superfluous long elevations should not be done as reason shows.[94]

Similar cautions had been raised in the thirteenth-century instruction on the Dominican conventual mass:

He should elevate the consecrated host not while leaning over the altar but rather gently inclining towards it and with both hands, so that it can be seen by those standing behind. He should not sway it, nor keep it elevated for a long time, but immediately replace it with both hands.[95]

---

[90] *Piers plowman: edition of the C text,* passus XVIII, lines 117–18, p. 283.

[91] Wenzel (1978), p. 184, lines 684–6.

[92] *Secreta sacerdotum,* fol. v^va.

[93] 'Dum autem more solito in elevatione sua erecta facie hostia diutius inspiceret vertiginem sensit in capite et incepit facillare quasi velit cadere', *ibid,* fol. a. v^vb.

[94] 'Sed illas versiones et longas elevationes superfluas reputo non debere fieri prout ratio capit', *ibid,* fol. a. vi^rb. For complaints against turning with the host by other writers, see Thurston (1901), p. 592.

[95] 'Hostia consecrata non super altare procumbens sed aliquantulum inclinans cum ambabus manibus ipsam elevet, ita quod possit retro stantibus apparere. Ipsam vero non circumferat, nec diu teneat elevata, sed statim cum utraque manu reponat', *Tracts on the mass,* p. 80.

Henry of Hesse's complaints fall in with the sort of contingencies envisaged and dealt with in penitential books as to the behaviour of negligent priests. He raised the problems inherent in the ritual, those of the exposure and vulnerability of what was claimed first to become and then to be, Christ's body. This type of eucharistic practice exerted inevitable pressure on the neatly designed mass of the liturgists and theologians. It exposes the living ritual not only in the material vulnerability of any sacramental exercise but through demonstration of the ways in which the clergy attempted to dramatise, vocalise, impress and cajole, in a complex dialectic of response to their audiences and to the exigencies of time and space. The balance of meanings presented in normative texts could never fully be achieved;[96] the symbol was bound to be appropriated not only in the minds, but in the handling, seeing, tasting of this very material artifact of divinity. Tracts like that of Henry of Hesse bear witness to the on-going struggle to redress the balance and to reappropriate the ritual into its designed form.

### TEACHING THE LAITY

In our search for the living ritual and the experiences which it engendered, manuals for the clergy inform us not only about clerical formation and ability to perform, but also about the types of formulations which were heard and possessed by the audience. Vernacular guidebooks included ready formulations and illustrative tales which could be immediately applied in teaching. Thus, although these texts cannot reveal the interpretations made by the audience as others can, they do reveal the contents of parochial teaching, of images which in turn appear in popular lyrics, and even in vernacular art. From the thirteenth century onwards texts were written by leading thinkers in the vernacular for the express use of the laity.[97] The *Manuale credencium* which may have been written by Richard Rolle, was 'in englisch tonge for lewid men þat nought understond latyn ne frensch'.[98]

Whenever the core of beliefs was explicated the eucharist was explicitly mentioned. Ranulph de la Houblonnière (c. 1225–1288) described

---

[96] Therefore studies based almost exclusively on normative sources, such as Bossy (1983), cannot capture the experience of a lived mass.

[97] At the beginning of a mystical tract in French Jean Gerson defended his undertaking: 'Aucuns se pourront donner merveille pourquoy de matiere haulte comme est parler de la vie contemplative, je veuil escripre en françois plus qu'en latin et plus aux femmes que aux hommes. Qu'en latin ceste matiere est donnee et traite tres excellenment es divers livres . . .', Jean Gerson, *Oeuveres completes* VII, no. 296, p. 16.

[98] BL Harley 2398, fol.

eucharistic belief as the very core of faith.[99] Mirk's summary of 'Quod sufficit scire in lingua materna' includes:

> 'Be-leuest also verrely
> Þat hyt ys goddes owne body,
> Þat þe prest ȝeueth the,
> Whenne þou schalt I-hoseled be,
> Leuest also in fulle a tent,
> How þat holy sacrament,
> Is I-ȝeue to mon kynne
> ·In remyssyone of here synne'.[100]

The eucharist was a central issue in the examination of a sick person before the administration of sick-bed communion, as in a fifteenth century English service-book:

Beleuyst þow in þe sacrament of þe auter, þat is cristes bodi whiche was born of Marie, wiche criste lefte her among us as for þe most precious iewel, whan he schulde departe be deth from his disciples?[101]

The eucharist also appears in the simple recitations of lists of sacraments, like those in the commonplace book of Robert Reynes (1430–c.1505) of Acle in Norfolk, as a set of simple questions:

How many are the church's sacraments? Seven. Which? Baptism, confirmation, eucharist, penance, extreme unction, ordination and marriage. How many are repeatable and how many not? Four are repeatable: eucharist, penance, extreme unction and marriage . . .[102]

Within the basic programme of instruction this central subject was discussed in a number of contexts, at the explanation of the sacraments and in the discussion of the *Pater noster*. An early work based on the Pecham syllabus, from the first half of the fourteenth century, discusses the eucharist among the sacraments:

Ye ferþe sacrament is godys body in forme of bred yt þe prest sacret at masse. Yat euerych cristenman schal by leue yat hyt is uerylyche godys body yt y bore of ye mayde marye & hengit on ye rode.[103]

---

[99] Beriou (1987) I, pp. 128–9, esp. p. 154: 'Ad huc ergo quod simus beati, oportet quod credimus firmiter . . . quando videmus sacramentum altaris, firmiter debemus credere et tenere quod ibi descendit ille totus integer qui natus fuit de virgine in die Natalis, qui passus et ascendit . . .'.

[100] *Instructions (a)*, lines 949–56, pp. 29–30.

[101] *English fragments*, p. 8.

[102] 'Quot sunt sacramenta ecclesie? Septem. Que? Baptismum, confirmacio, Heukaristia, penitencia, extrema unccio, ordo et matrimonium. Quot sunt [iterabilia] et quot non sunt? IIII$^a$ sunt iterabilia: Heukaristia, penitencia, extrema unccio et matrimonium . . .', *The commonplace book of Robert Reynes of Acle*, no. 38, pp. 180–1.

[103] CUL Dd.12.69, fol. 31$^v$.

By the 1370s the *Lay folk's catechism* taught the fourth sacrament:

> The ferthe is the sacrament of the auter,
> Cristes owen bodi in likeness of brede,
> Als hale as he toke it of that blessed maiden;
> Whilk ilk man and woman, that of eld is,
> Aught forto resceyve anes in the yhere,
> That is at sai, at paskes, als hali kirke uses,
> When thai er clensed of syn thurgh penaunce. . . .
> For he that takes it worthili, takes his salvation,
> And who-so unworthili, takes his dampnation.[104]

The eucharist was often discussed at the exposition of the *Pater noster*, in connection with 'our daily bread', as in the *Ayenbite of Inwyt* of *c.*1340:

Hit is ysed þeruore echedayes: þet eche daye hit is ous nydeuol and echedaye me ssel hit nyme oþer ate sacrement of þe wefde ase doþ þe prestes; oþer gostliche be riȝte byleaue.[105]

And again in the *Book of vices and virtues* of *c.*1375:

Now semeþ þan it is riȝt litle þing þat we biddeþ, but, forsoþe, it is not so, for we biddeþ many þinges . . . þat is þe bred of þe blessed couent, þe bred of heuene, þe bred of angeles, þe delitable bred, þe bred of lif wiþout endynge . . .[106]

Lydgate's poetic exposition on the *Pater noster* was not a simple pastoral aid, but it brings together elements which were current in parochial instruction:

> To thy dyscyplys for a memoryall,
> For a perpetuall commemoracyoun,
> Of thy flessh and thy blood, take in especiall,
> Of a pure maydyn thyn Incarnacioun,
> Thy meek suffraunce for our Redempcioun,
> With mynde also thow lyst for us be ded,
> That we may cleyme for our sauacioun
> Receyve thy boody among in forme of bred.[107]

He does not stress transubstantiation as much as parochial schemes do, but the biblical reference, the mention of Mary, and the salvific promise, were typical of the current vernacular pastoral manuals. So too was his interpretation of 'our daily bread':

---

[104] *Lay folks' catechism*, lines 316–22, 326–7, p. 66.
[105] *Ayenbite*, p. 112.
[106] *Book of vices and virtues*, pp. 108–9. In *Pupilla oculi* the Pater noster is discussed in the fourth part on the mass, Ball (1976), pp. 265–6.
[107] *Lydgate's minor poems* I, lines 201–8, c. 26, pp. 66–7.

Our daily bred, our Restauracioun,
Our foode, our manna, geyn fendis violence.[108]

Conventional schemes for the discussion of vices and virtues were also used for eucharistic discussion. In *Handlyng synne* the vice of gluttony provided the occasion:

Me þenketh þey trespas ful yl,
Þat any day ete, are þey here messe,
But ȝyf hyt be þurgh harder dystresse . . .
Þat swych a preste doup glotonye,
Þat leuyþ hys messe on þe auter
For to go to a dyner.[109]

The *Book of vices and virtues* was similarly structured but discusses unworthy reception of the eucharist as the second branch of the vice of pride:

And after, how þou to litle hunouredest Goddes body whan þou seye it or whan þou receyuestest it, as whan þou were not worþy, for þou ne were nouȝt tiȝt wel y-schryue ne repentaunt.

Or else, worst of all:

ȝif þou receyuedtest hym in dedly synne by þy witynge, for þat is a gret despit to God.[110]

In *Handlyng synne* of *c.*1303 Robert Mannyng devised a correspondence between the characteristics of the host and the seven cardinal sins, using a mnemonic device which related a material aspect of the host with the abstract knowledge to be imparted. Applying common colour symbolism he described the host, the remedy to all manner of evil and sin:

The uble is small, so should we be little in will,
Of wheat – loveliest corn man makes – so meek and lovely,
Its paste not of sour dough – so we shouldn't be envious,
As wheat does not prick like barley and oats do – we should not have thorns of idleness,
Paste not mixed with other corns – so we should not mix with avarice,
As the uble is not thick we must not be gluttons,
White – we must not be blackly lecherous.[111]

---

[108] *Ibid,* lines 213–14, p. 67.
[109] *Handlyng synne,* lines 7,312–14, 7,318–20, p. 234.
[110] *The book of vices and virtues,* p. 16.
[111] Paraphrased from *Handlyng synne,* pp. 314–16, lines 10,079–142. Some of these themes were taken up in Corpus Christi sermons which were often purely eucharistic expositions, see below, pp. 213–25.

The *Fasciculus morum,* composed by a Franciscan in the fifteenth century, includes a short verse in English and in Latin versions, describing the properties of the host, under the vice *accidia*:

| | |
|---|---|
| In figura rotunditatem | Ronde in schapyng |
| In pressura tenuitatem | Thynne in þe bakyng |
| In aspectu albedinem | Whyte in þe seyng |
| In gustu dulcedinem | Swete in þe smackyng or tastyng |
| In una parte dulcis descriptio | On þe to halfe wel y-wrete, |
| In alia parte levis percussio | On þe þother halfe þynne ysmete.[112] |

The schemes of vices and virtues and the list of seven sacraments were the building blocks in both clerical and parochial instruction; and their merging is witnessed in their entry into visual representation. Besides the simple relation between the crucifixion, the source of grace, and the sacraments, the seven channels of grace, schemes relating the sacraments to particular virtues were being developed, built on edifices of scholastic method. Vincent of Beauvais (*c.*1190–*c.*1264) produced the standard set of correlations, which can be seen in the Dominican Belleville breviary of 1343.[113] Here the sacraments and their related virtues were accompanied by a biblical scene exemplifying them, and fitting them into the seven canonical hours. The sacraments were related, as Aquinas had shown in his *De sacramentis,* to the three theological and four cardinal virtues: baptism to faith, extreme unction to hope, eucharist to charity, ordination to prudence, confession to justice, marriage to temperance, confirmation to fortitude. And the biblical scene used to exemplify the fusion of eucharist and charity was the story of Cain and Abel, a story uniting Abel's offering with the sacrifice of his life.[114] Another example, which is now lost but is fortunately recorded in drawings, is the late-fourteenth-century wall-painting in the north aisle of the church of Kirton-in-Lindsey (Lincolnshire). The scene of the crucifixion with Mary and John the Evangelist forms the uppermost images, and from the wounds of the crucified body blood flows in seven trickling lines which create a semi-sphere radiating into scenes of the seven sacraments.[115] A very similar composition was used in the stained glass window now in St Anthony's Chapel, Cartmel Fell (Lancashire), and which dates from the early sixteenth century. Red lines of blood issue from Christ's body to the

[112] Oxford Bodleian Rawlinson C670, fol. 88ʳ; Wenzel (1978), pp. 69–70, 182–3, on this digression in the discussion of *accidia*.

[113] Paris BN 10483–10484.

[114] Godwin (1951), esp. p. 612.

[115] Peacock (1866), pp. 24–6, plate I for a drawing. This drawing may have been related to the activities of the local Corpus Christi fraternity.

three surviving group scenes: the mass, ordination and marriage.[116] An iconography of the sacraments was also developed in the sculpted decoration of English octagonal baptismal fonts (most of which can be dated to the fifteenth century). Here, eight panels were available for decoration: a crucifixion scene and the seven sacraments, inspired by the type of idea which had motivated the painter in Kirton.[117]

The laity was offered a symbolic system, a sacramental world-view, taught in word and image and sound, through teaching which culminated in the ritual which was meant to be uniform and universal, and equally efficacious at every altar in Christendom. So a variety of stimuli were combined with writings aimed particularly to the laity to support and complement parochial instruction. The laity, and this term covers a variety of social and cultural positions, were taught the faith and relevant images, and their relation to the eucharist during the liturgy as well as outside it. Mirk's instructions to priests included guidance for parishioners in their postures at the various stages of the mass.[118] If wine was to be drunk after swallowing the host, this was in order to wash away the crumbs lodged between the teeth; and it was not consecrated wine. Priests were supposed to stress the intention and the appropriate signs of it in external behaviour:

> Ne non in chyrche stonde schal,
> Ny lene to pyler ny to wal,
> But fayre on kneus pey schule hem sette,
> Knelynge doun up on the flette
> And pray to God wyth herte meke
> To ʒeue hem grace and mercy eke.[119]

The priest was to teach them to stand at the reading of the gospel, to kneel after it for sacring with clasped hands, and to salute God in the sacrament.[120] Lydgate's 'Interpretation and virtues of the mass' recommends to the lay person to anticipate and understand the action at the altar. He directs his explanation of the significance of clerical gestures, vestments, words, to an active and well-informed participant, who is led from the moment of entry into the church and until the *Ite*, with a

---

[116] Fowler (1912), esp. pp. 298–9 and the mass scene with Christ standing on the altar as the Man of Sorrows, colour plate 1. Anne Nichols suggests the date *c.* 1520 for this glass; for a very similar iconography of the crucified Christ with three sacramental scenes see a glass window in St James' church, Rothenburg (Bavaria), of *c.* 1420, Wadell (1969), plate 6, no. 12, pp. 21–2. A Seven Sacrament window existed until 1730 in St Sampson's church, York, *York art*, p. 182.
[117] Fryer (1902). On other compositions with the seven sacraments, see Rushforth (1929).
[118] Bettey (1979), p. 21.
[119] *Instructions (a)*, lines 270–5, p. 9.
[120] On salutations, see below, pp. 156–63.

clear high-point at the consecration. Priest and lay participant are exhorted here as they receive cues from and keep a vigilant eye over each other's actions.[121] Similarly, the *Lay folks' mass book*, manual which originated in the province of York in the late twelfth century, and which was probably translated into English in the late thirteenth century, stressed the importance of the elevation as a moment for the expression of wishes. Just before the elevation:

> Yet shall ye pray for anything
> between the *sanctus* and the sacring.[122]

An anonymous early-fourteenth-century English tract based on Pecham's programme gave this instruction to one encountering the eucharist:

As ofte as any cristene man þt blessude body seyy at masse or y bore in prestis hondys to any syke he schal devotly knele a doun & worschepe hys god, bydde hys pater noster or what prayȝer þat he best can.[123]

The elevation reminded Mirk to suggest appropriate behaviour for all eucharistic occasions, such as the processions with the *viaticum* to the sick:

> Teche hem also, I the pray,
> That whenne þey walken in þe way
> And sene þe preste a-gayn hem comynge,
> Goddes body wyth hym berynge,
> Thenne wyth grete deuocyone,
> Teche hem þere to knele a-downe.[124]

A genre of tracts for the laity developed early in France producing by the mid-thirteenth-century books such as Joinville's *Credo*.[125] This work, written by 1250–1, described the sacraments with large and detailed pictorial illustrations.[126] Books of Hours sometimes contained sections of guidance on the mass, followed by the appropriate prayers. The Taymouth Hours of *c.*1325 provided 'Maner coment hom se deit aver en touz pour a la messe', together with prayers for every stage of the mass.[127] English works for the laity were often translations from the French, such as the magisterial *Handlyng synne*, a manual for the priest and for the lay person who was likely to possess and enjoy such a

---

[121] *Lydgate's minor poems*, pp. 87–115.
[122] *LFMB*, p. 141.
[123] CUL Dd.12.69, fol. 31ᵛ.
[124] *Instructions (a)*, lines 304–9, p. 10.
[125] Paris. BN nouv. acq. fr. 4509–10.
[126] *Joinville's Credo*.
[127] BL Yates Thompson 13, fols. 7ʳ–14ʳ.

book.[128] In it instruction and confession were linked through a process of self-examination in which the lay person was meant to use the book as a guide.[129] A devotional miscellany of c.1310–20 includes instructions on the mass in Anglo-French: thirteen miniatures show the priest, the servers and the congregation at various stages of the ritual with explanatory captions.[130] The work's purpose is expressed at the beginning, to teach: 'Ceo qe vous devez fere & penser a chascun point de la messe'. The *Poor Caitif* later in the fourteenth century is an original English work containing the usual sections on the creed, the *Pater noster* and the ten commandments together with more devotional material from Richard Rolle,[131] and the Counsels of Christ, the Charter of Heaven, devotional texts which were very popular in the late medieval vernacular milieu.[132] The fifteenth-century *Jacob's well* is a good example of this late medieval vernacular genre which combined exposition on the Pecham syllabus with guidance literature for the laity such as William of Wadington's *Speculum vitae*, and always with a sprinkling of illustrative tales from main stream *exempla* collections.[133]

The aim of manuals for the laity, as of all instruction, was to build a horizon of images, a vocabulary of associations, which would conjure each other, a train of symbols which followed from recurrent visual stimuli created by ritual or by private reading. Most people did not use manuals and prayer-books, and even had they done, a large area of *Rezeption* was bound to be undetermined, open to fantasy, imagination, extrapolation, creating new and reproducing old interpretations. Teaching, none the less, attempted to anticipate and to create *clusters* of images which would come to mind through habit and repetition, and supported by an internal logic. Thus, the *Lay folks' mass book* while recommending personal prayers for the mass which were to be told in a position of kneeling and with raised hands, still recognises personal diversity:

> Kneland halde up thy handes,
> And with inclinacyon
> Behalde þe Eleuacyon.
> Swylke prayere þan þou take,

[128] On the ownership of Books of Hours, see Reinburg (1985), pp. 25–104.

[129] Robertson (1947), pp. 163–8, 183.

[130] For reproductions of the images and discussion, see Wormald (1966–8); (BN fr. 13442, fols. 45ʳ–48ᵛ). See also *Gothic manuscripts 1285–1385* II, pp. 67–8. The elevation is represented fittingly, across a double opening, fols. 46ᵛ–47ʳ.

[131] Brady (1954), pp. 529–42.

[132] Pfander (1936), pp. 251–2. This highly popular work was associated in the fifteenth century with Lollard material, Hudson (1988b), p. 425.

[133] *Speculum vitae*: Gregg (1977), pp. 359–61.

> As the likes best forto make.
> Many men prayes sere,
> Ilke men prayes on his manere.
> Schorte prayer soulde be with-owten drede
> And þere-with a pater-noster and crede.[134]

The book provides for those without a ready prayer in mind:

> Welcome, lorde, in fourme of brede
> For me þou sufferde herd deede;
> Als þou bore the crowne of thorne
> Þou suffer me noghte be forlorne.[135]

A dominant image offered for reflection during the mass, and particularly at the elevation, was the Passion, the moment of utmost suffering and giving, with its generative and generous nature, always in relation to the gift of grace which it imparted to the eucharist. In the words of the *Meditations on the life and passion of Christ*,

> Þou madest a feste, prynce of prys,
> That passeth alle maner delys;
> Þin oune body þou ȝef hem alle
> Þat eton þanne wiþ þe in halle . . .
> And alle þo þat with þe ete
> Also weron fed with loue swete.[136]

Lydgate's poem *On kissing at Verbum caro factum est* (c.1430–40) concludes that the kissing of an object, the pax,[137] is only a spur to memory:

> Kyssyng the tokenes rehersyd here toforn,
> And euer haue mynde on Crystes passion
> Whyche for your sake weryd a crowne of thorne.[138]

The poem *The sacrifice of the mass* in Richard Hill's early-sixteenth-century common-place book similarly explains the foundation of the eucharist and its importance above all sacraments through the image of the sacrifice:

> But now þe blode of Crist, by doble halff
> Lechith þe people, and clensith well more,
> Which dayly at þe auter, his prist beffore,
> Consecrate with worde and mynde of entent

---

[134] *Lay folks' mass book* text C, pp, 38–40, lines 224–32.
[135] *Ibid*, p. 40, lines 237–40.
[136] *Meditations*, lines 257–60, 263–4, p. 8.
[137] See above, pp. 74–6.
[138] *Lydgate's minor poems*, p. 117, lines 30–2.

Wher God, in fowrm of bred, his body doth present.[139]

A summary of all that was necessary and useful in eucharistic lore could be found in the poem 'Of the sacrament of the altar'.[140] After establishing that 'holychirche' is made of 'goode men', and must remember and praise its saviour (lines 1–16), it proceeds to speak of Easter-time when 'Lyueliche quyk bred is put forþ þis day' (line 18). The Last Supper is invoked as the occasion on which light removed darkness, when Christ ordained the consecration of bread and wine through which:

> Lore is ȝoven to cristen men,
> In-to flesch passeþ þe bred;
> As holychirche doþ us kenne,
> Þe wyn, to blod, þat is so red.[141]

And this was said to happen without any noticeable, visible change, which can be discerned by the eyes,[142] only that which can be seen by the eyes of faith.[143] After transubstantiation, concomitance is taught, that Christ resides in both the species and in their tiniest parts:

> Þouȝ a thowsand take at o sete,
> Alone on takeþ as moche o prys . . .
> Þouȝ it a þousand peces seme broken,
> Nes parted ne wasted, but al holl take.[144]

The poem then teaches that this body is not always received worthily,[145] but also reiterates that every section of it has sacramental value, and the wholeness of the body in the broken host is restated:

> Þouȝ þe prest þe sacrament clyue
> In a þowsand peces and þre,
> Þe state, ne stature, ne myȝt doþ myue,
> Ne leseþ ne lasseþ of his pouste.[146]

And while the Jews eat lamb at Easter, Christians eat living bread 'qwyk bred', under the new law 'And kepen boþe by Goddis red' (line 104).[147] The poem ends with an invocation to God for forgiveness in the *Pater noster* formula, and calls for strengthening of faith over sense

---

[139] *Songs, carols*, no. 71, pp. 68–71; lines 17–20, p. 69.
[140] *Twenty six political poems*, pp. 103–7.
[141] *Ibid*, p. 104, lines 41–4.
[142] *Ibid*, p. 105, lines 45–8.
[143] *Ibid*, p. 105, lines 49–56.
[144] *Ibid*, p. 105, lines 63–4, 69–70.
[145] *Ibid*, p. 105–6, lines 73–80.
[146] *Ibid*, p. 106, lines 89–92.
[147] *Ibid*, p. 106, lines 97–104.

perception. It closes with a series of eucharistic images: the sacrifice of Isaac, manna in the desert, the paschal lamb, and the sacrament itself – the eucharist.[148]

John Audelay's lengthy poem 'De meritis misse, quomodo debemus audire missam', of the 1420s, is really a verse sermon summarising points of doctrine, which dwells on the utility of the mass when properly observed. We have already encountered the stock of benefits accruing from the mass: the company of angels all day, freedom from the threat of being struck blind on that day or suffering death, and from the need for food or drink.[149] Belief in the sacrament is stressed, as well as proper kneeling at the sacring with clasped hands and with thoughts intent on Christ.[150] Here, the reader is reminded that the eucharist was founded at the Last Supper by Christ and that Judas had received it unworthily. At elevation he instructs the reader to thank God for his grace, perhaps in words of another of Audelay's poems comprising thirty-two Hails to Christ, 'De salutacione corporis Jhesu Christi'.[151] Audelay also requires sinlessness, a state of charity, and gives the participant in communion an active role, reciting the *Pater noster* and the *Ave Maria*; he also surveys the rudiments of knowledge codified by Pecham in the Lambeth Council of 1281.[152] He then returns to the body of the mass with instructions on deportment, prayers for kin and prayer which at this moment is particularly efficacious for the dead.[153] He also tells a tale against speaking during the mass, suggests appropriate prayers and concludes with an indulgence of 100 days.[154] This comprehensive poem stresses more the lay person's behaviour than doctrinal instruction. It was a useful guide which could prevent the usual lapses, a religious poem and a manual in one.

### TEACHING THE EUCHARIST WITH MIRACLES

Yet, whatever the effort put into teaching from parochial guidebooks which repeated the basic doctrines and prayers, the effective dissemination of a set of ideas, symbols and practices could be achieved only through penetration into the domain of the daily, the usual, the habitual, through the demonstration of its relevance to the experiences

---

[148] *Ibid*, p. 106, lines 121–8.
[149] *The poems of John Audelay*, p. 67.
[150] *Ibid*, p. 69.
[151] *Ibid*, pp. 62–5.
[152] *Ibid*, p. 70.
[153] *Ibid*, pp. 72–4.
[154] *Ibid*, p. 79.

which large groups of people lived. *Exempla* provide us with the material designed, quite self-consciously, to capture the 'popular mind'; an example is found in Chaucer's pardoner:

> Thanne telle I hem ensamples may oon
> Of olde stories longe tyme agoon.
> For lewed people loven tales olde;
> Swiche thynges kan they wel reporte and holde.[155]

This concept was a cultural construct which was fed by ideas about status, about the otherness of the peasantry, the artisans, the working unlettered people who constituted the audience for most vernacular preaching. From the thirteenth century parochial instruction was supplemented in towns by the preaching of the friars, the 'professionals' who were wholly occupied in the task of preaching, converting and confessing.[156] The friars acted as the spearhead of the mission of preaching and teaching on which a transformation of the *societas christiana* depended. Writers of both major mendicant orders concentrated their efforts from the second quarter of the thirteenth century upon the preparation of preaching material, and above all on the collection of tales which could be used in the lively mendicant sermons.[157] The Dominicans, who were especially involved in fighting heresy, developed a number of tools for this task, ranging from instructive hagiography, like the five *Vitae* written by Thomas of Cantimpré exemplifying the life of women known for eucharistic devotion, to pocket bibles accompanied by lists of biblical quotations for the refutation of the central heretical claims.[158] The writing of sermons came to be facilitated by the great collections of tales, many of which predated the mendicants: Caesarius of Heisterbach's *Dialogus miraculorum* of 1223–4, James of Vitry's *exempla* from sermons of 1227–40, the *Bonum universale de apibus of 1256–61* by Thomas of Cantimpré,[159] and Stephen of Bourbon's *De septem donis spiritus sancti*,[160] as well as the massive hagiographic collection, the *Legenda aurea* of c.1255.[161] These

---

[155] 'The Pardoner's prologue', in *The Riverside Chaucer*, lines 435–8, p. 195. For an introduction to exempla, see Bremond, Le Goff and Schmitt (1982). On *exempla* research, see Oppel (1972).
[156] d'Avray (1985), pp. 13–63. On preaching to the laity in the later Middle Ages, see Zafarana (1983).
[157] Schmitt (1977).
[158] Light (1987), esp. 279–85.
[159] Murray (1981), pp. 287–8.
[160] Almazan (1967), p. 291.
[161] Boureau (1984).

provided a stock of tales, imagery and iconography which was shared by preachers, painters and parish priests all over Europe.[162] It would be wrong to claim, though, that the vivid *exempla* were the exclusive creation of the mendicants; these were merely their great popularisers and users.[163]

Many of the most popular thirteenth-century collections and tales drew upon collections of the late twelfth or the early thirteenth centuries, emanating from Cluniac and Cistercian circles. These were collections and tracts written for the edification of novices, and for the general strengthening of belief, such as Peter the Venerable's *De miraculis* written mainly between 1135–44,[164] Herbert of Clairvaux's *De miraculis* of 1178, and the *Exordium magnum ordinis cisterciensis* from Clairvaux of 1193×1221 of Conrad of Eberbach.[165] These collections were summarised in the classic of the genre, the *Dialogus miraculorum*.[166] Additionally, a tradition of *magistri praedicatores* contributed to the pre-mendicant surge in preaching and preaching materials: Peter the Chanter's *Verbum abbreviatum*,[167] and Gerald of Wales' *Gemma ecclesiastica* so much influenced by him,[168] as well as Alan of Lille's *Summa de arte praedicatoria*,[169] and James Vitry's work.[170] The sources used by the composers of the tales and compilers of these collections were those which could be found in any library of a monastery or cathedral school:[171] Gregory the Great's *Dialogues*, Bede's *Ecclesiastical history*. A convenient collection of eucharistic tales was Paschasius Radbert's *De corpore et sanguine Christi* of c.831×3, where miracles were used to substantiate his physical interpretation of the eucharist.[172] But as new themes raised interest, these sources were combed for new tales, and imbued with new meanings, as in the twelfth-century Cistercian collections eye-witness accounts and the experiences of brother-monks often constituted the authorities for new

---

[162]  For a selection of *exempla* from medieval collections, see *Prêcher d'exemples*, and on them the introduction Schmitt (1985).

[163]  On use of *exempla* in contexts other than preaching, see a study of John of Salisbury's use in the *Policraticus*, Van Moos (1984), pp. 219–20, 250–61.

[164]  Torrell and Bouthillier (1986), pp. 107–35.

[165]  *Ibid*, pp. 220–8; Hontoir (1946), p. 143; Rode (1957), p. 7.

[166]  Bouthellier (1975).

[167]  *PL* 205, cols. 23–370.

[168]  Gerald of Wales, *Gemma ecclesiastica*, Dist. 1, cs. 1–11, pp. 12–164 on the eucharist is peppered with tales; on works which influences Gerald see Bartlett (1982), pp. xx–xxii and Boutémy (1946).

[169]  *PL* 210, cols. 109–98.

[170]  Forni (1981), p. 36.

[171]  Hontoir (1946), p. 143.

[172]  'De corpore et sanguine Domini', *PL* 120, cols. 1,319; Cristiani (1968), pp. 187–8, 233; MacCulloch (1932), pp. 156–8.

tales. This tendency to incorporate the contemporary, even when this was invested in age-old *topoi*, was to grow rapidly with the work of the new orders of itinerant preachers.[173]

Thus, while *exempla* were born of pre-mendicant activity, the material was amplified, ordered, systematised and sometimes selected for particular themes.[174] The mendicants spread the scope and frequency of preaching, and what is striking in their work is the degree of sympathy between their tasks as confessors and as preachers.[175] Berlioz has stressed the connection between preaching and confession,[176] that the fruit of preaching was reaped at confession, their collective noun in the later Middle Ages was, after all, 'a convertynge of prechours'.[177] Alexander Murray's suggestion of another type of connection is of special importance; it was their position as confessors which allowed mendicants to be so effective in the construction of edifying tales which touched on the very difficulties in the acceptance of the world-view offered by the church.[178] From the confessor's ear to the preacher's pen, those secrets of doubt, of abuse, the more obvious areas of tension in the interpretation and acceptance of the normative sacramental world-view could be charted, and to what better effect than through the use of some traditional and some new tales.[179]

We know of some forty-six *exampla* collections made between 1200 and 1500, and these seem to have been organised increasingly systematically.[180] A southern French Franciscan collection of 1272×97 is an example of the final form reached by the late thirteenth century.[181] It provided a guide to the cure of souls and a source for sermon writing in its 236 *exempla* culled from the experience of preachers, early medieval *Vitae*, and the writings of the Fathers. It contained a section of eight tales on the eucharist.[182] The work of compilation and edition continued in the next two centuries, which saw popular collections such as the *Alphabetum narrationum* with some 800 tales by the Dominican

---

[173] Boitani (1982), p. 2.

[174] Like the rhymed collection of Marian tales in the vernacular produced by Gautier of Coinci around 1220, Pouchelle (1987); Ringbom (1969), p. 161. On Marian collections, see Southern (1958). On organisation of preaching material, see d'Avray (1985), pp. 64–90.

[175] On Bernardino of Siena's use of *exempla*, see Delcorno (1976).

[176] Berlioz (1981), p. 300.

[177] Allen (1936), p. 604.

[178] Murray (1981).

[179] *Ibid*, p. 292: 70 per cent of Thomas of Cantimpré's tales were from the mouths of other Dominicans.

[180] Schmitt (1977), pp. 19–20.

[181] Paris BN lat. 3555, fols. 168va–212rb.

[182] Welter (1930), pp. 432–6. For an English example, of the second half of the thirteenth century see Manchester Public Library fo91.F.9.

Arnulf of Liège, c.1307, and which was translated into English as the *Alphabet of tales* in the early fifteenth century.[183] Much of this production took place in the Low Countries and northern France, and from there travelled in the pockets of preachers, and was translated by members of the same order in other countries. By the fifteenth century collections of *exempla* derived from a vast array of material mediated through the great thirteenth-century collections, as was the case of Jean of Hérolt and Jean Lirelot who based their fifteenth-century collection largely on those earlier works.[184] Only a small part of the tales in these later collections were really new; only 2 per cent of the *exempla* in the fifteenth-century *Speculum exemplorum* collected by a Dutch compiler were 'noviter conscripta'.[185] The genre depended to a large extent on the confirming and supportive recourse to familiar stories, or familiar miraculous procedures, and once all-important new subjects, such as the eucharist, were covered there was no pressing need to innovate and dazzle with new tales.[186] It is noteworthy, however, that the new tales when entered were often florid, dealing sometimes with lurid miraculous events which had left a great impression on contemporaries: often tales of host desecrations and their aftermath.

It has often been said that a 'miraculous mood' prevailed in medieval culture, that people tended, both individually and collectively, to seek, out coincidences and to string them into patterns which proved the existence of active protecting and punishing forces, of providence which rewarded virtue and took revenge of the iniquitous.[187] An Augustinian view of miracles which influenced clerical thought in the early Middle Ages saw them as manifestations of the inherent powers of nature which God chooses occasionally to draw out, as a sign to humanity.[188] The miraculous was widely perceived as part of nature which provided a paradigm for the explanation of the world and its apparent aberrations. But more popular interpretations saw miracles as instrumental occurrences, as weapons against adversaries, through the interpretation of irregularities in nature as divine intervention in punishment for their misdeeds.[189] Bearing this approach in mind, the

[183] *Alphabet of tales*; Gregg (1977), pp. 361–2.
[184] Ringbom (1969), pp. 161–2.
[185] Geremek (1980), pp. 168–9. Notes on 'recent' occurrences sometimes accompany miracles tales, see *Catalogue of romances* III, no. 31, p. 576.
[186] Some new collections were compiled for specific uses, like the fifteenth-century *Speculum hereticorum*, Cambridge Trinity B.11.23.
[187] Brooke (1961), pp. 28–9, and more recently Sigal (1985); for a review of this, see Platelle (1985), esp. p. 381. On *exempla* as miracle tales, see Oppel (1976).
[188] Ward (1982), pp. 3–9.
[189] Platelle sees pilgrimages as a sort of collective quest for miracles, Platelle (1985), pp. 78–9.

suitability of *exempla* and the reason for their widespread deployment in preaching becomes clear: a eucharistic miracle tale was not only a story about the host, it was a manifestation of just how regular and reliable intervention was.

Viewing a eucharistic miracle could influence understanding of sacramental claims more than many sermons, and tales abound of shaky belief which was strengthened by a vision, such as that told of the Patarins of Ferrara who were convinced of the faith when a lamb appeared in the host,[190] or that of a northern heretic, Gautier of Flos, who saw a baby in the host during a mass celebrated by St John of Cantimpré.[191] And it was to counter the nagging questions of doubtful believers, as well as of heretics, that miracles were reported, creating the setting for the use of *exempla* which retold a miraculous event; the story of a woman's pet monkey, for example, which strayed into a church and ate the host, and which was consequently burnt by its owner who found in its stomach the undamaged sacrament.[192]

Effective as the tales of miraculous events were for teaching eucharistic symbolism, medieval intellectuals were obliged to analyse the nature of miraculous phenomena as part of their preoccupation with sacramental action.[193] On the whole learned opinion accepted the existence of apparitions and visions,[194] but most thinkers were reluctant to accept that these were predictable in any way. Visions, which were miraculous to their beholder, were deemed by theologians to be illuminations sent to bolster or reward faith, or to cure doubt. Although the change in substances during sacramental action was internal and invisible, God might reveal it to counter doubt or to benefit the virtuous,[195] but these remained subjective visions. Hugh of St Victor (d.1141) called the sacrament a *miraculum,* and Simon of Tournai (d.1201) saw the transubstantiation as miraculous, since it acted 'contra naturam', concluding that the sacrament was a miracle but most visions were merely showings.[196] In this vein, when Bishop Hugh of Lincoln was called to see a eucharistic miracle he answered that he experienced a true miracle daily at the altar:

---

[190] Gerald of Wales, *Gemma ecclesiastica* I, 11, pp. 40–2.
[191] Godding (1981), pp. 264–5 (*Vita Johannis Cantimpratensis* I, 10).
[192] In a collection of religious tales from the later fourteenth century, BL Harley 2316, fol. 12ʳ.
[193] On the theory of miracles, see Browe (1929d).
[194] On illusory visions, see Walter Map, *De nugis curialium,* c. 11, pp. 148–64: 'De apparicionibus fantasticis'.
[195] In the thirteenth century *Queste del Graal* only the elect were able to see Christ in the grail, Hamilton (1942), p. 108.
[196] Ward (1982), p. 15.

Why should we gape at a sensory image of this divine gift, when every day we behold by faith this heavenly sacrifice, whole and entire.[197]

Similarly, a thirteenth-century story, known to St Louis and recounted by William of Mailly, told of the Count of Montfort who refused to go to see a miraculous host for that reason.[198] Only when it could be proven that a large number of people had witnessed the miraculous transformation, say from bread to flesh, was Alexander of Hales willing to concede that divine intervention had changed the laws of nature in aid of faith, a view shared later by Thomas Aquinas. And even this posed a problem in practice: what was to be done with the changed materials? Albert the Great followed the distinction between a miracle seen by all or only by few:

If it is transformed in the sight of all, then it seems to me that it should not be consumed, but rather kept as relics and another should be consecrated.[199]

And what was to be done with the eucharist if it turned into a child?[200]

A basic problem remained: sacramental religion meant that the eucharist celebrated thousands of times every day all over Christendom was efficacious once the words were pronounced over a proper species and by an ordained priest. It contained a miracle become rule, a procedure *ex opere operato*, which went against the grain of the miraculous (God's willed and deliberate intervention for the just), at the same time opening the eucharist to assimilation into the world of artifact and mechanical procedure.

The very pervasive 'miraculous mood' meant that the most important and widespread consideration of the natural and the supernatural was articulated through the examination of an 'economy of miracles'. The pool of miraculous lore became the main tool for popular instruction.[201] *Exempla* attempted to locate the miraculous within the immediate surroundings of their audience, and tales acquired local place-names, their protagonists came to speak the regional dialect, and adhered to local customs. The *exempla* sharpened the existing stock of miracle tales, to make them serve the exemplification of a particular point more effectively, and they tended to be streamlined into short

---

[197] 'Num miramur particulares ymagines huius divini muneris, qui totum et integrum hoc celeste sacrificium cotidie intuemur fidelissimo aspectu mentis', Hugh of Lincoln, *Life* II, pp. 92–5; p. 95.

[198] Bériou (1987) I, p. 87, II, p. 388 and n. 7.

[199] 'Si autem transfiguratur quoad visum omnium, tunc non videtur mihi esse sumendum, sed pro reliquiis habendum et aliud consecrandum', Albert the Great, *IV Sent.* d. 13, a. 38. See also *ST* III q. 82, a. 4.

[200] Browe (1929d), pp. 308–9.

[201] Berlioz (1981).

pieces, univocal, universal in claim, and authoritative in tone.[202] Thus, tales conveying the most universal and wide-ranging claims of Christian culture were presented as a 'microcosm of human experience'.[203] Be it in Poland or in England, the context of familiarity and immediacy supported a superstructure of all-embracing claims for mediation and exclusivity.

*Exempla* were also manipulated in the ruling 'miraculous mood'. A good example is one told by James of Vitry about a priest who discovered that one of his parishioners was offering defective coins to the altar. The priest waited until Easter to punish the sinner, and when the man knelt at communion expecting the taste of the wafer on his tongue, he felt instead a false coin. He leapt in horror exclaiming that the wafer had turned into a false coin in his mouth, and repented.[204] The miraculous explanation was the one which came to his mind, inspired by guilt, and the priest was not suspected. The miraculous was the obvious story-line.

What can we make of these tales in our investigation of the dissemination and interpretation of eucharistic lore? Inasmuch as a political end motivated the whole exercise of teaching, the creation and support of a sacramental world-view, and the acceptance or adherence to the church as prime and single cultural mediator and channel to salvation and well-being, there was a conscious attempt to reach as far as possible. Motivated by this end, and also with the working knowledge of the most vexed areas, the most common 'abuses' and 'mistakes', the most frequently sounded heretical jibes, teachers and preachers operated not only by insight, but also according to some major overarching guidelines about the nature of their project. And this was not casuistry, the exploration of the reaches and particularities of eucharistic error (few casuists collected *exempla*, Peter the Chanter being a unique case). Rather, it was an exercise in response and provision, a creation of rhetorical rules to correct the observed and on-going uses of the eucharistic idiom.[205] Thus, despite the fact that they were written largely by celibate men living in religious orders, *exempla* were what has been recently called 'lieu privilégié de la recontre entre la culture savante et al culture populaire ou folklorique',[206] even if one does not

[202] This is Berlioz's analysis, Berlioz (1980), pp. 118–22; Berlioz (1981), p. 305.
[203] Boitani (1982), pp. 2–4.
[204] James of Vitry, *The Exempla*, no. 198, pp. 82–3; see other versions: *Alphabet of tales*, no. 577, pp. 385–6; BL Arundel 506, fol. 40r; BL Harley 1288, fol. 57r.
[205] On the development of techniques of comparison and exemplification, see Bataillon (1985).
[206] Berlioz and David (1980), pp. 26–7.

accept the dichotomy of learned and popular cultures. *Exempla* are thus a privileged site for an ethnographic exercise in teasing out areas of conflict and tension within the symbolic system and even, through the disapproving tone and sometimes the erroneous interpretation of their teller, for an ethnographic gaze at the living, used, interpreted, eucharist.

But what of the eucharistic theme in these tales? Can one clearly say that the eucharist produced and consumed more tales in the mid thirteenth century than in the mid twelfth? The collections are not amenable to any simple quantitative analysis by theme. A tradition of eucharistic tales existed from the very early Middle Ages, such as the miracles in Gregory the Great's *Dialogues*,[207] and in Bede's *History*.[208] These were used by Paschasius Radbert when upholding his arguments on the nature of Christ's presence in the eucharist.[209] He included four eucharistic tales: that of the old man of Scete in which an angel broke Christ's body just as the priest was breaking the wafer; the story of St Basil and the Jew, where a child appeared in Basil's hand at mass and bits of it were distributed to communicants, and led the Jew to conversion; the story of St Gregory's mass in which a woman's doubt was removed by the appearance of a bloody finger in the host; and the story of Plecgils who doubted and to whom Christ appeared as an infant in the host. Some elements of the later eucharistic tales are already present; the need to counter doubts in the minds of clergy and lay folk, the cure of simple disbelief. The eucharist thus appears in the work of twelfth-century collectors of tales: Peter the Venerable had eleven tales in his *De miraculis*.[210] In the twelfth and thirteenth centuries the eucharist rises in importance, even if it never overwhelm the miraculous repertoire. In the next century Caesarius of Heisterbach's collection included a whole section on the 'Sacrament of Christ's body and blood', the ninth of the twelve books in his *Dialogus miraculorum*, and the only one dedicated to the discussion of a sacrament.[211] Those needing support in faith were still the clergy, the laity and monastic novices, but now the audience also included more pointed critics, heretics who rejected and ridiculed, and against whom powerful and new proof was needed. In the *Gemma ecclesiastica* Gerald of Wales presented two of Paschasius' eucharistic classics, the story of St Basil

---

[207] For those on the mass, see de Vogüé (1986), p. 125.
[208] Like the tale on the efficacy of the mass recounted below, p. 221; on its occurrence in Anglo-Saxon literature, see Jolly (1985), pp. 286–7.
[209] *PL* 120, c. 14, cols, 1,316–21.
[210] Bouthillier (1975), pp. 337–8.
[211] *DM* II, pp. 103–69. Cristiani (1982), p. 188; MacCulloch (1932), p. 156.

5 Miracle of the child in the host, revealed to Edward the Confessor

and St Gregory's mass together with contemporaries accounts of refutation of heretical error in Arras, Chartres and Ferrara.[212] Collections of tales often contained a section of the eucharist, by no means the largest section, but the impact of such material cannot be measured in numbers alone. The English thirteenth century collection of tales, the *Speculum laicorum*, had a section entitled 'De eukaristia et ejus virtutibus' with seventeen tales; the section opened with a short summary of eucharistic tenets.[213] Another English collection of *c.*1300, contains twenty-one tales in a section entitled 'Incipiunt exempla de virtutibus Eucharistie, et eiusdem contemptu'.[214] Vernacular, didactic writings used these tales to enliven the catechism, as in Robert of Brunne's *Handlyng synne* and in the *Ayenbite of Inwyt*. I believe that the rise in eucharistic sensibility was related to the greater and clearer claims made

[212] Gerald of Wales, *Gemma ecclesiastica*, Dist. I, 11, pp. 38–43.
[213] *Speculum laicorum*, c. 32, pp. 51–5.
[214] BL Harley 2851, fols. 105ʳ–117ʳ.

for it, which in turn opened up new possibilities for both orthodox and heterodox practices and interpretations. Many tales were bred in the fight against heresy, but they were told and retold in innumerable encounters with those who did not intentionally threaten or challenge the whole symbolic system.[215]

Eucharistic *exempla* can be divided into many groups and sub-groups.[216] Here they are presented in three categories according to the type of story-line pursued:

1. A vision of the real substances, or other unusual sensations, such as smell, taste or sound, as a reward for faith and piety *or* such revelations used to counter trivial doubt;

2. Some unusual behaviour of natural elements, animals and humans, arising from awe of the eucharist or from sheer proximity to it;

3. The appearance of eucharistic properties, usually flesh, blood or the Man of Sorrows, to a knowing abuser – a Jew, a witch, a thief, a negligent priest – and the ensuing punishment.

The first type is very well-known.[217] The properties of the eucharist are revealed in their various equivalent symbolic forms – as raw flesh, blood, a child Christ, the crucified body – only to confirm what the good believer already knows. Christ sometimes appears in his vulnerable childish form, as in 1116 to a monk of Déols.[218] According to Matthew Paris in *La estoire de sent Aedward le rei*, Edward the Confessor saw a child between the hands of the celebrating Archbishop Wulfstan (figure 5).[219] A variant on this has a child as visionary, perhaps not by its piety but by its purity, as in the story told by Thomas of Eccleston *c.*1258–9 of Brother Peter of Tewkesbury who was a frequent visitor to the household of Geoffrey le Despenser, and a special favour-

---

[215] It has been suggested that the rise in awareness of the *imago pietatis* produced the many eucharistic legends in thirteenth-century Germany, Bauerreiss (1931), pp. 325–7. This is a limited formulation of the general truth of greater awareness of the implications and problems inherent in a sacramental world-view.

[216] Browe (1938) has suggested eight such categories.

[217] The revelations with which the holy women were blessed have been lovingly described by Caroline Bynum and need not be repeated here, Bynum (1986).

[218] 'In Dolensi coenobio cuidam monacho missas agenti apparuit puer super altare loco hostia ante calicem', *Monumenta Vizelliacensia*, p. 224.

[219] Brieger (1957), p. 153; Vaughan (1958), pp. 173–6 argues that Matthew Paris was the author of the tale even if he based it on older stories, CUL Ee.3.59, p. 37; for another version see *Speculum laicorum*, no. 262, p. 53. Another 'royal' vision is that of Eleanor, sister of Henry III and wife of Simon of Montfort, on her visit to Waverley abbey in 1245, when she saw Christ in the host as she entered the chapel during celebration, 'Annales de monasterii de Waverleia', p. 336: 'cujus amor eam illuc adduxit benignissima Ipsius presentia prompte se offeret requirenti'.

ite of the son John. The boy recoiled from Friar Peter in horror after having attended a mass celebrated by him, and when asked to explain his behaviour the boy said 'That he had seen him [Peter] devour a child on the altar in the chapel, and feared lest he would do the same to him'.[220] The purity of little John reinforces the innocence of Christ the child in the sacrificial context, and underscores the eucharistic story of sacrifice and mediation.

The related tales of reward for worthy reception of the sacrament could also be quite complex, like the story told by Caesarius of Heisterbach and often thereafter, of Raynald the Justiciar who had killed his sinful and criminal son, and was thus not given communion by his priest. When he asked to see the eucharist at his death-bed he begged Christ 'Lord Jesus Christ I have called to you, show me your judgement', and Christ's body lifted itself into the air and 'attached itself to his mouth'.[221] Sometimes the host revealed its power without obvious prompting and this type of tale fed ideas about the host's mechanical power to work good or harm, like the tale of a ship which was saved from sinking when the host was elevated.[222] The recipients of these visions could be simple folk who were rewarded for their belief,[223] or in support of a just cause, as in the case of a knight who, defending his honour in a duel performed before Frederick Barbarossa, triumphed through the presence of the host.[224] A papal legate forced King Roger of Sicily to submit to ecclesiastical discipline by carrying a newly consecrated host (note the notion of 'freshness' stressed here) to him and daring him to resist the body of Christ which was the church and its authority.[225]

But most frequently visions occurred to people with a special vocation, a eucharistic attachment which turned communion into a momentous event. Then the taste of honey, or sweet smells, suffused the eager communicant.[226] When by mistake an unconsecrated host was offered to Bishop Maurice of Sully on his death-bed, he refused to

---

[220] 'Quod viderat eum devorasse infantem in capella super altare, et timuit ne faceret sibi similiter', in 'De adventu fratrum', p. 67. A similar story is told in the early twelfth century by Guibert of Nogent, about the privileged eucharistic vision of a child, who was taken to church with his mother and saw a beautiful boy in the host, which she could not see, 'De sanctis et eorum pignoribus', I c.2,I, on which see Erikson (1976), p. 10.

[221] 'Domine Jesu Christe, ego ad te appellavi, ostende nunc iudicium tuum', 'ori suo se adiunxit', *DM* 9,38, pp. 140–2; :*Erzählungen des Mittelalters*, no. 134, p. 336; BL. Add. 18364, fol. 41ʳ.

[222] *Speculum laicorum* no. 259, p. 52, based on a tale told by Gregory the Great.

[223] For example, by seeing the host radiant, *DM* 9,33 and 9,34, pp. 135–7.

[224] *DM* 9,48, pp, 151–3; *Alphabet of tales*, no. 163, p. 113–14.

[225] BL Add. 11872, fol. 93ᵛ, in an Italian Franciscan collection of c.1400.

[226] *DM* 9,46, pp. 149–50; Bynum (1984), p. 182.

receive it, and died happily merely looking at the host.[227] Another tale concerned Count Albert who, suffering from nausea on his death-bed, received the host miraculously through an opening in his side.[228]

Caroline Bynum has discussed with compelling insight the eucharistic miracles of reward experienced by *mulieres sanctae*, and has shown that in their *Vitae* eucharistic miracles were more plentiful and more intense than in those of men. Two types of experience were associated particularly with women: seeing a child in the host, and living on the host alone.[229] Religious women, Cistercian nuns, and especially the beguines were particularly susceptible to eucharistic visions, and especially to being given communion directly by Christ; forty-five of fifty-five such known miracles occurred to women.[230] Special sensations accompanied their communions, as well as an ability to distinguish consecrated from unconsecrated hosts. Bynum places these types of miracles within the realm of female experience, with the heightened awareness of food, preparation and consumption, on the one hand,[231] and the sensibility to pain, bodily suffering and the possible incorporation of discrete bodies, on the other. These women inspired such arch-storytellers as James of Vitry and Thomas of Cantimpré, who sat at their feet, and collected their miracles for further didactic use, and especially in preaching against heretics.

These women's miracles form a sub-group of the tales of miraculous reward. They often centre on questions of authority, the women being blessed by communion which obviates parochial routine and its limitations. A tale in the book written by Geoffrey de La Tour *c.*1371 for the education of his daughters, tells of a host which flew into the mouth of a holy woman 'in maner of a lytel bryght clerenes'.[232] His next story described an angel celebrating mass for a lady in the absence of her chaplain.[233] These were the stories which could feed the suspicion and

---

[227] *DM*, 9,43 and 9,44, pp. 147–8; Gerald of Wales, *Gemma ecclesiastica* I,9, pp. 32–3; James of Vitry, *The Exempla*, no. 7, pp. 101–2; *Alphabet of tales*, no. 310, pp. 212–13.

[228] As witnessed by two Franciscans and reported in 1267, included in a fourteenth-century manuscript of the Dominican Robert Holcot's collection of preaching material 'Convertimini', BL Royal 7 C I, fols. 93ʳ–121ᵛ; at fol. 109ᵛ.

[229] Bynum (1984), pp. 182, 188–9. Bynum (1974a) traces the development, from the twelfth century, of female attributes in the increasingly human representations of Christ and the analogy between the body of Christ both suffering and nurturing, and the female body.

[230] Bynum (1985), p. 3.

[231] *Ibid*, p. 8.

[232] In Caxton's English translation, *The book of the knight of the tower*, pp. 53–4. This is reminiscent of the tale of St Catherine's communion, when a piece of the host broken at the altar by her confessor Raymond of Capua flew into her mouth, for a representation of which see a *predella* painted by Giovanni di Paolo of *c.*1449, *Painting in Renaissance Siena*, pp. 234–5, plate 38g.

[233] *The book of the knight of the tower*, p. 54.

rumour about religious women, that they did not recognise sacerdotal mediation or parochial discipline.[234] This can explain the choice of a beguine as the protagonist in Stephen of Bourbon's tale about a quarrelsome beguine who had been warned to mend her ways before taking communion, but who still quarrelled after her Easter communion, and did so repeatedly, until once at communion a napkin with the eucharist which had been seen going into her mouth, came out of it and went to heaven.[235] Women were prominent in the eucharistic discourse; their position was, however, more precarious than has hitherto been recognised.

Another sub-group of the tales of reward represented the doubts of simple folk, the doubts and errors of those who were misguided by an alleged simplicity, who wished to believe and simply could not. These tales repeated questions about worthy reception, of the dilemma of those who wished to receive, and yet did not properly believe that they were receiving the very body and blood of Christ, and therefore attempted to rid themselves of the host. Women feature prominently in such tales, as in the English poem *The lady that was in despair*: a lady hid a consecrated host in a pear tree since she could not bear to swallow it in her state of doubt about transubstantiation.[236] The pear tree miraculously blossomed out of season, and on investigation, a baby was found in place of the buried host. Here the refrain is 'That very God was in fourme of bredd', a tag common to eucharistic salutations.[237] The German mystic, Christina of Stommeln (1242–1312), doubted transubstantiation until a child was revealed to her in the celebrant's hands.[238] The most popular of these tales was the miracle of St Gregory's mass, which first occurred in the eighth-century *Vita* of Gregory the Great by Paul the Deacon, and thence entered a ninth-century *Vita* and later the *Legenda aurea* in the mid thirteenth century.[239] While Gregory was celebrating mass a woman in the congregation chuckled before the reception of communion.[240] When he asked her how dare she laugh, she answered that she herself had baked the bread, how could she believe that God resided in it? Gregory prayed for a sign, and this came in the form of a bleeding finger.[241] Here again, a

---

[234] Kieckhefer (1984), pp. 171–3; Bell (1985).
[235] *Anecdotes*, no. 380, p. 335.
[236] CUL Ff.2.38; Ff.5.48.
[237] See below, pp. 156–63.
[238] MacCulloch (1932), p. 159.
[239] On the history of the tale, see Endres (1917), and for the original tales *AASS* March III, pp. 133–4, 152–3.
[240] For images, see *Die Messe Gregors des Grossen*.
[241] For an early fifteenth century version in a Corpus Christi sermon see *Festial*, p. 173: 'And fonde þe ost turnet into raw flesch bledyng'.

woman is the vehicle of doubt, exposing the areas of sensitivity at the heart of a symbolic system.[242] In the later Middle Ages the story came to depict the appearance of Christ himself on the altar, and ultimately, of his appearance as the Man of Sorrows surrounded by the *arma christi* (figure 6). This was an elaboration of the original tale which followed from an image of the Man of Sorrows popularised in Rome during the jubilee of 1350, and which spread in the rest of Europe with the return of pilgrims from the City.[243]

Priests are prominent in this mode of tale, like the learned priest who believed that the host could not be the real body of Christ, but merely a symbol thereof.[244] A similar punishment occurred to a priest who celebrated in mortal sin, as told to Bishop Hugh of Lincoln and reported in his *Vita*. When the priest broke the host in three before consuming it

Immediately blood began to flow copiously through the break, and the middle part of the host which I held in my hand suddenly took on the appearance of flesh and became blood-red.[245]

He dared not communicate, but was moved to confess his sin, do penance and receive absolution. Jews appear in these stories in their traditional role as witnesses to the faith: they were confronted with a miracle and were thus compelled to accept conversion, sometimes in groups. The classic story is that of the mass of St Basil in which a Jew entered a church and saw instead of the host a child torn asunder: the Jew was convinced of the truth of Christianity and converted. But Jews were increasingly being associated with vicious and wilful attacks against the host, just as the theological interpretation of their culpability in the crucifixion was being rethought by mendicant theologians. New stories were reporting vicious abuse and gory punishments for it.[246]

The second group of tales involved miraculous breaches in the rules

---

[242] See examples of the tale in Bromyard, *Summa praedicantium*, a.7 example 5; *Alphabet of tales*, no. 309, pp. 211–12. It was also used in a series of eucharistic tales embroidered on the tapestry of the monastery of Ronceray, in Angers, Tervarent (1933), p. 80, fig. 2.

[243] See example of this version of the story in *Speculum laicorum* c. 32, no. 258 p. 52.

[244] *DM* 9,56, pp. 160–1. This story is represented in a wall-painting in the Corporal Chapel of Orvieto Cathedral, where the doubting priest faces the viewer and a child holding a cross appears in the host; reproduced in Camporesi (1989), p. 220. And similarly in the preaching of Ranulph de la Houblonnière in 1273, Bériou (1987) II, p. 53.

[245] 'Mox cruor liquidissimus per fracturam effluere cepit, qui mediam hostie partem quam manu tenebam in carnis speciem subito conversam rubore sanguineo infecit', Hugh of Lincoln, *Life* II, p. 94.

[246] See pp. 336–7.

6 The mass of St Gregory

of nature – evidence that Christ's body exerted an influence which mere bread could not. Within this group there is a type in which simple beasts attest the divinity of the host where blind or vicious humans do not, instances of the devotion of animals. A ubiquitous *exemplum* tells of the woman who stole the host after communion to fructify her bees: she put it in the hive, only to find when she returned to check the results that the bees had erected an 'ecclesiula' in its honour and were venerating it.[247] Caesarius also tells of a host stolen from a church and hidden by a thief in a field; but his oxen-team refused to plough over it, and knelt and adored the burial spot.[248] In another version, a number of thieves robbed a church in the diocese of Canterbury during Archbishop Boniface's office (1243–70), and left the pyx in a field, only to find that the swine lay prostrate in front of it.[249] Sometimes a Jew, as a typical wrongdoer, is inserted into this type of tale, as in the case of the one who fed the eucharist to some pigs in disrespect and found that they refused to eat it;[250] a Jew offered a host to his dog and the animal refused to eat it and finally attacked the Jew.[251] The story of St Anthony of Padua (d.1231) and the mule is a good example: a heretic with whom Anthony was arguing in Toulouse was convinced of the truth of transubstantiation only after an experiment involving a mule. The animal was starved for three days at the end of which he was offered a basket of oats in one hand, and a host in the other. Rather than rushing to the oats, he knelt in adoration of the eucharist.[252]

The forces of nature could change their course when faced with the eucharist, and especially when it was endangered. A wafer fell out of a priest's hands and left an impression on the stone floor, and then emerged and rose up to the altar; in another tale a number of neglected hosts arranged themselves in a cross over the altar.[253] A popular tale told in Marian as well as in eucharistic collections, which circulated from c.1150, is that of a young monk of a monastery of Chiusa who had spilt the sacramental wine only to see it removed by the Virgin.[254] The miracle of Douai reported by Thomas of Cantimpré happened in St Amand's Church where a fallen host rose to the altar and appeared to some in the form of a child.[255] A tale worthy of the title *exemplum* was entered in the register of Bishop Philip Repyngdon of Lincoln in 1405:

[247] See a Middle English version *Alphabet of tales*, no. 695, p. 465.
[248] *DM* 9,7, pp. 113–14.
[249] *Speculum laicorum*, no. 265, pp. 52–3.
[250] *Ibid*, no. 269, p. 53; a fourteenth-century German collection Arundel 506, fol. 3[rb]; and similarly *Exempla aus Handschriften*, no. 77, p. 62.
[251] *Speculum laicorum*, no. 264, p. 52; in a late fourteenth-century English collection, BL Burney 361, fol. 149[rb]; and in a fifteenth-century sermon, *Middle English sermons*, pp. 128–30.
[252] 'Mirabile certe! nam animal tam fame cruciatum, in conspectu Christi, post verba S. Anthonii, cibus parvipendens, statim capite usque ad poplites inclinato, coram sacramento vivifico genuflexit', 'Legenda alia seu liber miraculorum', *AASS* June II, no. 5, p. 725. For a lovely illumination of this story from 1485 see *Les Tres Riches Heures du Duc de Berry*, plate no. 103. For another story of eucharistic proof against heretics, see Thomas of Cantimpré, *Bonum universale de apibus*, book 2, c. 57, no. 23, pp. 553–5.
[253] *DM* 9,14 and 9,15, pp. 119–21
[254] Southern (1958), pp. 190–1; Brooke (1961), p. 29. See a version with illuminations from c.1310–20 in the Queen Mary Psalter, BL Royal B VII 2, fol. 124[v].
[255] *Bonum universale* book 2, c. 40, no. 2, pp. 399–401.

fourteen days' indulgence were granted to those contributing to the rebuilding of Yarborough Parish Church (Lincolnshire) which had been destroyed by fire. It was especially worthy of help since a miracle had occurred there: the silken pocket containing the host remained miraculously unharmed, while the inner and outer, ivory and copper receptacles were burnt:

> the furious blaze burnt everything that it could find on the altar, even the double conical pyx, of ivory without and within, containing with great care this vital bread . . . and only that bread enclosed within a little silken compartment which could not have withstood such a fury remained miraculously whole.[256]

And we have already encountered the eucharist which saved a ship from wreckage in a storm.

The third type of eucharistic miracle tale is that which reported knowing, intended and malevolent abuse of the elements. The host rebelled violently against breaches of the eucharistic code. For celebrating the mass unworthily a priest was punished when the host turned to coals in his mouth;[257] another undeserving celebrant had the host removed from his hands by a human figure which descended at the moment of elevation, and he was moved to confess before continuing the mass; one version places the tale in Oxford in 1356.[258] One of St Bernard's monks was said to have received communion despite his confessor's warnings of his unfitness, and then fell dead upon reception.[259] A monk who usually tasted honey in his mouth at communion, tasted wormwood when he once received it in anger.[260]

Abuse of the host through unworthy reception by lay people forms another common story-line. A woman who had killed her husband by burning their house down on him, choked to death on the host.[261] A quarrelsome woman who had feigned reconciliation received communion at Easter and the host leapt out of her mouth.[262] Similarly, Friar Mansuetus told Thomas of Eccleston of an event he had witnessed at

---

[256] 'Ignis huiusmodi furoris . . . omni quod super altare repperiri poterat comburendum, duplici que pixide cuneo, videlicet exteriori interiorique eburneo infra quos panis ipse vitalis omnia pugilla continens . . . solus ipse panis loculo conclusus serico qui vim tanti furoris verisimiliter evitare non poterat intactus remanserat miraculose satis', *Reg. Repingdon* I, pp. 14–16, on p. 15.

[257] *DM* 9,54, pp. 158–9; 9,63, pp. 165–6.

[258] *Speculum laicorum*, no. 436a, pp. 89–90.

[259] *Speculum laicorum*, no. 269c, p. 55; John Bromyard, *Summa praedicantium*, tit. Eucharistia, col. 255r. On an undeserving recipient who vomited to death, see *Liber exemplorum*, no. 14, p. 8.

[260] *DM* 9,39, p. 142.

[261] BL Harley 2851, fol. 106ʳ.

[262] From a late fourteenth-century English collection, BL Harley 2316, fol. 11ᵛ.

the communion of a well-known sinner, who swaggered back to his place in disrespect after reception, only to see the host leap out of his mouth to the floor, to be rescued later by the priest.[263] A count who had received communion at his sick-bed without proper confession of his many sins was grabbed by demons:

> Having dared to receive the body undeservingly, he lost the spirit . . . and the demons dragged him horribly chained in fiery chains.[264]

Stories of abuse by Jews proliferated from the late thirteenth century, eventually replacing the tales which had survived from the early Middle Ages and which spoke of blind doubt and ridicule rather than vicious and intended abuse. They tell of a Jew and later of a group of Jews, who procured a host, often through a Christian maid or debtor, and attacked it with knives and axes and fire. The host bled, and survived all manner of attack; finally, the Jew was led to execution, the miraculous host was revered, a chapel built in its honour, and processions, hymns and memorials created for it. The prototype is the story of the Rue des Billettes, the miracle of Paris of 1290, which spread in the chronicle, art and drama of the fourteenth and fifteenth centuries.[265] These tales proliferated in different contexts and both fashioned people's eucharistic sensibilities and refashioned the eucharistic repertoire, the story inspiring similar miracles in many localities.

Exemplary stories also surrounded the ritual of bringing the eucharist to the sick, a public event which brought the eucharist into the public domain and which was fraught with potential dangers. Most common were tales of miraculous intervention and reward for piety, such as the tale which appears in the *Dialogus miraculorum* about the knight who had knelt in devotion to the passing eucharist, thus dirtying his clothes, only to find them miraculously restored to their original state.[266] From a neighbouring milieu arose the tale of Thomas of Cantimpré in a *Vita* composed by him *c.*1239: of a rich man, John of Montmirail, who during a visit to Paris, fell to his knees at the sound of the visitation bell. His clothes remained, none the less, unsoiled.[267] In England the story

---

[263] 'De adventu fratrum', p. 67, written *c.*1258–9.

[264] 'Ausus fuit indigne continere corpus, emisit spiritus . . . demones ducebant virum horribiliter cathenatum ignea cathena', *Erzählungen des Mittelalters*, no. 14, p. 241, in the collection of a Dominican of Breslau *c.*1485.

[265] Lavin (1967), esp. pp. 2–10.

[266] The story was reported as being told by the bishop of Palestrina on his mission to Cologne in 1201, *DM* 9,51, pp. 155–6.

[267] Godding (1981), (*Vita Johannis Cantimpratensis* 2, 8,2).

was popularised in the *Alphabet of tales* translated in the early fifteenth century.[268]

Other types of reward were granted to those who venerated the eucharist when it was taken to the sick. A woman who was pouring wine when she heard the visitation and left the cask with the spigot in hand, knelt and venerated, returned to find that not one drop of wine had been lost.[269] Improper veneration was shown to be punished, as in the story of the group of revellers who followed a procession with the *viaticum* with music and song, and when they reached a bridge it collapsed drowning them but leaving the priest, acolyte and eucharist unharmed.[270]

Another common tale about the taking of the eucharist to the sick stresses rather more the aspect of Christ's presence in the sacrament. It developed out of a Byzantine tale of John Moschus and was taught in a Thuringian version by the late twelfth century.[271] It tells of a prostitute who met a priest in a mountain pass carrying the eucharist to the sick, and thought:

If the Christian faith is true, and if that which the priest is carrying in the pyx is the saviour of the world . . .

Then he was worthy of her petition which followed:

Lord Jesus Christ, son of the living God, if you are he who has created all things, born of the Virgin Mary, suffered and buried, risen to heaven, sitting on the right of God the almighty father, and will judge the living and the dead, if it is you that the priest carries in the pyx, I beg you by your ineffable mercy, to forgive me all my sins.[272]

The woman was voicing a mixture of faith and doubt, to which she received Christ's answer from the pyx, and in Latin, to which she

---

[268] *Alphabet of tales*, no. 492, p. 335. The *Book of vices and virtues* combines the eucharistic message with the charitable one in its inclusion of stories about Mary of Oignies' ministration to lepers while expounding on the importance of visitation of the sick; Mary was after all a very famous 'eucharistic' saint; *The book of vices and virtues*, p. 207.

[269] See the fifteenth-century French collection of Jean Mensel, BL Royal 15 D 5, fols. 344[vb].

[270] See together with the accompanying woodcut in the version of the *Nürnberg chronicle*, printed in 1493, *Illustrations*, fig. 25, pp. 46–7.

[271] *Patrologia graeca* 87, col. 2,879.

[272] 'Si fides christiana vera esset, et si ipse esset salvator mundi, quem sacerdos portavit in pixide . . .', 'Domine Jhesu Christe, fili dei vivi, si tu es ille, qui omnia fecisti, natus de Virgine Maria, passus et sepultus, ascendens ad celos, sedens ad dexteram dei patris omnipotentis, iudicaturus vivos et mortuos, si te talem portat sacerdos in pixide, rogo te per ineffabilem misericordiam tuam, ut ignoscas michi omnia peccata mea', *Erzählungen*, no. 68, pp. 268–9.

answered: 'Lord, I do not understand Latin, I ask you to speak German to me.' Which He did and helped her to convert to a better life.[273]

On the *Rezeption,* and the hearers' response to these tales, we have few explicit statements. As we have seen, miracles and their retelling were thought to affect belief and to counter doubt. *Exempla* often report this very transformation, like the conversion of Jews or the return of heretics to orthodoxy. A preacher who did not tolerate Margery Kempe's noisy devotions and who preached against her in St James' church in King's Lynn, changed his mind and turned to Margery after having read the *Vita* of Mary of Oignies, a holy woman and saint who had also been deeply attached to the eucharist.[274] *Exempla* very clearly provided the story-line in actions against the Jews during accusations of host-desecration. *Exempla* provided material for use in other media: eucharistic tales adorned the walls of the Corporal Chapel in Orvieto Cathedral decorated in $1357 \times 82$,[275] they were developed into vernacular poems, such as the one about the 'Lady that was in despair',[276] and a Sienese *predella* panel by Sassetta of $1423 \times 6$ depicted the eucharistic miracle as the host started bleeding when a young monk in a state of sin (the devil was clawing at him) was about to receive communion.[277] A series of tapestries made in the early sixteenth century for the abbey of Ronceray in Angers depicted thirteen eucharistic miracles, some local and some from the general lore.[278] These uses show that *exempla* were accessible and repeated, and that they addressed a multitude of eucharistic interpretations. Their singular value for the investigation of eucharistic symbolism is in the ethnographic gaze they make possible by reporting and correcting abuse and malpractice, confusion, error and doubt, before their rhetorical transformation into an example of orthodoxy.

This brief survey of the arsenal of eucharistic miracle tales, most of which were told as *exempla,* suggests that every area of injunction, restriction and practice, and every custom, ritual and demand which could be mistaken, neglected, misunderstood or manipulated, was countered by an appropriate tale. The tales invariably present a protagonist in one of the situations of doubt, abuse or error; most frequently the protagonist is a marginal character: a Jew, a woman, a *rusticus.* In

---

[273] 'Domine, non intelligo latinum, rogo te ut loquaris teutonicum'. See another version of the late thirteenth century in a collection of Marian tales from north Germany, BL Add. 18929, fol. 84[vb].

[274] Atkinson (1983), pp. 152–4.

[275] Lazzarini (1952), pp. 51–5.

[276] *Ancient metrical tales*, pp. 134–44, CUL. Ff.2.38.

[277] *Painting in Renaissance Siena*, pp. 72–4, plate 1c.

[278] Tervarent (1933).

stories involving active abuse, it is a Jew, a heretic, a witch – characters from whom, and from whose practices, the audience would willingly distance itself.

Following the code of eucharistic propriety the tale began with a pure, wheaten, white host which had been transubstantiated, and proceeds to expose it to the world. A tale of Caesarius of Heisterbach even tells of imperfect baking, when a worm baked in the host miraculously jumped off the altar before consecration.[279]

## FURTHER IMAGING OF THE EUCHARIST

The images incorporated in the sacramental world-view were fed from a variety of traditions which have surfaced in the teachings, discussion, objections, tales and miracles of the eucharist. The exact source of these images cannot always be traced, but they determined the representations in art and in vernacular literature, and they spoke to priests and teachers from the historiated initials on the pages of liturgical books.

### Biblical correlations

In the early thirteenth century biblical imagery related to the eucharist could be learnt in a number of contexts in the clerical literature and in that designed for the laity; and especially in such texts as the *Biblia pauperum* which have pictures apparently for the laity but texts, and sometimes complex iconographies intelligible only to the clergy. The *Biblia pauperum* taught the Christian tale through the linking of Old Testament tales with their fulfillment or realisation in the New Testament. These correlations exploited similarities in appearance but contrasted the scenes, one of which had taken place before, and the other after, the arrival of grace.[280] The correspondences provided schemes for representation in all the media through which Christian symbolism was conveyed; in the ornamentation of other books, and in buildings, and could be transposed into vivid material for preaching. As the *Biblia pauperum* included a text and its related image, it drew out a story's moral vividly.[281] The image of Melchizedek, priest and king, as a precursor to Christ, was visually popularised in the *Biblia pauperum* and in the more allegorical *Bible moralisée*, in correlations such as:

---

[279] *DM* 9,65, pp. 167–8.
[280] Eleen (1982), p. 148.
[281] On the influence of the *Biblia pauperum* on other didactic genres see Brooks (1936).

| Melchizedek | Last Supper | manna |
| Sacrifice of Isaac | Christ on Cross | Moses and bazen snake[282] |

Occasions for eucharistic interpretations, loosely based on the traditional exegesis but exploring them with new interest, were numerous
and were created anew. In a French *Bible moralisée* of the mid thirteenth century (by 1240) Abraham is shown with Sarah making offerings to two clerics celebrating mass, evoking their offering at Mamreh
to the angels, and a few folios later another eucharistic connection
appears: Aaron's rod and the miraculous serpent appear near a priest
holding a chalice at the altar.[283] The Passover scene corresponds to
communion, and in a resonant image Christ faces three men in peaked
hats, Jews, set in parallel with a priest raising the eucharistic wafer.[284]
The opposition is echoed in the fifteenth-century English poem, 'Of
the sacrament of the Altar', which tells that in olden days Jews ate lamb
at Easter, but:

> Is ouer put in newe lawe now
> At estre we, eten quyk bred.[285]

The theme of sacrifice receives further eucharistic meaning as it is
related to the elevation: an English psalter of the early fourteenth
century in the *Biblia pauperum* tradition contained an elevation scene
which was explained:

> The sacrifice which is offered to the Lord in justice signifies the most precious
> sacrifice of Christ's body offered by the hands of the priest, and through which all
> faithful people will be found just, and saved.[286]

Another early-fourteenth-century *Biblia pauperum* from Weimar
shows Melchizedek offering a chalice and a host: the priest represents
Christ, and the bread and wine his flesh and blood.[287] Another English
psalter in this tradition has Melchizedek depicted as offering Abraham
a chalice and a host, in place of the biblical bread and wine.[288] Ambrose

---

[282] Anderson (1971), p. 241; also in other media listed in Anderson (1963), p. 209. See the use
of the theme of Melchizedek in the preaching of Ranulph de la Houblonnière in Paris in
1273, Bériou (1987) II, p. 68.
[283] Oxford Bodleian Bodley 270b, fols, 12ʳ, 41ʳ; Eleen (1982), pp. 119, 124, 134, 138, fig. 273.
[284] Oxford Bodleian Bodley 270b, fol. 46ʳ. See also the Hush psalter from Lincolnshire of
c.1280, BL Add. 38116, fols. 8ᵛ–13ᵛ. On pictorial aids for instruction, see Saxl (1942).
[285] *Twenty six political poems*, lines 99–100, p. 106.
[286] 'Sacrificium quod offertur domino in iusticia significat preciosissimum sacrificium corporis Xristi oblatum per manus sacerdotis per quod fideles omnes iustificantur et salvan-
tur', BL Add. 18719, fol. 224ᵛ.
[287] Lane (1984), pp. 107–8.
[288] Cambridge. Trinity College B.11.4, fol. 10ʳ.

had called Melchizedek the 'auctor sacramenti', that is, the author or authority or prototype of the priest of the sacrament;[289] and that is how he is shown, the first in an order of priests, as put by Paul, 'following the order of Melchizedek'.[290] He was placed within the visual scheme of missal decoration, at the Initial of 'Te igitur', at the beginning of the canon of the mass, in Sarum missals of the fourteenth and fifteenth centuries.[291] Melchizedek entered the imagery of priesthood related to the feast of Corpus Christi, as in the initial of the mass for the day in a Chester breviary of 1414×43, where his encounter with Abraham, the offering of a chalice and a wafer, is shown.[292]

Understanding of the correlations suggested by the *Biblia pauperum* was not confined to the literate, clerical or lay: this can be demonstrated, even if only rarely can we trace the routes of transmission. The parishioners of Friskney in Lincolnshire attended their mass in a church, the north wall of which was painted with scenes from the life of David and of Christ. Even more significantly, the south wall presented a selection of eucharistic scenes and miracles, showing the Israelites gathering manna, the marriage in Cana, the story of the laughing woman in St Gregory's mass, and a tale of the desecration of a host by a Jew.[293] A certain fruition and cross-fertilisation of the genres from very different traditions had reached the smallest of social and cultural frameworks, the rural parish.

## Elevation scenes

The elevation was a token both of sacramental meaning and of the exclusive priestly power in its mediation and it becomes common in the decoration of the text of the mass in missal.[294] Awareness of the symbolic meaning of the scene of the elevation is demonstrated in its choice for the illumination of the initial I of the third book of the *Decretals*, 'Incipit liber tercius de vita et honestate clericorum'; in sumptuous books the scene could occupy half a page. In a thirteenth-

---

[289] 'Quis habuit panem et vinum? Abraham non habuit. Sed quis habuit? Melchisedech. Ipse ergo auctor sacramentorum', Ambrose, *De sacramentis* IV c. 3,10, *PL* 16, col. 457. This image also appears in Gilbert Crispin's 'De sacramento altaris' of *c.* 1093, *The works of Gilbert Crispin*, p. 105.

[290] Hebrews, 5,6; 6,20; 7,17.

[291] See, for example, Oxford Oriel 75, fol. 143[ra].

[292] London Lambeth Palace 69, fol. 148[vb]. The image also appears in the full-page illumination painted in 1485 in *Les Tres Riches Heures du Duc de Berry*, plate 103, together with other eucharistic figures, Moses and Elijah.

[293] Anderson (1955), pp. 183–4.

[294] It was also represented in monumental art; see the stained glass window in St Michael's church, Doddiscombsleigh (Devon), Whiting (1989), p. 19, figure 1.

century miscellany of canon law two priests are shown at a draped altar,[295] and a Bolognese manuscript of 1241 shows the elevation with attendants and an audience of four men.[296] By the fourteenth century the elevation scene could be very elaborate; it was a favourite choice for the illustration of canon law texts dealing with liturgical practice. An elevation scene was often chosen for the decoration of the third part of the *Decretum*, 'De consecratione'.[297] It was also used to illuminate the beginning of the third book of the *Decretals* when it opened 'De vita et honestate clericorum', as in the splendid half-page illustration at the beginning of John Andrea's *Novellae,* a commentary on the third, fourth and fifth books of the *Decretals,* illuminated in Bologna in 1353–4,[298] and an English copy of the *Clementines* from the first half of the century contains an elevation scene with priest and acolyte at the initial D of 'Diocesanis'.[299] The elevation was perceived as the essence of clerical office, the focus of the liturgy, the epitome and justification of clerical privilege.

As eucharistic sensibilities grew eucharistic imagery became more pervasive, colonising scenes which were previously not used in this way. An example is the decoration of the initial C of psalm 97, 'Cantate domino canticum novum quia mirabilia fecit', traditionally decorated with a scene of two or more monks chanting at a lectern.[300] But in the Worcester psalter of *c.*1210 a eucharistic theme is added, with five clerics at a lectern placed before a draped altar with a chalice,[301] and an English psalter of the mid thirteenth century has a priest elevating a wafer at a draped altar at this position.[302] Some thirteenth-century psalters, of the group known as the Lambert-le-Begue psalters, display a variety of interpretations of this scene: in one two clerics at a lectern are present as a priest elevates the host above a chalice, in another a deacon rings a bell for elevation, and in yet another the priest elevates the host in the presence of three figures.[303] The scene of the mass at this initial becomes even more popular in fourteenth- and fifteenth-century

[295]  BL Royal 10 d VII, fol. 165[ra].
[296]  Oxford Bodleian Th.b.4, fol. 101[ra].
[297]  See Cambridge Fitzwilliam Museum 262, fol. 139[r]; and many examples in *The corpus of miniatures of the manuscripts of the Decretum* III, figure 35 (Vatican lat. 2492, fol. 36[v]); plate 3 (Vatican Archivio San Pietro A 25, fol. 300[r]).
[298]  Vatican Vat. lat. 2534, fol. 1[r]. Cassee (1982).
[299]  Oxford Corpus Christi 70, fol. 55[vb]; see also the Brewes-Norwich commentaries on Boniface VIII's *Liber sextus* of 1335×50, Cambridge St John's A.4(4), fol. 46[va].
[300]  See for example the Benedictine psalter of Worcester diocese, Cambridge Queens' 17(H.29), fol. 98[r].
[301]  Oxford Magdalen lat. 100, fol. 114[v].
[302]  The Carrow psalter of *c.*1250–60, Baltimore Walters Gallery W34, fol 78[r], *Early Gothic manuscripts* II, no. 18, pp. 88–90.
[303]  Oliver (1988) I, pp. 54–61, 72–4.

7 Elevation of the host; decoration to Psalm 97, 'Cantate domino'

psalters (figure 7).[304] In a psalter of the monastery of St Peter of Ghent of *c.*1320–30 decorated in the style of the Ile-de-France the image recurs with a clerk placing the host in a man's mouth, and at psalm 101, 'Domine exaudi', David is shown clasping his hands at a draped altar with a chalice.[305] The psalter and hymnal of St Augustine's, Canterbury, of *c.*1210–20, expresses the redemptive nature of the eucharist in the initial E showing Christ with a host and chalice in the upper register, and the church in the lower register with the explanation, 'At this psalm the Church gives thanks'.[306]

The process which emerges is one in which in the search for an iconographic scheme for a subject which was growing in interest, scribes, illuminators and writers used existing images and correspondences in new ways. Romanesque wall-painting of the eleventh century

---

[304] CUL Ee.4.24, fol. 25$^r$, and at other initials on fols. 7$^r$, 7$^v$, 14$^r$, 22$^v$.
[305] Oxford Bodleian Douce 5–6, fols. 99$^v$, 44$^r$. For similar decoration of the latter psalm see Cambridge Fitzwilliam 12, fol. 139$^v$.
[306] 'In isto psalmo ecclesia gratias agit', Oxford Ashmole 1525, fol. 32$^v$.

usually showed the Last Supper as a paschal meal attended by Christ and the Apostles with meat and herbs and bread on the table, such as the image in the basilica of Sant'Angelo in Formis (near Capua) painted in 1072×87.[307] By the thirteenth century the theme was sometimes imbued with greater eucharistic tones: by 1230 at St Mary, Neuerbeken (Westphalia) the scene of the Last Supper shows a long table on which stood a large chalice in front of a sacerdotal Christ. Each participant had a round bread and a chalice – nothing else. This was less of a teaching, feasting mode, but a liturgically ordered scene.[308] This may mark a shift in the associations, with the rise in the prominence of the eucharist and a greater awareness of its import.

### Historic communions

The imagery connected with 1 Corinthians in bibles and in collections of Pauline epistles is a good example of this trend. The commonest scene is that of Paul as priest placing a host on the tongue of a layman who was situated on his left.[309] This scene was expanded in the early thirteenth century to include the man's wife at his side and a chalice on the altar behind Paul, perhaps displaying greater attention to the details of the mass than before.[310] But another change occurs with the withdrawal of the chalice at mid-century in some of the representations of this scene, perhaps reflecting the decline in communion in two species to the laity.[311] In scenes of the mass carved on fifteenth-century English octagonal fonts the elevation is the predominant choice for decoration of the panel on the mass. It is interesting to note, however, that about a third of the East Anglian examples show the elevation of the chalice, rather than that of the host which dominates in other types of representation of the elevation.[312]

Representations of historic and miraculous masses and communions creep onto the pages of liturgical and devotional books and by the fifteenth century appear on painted panels, but they are far less pervasive than scenes of elevation. These are representations of masses such as the mass of St Giles, the scene from the life of Charlemagne, who had asked for St Giles' prayers since he dared not confess his sin of incest

---

[307] Demus (1968), plate x top. See also the painting in San Braudel de Berlanga (Catalonia) of the 1120s–30s, plate 171.

[308] Demus (1968), plates 216 and 217.

[309] Eleen (1982), pp. 129–31, 147.

[310] For examples see Eleen (1982), plates 250–3.

[311] *Ibid*, p. 131.

[312] I am grateful to Anne Nichols for pointing this out to me and for discussions on the Seven Sacrament fonts.

with his sister Gisela. The holy man's intercession procured pardon for Charlemagne in the form of a parchment delivered by an angel at a mass celebrated by him and attended by the Emperor. Psalters from the area of Liège turn the scene of the mass of St Giles into a eucharistic scene for the decoration of the initial to psalm 97.[313] The communion brought by Christ to St Denis in his prison cell before his martyrdom showed Christ in the position of officiating priest, as in the panel of the Communion of Saint Denis painted by Henry Bellechose *c*.1416, with the crucifixion in centre page and the communion on the left,[314] and in a Parisian missal of the same period showing Christ in this scene holding a chalice served by an angel-acolyte.[315] In the late fifteenth century the theme of the last communion of Jerome, based on a fourteenth-century legend grounded in an early medieval text, described Jerome's privileged vision of the real presence of Christ's body in the sacrament.[316] By the fifteenth century private scenes of communion enter the Books of Hours and devotional works, such as the communion of Margery of York, the wife of Charles the Bold, at the beginning of a collection of moral treatises. Another miniature of the Flemish school shows Philip the Good, Duke of Burgundy, in his oratory, at the beginning of a commentry on the *Pater noster* of 1457×67.[317]

## The child in the host

An image closely related to Christ's presence in the host is that of Christ the child, the immolated innocent which we have encountered in eucharistic miracle tales. One of the oldest tales in the eucharistic repertoire was that told in the *Vitae patrum* of an old man who suffered from doubts and who was convinced by seeing a child at the moment of consecration, a scene which disappeared once the old man professed his faith.[318] This image which was designed to evoke compassion came to inhabit a very central place in eucharistic symbolism: the child, viewed, chewed, adored, sacrificed, appears again and again in various eucharis-

[313] Oliver (1988) I, pp. 73–4. See an *exemplum* based on it, Bériou (1987) II, pp. 96–7.
[314] In the Louvre; on this theme Oliver (1988), I, p. 49.
[315] Paris Arsenal 621, fol. 442ʳ, *Les Sacrementaires et les missels manuscrits* plate volume, plate 82; see also Communion of St Denis decorating the memorial of St Denis in the Book of Hours of King René, BL Egerton 1070, fol. 90ᵛᵃ.
[316] Pseudo-Eusebius, 'De morte Hieronymi', *PL* 22, c. 52, cols. 274–5; Rice (1985), p. 144. See Botticelli's painting of *c*.1491 in which the host is put in St Jerome's mouth by a priest in the presence of two acolytes, *Italian painting: a catalogue of the Metropolitan Museum of Art*, pp. 159–62, plate facing p. 160.
[317] *Medieval manuscripts from the department of manuscripts*, pp. 172–5, 192–5, (BN fr. 9492, fol. 9).
[318] Told by Humbert of Romans among many others, *Sermones*, no. 44, p. 59.

tic registers and contexts. The image brought together two strains in eucharistic symbolism, one which stresses the presence of a real human, suffering body, a historic Christ born to a Virgin, and the other, which stresses redemption through sacrifice; and what dearer than the sacrifice of innocence, of the dearest, son by father?[319] In terms of biblical prototypes the imagery of sacrifice was well established; the *Biblia pauperum* provided a stock of correlations with the Sacrifice of Isaac, the Presentation at the Temple and other juxtapositions of the child on the altar. In an Italian New Testament of *c.*1220 the scene of the Presentation has Christ the child in Mary's hands at a draped altar on which were a chalice, an open missal and three white hosts.[320] A link between the sacrifice of the child and the institution of the mass is displayed in an early-thirteenth-century German psalter where a chalice and a child Christ are laid on the table at which Christ and the Apostles were seated for their Last Supper.[321] Similarly, an illumination in the psalter of St Peter of Ghent of *c.*1320–30 shows the child Christ of the Presentation, holding a host in his little hands.[322] More explicitly, an illumination in a Flemish manuscript of the *Queste del saint graal* of 1351 shows the Apostles flanked by kneeling angels around the table of the Last Supper, on which stands a chalice containing the nimbed Christ child![323]

The use of the child in these contexts linked the Nativity and the Passion, birth and death, building on the growing awareness of the historic and moral dependence between the two, as merged and inscribed in the eucharist.[324] That which was expressed through the liturgy is shown in the vernacular literature, as in the fourteenth century poem on the sacrament of the altar:

> When abraham of Ysaac his offryng made,
> For a ffygure he lykned is
> To angels bred, oure fadres hadde
> Þat God fed hem in wyldernes . . .
> In stede of þat, oure soules to glade
> We resceyve oure housell, god oble.[325]

The Sacrifice of Isaac came to be one of the commonest themes for the

---

[319] Shahar (1990), pp. 134–9.
[320] Vatican Chigi A IV 74, fol. 58^va.
[321] London BL Add 18144, fol. 13^r.
[322] Oxford Bodleian Douce 5, fol. 12^v.
[323] See Loomis (1963), plate 341 (Paris Arsenal 5218, fol. 88^r). The *chronotopos* of these tales can shift a number of times with Christ appearing as child, lamb, crucified, in succession, as in *DM* 9,3, pp. 110–11.
[324] Rode (1957), pp. 13, 54–60. On the liturgical link between Nativity and Passion, see Cassee (1980), p. 35.
[325] Oxford Bodleian Digby 102, fol. 124^r.

8 The sacrifice of Isaac; initial of the canon of the mass

decoration of the initial P of 'per omnia' of the canon of the mass in Sarum missals (figure 8).[326] A rare but related scene is the Circumcision of Isaac, again showing a child on the altar under a wielded knife, as in a late-fourteenth-century misericord of Worcester Cathedral.[327] Of course some contemporary representations are more benign, such as Robert Campin's *Madonna and child before a fire screen,* where Christ is handled in a gesture of offering but is surrounded by a domestic setting without the sign of blood or the threat of violent instruments.[328]

So used did the eye become, so trained was the mind, to think of the transubstantiated host as the real Christ, and in one of his suffering personas, as a sacrificed child, that horrific tales of a bleeding child Christ in the host were tolerated within the culture, and could circulate in *exempla.*[329] We have already met the boy who complained he was horrified by the view of Friar Peter devouring an infant at the altar.[330] The vision which appeared to Jane Mary of Maillé (d.1414) showed the child Christ with five wounds gushing with blood in the elevated

---

[326] The missal of *c.*1430, Cambridge Trinity B.11.11, fol. 151[ra]; and at 'Per omnia' in the early fifteenth century missal, Oxford Oriel 75, fol. 141[ra].

[327] Misericord no. 14 on the south side, Remnant and Anderson (1969), p. 172.

[328] London, National Gallery, Lane (1984), pp. 1–10. Here the Marian discourse predominates, Bynum (1986), pp. 424–5.

[329] As in Bors' vision in the *Queste del seint graal,* Matarasso (1979), p. 183, the Christ-child turns into Christ as the Man of Sorrows.

[330] Thomas of Eccleston, 'De adventu fratrum', p. 67; see above, pp. 118–19.

host.[331] Concurrently, the habit of transposition of the child and the host led to some iconographic innovations. The opening illustration in the missal is that of the letter A of 'Ad te levavi animam meam' of psalm 25 at the beginning of mass for the first Sunday in Advent. This was traditionally decorated with a scene of David kneeling in the wilderness, raising his hands with which he offered his soul, in the form of a swaddled baby, to the Godhead peering from a cloud.[332] From the thirteenth century David is increasingly shown in missals as kneeling at an altar dressed with vessels and liturgical books, David as a priest.[333] By the mid fourteenth century this had developed into a priest raising a soul-child to God at an altar, perhaps David as priest, as in the missal of Jean Tixerdarent, bishop of Rieux (1322–48),[334] and it is clearly David as priest in a Flemish Franciscan missal of c.1400.[335] The image of the priest at an altar elevating a child was neatly superimposed upon the common image of the elevation,[336] and by the early fifteenth century the mental leap required from a Parisian illuminator to move from 'Ad te levavi' to 'elevatio' was very small indeed, through the image of the child in the host, the child-offering, the swaddled child-soul of the traditional image – Christ in the elevation scene. So an early-fifteenth-century missal of Paris is decorated by an elevation scene inside a Gothic church,[337] while an Autun missal shows a priest elevating a host between index finger and thumb at an altar on which were a book and a chalice and surrounded by an admiring group of lay folk.[338] A typical elevation scene came, in stages, to replace the psalmist's commendation of his soul to God through the identification between visual images and gestures. A missal of the Use of Paris decorated by the Boucicaut workshop c.1415 shows a priest bowing at an altar during the celebration of mass, not even an elevation scene any more.[339] And even a

[331] Kieckhefer (1984), p. 171.
[332] Dumoutet (1925–6); see also the fifteenth-century Venetian manuscript Venice Marciana library lat. 46(III)2099, fol. 157[va].
[333] See a Paris missal of after 1228, Paris. University library 177; a missal of Sens of the early thirteenth century, Paris BN lat. 10502, fol. 14[rb]. A Flemish Book of Hours of c.1300 at the psalm 'Ad dominum' had David kneeling and raising a naked child (soul) near an altar on his right, on which stood a chalice and corporal, Cambridge Trinity B.11.22, fol. 99[r].
[334] *Les Sacrementaires et les missels manuscrits* II, no. 394, p. 221 (Toulouse Municipal Library 90, fol. 246v).
[335] Bodleian Can. lit. 389, fol. 7[ra].
[336] Rode (1957), pp. 49–54.
[337] Paris Mazarine Library 406, fol. 7[r].
[338] Lyon Municipal Library 517, fol. 8[ra].
[339] Meiss (1968), plate 356 and pp. 100–1 (Lucca Bibliotheca Governativa 3122, fol. 7[r]). Other scenes include Bishop James of Châtelier (1427–38) elevating at an altar, Paris Arsenal 621, fol. 1[ra]; *Les Sacrementaires et les missels manuscrits* III, pp. 37–8; Dumoutet (1925–6), p. 35; and Paris Arsenal 623, fol. 1[ra], with a priest elevating a child at a draped altar in the presence of kneeling layfolk.

simple scene of Nativity at this place in the missal, so obvious a choice for the first Sunday of Advent, would come to resonate richly with the eucharistic overtones that it was gradually acquiring.[340]

The child on the altar was a potent image, one which seems to have gained in importance and frequency of representation in the thirteenth century; and it fed on the same trends which portrayed increasingly gory images of the crucified Christ.[341] The nature of the child's sacrifice is terrible, as an innocent child was immolated. The more didactically controlled interpretations were probably meant to stress the sacrifice and the father's loss and endless generosity.[342] But what seems to have developed is much more of an appreciation of the mother's loss, and the victim's suffering, as a pathetic child, or as sorrowing adult, as in some vernacular literature. The transgression involved in contemplating, viewing and representing scenes of infanticide within the eucharistic discourse provided sites for fantasy which could have hardly been tolerated in other reaches of the same culture.

### Grail imagery

Moving from the child to the suffering man, Christ's crucifixion and death were represented as prerequisites for the grace which passed through the eucharist, to promise regeneration and salvation. An aspect of the crucifixion and its aftermath was explored in legends about the grail into which Christ's blood was collected by Joseph of Arimathea, stories which circulated in written form by the late twelfth century.[343] It is, however, only early in the next century that the eucharistic meanings become fully pronounced in one of the versions of these legends, with the development of the narrative of the grail as a quest for the vessel used at the Last Supper which later contained the blood, in the *Queste del seint graal*.[344] The *Queste*, written around 1220 by a Cistercian monk,[345] created a quest which was a route towards self-discovery, in search for an ultimate reward. The terms in which both the route and the reward were described are couched with eucharistic meanings and associations, the grail being both symbol and object, like

---

[340] See the miniature of *Ad te* in a missal of the Use of Paris of the early fifteenth century which belonged to the hospital of Beaune and where the scene is one of a procession of three clerics to the altar, the approach to the altar at the beginning of mass, BL Add. 17388, fol. 7r (it is the only historiated initial in this book).

[341] See below, pp. 302–10.

[342] A parent's love was particularly precious, as the child was of their very *substantia* which did not apply for the child's relation to the parent, Lawn (1963), p. 151; Shahar (1990), pp. 169–70.

[343] Barb (1956), p. 40.

[344] Matarasso (1979), pp. 180–203.

[345] Stevens (1973), pp. 120–1.

the very eucharist, symbol and essence, even though it is never quite pinned down to one meaning being at once chalice, lamb, *ciborium,* and the Supper's tray.[346]

The *Queste* is related to the religious language of Cistercian spirituality; like the eucharist it is both symbol and vehicle for an unachievable mystical union.[347] The knights seeking the grail wish to fathom the truth behind the material veil, like the eucharistic moment of gazing at the host which subsumes under the accidents the substance of God.[348] The *Queste* is complex and convoluted, as complex and arduous as the spiritual quest of a mystic. It is of a very different order from the readily available efficacy taught in the literature of the 'Merits of the Mass'. This difference is captured in the high point of the *Queste*, the mass at Corbenic, when for all but Galahad the quest was over, fulfilled, just as for most people, participation in the eucharist was achieved through attendance at the mass,[349] here it is implied that for a few, this was bound to remain merely a stepping stone.[350] The grail quest points towards a eucharistic world which is overlaid with meanings and populated with numerous tasks, demanding and elusive. It emerges from the eucharistic sensibilities of the late twelfth century, and out of the turn-of-the-century grail epics in that privileged area of intellectual and spiritual activity of northern France and the Low Countries in which we have found the routes of so many of our eucharistic investigations. And it was popularised in the thirteenth century, a eucharistic elaboration with meanings particularly resonant in the aristocratic and knightly milieux.[351] It interpreted and gave new meanings to the most pervasive and potent religious symbol, creating within it areas of exclusivity through the implication and creation of tasks which only few would, or could, undertake.

The representations which accompanied the text of these romances are by necessity more concrete than many of the verbal allusions. The images were heavily overdetermined; showing a knight seated at Bishop Joseph's table was arranged like a scene of the Last Supper, with the chalice and the bloody lance on the table-altar and with angels and acolytes bearing candles to the seated host-celebrant.[352] The mysteries of Corbenic, where the grail was housed after its arrival in Brittany, are

---

[346] *Ibid*, p. 182. In Chrétien de Troyes' *Contes del graal* it seems to be a pyx, but remains a mystery, Brooke (1989), p. 184.

[347] Hontoir (1946), pp. 141–8; Rode (1957), p. 12, Hamilton (1942), p. 95.

[348] Matarasso (1979), p. 184.

[349] Hontoir (1946), p. 110, comments on the infrequency of communion in the *Queste*.

[350] Hamilton (1942), pp. 186–7.

[351] About knights' communion, see Sylvester (1897) and below, pp. 335–6.

[352] In a manuscript of 1351, Paris Arsenal 5218, fol. 88ʳ.

in the *Queste* highly, if not wholly, Christocentric, which in the symbolic world of the thirteenth century also meant sacramental, eucharistic.

The doctrine of the *Queste* consisted of the insertion of the eucharistic symbolism into a romantic-chivalric discourse. The grail was a symbol of the ineffable, that which could never be deserved; it was tantalising and thus attracted the Knights of the Round Table. It could be appropriately approached only once one was purged and prepared, through confession, obedience and celibacy, through a vocation which even surpassed the clerical. To those who are pure it may become visible, but no more, in the elevated host.[353] The grail was the romantic idealised extension of the host – one was to see/receive it, and then to die, like Galahad.[354]

These eucharistic romance images were popularised with the increasing dissemination and adaptation of the themes of the literature.[355] It is present in the didactic effect of the song, 'By a chapel as I came', which was based on a May song, 'Mery hyt ys in May mornyng', which tells of a meeting between Christ and his disciples:

> Oure lorde offeryd whate he wollde,
> A challes alle off ryche rede gollde.[356]

The warm colours of red and gold, majesty and blood, derive from the descriptions of the knightly halls of romance. These are richly displayed in the suggestive Corpus Christi carol of *c.*1500 copied into Richard Hill's commonplace book.[357] In this poem we are embarked on a journey combining the private and the mythical realms; the poem is at once a lullaby, a romance, a liturgical text and a riddle. It describes a man carried aloft, then laid, in a hall hung with purple and pall, on a bed of gold so red, a knight incessantly bleeding from his wound, besides whom a woman kneels crying. The journey is finally summarised if not resolved when we encounter at the end of the carol a stone inscribed 'Corpus Christi' – nothing more. Here, as elsewhere, eucharistic Christ is an end, a travellers' fare and a travellers' rest.[358]

This is a complex and rich picture, accomplished from the weaving of the chivalric imagery of the grail and the hall and the eucharistic Christocentric iconography of suffering. These images would have been read differently by different people, but the culture was suffused

---

[353] Matarasso (1979), pp. 183–4.
[354] *Ibid*, p. 181.
[355] On the eucharist in Middle English verse, see MacGarry (1936).
[356] *Religious lyrics of the xvth century*, no. 116, p. 183, lines 9–10.
[357] Of the early sixteenth century, but the material is much older, *Songs, carols*, no. 86, p. 13; Greene (1960); Gray (1972), pp. 166–7; Stevens (1973), pp. 114–15.
[358] See also Peck (1975), pp. 466–7.

in eucharistic symbolism, as one image conjured up another, never quite discrete, never quite the same; a symbol can serve as a focus for a variety of different positions and approaches, differences which are thus inscribed and celebrated in the symbol itself: lamb, child, man, tray, chalice, host . . .

## Mary of the eucharist

The correspondences between incarnation and passion in the eucharist have several resonances. We have already noted the prominence of the image of the child and the development of the theme of the crucifixion. The connection is also expressed in the use of Christmas collects as well as benedictions from Easter week in the Corpus Christi liturgy.[359] From the eleventh century, with greater interest in the reality of Christ's presence in the host, ideas about Mary's affinity to the eucharist developed, and their bearing on other areas of eucharistic lore was explored.[360] In vernacular literature a strong bond was created between the eucharistic body reborn at the mass and the original body born from a virgin womb, to produce the powerful image linked both to crucifixion and to nativity in the Virgin Mary.[361] But the child was never without his mother, Mary herself was augmented in the eucharistic context.[362] She became a mediator, celebrant, the person who had intimately constituted the sacred.[363] Nowhere is this celebrated more beautifully than in Hildegard of Bingen's poetry which marvels, as in 'O quam magnum miraculum', that the female form could contain Christ:

> O how great a miracle it is
> That into the humble female body
> A king has entered
> God has done this
> Because humility surpasses all.[364]

[359] On the mingling of Nativity and eucharistic themes in the Wakefield Corpus Christi cycle plays, see Robertson (1980), pp. 219–20.
[360] Paschasius had already dwelt on this connection in the ninth century, Laurentin (1952), pp. 38–40; and on developments from the eleventh century, see pp. 101–31.
[361] See Fulton (1987). See also Humbert of Romans' sermon 'In solemni communione' which draws this link, *Sermones*, fol. 59ᵛ.
[362] Fulton (1987), chapter 4, pp. 62–80.
[363] Laurentin (1952), pp. 127–31.
[364] 'O quam magnum miraculum est
    Quod in subditam femineam formam
    Rex introivit
    Hoc deus fecit
    Quia humilitas super omnia ascendit',

Newman (1987), p. 277, also pp. 193–4. See also 'O viridissima virga': 'quoniam viscera ipsius frumentum protulerunt', *ibid*, p. 279.

And the union of Christ and the church in the eucharist is likened by her to marriage, celebrated at the crucifixion.[365] The identification is expressed in another image, that of honey; the eucharist smelt like honey to those blessed by eucharistic visions, and in it Christ was miraculous honey produced, according to Bonaventure, by 'our bee the Virgin Mary'.[366]

The overarching symbol of salvation, the eucharist, was combined with another source of comfort, solace and healing, Mary, in an intersection of discourses. When Ranulph de la Houblonnière preached at the beguinage of Paris in *c.*1273 about Christ's daily presence, he described Christ's body simply in these terms: 'In his presence in flesh taken from the Virgin, on the table of the altar, he visits us by his grace.'[367] Mary appears here as the progenitor of the body which was subsequently reborn at the very altar which her image so often adorned. In a number of Venetian altarpieces of the late fifteenth century scenes of the Virgin were associated with those of the Passion and the eucharist, as in Bartholomew Vivarini's Madonna of 1482 in the Frari Church, where the central panel of the Madonna enthroned is crowned by a Man of Sorrows in the panel right above it.[368]

Eucharistic poetry and mysticism revelled in this myth, of a virgin mother and her divine son unceasingly born and unceasingly mourned. Ida of Nivelles (*c.*1197–d.1231), who was known for her eucharistic devotion had a vision of a newborn baby in the host during the Christmas mass.[369] A polyptych painted in the workshop of the Florentine Daddi in the 1340s for the Dominican church of Santa Maria Novella combines a strong eucharistic interpretation with a traditional composition of Madonna and Child flanked by saints.[370] The child in the Virgin's lap holds a scroll on which is inscribed 'Ego sum panis vivus qui de celo descendi' (John 6,51), and the four saints Peter, John the Evangelist, John the Baptist and Matthew in their separate panels carry similar scrolls with important eucharistic phrases, all of which include the word 'panis'.[371] The church of Santa Maria Novella was a

---

[365] *Ibid*, pp. 211–14.

[366] 'Jesus, decus angelicum, in aure dulce canticum, in ore mel mirificum . . . Hoc mel produxit nobis apis nostra Virgo Maria', Bonaventure, *Opera omnia* v, pp. 558–9. On experiencing the taste of honey in the host, see above, p. 119, and Bynum (1987), p. 131.

[367] 'Sua presentia in carne quem sumpsit de Virgine, in mensa altaris, et etiam visitat nos per graciam suam', Bériou (1987) II, p. 107.

[368] For this and other examples, see Goffen (1986), pp. 86–7 (figure 22), 215–16.

[369] Axters (1948), p. 28. On visions of the child Christ, see Rode (1957).

[370] *A critical and historical corpus of Florentine painting*, section 2, vol. 5, pp. 87–90 and adjacent plates. The polyptych was transferred to the Spanish Chapel *c.*1485 and is now in the Green cloister.

[371] *Ibid*, plates XVII 4, 5, 6, 7. The passages are 1 Peter 1, 18–19; John 6,59; John 1,34; Matthew 26,26.

venue for a eucharistic cult as early as 1294; in 1355, a decade after the polyptych's painting, the Spanish Chapel dedicated to the Sacrament was consecrated. This monumental altarpiece which was to adorn one of the greatest Dominican churches of Christendom represented the Virgin in the fullness of eucharistic promise. She was adorned with scriptural passages become liturgy, holding in her lap Christ the Child, the eucharistic bread.[372]

Nicholas Love's translation of pseudo-Bonaventure's *Meditationes vitae christi*, the very popular *Mirrour of the blessed lyf of Jesu Crist* of 1410, a work which gained Archbishop Arundel's approval for its orthodoxy, states in the section 'De sacramento altaris':

His mete that he ʒeueth to us in the sacramente of the awtere; for thereynne is he verreily And in that self body that was so merueylosly conceyuede by the holy goost aboute kynde and also merueylosely born of his blissed moder Marye with oute sorwe or weme of synne.[373]

In a fifteenth-century poem on the festivals of the church, the connection is vividly struck again in at the discussion of Christmas:

> Þe kirnell sprang at Cristenmasse,
> Þat now is crist in a cake clere,
> Þe preest drynkeþ blessyd bere,
> Goddis blood in sacrament.
> Almyʒty God omnipotent
> Hys blyssyd body haþ sent
> To fede hys frendys here.[374]

This image was taken up with great interest in less didactic material in the vernacular, in popular songs, as well as in formal iconography and theology.[375] It is even mentioned in passing in an elevation prayer which salutes God in the eucharist:

> I þe honoure wiþ al my miht
> In fourme of Bred as i þe se,
> Lord þat in þat ladi briht,
> In Marie Mon bi-come for me.[376]

Or in an early-fifteenth-century eucharistic prayer:

[372] In medallions above the saints' heads are scrolls containing passages from the Old Testament which carry eucharistic meaning: Exodus 16,15; Psalms 77,25; Wisdom 16,20; Genesis 49,20.
[373] *Mirrour*, p. 302.
[374] *Legends of the holy rood*, p. 211.
[375] Fulton (1987), chapter 4, pp. 62–80.
[376] Robbins (1942–3), p. 134; *Minor poems of the Vernon manuscript*, p. 25.

> Ey! My Lord in wom Ich leue,
> Sothfastliche God and Man,
> Þou art under bredid ewe,
> Also þou was born of woman.[377]

In a Corpus Christi song from the same century the eucharist is:

> It is bred from heuene cam
> Ffleych and blod of Mary it nam.
> Ffor þe synnys of Adam.[378]

The eucharist intervenes even more powerfully in the imagery which likened Mary to an oven for the baking of bread, as in the Franciscan John Ryman's carol of *c.*1492:

> This brede geveth eternall lyfe
> Bothe unto man, to childe, and wyfe . . .
> In virgyne Mary this brede was bake
> Whenne criste of her manhoode did take,
> For of alle synne mankynede to make,
> Ete ye it so ye be [not dede].[379]

Medieval embryology maintained, in the tradition of Galen, that the mother was an oven, or a vessel in which the foetus was cooked.[380] This understanding is present in the imagery we have encountered in these poems, as well as in a type of eucharistic devotional objects, the *vièrge ouvrante*, a pyx in the form of the Virgin with an opening.[381] These devotional artifacts for the reservation of the eucharist combined a statue of the Virgin with child, and a receptacle for the eucharist, making of her a worthy handler of the eucharist, as otherwise only priests were.[382] This type of association inspired the representation which showed Mary in priestly garb, at an altar, as the summoner and bearer of God that she was, in a mutual reinforcement of the clerical and Marian symbols.[383] The *Book of vices and virtues* put the connection between 'oven' and 'bread' in its exposition on 'our daily bread' in the *Pater noster*, moving, as it claimed from bread to bread-maker:

---

[377] Robbins (1942–3), p. 137.
[378] Fehr (1902), no. 43, p. 63; *Religious lyrics of the xivth century*, pp. 180–1, at p. 180.
[379] Based on John 6,50, *Early English carols*, no. 65, p. 216; in CUL Ee.1.12, fols. 49ᵛ–50ʳ.
[380] Bynum (1986), p. 421.
[381] See two examples in Lane (1984), p. 28.
[382] Forsyth (1972), p. 24. On the image of Mary as priest, see Bériou (1987) II (a sermon for Purification 1273), p. 55: 'possumus dicere quod ipsa fuit prima presbiterissa'.
[383] Lane (1984), pp. 71–2. On Mary as a symbol of transubstantiation in the art of the Counter-Reformation, see Mâle (1932), pp. 72–86.

Þᵗ is to seye þat a man or a woman schal record swetliche and in smale peces þe many smale þouȝtes al þe godnesses of oure lord and al þat Ihesu Crist suffrid for us . . . And al þat doþ þe vertue of þis bred . . . Þis bred we clepen oure for it was made of oure deuȝh. Blessed þe þilke good womman þat leide forþ þe flour, þat was þe virgyne Marie.[384]

Moving from the breadmaker to the bread, we reach the host, in which the most outrageous benefits were said to dwell. The nature of this bread fascinated its recipients, who were perforce its bakers, makers, shapers, vendors and consumers. Carols and prayer-tags, perhaps the most nebulous literary forms, but resonant and widely known and used, were rich and explicit in interpretations and imagery. Like the poem *The sacrament of the altar* of c.1450, which tried to make sense of it:

> It seems white and is red;
> It is quike and semes dede;
> It is fleshe and semes bred;
> It is on and semes too;
> It is God body and no mo.[385]

This poem used the rhythm of a riddle with oppositions and mock numeric precision.[386] And this little poem was very popular; it is to be found inserted into other poems, as the second of three stanzas in the 'Mirabile mysterium', a poem devoted to the eucharist, and in the collection of poems and carols of John Ryman of c.1492.[387] It also appears in less than obvious contexts; in an astronomical calendar,[388] and a Latin treatise.[389]

The bread of the eucharist fascinated by its simplicity of texture and the power of its transubstantiated substance. A fourteenth-century English compendium for preachers used it as a metaphor describing all things that can be offered as spiritual remedy. There are five loaves in the 'goostly pantere': the word, penance, temporal goods, the eucharist, and eternal life.[390] A fifteenth-century sermon for the fourth Sunday in Lent in an English manuscript which displays some Lollard tendencies links the progression of Christ's life with the process of

---

[384] *The book of vices and virtues*, pp. 109–10.
[385] Robbins (1939a), p. 344; BL Royal 17 A 16, fol. 27ᵛ; see *Index*, no. 1640 for further examples of this tag.
[386] Robbins (1939a), p. 344; Gray (1972), p. 159.
[387] CUL Ee.1.12, fols. 49ᵛ–50ʳ.
[388] BL Royal 17 A 16, fol. 27ᵛ mentioned above.
[389] Durham Cathedral V.1,12, fol. 65ʳ; Robbins (1939a), pp. 344–5.
[390] Von Nolcken (1981), p. 280. On bread as a symbol see Ferguson (1954), p. 38.

bread-making. Christ's body was sown in the Virgin, rinsed at the Passion, reaped by enemies, threshed at the scouring, winnowed in foul words, ground in the mill of gentiles and made into pure flour and blood cooked in the sepulchre for three days – from which a loaf came forth from which Christians were to be fed.[391] The less learned material presents less intricate, but direct images. In a mid-fifteenth-century manuscript collection of carols are the lines:

> Of alle þe spyces þat I knowe
> Blyssed be þe qwete flour.[392]

In this carol the richness of the sacramental bread is deduced from its superiority over all manner of rich spice, since from white flour Christ was born:

> Qwete is kyng of every corn,
> Jesu hymself for us was born
> In qwete is proceywid Gods face
> Of qwete is made þe bred of lyf . . .

And in the closing stanza:

> Jesu Cryst þat sit on heye,
> Ne let us never for hunger dey,
> So blyssid be þe qwete flor.

The poem expresses the fascination shared by rural and urban folk alike with the fine bread made of white flour which was too expensive for frequent consumption by the majority of the population.[393] Wheat was usually grown as a cash crop which was sent to the market while those who produced it ate darker bread. Imaginative literature often mused upon and expressed a wish for regular consumption of white bread in a utopian world. The eucharist, the small wafer made of the finest wheaten dough, was transported into that realm of fantasy.

## COMMUNION AND ITS SUBSTITUTES: FREQUENCY, MEANING AND PARTICIPATION

But the bread was not simply accessible, and was not frequently to be consumed. Communion was taught as an annual duty, which could be

---

[391] Oxford Bodleian Laud. Misc. 200, fol. 92; see Von Nolcken (1985–6), pp. 245–6.
[392] BL Sloane 2593; Fehr (1902), no. 34, p. 53.
[393] On white bread in the medieval diet, see Dyer (1983), pp. 205, 216.

taken perhaps thrice a year on the major feasts of Christmas, Easter and Pentecost, but only after due penance and preparation (plates 2 and 3). As the reality of Christ's body in the eucharist was more clearly formulated and taught, the occasion for the reception of that body became as awesome as it was full of promise. It also exerted demands on faith, as shown in a verse on the eucharist in a collection of works by Robert Grosseteste:

> The bread changes while the original species remain,
> And it is not that which is felt in the mouth.[394]

The proper preparation necessary before communion was reiterated in the preaching and teaching. Stephen of Bourbon encouraged communion after proper confession, and followed this with three *exempla* about unworthy reception.[395] It was stressed that gazing was not sufficient and that communion was not merely a duty, but a real need; since the host itself 'informs, calls to memory, sustains, strengthens and increases'.[396] The requirement of worthy reception could rarely be tested by external signs, which made it difficult to enforce. Stories proliferated, therefore, about the consequences of undeserving reception. Hildegard of Bingen (1098–1179) had a vision in which the communicants approaching the altar were transformed into five categories: those shining in purity and with souls of fire, those with pale bodies and dark souls, those with rough and hairy bodies and dirty souls, others who looked as if surrounded by thorns and with souls emaciated by leprosy, and those dripping blood with souls that smelt terribly like decaying corpses.[397] The enormity of undeserving reception of Christ's body was made increasingly clear and led to a decline in frequency of communion combined with a rise in other eucharistic practices. But James of Vitry explained the reason for this decline in a different manner:

Nowadays, however, since sins have so multiplied in the land, it is permitted that communion be received by the laity only once a year, that is at Easter.[398]

In order to link the eucharist to the maintenance of social order, it

---

[394] Cambridge Trinity College B.15.20, fol. 131[vb].
[395] Berlioz (1981), p. 317.
[396] Cambridge Gonville and Caius College 112, fol. 14[v]: 'Informat, memorat, sustentat, roborat, auget hostia'.
[397] Hildegard of Bingen, *Scivias*, Part 2 vision 6, cs. 51–6, pp. 272–5; also c. 57, pp. 275–6.
[398] 'Hodie tamen, eo quod multiplicata sunt peccata super terram, permittitur, quod semel in anno scilicet die Pasche laici corpus Christi recipiant', James of Vitry, 'De sacramentis', p. 244. For an English sermon on undeserving reception, of 1389×1404, see, *Three Middle English sermons*, no. 3, pp. 71–2.

had to be received in a unit which possessed real power over participants in the mass. Communion was to be received in the parish of
domicile where people were known and only in a state of reconciliation with the church, and after the proper payment of tithes.[399] Reconciliation with the community was also effected through the mass in
cases where public penance culminated in the parochial mass. In 1468
Thomas Wortby confessed his misdeed, the pollution of the Grantham
churchyard during a scuffle, and was made to go 'with bare shins and
feet' to the consecration of the churchyard. He was then struck with a
rod by the priest during the procession on the feast of the Purification
and was to place a taper on the altar during the offertory of the mass.[400]
But the requirement for communion in one's parish was obviously
open to abuse; the acts of Ripon Minster record an accusation made in
1481 against Isabel wife of Robert Greve, who had not confessed
during Lent, nor taken communion at Easter. Isabel claimed that she
had communicated at a chapel nearby, *le Masyndew*, what must have
originally been a hospital chapel, but this was proven to be false. She
then claimed to have confessed and received communion at St John's
parish in Falkirk near Thirsk, but failed to produce adequate proof,
and was finally excommunicated.[401]

A widespread uncertainty about the appropriateness of sexual intercourse before eucharistic reception is also evident.[402] It was understood that communion must follow confession and be taken in purity,
and there seems to have been a tacit acceptance that menstruating
women should abstain.[403] Breaches of the elaborate code for communion could happen in many ways, and such cases can convey the extent
of normative teaching about communion – for example, the interesting
case of 1529 brought by the churchwardens against Joanna Carpenter
of the parish of St Mary Queenhith, London, who was accused of
disturbing the communion of her neighbour Margaret Chamber.
Joanna was accused of having grabbed Margaret by the arm while the
latter was kneeling at the altar, about to receive communion, and
saying to her: 'I pray you let me speke a worde with you, for you have
need to axe me forgyvenes, before you rescyve your rights'.[404] This is a
late case, but it offers useful evidence of how the requirements of

---

[399] See the statutes of the synod of Paris, *Statuts synodaux* I, c. 66, p. 77; Canterbury I, *CS* II,
  I, cs. 46–7, p. 33; Bordeaux, *Statuts synodaux* II, c. 98, p. 88.
[400] And this was to be repeated a number of times ending with his final plea for forgiveness
  from the parish, *Lincoln diocesan documents*, pp. 126–8.
[401] *Acts of Ripon*, p. 186.
[402] Browe (1932), p. 376.
[403] For examples from late antiquity, see Brown (1988b), pp. 146, 433.
[404] *Series of precedents*, no. 340, p. 108.

communion could be understood. Joanna had chosen her moment well: she obviously knew that the need to take communion in a state of charity rendered her intervention especially potent. Yet it was she who was presented, either because the disruption of the ritual took precedence in the eyes of her parish priest, or perhaps because her claim against the neighbour could not be sustained.

As it became thought a fearful thing to receive Christ's body, and with the growing appreciation of the quasi-sacramental value of gazing at the present Christ, notions of 'spiritual communion' developed. Already in 1117 Anselm of Laon discussed it and by the end of the century Peter the Chanter recognised such 'communion' as effective and beneficial.[405] A mental concentration on the eucharist during elevation with attention to future redemption could bring one into a state of charity.[406] Still, there was the danger that people might obviate parochial and clerical authority in adopting the practice of spiritual communion. It was particularly suspect when adopted by groups which seemed to question priestly authority in other ways, such as some beguines or those taken to be adherents of the movement of the Free Spirit. But the danger also dwelt in widespread understandings entertained by the laity that gazing was as good as reception.

In the interpretation of communion there were two ideas at work, often at variance: first, that Christ himself was present at the altar – with all the implications which this had for the handling of the eucharist and for the exclusivity of access to it; and secondly, that the eucharist was necessary and useful, that it could do good and was powerful, thus creating a potential entry into lives, minds and aspirations. The first could exert pressure leading to infrequent and awesome communion, and the second made it a desired object and locus of power which was tantilisingly offered and longingly pursued. A strong 'vicarious' procedure thus developed, one which reflected understandings of sacramentality, of the natural and of the supernatural, and which dwelled in the *participant's* elevation, designed as a liturgical moment, and lived in a variety of ways (figures 7 and 9).[407]

Once the elevation emerged as a moment sufficiently powerful and

---

[405] But this remained unresolved until the mid thirteenth century, Macy (1984), pp. 73–4, 100–1.

[406] Dumoutet (1928), pp. 190–3.

[407] For a powerful image showing the elevation as it was seen by the viewer from the nave see the bas-relief made by Giotto and Andrea Pisano for the bell-tower of the Duomo in Florence. The elevating priest, kneeling acolyte and burning taper are powerfully juxtaposed. See the deep view inwards from the back of the nave, the vantage point chosen in Rogier van der Weyden's (1399/1400–1464) Altarpiece of the Seven Sacraments, Lane (1984), figure 52.

9 Elevation of the host in the presence of acolyte and woman; initial to the prayer 'Deus qui' of the Corpus Christi mass

useful in its own right people naturally concentrated their attention on it, and neglected other parts of the mass. William Durand complained in the late thirteenth century that people ran into church at the sound of the elevation bell.[408] Requirements to remain until the end of the mass abound. An early-fourteenth-century Florentine synod ordained that 'integram missam audiant',[409] as in the following Latin ditty, the last line of which circulated as a proverb:

He who wishes to hear the mass, ought not to leave
While it is said, and he will profit from it all.
If you are there at the start but do not remain till the end,
The part will not be granted to you, because the benefit accrues at the end.[410]

A mid-fourteenth-century poem refers to simple folk lacking in refinement:

Nu le fois sont a l'Introite
Encore sont il mains a l'Ite.[411]

Similarly, Lydgate's 'Interpretations and virtues of the mass' stresses, albeit less directly, that those who stayed until the end of the mass would enjoy grace:

Tyll *In principio,* conclusions of the masse,
Grace shall guyde hym, and conducte hys presence,
Agayne all hys foon of hygh estate or lasse.[412]

The promise of special grace brings us back to the very common genre of teachings on the 'merits' or 'meads' of the mass. In Caxton's translation of the fourteenth-century French *Livre des métiers* of 1349, a book of manners and conversation, the mass is recommended:

Men ought to here masse
And all the houres of the day,
Whiche is at his ease atte leste
God see the sacrament
Is a good brekefest.[413]

The benefits of the mass were so closely linked to the moment of the

---

[408] Adam (1964), pp. 249–51.
[409] Trexler (1964), p. 30.
[410] 'Qui vult audire missam, non debet abire,
Donec dicatur et totum preficiatur!
Si primo fueris et non in fine manetis,
Pars tibi nulla datur, quia laus on fine probatur',

*Sententiae,* no. 24940; see also no. 24282.
[411] Adam (1964), p. 251.
[412] *Lydgate's minor poems* I, lines 590–2, p. 112.
[413] *Livre des métiers,* p. 51.

elevation, when Christ was in presence, that it is not surprising that the lengthy ritual that followed it was felt to be an anti-climax.[414] A fourteenth-century clerical manual made the following promises:

Eche man yat williliche desireth to se godis bodi ofte schal have yese mede God grauntith hym nedful liflode her idel oyys and forȝete synnes buth forȝeue. He schal not lese ye sith of hys eien yat dai ne yat dai schal bi falle hym no sodainy deth; he schal not eldi in yat tyme yat he herith or seith hys masse.[415]

It was a help in the on-going battle against the devil, as put in an English sermon: 'A reseyuyng of heuene-fode to strygth þe to with-stonde þe fyndis wille'.[416] A cluster of benefits was offered in an exposition on the eucharist copied into Richard Hill's commonplace book, based on the traditional authority of Augustine on this point. It teaches the good which could accrue to the living and the dead:

> For all þat at þe messe stondith a-bowte,
> & for all Cristyn people, þat be well moo,
> Þat labowr þe comen vele in þe world a-bowt,
> Then to pray for thy frend haue þou no dowt.[417]

The mass's efficacy for the dead was debated by theologians, but in its teaching there is no such ambiguity.[418] It was so useful that souls were said to return and haunt their relatives and request masses.[419] A famous tale in *Handlyng synne*, the tale of the man of Suffolk, de-scribes such demands reiterated by a dead husband until his wife provided proper personal masses in his memory.[420]

In parallel to the teaching and poems on the virtues of the mass there are those which warned about the dangers of disrespectful behaviour during the ritual. The mass is discussed in a book of advice written by a bourgeois of Paris *Le ménagier de Paris* for his young provincial wife c.1393. Among the sins which must be confessed he mentions unsuit-able thoughts during the Hours, chatter during the mass, and even sleep while others were praying.[421] In a similar book of guidance written by John Barbour (d.1395) for his daughter he advised:

[414] Dumoutet (1926), pp. 30–4.
[415] Oxford Bodleian Bodley 110, fol. 161r. Similarly in *Manipulus curatorum*, p. 21.
[416] Wenzel (1978), p. 76, from a sermon in BL Harley 331, fol. 22r, on III Kings 19,5.
[417] 'The sacrifice of the mass', in *Songs, carols*, no. 71, pp. 68–71, esp. lines 65–8, p. 70.
[418] An early tale supporting the mass' efficacy for the dead is told in Gregory the Great, *Dialogues*, IV.57; de Vogüé (1986), p. 125.
[419] See tale in Oxford Trinity 7, fol. 49.
[420] *Handlyng synne (a)*, pp. 259–62.
[421] *The goodman of Paris*, pp. 79–80.

> And in the kirk kepe our aall thing
> Fra smyrking, keking, and bakluking.[422]

A fifteenth-century poem employs the burden:

> I consaylle you bothe more and lesse
> Beware of sweryng by þe masse.

It continues to stress the dignities which the mass merited, since it was attended by angels, and chided its readers and hearers:

> Why swerist by þe masse, þou man so wode,
> Wher is thy helth, thy lyves fode,
> Cristis body, his precyus blode,
> All thy saluacion, no thynge but good.[423]

A story disseminated among the *exempla* of James of Vitry and of Stephen of Bourbon told of a devil by the name of Tutivullus who attempted to write down the words idly spoken by those attending the mass, and ran out of parchment.[424] It is also told in John Audelay's poem 'De meritis missae, quomodo audire missam' of the 1420s, as the only *exemplum* expounded in this didactic piece.[425] Here it is told by a witness about St Augustine of Canterbury to whom sayings recommending silence at the mass are attributed, and ends with the tale's *moralitas*:

> Kepe ȝou out of Godis wreke
> Fore þer is no word þat ȝe speke,
> Bot ȝe don syn.[426]

And the devil is carved onto a bench-end with a rolling scroll of parchment in the parish church of Charlton Mackrell (Somerset).[427]

The criticisms by clerics are more difficult to assess; they often seem directed at the idiom, gesture and language of whole social groups rather than at particular abuses. A tract named *Ignorantia sacerdotum* of the fifteenth century describes the happenings during religious service:

Þei come not to matyns thries in a yere . . . þei iangle, þei iape, þei kysse wymmen,

---

[422] *The Bruce* III, p. 203.
[423] *Songs, carols*, no. 52, pp. 42–3, lines 19–22 at p. 43.
[424] James of Vitry, *The exempla*, no. 239, p. 100; *Anecdotes*, no. 212, p. 184. See also *Erzählungen des Mittelalters*, no. 33, p. 258.
[425] *The poems of John Audelay*, pp. 65–79, this tales on lines 266–341, pp. 74–7.
[426] *Ibid*, lines 339–41, p. 77.
[427] Anderson (1963), plate 24d; Camille (1985), p. 40.

and heere no word of þe service, but scorne þe preeste, saynge þat he slepeþ in his masse, and tarieþ hem from her brekefast.[428]

But some of the vernacular salutations of Christ may well have been deemed to be noisy, unsuitable, uncontrolled.

## EXCHANGE AND ENCOUNTER: PRAYER AT ELEVATION AND COMMUNION

Since so much that was tangible could be gained from the mass and especially at the moment of elevation, that moment of gazing was marked with the stamp of an exchange. Petitions and requests were made at the elevation in a pandemonium of vernacular prayers and salutations, exchanging faith and acceptance of the host as God, for a large variety of benefits.[429] Rituals of petition and complaint, such as the monastic *clamor*, were grafted onto the moment. The *clamor* was a ceremony which developed particularly in Cluniac houses in the eleventh and twelfth centuries, in which a monastic community cried for help after the consecration of the host, displaying their most precious relics and books, and pleading for help in Christ's presence.[430] Nicholas of Clamanges (*c.*1360–1432), curial official and reformer, critically records such views:

Those who have looked at the body of Christ during the elevation, judge him for that reason to be in their debt and boast it like a great sacrifice.[431]

Proper humility was recommended at this moment, when people were to kneel and gaze at the body and blood.[432] This is the attitude most commonly shown in visual representations of the elevation, a group of men and women with clasped hands, and sometimes holding their hands to their mouths in a gesture of awe, kneeling behind the servers and priest. They are most frequently shown to be clasping their hands

---

[428] Bodleian Eng. Th. c. 57, fol. 48ᵛ. To control such behaviour it was the custom in some churches to separate between men and women, as reported in *Rationale* lib. 1, c. 1, no. 46, p. 18: 'In conventu Ecclesiae mulieres et viri seorsum habitant . . . masculi autem in australi, foeminae autem in boreali, sive in aquilonari parte manent . . . causa autem divisionis est quia caro viri et mulieres si proprius accesserint ad libidinem accenduntur.'

[429] On eucharistic poetry up to the thirteenth century see Breuer (1970). On the accretion of salutation prayers after the elevation, see Hughes (1982), pp. 91–2.

[430] Geary (1979), esp. pp. 28–33; one formula of address was: 'In spiritu humilitatis et in anima contrito ante sanctum altare tuum, et sacratissimum Corpus et sanguinem tuum, Domine Jhesu Redemptor Mundi accidimus', p. 30, see another formula on p. 31.

[431] 'Qui vero corpus Domini cum manibus sacerdotis elevatum, conspixerint, Christum ea re sibi maxime obstrictum arbitrantur, magnificeque super caeteros, quasi de magno sacrificio gloriantur', Nicholas of Clamanges, 'De novis celebritatibus non instituendis', in *Opera omnia*, p. 143.

[432] *Lay folk's catechism*, p. 38.

in a gesture which becomes increasingly common in thirteenth-century representations, one which we nowadays think of as natural for private prayer.[433] At this moment of arrival, people were encouraged to express themselves in salutations and addresses and a whole genre of eucharistic salutations in the Latin and the vernacular developed producing hundreds of suitable prayers.

The earliest known clusters of prayers for those attending mass, rather than celebrating it, are in Latin, like the prayers which appear in psalters used by the beguines of Liège in the thirteenth century.[434] Dumoutet has suggested that eucharistic salutations evolved from communion prayers for the use of the celebrant, and which appear in missals by the thirteenth century.[435] Some of these Latin prayers were based on famous prayers in the canon, like those of Augustine, Anselm and Bernard.[436] But the moment of the elevation created an impulse for new compositions. New Latin prayers became very widespread like the *Adoro te* attributed to Thomas Aquinas,[437] and the *Ave verum corpus natum* written by Innocent VI (1352–62), and the *Ave principium noster redemptionis*. The Book of Hours of the Use of York includes thirty prayers for many occasions, and recommends for the moment of the elevation the *Anima christi*, *Ave verum corpus natum*, *Ave Ihesu Christe verbum patris*, *In presencia* and Boniface VIII's prayer *Domine Ihesu Christe qui hanc*.[438] By the end of the fourteenth century most of these Latin prayers were translated into the vernacular, but as we shall see there was a parallel veritable explosion of vernacular eucharistic prayers.[439] In the fifteenth century one often finds a mixed set with English and Latin prayers set side by side in Books of Hours.[440]

Books of Hours were, on the whole, for the use of the religious, the aristocracy, the gentry, and of wealthy merchant families (figure 10). They reflect, therefore, milieux in which some Latin could often be read, but in which Anglo-French was current, as well as vernacular

---

[433] Ladner (1961); on the development of devotional gestures in artistic representations, see Lane (1970). And for text and illustration of a twelfth-century prayer manual, see Trexler (1987).

[434] Oliver (1988) I, pp. 5–8.

[435] Dumoutet (1931), pp. 421–6. For a classic discussion of eucharistic salutations, see Wilmart (1932), pp. 361–414.

[436] See, for example, the prayers in Oxford Trinity 89.

[437] This attribution is mistaken according to Wilmart (1932), pp. 361–414; Szöffervy (1964), pp. 253–4.

[438] *Horae beatae Mariae virginis*, pp. 108–11.

[439] Zeeman (1957–8); on the *Adoro te*, see Doyle (1948), pp. 229–33, and for the English version see *Minor poems of the Vernon ms.*, pp. 26–9.

[440] See Lambeth 546, fols 57ʳ–78ʳ; with additions in French on fols. 57ʳ–80.

English.[441] The Latin prayers which proliferated in the more costly Books of Hours and prayer collections were drawn into the frenzy of indulgence acquisition. The prayer *Anima christi* was published by John XXII at Avignon in 1330, came to be related to the elevation, and was translated into the vernacular soon after.[442] This very popular prayer for communion was drawn into use at elevation; its words, which were written for reception, were now transposed onto the moment of communion through gazing:

> Hide me between your wounds
> And do not let me be separated from you.[443]

An English Book of Hours of 1413 × 16 had a rubric which attached 3,000 days' indulgence to this prayer.[444] An Italian Book of Hours attached to the most popular prayer *Ave verum corpus natum* three years' indulgence for those who recited it devoutly at the elevation.[445] Boniface VIII's *Domine Iesu Christi qui hanc,* was written for King Philip IV, and for its recitation after true confession 2,000 years' indulgence were granted.[446] It was so effective a prayer that it was sometimes copied apart from other eucharistic prayers, as in the book made for a group of nuns in the diocese of Norwich c.1400.[447] The prayer was primarily for salutation during the elevation, addressing the crucified Christ hanging on the cross, and evoking the symbolism of Passion and sacrifice. Yet, although this prayer was immensely popular on the Continent, it never acquired an English translation: as we shall see, a very independent English tradition was being created.[448]

A typical set of Latin eucharistic salutation prayers can be found in a Book of Hours made in Flanders for English use in the early fifteenth century:

> Ave domine ihesu christe . . .
> Ave corpus verum natum . . .
> Ave caro christi cara . . .
> Anima christi . . .
> followed by Boniface VIII's prayer . . .[449]

---

[441] On Books of Hours, see Backhouse (1985); Leroquais (1927–43). See the Teymouth Hours for a section of guidance on the mass and prayers for it, BL Yates Thompson 13, fols. 7ʳ–14ʳ. On the use of French Books of Hours see Reinburg (1985).

[442] Baix and Lambot (1946), pp. 102–4; Dumoutet (1931), pp. 419–20.

[443] 'Intra tua vulnera absconde me,
Et ne permittas me separari a te', *Ibid*, p. 419.

[444] BL Add. 43437, fol. 117ʳ.

[445] BL Add. 10826, fol., 140ʳ.

[446] Reinburg (1985), pp. 301–5.

[447] *Medieval manuscripts* III, p. 196; Liverpool Cathedral 36, fol. 150ʳ.

[448] Robbins (1942–3), pp. 139–40; for an example from England, see Durham. Dean and Chapter Hunter Library 98, fol. 31ʳ.

[449] *Medieval manuscript* II, pp. 42–3 (Ampleforth Abbey 277, pp. 92–4).

A similar set was provided in a Sarum Book of Hours made in the Netherlands *c*.1450 and which includes:

> Ave domine ihesu xristi . . .
> Ave principium noster redemptionis . . .
> Ave verum corpus domini nostri . . .
> Ave caro Christi cara . . .
> followed by Boniface VIII's prayer . . .[450]

Books of Hours included French prayers which were close to the Latin tradition, quite sophisticated and lengthy prayers.[451] The French prayer in a fifteenth-century Book of Hours is didactic and formal in tone, a veritable recitation of the creed:

Je confesse de bouche et de cuer que tu es le vray corps de ihesu crist offert a dieu le pere en larbre de la crois pour le salut de lumain lignange. Hostie sainte hostie sans tache. Hostie et sacrefice bien plaisant a dieu.[452]

Such French prayers reached England in Books of Hours, but at the same time salutations and prayers were being composed in vernacular English with very different structure, scope and imagery.[453] These prayers were used by those who read English, and for those who could not read at all, but were taught their salutations. This in turn inspired a profusion of carols, riddles and poems for the elevation which reappear in amulets, scribbled onto fly-leaves, and which were no doubt also used by those who had Latin and French prayers at their disposal; sometimes the only vernacular prayer in a Book of Hours is the eucharistic one.[454]

Books of Hours were produced in great number for the market by the fifteenth century and display a wide range of tastes; some had pictures describing the mass with obvious didactic purposes.[455] Lydgate's composition for Alice, Countess of Suffolk, *The virtues of the mass* of *c*.1430–40s, relied on her ability to follow the mass in a private book, and concentrated on linking the priest's gestures to a number of vernacular prayers, the Creed and the *Pater noster*.[456] They included formal prayers from the Latin repertoire or their translations, as well

---

[450] Oxford Bodleian Laud lat. 15, fols. 70$^r$–71$^r$.
[451] Reinburg (1985), pp. 227–8.
[452] BL Harley 2592, fol. 46$^r$.
[453] For eucharistic hymnody written in England see John Pecham's (d.1292) *Ave vivens hostia* and *Hostia viva vale*, *AH* 50, pp. 597–8. See also in Raby (1927), pp. 398, 425–9.
[454] Robbins (1942–3), p. 133.
[455] Like the magnificent English Carew-Poyntz Hours with French prayers accompanied by pictures of every stage in the mass, Cambridge Fitzwilliam 48.
[456] Pearsall (1970), p. 162.

as more private prayers, such as this 'good praier' from the Sarum Hours:

O gloriouse Jhesu! . . . The holy body of crist ihesu be my saluacion of body and soule. Amen. The gloriose bloode of cryst Jhesu bryng my sowle and body in to the euer lastynge blysse.[457]

Popular prayers in all three languages from these traditions appear in a later hand in the thirteenth-century missal from Chichester:

> Welcome louerd in likinge of bred
> For me on rode þou woldest bo dede
> Of mine misdede þou red me red
> Schrift and husle ar ih boe dede
> Tiþe me for thi milsfulhed.

And it is followed by the Latin *Te veneranda caro Christi*, and by the French:

> Sire dieu omnipotent
> Si come ieo crey verrement
> Ke li prestre tent en present
> Vostre seynt cors en sacrement
> Issi verrement moy donez garison
> Et devant ma mort verreye confession. Amen.[458]

The English prayer revels in the notion of Christ's bodily presence, while the French prayer is more formal; here as in other cases, the English salutation cannot be traced to a Latin eucharistic repertoire.[459]

The vernacular salutations tend to be direct addresses to a guest, and the *Lay folk's mass book* abounds with such tags, which were supposed to be taught by parish priests. Their use is attested in Lydgate's words:

> At lyftyng up of the holy sacrament
> Seythe 'Iesu, mercy!' with holly affeccion,
> Or seythe som other parfyte oryson,
> Lyke as ye have in custom devoutly.[460]

For those who had no such 'parfyte oryson' he provided a 'compilacion', his 'Praier to the hooly sacrament'.[461] The elements most frequent in the English salutations are the invocation, 'Hail!' or 'Welcome!'; an appeal to Christ's life and its salvific meaning; then an

---

[457] *Lydgate's minor poems* I, p. 29.
[458] Cambridge Emmanuel 27, fol. 162ᵛ.
[459] Robbins (1942–3), p. 140.
[460] *Lydgate's minor poems*, lines 315–18, p. 101.
[461] *Ibid*, lines 321–92, pp. 101–4.

appeal for health, help or protection; and a final petition for future bliss, *beatitudo,* a state of future harmony and well-being. Such a short salutation comes from the mid-fourteenth-century manuscript:

> Jhesu, lord, welcom thou be,
> In forme of bred as I thee see
> Jesu, for thyne Holy Name,
> Shield me today fro synne and shame . . .
> Grant me shrifte, housil and good ending.[462]

Similarly, John Audelay's *De salutacione corporis Jhesu Christi* is a didactic edifice. It begins by instructing the reader to kneel, and develops a series of thirty-two 'Hayle's to Christ in various appellations, such as:

> Hayle! I beleve fayþfule ȝe beþ fader omnipotent . . .
> Hayle! graunt me grace goostelly
> To reescayve þi blessid body
> In parfyte love and charite
> Þat is here present.[463]

And ends with an *adoremus te* and lauds to God, and with an invocation of the Holy Spirit.[464] Another prayer, reminiscent of Lydgate's description of salutations, shares the same components:

> O merciful Iesu, for mercy to The,
> I crie, swete Iesu, have merci on me,
> Lord Jesu, forȝeue me mi misdede,
> And helpe me, Iesu, at mi nede.
> Lord Iesu, if yowr swete wil be,
> Graunt me thingis thre:
> That I may have love, grace and charite.[465]

The excessive insistence on worthlessness is encountered particularly in Latin communion prayers. But even though sinfulness is acknowledged, the sense of an exchange is always retained, introducing an overall optimistic tone:

> Welcome be þou, soule fode,
> Bo þe, Iesu, God and Manne,
> For me þou honge apon a þre Roode,
> Þi bodi blike and wonne.

[462] *Medieval English lyrics,* no. 39, p. 115; lines 1–4, 10, BL Egerton 3245, fol. 180ᵛ. For another version see CUL Ii.6.2, fol. 98ᵛ.
[463] *John Audelay's poems,* lines 39, 51–4, p. 63.
[464] *Ibid,* p. 65.
[465] Robbins (1942–3), pp. 135–6 (Lambeth Palace 559, fol. 24ᵛ).

> The water and þe blod out of þi side ron,
> Of my sinnes, Lorde, do me bote,
> Jesu, God and Mon,
> Graunt me þat I þe love mote . . .
> I am sinneful, as þou wel wost,
> Jesu, þou have merce on me,
> Ne suffur never þat I be lost,
> For whom þou dyest upon a tre.[466]

This salutation had a number of versions, all speaking to a 'lord in bred', who suffered on the rood and brought the grace in which the supplicant wishes to share:

> Lowod be þou, kyng,
> And blesseud be þou, kyng,
> Of all þi gyftus gode,
> And þonkud be þou kyng,
> Ihesu all my Ioyng
> Þat for me spylt þi blode,
> And dede for me upon þo rode.[467]

More intricate in its imagery of Christ, and less explicit perhaps in its demands, is the following very popular 'orysun', in its version from the Gurney manuscript of devotional texts:

> Welcome lord in forme of bred!
> Ffor me þou þolidist peynful ded.
> Blisful body sacrid me beforn,
> Haf mercy on me I be nouht lorn.
> Heyl! Iesu Crist, Saueour of þis world,
> The ffadris Sone of Heuene,
> Holy, oft sacrid, lyfliche in flesch,
> Soþfast god and verrey man:
> The, þe precious body of Iesu Crist
> With al my herte I wurchipe.[468]

This prayer addresses Christ as God and as man, the duality which was the secret of eucharistic power. Yet some exceptions to the mood of balanced and harmonious exchange do exist in such prayers of self-abnegation as:

---

[466] *Ibid*, pp. 138–9 (BL Add. 37787, fol. 12ʳ).
[467] *LFMB*, Text E, lines 425–31, p. 41. See another version in a fifteenth-century book CUL Gg.5.31, fol. 4ʳ.
[468] Robbins (1939a), pp. 373–4.

And as I am wirmis food,
Mad of slim and clay –
Soo indirly I cry þe mercy:
Þou graunt me grace to liue clenly . . .[469]

And in a similar tone:

I þank þe, Jesu, of al þy goodnesse
I cry þe mercy for all my wickednesse
Jesu for þy Passiun
Þou kep me fro temptaciun
Save þou me fro helle
And bryng me þi ioye into dwelle. Amen.[470]

But the story of sacramental mediation which allowed contact with God through a mere gaze, could never be a sad one; it made possible many happy, hopeful endings.

It was this space for fantasy and hope, the fluid images which reflect orthodox formulations, but which definitely stress a certain strand of knowing and tentative engagement, that made the sacramental language of religion so useful. Like so many prayers, these reveal what is vital and worthy of exchange; as such they are social acts, which express areas of doubt, hope and fear.[471] The language was also flexible and easily encompassed new interests, like the growing late medieval devotion to the Name of Jesus:

O Iesu, Lorde, Wellcum thu be
In fforme of brede as y the se
O Iesu for Thy Holy Name
Schelde me thys day fro sorro and shame.[472]

The genre could encompass mystical flights, such as the salutation composed of an *Ave* and thirty-five names of Jesus, describing every aspect of his image.[473] It also blended into the world of eucharistic carol and hymn, a good example of which is the lyric which opens:

Welcom lord in forme of bred,
In ye is both lyffe and ded.[474]

and which continues to develop seven stanzas each opening with 'Heyll!', incorporating romance images of knights, kings and emper-

[469] *Ibid*, p. 374.
[470] *Ibid*.
[471] Khare (1977), pp. 295–317; Reinburg (1985), pp. 11–12.
[472] CUL Ii.6.2, fol. 98[v].
[473] BL Add. 16975, fol. 263[v].
[474] Oxford Bodleian Ashmole 61, fol. 26[r].

ors as signs of dignity due to the host. Similarly, the poem 'Welcome, Lord, In fourme of Bred!' in the Vernon manuscript opens with a salutation hailing Christ as 'godus sone', as well as blossom on a tree, fruit, flour, knight, duke, emperor, flesh and blood, a man of 'mylde mod', a rose, exploring every possibility offered by the eucharistic imagery which had been developing for some three hundred years.[475]

[475] *The minor poems of the Vernon ms.*, pp. 24–5.

# CHAPTER 3

# A feast is born: Corpus Christi – the eucharistic feast

## LIÈGE – THE BIRTHPLACE

Situated in a part of the Empire which enjoyed prosperity and a certain political autonomy, Liège had flourished from the tenth century under its prince-bishops with their dense network of ecclesiastical patronage.[1] By the thirteenth century the town boasted, besides its cathedral, seven collegiate churches, twenty-six parish churches, two Benedictine monasteries – St James and St Laurence – an Augustinian house of St Giles, the Praemonstratensian community at Mont-Cornillon, and a Cistercian house, Val-St Lambert. In the many schools of Liège some of the finest biblical learning of the day was being pursued. There was a great cathedral school at St Lambert's, schools at both Benedictine abbeys, and further in the hinterland were those of Stavelot-Malmédy, Lobbes, Gembloux, St Hubert and St Trond.[2] In all, some 300 clerics and monks lived and studied in the town's collegiate and regular houses.[3] In political matters the bishops succeeded in striking a balance between Empire and papacy from a position of strength. The Gregorian reform was applied to the diocese in moderation, and the products of its schools never lacked patronage from the highest circles of church administration well into the twelfth century.[4]

Yet, although Liège remained safe on the fringes of the Empire, it was effected by the general decline of the Church within its boundaries in the years of struggle between Empire and papacy, and this eventually took toll of the standing of Liège's prelates and religious houses. Liège's prosperity in its central position in the Mosan trading sphere started to decline when commerce moved to the Cologne–Louvain–Bruges line.[5]

---

[1] On the school of St Lambert in the tenth century, see Shrader (1973), pp. 189–91.
[2] Uyttebrouck (1978).
[3] Dereine (1951), p. 84.
[4] Kupper (1981), p. 381.
[5] Silvestre (1951), p. 113.

These political and economic shifts, and the political and economic growth within the kingdom of France moved the centres of scholarship from Lorraine southwards to the French schools, where new sources of patronage produced new learning and the rise of the schools. By the thirteenth century Liège was a fairly prosperous middling trading town, sustained by lively local trade, by the proliferation of craft and manufacture within it, and with a sufficiently robust religious institutional network to draw reformers, patrons and new religious orders. These forces also resulted in competition between new and old urban sectors, and the realignment of the areas of influence of old feudal families, burgesses, the religious, the bishop and combative chapter, the gilds and the lower clergy.

Under the political and economic domination of a powerful bishop and chapter, the burgesses of Liège came to the business of securing their freedoms like western German towns, in the thirteenth century, almost a century after their neighbouring French towns had done. If no longer destined to be a commercial giant such as Cologne, Liège was diversifying its economic base in those areas where it was particularly strong and which had developed with the urban growth of the previous century.[6] It was not doing badly; its viticulture was developing through collaboration of territorial lords and urban traders,[7] and its metallurgy and textile crafts were expanding. Merchants and entrepreneurs populated new quarters which were incorporated into the town by the new walls of the early thirteenth century.[8] Within a stone's-throw from the episcopal palace and St Lambert's cathedral grew the *vinâves*, the new quarters of St Servais, Outremeuse, the quartier d'Isle. Throughout the thirteenth century, their inhabitants – drapers, tanners and metal-workers – struggled for the right to exact from the church contributions to the town's expenditure on fortifications, for the right to try offenders who inhabited the area of cathedral immunity for offences committed in the town, and for the right to tax urban properties of ecclesiastical institutions.[9]

Thus, throughout the twelfth century Liège remained an old and respected centre, but was no longer the leader in intellectual debates. It retained a reputation and a strong tradition of biblical exegesis, through the fame of masters such as Alger of Liège and Renier of St Laurent.[10] Their intellectual project aimed at the perfection of a theology which

---

[6] de Spiegeler (1979).
[7] Chaineux (1981), p. 70.
[8] Polain (1933); Lejeune (1948), pp. 273–9.
[9] Polain (1933), p. 167.
[10] Brigué (1936), pp. 57–60.

was strongly based in scripture through inspired allegorical interpretations,[11] while in the south new approaches to authority and truth, and new analytical categories were being developed and applied to all areas of human science.[12] In the twelfth century another important development took place with the arrival of the Cistercians who rapidly came to replace the Benedictines as leading teachers and recipients of patronage.[13] By the end of the century some fifty houses had been founded, and by 1300 there were some 100 Cistercian houses between the Meuse and the Rhine. As the newest reformed order in the region the Cistercians offered, for a while, a space for experimentation in religious life, and an openness to the interests of lay patrons.[14] The affective strains in Cistercian spirituality inspired those seeking new positions within a religious framework; lay brethren and religious women were attracted to what appeared to be a uniquely open religious order. So in and around Liège we witness not only the spring from which came an important new religious impulse, but also its convergence with currents in the interests of lay people, and particularly of women, which were developing, there and in other places.[15]

The attraction between these two groups – newly arrived, reformed and affective religious, and lay people who wished to undertake some communal aspects of religious life – was based on mutual needs and capacities. In an institutional and legal context which left women little scope for independent organisation, Cistercians could offer a framework and religious services that old orders could do with less ease. And in offering such cooperation the Cistercians displayed the same initial insight that had inspired the institution of lay brothers in their order. Thus Cistercians and Praemonstratensians took over the management and guidance of women's religious houses, enlarging their areas of influence and access to patronage.[16] For a number of decades Cistercian abbots were willing to accept female houses, but throughout the twelfth century and early in the thirteenth as it became clear that women presented an economic burden, Cistercians returned to their original opposition to the influx of women into the order. Similarly, the Praemonstratensians, who had been more open to women, reformu-

---

[11] Silvestre (1951), pp. 113–18.
[12] Liège was important in the Beregarian debate and in its aftermath, Baix and Lambot (1946), pp. 46–8.
[13] Axters (1948), pp. 23–4.
[14] Silvestre (1951), pp. 121–2.
[15] Roisin (1943), p. 377; Meersseman (1948), p. 78; Bynum (1984), (1985).
[16] Roisin (1943), pp. 346–57; Freed (1972), pp. 312–15 for patterns of affiliation with Cistercians and later with Dominicans; on beguines' choice of protection, see suggestions in Neel (1989), p. 339.

lated their priorities and limited the creation of new female houses.[17] Yet even when more stringent rules for assimilation of women into the order were enforced, there was ample possibility for mutual benefit and dialogue between the monks and women who were organising themselves in increasingly independent and loose communal formations. Even when they could not found monasteries, women inhabited quarters near Cistercian houses and used Cistercian confessors.[18]

The idiom of religion created by these women inspired a number of Cistercian monks and Augustinian canons who came into contact with them. James of Vitry was fascinated by Mary of Oignies, a devout lay woman who renounced her marriage and retired to live besides an Augustinian community.[19] Walter of Utrecht, abbot of Villers, told stories of visions which were immortalised by another Cistercian, Caesarius of Heisterbach;[20] Ida of Louvain's (d.1300) visions were recorded by a Cistercian, and Liutgard of Tongres (d.1246) accompanied the abbot of Aywières.[21] The men witnessed the spirituality of their female neighbours or charges and compared it with their own; some extraordinary friendships were struck between monks and beguines, and this mutual fascination was to develop further when the mendicant and beguine communities were to meet in the thirteenth century.[22]

As the number of women who wished to assume some religious rigour and to live, at least part of the time, in a community, increased, and as they could no longer be provided for within existing tutelage frameworks, new units for religious practice and work were created, some simply attached to a parish church.[23] Women who came to live lives of poverty and chastity and to follow a penitential life of prayer in this part of the world came to be known as beguines, and they were particularly numerous in the diocese of Liège, and in the whole archdiocese of Cologne and in the Rhine valley.[24] By 1240 there may have been some 1,500 beguines in the diocese of Liège, and their needs raised on-going problems of supervision and control.[25] Into this space the newly-arrived Dominicans entered with great willingness and with

---

[17] Roisin (1943), pp. 359–60; McDonnell (1954), pp. 104, 108; McGuire (1981); Simenon (1912), p. 37; Thompson (1978), *passim*, esp. pp. 227–30.
[18] McDonnell (1954), pp. 170–84. On relations between Cistercians and beguines, see Roisin (1943), p. 343.
[19] James of Vitry, *Historia occidentalis*, pp. 5, 9, 11, 286; Neel (1989), pp. 325–8.
[20] *DM* 2, cs. 19–20, pp. 98–100; Roisin (1943), pp. 369, 372, and on Villers, pp. 354–5.
[21] Roisin (1943), pp. 374—5.
[22] On beguines and tertiaries in the Low Countries, see Troeyer (1980).
[23] Like the handful of recluses near St Denis, Liège, *Liège, St Denis*, p. 43.
[24] Freed (1972); Freed (1977), pp. 7–8, 87–9; Stein (1977).
[25] Daris (1891), p. 205; Freed (1972), p. 313, table 1.

many suitable capabilities, and in German towns beguines placed themselves under Dominican guidance and instruction.[26] Margaret of Ypres (d. 1237) was guided by a spiritual mentor, a Dominican, Siger of Lille.[27] The Dominicans came to Liège by the invitation of Bishop John of Eppes in 1229, their settlement was approved by the general chapter at Paris in 1230, and they arrived in the next year.[28] They set up a convent and a school of theology and stayed in patrician households in the area while they awaited the building of their convents, enjoying the hospitality of those whose daughters, wives and widows they were to guide in religious matters.[29] The bishops of Liège encouraged their settlement in the town and commended them to burgess largesse.[30] In the centre of Liège their convent of St Catherine's was dedicated in 1242, and the Franciscans moved into St Anthony's next door two years later. In some towns, like Huy, the beguinage was practically run by Dominicans; in Liège, they were frequently mentioned in wills, they acted as confessors and they provided burial.[31] These women shared some aspects of the mendicant life: a life of poverty, of chastity within the world, of religious activity outside parochial boundaries.[32] With the Franciscans they shared a particular interest in the eucharist.[33]

The *Vitae* of Cistercian or beguine female saints reveal strong strands of eucharistic devotion in these circles, a fascination with the tangible, physical contact with the suffering Christ, through his offering of himself in so vulnerable a form to the world. Christ in the eucharist could be watched, adored, smelt, touched and taken into one's body; and for some of these experiences little mediation was necessary. The language of eating is common in mystical writing even outside the eucharistic sphere, as a metaphor for union through incorporation and submergence of the distance between mystic and God. But in the eucharist it was more than a metaphor, the host could become something sweet, satisfying and nurturing.[34] Christ was apprehended in it as a man, a husband, a son, resplendent in vulnerable humanity, in the feminine principle, not as a judge, or as paternal, majestic or lordly.[35]

---

[26] For an analysis of their activities in Cologne, see Stein (1977), pp. 205–38; Freed (1977), pp. 87, 95.

[27] Meersseman (1948), p. 70.

[28] Ansiau (1937), pp. 94–6.

[29] Meersseman (1948), pp. 69–72.

[30] Willmaers (1975), pp. 118–19.

[31] Meersseman (1948); Oliver (1988) I, pp. 114–15.

[32] On involvement of mendicants in the pastoral of the Parisian beguines, see Bériou (1978), pp. 162–94.

[33] McDonnell (1954), pp. 313, 318–19. Ida of Louvain was reported to have received *stigmata*, Bynum (1984), p. 184.

[34] Riehle (1980), pp. 107–9; Vauchez (1981), p. 446.

[35] Platelle (1979), pp. 486–92.

The strong erotic tones which suffuse the descriptions attributed to these women of their reception and incorporation of Christ into their bodies, drew from a long standing tradition of mystical imagery, but was also a new and direct erotic idiom of longing.[36]

Yet it is difficult to decide whether these writings reflect a feminine experience, even if one were to believe in such a concept, or whether it was projected onto them to a large extent by their viewers. We are largely confined here to hagiographical material written by men, and we must allow for an interpretational gap, for the construction of the female religious by her beholders. So neatly does the density of ascription of luxury and sensuality, the fantasy of female carnality, fall in with constructions of the female in the culture, that it needs to be asked whether women, even religious women, could ever escape it. The problem is particularly acute when one bears in mind the extent to which we are acquainted with these women through their male confessors and friends.[37] Christina of Stommeln (1242–1312) is known to us through records of her relationship with the Dominican Peter of Dacia, which spanned two decades. Every new apparition brought her one of his visits from afar, every extravagance an epistle in return.[38] We know little that comes directly from these women,[39] and yet the material is rich; we should, therefore, talk not of experience but of the relation between representations of such experience.

But there is no denying that eucharistic awareness was everywhere, and particularly in the circles of vocation and devotion around Liège, and in the thoughts and practices of the beguines. In their eagerness beguines are said to have sought frequent communion, to have fasted for long periods hungering only for the eucharist, and filling themselves with an affection for the crucified image of the sacrificed Christ.[40] Women such as Mary of Oignies, Juliana of Cornillon (c.1193–1258), Ida of Léau (d.1268) and Ida of Louvain (d.1300) fascinated and sometimes bewildered their contemporaries, and drew the attention of mendicants to them, as well as other ecclesiastical observers, who were bemused but not unimpressed. Thus there was a particular keenness and responsiveness at this time, and when Juliana, a famous saintly woman who served at the leper-hospital attached to the Praemonstra-

---

[36] Bynum (1984), pp. 179–88, 190, 257–9; Bell (1985), 20, 170–2; Roisin (1947), p. 111.

[37] On friendship, see McGuire (1981) and McGuire (1985).

[38] Thurston (1928).

[39] Even Margery Kempe dictated her *Book*, but this is more direct a link than in most cases; on her, see Beckwith (1986).

[40] Kieckhefer (1984), p. 38; also Ziegler (1987), pp. 31–2 on the development of the image of *pietà* in these circles.

tensian house of Mont Cornillon in Liège, had a eucharistic vision, there were openings for a serious consideration of its meanings.

In her vision Juliana was shown the full moon, a segment of which was darkened by a blemish:[41]

I tell you that a moon appeared to her in its splendour, with a little break in part of its sphere. She watched this for a long while, wondered a lot, and did not know what this might portend.[42]

This dream was repeated, and its meanings was finally revealed after some twenty years by Christ himself:

Then Christ revealed to her that the Church was in the moon, and that the missing part of the moon stood for the absence of one feast in the Church, which he would want his faithful to celebrate on earth.[43]

This message falls in with the symbolic tradition represented in the *glossa ordinaria*:

And there was a great and wonderful sign in the moon, that is, in the Church . . .[44]

An unusual historiated initial for psalm 109 in a mid-thirteenth-century psalter of Liège shows David kneeling before Christ who emerged from a cloud holding a 'defective' moon.[45]

In the Middle Ages dreams and visions often provided a seal of approval for human efforts, and in the high Middle Ages visions were increasingly reported from the mouths of layfolk and women, rather than the religious and mystics.[46] Juliana's dream, which probably first occurred *c.*1208, supported her campaign for the institution of a eucharistic feast as an apogee of eucharistic devotion,[47] and armed her supporters with an incontestible sign of divine approval: the message had after all finally come from Christ's own mouth. For years Juliana kept her secret, and finally revealed it to her confessor John of Lausanne, of St Martin's Church, who spread it further; from this point

---

[41] This is reported in her *Vita*, on which see Lambot (1946c), and for more on the *Vita* Balau (1903), pp. 438–43; Brouette (1960).

[42] 'Apparebat, inquam, ei luna in suo splendore, cum aliquantula tamen sui sphaerici corporis fractione; quam cum multo tempore conspexisset, mirabatur multum, ignorans quid illa portenderet', *Vita Julianae* II, c. 2, n. 6, p. 459.

[43] 'Tunc revelavit ei Christus; in luna praesentem ecclesiam, in lunae autem fractione, defectum unius solennitatis in Ecclesia figurari, quam adhuc volebat in terris a suis fidelibus celebrari', *ibid*.

[44] 'Signum etiam in luna, [id est] in ecclesia, magnum et mirandum fuit, quod ab hominibus indoctis et idiotis tantum principium habuit', *Biblia sacra cum glossa ordinaria* v, col. 400.

[45] Oliver (1988) I, p. 165, II, plate 165.

[46] Holdsworth (1963), pp. 142–7; on the use of dreams in contemporary romance literature, see Braet (1975).

[47] Roisin (1947), p. 113.

Juliana and her sisters were being watched closely by mendicants, Cistercian confessors and bishops.

We have already noted the interest which these religious women inspired in those intent on control of forms of lay religious involvement, which seemed to lead to error and which threatened the edifice of parochial discipline. For some of the powerful men around them these women provided a model for a lay person's simple faith, and through their eucharistic attachments, privileged sacramentality. Beguines definitely had some high-ranking admirers; Robert Grosseteste exalted the beguines from afar for their religious perfection and their productive way of life:

About which he said that the beguines were the most perfect and the holiest in religion, because they live of their own labour and do not burden the world with their needs.[48]

James of Vitry, who was suffragan-bishop of Liège in 1216×19, and Fulk, bishop of Toulouse, had sufficient knowledge and commitment to advise Honorius III to allow beguines to organise into communities when this was discussed in 1216.[49] In a century in which heresy and a chorus of discordant voices clamoured against an increasingly homogeneous world-view, the unthreatening religiosity of some beguines seemed to be an acceptable new type of orthodoxy.[50]

Orthodoxy was very much in the minds of ecclesiastical dignitaries, and explains the willingness exhibited by theologians, bishops and scholars in Liège to add to their usual administrative, intellectual, diplomatic and political preoccupations, the observation and chronicling of the lives and mores of these religious women.[51] Thus, James of Vitry wrote the life of Mary of Oignies in 1213–15,[52] William of Mechlin, prior of the Benedictine house of Wavre and later abbot of St Trond, translated the autobiography of Beatrice of Nazareth (d.1268), Thomas of Cantimpré wrote the life of Margaret of Ypres (c.1201–1270×80) based on her vernacular version, and of Liutgard of Aywières (1182×3–1246)[53] At this moment in the second quarter of the thir-

---

[48] 'Unde dixit quod Begine sunt perfectissime et sanctissime religionis, quia vivunt propriis laboribus et non onerant exactionibus mundum', Thomas of Eccleston, 'De adventu fratrum minorum in Angliam', p. 123.

[49] Callebaut (1926), pp. 547–8; Bolton (1973), pp. 81, 84.

[50] Axters (1948), pp. 29–31.

[51] Scholars of Liège had been deeply involved in the Beregarian dispute and its aftermath well into the twelfth century, Simenon (1946), pp. 4–5.

[52] *AASS* June IV, pp. 636–66; Willmaers (1975), p. 102; James of Vitry, *Historia occidentalis*, pp. 5–11; on his life Renardy (1981), pp. 137–9.

[53] Meersseman (1948), *passim*; Roisin (1947), pp. 63, 220–1; 51–2, 242–3.

teenth century in Liège, there was an opening for a religious woman of middling or humble origins to be heard on devotional matters.

The impact of Juliana's claim depended, of course, on the centrality of the eucharist in the theological and pastoral interests of the day. Given the growing centrality of the mass as a focus for lay participation, and as the ritual underpinnings of a whole symbolic system, a feast celebrating this very ritual would generate some interest for its didactic potential. From what the *Vita* tells us of the response to Juliana's idea it is clear that Juliana had struck a chord with her idea of public, regular, concerted celebration of the eucharist.

But the impulse towards a new major feast came at a sensitive moment in Liège politics. Politics in Liège always hinged on the question of episcopal appointments, which had traditionally been under the influence of the great Lotharingian families.[54] The twelfth century contests between supporters and opponents of the Emperor were finally resolved in the 1190s with the acceptance of what was at the time the rule in canon law, that the bishop was elected by the cathedral chapter, with recourse to papal arbitration. The shift away from the Empire was reflected in the appointment of a series of French-born bishops in the next century: Hugh of Pierrepoint, John of Eppes, and Robert of Turotte. More immmediately, the Empire was in turmoil, ruled by a weak anti-emperor, William of Holland, who was elected by the pope and the German bishops;[55] so after the break with the emperor the bishop of Liège ruled without *regalia*, and the town became a Guelph citadel at least for the period 1238–78. Rome appointed its bishops and exerted patronage over important local ecclesiastical appointments, granting prebends of the cathedral chapter to papal favourites.

With the concession of the power of appointment the cathedral chapter became even more powerful. But it was being challenged by the *échevins*, the officials of Liège who effectively administered the town as a sworn commune, and whose hands were tied by restriction and ecclesiastical taxes. And there was the additional tension between the new *métiers* and the established merchant patriciate who controlled access to civic office.[56] These tensions erupted in the period of relative external quiet, and the bishops were forced to react.[57] The town's

[54] Génicot (1968), pp. 241–58.
[55] Lejeune (1948), p. 53.
[56] Polain (1932), p. 176; Vercauteren (1967), pp. 45, 71–2; Lejeune (1948), p. 73.
[57] In 1253 Bishop Henry of Guelder (1247–74) and town officials reached an agreement on distribution of jurisdiction, taxation income and trading privileges, Vercauteren (1967), p. 48.

prosperous craftsmen and merchants were willing and able patrons of the new religious orders, who were attracted by patronage possibilities in areas burgeoning with urban religious life. St Francis was sufficiently well-informed to consider *provincia Francia* (Northern France and the Low Countries) as most devoted to the eucharist, and therefore, a suitable venue for his order:

> I choose the province of France, in which the people are catholic, especially because among other catholic members of the Holy Church they show greatest reverence for the Body of Christ.[58]

He considered visiting the area in 1217, and there was a Franciscan presence in the town from 1230.[59]

The bishop of Liège who was faced with the beguine campaign for a new eucharistic feast was the head of a diocese whose cathedral town was divided into sharp factions, and whose religious and social life had just experienced the arrival of the mendicant orders. When Robert of Turotte was elected in 1240, he was destined to be a bishop without *regalia*.[60] He was committed to the reform of religious houses in his diocese, and among other issues addressed himself to the patronage disputes over the leper house of Mont Cornillon, on the outskirts of Liège.[61] Drawn as he was into the life of Mont Cornillon and interested in the regulation of religious life, he would have been well acquainted with their member, the leading religious woman of the town, and with the claims which she made, by 1240, to have had a vision of significant implications.[62] Juliana's vision was conveyed by her confessor to the bishop, as well as to the Dominicans of Liège Giles, John and Gerard, who were so closely related to beguine religious life. Another important actor was James Pantaleon, the archdeacon of Campines in the diocese of Liège, who had been Robert's colleague when they were both canons of Laon, who had arrived with the new episcopal entourage in 1240.[63] The *Vita* tells us that since there was no opposition from the local Dominican scholars, the idea of the feast was passed on to the chancellor of the University of Paris.[64] When no objection was raised

---

[58] 'Eligo provinciam Francie, in qua est catholica gens, maxime quia inter alios catholicos sancte Ecclesie reuerentian magnam exibent corpori Christi', *Scripta Leonis*, no. 79, pp. 226–7; Callaey (1957), pp. 3–8; Callebaut (1926), pp. 545–6; at p. 545.

[59] Callebaut (1926), pp. 553–6.

[60] On his election, see Schoolmeesters (1906), pp. 4–8.

[61] Kurth (1909) 1, pp. 434–6. He finally granted the house new statutes in 1242, *Liège, St Lambert* 1, no 352, pp. 434–6.

[62] Simenon (1946), p. 4.

[63] On Robert of Turotte's early career, see Simenon (1946), pp. 1–4.

[64] A former Chancellor of the University of Paris, Guiscard of Laon, attended the 1242 consecration of the second Dominican convent.

Bishop Robert of Turotte established a feast of the eucharist in his diocese through his pastoral letter *Inter alia mira* of 1246.[65] The feast was to be celebrated 'feria quinta proxima post octavas Trinitatis', a moveable feast which could occur between 21 May and 24 June.[66] Soon after establishing Corpus Christi Bishop Robert died at the Cistercian monastery of Fosses on 16 October 1246.[67]

With the death of its official promoter it was far from clear that the feast would ever become a practised reality. Robert's successor, Henry of Guelder, repealed a number of his predecessor's acts. Henry restored the traditional control over presentation to the mastership of Mont Cornillon which had been altered by Robert, and furthermore supported a faction within the house which was opposed to Juliana and which finally ousted her from her position as prioress in 1247.[68] Juliana was thus forced to leave the town and spend the rest of her life travelling from one Cistercian house to another, living in them as a recluse. Her last station was Fosses to which she moved in 1256, the house where Robert of Turotte had spent his last days, and where she died in April 1258.[69] With the death of its promoters and the hostility of the founding bishop's successor, there may have seemed to be little hope for a fledgling liturgical innovation.

The Dominicans were receptive and supportive of the eucharistic initiative in Liège, and it was a Dominican who spread the feast beyond Liège when its own bishop showed no interest in it. Hugh of St Cher, the great Parisian scholar, regent master of theology from *c.*1230, author of the most influential *Sentences* commentary of his time and leader of an *équipe* of biblical commentators, was also master of the Dominicans of Paris from *c.*1233, provincial of the French Dominican province from early 1240, and cardinal by 1244.[70] Hugh was a scholar, preacher and high ranking ecclesiastical diplomat, combining these activities when he launched the preaching campaign in Aachen, the only town which had remained loyal to the emperor after his excommunication. This brought him into proximity with the archbishopric of Cologne, and to Liège, and closer still when he was appointed Cardi-

---

[65] *Textus*, pp. 21–3.

[66] There is some discussion on whether in Liège this date meant not the second, but the third Thursday after Pentecost, since the octaves in Liège ended on the Sunday night rather than the Saturday as in the Roman usage. The Roman usage was enforced in Liège by 1331, but in 1246 it may be that 'feria quinta proxima post octavas Trinitatis' was a week later in Liège than elsewhere, Lefèvre (1947), pp. 417–20; Lambot (1946a).

[67] Baix and Lambot (1946), pp. 16, 76–7.

[68] *Liège, St Lambert*, no. 207, p. 56; Kurth (1909) I, pp. 147–50.

[69] Hontoir (1946b), pp. 112–13.

[70] Renardy (1981), p. 276; Paravicini Bagliani (1972), pp. 256–65; Lerner (1985), p. 166.

nal-Legate to Germany in 1251.[71] It was as such that he arrived in Liège in the autumn of 1251 where he fell ill in October.[72] Before leaving the town he lent support to the new eucharistic feast which his brother Dominicans had nurtured from the start. He had the feast celebrated out of sequence in St Martin's church of Liège, the church of Juliana's confessor and first confidant, and of the recluse, Eve, her friend.[73] A legacy left by canon Stephen of Châlons in 1251 to the church of St Martin, was intended for the promotion of Corpus Christi, the feast which Hugh of St Cher had celebrated, and which he had promoted in his preaching.[74] On his legatine route Hugh continued to promote the feast, granting the monastery of Villers an indulgence of forty days for those attending the Corpus Christi mass, and finally instituting it throughout his legation of Germania on 29 December 1252.[75] His legatine letter is now lost, but it would have been at least partially disseminated in imperial lands from Lorraine to Pomerania and Bohemia. Hugh of St Cher's successor, the Cardinal-Legate Peter Cappocci, confirmed his letter and republished it in November 1254.[76] In Liège, however, there was resistance and hostility, even as Juliana's *Vita* was being written in 1262. The feast's fortunes were yet to be settled.[77]

It was taken further by a witness and partner to its foundation, Jacques Pantaleon, who was both active and powerful. A native of Troyes, he was archdeacon of Campines in the diocese of Liège from 1243–8.[78] The archdeacons of Liège were sometimes men of high birth and high ecclesiastical standing, people who proceeded to become bishops and even popes.[79] James was present in 1246 at the feast's foundation, and remained in the town for two more years after his patron's, Robert of Turotte's death, under Bishop Henry of Guelder. After 1248 he served on a number of papal missions to Prussia, and in 1252 became bishop of Verdun, and three years later, the patriarch of Jerusalem. It was in the Holy Land that he received the news of his

---

[71] Schoolmeesters (1907), p. 150.

[72] Lambot (1946b), pp. 215–16.

[73] Hontoir (1946a), p. 153; Callaey (1957), p. 7.

[74] As reproduced in Denis (1927): 'H. dei … gratia apostolice sedis legatus in ecclesia nostra solempniter celebravit predicando commendavit et auctoritate legationis sue volentibus concessit celebrandam'.

[75] *Textus*, pp. 24–6; *Liège, St Lambert* II, no. 511, pp. 32–4.

[76] Callaey (1948), p. 222; Callaey (1957), p. 24; *Liège, St Lambert* II, p. 32; Schoolmeesters (1907), p. 152.

[77] On the developments in Liège, see Baix and Lambot (1946), p. 80. Juliana was canonised only in 1869 by Pius IX.

[78] Renardy (1981), pp. 320–1; Renardy (1979), pp. 277–8; Paravicini Bagliani (1972), pp. 59–69. On his origins, see Sievert (1896).

[79] Like James himself, and then Theobald of Plaisance, archdeacon of Havant 1246–47 and later Gregory X, Sievert (1896), pp. 9–11.

election to the papal see and the summons to return to Rome, and he received the tiara on 27 August 1261, as Urban IV.[80]

ROME – THE FEAST'S EARLY SPREAD

Numerous men such as Jacques Pantaleon were attracted to the papal court in the thirteenth century: Frenchmen of undistinguished social origins, who had been to an episcopal school, and who provided the papacy with a learned background bureaucratic force. Like James of Vitry earlier in the century, and like the Dominican Godescalc of Maastricht who planned Gregory IX's offensive against heresy, after him, Jacques Pantaleon articulated and executed papal objectives for the unification and spread of orthodoxy all over Europe. When in Liège, he had probably been involved in Robert of Turotte's reforming campaign, sharing similar pastoral views and similarly engaged with the circle of *mulieres sanctae*. He wrote a now-lost work, *Libellus de regula et vita beginarum,* which contained advice on their discipline and spirituality, as well as a guide for the spiritual life of canons.[81] It is under the influence of these interests and connections that as pope some twenty years later the erstwhile archdeacon of Campines elevated the eucharistic feast founded in Liège to universal observance. And one of the first people he informed of this deed was Eve of St Martin, a beguine and a friend of Juliana of Cornillon, the beguine whose moonlit visions had put the process into motion.[82]

This was the first time that a universal feast was founded by a pope, yet given Urban IV's interests and connections since the 1240s it is not surprising to find them crystallised into the bull *Transiturus* in 1264. The attempt to link the foundation directly to the alleged miracle of Bolsena whose traditions are known only from the fourteenth century seems, therefore, to be perhaps misplaced.[83] *Transiturus* relates itself in word and in gesture to a pre-history of the feast far from Orvieto, and for that matter from Rome. It incorporates Robert of Turotte's episcopal letter, mentions Hugh of St Cher's confirmation, and the pope's own part and interest in these happenings.[84] Given his background, the incessant drive to establish and protect orthodoxy which animated all churchmen of this century, given his personal links with the feast's first

[80] On Urban IV's life, see Simenon (1934–35); and for another view, see Darsonville (1902).
[81] Lambot (1969), pp. 305–8.
[82] The letter is from September 1264, *Liège, St Lambert* VI, no. 113, p. 21; see also Lambot (1946a); on its history, see Lambot (1948).
[83] The traditional dating of the miracle emerged only in the early fourteenth century, Franceschini (1965), p. 219; Lazzarini (1952b), pp. 213–14. Cf. Pesci (1946).
[84] See the bull's analysis and text in Franceschini (1967).

founder, and with the milieu that had given rise to the idea, Urban IV's actions are clear and moreover, coherent. As pope he protected the religious houses of Liège, and surrounded himself with northerners.[85] Three of the four cardinals named by him were men of Liège: Bernard of Reamo, canon of Bruges, William of Basseyo, canon of St Denis of Liège who had accompanied Urban IV on his missions to Germany, and Michael of Liège, canon-priest of St Martin's of Liège, who had also been on the German missions.[86] One cannot establish a link between the local Orvietan miracle of an unknown date and the feast which had been in the making over a period of more than twenty years. Urban IV celebrated Corpus Christi in Orvieto, where the papal curia was located that year, celebrated it, again out of sequence, in September 1264, and died soon after.

With Urban IV's death, the impulse to make universal the new feast, which depended on a very personal commitment, all but died. The tens of copies of the bull *Transiturus* which were meant to circulate throughout Christendom, were never sent. Of a small number of special missives which were sent we possess the copies in the papal register: a general letter addressed to Patriarchs, Archbishops, Bishops and other prelates, 'Transiturus de hoc mundo' of 11 August 1264;[87] a letter addressed to the Patriarchate of Jerusalem, to Urban IV's successor, 'Transiturus de mundo', of the same date;[88] and a letter of 7 September to Henry Guleder, still bishop of Liège, whom Urban IV knew to be far from keen to support the feast, with instructions for immediate celebration.[89] A letter was also sent to Eve of St Martin informing her in a very personal tone that the feast had finally been instituted.[90] These were most probably accompanied by a small booklet containing a liturgy for the feast, as explicitly mentioned only in the letter to Eve:

And since we are sending you a quire enclosed together with this our bull, we wish and command you by apostolic writing, that you should receive and disseminate it with devotion, generously and willingly.[91]

[85] *Regesta pontificum romanorum* II, nos. 18,376, 18,380, p. 1,493.

[86] Paravicini Bagliani (1972) I, p. 2.

[87] *Regesta pontificum romanorum* II, no. 18,998, p. 1,538.

[88] 'Universis archiepiscopis et episcopis per Patriarchatum Ierosolymitanum . . .', *ibid*, no. 18,999, p. 1,538; *Registres d'Urbain IV* II, 1, no. 874, pp. 423–5.

[89] *Liège, St Lambert* VI, p. 618.

[90] *Regesta pontificum romanorm* II no. 19,016, p. 1,539; Lambot (1948), pp. 261–2.

[91] 'Et quia quaternum, in quo ipsius festi habetur officium, tibi sub bulla nostra per latorem presentium destinamus, volumus et per apostolica scripta tibi mandamus, quatinus quaternum ipsum cum devotione recipias et eius copiam personis illam petentibus exhibeas liberaliter et libenter', Liège Archives de l'Etat. St Martin no. 79. This is the office *Sacerdos in aeternum* which will be discussed below.

After these the papal chancery was silent on the subject of Corpus Christi. Copies of the liturgy of Corpus Christi existed in Boniface VIII's library in 1295:

> Item a quire, in which is the office of Corpus Christi
> Item, another, in which is the office of Corpus Christi
> Item, another with the same office . . .
> Item, 4 quires, in which is the Corpus Christi office, with notes.[92]

The papal library possessed copies of the liturgy prepared for Urban IV and circulated to some, but little else that demonstrates interest in the feast. No thirteenth-century liturgical book emanating from the *curia* makes any note of it: Gregory X's ceremonial of *c.*1274 does not mention it,[93] and in Clement V's missal of 1295 Corpus Christi and the Holy Trinity were added on a separate later quire, probably for the use of John XXII who elevated both feasts to universal usage.[94] Nor do papal accounts, which survive for some of Boniface VIII's years – 1299/1300 and 1302/3[95] – reveal any expenditure on the feast, and the accounts for the Avignon years are equally silent.[96] Nevertheless, a person who was particularly close to the *curia* and who was very keen and well-informed on both universal and local feasts and usages, William Durandus, was aware of the feast's history when he wrote his *Rationale divinorum officiorum c.*1298:

> And it is to be known that Urban IV has instituted the feast of Corpus Christi on the fifth day after that Sunday (Trinity Sunday) granting a great indulgence both for officiating clerics and for the people gathered for divine office, as is contained in the office ordained for it.[97]

---

[92] 'Item unus quaternus, in quo est officium de corpore Christi
  Item alius, in quo officium de corpore Christi
  Item alius, in quo est simile officium . . .
  Item iiij quaterni, in quibus est officium de corpore Christi cum nota',

*Historia bibliothecae romanorum pontificum. Addenda et emandanda*, nos. 289, 294, 295, 418, pp. 18, 23; one of these, probably the last, is BN.lat.1143, which originated from Boniface's library and must therefore date from 1264×95, and contains a noted office for the feast 'officium nove solemnitatis corporis domini nostri Jesu christi', with notes on the musical themes in the margins (fol. 1), Gy (1985), p. 312; (Boyle is sceptical, *ibid*). Interestingly, the library also possessed a copy of Mary of Oignies's *Vita*, *Historia bibliothecae pontificum romanorum*, p. 18.

[93] Schimmelpfennig (1973), p. 73.

[94] Dykmans (1972), pp. 451–8.

[95] *Libri rationum camerae Bonifatii papae VIII.*

[96] *Die Ausgäber der apostolischen Kammer unter Johann XXII.*

[97] 'Et est sciendum quod Urbanus papa IV statuit fieri festum de Corpore Christi quinta feria post hanc dominicam, et concedens magnam indulgentiam tam clericis officiantibus, quam populis convenientibus ad divina, prout in officio super hoc ordinato habetur', *Rationale* lib. 6, c. 115 ('De dominica I post pentecosten'), no. 6, p. 628.

The diffusion of the feast down to 1300 was stimulated by initiatives of particular bishops, like Durandus, in their areas of influence, but there was clearly no driving force from Rome.

The feast was somewhat more widespread in the area of its origin, but not accepted everywhere. Henry of Guelder would have received the letter sent to him in September 1264 within a few weeks, but no evidence of episcopal celebration or involvement survives, and St Lambert's chapter probably continued to oppose it. Some churches and religious houses which were related to the protagonists of the foundation or to the beguine milieu had celebrated it already in the 1240s and 1250s, such as St Martin's of Liège, which had received a testamentary bequest for use its celebration in 1251,[98] as well as the church of St Denis of Liège, which was given an indulgence for those visiting it on a number of major feasts, including Corpus Christi.[99] Monasteries such as Fosses, where Robert of Turotte and Juliana had died, and Tongres in the Namurois, observed it, and other Cistercian houses did when the order adopted the feast in 1277.[100] It was officially recognised in the diocese of Liège in the synodal statutes of Bishop John of Cambrai in 1287, in the section dealing with the calendar and feasts:

And on the Thursday of that week the feast of the eucharist will be solemnly celebrated, according to that which has already been instituted by our predecessors.[101]

It is hard to assess whether the impulse derived from the bull, or from the changes in the ecclesiastical politics of Liège, and the accession of a new bishop. Local political alignments had influenced decisions to encourage or to oppose the feast from its beginning; but even these were not pursued with great intensity throughout the century. Another difficulty about the feast is mentioned in Urban IV's bull, which must mean that it had some currency in Liège, the site of the early discussions of the feast; that is, the objection to a feast related to a ritual celebrated daily, and to a concept so fundamental that it could hardly be adequately celebrated in the mode of saints' days.[102] How could the basic claim on which Christianity had come to rest be commemorated in a single day's festivity? Similar objections had been levelled centuries earlier

---

[98] From the legacy of canon Stephen of Châlons: 'Volens eam cum proprio officio lectionum et reponsiorum quinta feria post Octabas trinitatis singulis annis in nostra ecclesia sollempniter duplicem celebrari', Denis (1927).

[99] *Liège, St Denis*, no. 27, p. 53.

[100] Lambot (1942), pp. 78–81.

[101] 'Et quinta feria ejusdem hebdomade fiat sollempniter festum Eucharistie, prout hactenus a nostris antecessoribus sunt statuta', *Les Statuts synodaux de Liège*, p. 44.

[102] Baix and Lambot (1946), p. 84.

against the attempts of Bishop Stephen of Liège (903–20) to found the feast of the Holy Trinity *c.*920 in his diocese.[103] In Urban IV's bull the answer was simple and functional: just as there was a day for every saint, so too Christ's body deserved one. It continued to argue that Corpus Christi was to be a sort of obverse of Maundy Thursday, celebrating the day of the institution of the eucharist not in sorrow in the Passion week, but on another, joyful, occasion.

The feast was received in and around Liège almost independently of the papal initiative. In 1287 John of Cambrai claimed to be implementing his predecessor's work. Cologne was closely linked to Liège economically and culturally.[104] It was easily within the sphere of the feast's development: the bishops of Liège had a palace there, and Hugh of St Cher had spent half a year there on the legation to Germany, and used it as his base on later missions.[105] St Gereon's Collegiate Church in Cologne, celebrated the feast in 1264×79, and its diocese of Osnabrück and Münster followed in 1276. In its dioceses of Paderborn the introduction of the eucharistic feast in 1299 was facilitated by a eucharistic miracle seven years earlier.[106]

Thus, the feast spread through a number of channels. It was a local feast observed by parts of the diocese of Liège; it was similarly taken up by a number of dioceses when the chapter of Cologne adopted it. Corpus Christi also spread through the Cistercian order; after the order instituted its observance in 1277, we see it celebrated in the next year in Heilbronn monastery (Würtemburg), in Bernstein (Brandenburg) in 1290, Wesserleben (Saxony) in 1294.[107] The Dominicans adopted the feast in 1304.[108] The feast also spread through personal contacts: a Corpus Christi sermon was delivered in 1265 at the Austrian monastery of St Lambrecht in Graz.[109] In this case it has been suggested that monastery emissaries sent to Rome in 1265 to supplicate for help after a disastrous fire which had struck St Lambrecht's, heard about the

---

[103] Cabrol (1931), pp. 270–6; Browe (1950); Axters (1948), p. 15. The feast was celebrated locally with a Trinity mass composed by Alcuin and spread throughout the Low Countries and France in the twelfth century, until it was raised to universal recognition by John XXII in 1334, Guillemain (1962), p. 99; Browe (1950), pp. 65–71. The beguine Ida of Nivelles (d.1231) was a particular devotee of the feast, Axters (1948), p. 27; on the liturgy and hymnody of the Holy Trinity, see Szöffervy (1964), p. 267; Raby (1927), pp. 389, 425–9.

[104] Wensky (1982), pp. 632–8.

[105] On the beginning of celebration in Cologne, see Schnitzler (1973).

[106] Fürstenberg (1917), p. 315; on the feast's spread in north-west Germany, see Jörres (1902).

[107] *Statuta* III, p. 182.

[108] Bonniwell (1944), p. 239.

[109] Kern (1954), pp. 49–50. Two books '2 hystori von unsers hern lichnam', belonged to the chapel of Tirol castle in 1300×20, *ibid*, p. 55.

feast and carried back its liturgy in its earlier version with the office *Sacerdos in aeternum*.[110] One of the earliest documents bearing directly on the feast's celebration comes from the collegiate church of St Gereon of Cologne. A document of 1275×7 allocated income from the manor of Oekoven for its expenses.[111] The feast was to be celebrated with a procession within the college close and into the neighbouring parish of St Christopher, and in it the canons marched in red capes and with the eucharist, the head of the martyr St Gereon, and with the Crown of St Helena.[112]

Another interesting example of early observance of the feast was in Venice. In 1295 the *consiglio* established the feast to be celebrated 'pro patria', being the only documented civic celebration of the feast in Italy in that century.[113] It may well be the case that knowledge of the feast travelled directly from Cologne (where it was celebrated in the 1270s) to Venice, the two cities being so closely bound through trade. Cologne was the renowned for the best quality linen yarn, the 'Cologne thread', and even more importantly, for the gold and silver threads produced by its skilled metal-beaters, the type of thread used in the production of high-quality brocade in the workshops of Venice and Genoa.[114] So Venetian merchants may have heard of the new northern feast, and introduced it to their pageant-loving city.[115] Venice illustrates the distance which ritual could travel, even when it was not promoted by a central authority. It also shows what will become increasingly clear, that Corpus Christi was taken up by different groups and fulfilled a variety of programmes as its traditions were being invented.

## AVIGNON – THE FEAST ESTABLISHED

Yet by the early fourteenth century Corpus Christi had become a universal feast. It spread with the papal letter *Si dominum* which was incorporated into the new canon law collection published in October 1317, the *Clementines*. It has traditionally been held that the bull *Transiturus* on which *Si dominum* was based, was repromulgated by Clement V at the council of Vienne which met between October 1311

---

[110] Kern (1954), p. 56; Morin (1910), p. 239.
[111] Schnitzler (1973), for the text and its analysis.
[112] *Ibid*, pp. 453–5.
[113] Muir (1981), pp. 223–4.
[114] Wensky (1982), pp. esp. p. 638, see also pp. 632, 635–6. There were also some Italian scholars in Liège in the thirteenth century, Renardy (1979), p. 272.
[115] The archbishop of Milan granted an indulgence to a fraternity devoted to the Virgin 'et pro culto sanctissime Eucharistie', but this does not mean that the feast was celebrated there, Tamborini (1935), p. 6.

and May 1312.[116] The council met in order to deal with questions of church reform, the religious orders, and more immediately, the Templars, and it was attended by the kings of France, England and Aragon.[117] It discussed many issues which touched on current errors and abuses in religious organisation, and especially in new forms of religious life. The *Clementines* is the last great medieval collection of canon law, and was published in late October 1317 by Clement V's successor. Drafts of the decisions of the council circulated all over Europe for consultation and reference, and at the same time canonists at the *curia* were engaged in revision and amplification, and the consideration of objections.[118] They were designing not a list of conciliar canons but a coherent legal collection, a *Liber septimus* which adhered to professional legal conventions and which would be amenable to future glossing, commentary and application. In 1312 Clement V recommended the destruction of existing drafts of the canons, lest unofficial versions circulate and be confused with the official, comprehensive and modified collection sent from Avignon.[119] He allowed two years for a post-conciliar commission's revision,[120] and finally presented the *Clementines* to his consistory at Monteux (near Carpentras) on 21 March 1314. But Clement V died only four weeks later, in April 1314, before the completion of authorisation with the dispatch of copies to the universities of Paris and Orléans could grant the collection the seal of approval.[121] In fact, Bernard Gui, a contemporary at the *curia* claims that it was never even sent to the universities.[122]

With Clement's death in 1314 the publication of the *Clementines* suffered another setback. After a vacancy which lasted two years John XXII was elected pope in August 1316 and was consecrated in Lyons in September.[123] According to John Andrea the new pope undertook a revision of the *Clementines,* changing and correcting the all but final text left by his predecessor. John XXII explained his aims in this collection in a letter which accompanied the copy sent to the doctors of

---

[116] Lecler (1964); Müller shows that a tradition which held that Corpus Christi was celebrated in Vienna in 1312 was not based on fact, Müller (1934), pp. 644–8. For comparison of the papal texts, see Franceschini (1965).

[117] On the council, see Hefele-Leclercq (1915) VI, pp. 643–717.

[118] Tarrant (1974) and Tarrant (1984–5).

[119] Ehrle (1888), p. 452; Tarrant (1974), p. 301.

[120] In April 1313 still dispatched copies of the *Liber sextus* when an updated canonistic collection was needed, Ehrle (1888), p. 455; also Kuttner (1964), p. 429.

[121] Tarrant (1984–5), p. 68.

[122] 'Et sic liber ille non fuit [tunc] missus ad studia generalia ut est moris, nec expositus communiter ad habendum, sed remansit et adhuc remanet involutus', Ehrle (1888), p. 457 (BN nouv. acq. lat. 1171, fol. 183ᵛ).

[123] Hefele-Leclercq (1915) VI, pp. 744–7.

Bologna: he had wished to rationalise the constitutions 'in one volume and under suitable headings'.[124] Out of 106 constitutions, only 38 are directly attributable to the council of Vienne's deliberations; for the rest it is impossible to decide whether they were additions or changes, and if either, on whose initiative.[125] But in one case where the editorial process can be traced an interesting change is revealed. The decree *Cum de quibusdem* passed at the council was a harsh measure against those beguines who were deemed to be spreading unorthodox views about the sacraments and about the clergy,[126] and this was immediately taken up by some German bishops for wide-scale persecution of these communities, on the morrow of the council. The decree *Ad nostrum* was added after 1312, and it was most probably added by John XXII, as a tempering influence against the excesses which *Cum de quibusdem* proved to have inspired.[127] He sent copies for approval to Paris and Bologna, the last possible obstacle on Corpus Christ's road to refoundation was to be removed.[128]

By November 1317 the new collection was ready for dispatch accompanied by the bull *Quoniam nulla*.[129] Urban IV's *Transiturus* was incorporated in *Si dominum* title 3.16.1 of the *Clementines*, under the heading 'On relics and the veneration of saints' (*De reliquiis et veneratione sanctorum*), and reproduces almost word to word the letter which he had addressed to 'to the venerable brethren patriarchs, archbishops, bishops and other ecclesiastical prelates' (*Venerabilibus fratibus patriarchis, archiepiscopis, episcopis et aliis ecclesiasticis prelatis*).[130] The papal expenditures on the preparation of these copies were:

for 20 dozen parchments bought by Master Raymund Barrerie for the writing and making of apostolic letters for the decretals or constitutions of the blessed Clement of good memory, at 8s9d of Tours per dozen, to be paid to John of Besenchis, a parchmenter of Toulouse £8.15s of the money of Tours.[131]

The administrative machine of the Avignon papacy was superior to that

---

[124] 'In unum volumen et sub congruis titulis', Ehrle (1888), p. 452, n. 1.
[125] Tarrant (1984–5), pp. 68–70.
[126] Lerner (1972), p. 478.
[127] Tarrant (1974), pp. 302–3.
[128] *Chartularium universitatis Parisiensis* II, 1, p. 211.
[129] Kuttner (1964), pp. 429–30. It included 106 chapters in 52 titles, repromulgating a bull of Urban IV and one of Boniface VIII. John XXII also initiated twenty other constitutions which were collected as the *Extravagantes*.
[130] For an analysis of *Si dominum* and its comparison with *Transiturus*, see Franceschini (1965), pp. 234–40.
[131] 'Pro 20 duodenis pergamenorum emptorum per Mag. Raimundum Barrerie pro decretalibus seu constitutionibus d. Clementis bone memorie scribendis et literis curie faciendis, 8s9d tur., pro duodena, solvi Johanni de Besenchis, pergamenario Tholose £8.15s tur. p', an entry for 14 October 1317, *Die Ausgäber*, p. 319.

which had functioned in Orvieto in 1264. Papal missives reached their destinations throughout the Christian world through the work of a few professional couriers attached to the merchant companies, and sometimes using the services of merchants and proctors on their way to and from Avignon. The collection which promulgated anew the letter that had founded the feast of Corpus Christi would have reached Paris in about a week, and Florence in a fortnight.[132] And it may be that when the papal treasurers paid John de Corbino and John de Porcis 'emissaries sent by our Lord with letters to the cardinals in England' on 3 January 1318, they were paying for the dispatch of the *Clementines* to England.[133] So major a collection would have been copied for diocesan use, sections would have been extracted for royal chanceries, but it would still take some time for some decrees to penetrate local usage.[134] The glosses followed soon after the publication; John Andrea's apparatus of 1322, which came to be regarded as the *glossa ordinaria*,[135] and the commentaries of Guy of Montlauzun of 1319, of Paul de Liazariis of 1322×30, and that of Josselin de Cessantis of 1323.[136]

Although the bull of 1264 was available in two copies in the papal registers and the liturgies for the feast were kept in the papal library, the feast seems not to have been celebrated by the curia before its revival by John XXII. As we have seen, no papal liturgical or ceremonial book produced before 1317 contains any reference to the feast in the original, nor do the few accounts of the papal chapel contain any note on expenditure on this feast, whereas other feasts were regularly recorded. Urban IV was obviously devoted to the idea and had been so for years before 1264: he had surrounded himself by men from Liège and its surroundings, even in important liturgical and ceremonial positions such as *clericus capellae* and *ostiarius* of the papal chapel.[137] But after his death the feast was forgotten. This was much less likely to have happened to a pronouncement from Avignon, a court steeped in bureaucratic procedure, much more centralised and close to the centres of European power.

But how to explain further John XXII's interest in renewing *Transiturus* and thus effectively instituting the feast of the eucharist? John XXII was a remarkable personality with original views on politics,

---

[132] Renouard (1937), p. 29.
[133] 'Nuntiis missis per dominum nostrum ad cardinales in Angliam cum literis', *Die Ausgäber*, p. 390; it was 8 in advance and 8 upon return.
[134] Cheney (1972–3), p. 79.
[135] John Andrea also began a later gloss in 1324×30, Kuttner (1965), p. 196.
[136] Tarrant (1984), p. 70. John Andrea had also started work on a commentary, Kuttner (1965).
[137] Schimmelpfennig (1971), pp. 85–6.

religion and society.[138] He was anti-Franciscan, and adamant in preserving ecclesiastical power and privilege; he was the pope who canonised Thomas Aquinas, a Dominican, bringing to fruition a process which had begun under his predecessor. From the material related to the canonisaton, he would have encountered the tradition about Thomas' liturgical composition for Corpus Christi.[139] Additionally, the pastoral reasons for the creation of an orthodox eucharistic pageant were, if anything, greater by the early fourteenth century than a century earlier. Challenges and digressions, doubts and explorations on sacramentality and clerical office were stronger and more diverse than ever. John XXII had also undertaken other liturgical initiatives, and displayed interest and belief that new feasts and their attendant offices could bolster 'faith', in fact revitalise the symbolic system. Without labouring the point, it is significant that the man who sweetened the conciliar decree against beguines was also the person who elevated a feast first conceived in a beguine's cell to universal observance.[140]

## THE LITURGY OF CORPUS CHRISTI

Who wrote the feast's office, and how was it disseminated and adapted to widespread use?[141] Thomas Aquinas' authorship of the Corpus Christi office had traditionally been accepted in general accounts of the feast. With more careful scrutiny of the sources underlying this view modern scholars have either dissented from or restated this attribution.[142] Those who dissent point to the fact that the tradition appears in the sources only from the 1320s, and that support for this view from outside the circle of Dominican disciples of Aquinas does not exist. Thomas' first biographer, Peter of Calo, does not mention the liturgy, nor was it recorded in the material initially presented at his canonisation process.[143] According to Bartholomew of Lucca (*c.*1236–*c.*1336), Thomas' disciple and confessor, who was still alive and in Avignon in the years 1312–17 when Corpus Christi was refounded, Thomas was the author of the liturgy. In a list 'opuscula fratris Thomae' in his

[138] Mollat (1965), pp. 39–71; on his background, see Guillemain (1962), p. 118.
[139] William of Tocco, who wrote a *Vita* of St Thomas, was the Dominican in charge of the collection of material for the canonisation process, Gerulaitis (1967), pp. 36–40; Weisheipl (1974), pp. 176–7.
[140] On his position on the issue of beguines, see Tarrant (1974), p. 308.
[141] On liturgy in general, see King (1957); on thirteenth-century liturgy with special reference to papal influence, see Van Dijk and Walker (1960).
[142] On Aquinas and the liturgy, see Walz (1966).
[143] William of Tocco, 'Hystoria beati Thomae de Aquino', in *Fontes Vita s. Thomae Aquinatis*, pp. 203–369; Thomas' writings are listed on pp. 328–31.

*Historia ecclesiastica nova* the liturgy was part of Thomas' vast writings, and was written at Urban IV's wish:[144]

> He composed the Office of Corpus Christi at Urban's demand, which is the second he made at Urban's request. He made it complete both as to the readings as to the whole office, both as for day and for night, and as the mass, and that which was to be sung every day. And if we look closely at the author's words in the History, we will find them to contain almost all the figures from the Old Testament, as adapted in admirable and singular style to the sacrament of the eucharist.[145]

He continues to claim that the feast was renewed by Clement V at the council of Vienne, contrary to John Andrea's claim that he did not.[146] As we will see, Bartholomew's description of the office, with its mention of its most unique feature – the abundance of biblical material – is accurate.[147] This version was later taken up by William of Tocco, who was in charge of the initial collection of the material for Thomas' canonisation inquiry in 1317–18, in his *Vita* of Thomas; 'scripsit officium de corpore Christi de mandato papae Urbani'.[148]

Corpus Christi was effectively reintroduced to universal Dominican observance in the Lyons chapter of 1319, following the feast's refoundation, and from the Barcelona chapter of 1323 on the order was to celebrate it with Thomas' liturgy, a copy of which was sent to the provinces.[149] Thus, a temporary office was replaced by a Roman one in 1323, the very year of Thomas' canonisation:

> We wish that the office of Corpus Christi claimed to be written by the venerable doctor Thomas of Aquinas, be entered into the books . . . of the whole order.[150]

Lambot and Delaissé hold the tardy reception of the Roman liturgy as a claim against Thomas' authorship.[151] But one must bear in mind that the feast had fallen into oblivion, even in the very *curia* within which it

---

[144] On Thomas in Orvieto and the foundation of Corpus Christi, see Walz (1966).
[145] 'Officium etiam de Corpore Christi fecit ex mandato Urbani: quod est secundum quod fecit ad petitionem Urbani. Hoc autem fecit completum et quantum ad lectiones et quantum ad totum Officium tam diurnum quam nocturnum, quam etiam ad Missam et quidquid illa die cantatur. In qua historia, si attendimus ad verba scribentis, quasi omnes figurae Veteris Testamenti in hoc Officio videntur contineri, luculento et proprio stilo adaptatae ad Eucharistie Sacramentum', Ptolmey of Lucca, 'Historia ecclesiastica', *RIS* xi, lib. 22, c. 24, col. 1,153–54; Dondaine (1961).
[146] 'Quod quidem Officium fuit postea sub Clemente V roboratum Anno Domini MCCCX in Concilio Viennensi', *ibid*, c. 25, col. 1,154.
[147] Father Zawilla (OP) had conducted a searching study of these images, and has revealed the structure of the office (1985).
[148] Gerulaitis (1967), p. 36; William of Tocco, 'Historia beati Thomae', *AASS* March 1, c. 18, col. 665.
[149] *MOPH* iv, p. 152; Gy (1980), p. 491.
[150] 'Volumus quod officium de corpore Christi per venerabilem doctorem fratrem Thomam de Aquino editum, ut asseritur, per totum ordinem . . . annotetur', *MOPH* iv, p. 152.
[151] Lambot (1942), p. 67; Delaissé (1950), esp. p. 221n; Weisheipl (1974), p. 182.

was founded, so the fortunes of its used liturgy could be similar.[152] But once the feast was refounded its liturgy and the circumstances of its creation would have given rise to interest; and we should not be surprised that it took four years for it to be re-established in the Dominican order. A Dominican breviary of Rieti incorporates what may have been the exemplar of 1323.[153]

Was Thomas a likely person to have written the office in 1264? After completing his first period of study and teaching in Paris in 1259, Thomas became the conventual *lector* of the Dominicans in Orvieto. He belonged to a circle of superior scholars and administrators sur-rounding Urban IV, and as a *lector* attached to the *curia* he was called upon to provide answers and advice,[154] as in his work *Contra errores Graecorum*.[155] The first book of Thomas' gospel commentary, the *Catena aurea*, completed in 1263, was dedicated to the pope, who in turn is said to have selected Thomas for the task of composing the liturgy for the new eucharistic feast.[156]

But besides rumour and traditions, and the circumstantial evidence relating Thomas to Urban IV at the appropriate time and in the appropriate role, the office of Corpus Christi is linked to him as a very special type of office. The exhaustive studies of Father Zawilla under the inspiration of Father Gy of the present Dominican convent of Paris, have revealed the close association between the biblical themes and passages which made up the office, and the application of biblical material in Thomas' own eucharistic writings. Zawilla's work has shown that material which was rarely used in eucharistic contexts were deployed by Thomas in the office, creating a personal signature, which can be traced in the *Summa* and in his writings during his second period in Paris (1269–72).[157] In a sermon for the second Sunday after Trinity, the Sunday in Corpus Christi octave, which used the sacrament as its theme, there are sixteen biblical quotations, twelve of which were in the office.[158] In his use of Luke 14, 16–24, Thomas could have been inspired only by the work of Hugh of St Cher's group, the foremost Dominican exegetical enterprise of the preceding generation.[159] His sermon on the

[152] Lazzarini (1952a).
[153] Vatican Barb. Lat. 400, fols. 88[va]–93[vb], and rubrics fols. 93[v]–94[r]; *Manuscrits liturgiques latins* I, pp. 107–8.
[154] On the position of *lector* (where no Dominican *studium generale* existed), see Weisheipl (1974), pp. 161, 389.
[155] Gy (1980a), p. 502; Catto (1976), p. 5.
[156] Weisheipl (1974), pp. 370–1.
[157] Zawilla (1985); Gy (1980), pp. 504–6.
[158] Bataillon (1983).
[159] Bataillon (1983), p. 358. We have already encountered on his missions to Germany in the 1250s, above pp. 174–5.

parable of the feast *Homo quidam fecit cenam magnam*, contains biblical texts which figure in the Corpus Christi office.[160] The concept of a heavily scriptural office was, moreover, unusual in this period when liturgy tended to use less scripture and more poetry and hymnody.[161] The liturgy conveys peculiarities which fall in neatly with what we know of Thomas' later work.

The Corpus Christi liturgy includes a mass and an office for the feast and its octave. It is most original in its sequence *Lauda, syon*, in the hymns and in the choice of readings, especially those for matins.[162] The feast is highly stylised; like its prayers which move from past (*Deus qui*), to the present (*Ecclesie tue*), to the future tense (*Fac nos*). It is an office strong in eucharistic statements articulated in Aristotelian terms, offering a corporeal understanding of a sacramental substance, not veiled but real, which the senses cannot perceive, but faith can recognise.[163] This eucharistic position diverges from a trend in eucharistic interpretation which we have encountered, one which stresses the symbolic and hidden nature of the eucharist, the position of Hugh of St Victor and of Bonaventure, and one from which Thomas differed. In the highly didactic second lesson for matins it is clearly stated that 'The accidents exist in it without a subject', the sort of statement which Wyclif would reject a hundred years later. The merging of philosophy and faith is reiterated in the words of the famous hymn for vespers, *Pange, lingua*.[164]

The tradition about Thomas' authorship of the Corpus Christi office was established by the early fourteenth century, and was even represented in a number of contemporary works of art,[165] such as the final enamelled panel of the shrine of the miraculous corporal of Bolsena, made in 1337×9, and kept in the chapel of the Corporal in Orvieto Cathedral.[166] Pope Urban IV is here shown on his throne and surrounded by cardinals and admiring layfolk, while Thomas kneels and offers his office in a scroll.[167] One of the six *predelle* on eucharistic

---

[160] Like Deut, 4,7, or the little quoted Job 31,31 in the office is related to Mat. 26,26 in the fifth response, and many more examples, see Bataillon (1974), p. 454.

[161] Gy (1984), p. 552.

[162] For an analysis of the legend, see Gy (1983), pp. 85–92.

[163] Gy (1982a), pp. 85–6.

[164] For text, see Baldwin (1959), pp. 204–5; on *Pange, lingua*, Ong (1947), pp. 16–20.

[165] *Liber de vita christi ac omnium pontificum* of c.1474 included a *Vita* of Urban IV in which it was said about Thomas: 'composuit et officium de corpore Christi, quo in opere plurimae figurae Testamenti Veteris continentur', *RIS* 3, col. 242.

[166] Harding (1988).

[167] In Orvieto this is, of course, linked to the local claims that the Bolsena miracle inspired Urban IV to found the feast of Corpus Christi, Fumi (1891), Lazzarini (1952), and above pp. 176–7.

themes painted by the Sienese Sassetta in 1423–1426 to accompany the altarpiece of the Wool Merchants' gild (*arte di lana*) shows Thomas Aquinas kneeling before a crucifix and offering it a book.[168] This is a scene reported in Thomas' *Vita* as having happened at the convent of St Dominic in Naples in 1273. Thomas offered to the image of Christ his writings on the eucharist as incorporated in the third section of the *Summa theologiae,* and Christ accepted the offering, saying: 'Thomas, you have written well of me, what would you have from me for your reward?'[169]

Thomas' office was a success, a popular office reflecting the more affective aspect of his later work.[170] But even accepting his authorship of the Corpus Christi liturgy there still are problems thrown up by the feast's protracted development. What is the relation between Thomas' office and the office which was composed for local celebration and used before 1264?[171] And how are the different versions of the office found in thirteenth-century manuscripts but unrelated to the office of Liège to be understood?

The *Vita Julianae* tells that the first Corpus Christi office, *Animarum cibus,* was written by John of Lausanne and sent by Robert of Turotte to the churches of the diocese.[172] This office, which has been reconstituted by Fransen and Lambot,[173] drew heavily on canonistic and theological authorities, and very little from scripture; almost half its material was taken from Alger of Liège's *De sacramentis.*[174] This office would have probably been available at the *curia* for Thomas' use, since part of it appears in a thirteenth-century papal sacramentary,[175] and only one of the responses in the Roman office diverges from those of the early office of Liège.[176] But the Roman office is quite different in tone, scope, aim and contents, and definitely in the quality of its hymnody.

The Corpus Christi office preserved in the Benedictine breviary of St

---

[168] *Painting in Renaissance Siena,* pp. 68–9.

[169] 'Thoma, bene scripsisti de me, quam recipies a me pro tuo labore mercedem?', William of Tocco, 'Hystoria beati Thomae de Aquino', c. 35, pp. 79–80; *Painting in Renaissance Siena,* pp. 71–2.

[170] Thomas Aquinas never wrote devotional texts and showed little interest in popular currents in religion, Lacroix and Landry (1979), esp. pp. 170–1.

[171] Lambot and Fransen (1946); this is a reconstruction of the office based on a manuscript from the abbey of Tongres, Brussels Royal Library 70, F4, *ibid,* p. 29.

[172] Callaey (1948), p. 226; Gy (1980a), pp. 493–4.

[173] See Lambot and Fransen (1946) for the chanted sections.

[174] Zawilla (1985), pp. 17–19; Gy (1980a), pp. 497–8; Cottiaux (1963), pp. 16–18.

[175] *Les Breviaires manuscrits* IV, no. 1,036, pp. 422–5, Gy (1980a), p. 424 (Avignon Municipal Library 100); Andrieu (1924), pp. 348–76; Gy (1980a), p. 494.

[176] Morin (1910), pp. 237–9.

Lambrecht's Graz is yet another version. The breviary dates from
1233×58, but contains additions on fols. 241–6 of 'officium novae
solemnitatis corporis Christi', which were made not long after the
book's production.[177] The arrival of the office in Graz may be connected with the house's efforts to raise money from Clement IV in
Rome in 1265 for the rebuilding of its church after a fire.[178] If its
emissaries came away with the office that entered their breviary, it was
not the final Roman office of Thomas' composition, but rather similar
to the office found in the fourteenth-century breviary of the Praemonstratensian house at Strahov near Prague, which opens with the legend
*Dominus Iesus ad Invisibilia* (DIA) of the office *Sapientia aedificavit sibi
domum* (SAS) quite different from *Animarum cibus*, but also somewhat
different from the Roman office *Sacerdos in aeternum* (SIA), which
spread from Rome with the legend *Immensa divina largitatis* (IDL), the
liturgy which followed *Transiturus*.[179] Thus, there were two Roman
offices: SAS with the mass *Ego sum*, which was used, as reported by
Thomas' biographer, for the purpose of initial celebrations and which
remained the liturgy in Urban IV's natal town of Troyes,[180] and a
slightly later office with the mass *Cibavit*. This can be found, attached
to a copy of the bull *Transiturus*, in a *libellus* in the treasury of St
Andrew's church, Bognanco (Novara).[181] Here the user was directed to
the bull *Transiturus* for parts of the reading at matins in the octave.[182]
An early-fourteenth-century copy of what must have been the prototype of the bull and liturgy for the feast, similar to the Strahov manuscript, is to be found in a manuscript which existed in Boniface VIII's
library, and now at the Bibliothèque nationale, a lectionary of *c.*1270
which includes the earlier version, to which the new readings were
added.[183] A thirteenth-century lectionary for the papal chapel of St
Nicholas in Lateran contains lessons for Corpus Christi using DIA for
the first nocturne, the readings from Gratian and from the *Sentences*.[184]

---

[177] Within the lifetime of the illuminator, Kern (1954), p. 46.
[178] See above, pp. 180–1.
[179] The Strahov ms. was edited in Lambot (1942).
[180] As in the breviary of Montier-la-celle, near Troyes, *Les Breviaires manuscrits* IV, no. 859,
    pp. 255–6 (Troyes Municipal Library 1974, fols. 434ʳ–438ʳ); Gy (1980a), p. 498.
[181] Zawilla (1985), p. 34.
[182] Bertamini (1968), pp. 29–30.
[183] Paris BN 755; Gy (1980a), pp. 495–6; Delaissé (1950), p. 42; and two more books
    identified recently by Gy (1980); pp. 498–501; Lambot (1942), pp. 112–33.
[184] Paris BN 1143; David (1936), p. 12. There is disagreement on the dating of this book. The
    decoration could be as early as 1260s, *Manuscrits enluminés* II, no. 161, p. 312; Gy dates it
    as 1264×95 and as containing the earlier version of the liturgy Gy (1985); Boyle in Gy
    (1985) and Lambot (1942), pp. 95–7 tend to think that it is later. See on this Zawilla (1985),
    p. 63.

This soon became obsolete, and in the very late thirteenth century additions were made in the middle of the readings, the legend IDL of Thomas' final office.[185] So the new lessons came to replace, fully or partially, the juristic readings which appear as hastily put together and which relied so heavily on the *Decretum*. But the earlier office, the legend of which is found in this papal lectionary, was otherwise very similar to the latter, in hymns and responses; the readings were obviously the part on which Thomas had worked hardest and last.

In fact, SAS and SIA are so close in their masses that we are led to think that in 1264 or 1265 the office was almost ready, that it circulated in a limited fashion, was celebrated by Urban IV in Orvieto before his death, and that only later the new legend IDL was added by Thomas.[186] The legend IDL is original and accomplished. In the bull *Transiturus* the legend unfolds in three parts: doctrinal exposition on the eucharist, explanation of the motivation for foundation, and instruction on its celebration and indulgences attached. There is a Christological affirmation in the first lessons for matins, a doctrinal statement on transubstantiation in the third lesson of the nocturne, a memorial of the Passion in a string of scriptural themes with sacrificial overtones, *Deus qui*, *O hostia salutaris*, and an eschatological perspective of the ever-renewed sacrament in *O sacrum convivium*.[187] The legend which was not quite ready in August 1264 is included in two books of papal provenance BN lat. 755 and Avignon Municipal Library 100, in addition to the earlier legend. Sections of the early office even reached as far as the *cantatorium* of the Dominican convent of Marienthal of 1269,[188] which includes responses from SAS.[189] So the office travelled quite widely in its original form, which included many parts retained in the final version, but which differed in the contents of the legend, Thomas' readings being expertly crafted to sustain a wide-ranging and developed eucharistic ecclesiology.

Perhaps the best known section of the Corpus Christi liturgy is the sequence *Lauda, syon*, which has been considered the perfect sequence.[190] Sequences became increasingly popular in the twelfth century, as openings for the entry of new non-scriptural devotional themes and verse sections related to particular feasts and their seasons.[191]

---

[185] David (1936), pp. 12–17.
[186] Gy (1983), p. 84; Zawilla (1985), p. 84. Delaissé (1950) and Pikulik (1974) remain sceptical.
[187] For a close analysis, see Gy (1983), pp. 85–92.
[188] Brussels Royal Library 139.
[189] Fols. 107–9; Delaissé (1950), p. 221; Lambot (1942), p. 68.
[190] Text in Brittain (1953), pp. 222–3; Raby (1927), p. 405.
[191] Szöffervy (1964), p. 248; Messenger (1953), pp. 47–8. The Sarum missal came to contain some one hundred sequences, *ibid*, p. 53.

*Lauda, syon* is sober in tone; it is a conscious attempt to expound eucharistic doctrine in a way which was more affective than Thomas' usual discursive tone.[192] Borrowing from the Victorine tradition, *Lauda, syon* uses the Easter hymn *Zyma vetus expurgetur* of Adam of St Victor (*c.*1100–*c.*1180), borrowing phrases but altering its structure.[193] The sequence is also reminiscent of a hymn on the cross, *Laudes crucis,* which exists in a manuscript which once belonged to Cardinal Matteo Orsini who was in Orvieto in the 1260s, and which Thomas may have seen,[194] yet this hymn of praise to the eucharist is quite original.[195] It is particularly stark on the meaning of communion:

> Though his flesh as food abideth,
> And his blood as drink – he hideth
> Undivided under each.
>
> Whoso eateth it can never
> Break the body, rend or sever;
> Christ entire our hearts doth fill.
> Thousands eat the bread of heaven,
> Yet as much to one is given:
> Christ, though eaten, bideth still.
>
> Good and bad, they come to greet him,
> Unto life the former eat him,
> And the latter unto death.
> Those find death and those find heaven,
> See, from the same life-seed given,
> How the harvest differeth.[196]

Thomas here answers all the questions about the nature of the sacrament, the circumstances of reception, the consequences of unworthy

---

[192] On its style, see Szöffervy (1964), pp. 249–51.
[193] Brittain (1953), p. 222.
[194] Szöffervy (1964), p. 248.
[195] Messenger (1953), pp. 50–1.
[196] Caro cibus, sanguis potus,
Manet tamen Christus totus
Sub utraque specie.

A sumente non concisus
Non confractus, non divisus,
Integer accipitur.
Sumit unus, sumunt mille,
Quantum isti, tantum ille,
Nec sumptus consumitur.

Sumunt boni, sumunt mali,
Sorte tamen inaequali
Vitae vel interitus:
Mors est malis, vita bonis:
Vide, paris sumptionis
Quam sit dispar exitus.

reception, the queries which we have witnessed as they arose from the practitioners and the audience, and which intellectuals attempted to counter and answer. In the *Summa,* when considering the question 'Utrum in hoc sacramento sit Corpus Christi secundum veritatem?', Thomas answered, just as in the sequence:

> Thus in faith the Christian heareth:
> That Christ's flesh as bread appeareth,
> And as wine his precious blood.
> Though we feel it not nor see it,
> Living faith that doth decree it,
> All defects of sense makes good.[197]

This appealed to faith at the moment of doubt. *Lauda, syon* was incorporated into the Chester Corpus Christi cycle, paraphrased by Christ himself when reflecting on the passage from the Old Law to the New.[198]

The sequence was a great success, and this is attested in the fact that few other sequences were composed or used in its place. There is a Bohemian sequence *Eia, laeta cantica* by the bishop of Prague, John of Jenstein of *c.* 1400,[199] and another, *In exitu miserae,* based on the Easter sequence *In exitu Israel,*[200] but these never really replaced Thomas' sequence. *Lauda, syon* was often chanted at eucharistic processions, and during the course of processions for the blessing of fields.[201]

The liturgy's most moving part is undoubtedly its hymnody, and particularly its hymn for vespers, *Pange, lingua.*[202] Borrowing from Venantius Fortunatus' sixth-century hymn to the cross its opening and its meter, *Pange, lingua* combines mysticism with doctrine, in a mode reminiscent of the great Franciscan of the age, John Pecham, who wrote a number of eucharistic salutations.[203] Moving between new and old, as in the *Lauda, syon* Thomas' hymn thrives on oppositions, in a manner most suited for the exploration of the paradoxes in the eucharist: the

---

[197] Dogma datur Christianis
Quod in carnem transit panis
Et vinum in sanguinem
Quod non capis, quod non vides
Animosa firmat fides
Praeter rerum ordinem.
[198] Stemmler (1970), p. 239; *Chester cycle* I, lines 69–80, p. 271.
[199] *AH* 48, pp. 421–2.
[200] *AH* 34, pp. 45–6; see also *AH* 40, pp. 55–6.
[201] Browe (1929b).
[202] For the text, see Brittain (1953), p. 224; Szöffervy (1964), pp. 251–2.
[203] Messenger (1953), p. 50.

incarnation of God in the word, and the word in the flesh.[204] Yet behind the play there is a strong assertion of the truths of sacrifice and redemption. In his poem *Piers plowman* of *c*.1375 Langland refers to a line from *Pange, lingua* when discussing the nature of the faith:

> Lord lete þat this prestes lelly seien her masse . . .
> Thogh hit suffice fo oure sauacioun soethfast blyeue,
> As clerkes in Corpus Christi feste syngen and reden
> That *sola fides sufficit* to saue with lewede peple.[205]

In the hymn for the nocturne, *Sacris sollemniis*, liturgical consideration focuses on the present, and the day's commemorative purpose is expounded, with a picture of the Last Supper as a humane scene in which Christ takes leave of his disciples:

> Now is recalled to mind
> That supper last of all,
> When Christ, as is believed,
> Gave to his brethren all,
> Both the unleavened bread
> And lamb that did fulfil
> Laws made of old for the Fathers
>
> . . .
>
> Thus does he institute
> That sacred sacrifice
> And its dread ministry
> To priests alone applies;
> Those, then, most fittingly,
> First should themselves partake,
> Later to give to all others.[206]

This is perhaps the least 'doctrinal' of the three hymns, but it mediates between the past of sacrifice, and the future of renewed possibilities for redemption through the eucharist, and ties the feast directly to this on-going process.

---

[204] Ong (1947). On Dominican hymnody, see Messenger (1953), pp. 49–50, 54–7; Dronke (1978), p. 34.

[205] *Piers plowman: an edition of the C Text*, lines 117, 119–21, p. 283.

[206] Noctis recolitur coena novissima
Qua Christus creditur agnum et azyma
Dedisse fratribus juxta legitima
Priscis indulta patribus.

. . .

Sic sacrificium istud instituit,
Cujus officium committi voluit,
Solis presbyteris, quibus sic congruit
Ut sumant et dent ceteris.

In his hymn for lauds, *Verbum supernum prodiens,* Thomas again used a well-known line from the Ambrosian Advent hymn – not an insignificant gesture given the liturgical and symbolic link between Christmas and Corpus Christi, Nativity and eucharist.[207] The treatment of the eucharist is here completed with the interpretation of the eucharist's lasting redemptive power, Christ's enduring sacrifice:

> To whom beneath a twofold sign
> He gave his blood, his flesh to eat.
> That of the double substance there
> He might replenish man complete.
>
> At birth, He gave himself as friend,
> At table, then, our food to be,
> At death, as ransom for mankind,
> Enthroned, as prize eternally.[208]

The hymn was translated into English in the fifteenth century as 'Godys sone passyng frome place supernall'.[209]

The office of Liège was naturally a combination of old forms and new concepts and emphases. The hymns and masses which circulated with the few copies of *Transiturus* were a new departure, but the readings attached to them were far from original; only in their final compilation and gradual attachment and entry into liturgical books, for real usage does the liturgical whole coalesce. Local variations on almost every section of the liturgy were created, special *Kyries, sanctus* phrases, sequences and hymns for Corpus Christi proliferated, but they were secondary to the popular Roman office.[210]

The *Clementines* spread the feast to every province, diocese, parish, religious house, and thus helped turn it into a reality. In the thirteenth

---

[207] See above on the symbolic link between the two, pp. 142–5.
[208] Quibus sub bina specie
Carnem dedit et sanguinem
Ut duplicis substantiae
Totum cibaret hominem

Se nascens dedit socium
Convescens in edilium
Se moriens in pretium
Se regnans dat in praemium.

The last stanza of the hymn is the O *salutaris hostia* of the benediction in the Corpus Christi mass.
[209] Patterson (1927), pp. 433, 446–8.
[210] Translations into English of the Corpus Christi Latin hymns were made in the fifteenth century, as in BL Add. 34193, fols. 107$^r$–119r$^v$. On the development of other rhymed offices see Hontoir (1942), p. 68. In a list of Dominican writings of 1414 Albert the Great is said to have composed an office for the feast: 'Item scripsit unum officium de corpore Christi, quod non est in usu communi Ecclesiae, cum diversis prosis de eodem sacramento', Scheeben (1931), p. 245.

century it was known in Liège, around Cologne, in German Cistercian houses, in some towns of the south of France, in an Austrian monastery, and in Venice. The eucharistic feast received an impulse in 1317 which brought it to everyone, everywhere, reaching as far and wide as the sacrament it celebrated.

### THE ENTRY INTO LITURGICAL BOOKS AND ICONOGRAPHIC DEVELOPMENT

The incorporation of a new feast, and especially of a moveable feast, into local usage through liturgical books could happen in a number of ways: it could be added to the last folios or added as a separate quire at the front or at the end of a book. The feast of Corpus Christi was initially added at the end or copied onto blank spaces in books. When it was finally incorporated into a missal it was usually placed after the feast of the Holy Trinity, but it was often copied outside its temporal sequence. It sometimes entered a missal together with a number of other new offices, as it was in a turn-of-the-century hand to a Franciscan breviary of 1263, together with the Holy Trinity and the Visitation.[211]

The entry of the feast into liturgical books took different forms in different places. A number of thirteenth-century Italian books have it as an insertion, and in a few cases it is clear that it occurred before 1317.[212] It was an addition in the Venetian missal for Franciscan use of *c.*1290,[213] and one which occurred soon after the completion of an early-four-teenth-century gradual of the Augustinian house of Certaldo;[214] a Roman breviary of *c.*1300 (inserted before 1308) which belonged to a house of hermits of St Augustine included added offices of Corpus Christi, of St Mary *ad nives,* and of the Conception of the Virgin.[215] But as late as 1323×66 an Italian Roman missal could still be produced without the Corpus Christi mass.[216] One of the first liturgical books to include Corpus Christi as an integral element is the collectory of the

[211] Vatican Lat. 12992, fols. 243$^{rb}$–6$^{rb}$.

[212] A Corpus Christi liturgy was adopted by the Praemonstratensian order in 1322, Lefèvre (1957), pp. 50–1.

[213] *Medieval and Renaissance illuminated manuscripts in Australian collections*, pp. 28, 37–8: Box Hill (Victoria), St Paschal's College, fol. 252, and a sequence for Corpus Christi with additions at fols. 390$^r$–4$^r$. It is also a later addition to a later thirteenth-century gradual of the Cistercian abbey of St Stephen in Cornu (Lodi diocese), *ibid*, pp. 27–8 (New South Wales State Library Dixson Q3/1, fol. 195r).

[214] Cambridge Fitzwilliam Museum CFM 5, fols. 295$^r$–300$^r$.

[215] Vatican Ottob. Lat. 140, Corpus Christi on fols. 368$^{vb}$–72$^{vb}$; also an even younger office of the Visitation, fols. 377$^v$–80$^r$.

[216] BN lat. 838, it is a later addition.

metropolitan church of Genoa of $1313 \times 21$.[217] Thus in Italy the feast was added to numerous thirteenth-century books, and becomes integrated into the *temporale*, the sequence of regular feasts, fairly soon after the feast's revival in the early fourteenth century.[218]

In France as in Italy there are few cases of entry before 1317, and those occur in local pockets late in the thirteenth century. A missal of Bec of $1265 \times 72$ has no Corpus Christi office in the original,[219] nor does a late-thirteenth-century Trinitarian missal and breviary,[220] or a Cistercian missal of 1299,[221] or the missal of Sens of $1292 \times 1309$.[222] A number of early-fourteenth-century books do not contain the feast's office in the original – the Cambrai missal,[223] the Paris missal[224] – and the pontifical of Durandus contains no benediction for Corpus Christi.[225]

As the feast was adopted, it was sometimes introduced into some very old books, such as the fragmentary twelfth-century missal of St Etienne of Caen, to which it was added between the calendar and the temporal in the fourteenth century.[226] The Corpus Christi office was inserted into the missal of Notre Dame of Paris of *c.* 1200, at its very end,[227] as it was in an early-thirteenth-century Evreux missal, after the section of votive masses and the mass for the dead.[228] The mass was copied into a blank quire after a section of proses in a Paris missal of mid thirteenth century (after 1247),[229] and the whole office was added in a series of additions at the end of a thirteenth-century Chartres breviary together with masses for St Anne and St Fiacre.[230]

The first examples of organic incorporation into liturgical manuscripts of French origin probably predate the feast's refoundation, as in a missal of St Trophime of Arles, written under Bishop Fougères (1308–17), where the mass and office appear in their proper temporal sequence

[217] Cambiaso (1917), p. 63.
[218] We must, of course, remember that Venice celebrated the feast from 1295, Muir (1981), pp. 223–4.
[219] BN lat. 1105.
[220] BN lat. 1022.
[221] BN lat. 9444; it is added on fol. 4 before the beginning of the text in a hand not much younger than the original.
[222] *Les Sacramentaires et les missels manuscrits* II, no. 356, pp. 172–3 (Auxerre Cathedral treasury 8).
[223] BN lat. 17311.
[224] Paris Arsenal 203; it was added later on fols. $35^r$–$36^r$.
[225] This was added at the end before the table of contents, in a later hand, on fols. 193–4.
[226] BN Nouv. acq. lat. 1590, fols. 7–8; before the calendar in a French Franciscan missal, Vatican ASP E 9, fols. $2^{va}$–$3^{va}$.
[227] Cambridge Fitzwilliam Museum 84–1972; and in an appendix after a paschal table at the end of a French breviary of Carpentras, Vatican Burgh. 53, fols. $386^{ra}$–$92^{vb}$.
[228] BN nouv. acq. lat. 1773, fol. 280.
[229] BN lat. 9441, fols. $430^r$–$2^r$.
[230] Vat. lat. 4756, fols. $358^r$–$69^v$.

after the feast of the Holy Trinity.[231] A breviary of Apt of 1317×23
includes the feast, and it may have been known there as early as 1277
when it was used in a dating clause.[232] Some early-fourteenth-century
examples which cannot be precisely dated may also have antedated the
year 1317, like the pontifical of Durandus with Corpus Christi in the
temporal, as well as after the mass of the feast of dedication,[233] or the
Arles missal where the office appears in a miscellaneous section after the
votive masses.[234] There was obviously a penetration of the feast in
southern France, in areas of papal influence, already before 1317. In
other early-fourteenth-century liturgical books the proper place for the
new office and mass was being sought: the Carmelite missal has it
between two votive masses,[235] a Paris missal of 1313×17 had it at the
very end,[236] the 1321 missal of St Arnoul of Metz places it properly in the
temporal after the feast of the Holy Trinity,[237] as does the 1325 missal of
Châlons-sur-Marne.[238] Thus, by the mid fourteenth century the
Corpus Christi office had become an organic part of the French
missal.[239] Other liturgical books were also quick to adopt the feast:[240] a
Book of Hours of 1330 included hours for Corpus Christi,[241] the 1337
psalter-hymnal of Aix-en-Provence already included a set of Corpus
Christi hymns with notes, in its proper temporal sequence,[242] and a
breviary of the diocese of Rodez of after 1360 incorporated John XXII's
rubric for the feast.[243] Yet even in the later fourteenth century there are
examples of Corpus Christi offices placed out of sequence, like a Paris
missal of after 1348 where the 'officium nove sollemnitatis corporis
Domini' was placed after the votive masses,[244] or the Châlons-sur-
Marne missal of 1392 which has it at the end of the temporal.[245]

In books of northern Germany the feast took its place in the liturgical
routine early on and with comparative ease. To an eleventh-century
psalter of St Mary's abbey near Heidelberg a Corpus Christi sermon was

[231] BN lat. 875, fols. 122$^{va}$–5$^{rb}$.
[232] Saxer (1971), pp. 118–19.
[233] BN lat. 733, fol. 158$^r$ and 166$^v$.
[234] BN lat. 839, fols. 157$^{vb}$–8$^{rb}$.
[235] BN lat. 884, fols. 328$^{va}$–29$^{vb}$.
[236] Paris Arsenal 601, fols. 429$^{ra}$–31$^{vb}$.
[237] *Les Sacrementaires et les missels manuscrits* II, no. 382, p. 206 (Metz Municipal library 133, fol. 139$^r$).
[238] BN lat. 842, fol. 103; *Les Sacrementaires et les missels manuscrits* II, no. 385, p. 209.
[239] See also BN Nouv. acq. lat. 1689.
[240] Like the breviary BN lat. 1052 and the hymnal BN lat. 767.
[241] Vatican Chigi D V 71, fols. 78$^v$–90$^v$. See Dumoutet (1932), pp. 135–6.
[242] BN 764, fols. 129$^v$–31$^r$.
[243] *Medieval manuscripts* III, p. 169 (Liverpool Cathedral Library 11, fol. 101$^r$).
[244] BN lat. 835, fols. 287–8.
[245] BN lat. 885, fols. 155$^{ra}$–56$^{ra}$.

added sometime in the thirteenth century.[246] By 1314 a collectory and a missal contained the mass in its temporal sequence.[247] Since Liège was in the archbishopric of Cologne, the feast would have reached Aachen early on; it was used for dating in 1302.[248] The feast was entered in the original hand of a fourteenth-century Cistercian missal of Cologne, albeit in an unsettled position, at the end, between the temporal and the creed.[249]

As to the spread in England, there is no trace whatsoever of the feast before the arrival of the *Clementines*. Numerous sources attest this *ex silencio*. The statutes of London of 1245 × 69 do not include it in the list of feast days,[250] nor does a list of 'festa indici debeant et observari' of the Exeter council of 1287 have it, but a fourteenth-century copy of these canons already does.[251] The book of Ralph of Baldock (1294–1305), dean of St Paul's, which is incorporated in a fifteenth century St Paul's customal, lists the order of procession on Christmas, Epiphany, Easter week, Pentecost, and on the feast St John the Baptist, and of Sts Peter and Paul, but omits Corpus Christi which, once instituted, was a major processional feast.[252] The arrival of Corpus Christi is not mentioned in the annals of St Mary's, York, which cover in detail the years 1258–1326,[253] nor was it listed in 1341 × 8 as one of the feasts on which the dean provided festive gifts of food to the clergy of Salisbury Cathedral.[254] The feast is not mentioned in the thirteenth-century Franciscan missal,[255] nor in the hymnal of St Augustine's, Canterbury, of *c.*1299.[256]

### THE FEAST'S ARRIVAL IN ENGLAND

By 1318 the feast had safely arrived in England. The mandate from Canterbury is not known, but other early diocesan references survive. On 4 June 1318 Bishop John Droxford of Bath and Wells sent a mandate

---

[246] Vatican Pal. lat. 39, fol. 1.
[247] Aachen Cathedral 40, fols. 92ᵛ–93ᵛ; Vatican Pal. lat. 500, fols. 113ᵛ–14ᵛ. See also Aachen Cathedral 33, pp. 122–32, and Aachen Cathedral 15, fols. 25ᵛ–8ᵛ, both of 1330, and on them, Gatzweiler (1924).
[248] *Ibid*, p. 201.
[249] Oxford Keble 54, fols. 281ᵛ–3ʳ.
[250] *CS* II, 2, pp. 655–6, c. 104.
[251] *CS* II, 2, c. 23, p. 1,022. The manuscripts of the Hyde Abbey missals of *c.*1270, *c.*1275 and *c.*1300 omit the feast, BL Harley 4664, CUL Ll.4.20, Oxford Bodleian Rawl. lit. e. I*.
[252] *Registrum statutorum et consuetudinum*, c. 43, p. 51.
[253] *St Mary's York*.
[254] *Hemingsby's register*, no. 313, p. 165, this is the earliest Salisbury Chapter act book of 1329 × 49.
[255] Oxford Bodleian lat. lit. f. 26.
[256] Cambridge SJC 262 (K21). For a list of surviving missals, see *Tracts on the mass*, pp. xiv–xv.

to his Official ordering him to publish the institution of Corpus Christi by the pope, and to establish it as a great solemnity, an occasion on which layfolk were exhorted to do penance and give alms, a day recommended for communion.[257] In 1318 St Peter's Monastery, Gloucester, already celebrated the feast:

In the year of the Lord 1318 the general celebration of the festivity of Corpus Christi was begun throughout the whole English church.[258]

In 1320 Bishop Walter Stapledon of Exeter included its celebration in a corrective ordinance for the priory of Polslo (Devon), following a visitation of the house:

Item, qe le servicz du Corps et du Sanke Nostre Seigneur Jhesu Crist soit fait od graunt solempnite entre vous chescun an, le Judi prochein apres la Trinité et par les Oytaves siwantes, si autre Feste de plus graunt solempnite ne viegne dedenz les ditz Oytaves si come en la constitucion del derein Concil de Vyene est establi et ordine.[259]

A few years after Canterbury the new feast was established in the York province; in June 1322 Archbishop Melton recommended it:

The glorious feast of the most precious sacrament of the flesh and blood of our Lord Jesus Christ (will be celebrated) on the Thursday after the Pentecost octaves every year, following the tenor, form and effect of the holiest Urban IV's letter published on this matter, . . . which was renewed by pope John XXII.[260]

In 1325 the chapter of the English Augustinians assembled at Northampton and instituted Corpus Christi as a double feast after the Canterbury usage,[261] and it appears in a list of *festa ferienda* in the statutes of Archbishop Simon Islip.[262]

As on the Continent, the feast was inserted into English liturgical

[257] *Reg. Dronkesford*, p. 13.
[258] 'Anno Domini millesimo trecentesimo decimo octavo incoepit festivitas de Corpore Christi generaliter celebrari per totam ecclesiam Anglicanam', *Historia monasterii sancti Petri Gloucestriae* I, p. 44.
[259] *Reg. Stapeldon*, pp. 316–17.
[260] '. . . gloriosum festum preciosissimi sacramenti corporis et sanguinis Domini nostri Jesu Christi quinta feria post octabas Pentecostes singulis annis juxta vim, formam et effectum sanctissimi . . . Urbani pape IIIIti dudum super hoc edite, ac per dictum . . . J. papam ut predicitur XXII innovate', York Borthwick Institute Reg. Melton, fol. 514$^r$.
[261] *Chapters*, p. 12.
[262] At Mayfield council, *Concilia* II, p. 560; on the attribution of these statutes, see *Lincoln Cathedral Statutes* III, pp. 542–5.

books in a variety of ways, but these were all later than 1317.[263] A whole section of fourteenth-century additions was appended to a summer missal for Benedictine use, of c.1200, including Corpus Christi.[264] Similarly, the two liturgical volumes of Gilbertine use bound together in the mid thirteenth century, later received into some empty space the mass of 'the feast of the transubstantiation of Christ's body' ('In festo transsubstanciacionis corporis Christi').[265] The office was added in a fourteenth-century-hand to a mid-thirteenth-century breviary-missal of Lewes Priory (Sussex),[266] and two fourteenth-century quires with the mass of Corpus Christi and of some other feasts, were added to a thirteenth-century Sarum missal.[267] A Sarum missal of c.1300 of the Augustinian canons of Hanlet Castle priory (Worcestershire) was updated as late as the fifteenth century to include the chants 'on the day of the new feast of Corpus Christi, at the procession' ('In die sollemnitatis nove corporis Xristi ad processionem'), and the mass of the day.[268]

Even in the fourteenth century new books were being produced without the Corpus Christi liturgy, such as the breviary of Hyde Abbey of c.1300, into which eight folios containing the feasts of the dedication, of Corpus Christi and of the Holy Trinity, were inserted.[269] Episcopal decrees must have included a copy of the Corpus Christi office, a quire which would have been used, or copied into the missal or breviary books, as the first stage of incorporation. Even when a book was copied afresh the new feast might linger for a while longer on the fringes of the temporal, when a book was copied without revision. In the visitations of Norwich of 1368 some parishes were reported as having separate books of the office, as in the case of Postwick (Norfolk) which had a 'quaternus de servicio corporis xristi', or Little Plumstead with 'unus quarterius de servicio corporis xristi'.[270] In some parishes the use of the separate book persists; the churchwardens of Sts Edmund and Thomas, Salisbury, paid 2s 4d in 1473/4 for 'j queyre bought with the story of Corpus Xristi'.[271] The provision of new liturgical books was the parishioners' duty, and

[263] Corpus Christi was not included in additions to the ordinal of Risby church (Suffolk) in 1278, BL Harley 1001, at fol. 162r.
[264] CUL Gg.3.21, fols. 153–256; Corpus Christi is at fol. 255ᵛ.
[265] Lincoln Cathedral Library 1.5.5 (155), fols. 74ᵛ–75ʳ.
[266] Cambridge Fitzwilliam 369, fols. 59ʳᵇ–74ʳᵇ.
[267] Arsenal 135, fols. 292ʳ–315ʳ.
[268] CUL Kk.2.6, fol. 112ʳ.
[269] Oxford Bodleian Rawlinson lit.e.1*, fols. 171–8.
[270] London PRO.E164.30. A transcript of this visitation report exists in the Norwich and Norfolk Record Office, NRO.MC16/8.
[271] *Salisbury, Sts Edmund and Thomas*, p. 15. See the inventory of St Stephen's, Genoa, with 'Duos quaternos de officio Corporis Xristi et aliud quaternum de corporis xristi ad legendum in nocte', Cambiaso (1917), p. 63.

10 Celebration of the mass in a private chapel

occasionally fell into neglect, with frequent complaints in the fifteenth century that for many new feasts the liturgy was not properly available.[272] The feast's absence from a missal need not mean that the feast was not celebrated in a parish; it could have been followed, as late as the fifteenth century, from a psalter 'cum servicio corporis Xristi', such as the one which Robert Samson, a married cleric of St Mary Castlegate, York, passed on after his death in 1463 to Terrington church near York;[273] from a didactic collection for the use of a parish priest, such as the mid- to late-fifteenth-century book bound with Mirk's *Festial* which included a selection of sequences among which was *Lauda, syon;*[274] or from the 'oon rede quire with certen masses and history of Corpus Christi', mentioned in the 1519 inventory of Rotherfield (Sussex), some 200 years after the feast's institution.[275]

Corpus Christi entered early into English liturgical books, such as at the very end of the Sarum missal of Sevenhampton (Wiltshire) of 1319×22.[276] But the spread was not uniform; the beautiful East Anglian Tiptoft missal of 1311×19 contains a lower marginal note at the office of the Trinity 'here the Corpus Christi service is missing' ('hic deficit servicium de corpore Christi'); presumably a separate quire was used.[277] The Corpus Christi mass also appears in a number of early-fourteenth-century liturgical books which are not precisely datable, but which are probably post-1318, such as a Franciscan missal with English decoration,[278] or in the partially surviving Chertsey breviary which includes an incomplete Corpus Christi office.[279] It was still a novelty to the copier of the Exeter ordinal of 1337,[280] but in the second half of the century was usually safely located within the temporal. It was added to the missal of St Peter's, Hereford, of 1358,[281] as in the hymnal section of a Cistercian breviary of *c.* 1360.[282] Yet even then, and as we have seen for Continental

[272] Pfaff (1970), p. 80. Archbishop Warham's visitation of Kent in 1510–11 reported such defect: Easter church lacked books for the Transfiguration and for the feast of the Name of Jesus, and at St Clement's, Sandwich, where books for the new feasts were lacking, these were soon provided by the parishioners, *Warham visitations*, pp. 100, 110–11.

[273] York Borthwick Institute Prob. Reg. 2, fol. 587ᵛ. Jeremy Goldberg kindly brought this to my attention.

[274] Leeds Brotherton Collection 502, fols. 117ʳ–38ᵛ.

[275] *Rotherfield*, p. 28.

[276] CUL Ee.2.2, fols. 201ᵛᵃ–202ᵛᵇ.

[277] *Gothic manuscripts 1285–1385* II, no. 78, pp. 84–6; (New York Pierpoint Morgan Library 107, fol. 176ᵛ).

[278] BN lat. 1332, fols. 280ᵛ–4ʳ. See also CUL Ff.2.31, fols. 130ʳᵃ–1ʳᵃ.

[279] Oxford Bodleian lat.lit.e.39, fols. 178ᵛᵇ–87ᵛᵇ.

[280] *Exeter ordinal*, pp. 129–33: 'officium nove sollempnitatis corporis domini nostri Iesu Christi celebrande singulis annis'.

[281] BL Add. 10926, fols. 64ʳ–5ᵛ.

[282] BL Burney 335, fol. 329ʳ.

liturgical books, the office can be oddly absent or strangely located, as in the missal of the parish of Shepton Beauchamp (Somerset) of the second half of the century which had the feast at the very end,[283] and its contemporary, a breviary to which the Corpus Christi office was added in a later hand, over an erasure and on the following five added leaves.[284]

The missal with the mass, and the breviary with the offices for the canonical hours for feast and octave, came to include the feast's liturgical rubric. This was provided already by John XXII, and confirmed by Clement VI (1342–52) who was forced to respond to complaints about the damage caused to the cult of saints whose feast-days occasionally coincided with the moveable feast of Corpus Christi or its octave. An especially difficult case was the feast of St John the Baptist, 24 June: the rubric recommended its deferral to the morrow when Corpus Christi coincided with it, and commemoration of the saint in the second vespers of Corpus Christi and during its octaves.[285] Yet the difficulties involved in the dissemination and incorporation of new liturgies meant that Corpus Christi was often referred to as a new feast even in the fifteenth century, as in the collection of new offices made for the monks of St Albans, together with the feasts of St Anne, St Oswyn, the feast of 10,000 virgins, the Name of Jesus, the Holy Cross, and St Gregory's feast.[286]

## IMAGES OF A NEW FEAST

Corpus Christi also forced illuminators to create an iconography for the decoration of the office of the eucharistic feast.[287] As long as the feast was added into books there was little scope for decoration, but with its entry into the liturgical sequence by the middle of the fourteenth century, new conventions emerged. The initial C of the introit of the mass 'Cibavit eos ex adipe frumenti' and its environment were the usual spaces for decoration.[288] By far the earliest and most widespread choice was a scene of the elevation of the mass, already the favourite choice for the decoration of the canon of the mass.[289] Thus, the elevation decorated the Roman missal of Toulouse before 1344,[290] appeared in the Bolognese

[283] Liverpool Cathedral 29, fols. 231ʳ–2ᵛ, rather than after the Trinity, fol. 137ᵛ.
[284] Liverpool Cathedral 37, fols. 143ᵛ, 144–6, 146*, 147.
[285] *Le Cérémonial papal III: les textes avignonnais*, cs. 7–8, pp. 18–19, 256–7.
[286] Cambridge SJC 137**(E36), fols. 1–27.
[287] On the iconography of the eucharist in Belgian manuscripts, see de Boom (1946).
[288] Only rarely is the D of the prayer 'Deus qui nobis' chosen, as in Venice Marciana Library lat. 111(III)2116, fol. 177ᵛ; or in the English breviary, Oxford Bodleian Laud. misc. 3a, fol. 153ra.
[289] See above, pp. 131–5.
[290] *Les Sacrementaires et les missels* II, no. 394, pp. 220–1 (Toulouse Municipal Library 90, fol. 246ᵛ).

missal of 1340–60,[291] and persisted throughout the century, as in a Roman missal of before 1370, said to be that of Clement VII,[292] in a Book of Hours made for Philip the Brave, Duke of Burgundy after 1370,[293] in Charles V's breviary of 1380,[294] and in the English Carmelite missal of c.1393.[295]

A choice especially favoured in the Italian tradition was the scene of the Last Supper for the decoration of the feast which exalted the creation of the eucharist. Here the illuminators could draw from a firm tradition of representation in the *Biblia pauperum,* which laid rather greater stress on the paschal parallel, the presence of lamb, bread and wine on the table. In the context of Corpus Christi the eucharistic, rather than sacrificial, aspect was stressed, with only the host and the chalice, the eucharist as it was left to the world in the model of the Last Supper. It appears in a fragment of a fourteenth-century Florentine missal,[296] and in a Bolognese missal of c.1340–60 where Christ holds the host and chalice in his hands.[297] In an English example, the Carmelite missal of c.1393, the initial C was divided horizontally into an upper and a lower register, one occupied by the Last Supper, and the other by an elevation scene (figure 19). This juxtaposition invoked the causal link between the two events, through a real reconstruction of the historic event, with bread and a bowl on the table, and two ribbons containing the words: 'Take and eat this is my body' ('Accipite et comedite hoc est corpus meum') and 'This chalice is the new testament in my blood' ('Hic calix novum testamentum meo sanguine').[298] Around 1412×13 a Flemish illuminator combined the themes of the Last Supper and communion in the initial C in the Turin–Milan Hours.[299] A Sarum breviary made for Margaret of York in the 1470s and decorated in Ghent, has in the initial S of the Corpus Christi vespers a scene of the Last Supper showing Judas with the sop.[300]

The letter S of the vespers opening with 'Sacerdos in aeternum' gave

[291] Vatican ASP B 63, fol. 227ᵛ.
[292] *Les Sacrementaires et les missels manuscrits* II, no. 496, pp. 324–5 (Avignon Municipal Library 136, fol. 152ʳ).
[293] It followed the Use of Paris, Cambridge Fitzwilliam Museum 3–1954, fol. 189v.
[294] BN lat. 1052, fol. 157rb, for a reproduction see Calkins (1983), plate 126, p. 231.
[295] BL Add. 44892, fol. 38ʳᵇ; admittedly here it is joined with a scene of the Last Supper, on which more below, pp. 298–302.
[296] *Italian manuscripts in the Pierpont Morgan Library,* plate 29; (New York Pierpont Morgan M653–4).
[297] Vatican Archivio San Pietro B63, fol. 227ᵛ.
[298] BL Add. 44892, fol. 38ʳ; Rickert (1941).
[299] On the manuscript, see Panofsky (1953) I, pp. 45–50 (Turin Civic Museum, fol. 90ʳ).
[300] Cambridge St John's College 215 (H13), fol. 57ᵛᵃ; this scene is one of only two miniatures in this fine book.

rise to representations of Christ as priest.[301] This theme is consonant with the growing tendency to turn the Last Supper into a eucharistic event in the context of Corpus Christi. A late-fourteenth-century French breviary has Christ as priest performing the elevation at the table of the Last Supper, thus transporting the eucharistic ritual to the first eucharist.[302] Christ holds the host in front of a table with a chalice in a summer breviary of the Use of Paris of 1409×15, made for the King of France,[303] and a Venetian missal of 1456 shows Christ as a priest at an altar in the initial C of *Cibavit*.[304]

While the elevation was the earliest choice which seemed to capture the feast's intent and symbolic meaning, the experience of celebration, as it developed in the first decades following the foundation of Corpus Christi gradually entered the feast's iconography. Scenes of processions are represented in the initials of the mass by the 1340s: one early example is a missal of the Use of Rome produced during the episcopate of John Tixeradent, bishop of Rieux between 1322–48,[305] and is similar to an image from a festive French missal of mid-century,[306] and to a missal of the Hospitallers of Autun of the second half of the century.[307] The procession remained the dominant theme in French illumination, and a very popular one in Italian manuscript throughout the fifteenth century; it sometimes showed a priest or a bishop carrying the monstrance, often a transparent cylinder containing the host. It sometimes had a group of lay dignitaries carrying a canopy under which a priest carries a monstrance, or alternatively just two priests carry the monstrance on staves, like the missal of 1362 made for the Augustinian hermits of Toulouse.[308] Some scenes simply show a priest preceded by a lay person carrying a banner and followed by one of two acolytes – more of a parochial scene – reminiscent of processions with the *viaticum*;[309] but

---

[301] The fragment of an Italian service book, an historiated initial S, shows a priest at elevation, and may have been the initial of the Corpus Christi office *Sacerdos*, Manchester John Rylands Library 14, miniature no. 26.

[302] New York Pierpont Morgan 12, fol. 302[r].

[303] *Les Breviaires manuscrits* I, no. 187, pp. 315–22 (Châteauroux Municipal Library 2, fol. 113[v]).

[304] Venice Marciana Library III(45)2444, fol. 196[va]. Drawing on the growing processional imagery of Corpus Christi, a Westphalian Augustinian breviary of 1464 shows a priest holding a monstrance, Oxford Bodleian Can. lit. 286, fols. 164[va]–7[rb].

[305] *Les Sacrementaires et les missels manuscrits* II, no. 394, p. 221 (Toulouse Municipal Library 90, fol. 246[v]).

[306] Vatican Archivio San Pietro B 76, fol. 32[v].

[307] BN nouv. acq. lat. 1689, fol. 170[ra].

[308] Example: Toulouse Municipal Library 91, fol. 147[r]; on the use of the canopy, see Guenée and Lehoux (1968), p. 15, and below, chapter 4, pp. 251–5.

[309] See missal of St Maur-les-Fossés of the second half of the fifteenth century, Paris BN lat. 12061, fol. 98[rb].

most processional scenes became increasingly ordered and splendid. The missal of Etienne Loypeau, bishop of Luçon between 1388–1407, shows against a stylised checkered background so typical of the international Gothic style two priests in copes carrying the monstrance on staves covered with a red cloth, preceded by two banner-carriers and followed by two clergymen and three laymen, one of whom was obviously a nobleman.[310] A missal of Rennes of the early fifteenth century shows two bishops carrying a church-shaped tabernacle on staves, followed by three laymen.[311] The English Fitzwilliam Missal, which was produced in Yorkshire c.1470, has an initial C at the beginning of the Corpus Christi mass, filled with an image of a church-shaped tabernacle upon draped staves.[312] This depiction of Corpus Christi shows the feast as it came to be lived in towns and countryside, in big and small, secular and religious communities, reflecting the ubiquity of processional ceremonial in the feast's celebration and the increasingly civic and sumptuous nature of the procession. The processional mode became an important image in the eucharistic symbolism, but its representation differed slightly in the various cultural spheres. It was the commonest choice in French manuscripts, not unusual in England, and less common in Italian and German iconography.

In Italy and Germany other iconographic themes were developing, and these tended to be more devotional in nature, such as the Man of Sorrows.[313] A fifteenth-century Venetian school of illumination produced a number of missals used in San Marco and for some Venetian religious houses, and decorated the Corpus Christi mass with the Man of Sorrows.[314] Other northern Italian books, such as the fourteenth-century Venetian[315] and the Roman,[316] and the missal made for Matthew Corvin, king of Hungary (ruled 1462–90),[317] show a scene of communion, but the majority still chose the elevation (figure 3). Other devotional themes, such as the Mass of St Gregory and the monstrance on an altar, were developed on the pages of Books of Hours, and will be discussed in connection with eucharistic devotional practices.[318] An interesting combination of themes on a single page of the sumptuous Turin–Milan Hours brought together a scene of the Last Supper at the

[310] Paris BN lat. 8886, fol. 325ᵛ.
[311] BN lat. 1098, fol. 149ᵛᵇ.
[312] Cambridge Fitzwilliam Museum 34, p. 212; see plate in *York art*, p. 71.
[313] On the Man of Sorrows in Italian art, see Eisler (1969).
[314] Venice Marciana III(18)2283–4, fol. 58ᵛ; III(120)2478, fol. 191ᵛᵃ.
[315] Venice Marciana Library III(111)2116, fol. 176ʳ.
[316] Vatican Rossiano 178, fol. 121ʳ.
[317] Vatican Urb. lat. 110, fol. 128ᵛ.
[318] Below, pp. 288–94, 308–10.

top, followed by an initial C showing a monstrance opening the mass, and a scene of communion at the bottom of the page.[319]

Corpus Christi was also taken up within existing liturgical practice in the celebration of votive masses which was growing in the thirteenth and fourteenth centuries.[320] It was included in missals such as the Flemish Franciscan missal of *c.* 1400 which had a section of votive masses.[321] In some cases it was inserted, as it was in the fifteenth century, into the front of a missal of *c.* 1300 belonging to the hermits of Monte Fiascone.[322] Corpus Christi's office was also arranged as a mass for Thursdays at Clare Hall, Cambridge, by 1359,[323] as it was in the use of an English monastic house in the late fifteenth century.[324] We even find it on the dorse of a role containing carols, where a number of masses including *Cibavit* and the masses for Holy Trinity, the angels and the Holy Ghost, were copied out.[325]

### FUNDING AND ADMINISTERING THE NEW FEAST

Being a moveable feast the date of Corpus Christi was harder to recall. The *Livre des métiers,* a French poem of conversation and manners of 1349, praises the maid Agnes who knew her moveable feasts:

> Agnies no meskine
> sciet bien nommer
> le v festes qui ne sont mie
> escriptes ou calendrier . . .
> La feste de pasques,
> L'Ascension, le Penthecouste,
> le Trinitet et le sacrement . . .[326]

The calendar of the priory of St Victor of Marseille was updated in the early fourteenth century and at the entry for the date 25 May it had an addition related to Corpus Christi:

---

[319] Lane (1984), plate 74 (Turin Civic Museum Hours of Turin–Milan, fol. 90ʳ).
[320] Dumoutet (1924–5).
[321] Oxford Bodleian Can. lit. 389, fols. 228ʳ–9ʳ.
[322] In a section of miscellany at the beginning which also included a paschal table, calendar and other votive masses, Vatican Rossiani 199, fols. 1–12.
[323] Clement Maydstone, *The tracts,* p. 175.
[324] CUL Hh.6.15, fols. 5ʳ–7ʳ.
[325] Cambridge Trinity O.3.5.8, dorse.
[326] *Livre des métiers,* p. 24. The whole household would have celebrated Corpus Christi together in households of the nobility and the gentry, such as described in Mertes (1987), p. 132.

Note that on Thursday after the octave of Pentecost, the feast of the holy eucharist will always be celebrated in copes and it will have a simple octave.[327]

and noted on the following Sunday, at 28 May:

On the first Sunday after the octaves of Pentecost, which is in the octave of the Eucharist, there will be a full [office] of this octave including the Sunday.[328]

Its placing in the calendar was an intrusion into the liturgical routine, and rubrics were formulated to regulate possible clashes. John XXII, followed by Clement VI (1342–52), provided rubrics with solutions for such difficulties, and these were supplemented by local usages.[329] Clement Maydstone evolved a system in the fifteenth century for followers of the Sarum Use, which settled the problem of superimposition of the octave of Holy Trinity and the Sunday in Corpus Christi.[330]

Established in liturgical books, and indicated in calendars, the feast was gradually blended into the routines of religious houses and parishes, and we tend to know more about the former, through their customals and statute books. Sources of income were ear-marked for the celebration of the new feast, models for its celebration were to be determined, such as befitted it and the house's traditions, and responsibilities for its organisation and celebration were allocated. About 1301 the abbot of St Godeschard in Hildesheim allotted one mark from the wine-tax paid by the town towards the expenses of the new feast.[331] By 1319 Corpus Christi was observed by the canons of Zurich Cathedral, who contributed one mark of their annual income to its maintenance.[332] The chapter statute book of 1346 allocated the responsibilities connected with the new feast: the sacrist was in charge of bell-ringing, the doctor in charge of poor scholars supervised their attendance, and the chamberlain distributed the same lavish pittances as were customary on the feast of the patron saints Felix and Regula: measures of wheat, of loaves of bread and of pennies.[333] Recognising the new needs which a major feast created, and the benefits accrued by supporting it, bishops, the clergy and the laity offered support in legacies and gifts attached to the feast:

---

[327] 'Nota quod feria v post octabas Pentecostes semper celebratur festum S. Eucharistie in omnibus capis et habet octabas simplices', Saxer (1966), n. 23, p. 279.

[328] 'Dominica prima post octabas Pentecostes, que est infra octabas Eucharistie, fit totum de ipsis octabis et cum de dominica', *ibid*, n. 24, p. 479; see also Guillereau (1911–13), p. 394.

[329] *Le cérémonial papal* III, pp. 254–8.

[330] Clement Maydston, *The tracts*, pp. xx–xxi, c. 21, p. 34; p. 126.

[331] *Urkunden der Stadt Hildesheim*, no. 558, p. 306.

[332] *Zurich cathedral statutes*, pp. 114–19. The entry payments of one mark made by entrants to the community were also allocated to Corpus Christi expenditure.

[333] *Ibid*, pp. 44, 57, 267.

Catherine Ibsung left property in Augsburg to the cathedral for due celebration of the Corpus Christi procession.[334]

The feast was properly established at Rennes cathedral in 1318.[335] At St Victor's in Marseille, All Saints' was used as a model for the celebration of Corpus Christi when it was introduced in 1324: similar lighting and ornaments were provided on the vigils and an octave, and a full office on the Sunday in the octave; it shared All Saints' precedence over other feasts even if not its fixed place in the calendar.[336] In the statutes of the collegiate church of St Mary Ottery, Exeter, of 1339, Corpus Christi is a major double feast, celebrated not as a principal (Christmas, Epiphany, Pentecost, All Saints) but as a secondary feast.[337] In Florence the synod of 1327 urged priests to encourage the laity to come to church, especially on the feasts of the town's patrons, Sts Zenobius and Reparata, and on Corpus Christi.[338]

## DEDICATIONS AND INDULGENCES FOR CORPUS CHRISTI

Thus, Corpus Christi was finding its way into not only liturgical books, calendars and customals, but into a wide array of uses in which its symbolic content was applied. Since by 1200 the English parochial system was largely established, we should not expect the new devotional interests to be reflected in the dedications of parish churches. Only one case is known in England, St Mary and Corpus Christi in Hatherley Down (Gloucestershire).[339] In Germany, and especially in Bavaria, there are tens of churches dedicated to Corpus Christi, some of which acquired their titles after a local eucharistic miracle.[340] Corpus Christi would seem more likely to be chosen for new religious houses, but there are not many examples of this kind. Strikingly, it was adopted by an academic college in both Cambridge and Oxford. In Cambridge the college was related to a fraternity which founded it in 1351–2 from the inherited wealth of its deceased members, decimated by the Black Death, and through the efforts of the surviving members of this patrician fraternity.[341] Its counterpart in Oxford was founded in 1513, by a notable devotee of 'conservative' religion.[342] A licence granted in 1348 to

---

[334] Kellner (1908), p. 124.

[335] Guillotin de Corson (1879), p. 6.

[336] Guillereau (1911–13), p. 394. See above about rubric for regulation of clashes, p. 204.

[337] *The collegiate church of Ottery St Mary*, statute 77, c. 11, p. 242.

[338] Trexler (1964), pp. 10, 32.

[339] Arnold Forster (1899) I, p. 35. It was common to dedicate to Mary and to another saint.

[340] For analysis of German dedications, see Bauerreiss (1931), pp. 36–75.

[341] On these foundations, see below, p. 234.

[342] Richard Fox chose to place his chantry next to the shrine of St Swithun in Winchester cathedral.

the provost of Beverley Minster allowed him to found a chantry and a
Corpus Christi altar in it, to be endowed in the hands of the Corpus
Christi fraternity, to which the chantry founder had belonged.[343] In
1400 a chantry was founded at the Corpus Christi altar of Newark
Church, similarly related to a local Corpus Christi fraternity.[344] The
existence of a Corpus Christi fraternity encouraged the creation of
Corpus Christi altars in churches, such as in Holy Trinity Church,
Hull.[345] Other dedications are a chapel of Corpus Christi in the college
of St Laurence of Pountenay in London, which existed by 1347, when
the bishop of Rochester entered an agreement to farm Speedhurst
Church to 'magister sive custos capelle collegiate corporis Christi,
London',[346] and which was held by Nicholas Mockyng, subdeacon of
Wells, by papal licence of 1411.[347] There was a Corpus Christi house of
the Augustinian friars in Benfada, diocese of Achnory, c.1444/5.[348]
Corpus Christi did not suggest a sufficiently familiar and local, an
intimate focus of patronage, in its abstract and all-encompassing meanings. So universal in its implications, it lacked familiarity that could be
developed in relation to the image of a saint.

Corpus Christi was a new feast, and as such required some help and
encouragement. The bull of foundation granted a moderate forty days'
indulgence to those who attended its office, and as its processional aspect
developed and required widespread participation, processions too were
furnished with such rewards.[349] Pope Martin V (1417–31) and later
Eugenius IV (1431–47), granted indulgences which were attached to the
procession.[350] Besides papal grants there was a myriad of indulgences by
bishops and for the benefit of particular religious houses: the visitors of
the Augustinian priory church of the Holy Trinity at Mottisfont, in
Winchester diocese, on the feast of its dedication and other major feasts,
including Corpus Christi, would enjoy an indulgence granted in
1457.[351] That the feast was an effective occasion to display an indulgence

---

[343] *IqD* 22 Ed 3, no. 34; *Beverley minster*, p. lx; Leach (1893–5).

[344] *Reg. Scrope* I, no. 56, p. 80. On the fraternity, founded c.1351, see Westlake (1919), return 385, p. 222.

[345] Heath (1984), p. 223.

[346] *Reg. Hethe*, pp. 825–6, and in 1349 he instituted a vicar, p. 886.

[347] *CPL* VI, p. 292.

[348] *CPL* IX, p. 455.

[349] See the text in Franceschini (1965), p. 239. John XXII extended this indulgence to the burgesses of Tolouse in 1318, John XXII, *Lettres communes* II, no. 7296; see also III, no. 11366.

[350] Eugenius IV's *Excellentissimus* was published in May 1433 at the council of Basle and it doubled the indulgences granted by Urban IV to those attending the Corpus Christi offices, Kellner (1908), p. 124. The bull was appended to Caxton's 1498 edition of Mirk's *Festial*.

[351] *CPL* XI, p. 146.

is made clear at least in the case of St Leonard's, Hythe (Kent), which recorded the income from its indulgences: Corpus Christi accounted for the highest collection, 5d out of a total of 16d in 1412/13, while only 3d were collected on either All Saints' or the Assumption.[352] Indulgences could be acquired by influential people for particular aims; Joan Holland, duchess of Brittany, need not have gone to church to enjoy the benefits of Corpus Christi preaching from 1369 on, since a hundred days' penance were relaxed for her by Urban V's indulgence, which applied on the occasion of preaching, even in her chapel, in her presence on Corpus Christi.[353] Interest in Corpus Christi is reflected in another papal indulgence of 1391 granted to All Saints' Church in Moulton in Lincolnshire, relaxing the penance of those visiting it on the feast and contributing to its repair.[354] Continental examples are very numerous, as traffic in indulgences was, on the whole, more lively there than in England; as early as 1283, the visitors to the Dominicans of Warburg on Corpus Christi and other feasts were granted forty days' indulgence,[355] and the feast was commonly mentioned among the great feasts on which those attending the office were granted indulgence of enjoined penance.[356]

Corpus Christi was becoming part of the ritual rhythm of the year, its liturgy assimilated, the tasks of its celebration allocated, its hymns learnt, its images considered and thought out. As its meanings, possibilities and associations within the symbolic system were recognised and interpreted, it developed into a living feast. Its eucharistic currency was becoming recognised, realised, and thus negotiable, communicable, and most strikingly – exchangeable for *power*.

[352] *Hythe, St Leonard's*, p. 246.
[353] The original was granted in 1369, and was renewed in 1371 as in *CPL* IV, p. 165.
[354] *CPL* IV, p. 392.
[355] Fürstenberg (1917), p. 315.
[356] See, for example, the study of indulgences to Belgian houses, Delehaye (1926–27).

# CHAPTER 4

# The living feast: sermons, fraternities, processions and drama

## PREACHING ON CORPUS CHRISTI

Like all major feasts, and especially as a summer feast which drew crowds, Corpus Christi was seen as a suitable occasion for public preaching.[1] The centrality of the symbol which it celebrated meant that some of the most fundamental claims of the sacramental world-view were addressed in Corpus Christi sermons. If Easter week was the annual occasion for teaching the articles of faith and for sermons which dealt with events in Christ's life culminating in the Passion, Corpus Christi was a time for more explicit instruction on the sacraments, particularly on the eucharist. We encounter Corpus Christi sermons from about the mid fourteenth century; it was one of the four *dies praedicabiles* of the University of Cambridge when sermons were preached in Great St Mary's.[2] The preaching diary of Archbishop Richard FitzRalph of Armagh, which covers events in the period 1344–1359, records sermons on Sunday in the octave of Corpus Christi 1355 'ad populum' near Greenock in the diocese of Dublin, and at St Paul's, London, on Sunday in the octave in 1356.[3] Indulgences were sometimes attached to attendance at Corpus Christi sermons, which were becoming increasingly public events.[4] Corpus Christi was deemed sufficiently popular and public in Oxford in 1382 for Philip Repyngdon to voice his views on the eucharist on it, with the support of the University

---

[1] For basic orientation in the study of sermons, see Bataillon (1980). Although the day called for preaching, when its other ceremonial vestiges became too elaborate or lengthy, the sermon could be eliminated, as happened in the fifteenth-century papal curia, Dykmans (1985), pp. 14–15.

[2] Corpus Christi was added as a preaching day to clause 168 of the *Statuta antiqua* (after 1304) besides the first Sunday in Advent, Septuagesima Sunday and Ash Wednesday, *Documents relating to the university and colleges of Cambridge* I, p. 398; Hackett (1970), p. 242, n. 1.

[3] Gwynn (1937–38), no. 49, p. 53; no. 60, p. 54. Another entry on an English sermon preached to some nuns in London on Corpus Christi 1355 must be wrongly dated since FitzRalph was in Ireland at the time, *ibid*, no. 59, p. 54. On FitzRalph's preaching see Owst (1926), p. 13.

[4] *CPL* IV, p. 165.

chancellor, and conversely for a harsh attempt to deny him the opportunity in a letter of denunciation of Archbishop Courtenay.[5]

As they became an established practice, sermons were performed in a variety of venues, and were financed in many ways. The 1388 statutes of the Corpus Christi fraternity of Belluno (Veneto) required that a sermon be preached on the feast and discuss amongst other matters 'that salvific sacrament of the body and blood of Christ', and all members were required to attend.[6] In 1468 the council of the city of York paid for a sermon to be delivered in the minster chapel on the morrow of Corpus Christi.[7]

Thus, some of the great late-medieval sermon cycles included a sermon for Corpus Christi, such as those of Eckhart, Peregrinus of Oppeln, John Mirk, Gabriel Biel; but by no means all. A number of Sunday cycles which included sermons for the major feasts such as Christmas and Easter also provided a Corpus Christi sermon.[8] Well into the fifteenth century temporal cycles of sermons for the feast failed to provide a Corpus Christi sermon, such as the cycle of sermons in 1432 which belonged to a Praemonstratensian house in Nottinghamshire.[9] Like the liturgy, Corpus Christi sermons may have circulated in separate books and quires before being incorporated into books of sermons.

The absence of specific preaching material for the most doctrinal of feasts may have been due to the fact Corpus Christi was often served by pre-existing material. It was an attractive occasion for preaching, but the theme of Corpus Christi raised the problem inherent in its character as a feast of a symbol, a concept, a world-view rather than of a saint, or a commemoration of a particular historic event. After a period of experimentation when obvious material from Maundy Thursday preaching was used, some themes arise, like an exposition on transubstantiation for lay audiences,[10] and a symbolic exegesis on one of the 'eucharistic' biblical texts, for the Latin preaching to clerics.[11]

---

[5] *Fasciculi zizaniorum*, pp. 299–301. Kightly (1975), p. 48; Hudson (1986), pp. 69, 71–2; Hudson (1988b), pp. 70–1, 97.

[6] 'De eodem salutifero sacramento corporis videlicet et sanguinis Christi', Barbiero (1944), c. 14, p. 252.

[7] *REED: York* I, p. 102, 3s 4d were paid for it 'curialitate datis cuidem fratri Augustino predicanti in crastino dicti festi in Capillo Ecclesie Cathedralis'; Johnston (1973–4), p. 58. On processional preaching, see Owst (1926), pp. 195–221.

[8] See for example Oxford Bodleian e Musaeo 180 which includes sermons for Ascension, Christmas, Circumcision, Epiphany, Ash Wednesday, Dedication and Corpus Christi.

[9] Manchester. John Rylands Library Eng. 109 and Norwich Cathedral 5.

[10] Like Mirk's choice in *Festial*, pp. 168–75.

[11] These spheres are definitely not separate, see Erikson (1976), pp. 80–2, on the combination of vernacular and exegetical imagery. See above an example of a clerical sermon

The most commonly used were sermons 'De Corpore Christi' or 'De eucharistia' written for Maundy Thursday, when the theme of the foundation of the eucharist at the Last Supper was addressed. The series of sermons written by Thomas Brinton, bishop of Rochester, includes no item specifically devoted to the feast, but all three Maundy Thursday sermons for 1375, 1376 and 1378 were dedicated to the eucharist.[12] In these the background for the institution of the eucharist is discussed in terms of the link between the historic Supper and the daily celebration of mass. In his Easter sermons Brinton also dwelt on the effects and merits of attendance at mass and reception of communion. In the Easter sermon of 1375, the mass is considered as a test of faith, since 'all senses are deceived in this sacrament, except for the sense of sound' ('omnes sensus in hoc sacramento deficiunt, excepto audito'), a theme much discussed in the Corpus Christi liturgy.[13] The merits of the mass are spelt out here: it liberates from evil, confirms virtue, deletes venial sins.[14] In his Easter sermon of 1374 Brinton also invoked the eucharist at the end of his discussion of Christ's shedding of his blood, the main theme of the sermon.[15] A similar exposition was made by Pier Filippo Pandolfini in his sermon to the Company of the Magi of Venice on Maundy Thursday 1476. He stressed that the eucharist was a memorial, and that the bread and wine are mere figures of the flesh and blood which were given not only to Christ's disciples at the Last Supper but to the confraternity members: 'Our travel-fare to lead us to the real and true confines of the celestial land where he who is alive reigns'.[16] Thus, a store of issues which were related with the eucharist's foundation and to the nature of reception of communion had already been created for the Maundy Thursday and Easter sermons; some of these formed the basis of Corpus Christi preaching, and seem to have provided material for many preachers until the purpose-designed vernacular Corpus Christi sermons such as Mirk's appeared. Such material would have been used to create the Middle English Easter sermon on the eucharist based on John 6,59 ('Qui manducat'), where a store of *exempla* together with doctrinal formulations on eucharistic matters were combined in an extensive exposition on the sacrament.[17] Thus, the peculiarity of a

based on 'Hoc est corpus meum' for the mixed fraternity of Corpus Christi, York, discussed below on p. 242.

[12] Thomas Brinton, *Sermons*, no. 55, p. 248–51; no. 67, pp. 304–306; no. 97, pp. 445–8.

[13] *Ibid*, no. 40, pp. 177–80, at p. 178.

[14] *Ibid*, p. 179, also pp. 251, 305, 371.

[15] *Ibid*, no. 37, pp. 157–62, at p. 162.

[16] 'Nostrô vjatico a condurci a quello vero e perpetuo convito nella patria celestiale dove regna coluj che è vivo', Hatfield (1970), p. 156. See a Milanese example Tamborini (1935), p. 7.

[17] *Middle English sermons*, pp. 125–33.

feast which celebrated all that was salvific, hopeful and efficacious and yet which lacked models for its pastoral exposition baffled sermon writers, who were forced on this occasion to adopt kindred material to good effect. Nevertheless, we do know of some sermons written for the day and which considered the feast as a special event which required particular intellectual consideration, as a living eucharistic affirmation, not merely as a memorial of the Last Supper or Passion. These sermons will now be examined in detail.

Such a separate composition for Corpus Christi was the English vernacular treatise-sermon which survives in three versions, the 'Sermo de corpore Christi'.[18] Each version enshrines a stage of its development from a model sermon, through extrapolation and exemplification, into a veritable tract on the eucharist, transubstantiation, the ten commandments, and the foundation and significance of the feast.[19] This sermon became truly encyclopaedic.[20] It opens with the story of Exodus, God's providence and the protection He gave the Jews in the desert, where manna was provided for their sustenance:

> God dude lete reyne a-doun
> As hit were flour gret foysun,
> Manna, o hit is I-write,
> And is I-clept Angeles Mete.[21]

Here a digression occurs to warn against usurers and regrators, likened to those who gathered more manna than was necessary for a day's fare, showing their lack of faith in God's provision:

> Þerfore god wroþ was
> Þat þei trist not to his gras.[22]

Returning to his main narrative, the writer passes to the Christian era, when God's love became even greater, and the food He provided even better – God's body itself:

> Now is wel sene to-day
> Þat he loueþ us more þen þay
> Ffor he ne sende hem but Angel brede,
> Þat lasteþ but a day to nede,

---

[18] The three versions are collated in *The minor poems of the Vernon ms.* I, pp. 168–97, and is followed on pp. 198–221 by 'septem miracula de corpore cristi', a section of *Handlyng synne,* which follows the sermon in the Vernon manuscript. On English sermons in general, see Heffernan (1984).

[19] The progression is from the oldest manuscript, a northern version, BL Harley 4196, through CUL Dd.1.1 and into the fullest version in the Vernon ms.

[20] On this development, see Owst (1926), pp. 282–4.

[21] *The minor poems of the Vernon ms.,* lines 37–40, p. 170.

[22] *Ibid,* lines 103–4, p. 173.

> He haþ send us a Ricchor sonde:
> His owne bodi, ich understonde.[23]

Next follows a classic *exemplum*, still bound in the opposition of Old and New Testament. A Christian and a Jew travelling together enter a church, and only the Jew is visited with a vision of the bleeding Christ in the hands of Christians. To the question why only he could see it the answer is given:

> And þy kun made hym dye,
> Þerfore al blodi þou hym seȝe.[24]

The miracle is explained as proving that the bread 'is godus flesch', and although it is divided it remains whole, like the image on the fragments of a mirror (line 205). And this type of bread has useful qualities arming one for the battle against sin: its whiteness against lechery, its thinness against sloth, its sweet wheat against bitter wrath, its unleavened quality against envy (which makes men swell), the pureness of its wheat against covetousness, its cleanness and smallness against pride.[25]

From the personal to the collective, discussion now returns into the orbit of Christian history as the eucharist is considered for its place in the Christian world. Through the Last Supper, when God said 'Do þis in þe muynde of me', communities were created; those who received it worthily and those who did not. The words of St Paul in I Cor. 11, 29, the epistle for the feast, are paraphrased:

> Whose unworþiliche ȝode
> To fonge Godus fflesch and blode,
> Þere he fongeþ his owne dome.[26]

And in the words of John's gospel (John 48, 56–9), read on the feast, the bread is described as a source of life, the flesh in it is food and the blood in it is drink.

Having established the historic link between the Last Supper and the ever-repeated eucharist which Corpus Christi celebrated, and its scriptural basis, the sermon proceeds to explore the salvific nature of this sacrament which was passed on to the Church for posterity. Difficult as it may seem it exhorts:

---

[23] *Ibid*, lines 115–20, p. 174. This theme of 'how much better' is also explored in an Easter sermon preached by Pandolfini in 1468: 'E nostri antichi padri del Testamento Vecchio non potrebbono havere questo singularissimo dono, se nonn per modo di similitudine et di figura', Hatfield (1970), pp. 153–4.

[24] *The minor poems of the Vernon ms.*, lines 197–8, p. 177.

[25] *Ibid*, lines 221–46, pp. 178–9.

[26] *Ibid*, lines 269–71, p. 180.

Þis bred mihte neuermore be spende
Til God hym-self on eorþe hit sende
To same mon fro pyne of helle,
So þat he kepe hit welle.[27]

And the importance of worthy reception re-emerges quite clearly from
this; it is a prerequisite for an effective benefit from the salvific treasure.
Although in the past communion was taken every Sunday, it was now
enjoyed only thrice a year, or the very least, once.[28] This is made even
clearer by 'a luytel ensaumple' which tells of a sinful English priest who
had a vision on his sick-bed in which a child brought him a basket of
burning sacramental wafers, wafers which he understood to represent
those he had consumed unworthily. When one of the wafers was placed
on his hand it burnt it through and this taught him to live cleanly
thereafter.[29] The *moralitas* is given as:

I holde þe Mon more þen mad
Þat takeþ his bred and nis not drad
Of þe wreche þat mihte bi-falle.[30]

The sermon next turns to the historic development of the mass
liturgy from Christ's message to the apostles, which was a simple *Pater
noster* over bread and wine, without any vestments or precious vessels:

And in vessels of treo –
Non oþur chalys hedden heo.[31]

Later, through the work of popes which is described in detail, the
chalice and paten, the prayers, the *kyrie* and *gloria,* the vestments,
corporal, prefaces, *sanctus,* the *Pater noster* in the canon, were all
added. Here an opportunity was taken to repeat the *Pater noster* in
English, and to list the gifts of the Holy Spirit enfolded in it.[32] The
further layers of the mass liturgy, the memorials and invocation of the
Virgin, of martyrs and saints, is explained as a tribute to those who had
died for the sacrament!

Cecili, and Agnes, and Agace
Diede for þis bred of grace
Þerfore is riht heore names to be

---

[27] *Ibid*, lines 325–7, p. 182.
[28] Lateran IV requires annual communion, but most English synods attempted to enforce
three reception a year, see above, p. 69.
[29] *The minor poems of the Vernon ms.*, lines 351–90, pp. 183–5.
[30] *Ibid*, lines 391–3, p. 185.
[31] *Ibid*, lines 413–14, p. 187.
[32] *Ibid*, lines 464–90, pp. 189–90.

Nempned in þe Canone.[33]

Having surveyed the development of the mass from its historical source through its liturgical development, the sermon returns to its theme 'Panem angelorum manducavit homo', which in two of its versions appears at the head of the text. An apocalyptic perspective is given to the sacrament, as it is promised to secure one until Resurrection and until the heavenly feast with the Trinity. But more immediately, the earthly feast was an occasion for benefits, since honouring the sacrament on Corpus Christi was rewarded with Urban IV's indulgences. The later version of the sermon also mentions that John XXII had doubled this indulgence's fruits, and that Miler le Poer, bishop of Loughlin, granted forty additional days of pardon.[34] The sermon ends with a prayer that all men and women should be led to heaven.

This sermon was written for Corpus Christi sometime in the second quarter of the fourteenth century and copied soon after, about 1350, into the source of CUL Dd.1.1. It was eventually developed into the tract-version found in the Vernon manuscript of *c.*1390, which also includes a treatise 'Seven miracles of Corpus Christi', taken from Robert Mannyng of Brunne's *Handlyng synne.*[35] Mannyng's work is an English version of William of Wadington's *Manuel des pechez*, a thirteenth-century treatise on the vices and virtues, the articles of faith, the sacraments, following what we have identified as the Pecham programme. Mannyng's version is rich in *exempla* with particularly English flavour, few being drawn from the stock of Continental tales. In them Mannyng first deals with the thorny issue of transubstantiation, arguing that God who created all things had accomplished far more arduous tasks than it, after all:

> And some haue seye hyt bodyly
> To whom he shewed his mercy.[36]

A stock tale from the early Middle Ages follows: a doubting monk was not persuaded of the eucharistic power by argument, and only the miraculous appearance of a bleeding child on the altar convinced him.[37] Next, the unique qualities of the wafer render it effective to counter sin, a shorter version of this we have seen in the 'Sermo'.[38] But the wafer

---

[33] *Ibid*, lines 553–6, p. 194.
[34] *Ibid*, lines 587–622, pp. 195–7.
[35] On *Handlyng synne*, see above, p. 89.
[36] *Handlyng synne (a)*, lines 10,003–4, p. 249.
[37] *Ibid*, lines 10,006–82, pp. 249–50.
[38] *Ibid*, lines 10,089–146, pp. 252–3.

is also a paradigm for charity, the spirit in which the wafer, now soundly established as the real flesh and blood, is to be received:

> A3ens þys sacrament þan do po
> Pat are yn synne and þar to go,
> Or are yn wyl a3en to wende
> To synne and hemself shende.[39]

And an example follows concerning a priest who was granted insight into his parishioners' moral state by looking at their faces. There were bright ones (the pure) and black ones (the lechers); some were red (the tyrants), some swollen (the envious), some prickly (the back biters), some like lepers (who did not love God sufficiently) and some like idols (the worldly). This is to teach that one must prepare, repent and confess all these sins before taking the sacrament, and that this applies to priests as well.[40]

The third 'point' applied to the merits of the mass, particularly its power to help souls in purgatory, and is exemplified in a tale by St Gregory. A priest called Felix was asked by a man in his service to commute his wages for two loaves to be offered at the altar and to thus procure bliss for him; but the tale gave warning that although the power of the eucharist is very great in many things one should beware of payment to a bad priest whose prayers are of no avail.[41] And another tale is told of a man of Suffolk who died at Sudbury and who was allowed to visit his wife after his death and to ask for masses for his soul. The widow offered the commemoration in a common prayer for the dead at mass, but he reappeared to ask for particular and individual prayers, so the widow hired a friar to sing for her dead husband alone, and when he appeared the third time it was to confirm that this had brought him eternal joy. The conclusion is:

> In þis tale schewed is:
> Of alle þing good is þe mes,
> Pe sacrament of þe auter
> Ouer alle passeþ his pouwer.[42]

Mannyng employed two further tales, perhaps against existing scepticism, on the subject of the merits of the mass and the idea that prayers for the dead discriminated against the poor and lined the pockets of

[39] *Ibid*, lines 10,151–54, p. 253.
[40] *Ibid*, lines 10,221–56, p. 255.
[41] *Ibid*, lines 10,325–96, pp. 257–9.
[42] *Ibid*, lines 10,403–506, pp. 259–61.

priests and friars.[43] And after benefits to the dead, those to the living follow:

> Nat only for soules is he herd,
> But also for us here yn þe werld.[44]

A story told by Bede illustrates the point; and this was a tale of the knight Iumna taken prisoner by King Eldred. Thinking his brother Iumna dead, the Abbot Tumna sang a daily mass for his soul; but these were not wasted since the masses which had the power to release souls from suffering, helped loosen the knots which bound Iumna, through the power which bound the brother in captivity. The redeemed knight returned to his brother and the mystery was described, as it was summarised to the audience:

> Þat þe Mess helpeþ us weyl here:
> For us lyvyng hyt makþ memorye,
> As weyl as for soules yn purgatorye.[45]

The last point follows logically from practices of buying masses and paying for them in money and gifts; it discusses offerings to the altar and their rewards:

> Þe offrynge ys also a present
> Þat hyt be oure helpe þe sacrament,
> To þe fader of heuene bysyly
> For whom þou offrest, to haue mercy.[46]

The story that follows tells of a miner who fell into a pit and who survived only by virtue of his wife's offerings at the altar. And yet, the audience is encouraged *not* to rely on wives and children, who are only rarely truly good, but to act before death and to provide offerings generously during their lifetime:

> Truste ȝet nat moche on ȝoure wyues,
> Ne on ȝoure chyldren for no þyng,
> But makeþ ȝe self ȝoure offryng.[47]

The treatise ends soon after with a short exhortation to pray:

> Þat þe sacrament oure sauueour,

---

[43] Ideas which later arise in Lollard writings, see Hudson (1988b), pp. 309–10, 348–51.
[44] *Handlyng synne (a)*, lines 10,515–6, p. 262.
[45] *Ibid*, lines 10,525–716, pp. 262–67; lines 10,714–16, pp. 266–7.
[46] *Ibid*, lines 10,729–32, p. 267.
[47] *Ibid*, lines 10,080–82, pp. 268–9. The implications of such teaching for prevailing ideas about household and family are, of course, interesting, and little explored, except for the very general treatment of Goody (1983). A similar understanding seems to inform membership in and especially gift-giving to fraternities, see Rubin (1991b).

Þat bodi and soule he wyl us saue,
And we hym loue and he us haue.[48]

This sermon-cum-didactic treatise was not delivered on a single
occasion to a particular type of audience; it is too long and repetitive.
But it did provide a variety of material from which a number of Corpus
Christi sermons could easily be constructed. It was useful in offering a
historically grounded explanation about the development from the
Last Supper, the eucharist's scriptural basis, to current day celebrations
in the parish church. The *exempla* were necessary for illustration and
for aesthetic effect. Thus, typically a Corpus Christi core sermon
would be expanded with new and useful connections and tales, which
turned it from homily to eucharistic tract.[49] A sermon created for 'the
new feast' would have been copied, and perhaps survived in sermons
such as the one for Corpus Christi in the *Speculum sacerdotale*, or in
Mirk's *Festial*. Such a sermon might serve as a basis for a more comprehensive tract for the feast which attached to the sermon suitable tales.
These were taken from pre-existing pastoral manuals such as *Handlyng
synne*, and from collections of biblical paraphrases, such as *Cursor
mundi*.[50] In its turn the complex treatise which the 'Sermo de corpore
Christi' became may have been based on a core sermon, and was a
source for shorter and simpler Corpus Christi sermons.

So the treatise-like 'Sermo' provided important pastoral material and
literary resources for a parish priest but what most people would have
heard is a short English sermon with many good tales. One of the most
frequently used sermons in fifteenth-century England was probably
Mirk's Corpus Christi sermon in the *Festial*, a sermon cycle compiled
in 1415.[51] John Mirk was a canon of the Augustinian house of Lilleshall
(Shropshire), and his vernacular cycle includes sermons for all major
feasts of the temporal and the sanctoral feasts of the calendar. The
Corpus Christi sermon opens with a general statement about the feast
as a celebration of the sacrament of the altar offered by God daily for
the living and the dead:

In remission of synne to al þat lyuen here in perfite charite and in gret secoure and
reles of her payne þat be in purgatori.[52]

---

[48] *Handlyng synne (a)*, lines 10,816–18, p. 269.
[49] Owst (1926), p. 284.
[50] Boitani (1982), pp. 23–5.
[51] *Festial*, no. 41, pp. 168–75. On the *Festial*'s popularity among the parish clergy, see
    Fletcher (1980), pp. 514–15; Spencer (1982), pp. 10, 18. On the *Festial*'s reception in the
    fifteenth century, see Steckman (1936).
[52] *Festial*, p. 168.

The circumstances of the feast's foundation are described, and especially Urban IV's particular devotion which led him to found it and to endow it with indulgences. Moving further back into history, the foundation of the sacrament itself is retold, presenting it as a token left by Christ in his memory before he proceeded to his death. Here, an interesting emphasis is given to the dignity of priests:

And so ȝaf hit to hem and to al oþyr prestes, ȝee and to al oþyr prestes, power and dignite forto make his body of bred and wyne yn þe auter, so þat eche prest haþ of Cristis ȝeft power forto make þis sacrament, be he bettyr, be he wors.[53]

Mirk stresses a point which was consistently attacked by Lollards, of whose criticism he was very mindful. As we will see below, in the context of sacerdotal efficacy, in quite different contexts from that of the mid-fourteenth-century sermon, the objection was after raised that offerings to a 'bad' priest were of no avail.[54]

Mirk then continues to discuss the utility of the sacrament according to four particular properties which he calls 'skills': to help Man, alive or dead; to bring to mind the Passion, the source of grace and remission; as a token of love between Father and Son and the love of Man for God, through faith; as a source of mead and grace through the testing of faith. These benefits are grounded in the theological and pastoral precepts which we have followed through the writings of the schools. They convey a middle-way in eucharistic understanding, between a gross physicality and an abstract identification. The eucharist is shown to be useful in diverse practical as well as spiritual ways.

The sacrament's first property is its utility for the living and the dead, and for the sick and dying who view it and draw strength from it. The second property of the eucharist is two-fold: on the one hand, it is conveyed in the reality of the blood of forgiveness shed on the cross and renewed at every mass, and illustrated in a tale of a doubting priest who was convinced of the reality of Christ's blood in the sacrament when he saw it trickle during the fraction of the host; on the other, it is present in the eucharist's power to bring to mind the all-important memory of the Passion, which is the key for sharing in grace and fighting the devil. Mirk digresses here to discuss the similar power of crosses and images to evoke the Passion, referring explicitly to Lollard criticism of them as artifacts of idolatry:

And þerfor roodes and oþyr ymages ben necessary in holy church, whateuer þes

[53] *Ibid*, p. 169.
[54] See below, pp. 328–9.

Lollardes sayn; for yf þay nade ben profitable, goode holy faders þat haue be tofore us wold haue don hem out of holy chirch mony a ȝere gon.[55]

An animal-example is offered concerning birds in a foreign land who, in memory of the Passion, abstain from singing between Palm Sunday and Easter Day.[56]

The third property of the sacrament is to give occasion to contemplate the exchange of divine love for the love of Man, an ideal explored in the Charter of Christ.[57] An example of eucharistic devotion follows, of a dying man who was vomiting and therefore feared to receive the eucharist and rather put it at his side, near his heart ('I lay þe on þe place þat is next myn hert, and so show þe my hert and my moue') and whose love was rewarded by an extraordinary reception of the host into his body through his side.[58] The fourth and last property of the eucharist is to increase virtue by providing a test of faith through belief in transubstantiation. To believe in it, in Christ's presence and in the Creed which Mirk paraphrases at this point, 'he getet hym gret merite'. The highly appropriate tale of the mass of St Gregory follows, the story of a woman who doubted the real presence of Christ's body and who was privileged with a miraculous appearance of flesh in the host through Gregory's intercession on her behalf.[59] A short summary at the end of the sermon exhorts men and women to worship God's body with all their might and to love Him wholeheartedly.[60]

Mirk's Corpus Christi sermon is a perfect piece of practical pastoral material. In simple language, peppered with tales, the eucharistic symbols and their interlocking relations are presented and explained. Acceptance of the eucharist is shown to have very practical and satisfying rewards, denied by and to those who doubt the priesthood which mediates it. This is a useful exposition of eucharistic orthodoxy which is also neatly linked to the historic circumstances of its generation, and the contemporary context of its celebration.

A shorter Corpus Christi vernacular sermon appears in the *Speculum sacerdotale* of the early to mid fifteenth century. Here, even less doctrine is expounded, but the practical utility is emphasised – the *need* for the eucharist – and most importantly the close connection between the feast of Corpus Christi and the foundation of the sacrament. The

[55] *Festial*, p. 171.
[56] *Ibid*, pp. 171–2.
[57] See below, pp. 306–8.
[58] *Ibid*, p. 172. For examples of reception from the side see above, p. 119.
[59] On the tale, see above, pp. 121–2.
[60] *Festial*, p. 175.

sermon begins with the history of the feast's foundation, and follows on to the eucharist's salvific value:

And þat is a nedefull poynte to oure beleue and to be trowed boþe for remission of venyall synnes and also to encresynge of perfeccion and of vertues.[61]

After establishing the link between the eucharist's institution on Maundy Thursday and the feast of Corpus Christi the sermon continues to explain the need for a separate eucharistic feast on another date in the very words of the bull *Transiturus*:

for that it may noȝt in that day be i-worschipid as it oweþ for the passion of oure lord, þerfore the blessid Pope Urban þe iiii. ordeyned that this feste schuld be halowid and hadde in worschep . . . in the v. ferie after the Sunday of the Trinite.[62]

And believers were encouraged to celebrate the feast in church at its services and with prayer.

Just as orthodox popular preaching centred on the transubstantiation and the validity of the scriptural-historical basis for the eucharist, the Lollard sermon 'In festo corporis Christi', which uses the theme from 'Caro enim mea vere est cibus' (John 6,56) attacks these very points. In opposition to Mirk's assertion that the sacrament on the altar 'þe same flessch and blod þat Crist toke in mayden Mary, . . . and aftur soffreth deth on þe crosse,[63] the Lollard writer claims that it is obscene to speak of Christ in this manner, 'Þes ben to ruyde heretikis þat seyen þey etyn Crist bodily',[64] ridiculing the belief in transubstantiation and claiming that 'a man brekiþ not Goddis body ne drynkiþ his blood wiþ his mouþ'[65] and thus returning to the age-old ridicule of the physical interpretation of the eucharist as enshrined in the oaths taken by Berengar.[66] The Lollard sermon continues in this vein:

And þus a mous etiþ not Cristis body, al ȝif he ete þis sacrament, for þe mous fayliþ gostly witt to chewe in hym þis bileue.[67]

So the preacher has turned to belief as an essential element in nourishment, not the eating of sacramental bread alone:

And he etiþ betere Goddis body þat hap bileue and pis good loue, þan he þat etiþ pis sacrament and fayliþ more in þis spiritual mete.[68]

---

[61] *Speculum sacerdotale*, p. 162.
[62] *Ibid*, p. 163. See for similar claims in a sermon Tamborini (1935), p. 17.
[63] *Festial*, p. 170.
[64] *English Wycliffite sermons* III, sermon 87, pp. 247–8 (BL Add. 40672).
[65] *Ibid*, p. 248.
[66] See above, pp. 19–20.
[67] *English Wycliffite sermons* III, p. 248; on such criticism, see Macy (1983).
[68] *English Wycliffite sermons* III, p. 248.

So Corpus Christi provided for Lollards an occasion for the exposition of their critique of the sacrament, and using some of the orthodox notions of test of faith, and love of God, turn these round to support a truer version through the loving 'goostly' eating of Christ's flesh and blood which are only 'sacramentaliche' in the bread and wine of the sacrament.

Intended for an altogether different audience was the Latin sermon for Corpus Christi found in a collection of material for preaching and instruction in Lincolnshire from the mid to late fourteenth century.[69] This is a collection of fifty-six sermons, copied in three hands, containing many *exempla*, and including bi-lingual passages.[70] The English enters in a number of ways, in vernacular prayers or tags, or in translation of Latin hymns or prayers in the sermons.[71] The author of only two of the sermons in this book is known, and the Corpus Christi sermon is anonymous. This sermon is constructed in the usual format of a clerical sermon of this period, with the invocation of 'Karissimi'; but its use of the vernacular, its vibrant reference to tale and allegory suggest that these sermons had wider audiences in mind, definitely different from that envisaged, say, for the sermons of Thomas Brinton. The Corpus Christi sermon is of especial originality and beauty, developing the theme 'Sic honorabitur quem rex voluerit honorari' ('Thus will be honoured the man the King desireth to be honoured') (Esther 6,7).

Starting with the phrase which refers to the honours showered on Mordechai, the writer expounds on the honours due to great personages, like emperors, and like Christ. He then turns to a parable about a lord who, before going on pilgrimage, entertained his friends at a banquet and gave them jewels by which they are to remember him. To his wife he gave a golden ring with the inscription:

> ay bitwene þou loken on me
> and þenc on hym þat ȝaf þe me
> hou I am broken for þy sake
> and neuere ne tac þou oȝer make.

and left on his journey. The *moralitas* follows: Christ who went on his long journey from the Holy Land to heaven had similarly left a ring:

His gelden ring, which is no other than Christ's body, which in its roundness is

---

[69] In a manuscript of *c.*1400, CUL.Ii.3.8, fols. 90ʳ–91ᵛ.

[70] On these, see Erb (1971), p. 56.

[71] On English in sermons, see Wenzel (1978).

apprehended by man as similar to the ring which you, Christian, receive on Easter in the form of bread.[72]

And since the church did not institute a full memorial of this gift at the time, it has now ordained 'That this honourable feast of Corpus Christi is Christ's final feast, celebrated by us every year'.[73] Again a writer for Corpus Christi dwells on its link to a historic event, and must ground its curious recent foundation in a larger scheme of things.

Continuing the thread of honour due to a chosen person, the writer returns to the scenes of the Holy Week beginning with Christ's reception on Palm Sunday to the sounds of the *Gloria, laus,* here in English translation.[74] And conversely, Christ himself honoured many people in this world, but since he surpassed them all he was still owed the greatest dignity of all. Here the tail-end of the tale of Esther is introduced, labelled 'historia' in the margin. King Ahasuerus asked his steward what should be done to a man the king wished to honour, and the answer was that 'He must be dressed in *kyngges clo3yngge* and must be put on a horse from the royal stable', and he must wear a diadem.[75] The king had his seneschal do all these things for Mordechai who was sitting at the palace gate. The parable is expounded: the king is God, Mordechai stands for Jesus, and the Christian is like the king's servant who was entrusted with the task of honouring Mordechai. Just like Mordechai was raised onto a horse from the king's stables, God has ordained the priest to raise Christ aloft in his hands. The equestrian ride is paralleled by the exposition of the host:

The priests who are this day with Christ our king *ladden hym abaute* led him around the city streets and entered with him in a procession. And Christians cried out in a loud voice *Thus will be honoured etc.* because they carried Christ like the boys of Jerusalem had done as I have told above.[76]

And the following English verse of welcome is inserted:

A lord crist of heuene blisse þou art kynge

---

72  'Anulum suum aureum quod non est nisi Corpus Xristi quod in rotunditate sic in visu hominis habet similitudinem anuli quem tu recepisti Xristiane die pasche in forma panis', CUL.Ii.3.8, fol. 90ʳ.

73  'Quod istud honorabile festum de corpore xristi sicut ultimum festum quod facimus de xristo tocius anni', CUL.Ii.3.8, fol. 90ʳ.

74  *Index* no. 1803; see another translation in *Religious lyrics of the XIV century*, pp. 16–17. On Palm Sunday processional liturgy, see below, pp. 244–5.

75  'Debet indui in kyngges clo3yngge et deberet poni super equum de sella regis', CUL.Ii.3.8, fol. 91ʳ.

76  'Religiosi qui fuerint hodie cum xristo rege nostro ladden hym abaute duxerunt illum circumquaque per vicos civitatis inierunt prope cumeo in processione et xristiani clamabant eum magna voce *Sic honorabitur etc.,* quia ipsi portabant Xristum sicut pueri ierusalem fecerunt sicut prius dixi', *ibid.*

þou art þe faderes sone of heuene wythouten endynge
of a mayde þou toke oure kende and were y bore
for man to deye þat þoru is senne was for lore.[77]

From the entry to the City we are led to the Last Supper and to a direct address to the audience 'tu Xristiane!', a reminder that when the priest says the words of the sacrament 'Christ is wholly present in body and in soul and divinity there in the sacrament of the altar both in the form of bread and in that of wine'.[78] Christ's human nature is likened to the beast with a human face seen by Ezekiel: its two wings are like the bread and wine which envelop Him, and which are misleading to four of the senses: 'All your senses are deceived in this sacrament except your hearing, because when you hear the words of the priest . . . you hear a real thing.'[79] Thus at the moment of abandonment of the senses to faith, following Thomas' assertion in the feast's own liturgy, a careful and unambiguous reiteration of the priest's vital function is stated. The words of the consecration are not deceptive, Christ is reborn in the words of consecration, just as the Old Testament prophecies had foretold the incarnation in Mary's womb: 'Because immediately as the priest says the words, the holy materials turn immediately into Christ's body by the power of the bread.'[80] And the sermon ends with reference to the day's gospel reading from John, 'Qui manducat meam carnem' (John 6,55).

This sermon was not amenable to immediate use for parish preaching,[81] but it could have been used in religious houses, in private oratories, and above all it could form a basis for the composition of vernacular sermons. It is more subtle than the didactically orientated sermons and it draws from a variety of sources, from both Latin and vernacular imagery in hymnody, homiletic lore, biblical exegesis and tale. It uses the technique of relating Old and New Testament to create a sense of the unfolding Christian story, a narrative of providence and divine commitment, which creates a magnificent plan realised in the eucharist. The biblical allusions are not opaque but rather designed to create an affective mood: Mordechai bedecked in crimson, and Christ mocked in crimson on his way to the crucifixion; the touching moment of parting between lovers, and a token of love is the eucharist offered

---

[77] *Ibid*; *Index* no. 10.
[78] 'Quod xristus plene in corpore et anima et deitate est ibi in sacramento altaris *boye* in forma panis et vini', CUL.Ii.3.8, fol. 91ʳ.
[79] 'Omnes sensus tui decepti in illo sacramento excepto auditu tuo quia quando audis verbum sacerdotis . . . audis rem veram', *ibid*.
[80] 'Quia sacerdos quando cito dixerit verba sacra materialia quod panis virtute domini vertitur statim in corpore xristi', *ibid*.
[81] For a discussion of parish preaching, see Spencer (1982), p. 25.

for those Christ loves. A lay public versed in biblical paraphrase of the type which informed the understanding of much of the Corpus Christi drama would have appreciated a vernacular rendering of these themes.[82] Once again a universalising drive is apparent; the eucharist could hardly be discussed without reference to a whole number of stages in the Christian myth.

The last sermon to be examined here is the product of the borrowing and working of materials from the didactic sermon with *exempla*, from a mastery of Latin clerical learning, and from the energy and rhythm of the Corpus Christi plays which we have just mentioned. This is a sermon only in name; it is actually a report on the Corpus Christi procession as celebrated in London in the mid fifteenth century with *tableaux vivants* and organised under the auspices of the skinners' guild.[83] It is a poem of twenty-eight stanzas by John Lydgate, the monk of Bury St Edmunds,[84] court poet and widely-read devotional writer, and prefaced by 'followeye an ordenaunce of a processyoun of þe feste of corpus cristi made in London by daun John Lydgate'.[85] It is a didactic and explicatory piece, and it follows the tradition which developed around the feast in its discussion of the history of the sacrament, and in use of stock Old and New Testament parallels. He describes the biblical pageants as they passed by:

> In youre presence fette out of fygure,
> Schal beo declared by many unkouþe signe
> Gracyous misteryes grounded in scripture.[86]

No elaborate doctrinal schemes are constructed: he merely tells the Christian tale which ends in the eucharist. Adam's sin called for redemption, Melchizedek was priest and king like Christ to come; Abraham who offered bread to angels:

> Set to hem brede with ful gladde chere,
> Of gret counforte, a token who list see,
> Þe sacrament þat stondeþe on þe awter.[87]

From Abraham issued Isaac, blessed by God, and from whose seed Mary would be born; then Jacob whose dream revealed wheat, corn

---

[82] On drama see below, pp. 271–87.
[83] Cambridge Trinity college R.3.20, pp. 349–56; *Lydgate's minor poems*, pp. 35–43; Gibson (1981), pp. 81–4. On the Skinners, see Unwin (1963), pp. 105–6, 227; Barron (1985), p. 15.
[84] For more on the literary milieu of Bury, see Gibson (1981).
[85] Pearsall (1970), p. 188.
[86] *Lydgate's minor poems*, lines 6–8, p. 36.
[87] *Ibid*, lines 30–32, p. 36.

and a host in the midst; then Moses through whom God gave manna to his people, with the following meaning:

> To us figureþe in oure Inwarde sight
> A symilitude of þe sacrament.[88]

Then came Aaron, first true priest of the Old Law, who sacrificed lambs to God and who:

> Is token and signe of Cristes pasyoun,
> Spirituel gladnesse & mooste fer to habounde
> This day mynisterd til oure Reffeccion.[89]

Next came David who was victorious over Goliath, like Christ who triumphed over his wounds; and Ecclesiastes is treated like a person, with its enclosed garden, symbolising Mary who was visited by the Holy Ghost in Nazareth. Jeremiah followed with his vision of being pressed like a grape into a chalice, and of wheat being made into bread, and he prefigured:

> A gracyous fygure þat a pure virgyne
> Shoulde bere manna in which lay al our speede.[90]

Isaiah too had seen a feast in a vision, a token of the joy which was to issue of Jesse's line, and Elijah's repast of bread and water on his journey of forty days reminded Lydgate of the sacrament, man's fare for a journey on earth. Here, Lydgate passes to the figures of the New Testament, presenting them actors fulfilling the prophecies of the Old. He mentions Zachary, the priest, whose incense rose to heaven like a prayer which is as refreshing and healing to the soul as sacramental bread 'Ageynst þe sorowes of worldely pestylence'.[91] John the Baptist carried the lamb of God, who was crucified and who then arose to act as a balm, 'ageynst seeknesse our Restauracyoun'.[92] Then come the four evangelists, each with his version of the Last Supper and the words said at it, with pride of place given to Luke:

> Lucas confermeþe of þis hooly bloode,
> Tavoyde aweye al Ambeguytee,
> 'Þis is my bodye þat schal for man beo ded,
> Him to delyver from infernal powstee; . . .
> By Cryst þat suffred a spere to perce his syde'.[93]

[88] *Ibid*, lines 55–6, p. 37.
[89] *Ibid*, lines 62–4, p. 37.
[90] *Ibid*, lines 87–8, p. 38.
[91] *Ibid*, line 110, p. 39.
[92] *Ibid*, line 120, p. 39.
[93] *Ibid*, lines 145–8, 152, p. 40.

And Paul's words in the epistle to the Corinthians (1 Cor. 11,27)
explicate the message of the gospel, in warning against unworthy
reception, one of the three moments when doctrine is discussed in this
poem:

> Yif þere þeo founden any creature
> Which þat þis bred resceyveþe unworþely,
> He eteþe his doome most dampnabully,
> For which I counseyle, and pleynly þus I mene,
> Ech man beo ware to kepe him prudently,
> Not to resceiue it, but yif he beo clene.[94]

The link with the contemporary church is then made through the
masters of the central Middle Ages who interpreted these messages.
First is Peter Lombard, 'He þat is cleped maystre of sentence' – master
of the *Sentences* – who established the basic tenets of sacramental
theology:

> Þis sacrament affter his doctryne
> Is Crystis body, Repaste of our passage,
> Be þe Holly Gooste take of a pure virgyne.[95]

Jerome is remembered as another Father of the living church, to whom
is attributed the doctrine that Christ's body existed in every part of the
host, a view which was hotly discussed by theologians from the twelfth
century on,[96] 'Howe þat þis hoost is hole in ech partye', a view
especially important in refuting heretical ridicule of the sacrament.[97]
Gregory the Great is remembered for having written that Christ's flesh
was taken from a pure virgin and was thus powerful as 'Geynst al
seeknesse our cheef restauratyff', as already mentioned by Lydgate.[98]
Augustine contributed to the eucharistic tale by formulating the sacrament's many remedies against the ills of the world, benefits which came
to be known as the 'Meads of the mass'.[99] Similarly, Ambrose taught
that the sacrament could strike blows against Satan and make Man
victorious in his mortal wars against the devil:

> Þe sacrament is Justely consecrate
> Oure daily foode, Renuwyng oure estate,
> Recounseylling us when we trespas or erre,

---

[94] *Ibid*, lines 155–60, p. 41.
[95] *Ibid*, lines 166–8, p. 41.
[96] See above, p. 70.
[97] *Lydgate's minor poems*, line 172, p. 41.
[98] *Ibid*, line 182, p. 41 and before line 120, p. 39.
[99] Sermon 131 'Corporis et sanguinis Christi sacramentum', caput 1, Augustine, 'Sermones',
*PL* 38, cols. 729–30.

And maþe us mighty with Satan to debate
To wynne tryumphe in al his mortal werre.[100]

A curious section next follows in which the 'master of history' holds a chalice aloft, and above it glorious is the mourning figure of *pietà*, Mary suffering over her son's death 'Whan he for man þe Raunsoun on him tooke'.[101] This does not fit any particular iconographic or exegetical scheme of the eucharist, but rather derives from the fundamental convergence of Passion and Eucharist, of Incarnation and sacrifice at the altar, which informs the eucharistic symbol. This convergence placed Mary in a special position as fellow-sufferer with Christ through their special *substantial* likeness.[102] But the sermon ends with a great eucharistic hero, and a particular protagonist of the eucharistic feast of Corpus Christi, Thomas Aquinas. One of his eucharistic visions is recounted, and he finally links the eucharist with the feast, the day on which this sermon commentary was delivered.

Having heard, and in some cases seen in pageant form, the unfolding Christian tale the audience is exhorted to show reverence:

> Þis bred of lyfe yee kepe in Remembraunce . . .
> Youre restoratyff celestyal manna,
> Of which God graunt eternal suffysaunce
> Where aungels sing everlasting Osanna.[103]

Lydgate, the monk of Bury, pursued here a rather interesting path marked by the pageants which in themselves were informed by the sermons for the day. This seems like a journey through a Book of Hours, where full-page figures of saints were meant to conjure up memories of moral examples and to shape future behaviour. But here is a living poem which was linked to a public, out-door, didactic as well as artistic event. None the less, it is a sermon in its assumption of the conventions of didactic structures. It was preoccupied with bolstering the symbolic system with the eucharist at its heart, and addressed itself to the sort of difficulties and misunderstandings which the eucharist, and the day founded for its celebration, could engender.

## CORPUS CHRISTI FRATERNITIES

The new feast was established in calendars and provided with a liturgy; it became an occasion for teaching and was increasingly an opportunity

---

[100] *Lydgate's minor poems*, lines 196–20, p. 42.
[101] *Ibid*, line 208, p. 42.
[102] Fulton (1987), *passim* esp. pp. 63, 73, 78; Shahar (1990), p. 169.
[103] *Lydgate's minor poems*, lines 220, 222–4, p. 43.

for experiment among groups and institutions, negotiating its meanings with regard to pre-existing cultural modes. Fraternities in which a variety of social-religious activities were organised offered a framework for the celebration of the new feast, while the increased interest in the eucharist inspired by the feast suggested it as a focus for a variety of social, economic and political activities. Let us begin by looking at the voluntary bodies which chose to organise their various activities of mutual help, commemoration and sociability around the eucharistic feast and the symbol at its heart.

A considerable rise in the number of fraternities which becomes apparent after the second half of the fourteenth century has been explained in two ways. Some have perceived an explosion of lay piety, others an orphaned humanity huddling together after the ravages of plague and the dislocations it caused.[104] As an explanation of the fraternities which dedicated themselves to Corpus Christi – the idea and the feast – neither approach seems particularly useful. Admittedly, there was a greater interest in eucharistic practices; but the word piety hardly informs us of the nature of this evolution and the reception of the symbol. Nor do notions of psychological disorientation seem to explain the degree of planning, attention, common sense and mutual bargaining which made fraternities flourish throughout society. Let us try to understand fraternities as providers of essential personal, familial, religious, economic and political services, as providing security in some essential areas of life; and let us see these activities as articulated most frequently in symbols from the language of religion. These could be cults of saints, particular practices such as flagellation or charity, or a concept much discussed and prominently experienced through an essential ritual, the eucharist. The motives for interaction and the strength and character of the bonding within fraternities differ widely; what we will try to trace is the way in which the eucharist was used and deployed to formulate these relations.

Fraternities are known to us from their statutes, from rentals and accounts, from lists of members and records of benefactions to them in wills. They occasionally surface in material generated by other institutions, such as the great inquest into guilds and fraternities of 1388, a royal inquiry made under Richard II, the returns of which were received in Chancery by the spring of 1389.[105] Thus for the Corpus Christi fraternities we have a picture of the situation some sixty years

---

[104] For the first view Brigden (1984), pp. 94–7 (suggestion that animosity to parochial religion contributed to it, p. 95), Scarisbrick (1982), pp. 19–39, a less committed view in Barron (1985), pp. 36–7; and for the second most notably Chiffoleau (1980), pp. 429–35.

[105] Tuck (1969); *Parish fraternity register*, pp. ix–x.

after its foundation, a period long enough to allow some of the under-standings and uses of the new feast and its public potentials to have emerged. The returns cover most of the East Anglian counties, the East Midlands, London, and some of the West Country. Of the 471 fraterni-ties, 44 were dedicated to Corpus Christi and 31 of these have a known date of foundation, giving the following sequence of foundation:

| | | | |
|---|---|---|---|
| before 1320 | 2 | 1351–1360 | 7 |
| 1321–1330 | 2 | 1361–1370 | 3 |
| 1331–1340 | 2 | 1371–1380 | 7[106] |
| 1341–1350 | 8 | | |

There was a clustering of foundation in the years in and around the plague.[107] But this picture, even for the counties which are well repre-sented, omits those foundations which were founded and dissolved between 1320 and 1388; fraternities could have literally died out during the Black Death, their funds being used for other ends. A good example of such a transformation is the prominent Corpus Christi fraternity in Cambridge, which after the Black Death was burdened with interces-sory obligations and related properties. It decided to fulfil these duties through the foundation and endowment of an academic college, of which there were already a few in Cambridge.[108] Thus, it invested the properties in the new college which formally came into being in 1352 and which was obliged to commemorate the dead and living members of the once flourishing fraternity. This would not have been recorded in 1389, and there must have been other similar cases. At the other end of the period, there is no comprehensive record of fraternities until their dissolution in 1542 and the creation of the Chantry and Guild Certifi-cates. But at least in one county, Cambridgeshire, we witness eighteen fraternities in the sixteenth century, whereas only five were recorded in 1389.

Corpus Christi fraternities exhibit traits which were common to most fraternities:[109] they provided funerary services and relief to members and their dependents, and organised feasts and dinners; some provided legal support, and all indulged in para-liturgical activities,

---

[106] These are based on the returns as tabulated in Westlake (1919), pp. 137–238, and checked against the originals in the PRO C47/37–48.

[107] There were 2 foundations in 1349, 3 in 1350, 1 in 1351 and another in 1352; this is, of course a very small sample. The pattern of foundation of Corpus Christi fraternities in the Avignon area shows that of the 28 foundations between 1324–1482 there is a clustering between 1376–1400, Chiffoleau (1980), annex II, pp. 448–53.

[108] See Brooke and Highfield (1988), pp. 92–100.

[109] We know much more about urban than of rural fraternities for a French rural fraternity of the eucharist, see Lestrade (1937).

those religious practices which went beyond basic parochial requirements. Most Corpus Christi fraternities held their annual meetings on
or around the feast day; these assemblies were often combined with
commemoration of dead members.[110] The tailors of Lincoln assembled
for a requiem on the morrow of Corpus Christi, as did the Northampton fraternity, while at Oxborough (Norfolk) the fraternity met at the
feast's first vespers and kept its lights burning until second vespers. Yet
the eucharistic interests exhibited by the Corpus Christi fraternities
never overwhelmed the basic routine of sociability and mutual help,
but rather enhanced it.[111] Some Corpus Christi fraternities founded
chantries, such as those in Beverley in 1352 and Hull in 1382;[112] others
developed quite different enterprises such as running hospitals, alms-
houses, visiting the sick, or even founding a college.[113] But these
practices always coexisted with a eucharistic interest, and the array of
practices which had been prescribed, or which had grown up around
the eucharist.[114]

Attempts were made to keep the eucharist safe and well-lit wherever
it was. Lighting was thus a basic feature of eucharistic interest on the
part of Corpus Christi fraternities: ten of the forty-four Corpus Christi
fraternities recorded in 1389 made special provision for elevation
lights.[115] In some places entry fees were paid in wax candles, and a
constant flow of wax was ensured through fines in kind. An agreement
of 1449 made by the master of the Corpus Christi fraternity of King's
Lynn, John Pygot, regulated the supply of wax candles by a local
chandler, William Marche, who was to provide candles out of the
company's stock of wax which was deposited with him; he was paid 5
marks and 10s for his work.[116] Corpus Christi fraternities often combined charity and eucharistic practice in fostering the practice of taking
the *viaticum* to the sick and dying.[117] The Wisbech fraternity had a

[110] Some celebrated the Corpus Christi mass as a group, as shown in the noted Corpus
Christi office from a kalends fraternity in Giebeldehausen near Göttingen of c.1400, BL
Add. 41506, fols. 1v–7v.
[111] This argument is developed in Rubin (1986), pp. 103–9.
[112] See above, p. 211.
[113] Westlake (1919), p. 54; Martz (1983), pp. 160–61; Dossat (1976), pp. 366, 372. On the
foundation of Corpus Christi college in Cambridge, see Cheney (1984) and above, pp.
210–11.
[114] A few surviving seals of Corpus Christi fraternities exhibit eucharistic imagery, and
especially a conventional image of the wafer over a chalice with or without a paten. A
sixteenth century emblem of the York fraternity also shows the inscribed wafer above a
chalice flanked by the wounded members of Christ in the four corners, a merging of the
Passion and eucharistic themes which had developed in the fifteenth-century symbolic
practice.
[115] See above about canonical requirement of lighting, pp. 59–60.
[116] Mackerell (1738), pp. 254–5.
[117] On this practice see above, pp. 177–82.

special torch which was carried on these occasions,[118] and the Corpus Christi fraternity of Lincoln (founded in 1350) provided that the torch which otherwise burnt at elevation should be used for visitations to the sick.[119] The Corpus Christi fraternity of King's Lynn was founded in 1349 and its return from 1389 claims that it was founded during the Black Death by a group of burgesses who were appalled to find that on the very many occasions of taking the eucharist to the sick in this sad year, the sacrament was provided with poor lighting. The burgesses combined to provide for proper wax lighting, and eventually others joined them and the group's activities expanded.[120] Taking the *viaticum* to the sick was a task which continental Corpus Christi fraternities took up as well; it was practised by such fraternities in the Avignon area,[121] and in the Languedoc.[122] A miniature in the *mariegola*, the book of statutes and membership, of a Venetian Corpus Christi fraternity, the *Scuola del Corpo di Cristo*, shows a scene in a sick person's house where a priest is offering communion, surrounded by members of the fraternity bearing candles.[123]

Three Corpus Christi fraternities recorded in the 1389 returns developed an interest in the ceremonies of the Easter sepulchre.[124] This was a liturgical drama or a ritual re-enactment of Christ's entombment and resurrection in English cathedrals and parish churches around a structure which resembled a tomb, and in which an effigy, which sometimes contained the host, was placed and then raised on Easter day. The ritual was attended by a vigil over the tomb which lasted until the Resurrection occurred. The fraternity at Caistor (Lincolnshire), founded in 1376, provided illumination on the procession to the tomb on the 'day of preparation', as Easter Friday was called. These were thirteen lights and fourteen candles around the shrine into which the eucharist, as Christ's crucified body, was being placed.[125] The Corpus Christi fraternity founded in 1350 at Lincoln also provided thirteen square candles which were to be placed around the sepulchre and left to burn throughout the octave, as well as three round candles which were to be

---

[118] PRO. C47/38/38.
[119] PRO. C47/40/135.
[120] PRO. C47/43/279.
[121] Chiffoleau (1980), p. 284.
[122] Dossat (1976), pp. 367, 373–4. A fraternity of St Mary in St Gudule's church, Brussels, acquired an indulgence in 1363 which relaxed the penance of those members who visited the sick with the sacrament, or participated in a Corpus Christi procession, heard mass at the fraternity altar, or listened to sermons, Delehaye (1926), no. 18, 375–6.
[123] Brown (1988a), plate 5, p. 18. On the activities of another Italian Corpus Christi fraternity, that of Bergamo, see Galizzi (1963).
[124] On Easter sepulchers, see Sekules (1986) and see below, pp. 294–7.
[125] PRO. C47/39/92.

lit only between the 'preparation' and the Resurrection.[126] The Holy Trinity fraternity at St Botolph's church, Aldgate, founded before 1374, was dedicated to Corpus Christi and undertook 'the maintenance of 13 torches burning around the sepulchre in that church at Easter'.[127]

As most towns developed urban processions in which the disparate corporation, fraternities and religious houses were represented in a variety of ways, Corpus Christi fraternities sometimes processed as a group within the wider processions.[128] Where smaller parochial processions co-existed with town-wide processions, or where village celebrations existed, fraternities could play an important organisational role. Of the forty-four Corpus Christi fraternities recorded in 1389, seventeen explicitly mention participation in a procession, ten of which also provided lights either to decorate the eucharistic tabernacle or to be carried by members. The fraternity of Stretham in the Isle-of-Ely provided 'to maintain twenty six tapers to be carried around Christ's body on the said feast'.[129] The Leicester Corpus Christi fraternity required each member to carry a torch of pure wax 'en la honour de dieu et la solempne feste de la consecracion'.[130] The Corpus Christi fraternity of Lincoln tailors decided that 'All brethren and sisters of the fraternity should attend the solemn procession once a year leading with a decent light'.[131] The fraternity at Caistor had forty candles carried by six brethren at the procession.[132] At Grantham the provision was even more elaborate: the fraternity assembled in the parish church before the procession where two priests in vestments carried the eucharist, and two boys in albs carried candles before them and the brethren and sisters followed up to the altar where they left some of their lights before joining the procession.[133] The Annunciation fraternity which met in St Mary's, Norwich, and which followed eucharistic practices, assembled on Corpus Christi at Sext and marched as a group in the procession.[134]

---

[126] PRO. C47/40/135.

[127] 'Ad sustentandum tresdecim cereos ardentes circa sepulcrum in eadem ecclesia tempore Pascha', London PRO. C47/42/210.

[128] On the role of fraternities in German Corpus Christi processions, see Zika (1988), p. 43, n. 53.

[129] 'Ad sustentacionem xxvi cereorum portandorum circa corpus cristi in predicto festo', London PRO. C47/38/31.

[130] PRO. C47/39/71.

[131] 'Omnes fratres et sorores eiusdem ibidem cum solempni processione semel in anno processionem generalem precendendo cum, lumine honorabili in festo corporis Christi', London PRO. C47/41/159.

[132] PRO. C47/39/92.

[133] PRO. C47/40/109.

[134] *Records of the city of Norwich*, pp. 296–8.

The mode of urban celebration of Corpus Christi often involved some pageantry and, especially in England, some dramatic show. There are the large cycles which were performed in whole or in parts on the feast day, and which will be discussed below. These elaborate enterprises, the production of the Corpus Christi cyclical drama, was undertaken by the craft guilds, the most substantial administrative, economic and political unit of late-medieval towns. Corpus Christi patrician fraternities were placed at the very heart of large processions, around the tabernacle, as at Leicester and York.[135] None the less, there are some examples of smaller scale dramatic activity in the fraternities. The chaplain of the Boston fraternity was called 'master of plaies'.[136] The Cambridge Corpus Christi fraternity spent 9d 'soluti Johanni Sekersteyn pro visers' in 1350,[137] and used some entry fines paid by a married couple in 1353 towards expenses 'in ludo filiorum Israel'.[138] The Holy Trinity fraternity at Shelford had minstrels playing on Corpus Christi in 1479–80,[139] that of Bury was recorded in 1389 as having an *interludium*,[140] and the York fraternity which came to such prominence in the procession by the fifteenth century had its own play of the Creed.[141] Similarly the fraternity at St Botolph's, Aldgate, which was dedicated to Corpus Christi, possessed a roll of vellum with various pageants which may well have been played on the feast.[142] The religious and social fraternity of the London skinners was dedicated to Corpus Christi and from 1393 it held an annual procession on the feast from its hall in Dungate Hill to St Antholin's Church in Watling Street.[143] By the 1440s these had developed a dramatic dimension which Lydgate immortalised describing it scene by scene in his poem on the Corpus Christi procession.[144]

But beyond processions and pageants, much happened on the feast day within the separate fraternity sphere. Few fraternity accounts have survived, but these sometimes offer a glimpse into the activities which were taking place. The accounts of the King's Lynn Corpus Christi fraternity show in 1387–8 that expenses were incurred in the purchase of thread and nails for the hanging of clothes in the hall, in payment to

[135] Johnston (1976).
[136] Owen (1971), p. 130.
[137] *Cambridge gild records*, p. 27, and in a separate entry later down recorded a vast expense in the procession, 56s 10d, which may have financed some dramatic show.
[138] *Ibid*, p. 51.
[139] Owen (1971), p. 130.
[140] London PRO. C47/46/401; Gibson (1981), exp. pp. 60–63.
[141] Johnston (1975).
[142] *Fraternity register*, p. 56.
[143] Unwin (1963), pp. 105–6.
[144] Discussed above, pp. 229–32.

bedesmen for prayers, and to clerks for transporting the tabernacle from the church to the hall, as well as in the purchase of bread, ale, cheese and candles.[145] The accounts of the fraternity of Holy Trinity and Corpus Christi of Wisbech for the late fourteenth century describe a mouth-watering variety of foods for the annual dinner on the feast day, as well as regular expenditure on commemoration.[146] The Corpus Christi fraternity of Cambridge feasted and entertained townsmen on Corpus Christi.[147] The Leicester Corpus Christi fraternity spent 2s 6d in 1493–4 on the 'bearing of the fertur and for torches on Corpus Christi day',[148] and in 1525–6 8d were paid 'ffor wedyng of the Cort & clensyng off the howse ageynst Corpus Xristi dynar'.[149]

Fraternities created loyalties between the members and the institution which were cemented by the promise of intercession and interdependence in moments of crisis, as well as through shared experiences in prayer, feasts and administration. Property was accumulated over generations and the richer fraternities were formidable institutions. The property of the Leicester fraternity produced an income larger than that of the borough,[150] and the Corpus Christi fraternity of Hull was an important land owner in the city,[151] with an estate built up from bequests such as that in 1349 of Nicholas Stut who directed that all his tenements in Monkgate go to the fraternity after the death of his wife and progeny.[152] Properties were accumulated in the late fourteenth and fifteenth centuries and new licences procured from Chancery for their acquisition: the Leicester fraternity applied for a licence in 1392 with some nineteen members, and around 1401 it was extended, the fraternity now naming sixty-four members.[153] Fraternities depended on special gifts or particular donations for extraordinary purchases; they were often left bequests of plate and hangings appropriate for the cult, and in the Corpus Christi fraternities, these usually had eucharistic connections. A silk baldaquin was left to the Hull fraternity by Asselia

[145] *The making of King's Lynn*, pp. 317–19.
[146] Wisbech. Wisbech and Fenland museum. Wisbech corporation archives. Accounts of the Holy Trinity gild.
[147] For evidence of its commensality, see the ceremonial drinking horn of this fraternity in Brooke and Highfield (1988), plate 58, p. 98.
[148] *Leicester, St Martin*, p. 343.
[149] *Ibid*, p. 225.
[150] Accumulated from bequests such as the 100s left in a will proved in 1405, *Reg. Repyngdon* I, p. 25.
[151] For the spread of properties in Hull see *The changing plan of Hull, passim*; and for holdings in Hull *c*.1445 *Selected rentals and accounts*, pp. 162, 164, and notes on pp. 182–3.
[152] The Corpus Christi fraternity was the second most frequently cited in Hull wills, after the Holy Trinity fraternity, Heath (1986), p. 223.
[153] *Leicester, St Martin*, pp. 193–6.

of Malton in her will of 1402 to hang on the day of her husband's obit, but which may have also served for a processional occasion.[154] When a chaplain, William of Clopton, entered the fraternity of Corpus Christi in Cambridge in 1350 he gave it a pair of organs and 'j almarie', perhaps an aumbry for the eucharist.[155] In 1497 Thomas Dalton left £8 to the Corpus Christi fraternity in Holy Trinity Church, Hull, for the purchase of a table of 'oversea work' for the altar,[156] and in 1449 Bishop Spofford of Hereford granted the York Corpus Christi fraternity, of which he was a member, a gilt silver shrine for the sacrament with images of the Virgin in pearls, all crowned by a steeple within which was placed the vessel containing the eucharist.[157]

Like the feast day, its liturgy and its procession, the eucharistic celebration was being incorporated into existing institutions and procedures, giving them and drawing from them new meanings and practices. The creative possibilities inherent in this occasion, when so powerful an image was displayed, were many – and were realised and expressed for as long as Corpus Christi was celebrated. Corpus Christi sermons were written, the ways in which small groups such as fraternities could coalesce around it were being explored, and new types of drama were developed for it. The feast's uses and traditions differed from place to place, from context to context with some recurrent features, which reflected local politics as well as some inherent meanings of the symbol. This interaction is nowhere more powerfully demonstrated than in the uses made by urban elites of the feast of the eucharist.

The feast which celebrated the eucharist, the most powerful symbol of Christian culture, and which came to be associated with public processional modes, in which the eucharist was venerated at the heart of a hierarchical display, spoke an idiom of privilege and lordship.[158] This attachment is not evident in the very first years of the feast after the feast's institution. But as its practices and traditions evolved these examined the symbolic rhetorical opportunities enfolded in the eucharistic language. An early example is the adoption of the Corpus Christi theme by the gild-merchant of Ipswich, the body which ruled the town since it had acquired its freedom from King John in 1200. In 1325 it adopted the Corpus Christi dedication for its fraternal aspect.[159] But

---

[154] Heath (1986), p. 218.
[155] *Cambridge gild records*, p. 30.
[156] Heath (1984), p. 223.
[157] *York, municipal records*, pp. 248–9.
[158] On the juxtaposition of royal pageantry and Corpus Christi iconography, see Guenée and Lehoux (1968).
[159] Westlake (1919), pp. 51–2.

when the patrician fraternities came to be integrated into the town-wide procession, this was done in ways which enhanced the group's claim to privilege and authority through its contact with the eucharist. The Northampton Corpus Christi fraternity assembled at the church of All Saints, and was the group closest to the eucharist in the procession.[160] In 1431–2 following a revision of the Order of celebration of Corpus Christi in York, members of the Corpus Christi fraternity were allowed to carry the eucharistic shrine, and to process around it, at the most privileged position for laymen. Last within the group walked the master of the fraternity in a silk cope;[161] the beneficiary of an honour which also entailed a contribution towards the expenses of such events.[162] The clergy followed the fraternity members who were the most exalted laymen on this eucharistic map.

As elites came to appreciate the power inscribed in Corpus Christi symbolism, they adopted it to existing political procedures in ways which were as varied as local custom. We find a relation between the business of running a town, and the spheres of symbolic interaction related to Corpus Christi. The Coventry Corpus Christi fraternity, which was founded in 1343, assembled in its livery and processed around the host. Charles Phythian-Adams has analysed the position of the Corpus Christi fraternity as a junior patrician group where younger members of office-holding families cut their teeth in political life and assumed their first public appointments, to progress later into the senior Holy Trinity fraternity once mayoral status had been achieved.[163] In Leicester the Corpus Christi fraternity was a social representation of the town council; it provided a venue for collegial correction and disciplining of the elected town officers within a fraternal framework. The *Hall book* of the Leicester corporation shows the Corpus Christi fraternity collecting fees for negligence or infringement of official duties and arbitrating between the members of the town council[164] who met in the Corpus Christi fraternity hall near St Martin's church in the second half of the fifteenth century.[165] The fraternity was an extension of the group which ran the town on a daily basis.

The attractions of the feast of Corpus Christi as an occasion for

---

[160] PRO. C47/45/380.
[161] *REED: York* I, pp. 50–2; Johnston (1976), p. 378.
[162] These occur regularly in the fraternity's accounts which survive from 1477, in *ibid*, p. 380.
[163] Phythian-Adams (1979), pp. 120–22.
[164] *Leicester records* no. 213, pp. 298–300; Wilshire (1979), pp. 196–8.
[165] Wilshire (1979), pp. 198–9. Similarly, the hall of the King's Lynn Corpus Christi fraternity was used as a location for the sale of goods by foreigners to burgesses by 1443, *The making of King's Lynn*, p. 266.

articulation and display of identity were apparent not only to the great and powerful of medieval towns, but also to the clergy. Fraternities, on the whole, had little or limited space for members of the clergy. They tended to hire them as chaplains, like the fraternity at Boston which maintained nine chaplains for the celebration of daily masses,[166] but to refuse them membership or halt their progress to office.[167] Thus clerical fraternities were occasionally created to provide mutual support, commemoration, sociability and relief, for a town's clergy. As the feast of the eucharist Corpus Christi had special meaning for the clergy, since it celebrated the ritual which encompassed their particular role; as we have seen the moment of the elevation of the mass came to represent the very essence of clerical life.[168] So it is interesting to witness the creation of clerical fraternities devoted to Corpus Christi, three cases of which are known. The fraternity of Corpus Christi in the collegiate church of St Mary-in-the-Fields, Norwich, celebrated daily masses for its members, and observed an annual procession in the octaves of Corpus Christi with a collegiate mass and a dinner.[169] The clerical fraternity of Beverley was founded by 1352 by a group of priests and prominent laymen, and its membership was made up of clergymen and of lay people of good reputation.[170] This Corpus Christi fraternity played a major part in the feast's procession: 'They should march in the procession in albs and with a stole and fan . . . with the other brethren, clerics and lay'.[171] In 1352 it was endowed with properties and charged with the administration of a chantry founded in the minster by John Wilton, under the supervision of the corporation.[172] The mixed fraternity of York was founded in 1408 by a group of priests and at the beginning of its register a Latin sermon was incorporated. This discussed the meaning of the sacrament as a symbol and a vehicle of unity, merging fraternal idiom and eucharistic symbolism at the moment of inception of this prestigous body.[173]

The acceptance, adoption and manipulation of the eucharistic symbol within the sphere of voluntary associations, and especially in that of patrician fraternities, was not necessarily tied to aggressive

---

[166] Owen (1971), pp. 129–30.

[167] On chaplains, see Barron (1985), p. 33.

[168] See above, pp. 131–2.

[169] Tanner (1985), pp. 75–6. The fraternity has been mistakenly dated as a Corpus Christi fraternity in 1278 in its return to Chancery, PRO. C47/43/291; Westlake (1919), p. 201.

[170] Horrox (1989), p. 47; based on PRO. C47/46/445.

[171] 'In albis cum stola et fanone incedant in processione . . . cum ceteris fratribus literatis et laicis', *ibid.*

[172] *Beverley minster* II, pp. lx–lxi; Leach (1893–5), pp. 103–5, 110–16.

[173] *The register of the Corpus Christi gild*, sermon on pp. 1–6; statutes on pp. 6–9.

orthodoxy. In Leicester in 1413 John Belgrave, a notorious Lollard preacher, was presented to the bishop of Lincoln for his heretical views. He was made to swear that he would no longer maintain his erroneous views and to call seven compurgators. These were men from Leicester's leading families, a number of whom were members of the Corpus Christi fraternity.[174] Yet these same men processed proudly at the side of the eucharist at Corpus Christi! This is only to say that fraternities exhibited the variety of understandings and uses of the eucharist which we have encountered elsewhere, and that one could borrow and apply particular readings of the eucharist rather than others, and align them with the practicalities of life, politics, the contingencies mediated through local knowledge. These practical orientations in the public arena will be even clearer once we examine the Corpus Christi processions.

## CORPUS CHRISTI PROCESSIONS

Corpus Christi was a summer feast, and the part of its celebration which did not have to be enacted within a church took place out of doors. Although the bull of foundation never strictly required a procession – it provided only for a mass and an office – by the early fourteenth century this was deemed the most appropriate mode of celebrating the eucharistic feast. By then numerous forms of eucharistic ritual had *processional* and *expository* features, and conversely, many aspects of civic life were ordered in such modes.[175] Thus within a few decades in most towns and parishes a processional enterprise dominated the day. Already the synodal decrees which spread the feast, and these were more explicit on the Continent than in England, decreed a procession. The earliest example is the council of Sens of 1320:

Around the solemn procession which takes place on the Thursday after Pentecost octave, clergy and laity should attend the carrying of the said sacrament which was instituted by divine inspiration, and we hereby enjoin that nothing in the devotion of clergy and laity should be left out.[176]

And this was repeated in other synods, such as the synod of Paris in 1323.[177] The feast was usually introduced through episcopal initiative,

---

[174] Crompton (1968–9), pp. 29–30.
[175] On eucharistic processions in Germany, see Niedermeyer (1974–5).
[176] 'Circa vero processionem sollemnem quae dicta quinta feria sit a clero et populo in delatione dicti sacramenti his diebus, cum quodammodo divina inspiratione introducta videatur, nihil quo ad praesens iniungimus, devotioni cleri et populi relinquentes', Mansi 25, col. 649.
[177] Mansi 25, c. 1, cols. 727–8. It was not discussed at London council of 1327.

as occurred in the second quarter of the fourteenth century all over Europe.[178] By 1336 the Milanese procession was ordered to include ecclesiastical dignitaries, hermits, friars, monks, secular clergy, and the archbishop on a white horse.[179] The ordinal of the collegiate church of St Peter, Louvain, of the early fourteenth century, did not include Corpus Christi, but a marginal note observed that the episcopal decree which applied to the diocese of Liège made celebration obligatory.[180]

Thus, the processional mode was recommended through episcopal legislation which brought the feast to diocese and parish. There was only one liturgical model for eucharistic public processions, that on Palm Sunday, an Anglo-Norman usage which may have been introduced to England from Normandy in the Rouen rite.[181] The procession was established by Lanfranc in his *Constitutions* of c. 1070–80, and it represented a re-enactment of Christ's entry into Jerusalem. After the sacrament, heralded with palm branches distributed by the sacristan:

Two priests come forward, vested in albs, to carry the shrine, which shall have been brought thither by these same priests a little before daybreak; in it the Body of Christ shall have been laid. Those who carry the banners and cross and the rest as above shall go straight to the shrine.[182]

Such a procession was celebrated at St Albans during the abbacy of Simeon (1160–83),[183] and is described in the customal of St Osmund's, Salisbury, of c. 1225:

And after distributing blessed branches, the tabernacle is prepared, with relics and with the Lord's body hanging from it in a pix, which is carried to the site of the station by two clerics, preceded by a lantern.[184]

At Norwich Cathedral Chapter around 1260 two priests carried the eucharist in procession in the cathedral court in front of the hospice preceded by two flags, two crosses, and incense, and followed by

---

[178] See on the introduction in the dioceses of Constance, Heilig (1936) and Zinsmeier (1953) and Bamberg, Haimerl (1937), pp. 32–58.

[179] Tamborini (1935), pp. 60–2.

[180] 'Nota quod statutum synodale dicit . . . quinta feria ejusdem ebdomade fiat sollempniter festum Eucharistie, prout hactenus a nostris antecessoribus sunt statuta', *Ordinaires des collégiales*, p. 128; on the ordinal pp. xiv, xxv.

[181] Bishop (1918), pp. 276–94; Browe (1939a), pp. 107–9.

[182] 'Exeant duo sacerdotes albis induti, qui portent feretrum, quod parum ante diem ab eisdem et Corpus Christi reconditum. Ad quod feretrum praecedant statim qui unexilla portant, et cruces, et cetera quae superius dicta sunt', Lanfranc, *The monastic constitutions*, pp. 23–4. Cf. Bishop (1928). This was not an Anglo-Saxon custom, but a definite Norman introduction, Bailey (1971), p. 116. On the liturgy, see Hughes (1982), p. 256.

[183] *Vetus registrum* I, p. 191.

[184] 'Et dum distribuuntur rami benedicti, preparetur feretrum cum reliquiis a quo Corpus Domini in pixide dependeat et ad locum stationis a duobus clericis . . . deferatur, lumine in lanterna precedente', *ibid*, pp. 120–22.

relics.[185] In Hereford in the mid fourteenth century the re-enactment was more elaborate. The sacrament and relics were carried from the cathedral on the morning of Holy Thursday outside the city walls and then were brought back in amidst chants and to the greeting and singing of five or seven boys from the top of the city gate.[186]

In the Palm Sunday processions we see a conflation of a number of important eucharistic elements.[187] As symbols of power the eucharist and the relics represented Christ in the enactment of the Entry. This layer of the ritual, which obviously predated the twelfth century, still conflated the meaning of the eucharist with that of the relics. In the early Middle Ages the eucharist was sometimes used for the consecration on altars. This was prohibited by the twelfth century[188] as the eucharist came to be reserved for more rigorous use than relics. Thus, by the later Middle Ages, a more widespread practice of re-enactment – the re-enactment of Christ's burial and resurrection in the Easter Sepulchre – used only the eucharist, buried and then risen, to represent Christ.[189] The Palm Sunday processions obviously continued in religious houses throughout the Middle Ages, but they represent an older perception of the eucharist. While they could have provided a model for processional celebrations on Corpus Christi in which the clergy carried the eucharist to the altar, Corpus Christi far transcended the scope of this traditional event.

The Corpus Christi procession developed in cathedrals, religious houses and parishes,[190] in clerical processions, or those which included both clergy and laity; there were village processions as well as processions arranged in craft-gild groupings.[191] But the shared element in these was the eucharist in whose virtue the orderings and hierarchies were being negotiated and displayed. It was the *raison d'être* of the procession, lending focus to the variety of features which were arranged around it. All those processing, from their differing but

[185] 'Eucharistia vero inter cantores et lucernam. Cantores in sinistra parte eucharistie. Reliquie ultimo retro in transverso', *Norwich customary*, p. 77. See mention of a Palm Sunday procession in the statutes of St Mary Ottery college of 1338, *The collegiate church of Ottery St Mary*, c. 48, p. 178.

[186] Bishop (1918), pp. 279–88. On Palm Sunday celebrations in Pisan parishes of the thirteenth century, see Ronzani (1980), p. 48.

[187] Stemmler (1970), pp. 196–9. Agnes Brown's gift of 1470 towards a canopy for All Hallows' Church, Stamford, was meant to be used on Palm Sunday and Corpus Christi processions, Peck (1785) I, p. 245.

[188] Hermann-Mascard (1975), p. 167; Geary (1978), pp. 28–9.

[189] For a discussion of this practice, see below, pp. 294–7.

[190] On the Genoese obligation to attend one's parochial procession, see Cambiaso (1917), p. 67.

[191] Browe (1939a), pp. 109–17.

interconnected positions, related symbolically to the eucharist on show.

Thomas Aquinas' office did not provide processional hymns for the feast since a procession had not been explicitly envisaged by the bull, but the hymn *Pange, lingua* with its suitable trochaic mode, was adopted in many cases, and a *Salve* chant was used on the processional route.[192] In some places the *hystoria*, the chanted sections of the feast's office, was used throughout the procession.[193] Some processional rubrics entered liturgical books together with the office, but religious houses increasingly entered the chants in processionals, a type of liturgical book which was increasingly in use from the thirteenth century.[194]

In England the Sarum processional provided the liturgy for Corpus Christi processions, which were categorised among 'Double . . . principle feasts',[195] and had an office of nine lessons.[196] The service was to be conducted in silk copes ('in capis sericis'), a category of liturgical decorum in monastic use.[197] This indicated for religious houses and parishes which followed the Use, that Corpus Christi should be celebrated with banners, reliquaries and silk copes, with a procession down the middle of the choir, out of the west door, around the church and back through the same door to the altar.[198] Since it was a eucharistic feast the sacrament was carried surrounded by clergy holding candles, to the sound of processional hymns such as the *Salve festa dies*, or less commonly, but taken from the Palm Sunday liturgy, *Gloria, laus et honor* or *Rex venit*, followed by the proper hymns of the day.[199] Most houses opened with 'Salve festa dies, toto venerabilis aevo' of which there were a number of versions.[200] For example, Syon monastery began with 'Salve, festa dies' and upon a return the choir intoned the antiphone 'Magnum hereditatis.[201] But there was variety in the way the feast was adopted in religious houses; the Gilbertine rite incorporated it

---

[192] Messenger (1953), p. 71. For German gradual hymns for placing the eucharist on the altar see *AH* 34, pp. 47–8; *AH* 47, p. 414.

[193] Klein (1962), p. 34. *Central European manuscripts* no. 42, pp. 56–8, plate 62.

[194] Gy (1960), p. 468.

[195] 'Festa dupplicia . . . principalia', *The use of Sarum*, p. 29. For the York processional liturgy, see *Manuale et processionale . . . York*, pp. 192–3.

[196] *Ibid*, pp. 111, 181, 198, 230–31, 236. The feast was added to fourteenth-century versions of the Sarum customary of 1278 (BL Harl. 1001), *ibid*, p. 68.

[197] *Ibid*, p. 213.

[198] Bailey (1971), p. 17.

[199] *Ibid*, pp. 174–5.

[200] See the York version *AH* 52, pp. 25–6; and another from York province from the turn of the fourteenth century, *AH* 43, pp. 34–5; and the Sarum hymn of *c.*1390 from St Osyth's, *AH* 4, p. 32; and in an addition to an Osney manuscript another hymn, *AH* 43, pp. 33–4.

[201] Cambridge SJC. 139(F2), fols. 48ʳ–51ʳ.

only in the early fifteenth century, with a eucharistic procession 'portetur corpus Christi in aliquo vasculo ab illo qui celebrat missam'.[202]

Nuns were not in orders and were therefore barred from handling
the eucharist.[203] Barking Abbey's ordinal, given to the convent by its
abbess, Sibille Fenton, in 1404 included the office for the 'solemnitas
nova festivitatis corporis Christi celebratur principalis'.[204] The abbess
led the chanting of 'Salve, festa dies' and then six sisters continued the
verses in mid-choir with responses from the whole community. A
procession without the eucharist then began and after it a sermon was
heard in the nave and then a festive mass was celebrated.[205] The
Bridgettines observed 'middis' in the choir during vespers, compline
and matins on the major feasts of St Mary and St Birgitta, and on
Christmas and Corpus Christi:

> On these celebrations two sisters will stand in the middle of the choir and begin all
> the chanted parts at Matins, Vespers, Compline as well as in the other hours at the
> mass.[206]

Responses were sung at vespers and matins and alleluyas were chanted
as mass by four sisters in the middle of the choir. But there seems to be a
more muted response on the matter of festive processionality, and
definitely some difficulty concerning the eucharistic exposition.

Corpus Christi processions also developed in the secular sphere,
outside religious houses, where they extended the impulse to construct
hierarchies around the supernatural power of the eucharist. Its presence
could hallow other spaces, such as fields and villages. In Germany the
custom of beating the boundaries of a village was particularly common,
and the procession with the host stopped at numerous important places
– trees, mills, crosses, bridges – and blessed them in turn,[207] a practice
which recalls the bringing of the host to the sick in procession, which
created, for a while, ritual occasions in secular spaces of towns and
villages. Corpus Christi processions enshrined common practices of
eucharistic reservation and exposition; the host was carried in a costly
and ornate vessel, carried by the clergy, and often covered by a canopy

---

[202] *Gilbertine rite* I, pp. xxiii–xxiv, 16, 55–6. A processional which may have served Castle-
acre priory opened the procession with *Immolabit*, and another Sarum processional had
'Respexit Elyas' upon return, Cambridge SJC. 151(F4), fols. 80ʳ–82ʳ.

[203] The nuns of Chester borrowed from both York and Sarum uses, *Chester processional*, p.
13.

[204] *Barking ordinal* I, pp. 407–17.

[205] *Ibid* I, pp. 143–6.

[206] 'In hiis autem festivitatibus stent due sorores in medio chori que incipiunt omnia cantanda
tam ad matutinis vesperas completorium et ceteras horas ad missam', *The Bridgettine
breviary*, n. 1, p. 117.

[207] *Der Liber Ordinarius der Essener Stiftkirche*, pp. 176–7; Fürstenberg (1917), p. 320.

of rich material held up by staves which were handled by prominent laymen. These elements were redolent symbols of power and well-being, so by the late fourteenth century most urban processions came to be controlled by secular civic authorities, and adopted hierarchies which, while always necessarily involving the clergy at the heart, were increasingly inscribed with local political meanings.[208] By reading the procession like a text as an exercise in self-portrayal which does not necessarily reflect consensus within a community, but rather juxtaposes symbols articulating one of many possible and competing visions of that community, we can gain some access into the rich processional life, full of variety, which developed around the feast of Corpus Christi.

Churchwardens' accounts record the expenses which were connected with all these aspects of the processions; they also fit in well with what we can see with our own eyes in miniatures and paintings of Corpus Christi processions.[209] The procession opened with the carrying of a cross, which as Durandus reminds us in the *Rationale*, warded off the devil.[210] As at the mass, bells were rung, and accounts show that ringing during the procession was also provided in some places. At (Saffron) Walden (Essex) in 1443, 2d were paid to bell ringers during the Corpus Christi procession,[211] and at Yeovil in 1457/8 a penny was paid to ringers on Corpus Christi 'dum processione ibat circa villam'.[212] In some cases clerics were hired for the job, such as William Pou, the sub-sexton of St Laurence's, Reading, who in 1508 was paid for ringing during the Corpus Christi procession.[213] Bell-ringers were sometimes given a breakfast of bread and ale for their labours, as were other people whose work contributed to the procession.[214]

Procession routes were strewn with grass and sawdust to reduce slipperiness,[215] and, as the procession progressed, often with flowers from the hands of children. This prepared the route, and heralded the arrival of the body of participants. The churchwardens of Bridgewater paid 2d in 1452/3 for collection of rushes for Corpus Christi,[216] and the

---

[208] The ceremonial life of Florence has been described as the creation of a theatre of the world, *Libro cerimonial*, p. 25.

[209] See images in Vatican ASP B76, fol. 32v; Cambridge Trinity College B.11.3, fol. 155rb; BN lat. 12065, fol. 177^vb; BN lat. 8886, fol. 325^v; BN lat. 865^a, fol. 340^ra; and in 1 *corali*, no. 227 (Siena Cathedral 23.8, fol. 132^r).

[210] *Rationale* lib. 4, c. 6, no. 18, pp. 160–1.

[211] *Walden*, p. 221.

[212] *Yeovil*, p. 140.

[213] *Reading, St Laurence*, p. 92, see also *Derby, All Saints*, p. 168.

[214] As in 1499/1500 in *Salisbury, St Edmund and St Thomas*, p. 51.

[215] Royal officials checked that the roads were in good repair before the procession at Guernsey, Berry (1815), p. 129. See also Guenée and Lehoux (1968), p. 16.

[216] 'Ad colligendum joncaria', *Bridgewater* IV, p. 65; see also in St Andrew Hubbard Parish, London, in 1522/3, *London, St Andrew Hubbard*, p. 176.

bailiffs paid John Mill 4d in 1455–6 for collecting rods on the feast.[217]
Roses were used in the Corpus Christi garlands of many English
parishes. In 1490/1 woodruff and rose garlands decorated the church of
St Mary at Hill, London, on Corpus Christi and on St Barnabas' day, in
1492/3 13d were spent on such garlands for the decoration of the choir,
while in 1519/20 three dozen garlands were ordered for the Corpus
Christi procession.[218] At St Andrew Hubbard's Church, London,
some 5–6d were spent on garlands annually in the 1460s and around 1s
on roses and woodruff in the 1490s.[219] Roses were popular elsewhere,
at that time of the year, but also since Corpus Christi's liturgical colour
was red. Italian miniatures show the priests and acolytes wearing
garlands of roses on their heads while processing around the host;[220]
and on the vigil of Corpus Christi of 1392 the young men of Senlis went
out 'ès jardins de ladicte ville pour ceuillir des roses pour faire des
chapeaux pour ladicte fete comme les jeunes hommes de ladicte ville ont
acoustumé de fere'.[221] In Jáen in Andalusia the itinerary of the Corpus
Christi procession was decorated with branches and French cloth.[222]

The processions were heralded by the sound of bells, and the sight of
flowers, and sometimes by men carrying flags or crosses (figure 11).[223]
At St Peter Cheap, London, churchwardens recorded payments for
flags and garlands,[224] and at (Saffron) Walden (Essex) in 1449, 20d were
paid to John Smith for making a fringe for one of the parish's seven
Corpus Christi flags.[225] Regular entries for the church of St Andrew
Hubbard, London, show expenses on flags and garlands from the 1450s
to the 1480s.[226] At St Edmund's and St Thomas' church, Salisbury,
boys carried the church's banner ('vexille dicte ecclesie') on Corpus
Christi, Rogation, Ascension and Pentecost Thursday.[227] In the early

[217] *Bridgewater* IV, p. 92.
[218] Cox (1913), p. 239.
[219] *London, St Andrew Hubbard*, 1466–8, p. 398; 1491/2 and 1492/3, pp. 393, 395.
[220] See BN. lat. 880¹, fol. 197ʳᵃ, missal of Sens (Use of Melun) of 1489.
[221] Vaultier (1965), p. 120.
[222] As described in the chronicle of the royal constable Miguel Lucas de Iranzo in 1463: 'La celebración de la fiesta del Corpus se hace adorando con ramos y paños franceses el itinerario que recorriá la processión', Contreras Villar (1987), p. 316. At Llanasaph green herbs and flowers were strewn on thresholds on Corpus Christi eve, Brand (1813) I, pp. 237–8.
[223] See BN. lat. 12061, fol. 98ʳᵇ, missal of St Maur-les-Fossés, of the second half of the fifteenth century; Paris Arsenal 623, fol. 165ᵛᵃ, missal of Santa Maria Maggiore (use of Paris) of early fifteenth century; Vatican ASP B 76, fol. 32ᵛ, missal of Avignon of mid fourteenth century; BN lat. 8886, fol. 325ᵛ, missal-pontifical of Etienne Loypeau, bishop of Luçon.
[224] In 1447, 1521, 1534, Cox (1913), pp. 262, 240.
[225] *Walden*, p. 222.
[226] *London, St Andrew Hubbard*, pp. 248, 400, 402, 534.
[227] *Salisbury, St Edmund and St Thomas*, see 1461/2, pp. 8, 9, 11, 13, 27, 29, 31; 1483/4, p. 31.

11  A Corpus Christi procession; initial of the Corpus Christi mass

fifteenth century St Paul's, London, listed amongst its possessions
'Banners and a cloth for the feast of Corpus Christi'.[228] The bearers of a
processional cross for St Ewen's Parish, Bristol, are mentioned in 1455/
6 and again in the 1510s,[229] and members of the clothiers' gild of
Worcester carried a cross-banner in a procession to the cathedral on
Corpus Christi in 1523.[230]

In some places the procession was announced by the purest of the
pure, by children, who by virtue of their pre-political being symbolised

---

[228] 'Banners and a cloth for the feast of Corpus Christi', *St Paul's*, p. 141.
[229] *Bristol, St Ewen's*, p. 120, earning 2d in the 1510s, p. 130.
[230] Hughes (1986), p. 25.

that which was virtuous within the community.[231] They feature at prominent positions, but usually led or heralded the oncoming mass of adults. At Grantham *c.*1339 two boys in albs led the Corpus Christi procession.[233] The boys of Parisian charity schools often accompanied the priest with the *viaticum*, but more particularly, the young scholars of *Ave Maria* college were required to take part in the Corpus Christi procession by the wish of the founder:

tenuz chacun an porter a la feste Dieu par deuant Nostre Seigneur j. cierge de j. quarteron de cire vierge chacuns.

The accompanying illustration shows six boys carrying candles and two others carrying the canopy over the priest with the monstrance.[233] Children representing angels sang responses at the Corpus Christi procession of Mainz.[234] Yet even this ritual object, the pure child, could be integrated into formations of difference; in Florence children represented their families in the *gonfaloni* as they assembled to accompany the host on Corpus Christi day.[235]

But the heart of the procession was the eucharist, the vessel containing it, those carrying it, the canopy over it, and the dignitaries, lay and ecclesiastical, who surrounded it. The rules of reservation which prevailed in the church, and when the eucharist was taken to the sick, applied also in the procession; the consecrated host on parade was kept in a precious vessel. In England closed vessels were sometimes used, but as elsewhere the expository moment called for a partly transparent vessel. The plate recorded in parish inventories often describes the sort of vessels used on Corpus Christi, and related elements of imagery. A Bridgewater inventory of 1447 records 'j demonstracion' for the sacrament, made of gilt silver, as well as a latten box for it and two cups.[236] In his will John Welborne (d.1381) left Lincoln minster:

one great Fertur silver and gilt w$^t$ one cross Iles and one stepell in y$^e$ Middle and one Crosse in y$^e$ toppe w$^{th}$ twentye Pinnacles and an Image of Our Lady . . . and it is set in a Table of wood, and athing in y$^e$ middle to put in y$^e$ sacrament when it is borne weighing xvij$^{xx}$ unces'.[237]

[231] On the significance of children in processional ritual, see Trexler (1974), pp. 245–6.
[232] PRO. C47/40/109.
[233] Gabriel (1955), pp. 158–9, fig. 14, plate xviii.
[234] Klein (1962), p. 34.
[235] Trexler (1974), p. 222.
[236] *Bridgewater* IV, p. 39.
[237] MacGarry (1936), p. 149.

Similar images suffused the iconography of the procession. In Spain dancers, sometimes dressed as angels, accompanied the host.[238]

Where it could be afforded – often by the gift of a rich individual or a corporation – the eucharist was carried within or on an elaborate structure, a tabernacle (figure 13). In his will made in 1449, William Bruges, first Garter King-at-Arms, provided for the construction of an elaborate 'feretory' of gilt wood and silver, adorned with jewels, and surrounded by angels carrying emblems of the Passion enclosing a silver gilt cup for the eucharist. The structure would be carried on Corpus Christi between the deacon and subdeacon of Stamford.[239] A very similar structure was used at Genoa Metropolitan Church for the same purpose; in 1356 it was described as:

Item a gilt wooden panel with figures of four angels on which Christ's body is carried processionally.[240]

In Bristol the iconography was combined with living people, when the wooden tabernacle of Corpus Christi was preceded by twelve children and four men dressed as evangelists, all of whom carried candles.[241] Thornton Abbey's tabernacle was sufficiently remarkable to be noted in the house's chronicle as an achievement of John Hoton's abbacy:

During the time of that abbot a bier was made in which the Lord's body is carried around the church on Corpus Christi day and on Palm Sunday.[242]

Setting up the 'bier' cost the churchwardens of Bridgewater regular sums for thread, pins and nails, and for storage.[243]

Visual representations of Corpus Christi processions often show the eucharistic vessel or tabernacle carried by one or more priests, and often have a canopy stretched above the group, usually on staves carried by four laymen or priests (figures 12 and 14).[244] The canopy was an important symbol of dignity to which we will return; it was also an

[238] Reynaud (1974), p. 140; Prado (1932), p. 10.
[239] Peck (1727) lib. xiv, p. 25. A similar bejewelled vessel belonged to the metropolitan church of Genoa as described in 1386: 'Item tabernaculum unum magnum cristalo cum pede argenteo deaurato munitum argento desuper et circumquaque cum lapidibus et perlis quo defertur processionaliter corpus domini nostri iesu christi', Cambiaso (1917), p. 65.
[240] 'Item tabulla una de ligno deaurato cum figuris quatuor angelorum super quo portatur Corpus Christi processionaliter', *ibid*, p. 69.
[241] *Bristol, All Saints*, p. 237.
[242] 'Tempore ipsius abbatis factum est feretrum in quo corpus domini defertur circa ecclesiam in die Corporis Christi et in dominica palmarum', Clapham and Major (1946), p. 176. I am grateful to Dorothy Owen for providing me with this entry.
[243] *Bridgewater* III, pp. 104, 106, 108, 109, 112, 143; IV, pp. 7, 64.
[244] The gorgeous miniature for Corpus Christi on the pages of the Lovel Lectionary of *c.* 1400 (figure 16), has sumptuously clad priests carrying poles over a bishop with a monstrance, and the carriers face each other – where were they going? BL Harl. 7026, fol. 13[r].

12 A Corpus Christi procession; initial of the Corpus Christi mass

expensive object, made of embroidered velvet, heavily decorated with fringes. In her will of 1470, Agnes Brown left a gift of 4 marks to All Hallows' Church, Stamford, to buy a silk and gold cloth with a valence, which was to be borne on four staves over the sacrament on Palm Sunday and for the worship of the Sacrament.[245] In 1475/6 the parish of St Thomas and St Edmund, Salisbury, had a new canopy consecrated, its total cost of £3 16s 10d comprising:[246]

| | | |
|---|---|---|
| 2½ yards and i nail of satin | 22s | |
| for silken fringe | 5s | |
| | | 2d |
| 3 ells of Garnsey cloth | | 20d |
| 3 yards of purple velvet | 48s | |

Similarly lavish was the canopy made in London in 1515/16 for the parish of Holy Trinity, Cambridge. It cost £9 5s 4d in material and labour and was made of black velvet with a valence of red velvet, and was embroidered with an image of the Trinity in silk thread.[247] Smaller communities spent less, as in the case of Ashburton (Devon) which

[245] Peck and Harrod (1785) I, p. 245.
[246] *Salisbury, St Edmund and St Thomas*, p. 20.
[247] Cox (1913), p. 103.

13 A tabernacle on staves; initial of the Corpus Christi mass

spent 6s 11d on a painted linen cloth to carry over the sacrament on Corpus Christi and Palm Sunday.[248] Canopies were expensive objects and as they became *de rigeur* for eucharistic processions, communities depended on benefactors to provide them as gifts.[249] The canopy of Bassingbourn (Cambridgeshire) was described in 1498 as follows:

Item a clothe off velewet off purpur colour ffor the canopy to be born over the blyssid sacrament with the ymage off the cruciffixe broydrid in the myddys of the seid clothe *and the namys off the gifferes in the iiij corners.*[250]

Equally elaborate was a canopy to be placed over the host, the gift of Beatrice Balle, John Ode and Marion Mason to St Peter Mancroft Church, Norwich, in 1458.[251] So precious an ornament which was taken out of doors needed frequent and costly repair. Among other expenses related to Corpus Christi, St Andrew Hubbard's Parish, London, spent 11s 5d in 1458–60 on railings for a canopy.[252] In 1490/91 a new stave was bought and three other mended (5d), in 1493–4 points

[248] *Ashburton*, p. 68.
[249] See the example of another gift for the enhancement of the Corpus Christi feast, the frontal of blue velvet given by Gilbert d'Umfraville to the Augustinian friars of St Mary, Kyme (Lincs.) before 1377, for use at Easter, Ascension, Pentecost, Holy Trinity and Corpus Christi, *Lincoln cathedral statutes* III, p. 252.
[250] CUL. Add. 2792, fol. 3ᵛ.
[251] Bloomfield (1806) IV, p. 213. See a similar gift in Genoa, Cambiasio (1917), p. 66.
[252] *London, St Andrew Hubbard*, p. 248. See also *Glastonbury, St John's*, p. 144.

for the canopy were bought (1d), in 1494/5 the old canopy was replaced and sold for 2s, and a new one, which must have been quite humble, was bought for 15s 3d; in 1497–8 nails and points for it were bought again (1½d).[253]

Under the canopy marched a priest with the eucharistic vessel, which was sometimes a monstrance (figures 11, 14 and 15). In Yeovil in 1457 linen was bought 'for 2 banners of the church to be carried around the canopy', which were dyed and carried on wooden poles.[254] The parish of St George, St Peter and St Mary, Nottingham, paid twelve bearers a penny each to carry banners and torches around the eucharist on Corpus Christi.[255] Lights appear in contemporary depictions of processions. In his will of 1366, Thomas Buckton, an official of the archiepiscopal court of York, left 100s for the Corpus Christi solemnity of the city, in particular for the maintenance of torches around Christ's body at the procession.[256] In 1428/9 the churchwardens of Bridgewater spent 6s 8d on two torches for the feast, and at that price they must have been large and ornate.[257] Heavy tapers were placed in latten bowls on major feasts before the high altar, whence processions usually originated. Between 1491 and 1511 the parish of St Andrew Hubbard, London, spent some 3–4s annually on the decoration of twelve to sixteen Corpus Christi torches[258] and paid each torch bearer a penny and some breakfast of bread and ale,[259] as did the parish of St Ewen, Bristol.[260]

The centre of the procession was the most ornate, the most densely decorated; and it included people whose rank was reflected and enhanced by proximity to the holiest of holies. The eucharist could not be handled by a lay person, so its receptacle was always carried by priests, but the canopy and flags around it were carried by layfolk, as if they were invented for this very end. In Coventry four burgesses bore the canopy;[261] in 1388 a legacy of 100s was used by Mayor William Selby to commission a processional shrine for York,[262] and from 1431/2 this was carried by members of the Corpus Christi fraternity, whose

[253] *London, St Andrew Hubbard*, pp. 391, 396, 398, 571.
[254] 'Pro ij vexillis ecclesie portandis circa canapis'; they cost in sum 2s 5d, *Yeovil*, p. 139.
[255] Regular entries appear in the churchwarden's accounts from 1473, *Nottingham, St George*, pp. 33, 34, 36, 43, 45–7, 49, 52, etc.
[256] *Testamenta Eboracensia* I, p. 77. On the involvement of the archiepiscopal household in arrangements for Corpus Christi, see Hughes (1988), p. 170.
[257] *Bridgewater* III, p. 101.
[258] *London, St Andrew Hubbard*, pp. 393, 397, 568, 571, 573, 575–7, 665, 675.
[259] *Ibid*, pp. 395, 397, 568, 577.
[260] *Bristol, St Ewen*, in 1516/17, p. 577.
[261] Phythian-Adams (1979), p. 137.
[262] Johnston (1976), pp. 373–4.

14 A Corpus Christi procession; decoration of the introit 'Ego sum' of the
Corpus Christi mass

15  A Corpus Christi procession; initial of the Corpus Christi mass

resident membership consisted largely of members of leading York families,[263] followed by the council of twenty-four and twelve aldermen who accompanied the mayor in procession with torches.[264] Later, after 1449, the fraternity members carried a new tabernacle, and paid 12d to four deacons who carried the canopy.[265] In Germany similar hierarchies established themselves: in Nürnberg in 1419 the carriers were six counts, in Hildesheim in 1448 members of the town council carried the canopy, in Regensburg in 1532, eight princes.[266] From the early fifteenth century the Genoese Doge, from Guano Barnaba on, carried the receptacle with the host – something no Doge had done before, and was quite unheard of elsewhere.[267] Prominent craft corporations also processed nearest the host, such as the Mercers of Rennes in the fifteenth century, whose inventory of 1437 recorded two basins of white iron to support torches on the feast of the sacrament.[268] In

[263] *Ibid*, pp. 378–82.
[264] Johnston (1973–4), p. 58.
[265] Johnston (1976), p. 379.
[266] Zika (1988), p. 41, n. 51.
[267] *Annali* II, p. 274.
[268] Leguay (1975), pp. 171–2, 176.

Beverley the procession developed by 1431 into a craft gild and fraternity procession, but the Corpus Christi fraternity, which was in this
town a predominantly clerical body, was charged with the procession's
organisation and led it through the town.[269]

The gradual insertion of local political meanings into the eucharistic
procession was at work everywhere. It was usually some time in the
second half of the fourteenth century, as the symbolic possibilities
inherent in the ritual unfolded, that the greater involvement of corporations, town councils and crafts becomes apparent in the urban milieu.
The process is shared by English and continental towns alike. The
Corpus Christi procession of Aachen existed by 1319, but enters town
accounts only from 1334/5.[270] In València there was a procession from
1355 under the auspices of the cathedral, which was entrusted by the
bishop for organisation by the town in 1372.[271] The *échevins* of Lille
controlled the town's procession which by the late fourteenth century
had developed on the basis of craft-gilds.[272] Corpus Christi was celebrated in Venice from 1295 and under the auspices of the *consiglio*, but
only in 1416 did the Doge choose twenty-four old and wise citizens
('antiquos et probos cives') and twelve others to follow them with
torches, as his representatives in the procession.[273] From 1443 the city
of Verona took over the regulation of streets and people during the
procession. Leading citizens supervised the occasion and the town
council elected twelve *gubernatores* or *procuratores* who selected ten
other citizens to oversee order and discipline during the procession and
to collect the contributions towards expenses levied from the town's
quarters.[274] A decision of the Aberdeen town council of 1512 ratified
and approved earlier ordinances which required that every craft have a
pair of torches, of 4 lb of wax each, to bear on Corpus Christi for
decoration and worship of the sacrament.[275]

When Milan settled its peace with the papacy in 1335 the Doge
Giovanni Visconti had a most solemn procession celebrated in honour
of the event.[276] Giovanni Villani reports in his chronicle that when the
plague hit Florence in 1340 the *Consiglio* ordained that an especially
great eucharistic procession should be planned for the Sunday in the
octave of Corpus Christi:

---

[269]  PRO. C47/46/445; Horrox (1989), p. 47.
[270]  Gatzweiler (1924), pp. 202–3.
[271]  Merimée (1913), pp. 9–10.
[272]  Platelle (1971), p. 299.
[273]  Cambiaso (1917), pp. 65–6.
[274]  Spagnolo (1901), pp. 6–7.
[275]  *Aberdeen* I, p. 442.
[276]  Tamborini (1935), pp. 54–5.

Almost all the citizens were there, men and women, with the relic of Christ's body which was kept at the church of St Ambrose, and they walked with it throughout the area at the hour of none and with more than 150 burning candles.[277]

When Montpellier was struck by the plague in 1407 the eucharist was mounted and taken around the town, and even outside it.[278] In Germany it was also a common practice to take the eucharist out to the fields, to carry it through them and fructify the seed-beds.[279]

What emerges, then, is the penetration of the secular and the civic-political into the eucharistic procession in two hardly separable ways. First, the symbolic meaning of eucharistic practices, and the eucharistic public procession, attracted those whose claims to power and privilege could be re-expressed, and celebrated on this special event. Second, as the event developed, and impinged on political relations, law and order, a controlling and regulating function was required from the town officials, just as it came to be exercised within the participating corporations themselves.

The iconography of power which developed around the eucharistic procession was also adopted in other contexts. Those using it wished to imply that the very same will which made God institute the eucharist and ordain its celebration also placed the monarch in his God-given position. Thus, the French kings took up some eucharistic trappings, and especially the canopy which came to be associated with notions of majesty.[280] Drawing from the eucharistic iconography the kings of France, England, Navarre and Aragon came to use canopies in their own ceremonies.[281] In the coronation city of Reims the French kings carefully superimposed symbols of royal authority onto the Corpus Christi ritual; in 1350 John II had his torches carried at the procession and a royal mass of the Holy Spirit was celebrated for the king and his predecessors on the morrow of the feast.[282] Majesty was the theme of the eucharistic procession, and just as in a royal presence, music was played 'videlen to love and to ere dene hilgen lichamen'.[283]

The entry of Corpus Christi into local networks of relations meant that existing relations and tensions found a field for inscription. It also

---

[277] 'Furono quasi tutti i cittadini maschi e feminine colla reliquia del Corpo di Cristo che sta a Santo Ambrogio, e andorsi con esso per tutta la terra inficio a ora di nona con più de 150 torchi accesi', Giovanni Villani, *Cronica* XI, 114. Many thanks to John Henderson for providing me with this reference.

[278] Coulet (1982), p. 389.

[279] Browe (1929b), pp. 743, 748–50.

[280] Guenée and Lehoux (1968), pp. 5–8.

[281] *Ibid*, pp. 17–18; Stemmler (1970), pp. 291–9.

[282] Galpern (1976), pp. 16–17.

[283] Fürstenberg (1917), pp. 321–3; p. 323.

meant the problems were forced towards resolution, when neat hierarchies had to be decided upon. The feast of Corpus Christi has been seen frequently and unproblematically as a feast of unity, reinforcing order and confirming hierarchy. The need to order spurred bodies and corporations to assert their power and position, and finally to negotiate as best they could. According to the 1325 ordinances of Ipswich the town's two leading religious houses, the priories of the Holy Trinity and of St Peter, led the procession in alternate years. Starting at 9 am, freshly shaved and groomed, and in rich hoods, they set out from their respective priories, with the parochial clergy carrying cross and banners, and with a tabernacle at the heart and then returned to the priory for the day's mass. At this stage the role of the Corpus Christi fraternity is as yet unclear, but later in the fourteenth century clear groups by craft emerged to give the procession its tone. Durham displayed a similar development of the merging of clerical and craft groups. By the fifteenth century the procession began at the new palace green, and involved the merging of two distinct groups, the craft with their banners and torches in the right-hand file, and the clerical procession with the tabernacle 'squared box all of crystall' held by four priests, on the left. These groups met at the abbey church whence they processed together into the church up to the shrine of St Cuthbert around which they marched, before carrying the tabernacle back to St Nicholas' church where it remained for the next twelve months.[284] Crafts were assisted by the friars in organising the Corpus Christi celebrations. After the Clothiers' gild amalgamated with that of the Walkers and Weavers of Worcester in 1522, the new gild drew up an ordinance about the feast, according to which all members were to assemble at the Dominican house and walk in procession together to the cathedral, and later in the day retire from the procession as a group.[285] In some continental towns two separate ceremonies developed. In Essen there was a procession of canons from the main church; and on the morrow there was a procession of townsfolk, led by a canon and scholars, which went out of the town gate and around its walls into the fields, which were then blessed, before moving back into the town.[286]

But as the procession gradually moved from a predominantly religious sphere to the public and secular space it was bound to change.

---

[284] *Rites of Durham*, p. 107.
[285] Hughes (1986), pp. 24–5. The Dominican inventory included four staves, a canopy and a cross banner, which may have belonged to the fraternity, *ibid*. In Coventry the crafts marched from the house of a senior craftsman, Phythian-Adams (1977), p. 112.
[286] *Der Liber Ordinarius des Essener Stiftkirche*, p. 177.

The liturgical core was maintained in most places, but around it developed a variety of arrangements ordering political groups around the symbolic power centre. In most English towns the unit for organisation became the craft gild, and the regulating body, by necessity, the town council, whose function in all town business was to arbitrate and mediate between disparate bodies. Craft-gilds were also the units which produced the Corpus Christi cycle plays in those towns which mounted such enterprises.[287] But such undertakings were usually later: in York the procession is recorded by 1325: dramatic celebrations – there is no evidence yet for full cycles – first occur in 1377.[288] In the fifteenth century the procession of York began with an assembly at 4.30 am before the gates of Holy Trinity priory in Mickelgate, and was led by priests and boys holding candles. Then followed the parish clergy, the host carried by two men under a canopy and surrounded by four clerks and six men bearing torches. After the host came the mayor, aldermen and officials, and for as long as the pageants were part of the procession, that is until 1426, they processed to the cathedral, and finally to the hospital of St Leonard.[289] The crafts were an obvious source for income to sustain the processions as indeed they helped certain other urban expenses, with their self-governing procedures and internal discipline. Thus in King's Lynn a portion of the fines levied from craft members for infringement of craft regulations were allocated for maintenance of the Corpus Christi procession. The statutes of the Tailors of Lynn of 1449 show that 40d of the entry fee for a non-burgess went towards 'sustentacion' of the procession, as did the 40d fine for keeping foreign apprentices, and the 40d fine for slander against another member's work.[290]

The variety in arrangements was very great. Not only did processions develop at multiple levels – York had a procession of the cathedral, of St Mary's Abbey, and of the town[291] – but even the form of participation within the processing whole could vary. In York and Beverley there were the full-length processions in which each craft filed separately;[292] elsewhere there were clusters of crafts, linked by the common interest of kindred occupations. By 1453 the Norwich Corpus Christi procession was ordered by craft: the smiths, tilers, masons and lumbermen under a banner; carpenters, joiners and wheelwrights; woollen-weavers, linen-weavers, fullers and shearmen;

[287] James (1983), pp. 12–14, 15–18; but also religious fraternities, Gibson (1981), pp. 77–8.
[288] When rent for the storage spaces for props is recorded, Johnston (1976), pp. 373–4.
[289] Cowling (1976); Johnston (1976), p. 377.
[290] *The making of King's Lynn*, pp. 266–8; at p. 267.
[291] Cowling (1976).
[292] Horrox (1989), p. 46.

16  A Corpus Christi procession; initial of the readings for Corpus Christi

fishmongers and freshwater fishermen; and finally, haberdashers, cappers, hatters, pinners and pointmakers.[293] Similarly, in Ipswich in 1492 clusters of crafts processed under a saint's banner: the goldsmiths, blacksmiths, locksmiths and bladesmiths under St Eligius' auspices; the barbers and wax-chandlers under St Thomas; tailors with St John;

[293] *Records of the city of Norwich* II, pp. 312–13.

glaziers, carpenters, painters, fletchers, bowers, patten-makers and scriveners under St Luke; and thus all crafts and after them fraternities, groups of friars: Carmelites, Franciscans and Dominicans, and finally the tabernacle itself.[294]

Questions of precedence and order were of the utmost importance in the processional setting. We have seen in Ipswich the priories of the Holy Trinity and St Peter's alternate in leading the procession; the chapter of Rennes and the abbey of Ste Melaine alternated annually in occupying the place right before or right after the eucharist.[295] A similar agreement about alternating primacy in the Corpus Christi procession was arbitrated by the bishop of Freising in 1428 between the dean of St Peter's of Munich and the priest of the parish of Our Lady.[296] The agreement reached in Chester in 1475 between the coopers and the fletchers, settled for the former processing before, and thus in an inferior position to the latter, each with their lights on both sides.[297]

This rhythm of gradual and mounting dignity, the claim that power was graduated along a *continuum* of positions, created the rhetoric of inclusion for the procession. But this order which 'rippled past',[298] was highly exclusive and tendentious. The story of Corpus Christi processions is also one of *dis*order, of law-suits generations long, of disputes over precedence and riots.[299] The Cordwainers and Weavers of York were traditionally at each other's throats over questions of precedence which reached the city council on numerous occasions throughout the fifteenth century.[300]

Beyond the strife and the tension structurally embedded in social relations, the element of disorder, the excitement of a populous event, percolated and erupted in a variety of ways. When the parishioners of Kempsey (Warwickshire) were at the Ascension Day procession of 1339, thieves were at work stealing an expensive leather-bound breviary.[301] Corpus Christi attracted people from the hinterland of a town

[294] IESRO C4/2 (White Domesday), fols. 1ʳ, 72ʳ, 72ᵛ.
[295] Guillotin de Carson (1879), p. 7. On precedence in later processions see also Muir (1981), pp. 37–8; Pullan (1971), pp. 52–3; Martz (1983), p. 167.
[296] Mitterwieser (1930), p. 16.
[297] *REED: Chester* I, pp. 15–16. On strife in Chester, see Morris (1893), pp. 50, 572.
[298] Darnton (1984), p. 123. For a very minute gradation in the Corpus Christi procession, set out by the city of Angers in 1513, see Uzureau (1933).
[299] Like that at York Minster on Corpus Christi eve of 1345, Johnston (1976), p. 374; and note Wat Tyler's progression onto Smithfield on Thursday 13 June, in 1381, *The peasants' revolt*, pp. 155–6, 159–60, 214.
[300] *York civic records* II, pp. 56, 59, 71, 96; Johnston (1976), p. 382.
[301] *Reg. Bransford*, no. 49, p. 9. The murder of the vicar of South Brent (dioc. Exeter), after the vespers of Corpus Christi eve 1436 may have been induced by the high spirits of the oncoming feast: 'in profesto solempnis diei sacratissimi Corporis Domini nostri Ihesu Christi . . . tempore vesperarum prefati profesti', for the excommunication mandate against the unknown murderers see *Reg. Lacy* II, pp. 8–10.

who swelled the crowds of spectators, the sections outside the ordered procession.[302] On her pilgrimage route in Germany Margery Kempe timed her arrival at Wilsnack to coincide with Corpus Christi 1426. On its eve, between Stralsund and Wilsnack, she could only find a bed of straw since the area was flooded by fellow-travellers to the eucharistic miracle-site for the eucharistic feast.[303] On Corpus Christi 1399 the prostitutes of Paris descended on Senlis for the business,[304] as they had also created business for the police of Lille in 1382.[305]

After the ordered procession more informal celebrations followed. Parishes, fraternities, religious houses, withdrew from the public scene to have their dinners. The fifteenth-century text-book from Oxford, for use in Latin–English translation, describes what must have been the experience in a village of a small urban parish:

Parishyns mete eche other, and if they fynde eny crose by the way, ther thei tary anone. After the gospell is done, thei fall to ther metes that the wyffys brought from home for the nonys.[306]

This sounds very much like a picnic! Some parishes, like some of the fraternities which we have encountered,[307] arranged a meal. St Ewen's, Bristol, spent some 3s 7d on its dinner in 1471/2: 16d on ale, 23d on beef, mutton, chicken, bread and spices, and 4d for the cook's wages and fuel; or again, in 1480/81: 6d on ale, ½d on mustard, 2½d on mutton, 8d on beef pieces and 6d on beef rounds.[308] In St John's parish, Bristol, an ordinance of 1472 recorded expenses concerning a Corpus Christi 'dinner to the parson priests and clerks that were at the procession with the parish 3s'.[309] When religious houses indulged in conviviality an official was required to allocate the pittances. At St Augustine's, Bristol, on Corpus Christi 1491/2, the pittancer granted the abbot a pot of wine, and each canon a quarter pot, as on other major feasts.[310] Gifts also flowed in other directions on this great day of celebration. Not only was ale distributed among cross and torch bearers but it was also

---

[302] As mentioned by William Melton in 1426 in his reordering of the York Corpus Christi celebrations: 'dicebat tamen quod cives predicte civitatis et alij forinseci in dicto festo confluentes ad eandem . . .' *REED: York* I, p. 43.

[303] *The book of Margery Kempe*, p. 234.

[304] Vaultier (1965), p. 121.

[305] Platelle (1970) I, p. 355.

[306] *School book*, pp. 25–6.

[307] Above, pp. 238–9.

[308] *Bristol, St Ewen*, pp. 87, 108. Such expenses ranging from 2s 6d to 3s 5d per feast were recorded throughout the 1470s and 1490s, like 1486/7, p. 120, 1490/91, p. 130. For expenses on calves, sheep, honey, salt and the wages of cooks, see the accounts of Great Dunmow (Essex), in 1538, *Great Dunmow*, p. 235.

[309] Bristol Archive Office, St John's Book, fol. 11ʳ.

[310] *Compotus roll*, pp. 165–6.

given as gift. The common bailiffs of Bridgewater regularly sent a gallon of wine to the master of St John's hospital and to the local Franciscans, and two gallons between the 1440s and the 1460s.[311] The town of Exeter gave its mendicant friars 4s worth of wine from sometime in the 1390s onwards, and it is recorded in 1407/8 as being for the procession on Corpus Christi, and as of custom.[312] These were rewards for help in organising the procession, for a sermon, for a pageant, or simply as a gift, as in the case the 4d *potellum* of wine sent to the vicar of Bridgewater in 1453/4.[313] The Dyers and Smiths of Coventry provided ale to their journeymen on Corpus Christi, Midsummer and St Peter's feast.[314]

Having examined some of the features which developed around Corpus Christi processions, we must also remember and consider that processions, like all rituals, can mean different things to different people. In their construction of images of the world and in their incitement to action, processions can bear messages that are contradictory, volatile, and determined by context. For that reason a characteristic Corpus Christi procession cannot really be described, only the sort of possibilities embedded in it. Rituals can go wrong;[315] wrong, that is, for their planners. In fact, ritual, and especially processional ritual, possesses an inherent destabilising element. The need to put into linear form social relations which are in their nature fluid and on-going exchanges, induced the choice of arbitrary format, one which necessarily distorts experiences. The relations between master and journeyman as experienced within a household embodied contractual as well as informal exchanges which were disrupted at the procession that separated them – who usually worked together – in obvious ways.[316] Robert Darnton has summarised this difficulty in connection with the *procession générale* of Montpellier of 1768, the sort of procession which was observed on Corpus Christi:

A procession could not be taken literally as a model of society, because it exaggerated some elements and neglected others.[317]

This seems more perceptive than the view that a Corpus Christi

[311] *Bridgewater* III, p. 148; IV, pp. 62, 69, 83, 98, 103, 111, 117, 123, 137.
[312] Little (1927), p. 26.
[313] *Bridgewater* IV, pp. 69; also p. 123.
[314] Phythian-Adams (1972), p. 65.
[315] As they did in Romans in 1579–80, Le Roy Ladurie (1980).
[316] The master-weavers of Chester beat up their journeymen on Corpus Christi 1358, *REED: York* I, pp. 5–6: 'cum polaxes baculis premotis baslardis et aliis diversis armaturis'.
[317] Darnton (1984), p. 122; these are *not* 'miniature replicas' of the social order, *ibid*, p. 121.

procession, or other civic ritual, is 'a mirror of the city'.[318] A procession which excluded most working people, women, children, visitors and servants,[319] was not a picture of the community. It cannot be said to be a moment which expressed, according to Mervyn James and after Victor Turner, 'an essential and generic bond without which there would be *no* society'.[320] By laying hierarchy bare it could incite the conflict of difference ever more powerfully sensed in a concentrated symbolic moment.[321]

The *déroulement* of a procession was undoubtedly an event of social significance, which attracted investment, exertion, and vigilant supervision by its participants.[322] But the nature of such events as expressions of an underlying *communitas*,[323] sometimes asserted rather than proven,[324] is open to argument. It may be that scholars have been deceived by the rhetoric of the organisers of the Corpus Christi procession. Public ritual which displays prestige, perhaps reflects an equilibrium as claimed by Heers,[325] but if so it is conditional, involving so limited a number of enfranchised and active players that to claim that 'the community in its entirety was literally defining itself for all to see' hardly captures the significance of the event.[326] Durkheim's followers posit a necessary relationship between religious ritual and a society's most salient values; but this has led some to ignore the very divergent interests and understandings which coexist within society, and which must, perforce, even in Durkheimian terms, be articulated in some *représentations collectives*.[327] Steven Lukes has suggested that most applications of Durkheimian notions of ritual:

fail to explore, not only different levels of symbolic meaning in the rituals, but also socially patterned differences of interpretation among those who participate in them and observe them.[328]

---

[318] Phythian-Adams (1979), p. 178.

[319] No 'new men' were part of the procession at Montpellier, Darnton (1984), p. 126.

[320] Turner (1969), p. 83; as used by James (1983), p. 11.

[321] Corpus Christi processions were occasions of violent outbursts between Catholics and Protestants in sixteenth century France, Davis (1973), pp. 73–4.

[322] In London the city-wide procession of crafts never developed, it was too vast an enterprise to imagine or execute. London's version of Corpus Christi pageantry was a succession of parish processions, and a civic procession handled by the elite company of the Skinners, see above, pp. 229–32 and below p. 275.

[323] See the classic Phythian-Adams (1972); Phythian-Adams (1979); James (1983).

[324] On community, see also Rosser (1988).

[325] Heers (1985), pp. 94–5.

[326] Phythian-Adams (1972), p. 58.

[327] Durkheim (1915), esp. pp. 275, 375, 379–81; for a codified but still insufficiently dynamic articulation of the approach, see Geertz (1982), pp. 121–36.

[328] Lukes (1977), p. 67. I have benefited from Ian Archer's advice and comments on this article.

But the problem of ritual efficacy is not only in the 'socially patterned meanings' of Lukes, which are not communal, nor inert, nor static. What Corpus Christi did *not* do is 'resolve such contradictions that appear in life, and in that respect it does not instruct'; rather, it propagated 'a particular view of the world' because to participate in it was 'to repeat patterns of interactions common to other domains of life'.[329] It is the symbols which are conveyed in ritual which always contain a range of meanings. And more than most the body; even in the Corpus Christi drama which progressed processionally with the climax at the scene of the Crucifixion, Christ's suffering body was not serene: its wounds, its interstices, fascinated large number in the dramatic, public presentation.[330] Thus, the processional mode can induce tension and rivalry rather than resolve difference into *communitas* through ritual.[331]

The processional route or itinerary expressed themes and meanings which predated the feast and its symbolism and thus expressed a more local identity. In York and Coventry the mystery plays followed the route of royal entries,[332] in Lérida the procession followed royal and episcopal entries,[333] in Goslar that of legatine entries.[334] Just as kings borrowed the majesty of the eucharistic canopy, towns chose routes which were marked out by external events or authorities, which were themselves part of the town's history. Processional routes differed greatly; parochial processions began at the church and walked around significant places in the parish, and in villages they most frequently followed the boundaries.[335] But the more complex the processing body and the more inclusive the procession, the more varied the narrative unfurled on the processional way which framed the social act. Itineraries fall into two main categories, those *demarcating* territories, and those *linking* them. The former is by far the commonest: it was used to trace village boundaries, and in urban processions to mark spheres of influence, seats of particular families. The Neapolitan procession continued to trace the spheres of influence of thirteenth-century families even centuries later by which time most were defunct.[336] In England the

---

[329] Paraphrased from the conclusion to a study of Javanese shadow theatre, Keeler (1987), pp. 206–7.

[330] Travis (1985); and on drama, see next section.

[331] See the use of Corpus Christi for the expression of difference between two sections of a twentieth-century Breton village, Gueusquin-Barbichon (1977).

[332] For York, see Tudor-Craig (1986).

[333] In Lérida the decoration of houses with hanging clothes was permitted only on the queen's entry and on Corpus Christi, see Very (1962), p. 16.

[334] Schiller (1912), n. 1, p. 27.

[335] Browe (1929b).

[336] Tutini (1641).

*linking* type is more common, and in the urban sphere, it sewed with a processional thread the periphery to the centre, the parishes to the cathedral, the suburbs to the market place.[337] The bishop of Lincoln ordered in 1419 that the Corpus Christi octave Sunday procession should lead from the suburb of Wickford 'in suburbiis dictae nostrae civitatis' to the cathedral.[338] Beverley had processional plays performed at stations along the High Street, the town's backbone. These passed through North Bar, the Billing (the north edge of the market), Cross Bridge, Fishmarket, the edge of the minster precinct, and the suburb of the Beck. In Durham it was a mixed craft and clerical procession which carried the tabernacle from St Nicholas' to the palace green through a number of stations, to the shrine of St Cuthbert and back again.[339] In York the procession began at the Holy Trinity Priory at the town's Mickelgate and went to the cathedral and ended at the hospital of St Leonard, the foremost charitable house, a corporate and civic enterprise. Similarly in Rennes the procession led by bishop and chapter and with the prominent Mercers' gild at the centre moved from cathedral through every parish church and back to the cathedral.[340] In Verona the council of twelve decided in 1450 that the itinerary should start at the cathedral and link the seven town parishes and the main public spaces, the Piazza dei Signori, Piazza Erbe, and finally return to the cathedral.[341] In Würzburg in 1381 the parish clergy gathered at the cathedral and led a procession through the market square, the bridge on the Main, the city gate, along the wall, back through another gate and by a number of parish churches, before returning to the market place and then to the cathedral.[342] This trail was also followed on St Mark's day (25 April), and on Rogationtide.

In an interesting variation which evaded explicit boundary and sphere demarcation, some French towns in the later Middle Ages chose to process along routes which were quite anachronistic, such as old lines of fortification or boundaries of settlement. In Marseille the procession followed the line where the eleventh-century walls had been.[343] In Aix-en-Provence in the mid fourteenth century the Corpus Christi procession reflected a trajectory uniting the Count of Pro-

---

[337] For a different type of related contestation, see disputes over the rights of passage along processional routes, *London assize of nuisance*, no. 43, p. 9; no. 639, p. 172.
[338] *Concilia* III, p. 396.
[339] *Rites of Durham*, p. 107.
[340] Leguay (1975), p. 171.
[341] Spagnolo (1901), pp. 2–4.
[342] Zika (1988), pp. 39–40; Mitterwieser (1930), p. 9.
[343] Coulet (1982), pp. 390–91; on anachronistic features of processions, see Darnton (1984), p. 124.

vence's section and the episcopal section, including no parish or suburb founded after the early thirteenth century; in fact it delineated the urban topography of *c.* 1200.[344] These survivals indicate the importance of some symbols to a collective experience. Whether long-forgotten boundaries or long-trespassed borders of influence, the routes nego-tiated on processional occasions represent areas which were beyond political immediacy. Like the Neapolitan procession they represented mythical–historical narratives which could sustain a basis for coexist-ence without compromising contemporary political options. They lie at the basis of the construction of identities; some itineraries reflected a rejection of the more obvious, disputed, here-and-now boundaries, and favoured those which contained deeper local knowledge. They reflected experience without limiting political options, and can thus be seen as one of the procession's most revealing aspects.

The emblems which were chosen for display are also revealing. Processions carried emblems which held specific local meaning. In Durham the banner of St Cuthbert was taken out on Corpus Christi,[345] in Cologne the head of St Gereon, the city's patron,[346] and in Besançon the procession led to the tomb of the patron saints Ferréol and Fer-geux.[347] In Orvieto, quite properly but not insignificantly, it was the most precious local relic, the reliquary of the holy corporal, which was displayed at the heart of the procession.[348] In Beverley the most important integrative event was not Corpus Christi but Cross Monday (Monday in Rogationtide) when the town's precious relic of St John of Beverley was paraded and watched by gild members from their respect-ive 'castles', the wooden booths that the more established of gilds were allowed to erect.[349] Here Corpus Christi took second rank as an integrative civic event despite its emergent corporate imagery.

We thus return to the question of ritual efficacy,[350] especially in rituals which deploy so seemingly natural a sign as the body.[351] The rhetorical use of the body always attempts to draw from its very *naturalness* an imputed and undisputed acceptance of that which is signified by it.[352] In the medieval context the body was a metaphor of

[344] Coulet (1982), pp. 388–9.
[345] *Rites of Durham*, pp. 95–6.
[346] Torsy (1972), p. 335.
[347] Galpern (1976), pp. 71–2.
[348] Harding (1988), pp. 8–9.
[349] Horrox (1989), pp. 46, 47–8.
[350] For some questions on this, see Scribner (1989), pp. 183–4.
[351] Just how 'impure' and 'unsimple' the body can be is explored magnificently for the culture of late antiquity in which Christianity developed in Brown (1988b).
[352] Douglas (1970).

metaphors, embedded in the sacramental cosmology as well as in personal experience. The continued recourse by late medieval patricians who supervised the Corpus Christi processions to the body image to describe their towns and their privilege within them, is an example of how particular representations and their readings can be promoted.[353] To the natural symbol of the well functioning and harmonious body, they added the symbol of Christ's body, which is both identical with and separate from the social body, and much celebrated for its power.[354] In the confusion between metaphor and metonymy, between the likening and the symbolising reading of Christ's body, lay the possibility to claim the power inherent in the sacramental mediation, and the harmony of the body of God. The mystical body had become so public, so exposed, so much a locus of desire and power, that it was a sort of public good, which patricians hastened to appropriate, at least on occasions which they controlled.[355]

The Christian theological tradition, however, held different views in the degree of cohesion which the body implied.[356] The body could be male or female, weak or strong, nurturing or vulnerable;[357] bodies were not only sites of order and sacramentality, but of degrading dependency and deprivation. Even within the eucharistic language the body was sometimes glorified, but other times torn asunder.[358] Does the juxtaposition of many groups, many 'members', necessarily imply a moral relationship of stable interdependence, as so many have claimed?[359] Bodies cannot be taken as possessing an essential meaning; like all meaningful signs they are culturally constructed. In a political discourse, the invention of their naturalness in particular contexts may or may not be accepted by those who observe it; and their attitude may depend on their position within the political, or their ability to imagine a different order of things. Thus women often related to Christ's crucified body in very singular personal and even anarchic and asocial ways; the Lollards rejected the orthodox understanding of Christ's body in the sacrament, and yet some of them could choose to process prestigiously near the host as a measure of their standing in the community. A procession, even with the eucharist at its centre, even when seen as a metaphoric body, will contain members in disagreement as to

[353] James (1983), pp. 10–11.
[354] Travis (1985), pp. 18–23.
[355] On the adoption of Corpus Christi as focus for patrician fraternities, see above, pp. 240–1.
[356] Michaud-Quantin (1970a), pp. 59–64.
[357] As explored in Bynum (1986).
[358] Travis (1985), p. 21. See examples in miracles tales, above pp. 123, 125.
[359] Heers (1973), pp. 196–7.

their appropriate hierarchical position as to who was the stomach, who the head, for how long, and why. Mervyn James' seminal article places the social body at the centre; I believe the time has come for its decentring.

Another area of creation and application of eucharistic symbolism in the public arena developed in those towns and in some villages through the staging of sequences of biblical dramatic plays, which have been called Corpus Christi 'cycles'. This form combined the processional, the didactic, the civic, the competitive, the creative and the fantastic – the array of configurations which only a cosmic theme could bring about.

## CORPUS CHRISTI DRAMA

The feast of Corpus Christi triggered a variety of creative activities: the writing of sermons, organisation of processions, formation of fraternities, interpretation of eucharistic themes in the silver and gold of monstrances and in the fine cloth of canopies, in the composition of hymns, and in the orchestration of town-wide ventures. It also gave its name to a dramatic type which developed in the North and the East of England,[360] a cycle of biblical plays made up in a sequence from the Old and New Testaments, which told the Christian story from Creation through the Fall, the history of the Jews, the Incarnation, Christ's life and ministry, the Crucifixion, Resurrection to the Day of Judgement. The name 'The Play of Corpus Christi' has loosely been used to describe a variety of such dramatic performances in the vernacular which took place in the summer around the feast of Corpus Christi (which could occur between 21 May and 24 June). The texts of elaborate cycles have survived from York, Chester and Wakefield,[361] and there are fragments from the cyclical plays of Coventry, Norwich and Newcastle. There is also a fifteenth-century manuscript of East Anglian provenance containing a very similar type of cycle, known as the N-town play, and which has recently been considered as originating from Bury St Edmunds.[362]

Attention to the cycles and the analysis of their contents have been abundant, from the interest of antiquaries in the eighteenth and nineteenth centuries,[363] to the modern scholarship by drama students and

---

[360] Craig (1914), p. 590; Taylor (1972), p. 148.
[361] *The York plays*; *The Chester mystery cycle*; *The Towneley cycle*.
[362] *The N-town plays*; Gibson (1971), esp. pp. 58, 82, 85–6, 89.
[363] Sharp (1825).

literary critics,[364] and more recently by historians interested in late medieval town-life.[365] By far the most influential and comprehensive of treatments is V. A. Kolve's *The play called Corpus Christi* which took a structural approach to the Corpus Christi drama, seeing it as a product possessing a neat internal structure embedded in the late medieval religious culture. Kolve suggested that the cyclical drama was meaningfully related to the feast's theme, the tale of sin and redemption encoded in the eucharist,[366] and identified a core-cycle of plays which provided a necessary skeleton of meaning which could be elaborated in various localities. By historicising the plays so brilliantly Kolve produces a model of Corpus Christi drama which fits three of the four elaborate cycles which we know from the English towns. But in fact, the dramatic enterprises which Corpus Christi inspired are increasingly being revealed as a far more heterogeneous and a less neatly classifiable lot. They were living events, bound by some aesthetic rules, but of a far less fixed meaning and form than has been appreciated.[367]

What cannot be doubted is that Corpus Christi inspired a dramatic celebration of varying size and frequency in a variety of communities: towns, villages, cathedrals, groups of villages, within fraternities. Like the procession, the drama was not prescribed by the bull of foundation. In the early decades of the fourteenth century the procession had developed as the main form of celebration of the new eucharistic feast, and civic involvement in it was increasing. By the second quarter of the fourteenth century we witness in England and on the Continent the beginning of formation of dramatic sections in the procession. In some places these were *tableaux vivants*, scenes arranged and moved on pageant wagons along the processional route.[368] Such scenes could be elaborated with a number of spoken lines by the actors, or with music, and they would have been produced by the groups which constituted the procession.[369] Another source of dramatic impulse was the ubiquitous preaching associated with Corpus Christi, the sort of Corpus

---

[364] Kolve (1966); Nelson (1974); Prosser (1961); Craig (1955); Gardiner (1946); Woolf (1972).

[365] James (1983); Pythian-Adams (1972).

[366] Following Craig (1914), see p. 594.

[367] The picture has become clearer following the pioneering work of the participant in the vast editorial project of REED, which has produced some ten volumes to date, and which has amassed material relating to smaller towns, and other dramatic enterprises to complicate the interesting picture of Corpus Christi drama considerably.

[368] Stevens (1972), p. 44; Kahrl (1973), p. 246. This was also happening in Europe, Stevens (1972), pp. 48–50.

[369] For a comparative tabulation of the variety of processional and dramatic programmes and a suggestion for an evolutionary pattern from procession to plays see Pierson (1915); conclusion on pp. 159–60; also Blair (1940), p. 84.

Christi homilies interspersed with *exempla* and relevant tales which developed the typology that linked the Old Testament and the New Testament material around the eucharist and which introduced the biblical didactic element into the heart of the exploration of the feast's meaning.[370] The feast, celebrated out of doors, was related to the central symbol of Christian cosmology, to the very heart of its myth; it told a tale of possible redemption.[371] That some towns developed full biblical cycles, that others had only a 'Herod's play', or the 'Play of the children of Israel', or a 'Creed' play or a play about a host desecration, like the Croxton *Play of the Sacrament*,[372] was determined by local variations of community structure, by the availability of funds and access to dramatic material. It was related to the structure of the civic and communal ceremonial year, to the niches which the Corpus Christi summer feast could come to fill.

All this variety leads us to chip away at some of the schemes which have been developed about the structure and meaning of the Corpus Christi drama in England. This will show us the eucharistic feast, again as a varied and diverse ritual event which while building around a shared symbol constructed and represented differing local interests, lore, traditions and capabilities between the fourteenth and the six-teenth centuries. To modern scholars the Corpus Christi play is a *type*, a neat and sophisticated structure; but in fact it seems far more change-able over time, sometimes even from year to year, and varied in its many manifestations. It was a living and a contingent enterprise. We may start with the working knowledge that Corpus Christi was a public processional feast celebrated in the summer,[373] that it involved ecclesiastical and secular spheres of organisation, and that it was related to the most powerful, widely taught and best-known of Christian symbols, so fundamental an image that its essence could be read out of almost every biblical tale.

The earliest reference to a play on Corpus Christi is in a discussion by Robert Holcot on the term 'plays' in his *Book of wisdom* of *c*.1335.[374] The first possible mention of a cycle of plays is from York in 1376,

---

[370] Craig (1975). See for example the 'Sermo de corpore Christi' examined above, and its version with *exempla* taken from the *Handlyng synne*, above, pp. 216–20.

[371] Taylor (1972), pp. 150–5, esp. 154.

[372] *Non-cycle plays and fragments*; Axton (1974), p. 199.

[373] Wickham (1981) III, p. 260 stresses the importance of Corpus Christi as a celebration before harvest.

[374] Wenzel (1977). Following Thomas Aquinas Holcot distinguishes between three types of plays: vile plays, joyful devotional ones, and plays which comfort the soul. He adds his own example when discussing the second type: 'alius est ludus devocionis et gaudij spiritualis qualem faciunt christiani in die corporis Christi', *ibid*, p. 390; for criticism see Young (1985), pp. 12–13.

followed by a series of entries in the craft ordinances of the 1370s and 1380s, and by council minutes from 1394.[375] In Chester the drama is discussed in the treasurers' accounts which begin in the 1420s.[376] A heated debate has raged between scholars as to the origins of the Corpus Christi drama. An earlier interpretation, associated with E. K. Chambers' seminal work on the medieval stage, took an evolutionary view of medieval vernacular drama as representing a stage in a process which saw the secularisation of drama, and the exit of elaborate drama from the interior of the church to the village green and market place.[377] An opposing and later view saw the Corpus Christi drama as the culmination of impulses within the liturgical drama which had produced by the High Middle Ages mini-cycles for Christmas and for Easter, ready for combination when the impulse was provided by the new late medieval eucharistic feast.[378] Neither one of these views has stood the test of recent research and comparative work on English and European drama; England had never developed a liturgical dramatic repertoire as vast as those of Northern Italy or Germany,[379] and yet it had produced the elaborate Corpus Christi cycles.[380] The Corpus Christi drama never 'left' the church, it always retained a liturgical component, and more importantly, a strong didactic orientation. Between the Corpus Christi feast and the dramatic performances of the day were interposed didactic and dramatic activities, capacities and interests of a great variety; mendicant or monastic writers, a lay audience such as could enjoy Langland and Chaucer.[381] Biblical drama was performed not only on Corpus Christi, and not only by towns and crafts. Lincoln Cathedral was an important centre for dramatic activity and in the fourteenth and fifteenth century it had an array of miracle and saints' plays.[382] It now seems more fruitful to view the dramatic enterprises as an expression of local religious culture within the bounds of local political and social relations. These events brought together variously the groups which constituted a medieval town, or a single village community, the cultural agents such as priests and friars,[383] the administrators, such as church-wardens and gild-masters, to work on material as rich as bible

---

[375] Meredith (1981), pp. 316–17.
[376] Salter (1955), pp. 45–6.
[377] Chambers (1903); for criticism, see Meredith (1981), p. 311.
[378] Hardison (1965), esp. pp. 226–7; Craig (1914), pp. 599–602; Craig (1955), pp. 100–1. For a survey of these views, see Kahrl (1973).
[379] Meredith (1981), p. 313.
[380] Axton (1974), pp. 162–9.
[381] Wickham (1981) III, pp. 191–2.
[382] Wilson (1969), pp. 226–7; Shull (1937), pp. 946–60.
[383] Priests were involved in the French Corpus Christi drama, Heers (1973), p. 73.

harmonics,[384] tales on the life of Christ,[385] and apocryphal tales.[386] Between procession and plays an intermediary form could also play an important part, the *tableaux vivants* which were less elaborate dramatic products but which could easily evolve out of the emblematic representation of groups marching along. Thus, in London the Skinners' Corpus Christi procession, the feasts's most comprehensive celebration in the capital, remained in the form of *tableaux vivants* well into the fifteenth century when it was immortalised by John Lydgate who described them in a sort of descriptive eucharistic sermon.[387] Similarly, in Spain the *auto sacramentál* which was the widespread form of Corpus Christi celebration, remained a sort of mimed sermon.[388]

Once we discard a view which imputes a necessary development of the Corpus Christi drama into full-cycle form we are better able to appreciate the variety of dramatic forms which evolved for Corpus Christi, and the ubiquity of dramatic creation. Eucharistic processions could inspire the expression of different identities by the processing groups: in livery, banners, distinctive instruments and emblems carried by craft or fraternity members.[389] Thus the accounts of the Boston fraternity of the Virgin (Mariners) for 1518/19 records expenses for paying eight men for carrying 'naviculum Noie' on Corpus Christi, and other feasts.[390] As late as 1499 a will of William Brokshaw of East Retford (Nottinghamshire) bequeathed a gilt crown 'for the statue of the Virgin Mary in the Corpus Christi procession', and for the 'Virgin Mary in the play of mankind'.[391] In the Corpus Christi procession at Beverley the crafts carried statues of their patron saints, and were fined for failure to do so, like the Fishermen who were fined 40s in 1449.[392] In Ipswich the crafts processed in clusters under the banner of saints such as St Eligius, St John, St George or St Luke.[393] London never developed a town-wide celebration for the feast, a project which is almost unthinkable in so large and varied a city, but rather had a series of processions

[384] Boitani (1982), pp. 4–7.
[385] Sheingorn (1982), pp. 111–14; Sticca (1973), esp. p. 83; McNeir (1951).
[386] Dunn (1973).
[387] See above, pp. 229–32.
[388] Parker (1943), pp. 58–66 on Calderón's *autos*; for a definition of the *auto*: 'una composición dramática 9èn una jornada) alegórica y relativa generalmente a la communión'.
[389] Craig (1914), p. 598. On the involvement of European fraternities in drama, see Le Bras (1940–1), p. 350, n. 5.
[390] Lincoln City Archives. Misc. Don. 169, fol. 8ʳ.·
[391] 'Lego unum certum, vocatum a serkelett, deauratum, et ornatum cum lapidibus, pro imagine Beate Marie, ad processionem in festo corporis Christi; . . . et pro virgine Maria in ludo de Mankind', Wenzel (1977), p. 393.
[392] Champion (19), p. 57.
[393] IESRO C4/2, fols. 1ʳ, 72ʳ, 72ᵛ.

related to parish churches, fraternities, crafts. The Skinners of London organised 'a grete play' on Corpus Christi which was described by *The great chronicle* in 1408,[394] and which is said to have lasted from Wednesday to Friday and with more celebrations on Sunday,[395] described by Lydgate in 'the processyoun of þe feste of corpus Christi made in London', which we have already encountered.[396] The scenes unfolded the eucharistic tale from its prefigurations in Jewish history, through the Last Supper, the early Christian history, papal and medieval theological and liturgical discussion, including figures such as Peter Lombard and Thomas Aquinas. This was a vast procession, which John Stow (c.1525–1605) describes as having over a hundred lights, with some 200 clerics and priests, the sheriff, the mayor's servants, the city council, the mayor and aldermen, and the skinners in livery.[397]

This was obviously a well-wrought piece of vernacular didactic composition, the sort which we have seen in creation from the thirteenth century with great attention and intensity.[398] Just as reading the bible was a great issue for contest and competition in late medieval England, and free access to it was denied both laity and clergy,[399] there were authorised versions of imparting the biblical stories through tale,[400] and drama.[401] The material which made the plays was a combination of popularised biblical tale,[402] as told in vernacular sermons,[403] and as represented in wall-paintings, on the one hand, and of paraliturgical material such as hymns, devotional themes and lauds, on the other.[404] It is in the convergence of these materials and the techniques related to their use that the influence of the mendicant orders was most acute, in the introduction of that which was not strictly biblical, but rather devotional and sometimes apocryphal layers of the religious language.[405] In Exeter the Franciscans and Dominicans were remuner-

---

[394] London Guildhall 3313, fol. 72ʳ.
[395] BL Harley 565, fol. 68ᵛ. I am grateful to Mrs Mary Rose McLaren for providing me with these references.
[396] *Lydgate's minor poems*, pp. 35–43.
[397] *A survey of London* I, p. 230.
[398] On instruction see above, pp. 98–129.
[399] Moran (1985), p. 186. The evidence of wills reveals only very few bibles in the possession of the clergy.
[400] Fry (1967).
[401] *Ibid*, p. 203.
[402] On the influence of the *Biblia pauperum* tradition on the text of German religious drama, see Brooks (1936).
[403] See link between a mid fourteenth century (before 1352) sermon by an Oxford Dominican and the *Fall* play of the N-town cycle and the Chester play of Eve and the Serpent, Brown (1934), pp. 394–6; on the use of Grosseteste's *Château d'amour*, Southern (1986), pp. 225–30.
[404] Dunn (1960), pp. 56, 61.
[405] *Ibid*, p. 59.

ated on Corpus Christi 1407–8 and paid 4s on the day,[406] while in Beverley in 1423–4 a Dominican was paid by the town keepers 6s 8d 'for making and composition of the banns before the proclamation of the Corpus Christi plays throughout the town'.[407] The mendicant emphasis is felt in the incorporation of many minute scenes related to the life of Mary, and in the introduction of scenes such as the legend of Veronica in the N-town cycle, a particularly Franciscan theme related to the Way of the Cross (*Via dolorosa*).[408] There was an interaction between producers and organisers of the plays through a religious culture in which everyone shared to a degree. Thus in 1420 the Masons of York were able to reject their part in producing the *Fergus* play, the story of the Jew who struck the Virgin's bier after her Dormition, a scene which caused much mirth and commotion.[409] They expressed their objection as being against a play not contained in holy scripture, and they were allocated Herod's play instead.[410]

Thus, material of a popular-didactic nature which had elements of exposition and of dramatic display built into them were already known and used and available for further use on the public summer feast. In those towns where political power and wealth were exercised through craft gilds,[411] like York, Coventry, Beverley, Norwich, dramatic cycles were supported and presented by the crafts, expressing both the processional-communal and the sectional elements in town life. This aspect of the drama was clearly expressed by the ordinance which regulated the Corpus Christi cycle of York in 1417:

That for the convenience of the citizens of that city and for all the foreigners who come to it on the said feast, all the pageants of the play called Corpus Christi play should be supported and produced by the artisans of the said city in their order, for the due honour and reverence of our Lord Jesus Christ and the benefit of the said citizens.[412]

[406] Little (1927), p. 26.

[407] 'Pro factura et composicione de lez banez ante ludum Corpus Christi proclamationem per totam villam', *Beverley town documents*, p. 33; Horrox (1989), p. 47. The Chester play which is rather less interesting than the rest, was written by a monk of St Werburgh's, Chester, Morris (1893), p. 116.

[408] Craddock (1950), esp. p. 388.

[409] Mill (1950), pp. 867–9.

[410] 'In sacua non continetur scriptura', REED: *York* I, pp. 47–8. It is, indeed, an apocryphal tale, from the *Legenda aurea* IV, p. 240.

[411] It was in craft-guilds rather than in fraternities that financial resources were concentrated, Nelson (1974), p. 189; except for the cases of patrician groups, like the Corpus Christi fraternity of York, which had its own play, Johnston (1975).

[412] 'Quod ab comodum ciuium eiusdem ciuitatis et omnium extraneorum illuc veniencium in festo predicto, omnes pagine ludi vocati Corpus Christi play sint sustentae et producte suo ordine per artifices dicte ciuitatis ob honorem precipue et reuerenciam domini nostri Jesu Christi et comodum ciuium predictorum', REED: *York* I, p. 28.

The cycles which developed were tailored to a town's needs: York had forty-eight plays in the fifteenth century, and Chester had some fifteen or twenty-five throughout the century. Coventry had seventeen crafts but we only know of ten plays, as gilds often collaborated in the productions. The stories could also be divided into strings of episodes: the Coventry Shearmen and Taylors produced the scenes from the life of St Anne to the Massacre of the Innocents, the Weavers presented the stories of Christ's early ministry, the Smiths were in charge of the stories of Christ's later ministry up to the crucifixion, the Pinners and Needlers showed Christ's death and burial, and the Cappers the scenes from the Resurrection to the Harrowing of Hell and the appearance to Mary Magdalene.[413] The Fergus play which the Masons had discarded in 1420 was reallocated to the Linen-weavers, and in 1485 it was dropped when they were ordered to join the Tapisters and Cardmakers in producing the play.[414] Nor was the structure of the cycles fixed; as crafts merged or separated in response to the vicissitudes of political and economic life these changes were perforce expressed in the dramatic civic enterprise.[415] In some cases the crafts could distinctly relate to the subject of their scenes: the only play which survives from the Newcastle cycle is the play of Noah which was produced by 1426 by the town's Shipwrights, just as the York Shipwrights presented the Building of the Ark, while the city's Fishermen produced the scene of the Flood. Sometimes the connections were more elusive – the Bakers of York and of Chester presented the Last Supper, the Pinners, the Crucifixion, the Chester Saddlers, Christ on the road to Emmaus. And it was the rich Mercers of York who produced the scene of the Last Judgement, one which was prestigiously positioned at the very end, a complex scene whose trappings included a hell's mouth, and whose exhortative message perhaps seemed particularly appropriate for the town's leading merchants . . .[416]

Thus, towns which included differentiated corporations built cycles which accommodated the different identities and the varying capacities of these groups. Conversely, in the rural hinterland of East Anglia communities came together to subscribe and join forces in the production of a play.[417] Thus, although not on Corpus Christi, Bassingbourn parish (Cambridgeshire) was supported by contributions from the vicinity in the maintenance of a St George's play,[418] and the plays at

[413] Wilson (1969), p. 233.
[414] REED: *York* 1, p. 110.
[415] See changes in the number of cycles at Chester: 17 in 1475, 25 in 1540, Salter (1935), p. 47.
[416] On it, see Johnston and Dorrell (1971), (1972).
[417] Beadle (1977).
[418] CUL Add 2792, pp. 75–80 (fols. 37ᵛ–39ʳ), on St Martin's day.

Boxford (Suffolk) were similarly financed in 1510–12.[419] A community such as Ashburton (Devon) raised funds for parish needs in 'ale plays', as did the parish of Thame in 1496 when it collected 14s at a Robin Hood play.[420] But parishes also had substantial expenses on the maintenance of the costumes and the hospitality for players. At Ashburton in 1479–80 2d were spent 'for ale on Corpus Christi day', and in 1492–3 they spent 8d 'In costage of bread and ale a Corpus Christi day to ye players',[421] while 20d in 1516–17 were paid for '4 Ratilbaggez & vysers for the players on the feast of Corpus Christi'.[422] In 1528–9 10d were spent on making the 'crestes' worn on the players' heads on Corpus Christi, and an entry of 1537–8 describes the Corpus Christi play as Herod's play (the Massacre of the Innocents).[423] Similarly, in Thame in 1523 a Resurrection play was performed in the church and 8d were spent for writing out the parts ('parcells') of actors in the plays of the Three Kings of Cologne (a version of the Magi tale) and of Herod for Corpus Christi.[424] For a similar play 11s10d were spent by the churchwardens of St Edmund's parish in Salisbury in 1469–70 on apparel for the players and 4d on a woollen shroud for 'le King play'.[425] In 1507 the churchwardens of St Laurence, Reading, made numerous payments in connection with the plays: on dyed flax for wigs, doublets, caps, ears, even a coat for Eve, and an expense of 8d directly mentions the feast day, the expense of 'makyng of a doublett of lethur and j payr of hosyn of lethur agaynst Corpus Xristi day'.[426]

While a variety of plays was considered appropriate for Corpus Christi,[427] even a single biblical story could be played year in and year out, as records of storage of costumes and props attest. Reading had a group of four plays: Kings of Cologne, Adam and Eve, Cain and Abel, and Resurrection,[428] and Ipswich had its Assumption play.[429] In some areas a number of communities supported this single effort collectively. The form of the drama, in big town or in village, its extent, content and symbolic impact, were deeply related to the social and political arrangements which characterised the host communities. And even this determination is not stable, it developed out of the processional and the

---

[419] Cox (1913), pp. 270–4.
[420] *Thame*, p. 49.
[421] *Ashburton*, pp. 1, 19; see also p. 27.
[422] *Ibid*, p. 55.
[423] *Ibid*, pp. 82–3, p. 102.
[424] *Thame*, col. 53. Thame also had a Robin Hood 'sporte', *Ashburton*, pp. 28–9, 30–1.
[425] Cox (1913), p. 64.
[426] *Reading*, pp. 269–70.
[427] Wickham (1981) III, p. 43.
[428] Mentioned in the churchwardens accounts from 1498, *Reading*, p. 233.
[429] Nelson (1974), pp. 215–17.

public aspects of the feast, out of the didactic drive of all religious ritual, but constituted a social event representing different rhythms of communal life, priorities and capabilities of allocations of resources towards spectacular display, dramatic performances, collective ritual – in their attendant, negotiated forms.

The history of the York plays demonstrates the dynamic of the development of the dramatic enterprise. We first hear of *pagina* (pageant) in 1376/7 in the York Memorandum Book,[430] which may have only been *tableaux vivants* in the procession, but by 1399 plays were certainly part of the processional celebrations.[431] In 1415 the *Ordo paginarum* was recorded by the town clerk Roger Burton, and shows just how far the elaborate cycle of biblical scenes had developed.[432] By 1426 the drama had so grown and so come to influence the character of the day that the reforming Franciscan friar, William Melton, suggested that the procession and the plays be separated, the latter to be celebrated on Corpus Christi eve, and the former on the feast.[433] The procession of pageants on wagons started at 4.30 am and was usually played out at twelve stations throughout the city.[434] Later still in the fifteenth century the plays were moved to the feast day, and the procession to its morrow.[435] Norwich followed a different trail, inasmuch as it developed a communal, shared craft celebration only very late in the day. By 1449 the Norwich crafts were obliged to accompany the mayor on ceremonial ridings with the mercers and grocers closest to him,[436] and the Whitsun dramatic celebrations were maintained exclusively by the fraternity of St Luke throughout the century. Only in 1524 did they apply to the towns assembly and demand that the crafts provide towards these summer pageants which included a procession 'with disgisinges and pageauntes as well as the liff & marterdams of divers and many holy saynts'.[437] Thus, from 1527 the crafts participated in a set of twelve pageants, a cycle from which only the Grocers' play has survived.[438] As in the procession, thus in the play cycle: the rich were in prominent positions: they opened the cycle with the Mercers'

---

[430] 'De uno tenemento in quo tres pagine corporis Christi ponuntur per annum 2s', REED: *York* I, p. 3. Similarly in Beverley in the same year, *Beverley town documents*, p. 45.

[431] Meredith (1981), pp. 318–19.

[432] *Ibid*, p. 321.

[433] Johnston (1973–4), pp. 55–6; Moran (1985), p. 32.

[434] See Beadle (1982), on the details on the York cycle; Nelson (1970–1), p. 221; Nelson (1974), pp. 42–3.

[435] Nelson (1974), pp. 45–6; REED: *York* I, pp. 42–4.

[436] *Records of the city of Norwich* II, p. 288.

[437] Dutka (1979), p. 108.

[438] *Ibid*, pp. 109–10.

Creation and the Grocers' Fall, and closed it with the Worstead Weavers' Last Judgement.[439]

The study of the York civic records makes it clear that the city council regarded the plays as an extremely important event,[440] which required constant attention to avoid disorder, incompetent performance and strife. It sought to control the texts of the plays, and granted plays and copies of their lines as need arose. City officials examined the players to ensure that the performance would be 'sufficiant in personne and Connyng to þe honour of þe Citie and Worship of þe saide crafts',[441] and entered agreements with crafts to allocate or reallocate plays. They could withdraw scenes after faulty performance or reappoint them conditionally: the Smiths of Beverley were thus fined 40s in 1392 and given a second chance to perform under the pain of a 100s fine.[442] Such was the case of the Innholders of York in 1484 when they undertook to perform the play of the Coronation of the Virgin for the next eight years.[443] As the status of a craft changed its contribution to the drama was reassessed. The Porters and Creelers of Beverley had no play in 1390, in 1452 they were granted the newly made Annunciation, and when they became a major organised craft in 1476 they were given the scene of the Graving and Digging of Adam and Eve.[444] In 1488 the Painters, Goldsmiths, Masons and Glaziers of Beverley amalgamated and were jointly allocated the play of the Kings of Cologne, but conversely when the Shipmen and Tilers joined forces as a gild, they still kept their old distinct plays. Towards the late fifteenth century the Corpus Christi fraternity of York developed its own drama, the Creed play which was performed once in ten years, under the pain of a £20 fine in 1495.[445]

The town council was often obliged to mediate between crafts over their respective obligations towards the maintenance of the plays. In Chester in 1422 the Ironmongers and the Carpenters fought over their entitlement to be assisted by the craft of Fletchers, Coopers, Stringers, Turners and Bowyers. The jury decided that the latter had their own pageant, 'paginam suam propriam eiusdem ludi, videlicet de fflagela-

---

[439] Harty (1981). By this time St Luke's had moved to a mediocre place in the middle.

[440] On integration into town life, see Grimberg (1974), pp. 222–5.

[441] REED: *York* I, p. 109. See also an example from Beverley where in 1425 a weaver was fined 6s 8d for failure to master his lines, Nelson (1974), pp. 93–4.

[442] Wilson (1969), p. 222, and another example on p. 223. For the treatment of crafts who mounted badly performed plays in Beverley see Horrox (1989), pp. 46–7. See also White (1984), pp. 18–19, 24.

[443] REED: *York* I, pp. 133–4.

[444] Horrox (1989), p. 42.

[445] REED: *York* I, p. 177; such fines went towards common civic needs, for an example of 1535 see Raine III, p. 172. On the play see Wilson (1969), p. 231, Moran (1985), p. 30.

cione Corporis Christi cum suis pertinenciis', a play which told the tale
from the Flagellation up to the Crucifixion, that the Ironmongers
should perform the Crucifixion and that the Carpenters should perform the Salutation and the Nativity.[446] Reallocations and merging of
efforts to produce plays were an ongoing and necessary adjustment to
the changing economic fortunes of crafts, particularly in the less auspi-
cious circumstances of the late fifteenth century. When in 1493 the
Mercers and Drapers of Beverley split, they were each given a new play:
Black Herod and Pilate's Judgement, respectively.[447] In 1468 in York
the Chamberlains subsidised by 2s the production of the Innholders'
pageant, which had previously been the responsibility of the Mayor.[448]
In Leicester in 1477 following a discussion of the expenses connected
with the Passion play the assembly decided to appoint a committee 'for
to have the gydyng and rulle of the seid play'.[449] When hardship struck
plays could be redesigned, like that of the Money-changers of Valencia,
who were meant to produce an *entrames* (interlude) of the Annunciation on Corpus Christi 1453. They gathered at the Franciscan convent
and drew up a report about their inability to meet the expense, suggesting that perhaps the scene could be simplified to contain the Virgin
alone with the angel, who would simply walk onto the scene, and have a
dove hovering over. They wondered whether this would be acceptable
as being adequate for the town's standards.[450] Coventry crafts applied
to the council repeatedly in the late fifteenth century complaining of
their inability to sustain the expenses which the plays involved.[451] The
town councils of these towns attempted to spread the responsibility
and expenses, as in Walsall (Staffordshire) in 1493–4 where the mayor
and his officials ('brethren') ordained rules of repair and maintenance of
garments between the town's crafts.[452] Some towns also subsidised the
plays from the central funds, as in the case of Ipswich which in 1442–3
allocated some income from town lands towards meeting the expenses
of the pageant.[453]

Whatever the arrangement – a series of plays performed by crafts, a

---

[446] Salter (1955), pp. 44–5; Salter (1935), pp. 7–8. Crafts also competed over a particularly
good play, like the journeymen of the parish of Ste Madeleine of Tournai in 1394 who had
enjoyed the *jeux* performed by the journeymen of St Brice parish on Corpus Christi, and
tried to acquire a copy from them. A fight broke out when they refused to hand over the
roll containing the text, Vaultier (1965), p. 121.
[447] Wilson (1969), p. 223.
[448] Dorrell (1971), p. 42.
[449] *Leicester borough records* II, p. 297.
[450] Merimée (1913), pp. 13–14.
[451] Phythian-Adams (1979), pp. 44, 112, 212, 263–4.
[452] *Walsall*, pp. 224–5.
[453] IESRO, S. Ipswich 352, p. 42. Thanks to Mark Bailey for transcribing this for me.

single play in a town or a village, a performance by subscription, or a play performed by a fraternity – it is undoubtedly true that the drama ranged from the excellent and entertaining to performances which were less accomplished and more limited in scope. It is easier to explore the dramaturgy in the larger cycles which provide more material and a varied set of *dramatis personae*. What is most striking in the vernacular drama is the interweaving of the didactic and the ludic, the tragic and the comic, the sublime and ridiculous, the holy and the profane.[454] Even contemporary observers like the author of *Dives and pauper*[455] regarded the plays on feasts as able to teach 'men to loue God þe more', also the view of Friar William Melton who attempted to refashion the Corpus Christi experience in York in 1426.[456] The juxtaposition of the didactic and the popular is nowhere more evident than in the Wakefield Shepherds' plays, the *prima* being a serious and holy recounting of the Annunciation to the Shepherds which is inverted by the interpolated *secunda* in slapstick scenes of Shepherds' mischief.[457] These, none the less, seem to celebrate Nativity and Incarnation only to underscore *their* order by the disorder and frailty of the ordinary lives of contemporary shepherds.[458]

Many have dwelt upon the cosmic nature, the narrative tension encompassing every beginning and every end in the cycles, and that this broad canvas upon which the contemporary viewer was positioned *in media res* must have lent great impact to the viewing of the cycles.[459] But we must also bear in mind that of their nature the cycles were never performed in so even a way, nor observed in such perfect circumstances so as to allow the narrative to flow unproblematically. We know that some cycles were not shown in full every year,[460] nor were the qualities of performance equal, and in some localities the array of plays was far from comprehensive. Granting that those who composed and combined the dramatic lore into the cycles were intent on creating an overarching narrative in many cases,[461] we are probably on safer ground when abandoning the search for overall schemata and looking

---

[454] Taylor (1972), p. 155.
[455] *Dives and pauper* I, p. 293.
[456] REED: *York* I, p. 44.
[457] Cawley (1955).
[458] Cowley (1955), p. 215. On the insertion of extra-scriptural, profane material into the biblical play, see the example of the scene of buying the ointment and haggling with the merchant which preceded the scene of the Visitation of Christ's Sepulchre by the Holy Women, Kully (1979), pp. 216–21.
[459] Nitecki (1981), pp. 61–2; Dunn (1960), pp. 77–8.
[460] Salter (1955), p. 46.
[461] See the analysis of the Fall play and the scheme connecting it to the Incarnation, Harty (1981), esp. pp. 89–90.

at the plays' surer accomplishments. It is clear that the vernacular religious plays spoke in a language of religion which most folk could understand, and further contributed to the elaboration and constitution of that language. They used material from the didactic stock and constructed human archetypes which appealed to the audience's life experiences: the hen-pecked husband, the scold, the unjust judge, the gossips, the older man and his young wife. The familiar biblical figures were further embellished as vehicles for satire, a play on human failings, fears and guilt.[462] The penetration into the diverse audience was also achieved through dramatic techniques which broke down the distance between stage and spectator: players went down into the crowd, and played around as well as upon the wagon-stage, while the Devil famously roamed among his prey.[463] The extreme contradictions between the lofty Christian tale and the humble crasftmen who presented it contributed to the creative tension, a tension also found in the very presentation of Christ's sufferings, as in the Chester and York Crucifixion plays, his body weak, bleeding, vulnerable and yet the source of the power of salvation, the very organising image of the day's events.[464] To some spectators this would have translated into affirmations of the story, the power and promise arising from this contradiction, just as it did from the counter-intuitive claims of the eucharistic sacrament; for others this must have been disturbing, while for all it was a focus for personal as well as authorised interpretation.[465] Looking at the plays as products which were used suggests that they exposed the very contradictions which the language of religion possessed, and which normative readings of it attempted to erase.

The interpenetration of materials in the plays is clearly exemplified in the music which they contained, from Latin sequences to vernacular folk-song,[466] such as the music which accompanied Christ's Resurrection scenes in the Chester and York cycles, the antiphon 'Christus resurgens'.[467] They sometimes paraphrased liturgical lyrics, like the sequence for Corpus Christi *Lauda, Syon* which was used in the Chester Last Supper play where Christ addresses the relation between the sacrifice in the Old Testament and the sacrifice which he established that day.[468]

---

[462] Nitecki (1981), pp. 63, 68–9.
[463] On audience participation, see Kolve (1966), p. 32.
[464] Travis (1985), pp. 25–9.
[465] Christ himself was depicted differently in the plays; that of the Chester Ressurrection was extremely active and stepped out of his sarcophagus boldly, Sheingorn (1982), pp. 117–18.
[466] Collins (1932), pp. 614, 617–18; Nitecki (1981), p. 64; Jodogne (1972), pp. 5–11.
[467] Sheingorn (1982), p. 116; Stemmler (1970), pp. 244–5.
[468] Stemmler (1970), pp. 239–41.

For this very reason – the admixture of cultural materials and languages which the vernacular drama created – it was also the subject of severe criticism from within the Church and from Lollards. In *Handlyng synne* (c. 1303) Robert Mannyng claimed that the site of a miracle play 'Hyt ys a gaderyng, a syght of synne',[469] and that clerics should only take part in drama which is celebrated in the church, the liturgical plays of Easter and Christmas:

> Pley þe resurreccyun –
> Þat ys to seye, how God ros . . .
> And he may pleye withoutyn plyght
> Howe God was bore yn 30lë nyght.[470]

More extreme was the opinion of the Lollard who wrote c. 1390 the *Treatise of miracles playing* and which totally forbad clerical participation

And þerfore to pristis it is uttirly forbedyn not onely to been myracle pleyere but also to heren or to seen myraclis pleyinge.[471]

This was merely a consequence of his trenchant critique of the medium itself, the exercise in similitude. The plays were misleading since they celebrated man in sin, detracted from and trivialised Christ and his works, and moved people to emotion over the spectacle, rather than to tears for their sins. The very attempt to reproduce and reiterate, repeat and simulate that which was real and unique was reprehensible, and the words of a fifteenth-century poem against the friars and miracle plays puts this clearly:

> Thai have done him onna croys fer up in the skye,
> And festned on him wyenges as he shuld flie,
> This fals feyned byleve shal thai soure bye,
> On that lovelych lord, so forto lye.[472]

The cycles have been seen as expressions of a working internal logic, a plot about God's providence and judicious intervention in the world, a struggle between good and evil, a story of sin and the long road towards its expiation, and these no doubt guided some in design of dramatic plays and cycles.[473] But we must also shift the emphasis to the performance, and this necessarily involves questions about their *reception*. The

---

[469] *Handlyng synne (a)*, line 4,640, p. 155.
[470] *Ibid*, lines 4,642–3, 4647–8, p. 155. On clerical participation, see Wickham (1981) III, pp. 140–2, 162–3, 233.
[471] *Selections of Wycliffite writings*, p. 101; the whole treatise is on pp. 97–104 with notes on pp. 187–8.
[472] *Reliquiae antiquae* I, p. 322.
[473] Taylor (1972), pp. 151–4; Wickham (1981) III, p. 84; on York see Harty (1981), p. 80.

drama was the product of joint enterprises which in towns brought together civic officials, friars, priests, chantry chaplains, craftsmen and sometimes professional actors,[474] and in villages, churchwardens, parish priests, villagers and sometimes travelling players. Thus the didactic vied with other impulses, such as the wish to impose particular order and to stress the role of certain groups rather than others.[475] And these are not dissimilar to the forces and interests which were brought to bear on the religious lore in any case, as it was wrought and designed to live and be received and interpreted within such communities. The final product also involved experiences and worlds of knowledge which influenced reception, horizons of meanings, and stores of associations which influenced the interpretation and experience of event.[476]

What can be learnt from comparison of the English Corpus Christi drama with the developments on the Continent? A similar growth is evident from a processional mode of celebration to more elaborate dramatic processional presentations, which combined with strong local traditions of liturgical drama, and especially scenes of the Resurrection and the Visitation of the Sepulchre.[477] Valencia had a procession from 1355, which became the town's responsibility from 1372, and by 1400 this was accompanied by musical accompaniment and a number of *tableaux* carried on wagons.[478] In some German towns cycles similar to the northern and eastern English type developed, but these usually contained mostly Old Testament scenes, sometimes including the Incarnation and Crucifixion.[479] The Kunzelsau Corpus Christi cycle included in 1479 ten scenes from the Creation, through the tales of Noah and the Patriarchs, David and Goliath and Solomon,[480] and it resembled the Old Testament section of the Chester, Beverley and York cycles, and the Cornish cycle.[481] The Corpus Christi play of fifteenth-century Eger included seventy-four scenes which were played on three days, from the Fall to the Resurrection.[482] In Freiburg the Corpus Christi drama was also made of scenes performed by the craft gilds: after a procession in which twelve gilds were led to the Minster square by the three most prosperous ones, the tailors, the shopkeepers and the

---

[474] On stage management, see Phythian-Adams (1979), pp. 144–5, n. 8.
[475] Grimberg has noted that Corpus Christi was not perceived as a carnevalesque ritual of inversion, it was never described or treated with disrespect, Grimberg (1974), pp. 216–17.
[476] Robertson (1980), pp. 219, 221–2.
[477] Kully (1979), pp. 211–12.
[478] Merimée (1913), pp. 9–11.
[479] Sengpiel (1932), chapter 3, pp. 106–17.
[480] Kretzmann (1916), p. 79.
[481] *The ancient Cornish drama.*
[482] *Egerer Fronleichnamsspiel.*

butchers, and there a dramatic cycle with scenes from Adam and Eve to the Resurrection was performed by gildsmen and journeymen.[483] In Zerbst in the late fifteenth century fifty craft groups processed on Corpus Christi between the cantors at the front and the clergy behind with the Sacrament, and pronounced a few sentences as they passed.[484] But this type of arrangement was not universal; as in England there were occasions when groups other than gilds performed; the Corpus Christi play of Innsbrück in 1391 was acted out by scholars, and that in fifteenth century Lucerne which was played by schoolboys rather than burgesses.[485] Thus we encounter the familiar processional impetus in the dramatic growth, but also a variety in the forms of elaboration of the biblical drama to suit a town's structure and capacities.

We also encounter on the Continent another characteristic type of Corpus Christi drama, much more akin to a miracle play, in stories about the eucharist itself, the dramatic version of wide-spread host miracle tales.[486] These were plays like the *Jeu de la sainte hostie* known in France by 1444, or the Italian *sacra rappresentazione* of this tale which inspired Paolo Uccello's *predella* paintings for the Confraternity of the Holy Sacrament of 1475 × 8.[487] A single version of such a tale which has survived in England is the East Anglian Croxton *Play of the sacrament* of c.1461, which may have been used as a Corpus Christi dramatic piece.[488] These were tales which celebrated the eucharist's power, the truth of eucharistic presence, through a story which had a Jew as protagonist in vicious attacks on the host. These were miraculously exposed to reveal the criminal, and more importantly, to reiterate the host's nature as Christ's body, in its very bleeding or transformation into flesh. On the Continent the presence of Jews helped produce embellishment of the scenes with words in Yiddish and distinctive Jewish costumes. Such tales relate directly to the lore which was used for teaching and explicating eucharistic matters. Like saints' plays in general, they were far more popular in France, Spain and Italy than they ever were in England,[489] while in Germany the para-liturgical Passion and Christmas cycles, and the Old Testament tales, were the most popular.

---

[483] Hsia (1988), p. 109; Michael (1972), pp. 31–2.

[484] Brooks (1933), p. 144.

[485] Kully (1979), p. 207.

[486] Which have been discussed above, pp. 108–28. The Augustinian college of Neustift near Brixen had a Corpus Christi play by 1314, but we do not know its contents, Kern (1954), p. 54.

[487] Lavin (1967), pp. 2–10.

[488] Axton (1974), pp. 198–9. The text is in *Non-cycle plays and fragments*, pp. lxx–lxxxv, 58–89. On the play, see Cutts (1944), Scattergood (1971), pp. 259–60.

[489] Mill (1950), p. 866.

CHAPTER 5

# *Symbols in motion: the many readings of the eucharist*

In a liturgy, a feast, processions, and in eucharistic visits to the sick, the eucharistic symbolic system was understood and applied through a myriad of meanings. We will find eucharistic interpretations in very different contexts, determined by aspects of experience, gender, region, age, occupation, but never in predictable or univocal ways. One trend pushed towards the exploration of the material aspect of the sacrament, another used it as a basis for the consideration of the limits of matter; in some contexts it represented some ideas about community, and in others it became extremely individualistic. No single eucharist is to be sought, and no single category such as class or gender can adequately capture the variety of eucharistic meaning. There was no essential 'feminine' meaning, even if some women were strongly attracted to it,[1] any more than a 'bourgeois' reading, or an aristocratic one.

The new images of the eucharist were usually traditional images transformed, revived, reread. Some of the readings were orthodox, even when they took orthodoxy to its limits, as Margery Kempe famously did, but others were deemed heretical. We are tracing here uses of this eucharist which transcended the normative code, and are searching for their meaning in the life-worlds of their users. Be they heresies, abuses, manipulations, extensions or extrapolations, different eucharistic utterances were testing the language, exposing its capacities, filling its spaces and spelling out its possibilities. Divergent and wide-ranging as these utterances will appear, the eucharistic language of religion provided the means and the rules for their construction.

## EXPOSITION OF THE EUCHARIST

The merits of observing the eucharist during the mass being more widely taught, and liturgical arrangements providing frequent

---

[1] Bynum (1986) attempts to establish one; critique in Beckwith (1986).

moments for gazing at the consecrated host,[2] an impulse was created for exposition of the host on other occasions, even outside the church. The principle formulated by Albert the Great, 'ostensio boni provocat ad bonum', ruled, and church authorities engaged in an attempt to define the occasions and forms in which this would be allowed. The danger was that the carefully designed protection of the host from abuse and accident, might be eroded, and it might thus be exposed to ridicule. The elements, human error, or jeering crowds, threatened the edifice of protective measures which the church had designed especially when the eucharist was out of doors. The sort of threats deemed most dangerous to the eucharist is revealed in accusations against the Jews made in the papal court of Avignon in the 1370s, against those who did not kneel to it, or who mumbled injurious words in Hebrew while it was carried in the streets.[3] The growing Corpus Christi processions expressed the impulse towards display of the host, and served both as expository event and as a model for other types of showing; it familiarised its audience with large-scale eucharistic ceremonial, created the pattern for their future multiplication, and whetted an appetite for sharing the presence of the eucharist.[4] Reformers agonised over this trend throughout the fifteenth century.[5]

One of the consequences of the teaching on the virtue of seeing the eucharist, and of the development of routines for exposition, was the growth of a notion of the *right* to see the eucharist, and attempts to enforce this right.[6] During the interdict of 1376 in Florence public masses were suspended, and town officials were excommunicated. An issue which soon pressed on the city's councillers, the *sapientes*, was the provision for exposition of the eucharist. The public could bear for a while the prohibition of celebration of public masses as long as the consecrated host was exposed for all to see on the altar. Although some defiant Florentines claimed that they would see Christ 'in their hearts',[7] there was mounting pressure to arrange for exposition of the host as was the custom, and the council was caught between it, on the one hand, and the fear of alienating the clergy by forcing an act so closely related to liturgy, on the other.[8] The chronicler Stefani described scenes of people trying to gain a glimpse of the host in open chapels and

---

[2] On the elevation, see above, pp. 53–62.
[3] Chiffoleau (1984), p. 204.
[4] Andrieu (1950), pp. 397–8.
[5] Zika (1988), esp. pp. 48–64.
[6] On the fruitfulness of *visio*, see Mayer (1938).
[7] Trexler (1974), pp. 117, 126.
[8] Trexler (1974), pp. 122–3.

through holes in church walls.[9] Similar keenness was displayed by Walter Doget of St Leonard's, Eastcheap, London, who owned the house adjacent to the parish church. In 1370 he was presented by the parish priest according to the Assize of Nuisance for tearing a window in the church wall, from which he watched the celebration of mass. It was resolved that since he had given his property for the chapel's erection in the first place, he should be allowed to enjoy the view.[10] The issue of access to the host was more pressing than that of communion, which in any case was experienced far less frequently. In the eyes of the Florentines the pope's perverse interdict denied them contact with a source of health, a symbol of power. Seeing the host at the elevation or contemplating it shown in a monstrance on the altar bespoke autonomy, virtue, well-being.

Although theologians insisted that it was *not* to be treated as a relic, veneration of the host followed patterns current in the cult of saints' relics.[11] The famous scene in the Bayeux tapestry showing Harold's oath has him using both hands in oath-taking, one placed on a portable reliquary and the other on an altar with hosts.[12] Here, the two seem to possess comparable and equivalent holiness.[13] The glass cylinder, encased within a structure made of precious metal became the favourite type of monstrance. This differed from the vessels which were ordained for reservation and for carrying of the host to the sick, vessels which we have found in the inventories of parish churches:[14] a closed pyx made of precious metal, covering another case in ivory or copper was designed for safety rather than for visibility. The monstrance, on the other hand, was a public vessel, its design was more intricate and its transparent chamber revealed the host inside. Monstrances were thus very similar to reliquaries, and indeed some vessels were used both for the display of saints' relics and for the exposition of the host.[15] Westminster Abbey received a bequest in 1387 from William, Duke of Gloucester, and his

---

[9] *Ibid*, p. 123.

[10] *London assize of nuisance*, no. 574, p. 143. On people making holes in church doors to see the host, see Browe (1933), p. 62.

[11] Andrieu (1950), p. 418. On the eucharist as relic, Geary (1978), pp. 28–9, 39–40; on the increasing removal of the host from common practices of relic worship, see Herrmann-Mascard (1975), pp. 160–1; Macy (1984), pp. 86–8, 91–2.

[12] Brooks and Walker (1978), pp. 4–5.

[13] For another interpretation of the 'altar', see Bernstein (1982), pp. 40–64; and for an opposing interpretation on this point, see Cowdrey (1987).

[14] See above, pp. 43–7.

[15] Andrieu (1950), pp. 399–408; on modes of relic worship in the eucharistic cult, see Catto (1985; p. 278. When a eucharistic procession was ordained in Florence under interdict in 1376 the Dominican prior managed to convince the *signoria* that it had better process with relics than with the host, Trexler (1974), p. 125.

wife Eleanor: 'A large cup made of beryl for carrying the eucharist, decorated in well gilt silver and splendidly worked'.[16] The inventory of Louis of Anjou (1326–82) describes a crystal barrel which was placed in a reliquary for use on Corpus Christi;[17] the churchwardens of St Donat's church in Bruges removed the images of the Virgin from the reliquary when it was used on Corpus Christi, and placed a crystal tube (*pipa*) in its place.[18] At Tavistock the monstrance was described in an inventory of 1470–1: 'One beryl set in silver and with a chain of silver to hang to the pyx with the body of Xrist on the principal feasts'.[19] In St Petrock's, Exeter, in 1483–4 there was a box of gold with a beryl to bare the sacrament, which weighed 18½ ounces and was valued at £24.[20]

Some monstrances were designed as veritable reliquaries, like those containing miraculous hosts: such was the reliquary of Hasselt-Herckenrode (Limburg) of 1280, which contained miraculous hosts, or was it a monstrance?[21] The three miraculous hosts of Wilsnack which in 1388 were found intact but bleeding after a fire in the local church, were kept in a crystal and shown to pilgrims who streamed to it as to any other great relic.[22] When Margery Kempe travelled through Wilsnack she was led by a friar to see the bleeding hosts, and her *Book* describes the experience: 'þe blisful sacrament in here chirche . . . & it stod opyn in a cristal þat men myth se it yf þei wolde'.[23] And they 'wolde' indeed. Wilsnack represents the merging of eucharistic interests with the forms of relic worship.[24]

If relics could work miracles and generate health and prosperity, surely God's body, the constant and ever-renewed miracle, was even more powerful. By the fifteenth century eucharistic processions were so common, especially in Germany, that legislation was established to bring the eucharist back into church. German and Bohemian councils ordered that the eucharist be shown only on Corpus Christi and its octave.[25] Thus the council of Mainz of 1451 criticised the custom as detracting from the reverence owed to the divine sacrament of the

---

[16] 'Unam grandem cupam de Berilla pro Eukaristiam in eadem deferendam ornatam argento bene deauratam et nobiliter operatam', Legg (1890), p. 285.

[17] Dumoutet (1926), p. 82.

[18] Andrieu (1950), p. 410.

[19] Cox (1913), p. 138.

[20] *Ibid*, p. 139.

[21] Dumoutet (1926), p. 81.

[22] Zika (1988), pp. 49–59. The 1421 statutes of Orvieto cathedral attempted to limit occasions of exposition of its miraculous host and corporal, *Statuti e regesti*, c. 3, p. 7.

[23] *The book of Margery Kempe*, p. 235.

[24] For a representation of a miraculous host, see the early fifteenth century Book of Hours of king Rene, BL Egerton 1070, fol. 110ᵛ; *Le roi Rene et son temps*, p. 41, figure A49.

[25] Dumoutet (1926), p. 85.

eucharist and 'lest the people's devotion cool down due to frequent viewing of it; from then on that sacrament shall not be carried visibly in monstrances except on the octave of Corpus Christi, and even then only during the divine office of that octave'.[26] The council of Cologne in 1452 decreed:

And for the sake of the great honour of the holy sacrament we ordain that from now on that holy sacrament will never be put or carried visibly in any monstrances, except on the feast of Corpus Christi and its octaves once a year in every city or town.[27]

This most explicit legislation was developed where exposition had become most frequent, in processions and in permanent exposition of the host on the altar as in Germany and Italy.[28] The Dominicans of Cosel in Bohemia decided in 1471 to refrain from such practices which were exercised by the secular clergy, 'iuxta morem secularium'.[29] Permanent exposition was demanded by some Florentine politicians under interdict – that Christ's body be shown in every parish and neighbourhood.[30] Where this practice was especially lively in Germany, the Low Countries and Bohemia, a particularly flamboyant type of church architecture was developed, the *Sakramenthaus*, a gabled Gothic structure often approached by steps and railings in which the eucharist was kept, but also exposed.[31] In the fifteenth century a carved tabernacle was developed in Italy consisting initially of small structures which increasingly became elaborate additions to the altar on which they stood.[32] Similarly, elsewhere on the Continent altarpieces were growing in size and in complexity of structure, a tendency which culminated in the next century. The Ghent altarpiece, dedicated in St Bavo's church in 1432, was an intricate array of panels which were ever moving, displayed in sections on various feast days, accompanied by music with

---

[26] 'Propter reverentiam divinissimo eucharistie sacramento exhibendam et ne populi fidelis devotio ex frequenti ejus visione tepescat . . . deinceps ipsum sacramentum visibiliter in monstrantiis preterquam in festo corporis Christi per ejus octavas deferri, et tunc non nisi sub divino officio octave ejusdem ostendi debeat', Mansi 32, col. 140.

[27] 'Item, ad majorem honorem sanctissimi sacramenti statuimus quod deinceps ipsum sanctissimum sacramentum, nullatenus visibiliter in quibuscumque monstrantiis ponatur aut deferatur nisi in sanctissimo festo corporis Christi cum suis octavis semel in anno in qualibet civitate aut oppido', Mansi 32, col. 149.

[28] For similar activities of other councils, see Zika (1988), p. 35, n. 30.

[29] *MOPH*, p. 381.

[30] Trexler (1974), p. 124.

[31] King (1965), pp. 104–8. See, for example, Lane (1984), plate 20, p. 30 for the sacramenthouse in St Peter's Church, Louvain, and another lovely example in Collon-Gevaert (1951), plate 59. In a painting by the Sienese Giovanni de Paolo of 1436×60, such a structure is placed on the altar of the temple in a scene of the Presentation, *Painting in Renaissance Siena*, p. 214.

[32] Caspary (1969).

the eucharist in a little recess at its base; this was practically an independent altar.[33] In England, on the other hand, such structures were not very popular, while rood-screens were. It was not the eucharist but the altar area which was increasing enclosed by the erection of intricate rood-screens from the later fourteenth century. These marked a clerical space distinct from that of the laity; however, dating these screens is rather difficult.[34] There is a clear trend, however, towards the building of more intricate and opaque screens between nave and choir in English parish churches, and whereas the earlier screens had open tracery in their upper parts, later ones became increasingly intricate in design and enclosing in effect.[35]

A development in the imagery related to the eucharist reflects another aspect of this removal of the eucharist from its liturgical bed, and its exposition on occasions other than Corpus Christi, the liturgical feast of the eucharist. Full-page illuminations in Books of Hours, at the Hours of the Sacrament, represent the host, not at elevation, but on its own, in a monstrance, unfettered by liturgical ties. An Irish book of the fifteenth century shows a kneeling pope, emperor, king and bishop adoring the sacrament through a glass monstrance, a scene perhaps inspired by the Mass of St Giles;[36] and equally free-standing is the scene in King René's Book of Hours of 1420×46 where a monstrance is held aloft by four angels.[37] A fifteenth-century Flemish Book of Hours from Utrecht has prayers for the eucharist, and a little pen drawing in the left margin depicts a monstrance with a host.[38] The monstrance also entered the pages of the eucharistic liturgy, in the decoration of the Corpus Christi office, as in a Sarum missal of *c.*1430 where the initial includes two angels in adoration of a host suspended above a chalice held in their hands (figure 17),[39] or in the gradual of Siena Cathedral of 1474 where the monstrance is shown carried by angels.[40] It reached an even more

[33] On the Ghent altarpiece, see Panofsky (1953) I, pp. 205–30 and plates in II, figures 274–83; Goodgal (1981).

[34] Brooke (1971), esp. pp. 178–81 (also p. 175); Bond (1916), p. 101; Bond (1908), *passim*. Some demanded better views through their screens; the chinks in a former rood-screen in Skenfrith (Gwent) Church may have been made for this end.

[35] For a screen which did not block the view although it definitely enclosed the altar see that of St Mary, Atherington (Devon), Whiting (1988), p. 85, figure 3.

[36] See above, pp. 134–5.

[37] *Le roi René et son temps*, p. 188; see also Glasgow University Library Gen. 288, fol. 28ᵛ. The historiated intial of a Corpus Christi office in a fourteenth-century Roman missal of St Mark's in Venice shows Christ holding a host and a chalice, standing in a 'sea' of giant hosts, Venice Marciana III(111)2116, fol. 177v.

[38] London Society of Antiquaries 712, fol. 56ᵛ.

[39] Cambridge Trinity B.11.11, fol. 197ʳᵇ. For a similar but later example, see Leo X's missal of 1509, BN lat. 17323, fol. 213ʳᵃ.

[40] *I corali*, no. 27, p. 68 (Siene Cathedral Cod. 101.7, fol. 63ᵛ).

isolated form in some books such as the Venetian Roman missal of the fifteenth century where a host *in vacuo* decorates the initial of the Corpus Christi office,[41] and at the initial I which opens the statute book (*mariegola*) of the Venetian Corpus Christi fraternity in the church of Santa Maria Mater Domini of the early sixteenth century.[42]

## PARA-LITURGICAL PRACTICES AND IMAGES

### *Easter sepulchres*

The re-enactment of the burial and resurrection of Christ during Holy Week was another eucharistic practice which was widespread in Germany and the Low Countries, and quite common in England, France and Italy.[43] Here we encounter the introduction of eucharistic themes into a pre-existing ritual; the early medieval liturgical drama and music which dramatised Christ's death and resurrection centred on the visit of the holy women to the tomb, the *Quem quaeritis* scene.[44] From the thirteenth century the *depositio* and *elevatio* were enacted in the placing of a consecrated host or a crucifix in a sepulchre on Friday, and in watching it until Easter morning when the tomb was found to be empty by the three Marys.[45] At St Laurence's Church, Reading, the sepulchre was situated under the central chancel-arch and on Good Friday the consecrated element was placed in it until Easter morning when it was removed and placed on the altar. The parish's churchwardens' accounts recorded such expenses as $2\frac{1}{2}$d paid to Sybil Darling in 1507 for nails for the sepulchre and for rosin for the Resurrection play.[46]

In England by the fifteenth century an image of Christ with a hollowed chest, a place for a container with the host, was sometimes placed in the Easter sepulchre.[47] Thus, a tradition of re-enactment of Christ's death and resurrection was reinforced by placing in the altar that which was the very body itself. A silver gilt image of Christ 'w^t hys wonds bledyng' had a space for a little pyx in its chest and a diadem on its head.[48] The tabernacle of Warkleigh parish (Devon) was an oak structure which leaned against a wall and with a space for the pyx which

---

[41] Venice Marciana Library lat III(46)2099, fol. 157^va.
[42] Illuminated by Pellegrino di Mariano, Brown (1988a), p. 19, no. 7.
[43] Forsyth (1970); Sekules (1986); on the practice in Germany see Scribner (1984), p. 61.
[44] Chambers (1903) II, pp. 379–80.
[45] For the liturgy, see Hughes (1982), pp. 247–8, 362–3.
[46] *Reading, St Laurence*, p. 12.
[47] Cardinal Beaufort granted one to Wells Cathedral in 1425 × 52, King (1965), p. 138. See for example, the sepulchre from Patrington parish (Yorks.), Anderson (1963), plate 9a.
[48] *Norwich, St Peter Mancroft*, p. 209.

17 Angels holding a monstrance with the host; initial of the Corpus Christi mass

seems like a surrogate sepulchre.[49] Lights were placed around the sepulchre during the vigil, such as those provided for St Nicholas' Church, York, by Richard Tong's will of 1471,[50] or the lights maintained at St Leonard's, Foster Lane, London, from an income of two shops granted to the parish.[51] The merging of the drama and eucharistic practices is revealed in the use of the Easter sepulchre as a setting for display of the host with overlapping symbolic functions.[52]

These practices which were enacted within the parish church have left traces in parochial records. The inventory of All Saints', Bristol, of 1395 recorded two 'toiles' painted for the sepulchre.[53] Payments made by the churchwardens of Bridgewater in 1417–18 were: 1d for pins to

[49] Cox (1923), p. 43; Baring Gould (1892), p. 129.

[50] *York art*, p. 90. See collection for maintenance of sepulchre lights in the churchwardens' accounts of St Margaret Pattens, London, in 1524, *London, St Margaret Pattens*, p. 260.

[51] *London and Middlesex chantry certificates*, no. 48, p. 36. We know of some ten sepulchres in the churches of York, *York art*, pp. 89–90.

[52] Barking Abbey had an Easter drama *c.*1400, Dolan (1975), pp. 121–40, and Lincoln Cathedral had a play of the Resurrection *Lincoln cathedral statutes* II, p. 15; on Lincoln see Sekules (1986).

[53] Nicholls and Taylor (1881) II, p. 106.

fasten bonds in the sepulchre on Corpus Christi day, and 2s ½d in wine to the chaplain for setting up the sepulchre on Corpus Christi.[54] At Holy Trinity Church, Coventry, the deacon watched over the Easter sepulchre until the Resurrection.[55] At St Ewen's, Bristol, expenses connected with the sepulchre were reported in 1459 and 1461.[56] In the accounts for 1418–20 6d worth of pins and linen were bought 'to make the sepulchre on Corpus Christi day',[57] and gilt clothes were hung around the sepulchre at St Paul's, London.[58] At Bassingbourn (Cambridgeshire) churchwardens paid 7d in expenses incurred over the years 1499–1501 for 'taking down off the sepulcur and setting uppe'.[59]

The structure used as a sepulchre was also used as a tabernacle on Corpus Christi. This interchange of uses based on a symbolic analogy is also manifest in the description of a tower-shaped structure given by Abbot Thomas de la Mare (1349–96) to his abbey of St Albans, 'a silver gilt tower in which Corpus Christi was carried and can be seen, with lower part scenes in silver of the Resurrection amongst angels and four guarding soldiers'.[60] Here the carrying of the host may refer to a ceremony of carrying the 'rising' Christ around the church after the *elevatio,* which was remembered in Durham after the Dissolution as a full procession with 'Christ' under a canopy, in the manner of carrying the eucharist on Corpus Christi.[61] But it may be that the tabernacle of St Albans was used for the Corpus Christi procession. Similarly, a gilt pyx recorded in an early-sixteenth-century inventory of St Peter Mancroft, Norwich, was a monstrance 'for the sacrament beryng' and decorated with the figure of Christ rising from his tomb, with figures of Mary, Peter and Paul, and crowned by an image of the Trinity.[62] As we have seen, a number of Corpus Christi fraternities took charge of the Easter sepulchre ceremonies as part of their eucharistic devotional practices.[63] At Genoa the custom was for penitential fraternities to keep vigil by the tomb.[64]

---

[54] *Bridgewater* III, p. 61. See also *Glastonbury, St John's,* pp. 148, 187, 189.

[55] Dolan (1975), p. 179.

[56] Nicholls and Taylor (1881) II, p. 251.

[57] *Ibid,* p. 68.

[58] 'Item pannos aureos pro sepulchro', *St Paul's,* p. 141.

[59] CUL. Add. 2792, fol. 25ʳ; in 1503–7 expenses on wax for the sepulchre torches are mentioned, fol. 31ᵛ.

[60] 'Una turris argentea et deaurata, ex dono ejusdem, in qua corpus Christi defertur, et perspicue videri potest a plebe. Habetur etiam in eadem turri, in parte inferiori, de argento deaurato, Resurrectio Christi, cum duobus angelis et quatuor militibus custodientibus sepulcrum', John Amundesham, *Annales monasterii Sancti Albani* II, p. 334.

[61] *Rites of Durham,* pp. 10–11, and it was left on the altar until Ascension, p. 107.

[62] *Norwich, St Peter Mancroft,* p. 212. A girdle was left in a will to beautify the sepulchre of St Cross Church, York, *York art,* p. 89.

[63] Above pp. 236–7.

[64] Cambiaso (1917), p. 69.

The sepulchre and its rituals remained part of the Easter drama; but it came to be endowed with more pronounced eucharistic themes.[65] The drama of Holy Week was heightened by the symbolic burial of an effigy, which had a piece of Christ's very body in the cavity of the chest, the heart.

## Hours of the sacrament

Corpus Christi and the sacrament were a theme for private devotion with the guidance of a Book of Hours.[66] Books of Hours usually provided the office of the Virgin, but they often included cycles of weekly Hours with themes for each day: the Sacrament on Thursday, the Cross on Friday, the Virgin on Saturday and variable subjects for the other weekdays.[67] The choice of Hours of the sacrament may be more of a personal choice than with other Hours since its inclusion was an addition to the Book's core of Marian prayers. The usage was most common in the Low Countries and northern France, although it was never ubiquitous. We thus find it in the Book of Hours of the Use of Tournai which belonged to Sister Marie le Cocq who served in the hospital of Lille in the mid fifteenth century.[68]

The iconography of these Hours of the sacrament displays the variety of eucharistic imagery which we have encountered. A Book of Hours of *c*.1330 includes besides the offices of St Catherine, the Holy Trinity, the Holy Spirit, Passion, and the Lamentations of the Virgin, those of Corpus Christi, decorated with a 2/3 page image of Jesus at the Last Supper, handing the bread/host to Judas.[69] Another evocation of the events of Maundy Thursday appears in a Parisian Book of Hours of 1497 where the Hours of the Sacrament are accompanied by the scene of the Washing of the Feet.[70] A French book of Tournai includes the Hours of the Sacrament and was decorated with an elevation scene.[71] In a mid fifteenth-century Book of Hours from north-east France, Thursday's Hours were dedicated to the sacrament and opened with a full-page representation of a monstrance held aloft by angels.[72] These

[65] Sekules (1986) must be corrected at p. 131, n. 52; Corpus Christi was not celebrated in England in the thirteenth century, the mistake arises from a misreading of the dating of section of St Paul customs.

[66] On Books of Hours, see Backhouse (1985).

[67] Hughes (1982), p. 157.

[68] Cambridge Trinity B.11.11, fols. 86ᵛ–87ᵛ.

[69] Vatican Chigi D.V.71, fol. 78ᵛ.

[70] Birmingham Public Library 091/MED/6, pp. 261–7.

[71] BN lat. 1366, fol. 142ᵛ.

[72] Glasgow University Library Gen. 288, fols. 28ᵛ–45ᵛ.

Hours were sometimes decorated with the powerful devotional image of St Gregory's Mass with its image of the Man of Sorrows on the altar.[73]

In the private prayers to the eucharist, which were said in oratories and chapels, the images are those which take the host outside its enclosure in the church: suspended loftily in space by angels, and integrated into moving images of Christ's suffering which called for identification. This was no longer the liturgical eucharist of the mass.

## The Last Supper

With the development of the sacerdotal-sacramental emphasis in the eucharist came a related interest in the Last Supper. Quite apart from its place in the cycles of scenes from Christ's life,[74] the validating value of the Last Supper as the significant guarantee of the eucharist's foundation and meaning was growing. This awareness is expressed in Thomas Hoccleve's (*c.*1370–*c.*1450) poem about Easter, which read the eucharistic connections of the Last Supper:

> On Thursday, a noble soper þou made,
> Where thu ordeyned first thi sacrament;
> But muche more it doth oure hertes glade,
> The worthi dyner of this day present,
> In which þou schewest thi self omnipotent,
> Rising from deth to lyue, it is ful trewe:
> Honorud be thu, blisful lord Ihesu![75]

It was appreciated in the English carol *Mirabile mysterium*:

> Man þat in erth abydys here
> Thow myst beleue withowten due
> In the sacrement of the auter
> That God made at hys soper.[76]

And in the late-fourteenth-century poem 'Of the sacrament of the altere' a stanza is offered about the eucharist's foundation:

> As ly3t li3teneþ ny3t, fro derkenes of kynde,
> So dede crist at þe holy sopere
> Bad pertely do so of hym mynde,
> By holy ordynaunce tau3t us to lere,

---

[73] On the Man of Sorrows see below, pp. 308–10.
[74] Like the prefatory cycles in psalters between calendar and psalms, Oliver (1988) I, pp. 46–50.
[75] *Hoccleve's minor poems*, no. 11, p. xlix, lines 22–28.
[76] *Early English carols*, p. 220.

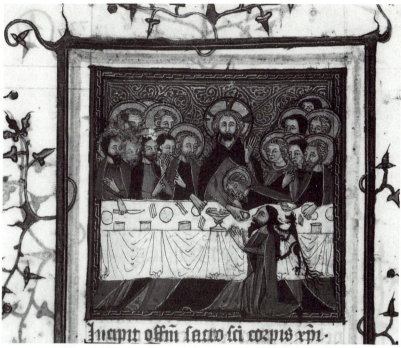

Juapit offin facto fci cozpis xpi·

18 The Last Supper; decoration of the office of the sacrament

> Halwe bred and wyn, by hys word and wynd . . .
> To liȝt of lyf, to shynen clere.[77]

The feast of Corpus Christi was itself a celebration of the foundation of the sacrament on that day, and Corpus Christi sermons often develop this 'historic' theme.[78] Already in *c.*1340–50 a painted glass window in the choir of York Minster depicted the eucharistic Christ at the Last Supper, with apostles on his side (and Judas standing alone). Christ blessed the table on which stood a *ciborium* full of hosts and a chalice.[79] According to Lollard crtique, scripture provides no basis for many current practices of religious life;[80] but the Last Supper was orthodoxy's support, the link between its central ritual of mediation and Christ's own life and words. An extremely illuminating example is the representation of the Last Supper in the Carmelite missal of *c.*1393, as part of the Corpus Christi initial, where the letter was divided into two: the elevation in the upper register, and the Last Supper, its source

---

[77] *Twenty-six political poems*, lines 33–7, 40, p. 104.
[78] Mirk's *Festial*; *Speculum christiani*; see above, pp. 222–5.
[79] Davidson (1977), plate VI.
[80] On the appeal to 'documentation' in medieval culture, see Stock (1983), pp. 59–87.

and support, in the bottom register (figure 19).[81] Here the iconography seems to reflect the denunciation of Wycliffite views at the Blackfriars council of 1382 at which the Carmelites played a prominent part. Carmelites and white dogs are shown at the Last Supper, signing this image of extreme orthodoxy, in a context which needed more than a conventional scene of the elevation – which cried for its guarantee, through the Last Supper.

It seems that the fascination with the theme of the 'law' of the eucharist, with the historic setting in which it was created and thus with its legitimacy, relates to some of the vexing questions about authority which are frequently found in late medieval English culture. As we have already seen, the Last Supper can be treated as a meal *tout court*, a theme promoted in Italy by the Franciscans, who were quardians of the *caenaculum*, the site of the Last Supper, in Jerusalem (figure 18). It was chosen thus for refectories, but also for a wide range of wall-paintings in churches.[82] Yet it was also being interpreted through the superimposition of eucharistic symbols such as chalice and host onto the table, thus turning the Last Supper into the story of the Institution of the Eucharist, to the Communion of the Apostles, rather than merely Christ's Paschal Supper with them.[83] Christ is here presented as priest, as the *Sacerdos in aeternum*, the first image of the Corpus Christi office,[84] as in the altarpiece painted by Dirc Bouts in 1464 for the fraternity of the Holy Sacrament at St Peter's Church, Louvain, where a scene of the Last Supper was turned into the Institution of the Eucharist, with chalice and wafer on the table rather than simple paschal fare.[85] Another famous altarpiece made by the Flemish Justus Van Ghent in the next decade for the fraternity of the Holy Sacrament in Urbino shows Christ as priest serving eucharistic bread to the assembled apostles, thus linking scripture and ritual fulfilment of its command.[86] In Leonardo's Last Supper painted in the 1480s the eucharist is blended into the promise of this communal feast.[87] But in

---

[81] BL Add. 44892, fol. 38[r]; Rickert (1941).

[82] See Brooke (1971), p. 179.

[83] See above, pp. 132–3, 205, and on the various types and their uses in the Italian sphere see Gilbert (1974), pp. 387–90.

[84] For such scenes in the illumination of the initial S of Sacerdos see the Sarum breviary Cambridge St John's College H.13, fol. 57[va], and in a Frenchy breviary of 1409×15 for royal use, Meiss (1968), plate 101 (Châteauroux Municipal Library 2, fol. 113[v]).

[85] Friedländer (1956), plate 81. On the altarpiece, see Dale (1984). Another example is the central *predella* panel to the altar of the Woolmakers of Siena painted by Sassetta in 1423–6, Pope-Hennessy (1939), pp. 6–7, 11–12; *Painting in Renaissance Siena*, pp. 64–7.

[86] Urbino National Gallery of the Marche; Friedländer (1956), plate 134; Lavin (1967); Lane (1984), pp. 115–17.

[87] Steinberg (1975).

19 Top register: the Last Supper; bottom register: the elevation of the host;
initial of the Corpus Christi mass

England the historic moment, the proof through scripture, informs another on-going and important debate, the one expressed in Lollard critique. This is perhaps the type of image which Robert Harryson had in mind when in 1520 he left in his will £10 'to depict the Corpus Christi story'.[88]

Some deep questions of authority which arose increasingly frequently in the fifteenth century, and which charged the eucharistic language, are thus reflected in the growing importance of the Last Supper and its transformation within the eucharistic discourse.

### CHRIST'S SUFFERING HUMANITY

Eucharistic imagery never overwhelmed the Book of Hours, but was a constant and growing presence in its pages. The miracle of transubstantiation was linked to liturgical and public manifestations. The eucharist was formally available only in public circumstances, and although we have seen it colonise the spaces of other rituals, it was meant to be contemplated in public spheres; even in a private oratory it required the presence of priest and servers. Its less formal manifestations will be explored, as the eucharist entered the most private fantasies, the most intimate prayers and desires. Thus, the private book of prayer had no obvious and necessary space for the eucharist, but it was sufficiently flexible to provide some niches for it.

### Christ's body and wounds

In the recesses of the Book of Hours the aspect of Christ's body most developed by private usages was that of the suffering Christ, the Christ of the crucifixion, of the vulnerable, bleeding, flesh of the Passion. Devotions to the wounds had developed in the monastic milieu in the eleventh and twelfth centuries, but spread more widely in the later Middle Ages, and especially in England.[89] The sort of identification which allowed this to happen is captured in an illumination of a Parisian Book of Hours of *c.* 1400–20 where to angels adore a round white host raised on a cross and dressed with a crown of thorns.[90] The suffering of the human Christ was the image most amenable to personal identifications, one of the most interesting was through its association with the eucharist. Let us consider the wounds: Christ revealed his wounds to

---

[88] Heath (1984), p. 223.
[89] Gray (1963), pp. 84–7; Gougaud (1927), pp. 80–91.
[90] BL Egerton 1070, fol. 110ʳ.

chosen holy people just as he provided them with private communion –
as to St Liutgard (d.1246), Ida of Louvain (d.1300), Catherine of Siena
(1347–1380) and to Julian of Norwich (1342–after 1416) in 1373.[91] This
theme is captured in Quirizio da Murano's (fl.1460–78) painting which
has Christ showing his wound and a host to a group of nuns.[92] The
interest in the wounds of Christ operated in a variety of ways; for
mystics they were literally an entry into Christ with whom they wished
to be united in the spirit, a 'refuge' in the words of Thomas à Kempis

> Rest in Christ's passion, and live willingly
> in His holy wounds. If indeed you escape into
> Jesus' precious wounds and stigmata,
> you will sense great comfort in your tribulation.[93]

Throughout the fifteenth century in the expensive Books of Hours as
well as in crudely drawn diagrams on amulets, pictures of the wounds
were represented in every possible way: five wounds in a semi-circle, or
the single wound of each limb saluted separately and uniquely side by
side, as in a Sarum Book for London use of *c.*1420.[94]

Christ's wounds were hailed as the essence of Christ's humanity
which was addressed in the mass, and thus entered the imagery of host
salutations.[95] Particularly privileged in its eucharistic and sacrificial
overtones was the side wound, the gash made by the lance, from which
flowed water and blood. In the eucharist this had determined the liquid
of the chalice as a mixture of wine and water, which became that
sacrificial blood and water.[96] A most popular salutation for the elevation, the *Anima christi*, begged 'O water from Christ's side, bathe
me'.[97] The other wounds were addressed in such vernacular cries as
'Mercy, mercy, mercy, mercy' addressed to 'þe v principall woundys'
in a Book of Hours of *c.*1440,[98] or in a request for forgiveness of sins
and good communion addressed to 'Lord, for þi woundes fyue'.[99] But
none of these appears before *c.*1300, before the making of the eucharis-

[91] Gougaud (1927), p. 114.
[92] Bynum (1987), plate 25, pp. 271–2, notes 65–6 on p. 411 (at the Venice Accademia Gallery).
[93] 'Requiesce in passione Christi,
et in sacris vulneribus eius libenter habita.
Si enim ad vulnera et preciosa stigmata ihesu devote confugis,
magnam tribulacione confortacionem sencies',

Thomas à Kempis, *Imitatio* II, 1, vol. II, p. 225.
[94] Oxford Bodleian Rawl. lit. d. 1, fols. 108ᵛ–10ᵛ; Gougaud (1927), pp. 164–5.
[95] See above, p. 157.
[96] On the eucharistic connotations of the side wound, see Gougaud (1927), p. 104–15.
[97] 'O aqua lateris Christi lave me'.
[98] Oxford Bodleian Lat. lit. e. 10, fol. 22ʳ.
[99] *Religious lyrics of the* XIV *century*, no. 124, pp. 219–22, p. 222.

tic into the strongest link to Christ, the surest promise of salvation.[100] Experience was drawn into Christ's vulnerable form, which was at once accessible through pity and also the source of all that was good. Again in the words of the host salutation:

> Sed sint tua vulnera tuique livores
> Pro nobis et hostia et intercessores.[101]

Or in the English version:

> Through virtue of your wounds v.
> That ȝsuffryd in ȝoure lyue
> Have mercy on me. Amen.[102]

And this is inverted in the *Fasciculus morum* as Christ cries out:

> Behold my woundes wide, man and se,
> My blod þat schedde in batayl for the.[103]

Masses dedicated to the wounds first appear from the early fourteenth century in sections of votive masses in missals, and in private books of prayer, often accompanied by appropriate pictures of open gashes.[104] Interest in the wounds developed into a special devotion; and further into a feast with its mass *Humiliavit* and indulgences in the fourteenth century.[105] This feast was encouraged by popes John XXII and Innocent VI in the next century by the grant of seven years' indulgence to those gazing at, wearing, or kissing a representation of the wound, the *mensura vulneris*, while Henry VI (1422–61) had a picture of the wounds at his bedside.[106] A prayer to the seven wounds was added to the Grey-Fitzpayn Sarum Book of Hours of *c.*1300.[107] A related devotion to the Sacred Heart, which was well established in the monastic mystical milieu,[108] a particular devotion of the nuns of Helfta,[109] spread rapidly in the milieu of the Books of Hours around

---

[100] There was of course much mystical contemplation of Christ's body already earlier, Gougaud (1927), pp. 105–7.
[101] *AH* 42, p. 8.
[102] CUL Ii.6.43, fol. 89ᵛ.
[103] Wenzel (1978), no. 27, p. 162.
[104] Oxford Bodleian Gough lit. 19, fol. 22ʳ; Gray (1963), p. 87.
[105] Gougaud (1927), pp. 82–3. The mass appears as early as 1314 in a French missal for Augustinian hermits, Vatican Pal. lat. 500, fol. 88ᵛ; *Manuscrits liturgiques latins* II, no. 315, p. 128.
[106] Gray (1963), p. 88; Gougaud (1925), pp. 99–100. On the development of the feast in England, see Pfaff (1970), pp. 62–83.
[107] Cambridge Fitzwilliam Museum 242, fols. 92ᵛ–3ʳ.
[108] Dolan (1897).
[109] Bynum (1984), pp. 181–2.

1400.[110] It produced images in Books of Hours that were as explicit as those of the wounds, and derive from that fascination with the redemptive meanings of the suffering of Christ.[111]

The fascination with the wounds was incorporated in a formal liturgy, with prayer and its provision with appropriate indulgences, but eucharistic meanings continued to develop within the language. Attention was drawn to the violations of Christ's body, as these were recorded and incorporated in acts of writing, measuring, wearing, eating: people carried the wounds around on a piece of parchment hanging from their necks, as amulets and as remedies.[112] An amulet containing a 'measure' of Christ's wounds was expected to stop the flow of blood, appealing to Longinus, the Roman soldier:

Longinus: who pierced the side and had blood flow – I dare you – in the name of Jesus Christ, so that the blood of Margery will stop flowing.[113]

A little parchment roll of the fifteenth century served as an amulet by virtue of the drawing of the cross and nails, the measure of Christ's wound, and bearing an inscription of the name of Jesus to which appeal is made for protection: 'He will be freed from all enemies and evil men, and be safe from other evil . . . Amen.'[114] The drawing symbolised but also recreated the Passion scene, in a sort of sacramental gesture. By referring to the accurate measurements of the wound, it thus could not but be beneficial. Such rewards were provided by a fifteenth-century amulet roll on which a carefully designed cross to a scale of 1/15 of the original was drawn: 'Þe schalt die no soden deth . . . þe shalt not be hurte nor slayne w$^t$ no maner of wepyn'.[115] Similarly, the number of drops of blood became a subject for speculation and attention, as shown in an entry in the commonplace book of Robert Reynes (1430– c.1505) of Acle, Norfolk, from the mid fifteenth century:

[110] For a tale about a recluse who wished to know Christ's wounds, see CUL Ii.6.43, fol. 98$^v$: 'Femina solitaria et reclusa numerum vulnerum xristi scire cupiens oravit dominum ut sibi revelaret', in an English vernacular miscellany of tales and prayers (with Latin rubrics).

[111] Such images which were even integrated into heraldic iconography, Dolan (1897), pp. 378–9. See the combination of devotional and heraldic in the self-portrait of Duke William of Hapsburg in a fifteenth century 'hystoria de corpore Christi', the office of the feast, with a ribbon inscribed with the salutation 'Ave verum corpus Christi', (Pierpont Morgan M853, fol. iv), see *Central European manuscripts in the Pierpoint Morgan Library*, no. 42, pp. 56–8, plate 62.

[112] Bühler (1964), pp. 273–4.

[113] PRO E163/22/2/82, my translation.

[114] 'ab omnibus inimicis et ab iniquo homine liberabitur et ab alio malo . . . securus erit . . . Amen', BL Harley roll T 11. Similar rolls contained the *arma christi* and although they were used as charms they may have had a didactic use as well, Robbins (1939c), pp. 419–20.

[115] BL Harley charter 43 A 14; this is the language of the 'merits of the mass', above, p. 108.

> The noumbre of thes dropes all
> I wyll reherse in generall:
> VC ml. for to tell,
> And xlvii ml. weell
> VC also gret and small.
> Here is the nombre of hem alle.[116]

The vulnerable bleeding flesh was encountered with pity, but also used and harnessed in search of security of life. Christ's body was a sought-after property, whose approximate dimensions, whose representations to scale, could be tested and applied for their efficacy.

Thus, the Christocentric fascination with sacrifice and bloodied passion was conflated with the eucharistic drive which posited the subject of identification in the host, and the blood of the wounds in the chalice. At the very end of the Middle Ages we find a fitting representation in an emblem on the roll of the Leicester Corpus Christi fraternity, showing an inscribed host above a chalice framed by two wounded hands and two wounded feet.[117]

### The Charter of Christ

A most striking development in the articulation of the Passion through eucharistic symbolism is the motif of the Charter of Christ.[118] Using the metaphor of a legal document, the promise made by Christ's suffering body was inscribed on a parchment, the undertaking to be renewed and to offer redemption. The Charter establishes an exchange of Christ's sacrificed body which brought the hope of redemption for Man's love.[119] It is a document inscribed on the crucified body, with the wounds as its script:

> How mony lettres þeron beon,
> Red, and þou miht wite and seon:
> ffif þousend foure hundred fyfti and ten
> Woundus on me, boþe blak and wen.[120]

The movement between metaphor and referent is dizzying. Christ is

---

[116] *The commonplace book of Robert Reynes*, no. 15, p. 152.

[117] Bridgettines wore five marks on their habits to commemorate the wounds, Gougaud (1927), p. 89. The related *arma christi* appear upon a shield in the emblem of the Cambridge gild of the Virgin Mary and Corpus Christi, which founded Corpus Christi college in Cambridge in 1352, Masters (1831), plate I, no. 6.

[118] On the Charter, see *The Middle English Charter of Christ*.

[119] *Minor poems of the Vernon manuscript* I, pp. vii–xii.

[120] *Ibid* II, lines 87–90, p. 644.

the parchment; one can smell the body in the parchment that had covered it, as in a fifteenth-century version of the Long Charter:

> Sone aftyr y-straynyd uppon a tre
> As parchement ow3t to be
> Herknyth and ye schall wete
> How this Chartour was y-wrete
> Of my face fill downe the ynke
> Whan thornys on my hed gan synke
> The pennys that the lettris were with wrytene
> Were skorges that y was with betyne
> How many lettris there-in bene
> Rede and thow myste wyte and seene
> With vmcccc fifty and ten
> Wowndis is my body blak and whane
> Ffor to schew the of my loue-dede
> My-sylue y Woll the chartor rede.[121]

Christ's skin is the parchment, the wounds, its letters, the blood, the sealing wax, and the eucharist, that section of the charter left for safe-keeping in the hands of those striking the legal transaction.[122] Copies of the Charter often show the wounds, crossing into the genre of *mensura vulnerum*.[123] This image surfaces in a Quinquagesima Sunday sermon of *c.*1400 where the body hanging on the cross is said to be inscribed like a charter with blood trickling down.[124] Hugh of St Cher's commentary on Apocalypse 10,9 drew out the eucharistic link: 'Indeed this book is the life of Christ . . . the sacrament of the church'. The simile is further developed by Peter Bersuire (*c.*1290–1362):

Christ is a sort of book written by the Virgin . . . spoken by the father . . . punctuated in the imprint of the wounds . . . illustrated by the outpouring of blood.[125]

The eucharistic theme informs the metaphor in other ways; it gives rise to the Last Supper as the setting, mentioned in the fifteenth-century poem:

> On a thorsday a soper y made
> With frendis and foys to make hem glad

---

[121] *The Middle English Charter*, pp. 58–60, lines 157–70; CUL Ii.3.26, fols. 235$^{vb}$–236$^{ra}$; Hughes (1983).
[122] The document is a chirograph, or indenture, which was a legal instrument written twice on the same parchment, which was then divided so that each party had an identical copy.
[123] Uzielli (1901).
[124] *Lollard sermons*, p. 113.
[125] Gellrich (1985), p. 17.

> Of brede and wyne the sacrament
> Euyr to be oure testament . . .[126]

This image of the Charter of Christ is sacramental symbolism carried to the limit; it operated with sacramental logic, through which signifier and signified dissolved into one. The eucharist is God, and his offering, the Charter, is at once evidence of a sacrifice, and the sacrificed body itself.

## The Man of Sorrows

The mournful interpretation of the sacrificed deity developed into the image of the Man of Sorrows sometimes surrounded by the instruments of the Passion. This is an image of Christ weary, bleeding, suffering, on whom are superimposed the crucifix and the wounds. It was developed in a number of settings and with multiple meanings.[127] The face of this Man of Sorrows was also an object of interest, as it appeared in Books of Hours,[128] and accompanied by prayers such as 'Salve sancta facies'.[129] In the thirteenth century the subject first emerged in scenes of the *pietà*, often in the chapels of beguines in Germany and the Low Countries where experiments in the language of religion were being conducted through the eucharist.[130] It developed into a major theme of late medieval Flemish painters,[131] as well as in the more intimate eucharistic context of liturgical books, in details such as the illumination of initials of the office of Corpus Christi in Venetian missals.[132] An English variation is apparent from the thirteenth century in sculpture and miniature illumination showing Christ pointing at his wounds, sometimes from the height of a tympanum, instead of the more traditional image of Christ as judge, as in Lincoln Cathedral,[133] or in the Carrow psalter.[134]

The Man of Sorrows converges with eucharistic themes in a very telling fashion in the late medieval visual representation of the Mass of St Gregory (figure 6).[135] This quintessential eucharistic tale, told from

---

[126] CUL Ii.3.26, fol. 238va (part of the 'Bona carta gloriose passionis domini nostri ihesu xristi', fols. 238[ra]–40[rb]).

[127] Mâle (1925), pp. 98–104.

[128] See an English Book of Hours of *c.*1460, Cambridge Trinity B.11.20, fol. 2[r].

[129] *Hours of York*, pp. 174–5.

[130] Kieckhefer (1984), p. 111; Ziegler (1987), pp. 31–3.

[131] Panofsky (1953) I, pp. 123–5 and figures 43–6.

[132] Venice Marciana Library III(12)2478, fol. 191[va]; III(18)2284, fol. 58[v].

[133] Roberts (1986), p. 142.

[134] Described in *Early Gothic manuscripts* II, no. 118, pp. 88–90; (Baltimore Walters Gallery w. 34, fol. 30[v]).

[135] On the image's development, see Endres (1917); and above pp. 121–2.

the seventh century, concerns St Gregory the Great who prayed for a miracle to occur to counter the doubt of a woman at a mass celebrated by him. His wish was granted and the host turned into a bleeding finger which dispelled the woman's doubt of Christ's presence.[136] This story was popularised in vernacular teaching from the thirteenth century,[137] and in the fourteenth century the miracle was told in a Roman version which had Christ as the Man of Sorrows appear on the altar in front of Gregory, an image spread by pilgrims to other parts of Europe.[138] This gave rise to an increasingly elaborate exploration of the Passion, showing Christ rising from a tomb on the altar, Christ surrounded by the *arma christi*,[139] and sometimes bleeding into the chalice on the altar, as in Robert Campin's famous panel.[140] In the fifteenth century it became a popular choice for the subject of altarpieces.[141] A panel from a collegiate church in Avignon of *c.*1460 goes further in stressing the Man of Sorrows within the tale: it shows St Gregory on the side of the panel together with a donor, with the centre occupied by the large piteous image itself rising from the tomb.[142]

The story further developed in a number of settings: it became very prominent in Books of Hours where it was related to eucharistic prayers. In an English Book it appears as a full-page scene facing the eucharistic prayer *Ave verum corpus natum*,[143] and in an English book of religious exercises the scenes were painted twice, once with the *Adoro te,* and once with the *Ave verum corpus natum*.[144] A late-fifteenth-century French Book of Hours depicted its owner, Jean le Meingre, viewing St Gregory's mass.[145] The scene sometimes appears in the decoration of the office of Corpus Christi,[146] but most often in the

---

[136] *AASS* March II, pp. 133–4. The story gained popularity in the thirteenth century and appears in many *exempla* collections such as John Bromyard, *Summa praedicantium*, tit. Eucharistia, a. 7, example 5, col. 255r. See above, pp. 121–2.

[137] Hirn (1958), p. 100.

[138] Réau (1958) III, 2, pp. 614–15.

[139] On the *arma christi,* see Berliner (1955).

[140] Lane (1984), pp. 129–30. Other examples of the image: a Book of Hours made in France for the English market *c.*1450 (Pierpoint Morgan 79, fol. 7ᵛ); *Die Messe Gregors des Grossen*, pp. 23, 44, illustration 15. For other examples, see the English treatment of *arma christi* in art, *York art*, p. 77; and on English *arma christi* rolls, Robbins (1939c).

[141] Eisler (1969).

[142] *Le roi René et son temps*, no. D14, pp. 202–3, 218 (now in the Louvre no. RF 1536); see also Marrow (1979), plates 42–3.

[143] Cambridge Fitzwilliam Museum 1058–1975, fol. 160ʳ.

[144] BL Add. 15216, fols. 20ᵛ, 103ᵛ.

[145] Meiss (1968), fig. 43; (Paris Jacquemart-André Museum 2, fol. 241ʳ).

[146] As in the fifteenth century Venetian missal and gradual Venice Marciana Library III (120)2478, fol. 191ᵛᵃ, also Marciana Library III(18)2284, fol. 58ᵛ. It was also placed at the beginning of the canon of the mass as in an early sixteenth-century missal of a Flemish Benedictine abbey, Glasgow University Library Euing 29, fol. 71ʳ.

commemoration of St Gregory himself.[147] The increased popularity of St Gregory as a focus of eucharistic devotion gave rise to a series of 'O's of St Gregory which were indulgenced prayers,[148] and were decorated in Books of Hours by the scene of the miraculous mass, as in a French Book where the Man of Sorrows is shown rising from his tomb.[149]

In the fifteenth century the Man of Sorrows became a popular theme for statues, reredos and altarpieces.[150] There are a number of English representations, such as the reredos of the chantry at Stoke Charity (Hampshire), the chantry of Bishop Oldham in Exeter Cathedral, and another in the Kirkham chantry at Paignton (Devon).[151] The last shows Christ in a form which developed in the late fifteenth century, appearing naked on the altar bleeding into the chalice. This seems to be a tradition which developed in Flanders and northern France,[152] and which travelled on the pages of Books of Hours produced for the English market.[153] These English monumental examples significantly appear in chantries and private chapels, the milieu for which private books and sophisticated devotions from the Books of Hours were cultivated. In Germany and Italy the scene was preferred to scenes of the Last Supper for the decoration of chapels of the Holy Sacrament, in these more public, but still restricted, spaces which were used predominantly for confraternal activities.[154]

### The pelican

An image which explored the sacrificial aspect of the Passion and the eucharist, linking it with traditional bird-lore, is that of the pelican.[155] The pelican was a bird which, according to popular legend enshrined in the *Physiologus* and the bestiary, wounded its own breast in order to feed its young ones.[156] This misconcepton arose from the fact that the she-pelican places fish in a skin-pouch in her breast to feed her young.

---

[147] As in fifteenth century additions to the Book of Hours of Philip the Bold, Duke of Burgundy, of after 1370, Cambridge Fitzwilliam Museum 3–1954, fol. 253ᵛ.
[148] Anderson (1975), pp. 57–8.
[149] Cambridge Gonville and Caius 670*/647, fol. 115ʳ; Cambridge Trinity B.11.20, fol. 1ᵛ – Man of Sorrows; fols. 2ʳ–9ᵛ – the Five 'O's.
[150] See examples of German statuettes of the late fifteenth century in Wadell (1969), plate 16 (nos. 32–4).
[151] Anderson (1955), pp. 43 (plate 20), 58, 59.
[152] Baltimore Walters Art Gallery 195, fol. 93ᵛ. See Paris Wildenstein Collection. Marmottan Museum, no. 139, scene of the 'Miracle of the holy host'.
[153] Manchester John Rylands Library 20, p. 16.
[154] Lefèvre (1933), p. 326.
[155] Ferguson (1954), p. 23; Rowland (1978), pp. 130–3.
[156] Based on Augustine's commentary to Psalm 101,7 'I am like a pelican in the wilderness'. For representations in misericords see Bond (1910), pp. 44–6.

In Alexander Neckam's *De natura rerum*, written in the 1190s, a number of allegorical parallels are drawn between the pelican and human history, one of them being between the pelican and Christ.[157] Thus, it was an image of sacrifice, but also of resurrection: the parents were said to strike their young ones so that they should not leave the nest, and then to repent and revive them by bathing them in the blood of their own breasts. Here there was scope for representing Christ as redeemer and as victim, or as God sacrificing his own. This bird-lore was popularised in the vernacular, providing a sort of scientific commentary on the natural world. The same image appears in one of the most popular eucharistic prayers, in the sixth stanza of the *Adoro te*, which is probably of the late thirteenth century, and which was widely translated into vernaculars:

| | |
|---|---|
| Pie pelicane, Jesu Domine, | Pious pelican, Lord Jesus, |
| Me immundum munda tuo sanguine, | Cleanse me the impure, in your blood, |
| Cuius una stilla salvum facere | One drop of which can save, |
| Totum mundum posset omni scelere.[158] | The whole world of all sin. |

The pelican is found most often in connection with the Passion: the missal of St Peter's, Hereford, of 1358, has a pelican eating its heart at the top of a crucifixion page.[159] An English collection of offices, prayers and hymns of *c.*1460, which was accompanied by drawings of the *arma christi*, had an image of the pelican feeding its young ones accompanied by the text:

> The pellicane his bloode bothe blede
> Therwith his birdis to fede
> It figureth that god with his blode
> Us fed hanging on the rode . . .[160]

And at the foot of the page there is a sketchy drawing of hosts. Thus, this image of Christ's sacifice with its emphasis on nourishment was given a eucharistic reading. In another manuscript which combines text and drawing, very much like the aviary from which bird-lore would have been derived, the symbols of the Passion are listed together with legends of the cross. Here the pelican is shown piercing its breast:

---

[157] 'Natura vero et consuetudines istius avis ad ipsum Christum referri solent. . . Triduo luget pellicanus natos suos, et Dominus triduo passionis quodammodo suos luxit. Latus aperuit haec avis, et sanguine respersos pullos excitat. Sic et de Domini latere aperto effluxerunt sacramenta nostrae redemptionis', Alexander Neckam, *De natura rerum*, c. 74, p. 119.

[158] Wilmart (1932), p. 394; on the *Adoro te*, see Doyle (1948).

[159] BL Add. 10926, fol. 192ᵛ. See it combined with the image of the Man of Sorrows in a German woodcut of the fifteenth century, Wadell (1969), plates 9–10, nos. 18–19.

[160] Oxford Bodleian Douce 1, fols. 54ᵛ–76ᵛ; at fol. 57.

Þe pelicane his blod did blede
Þer-with his briddus for to fede,
Þit be-tokenet on þe rode
Oure lord us fede with his blode
Wen he us bouht out of helle
In ioy and blis with him to dwelle
And bene our fadur and our fode,
And we his childurne and gode.[161]

In William Bonde's *Pilgrimage of perfection* of 1523, layfolk are instructed to meditate during the mass conjuring up the image of the pelican after the consecration and before the pax, with special reference to the eucharistic physical and spiritual feeding:

Therfore neuer forgeyt this moost tender louyng Pellycane, whiche of hys meyr marcy wolld wouchayffe not only to dye for to sawe hys byrdes but ouer that he haith ordenyd and dysposyd hys moost gloryouse and blyssyd fleyche and bloode to be our dayly foyde.[162]

The link between the pelican and the *Pater noster*, the commonest of prayers, illustrates the centrality of the image.[163]

The popularity of the image is also demonstrated in the art of the misericord, both in the extensive schemes of cathedral choir-stalls, and in those of a parish church such as Sts Peter and Paul, Wantage (Berkshire), with carvings of the pelican in piety.[164] A misericord formerly at St Katherine's Hospital, London, shows a pelican restoring its fledglings to life with the blood of its self-inflicted breast wounds.[165] Both academic colleges which were dedicated to Corpus Christi, one in Cambridge and the other in Oxford, incorporated the pelican in piety into their emblems.[166]

### *The Mill of the Host and the Mystic Wine Press and the Holy Blood*

Images of sacrifice which centred upon Christ's body were also developed in some more privileged contexts into metaphors which required careful reading. The Mill of the Host is an allegory on the eucharist as

---

[161] BL Royal 17 A 27, fol. 73ᵛ, in *Legends of the holy rood*, lines 21–8, p. 172 (another version is on p. 173 from BL Add. 22029). See the image on French seals, Demay (1880), pp. 354–6.
[162] *Langforde's meditations*, p. 27. Jan Rhodes has identified this tract attributed to 'Langforde' as a part of William Bonde's work; Langforde was the scribe. I am grateful to her for reading this chapter and illuminating me on this point.
[163] On eucharistic interpretations of the *Pater noster*, see above, pp. 100–101.
[164] Remnant and Anderson (1969), p. 4, plate 12d.
[165] *Ibid*, p. 93, plate 12c. For misericords, see also Bond (1910).
[166] See Masters (1831), title page: 2 shields with pelicans and two with lillies, for a college founded by the gild of the Virgin Mary and Corpus Christi.

bread, made into dough with Christ's blood, and shaped into hosts through a mill.[167] An earlier tradition which became popular in Romanesque art related the Old Law and the New in the image of Moses pouring grain into a mill, and Paul collecting the flour, as in the famous carved capital in the church of the Cluniac abbey at Vézelay, rebuilt *c.*1120–50.[168] The late medieval image is a dense one, incorporating disparate sections of the Christian myth. Four evangelists turn the mill in a gradual of St Urban's Monastery near Lucern of the late fifteenth century, with an Annunciation at the top, linking Nativity and eucharist yet again, on the very page of 'Ad te levavi', the first psalm in Advent.[169] Angels turn the mill in an altarpiece of the Franciscans in Göttingen of 1424: and it was as the theme for an altarpiece that this image was most developed, especially in the German sphere.[170] But this was not one of the images which was taken up in a variety of cultural forms; it was largely a monastic and clerical image, not of the explicit nature which we have encountered in other eucharistic developments.

The image of the Mystic Wine Press is another development,[171] building on an analogy made by Augustine between the grape in the press in Isaiah 63,3:

> I have trodden the wine press alone;
> of my people not one was with me.
> So I trod them down in my anger
> I trampled on them in my wrath.
> Their blood squirted over my garments
> And all my clothes are stained.[172]

and Christ's future suffering and bleeding, in his commentary on Psalm 23,5:

The first grape pressed in the press is Christ. After that [grape] was squeezed at the passion, and what remained after is thus 'my [excellent] cup runeth over'.[173]

Thus, the homely image of a wine-press, just like the comforting image of the mill, is here associated with the violence of the crucifixion, whose

---

[167] Mâle (1940), pp. 167–8.
[168] For a good reproduction, see Brooke (1974), plate 112. For another example of this image in a glass window of St Denis, which no longer surprised but which was described by Abbot Suger, see Panofsky (1946), pp. 74–5.
[169] Lucern Central Library KBP Msc. 19, fol. 1ʳ. On these images see above, p. 138.
[170] Rye-Clausen (1981), figure 11.
[171] Vloberg (1946) II, pp. 175–83.
[172] 'Torclar calcavi solus, et de gentibus non est vir meum; calcavi eos in ira mea, et adspersus est sanguis eorum super vestimenta mea, et omnia indumenta mea inquinavi'.
[173] 'Primus botrus in torculari pressus est Christus. Cum ille botrus passione expressus est, manavit illud unde *Calix inebrians quam praeclarum est!*', Augustine, *Ennarationes in psalmos LI-C*, on psalm 55, p. 680; Lavin (1977), p. 299.

meaning and value is in its bringing forth of a type of nourishment, wine and bread. The eucharistic connection was also appreciated by the illuminator of some psalters of Liège at psalm 80, 'Exultate Deo', which celebrates the Jewish feast of the Booths (*Sukkot*) and the harvest of grapes, and whose *titulus* was 'pro trocularibus'.[174] Through the eucharistic language the preparation of bread and wine were given meanings which transcended their traditional ones, and which also incorporated the eucharistic sacrifice in a series of workday and domestic settings.

The fascination with the eucharistic blood was never as pronounced in England, just as the fascination with miraculous hosts was rather limited, while both interests were particularly lively in Germany and common in Italy.[175] When Margery Kempe wished to see 'þat pre-cyows Blod whech be myracle cam owt of þe blisful sacrament of þe awtere', she was obliged to go as far as Wilsnack.[176] In England the Holy Blood cult was the product of a thirteenth-century royal initiative, and coincides with the circulation of Passion relics after the Fourth Crusade and the sack of the relics of Constantinople.[177] Following Louis IX's lead, in 1247 Henry III procured the relic of Christ's Holy Blood and placed it at Westminster Abbey.[178] Prince Edward followed suit in 1267, acquiring a relic whose authenticity had been guaranteed by no other than Urban IV, once Patriarch of Jerusalem.[179] Drops of the blood were deposited at Ashridge Monastery (Hertfordshire), and at Hales Abbey (Gloucestershire).[180] Hales developed into the only English pilgrimage shrine to the Holy Blood,[181] but the interest was not widespread; the blood was preferred as an image within a eucharistic setting of associated themes of humanity, sacrifice and regeneration. The blood was sometimes endowed with eucharistic overtones in its reliquary; represented as being elevated by angels, as in the widespread image of the host in the monstrance.[182]

---

[174] Oliver (1988) I, p. 71.

[175] Brückner (1958).

[176] Margery Kempe, *The book*, pp. 234–5. On Wilsnack fraternity, see Barron (1985), p. 17.

[177] On the relics brought from Constantinople to Venice see Pincus (1984), pp. 41–6 (for an image of the relics see p. 48). From there they spread throughout Europe. Passion relics were bought by Louis IX from the titular Latin Emperor in 1238, Jordan (1979), pp. 31, 107–8.

[178] Matthew Paris, *Historia Anglorum* III, p. 29 (on the relic of the impression of Christ's foot, see pp. 60, 310).

[179] For Grosseteste's opinion on a number of issues related to Christ's blood and resurrected body, see Matthew Paris, *Chronica maiora* IV, p. 644 and VI, pp. 138–44.

[180] Roberts (1986), p. 140.

[181] See a will of 1488 referring to the pilgrimage, *Ripon Acts*, p. 264.

[182] Browe (1938), pp. 139–59, 198; Pincus (1984), p. 41; about the monstrances, see above, pp. 290–4.

In England the emphasis, both in orthodoxy and in dissent, was upon the historic suffering of Christ and its implications – as in the Charter of Christ and the devotion to the wounds. The devotional texts emanating from Germany were consciously watered down in the process of translation into English;[183] and it is telling that an active spiritual traveller such as Margery Kempe was attracted to German pilgrimage sites. English Books of Hours concentrated rather on the mythical moment of the crucifixion and all its attributes, as in the pages of the Bohun Psalter-Book of Hours of *c.*1370–80, with images for contemplation of the *arma christi,* the crucifixion, the wounds.[184] The affective moment is related to the moment of sacrifice as in this prayer from a mid fifteenth-century Book of Hours:

> Ihesu for thy holy name
> And thy bitter passion
> Save me fro synne and shame
> And endles dampnacion
> & bring me to thy blis
> That never schal mys Amen.[185]

A widespread and peculiarly English development was the drawing at St John the Baptist into the eucharistic sphere, not only as a precursor of Christ, but as a sacrifice in his own right. A small alabaster carving of St John's head on a platter after Herod's banquet became one of the most popular religious artifacts, cheap and mass-produced in the thousands.[186] The severed head of the Baptist on a platter was an offering like a host on a paten, and for some could evoke the imagery of the grail as the platter of the Last Supper sacrifice.[187] The fifth reading on the feast of the Decollation of St John the Baptist in the York breviary makes this connection:

John's head on a tray signifies Christ's body, from which we eat at the holy altar, and which was given to the congregation of nations in salvation and remedy of souls.[188]

And it was adopted as a badge by such bodies as the Corpus Christi fraternity of York. The identification follows eucharistic language, as in

---

[183] Lovatt (1982).
[184] Begun for Humphrey de Bohun, Oxford Bodleian Auct. D.4.4, fol. 236ᵛ.
[185] Oxford New College 310, fol. 115ʳ.
[186] Stone (1955), p. 216; Weston (1923); Cheetham (1984), pp. 319–32, plate 243 and colour plate facing p. 41.
[187] Barb (1956), pp. 46–7.
[188] 'Caput Johannis in disco: signat corpus Christi, quo pascimur in sancto altari, et quod ecclesie gentium tribuitur in salutem ac remedium animarum', *York breviary* ii, col. 517. Stone (1955), pp. 216–17; Tudor-Craig (1986), p. 112–13.

the closing lines of the verse sermon, 'Of the sacrament of the altere' where the images of angels' bread, manna of the desert and sacrificial lamb, lead on to the eucharist as Christ:

> In stede of þat, oure soules to glade,
> We resceyue oure housell, god o blisse.[189]

### MYSTICISM

Mystical experience is personal and as such is difficult to communicate, and so to interpret. The mystic could pose problems to the liturgical and parochial routines, and thus to the symbolic system which they supported. This was not always so; Mechtild of Hackeborn (1207–1282×94) blended her contemplation with sacramental experience; in her *Liber specialis gratiae* she related the mystical and private Jesus to Christ of the eucharist, the past and ever-present saviour.[190] But for most mystics the sequence of mass, prayers, confession and communion was not enough; images recommended to the laity as aids to contemplation only detracted from Julian of Norwich's purity of mystical concentration.[191] She chose analogies from nature to describe her 'journey', rather than from an established orthodox vocabulary.[192] As John Tauler (*c.*1300–61) put it, on the threshold of *unio mystica* all that had previously helped now hinders, preaching, prayer, sacraments: 'Before, when [the pure nature] came, I had given it the body of God daily. Now I do so in no way'.[193] Frequent communion could help at the outset, but its benefits diminished as mystical progression occurred.[194] Aids which were useful to most people served mystics only at the beginning of their journey.[195] Removed from sacramental trappings and parochial rhythms, in its quest for unity with something else the soul is described by Gerson as being alone; it is never submerged in God like a drop of water in wine, it is independent and always separate.[196] In that sense the mystic sought a different niche in the symbolic language, not the normative idiom, but one which allowed for greater

---

[189] *Twenty-six political poems*, lines 127–8, p. 107.
[190] Haas (1983), p. 60.
[191] Julian of Norwich, *The book of showings*, p. 471; *Mirrour of simple*, p. 372.
[192] Bradley (1984), p. 207.
[193] Ozment (1980), p. 40, n. 4.
[194] Ritchie (1974), pp. 11–12.
[195] *Ibid*, pp. 7–11.
[196] Ozment (1980), p. 74; Gerson is, however, quite unique in the emphasis on the separateness of the soul.

freedom and less definition and determination in language usage. It is not surprising, therefore, to note that fourteenth-century mystics turned to twelfth-century pre-scholastic texts for inspiration. In them they found a less programmatic language; so it was to Hugh of St Victor, to Anselm, to Bernard of Clairvaux, that Geert Groote, Ruysbroeck and Thomas à Kempis were particularly attracted.[197]

The eucharist was used by mystics as the trigger for contemplation and absorption, ever closer to an immersion in God. Caroline Bynum has explored the ways in which the 'eucharistic' Christ appealed to the sensibilities and consciousness of medieval religious women, as a point of entry into such union with the supernatural.[198] The language of incorporation and submergence and their identification with the suffering body of Christ produced an affective link and its very site of fulfilment. The ultimate site of mediation was incorporated into the world of the nuns of Helfta – God-Man in the host, a Christ who bleeds and offers himself, who beckons through identification, who opens his body to the rising mystic.

Medieval mystics have often been seen through the eyes of their confessors, parish priests, and suspicious inquisitors: those who wished to control and correct what often seemed to be aberrant and dangerous innovations. Students of Margery Kempe have been side-tracked by assessments of her possible hysteria, while it is more fruitful to listen to her language of religion, and to ponder the meaning constructed by her.[199] The mystic speaks the language of religion and imbues it with different meanings.[200] To impute an essential female mysticism on the one hand, or to locate it in the realms of the aberrant, pathological or psychotic, is equally to evade the phenomenon.

Thus the type of symbolisation which animated the mystical experience was at odds with the routinised normative practices and the formal closure of meanings recommended in teaching and ritual. What seemed most threatening to the routines and procedures of mediation, particularly when practiced by women, was the transcendence of a whole range of norms regulating family life, privacy, motherhood, parochial adhesion. What worried was the romance which some women actually made of the suffering Christ as an object of their desires.[201] Margery Kempe identified with Christ as an eternal object, the bearer of consequences of human weakness and sin. The unsettling way in which she

---

[197] Constable (1971), pp. 5–18.
[198] Bynum (1984), (1985), (1987); see also Carmichael (1989), p. 635–9, 644.
[199] Beckwith (1986) offers a critique of these approaches.
[200] Kieckhefer (1984), pp. 165–6.
[201] Beckwith (1986), p. 48–54.

constructed Christ at once her son, lover, father, spouse and child attracted criticism and bewilderment.[202]

Attempts to identify feminine mysticism through the qualities of a 'female body', long-suffering, nurturing, given to dramatic transformations, and tending to cleave to other bodies, can easily be exaggerated, and make to simplify what was a complex and shifting array of meanings. Religious women do, however, show a great preoccupation with food. And we have come to appreciate the meaning of Catherine of Siena's frequent taking of communion and refusal of other food.[203] Liutgard of Aywières's (d.1246) second period of abstention from food was directed to the benefit of all sinners, to nurture them.[204] The Dominican Columba of Rieti (d. 1501) was allowed to take frequent communion: she fainted whenever she was deprived of it, and lived on nothing else for twenty years.[205] These practices are attempts to come to grips with, to negotiate a position in, their surroundings, to create an idiom within a language of religion. But the eucharist was not only the focus for women; communion was central to many male mystics, offering a privileged meeting with Christ. In the *Imitatio Christi* Thomas à Kempis derided those who rushed to see saints' relics when contact with God himself could be achieved:

And thus you are present here near me on the altar, my holy God . . . creator of saints and Lord of angels, to be seen in such things that are new and wondrous to wo/men . . . Here you are fully present my God, as man, Jesus Christ, in the sacrament of the altar: where the abundant fruit of eternal salvation is received whenever you are decently and devoutly consumed.[206]

Nicholas Love, prior of Mountgrace (Yorkshire) between 1409–21, appended a 'tretys of the hiʒeste and most worthy sacrement of Cristes blessed body' to the *Mirrour of the blessed lyf of Jesus Christ*, his English translation of *Meditationes vitae Christi*, a popular mystical text which had been attributed to Bonaventure. In this treatise he translated a eucharistic prayer of the German mystic Henry Suso

---

[202] Dronke (1984), pp. 215–27. On Margery Kempe, see also Fries (1984).
[203] See above, p. 120, n. 232.
[204] Hendrix (1978), p. 187.
[205] Bynum (1987), pp. 147–8.
[206] 'Et ecce tu presens [es] hic apud me in altari deus meus sanctus . . . sanctorum creator et dominus angelorum sepe in talibus videndis curiositas est hominum et novitas invisorum . . . Hic autem in sacramento altaris totus presens es deus meus homo Christus Ihesus: ubi et copiosus percipitur eterne salutis fructus, quocienscumque fueris digne ac devote susceptus', Thomas à Kempis, *Imitatio* III, 1, vol. II, pp. 30–2; Heimpel (1972), p. 49; Post (1968), pp. 2–5.

(*c.*1295–1366), which he deemed to be both effective and necessary to those embarking on mystical experiences.[207]

Thus, both men and women could use the sacrament as a departure, or see it as a distraction; they could join in Christ's suffering identifying with it either as the sympathetic vulnerability of a weak feminised body exuding tears, blood and milk, or in terms of a submission to trial, as it could have been for the male recipients of *stigmata*. The mystic's sense of self-obliteration, the merging into another body, the annihilation of the self, is present in some expressions of female mysticism. This image of wounds of love was Gertrude of Helfta's (1256–1302) interpretation of her *stigmata*.[208] Meanwhile, men were recipients of *stigmata*,[209] and were also creators of eucharistic worlds. Jan Ruysbroeck's instruction in mystical contemplation of 1377×1408, translated into English as *The chastising of God's children*, was grounded in eucharistic images such as the Name of Jesus and the Wounds which still retained the importance of prayer and good works.[210] He distinguished between those beguines who were vain and hard-hearted, and those who adhered to God in charity through the routines of the church's sacraments, and particularly through the eucharist.[211] He was thus addressing an existing tension between sacramental religion and the reaches of mystical experience.

Mystics constructed the most intractable life-worlds about which we are comparatively well-informed. But even when steering away from norms, they were speaking the language of religion, which they could never escape. Rather, in their intense creative use of senses and bodies they reproduced the symbolic system's very fissures.

## HERESY

Heresy is, or course, a term laden with judgements which we will try to turn into a tool for the examination of utterances and practices which incurred disapproval, by emphasising their place within the symbolic order. What has become extremely clear in the study of the sacramental language of religion is the inexorable nature of its critique, demonstrating the dialectical and necessary relation of any meaning-creating statement to the possibilities which it both constituted and excluded. And I say critique, rather than heresy, since heresy is the institutional and legal definition of those areas which at any given

---

[207] Zeeman (1958), p. 113, the text of the prayer is on pp. 114–16.
[208] Bynum (1982b), p. 192. See also Bynum (1986), pp. 423–4.
[209] Vauchez (1981), p. 514.
[210] *The chastising*, pp. 79–80, 203–14.
[211] Epiney-Byrgard (1984), pp. 69–70.

time are particularly implicated, out of a wide range of ideas and practice which erode and subvert the symbolic system. Critique developed at those points in the structure which were weakest, not in terms of the robustness of the ecclesiastical structure, but in terms of the philosophical claims which they made. These were often questions which troubled theologians and for which answers and remedies were repeatedly formulated by intellectuals.[212] Thus, although the definition of heresy changes over time and space, the areas open to critique are structurally embedded within the symbolic system and its statements, and we can expect to hear them from the lips of an illiterate villager as in the finer words of a theologian or a dissenting priest.

The fascination with the white sphere which was claimed to be God bred scrutiny and doubt. Already in the tenth century theologians discussing the nature of the eucharist were arguing against particular errors, heresies. Heriger of Lobbes refuted a distinctive error held by the Stercoranists, people who claimed that Christ's body in the eucharistic host was digested and incorporated into human bodies just like ordinary food.[213] From the twelfth century onwards a stream of diverse accounts attests to a growing problem in the reception of the claims made by the invigorated sacramental system. Dissent developed in a number of regions throughout Europe; in the twelfth-century diocese of Utrecht St Norbert countered Tanchelm, one who denied the power of the eucharist and of other sacraments.[214] Tanchelm was an ardent Gregorian but his claim against sacraments celebrated by underserving priests had clear anti-clerical implications. Elsewhere, new types of dualist dissent, such as catharism in the south of France, had a rigorous anti-sacramental critique, inasmuch as matter could never be conceived of as containing spirit, and definitely not as being capable of transformation into God.[215] The claim which recurred throughout the Middle Ages was of this type:

They believe that Christ's body and blood is in no way created by our consecration, and that it cannot be received by us by communion.[216]

Or in words which totally disposed of a priest, put into the mouth of a heretic by Caesarius of Heisterbach:

---

[212] Jones (1973), p. 48.
[213] Heriger of Lobbes, 'De corpore et sanguine domini', *PL* 139, col. 188.
[214] Russell (1965), pp. 56–68; Lambert (1977), pp. 55–7.
[215] Wakefield (1973), pp. 31–2.
[216] 'Corpus Domini et sanguinem nullo modo nostra consecratione fieri, aut a nobis per communicationem percipi posse credunt', Eckbert, 'Sermones contra catharos', col. 15.

That any peasant can make Christ's body at his own table and of his own bread which he eats.[217]

So the bread of the host did not differ from any other bread. Such objections were sufficiently credible to make good didactic tales: an *exemplum* described a woman's defiance in treating the host as bread, to be baked in her oven.[218] More extreme was the claim by a suspected Cathar examined by James Fournier Bishop of Pamiers (1317–26): 'That which the chaplains elevate in the mass is just some type of turnip'.[219]

The claim which ridiculed the host applied the common sense of conservation of ordinary matter to this putative divine matter, as in the early-thirteenth-century version in the *Historia Albigensium*:

They teach that the host of Christ's body does not differ from lay bread; instilling such blasphemy in the ears of simple folk, saying that even if Christ's body was as large as the Alps, it would have already been consumed by those eating it, and would have been totally annihilated.[220]

Such claims were found around Toulouse even late in the thirteenth century among people who had no apparent Cathar connections and a generation after the formal extinction of the Cathar church.[221] The merchant Durandus claimed in 1273 that even if Christ's body were as large as a mountain it would have been consumed by then;[222] the peasant Bernard claimed in 1276 that the eucharist was made of dough and that even if the body were as big as Mount Vinha (near Montauban) it could not be sufficiently large, nor would have God put himself in the hands of false priests.[223] This is expressed in the words which Beatrice Lagleize of Adalon near Montaillou was reported to have said: 'if the thing which priests held at the altar was Christ's body, and even if it were as big as this mountain [showing a mountain called Domergali], it would have already been eaten up even by the priests alone'.[224] So two

[217] 'Quod rusticus quilibet in mensa sua, et de pane suo quo resceretur, conficere posset corpus Christi', *DM* 5,19, pp. 298–9.

[218] In a fourteenth century collection, BL Harley 2851, fol. 106ᵛ.

[219] 'Quod elevant capellani in missa similatur pelalha de nep vel de rappa', *Reg. Fournier* III, p. 464; Duvernoy (1976), p. 207.

[220] 'Sacrosancti corporis Christi hostiam, a pane laico non differre publice dogmatizarent; simplicium auribus hanc instillantes blasphemiam, quod Christi corpus, etsi magnitudinem Alpium se contineret, jamdudum consumptum a comedentibus et annihilatum fuisset', Peter of Vaux Cernay [Vallium Cernaii], 'Historia Albigensium', cols. 546–7.

[221] Wakefield (1973).

[222] *Ibid*, pp. 25–6. See also Dossat (1968), p. 79: 'Si corpus domini nostri Iesu Christi esset ita magnum sicut mons, modo est comestum'.

[223] Wakefield (1973), p. 27.

[224] 'Creditis quod illud quod tenent sacerdotes in altari sit corpus Domini? Certe, si esset corpus Domini, et fuisset ita magnum sicut est mons iste (ostenso monte vocato Domergali) comestum fuisset iam a solis sacerdotibus', *Reg. Fournier* I, p. 215; Dronke (1984), pp. 212–3. For similar materialist criticisms see Merlo (1977), pp. 54, 61.

central objections are here combined, as described earlier in the century in a list of attitudes which James of Vitry titled 'objections and opinions' in his treatise on the sacrament of the altar: how could Christ be eaten by the apostles before his Passion and then suffer on the cross? When he suffered on the cross was Christ not also in the pyx of the Last Supper? These are questions which attempted to defend the claim that Christ's body resides in the sacrament against notions of materiality applied to other objects. Whenever necessary, James of Vitry answered by invoking miracles.[225] Similarly, in 1374–5 Thomas Brinton, bishop of Rochester, turned this point on its head to confirm a miraculous strength in the eucharist: 'Why is this sacrament miraculous in its multiplication? because every day it is made, eaten and not consumed'.[226]

These were not simply questions about the location of the crucified body in the host; these were also questions of authority. With greater circulation of Bibles in the vernacular in the twelfth century, an intimate knowledge of the gospels and the acts of the apostles was generated and induced in more people a willingness to accept only those explanations of religious practice based on scriptural proof.[227] Tested against understandings of nature and common sense the claims made about the nature of the eucharist on the altar were hard to accept. This is reflected in the type of fantastic-incorporeal formulations discussed by John XXII in a directive to the bishop of Draschitz and the Bohemian Inquistion of 1318:

> They preach according to the damnable heresies of the heretics that our saviour Lord Jesus Christ has not a human body but an imaginary one.[228]

The Italian inquisitors encountered similar claims: 'That [he] is not in the sacrament of the altar as Christian teach and believe, but always in heaven'.[229] Or 'God does not descend into the host which the priest elevates'.[230] Although these objections were often countered by appeal to the eucharist as a miracle which defied the rules of nature, it was in danger of becoming a miracle *ex opere operato*, one which constrained God's action. A scholarly attempt to combine an omnipresent God operating in total freedom was formulated by Amalric of Bène, lecturer

---

[225] James of Vitry, 'De sacramentis', pp. 238–9.
[226] 'Quid hoc sacramento mirabilius in sui multiplicacione? Nam cotidie conficitur, sumitur, et non consumitur', *The sermons of Thomas Brinton*, sermon 9, pp. 200–6, at p. 200.
[227] Bibles were owned by some of the suspects in Wakefield (1973); Rando (1983) on Italian Bible ownership.
[228] 'Salvatorem nostrum dominum Iesum Christum juxta dampnatas hereticorum hereses non corpus humanum, sed fantasticum predicant habuisse', Patchovsky (1975), p. 86.
[229] 'Quod non est in sacramento altaris sicut docent et credunt Christiani, sed est semper in celo', Merlo (1977), p. 28.
[230] 'Deus non descendit in hostia illa quam sacerdos elevat', *ibid*, p. 53, n. 100.

at the University of Paris in the late twelfth and early thirteenth century. Amalric saw God in all things, and especially in the members of the Church, and thus the words of the consecration did not transubstantiate the bread and wine, but rather brought forth God's presence in them, a presence which inhered in them as part of God's creation.[231] His views were condemned by Innocent III in 1209 since such pantheism and relativism could not be tolerated, but this is yet another attempt at the accommodation of the different discourses which intersected in the eucharistic symbol.

The movement of the Free Spirit also challenged the absolute necessity to attain grace through the mediation of sacraments, and of those who performed them, the priests.[232] Such views were attributed to beguines, the sort of women whose lives provided stories about taking the host to their cells for private devotion, subsisting on nothing but the host, and of turning the elevation into a sacramental substitute.[233] Their idiom verged on the mystical, and exerted pressure on the edifice of sacramentality offered by the church in their questioning of the need for extensive priestly mediation and clerical assistance.[234] Such views among religious women threatened the demarcation between the sacred and the profane, and it obscured the ritual privilege of priests. The decree *Ad nostrum* in the *Clementines* imputed to beguines the belief in their ability to become so perfect as to have no need for prayers and fasts, good works or veneration of the host.[235] Gerson reported that even some rather moderate mystics simply abstained from parochial communion when they knew the priest to be incontinent.[236] Such views converge with some anti-clerical attitudes, as in the repeated Lollard claim that a learned lay-person, even a woman, was as worthy a celebrant as any priest.[237] But they also echo ambivalence within orthodoxy; was it not in a vision to Gertrude of Helfta that Christ appeared and reassured the nun that priests gained nothing by handling Christ's body daily, that it was those who received worthily (like Gertrude) who shone in glory?[238]

The critique of the eucharist was an attack at its weakest points:

---

[231] MacCulloch (1932), pp. 206–7; Ferruolo (1985), pp. 290, 307.

[232] Lerner (1972); little is known of the effect of the movement in England, *ibid*, p. 195, n. 46.

[233] *Ibid*, pp. 138–40.

[234] See reference to such views in a sermon preached by Ranulph de la Houblonnière in Paris in 1273 against those who ask: 'Quale privilegium habent isti qui sunt de genere Levi, qui ita vadunt circa altare et incendunt solithus Deo?', Bériou (1987) II, p. 78.

[235] Tarrant (1974), p. 305.

[236] On such criticism of beguines, see Lerner (1972), pp. 57, 81–2.

[237] Cross (1978), p. 371.

[238] Bynum (1982b), p. 207.

where it claimed to conjure God under the guise of matter, where it claimed that this could even be done by a priest who was a sinner, and in its claim that no amount of virtue could free a person from dependence on the mediating sacramental channels. It was also the difficulty of accepting the fruitful or indeed possible mediation of power through an image, which was not exactly the sacramental claim, but rather the way the claim was posed.[239]

Criticism of images informed many of the dissenting views about the eucharist, and it achieved perhaps the most articulate and clear formulations in Wycliffite and Lollard positions.[240] John Wyclif's criticism of transubstantiation was a product of his studies in logic, optics and physics, on the one hand, and on his biblical inquiries, on the other.[241] It was also informed by traditions of anti-sacramental thinking, which in turn explain the widespread reception of his views. God was understood to dwell in his creation, to be committed to its laws, but not in man-made artifacts and procedures, unless they were really God-made, ordained by God's word, in scripture. And yet Wyclif did use the image, without ascribing inherent efficacy, in describing Christ's relation to the sacrament, which was *not* his very body: 'it is in anoþer maner godus body þan it is in heuene', and that manner is that of a token:

as a man leeves for to þenk þe kynde of an ymage . . . and settys his þou3t in him of whom is þe ymage, so myche more shuld a man leue to þank on þe kynde of brede:[242]

So images were rejected in their ascribed, almost sacramental role, the images of saints, the image of bread, since they could be no more than what they were; but they could induce thoughts and inspire moods, and as such were not without importance.

Wyclif's critique of sacramentality was articulated in the terminology of contemporary theological and philosophical scholarship. But it was transmitted and disseminated by knowledgeable clerics in town and countryside, so that in Lollard views we can often recognise, even decades after his death, terms and formulations which originated in Wyclif's writings.[243] Wyclif was a Thomist at heart. He thus recoiled from nominalist formulations such as Scotus' introduction of the term annihilation according to which God destroyed being in the eucharist. His view also differed from Ockham's method and its dogged pursuit

---

[239] Some contemporaries held that belief was essentially acceptance of the invisible, of that which cannot be tangibly proven, Schmitt (1981), pp. 337–61.
[240] On iconoclastic views, see Aston (1988).
[241] Keen (1986a), pp. 12–15.
[242] *Selections*, p. 17; on the eucharist as keep-sake, see above pp. 226–7.
[243] Hudson (1988c); Keen (1986b).

of the observation through the authority of the senses. As a realist Wyclif insisted that accidents could never be without their substance, which in turn was linked to abstractions that lay beyond sense perception. Thus, the substance of the bread and wine remained after the consecration, even if sacramental change had also introduced other qualities in them. Whatever the nature of Christ's presence on the altar, it could not simply be claimed to be the physical historic body[244] – it could, however, be accepted as a holy memorial.[245]

Wyclif never stripped the eucharist of meaning, as some Lollards did, nor did he deny its benefit for the participant in the mass. Rather he abhorred the notion of transubstantiation and its claims which contradicted unnecessarily the laws of nature, and insisted that on the altar after consecration the substances of bread and wine did remain. He could not accept that substance was simply transformed without an appropriate accidental change, and that this happened by virtue of a priest's words. Wyclif's formulations fed into pre-existing types of doubt and criticism, which, in England, had been fairly muted until then. Lollards were not merely 'nay sayers'; Lollardy was informed by a range of critical positions which coalesced through particular scholarly formulations which animated the participation of a learned preaching clergy.

So doubts about sacramentality were directly linked with a critique of images, particularly the use of images to explicate the nature of eucharistic signification.[246] William Woodford's *quaestio* of 1384 identified the Wycliffite difficulty with the eucharist as related to an understanding of eucharistic worship as a form of image worship of Christ, a position we have already found in Wyclif's views.[247] Lollards could describe the poor as 'quicke images of God', whereas they would not accept the consecrated bread as so closely bound to Him.[248] In response to Lollardy, arguments favouring images were marshalled, such as that of the *Dives and pauper* of c.1405–10:

Þey seruyn of thre thynggys. For þey been ordeynyd to steryn manys mende to thynkyn on Cristys incarnacioun and of his passioun . . . Also þey been ordeynyd to steryn mannys affeccioun and his herte to deuocioun . . . Also þey been

[244] Hudson (1978).
[245] See such a view expressed at a trial in Lincoln diocese in 1521, Aston (1977), p. 362.
[246] Aston (1988), pp. 7–8.
[247] Catto (1985), pp. 270–1; Aston (1988), p. 103, n. 26, 124. On Hussite sensitivities to this point, see Cook (1973), pp. 336–7.
[248] For a similar view echoed in a claim made to inquisitors in Italy in the 1380s: 'Christus in ostia per graciam non in carne et ossibus, sed eo modo quo dicitur in Evangelio: ubicumque fuerint duo vel tres congregati in nomine meo, in medio eorum sum, per graciam', Merlo (1977), p. 53.

ordeynyd to been a tokene and a book to þe lewyd peple, þat þey moun redyn in ymagerye and peynture þat clerkys redyn in boke.[249]

The third function was not so problematical, but the first two were, for they claim for images the function of calling sentiments into memory through sensual stimulation, and this smacked of luxury for the more extreme iconophobic Lollards.[250] Nor were the difficulties over images, pilgrimages, cult of saints and eucharistic worship vexing to Lollards alone; bishops, reforming friars and theologians marshalled arguments against the abuse of such practices, argument which did not differ from Lollard complaints. Archbishop FitzRalph attacked image-worship which was of local and limited appeal rather than of universal appeal within the church.[251] But Lollardy attacked the very epistemology which did not differentiate sign from signified, and thus attacked the basis for sacramentality, the linking of matter and God in the reception of a singular host, which was also the body of the church.[252]

The most dangerous and frequent stand taken by Lollards was that against transubstantiation. Wycliffite understanding of the transformation is captured, albeit not very clearly, in the term remanence or consubstantiation.[253] This view admits that through consecration the bread and wine underwent a spiritual change, one which now incorporated Christ's sacramental, spiritual and yet *real* presence: 'But þis sacrament is boþe brede and God togedre, as Crist is verre God and verre man'[254] and no other thing should be believed, since it could have no basis in scripture:

For in al þis tyme Crist tauȝt neuer þat þe sacrament of þe auter was an accident wiþoute subiecte and in no maner Cristis body.[255]

Even though Wyclif and the first generation of his followers were not thoroughly anti-sacramental but rather assigned subtle symbolic value to the eucharist, their fine distinctions were lost throughout the fifteenth century as strong anti-sacramental attitudes became increasingly pronounced.[256] It was only when Wyclif significantly commented

[249] *Dives and pauper*, p. 82; Gray (1972), p. 44–5; *Festial*, p. 171.
[250] Jones (1973), p. 36. See the rejection of images and of faith in the eucharist by two painters from the diocese of Coventry and Lichfield in 1511, Aston (1988), p. 141.
[251] *Ibid*, pp. 28–9. By the sixteenth century, as new artistic techniques produced dramatic and 'life-like' images and scenes, these were taken to be dangerous and subversive for possessing a persona which transcended their significatory function, images seemed to be 'taking over', to appeal to the senses, and were thus criticised, Arasse (1981), pp. 135–9.
[252] Van der Lof (1964), p. 296.
[253] Keen (1986a), pp. 12–13.
[254] *Selections*, p. 110.
[255] *Ibid*, pp. 111–12.
[256] Kightly (1975), p. 2.

upon the eucharist that he became really dangerous, and only then that he lost his position in Oxford and his patron.[257] In his *Chronicon* Henry Knighton (d.1396) reported that the Blackfriars council of 1382 placed the acceptance of eucharistic orthodoxy at the centre of the requirements made of suspected Wycliffites:

and afturwarde to wam [we] were requirede to say our beleve of þe sacrament of the autere, as to ȝoure understondyng outher the peple we knowlechene fyrst þat þe prist takus in his hondes, þorowe the vertue of the sacramental wordus, is made and turnyde veralyche into Christus body, þe same þat was taken and ben of þe mayden Marye, and þat sufferide deþ on the crosse for man kynde, and þat lay in the sepulcre, and þat ros fro deth . . . furthermore we beleve þat þe hole body of Christ is hole in þe sacrament, and hole in everyche partye of þe sacrament of þe autere.[258]

Views on the eucharist were thus the very central area of criticism, and the one which the Church could least allow to pass uncorrected. When Margery Kempe attempted to rebut accusations of heresy brought against her, she addressed these same issues, asserting her belief 'þat it is hys very flesch and hys blood and no material bred ne neuyr may be unseyd be it onys seyd'.[259] Anti-Lollards tracts such as the Dominican John's *Ferretra sacramenti* of c.1380 were often devoted solely to combating Lollard eucharistic error.[260]

Wycliffite formulations travelled wide and on the way shed some of the subtler aspects of remanence. Such a popular preacher as William White (burnt 1428) would have taught that the bread was not only *verus panis in natura* but also Christ's body.[261] But by the fifteenth century most formulations outside the intellectual circles had become far simpler, such as that attributed to William Mundy of Wokingham that the body of Christ consecrated by the priest at the altar was blessed bread and nothing more.[262] The formula which Lollards tried in Norwich in 1428–30 were made to use in their confessions touched on sacerdotal efficacy and on transubstantiation: 'that aftir the sacramental wordes said of any prest at messe ther remayneth nothyng but oonly a cake of material bred'.[263] Chaplain Simon Green of St Mildred's Poultry, London, it was claimed, taught Thomas Byrt's wife in 1496 that the sacrament of the altar was like material bread.[264] Criticism of the explanations on the quality and locality of the sacramental bread

---

[257] Catto (1985), p. 269.
[258] Henry Knighton, *Chronicon* II, p. 171.
[259] Margery Kempe, *The book*, p. 115.
[260] CUL Ff.6.44, fols. 60ʳ–104ʳ.
[261] *Fasciculi zizaniorum*, pp. 418, 424.
[262] *Reg. Hallum*, no. 1,142, p. 219.
[263] *Norwich heresy trials*, see for example the case of Richard Knobbyng of Beccles, p. 115.
[264] *Series of precedents*, no. 195, p. 55; Cross (1978), pp. 360–2.

put forth by a concept of transubstantiation was raised already by Cathars, as we have seen above. It also resounds in testimonies about Lollards. In 1428 the yound maid Agnes Bethom testified against Margery Baxter of Martham (Norfolk) and claimed that Margery had derided her faith and had said:

You believe wrongly, since if every such sacrament were God and Christ's real body, then gods would be infinite in number, because a thousand priests and more confect a thousand such gods every day and then eat them, and once eaten emit them from their back side in filthy and stinking pieces . . . such a sacrament is ordained falsely and deceitfully by the priests in church.[265]

If sacramental bread were like any other bread, then the priestly function, the particular sacerdotal efficacy which justified priestly privilege, and ultimately the whole ecclesiastical structure, was put into question. This is a problem which had been dealt with repeatedly, especially from the period of Gregorian reform, in questions such as that answered by Gilbert Crispin in his 'De sacramento altaris' of *c.* 1050:

If a simoniac who possesses no grace to bless can celebrate the mass and consecrate the Lord's body, for what reason does a lay person not have that grace to bless, nor the right to celebrate mass and consecrate the Lord's body?[266]

Following the rejection of sacerdotal-sacramental efficacy to its logical end could produce further crtitical views on the laity's need for the clergy. It could lead to a claim such as that attributed to John Godesell, a parchmenter from Ditchingham (Norfolk), in the trial in 1428 'every faithful man and woman is a priest and has full power to confect Christ's body as much as any priest'.[267] The link between the rejection of transubstantiation and anti-clerical attitudes is made clear in the type of view for which John Badby was burnt on a pire at Smithfield in 1410 – or so at least it appeared to Thomas Hoccleve:

> The precious body or oure lorde ihesu
> In forme of brede, he leued not at al;
> He was in no þing abassht, no eschu
> To seye it was put rede material;

---

[265] 'Tu male credis quia si quodlibet tale sacramentum esset Deus et verum corpus Christi, infiniti sunt dii, quia mille sacerdotes et plures omni die conficiunt mille tales deos et postea tales deos comedunt et comestos emittunt per posteriora in sepibus turpiter fetentibus . . . tale sacramentum fuit falso et deceptorie ordinatum per presbiteros in Ecclesia', *Heresy trials of Norwich*, pp. 44–5.

[266] 'Si ergo simoniacus qui gratiam benedicendi non habet, missam celebrare et corpus Domini consecrare potest, qua ratione laicus qui gratiam benedicendi non habet, missam celebrare et corpus Domini consecrare non potest?', Gilbert Crispin, 'De sacramento altaris', c. 58, pp. 133–4; see also c. 48, p. 132.

[267] *Heresy trials of Norwich*, p. 61.

He seyde, a prestes power was smal
As a Rakers, or swiche an oþer wiȝte
And to mak it, hadde no gretter myȝt.[268]

Using the human attributes associated with the suffering Christ as man, the priestly claim was derided by John Burrell, servant of Thomas Mone of Loddon (Norfolk), in 1429:

God created all priests and each priest has a head and eyes for sight, ears for hearing, and a tongue for speech, and all parts of such a man; and that sacrament which these priests claim to be Christ's real body does not have such eyes for seeing, ears for hearing, but is a cake of bread made of wheaten flour.[269]

Or even greater degrading of the clerical function in the words of William and Richard Spark in 1457, which claimed not simple clerical inefficacy, but rather the detrimental effect of consecration:

Also that a priest has no greater power to confect Christ's body than a blade of straw or a stick does. But that after the words of the priest real bread still remains, and that they make the bread over which the words of incarnation were uttered – far worse than it was.[270]

What followed from the criticism of the priest's sacramental efficacy was a further examination of his other claims to exclusivity and privilege, such as his role as teacher. Thus, Lollards could boast of possessing superior learning, as did the daughter of John Phip of Hughenden who claimed that she was more learned than her parish priest, and therefore could teach more authoritatively than he.[271] Accusations were made that Lollards allowed women to celebrate mass, but although there is no trace of such a practice in Lollard writings[272] such claims illustrate the sort of possibilities which were created, at least symbolically, once the sacerdotal taboo was broken.[273]

The church responded by attacking what it deemed to be the sources

---

[268] *Hoccleve's minor poems*, p. 11, lines 288–94.

[269] *Heresy trials of Norwich*, p. 73.

[270] 'Item, quod sacerdos maiorem potestatem conficiendi corpus Christi non habet quam stramen vel festuca conficere possit. Sed quod post verba sacerdotis verus panis semper manet, et eo longe peior atque deterior efficitur ille panis quo super eo huiusmodi incarnationis verba proferuntur', *Lincoln diocesan documents*, p. 91. And similarly, it is better to see the face of a woman, God's creature, than the sacrament of the altar, as claimed by William Colyn, a skinner from South Creake (Norfolk) in 1429, *Heresy trials of Norwich*, p. 91.

[271] Cross (1978), p. 371.

[272] Hudson (1988b), p. 151.

[273] This sort of levelling between the ranks of laity and clergy is also expressed in views reported in late fourteenth century Bohemia: 'Isti errores sunt inventi in Bohemia . . . Alii dicunt, quod in sacramento altaris non sit verum Corpus Christi, sed significativum, et quod sufficit, quod sit iustus homo qui conficit, et quod non sit differencia inter sacerdotes et episcopos et laycos iustos quoad confeccionem corporis Christi', Patchovsky (1975), p. 90.

of alternative readings of its symbolic system. It identified interpretation as the source of error; bad teaching failed to convey the harmonious whole of the symbolic universe which it offered. But having done so, it also curtailed the areas of teaching, by directing priests to teach only those issues which were not controversial. Archbishop Arundel's 1409 constitutions limited those subjects open to parochial instruction to the contents of *Ignorantia sacerdotum* the syllabus of 1287, evading disputation and confrontation over the eucharist, marriage and baptism.[274] This was, of course, impossible, since the catechism itself was full of eucharistic connections which had become embedded in the teaching apparatus. Neither could interpretation be prevented any more than could the dissemination of texts in which Lollard views were constructed. The church could hardly rid itself of those concepts and formulae which expounded orthodoxy. And these very claims which so attracted criticism were voiced repeatedly, simply and without change. In the early fifteenth century Thomas Netter (c.1370–1430), the Carmelite Provincial Prior of London, required belief in the unbelievable in his anti-Lollard work, *Doctrinale fidei catholicae*:

That is, that which at the outset is pure bread without a body, is at the end of the prayer a pure body without bread . . . from one nature to another, from one substance to another.[275]

Defenders of orthodoxy came to insist all the more upon the real presence of Christ's body at the altar.[276] Nicholas Love's translation of pseudo-Bonaventure's *Meditationes vitae Christi*, of c.1410, the *Mirrour of the blessed life of Jesus Christ*, is a characteristic product of this trend. It adapted a popular devotional work to the most pressing problems discussed by the English audience.[277] It gave a compassionate account of Christ's life and death, stressing throughout its pain, its sacrifice, and its relation to the eucharist. Christ in the eucharist is recommended as a focus since 'contemplacioun of the manhede of Christe is more lykynge more spedeful and more siker than is hiȝe contemplacioun of the godhede'.[278] Another approach was to deride heretical claims one by one, as in the *Doctrinale fidei catholicae* of Thomas Netter. By the early fifteenth century the ramifications of

---

[274] *Reg. Hallum*, no. 955, p. 144. See above on the syllabus, pp. 88–92.

[275] 'Sicut ergo hic in exordio est panis purus, sic in fine orationis corpus purum sine pane . . . de natura ad naturam, de substantia in substantiam . . .', Thomas Netter, *Defensor fidei*, III, col. 239.

[276] For earlier treatments of heretical views, see lists of counter-arguments in Humbert of Romans, *Sermons*, fols. 59r–60v, with six refutations of attacks on the mass and the sacraments.

[277] For its use see for example the library of Cicely, duchess of York, Armstrong (1942), pp. 79–80. On this and other translated works, see Ball (1976), p. 262.

[278] *Mirrour*, p. 8.

Wycliffite eucharistic teachings had become apparent not only in Lollardy but on the Continent in the Hussite movement. Thus, Thomas Netter criticised the practice of communion in both species which they upheld, and reasserted orthodox practice: 'Catholics do indeed consume the eucharist wholly according to its sacramental nature [*res*] in either one of the species'.[279] This work combined counter-arguments with edifying miracle tales and with simple parodies which ridiculed Lollard beliefs.[280] Netter was summarising some thirty years of argument, and placed the authorities within a longer tradition of patristic orthodoxy, and finally bolstered them with miracle tales. In this he was following the lead of some earlier works such as the *Ferretra sacramenti* by the Dominican Friar John of the 1380s, where miracles, scripture and patristic argument against Lollardy on the issue of the eucharist were synthesised.[281] Against Lollard texts studded with scriptural reference such works provided priests with answers, and preachers and teachers with stories of miracles designed to disprove challenging views.[282]

But beyond polemical literature mechanisms for examination and punishment were developed, and have provided much of our material about heretical as well as orthodox uses of the language of religion.[283] Formulae for examination were devised by ecclesiastical lawyers and theologians,[284] and paint our sources with a brush of misleading uniformity. We can hear the claims about the eucharist which were ascribed to Lollards in examination formulae, such as the list copied into the register of Thomas Polton, bishop of Worcester (1426–33), and which recommended the following questions when examining a suspect about the sacrament:

Whether a properly consecrated priest makes Christ's body;
Whether the body thus made is Christ's natural body on the earthly altar and not natural bread and wine;[285]

---

[279] Thomas Netter, *Doctrinale fiedei catholicae* III, col. 522. See also Keen (1986a), pp. 15–16.
[280] Hudson (1988b), pp. 50–3; as well as associated Hussite excesses, Thomas Netter, *Doctrinale fidei* II, cols. 120, 971.
[281] CUL Ff.6.44, fols. 60ʳ–104ʳ; it contains four dozen miracle tales, fols. 83ᵛ–104ʳ.
[282] On the anti-Lollard literature see Hudson (1988b), pp. 55–8, 454. The Croxton *Play of the Sacrament* of *c.*1461 may have been mounted as a miracle play vindicating the much attacked eucharist, on it Cutts (1944).
[283] And served as the basis for the studies of the religious culture, Le Roy Ladurie (1979), Ginzburg (1980). About the machinery of persecution in England, see *Heresy trials of Norwich*, pp. 1–31, esp. pp. 22–5.
[284] McHardy (1972); Hudson (1973), pp. 151–2. On the genre of inquisitorial manuals, see Dondaine (1947).
[285] 'An sacerdos rite consecratus conficit corpus Christi?
An corpus sic confectum sit in altare terrestri Corpurs Christi naturale et non panis naturalis neque vinum?', *Reg. Polton*, p. 155. For Bohemia see *Modus procedendi inquisitorum*, for similar questions, Patchovsky (1975), pp. 104–5.

So we cannot use these as straightforward sources for the interpretation of utterances and practices, merely as evidence that certain types of practices and ideas were sufficiently current to draw the attention of ecclesiastical officials. And these allow us to map some of the areas of the symbolic system at work, in the struggle between normative pronouncements and those challenges and critiques which insistence upon them created.

Lollardy was confined neither to a particular social group nor to a specific cultural milieu.[286] The centrality of vernacular reading for persuasion, conversion and maintenance of the Lollard world-view is striking.[287] Lollards created social and 'textual-communities', to use Brian Stock's phrase,[288] which were heterogeneous but which necessarily combined reading, sociability and mutual support.[289] The texts as sources of knowledge and The Text, scripture, as the authority for all knowledge, are here linked. As argued by a Lollard:

For in al þis type Crist tauȝt never þat þe sacrament of þe auter was an accident wiþoute subiecte and in no maner Cristis body . . . Lord! whiper men shul forsake Cristis owne wordis and take straunge wordis unknowen in holy writt and aȝens resoun.[290]

Congruity of practice with some scriptural base was the underpinning of the critique and the source for an evolving world-view. The possession of books could lead to suspicion of Lollardy as texts were presented either as instigators of dissent, but they also served as eye-openers. Reading was stressed in abjuration oaths imposed on suspects, as in the case of the brothers Richard and William Spark whose oath was taken before the bishop of Lincoln in 1457:

nor I shal hoolde not receyue doctryne, bokes, quayers, nor elles, concernyng heresyes, errours or opinions of hem, nor theym use.[291]

The Bible not only created a different source of authority, an alternative point of reference, but perhaps encouraged people to think about the nature of procedures which were clearly outside the text, like the sacraments.[292] It produced the sort of seemingly sensible question based upon biblical tales which could only baffle examiners who must

---

[286] For later period, see Plumb (1987), chapter 9 (conclusion), pp. 325–40, esp. pp. 328, 335–7.

[287] Aston (1977), pp. 351–6.

[288] Stock (1984), esp. pp. 88–240.

[289] Hudson (1988b). Particular books were sometimes cited as influential in converting Lollards. See such a claim about the *Shepherd's kalendar* in 1521, Aston (1977), p. 362.

[290] *Selections* 21(1), p. 112.

[291] *Lincoln diocesan documents*, p. 97.

[292] Cross (1975), p. 273.

have encountered difficulty in providing appropriate answers in the idiom of orthodoxy. Such a question was attributed to the brothers Spark in 1457: if thirty wafers are sold for ½d, how can it be that Judas sold Christ, the eucharist, for 30d?[293]

Thus, the alternative, Lollard, language of religion ws dialectically related to that of sacramental religion. Already in the thirteenth century Humbert of Romans (d.1277) wrote that simple doubt should be corrected, but that 'those, like heretics, who are drawn to it not by simplicity, but by intellectual pride' and who used distorting arguments, were to be treated quite differently.[294] But telling them apart was often a difficult matter; they raised familiar questions ingenuously, and they often used established procedures to undermine orthodoxy. Lollard writers used exising didactic tokens and formulae, not only in order to exploit their mnemonic value, but to emphasise their own difference.[295] The psalter which was translated into English in the early fourteenth century was given a Lollard version,[296] as was the *Pater noster*,[297] and the *Lay folk's catechism*.[298] In the *catechism* some areas were reworked, and some left as in the original, thus enhancing the message through selective divergence from the basic and well-known texts of parochial instruction. And then there are texts which were labelled heretical at various times, such as *Dives and pauper, The Pricke of conscience* (even *The Canterbury Tales*), but which can be appreciated better as reflecting the Lollardising effect of the encounter between the two world-views.[299]

The contending world-views can be distinguished broadly as the *sacramental* and the *metaphorical*, and the critique of the former held the clergy and the institution of the church guilty of upholding an epistemological fallacy.[300] In Lollardy the critique centres on the search for an appropriate metaphor to express the relation between supernatural power and earthly authority, between the sacred and the ritual practice. And this is evident in claims such as 'That Christ's body in the sacrament of the altar is only a mirrour-image of Christ's body in heaven'.[301]

---

[293] *Lincoln diocesan documents*, p. 91.
[294] 'Quos non simplicitas, sed superbia intelletcus ad hoc inducit, ut Haeretici', Humbert of Romans, *Sermones*, fol. 58ᵛ.
[295] See for example the late fourteenth century verses in Cambridge Trinity B.14.50, fols. 56ʳ–58ʳ.
[296] See the Lollard Sarum prymer, BL Add. 36683, of c.1425.
[297] Aston (1977), p. 363.
[298] Hudson (1985), (1988a).
[299] Aston (1977), pp. 361–2.
[300] Aston (1988), pp. 6–8.
[301] 'Quod corpus Christi in altaris sacramento est solum speculum ad corpus Christi in coelo', in the *Fasciculi zizaniorum*; Hudson (1988b), p. 87.

Besides the doubts and criticisms whose carriers remained none the less committed to orthodoxy, Lollards exposed in large areas of the symbolic order an ironic disparity between the normative narrative, and between the view and dictates of common-sense shaped by a substantial number of its users. There was a struggle over the authority to establish the apt metaphor, and to instruct on the practices which it implied, which was in many ways a questioning of necessary mediation of grace by a clergy through ritual practice. In turn, this right was defended by the vigorous formulations of scriptural justification for the eucharist in some representations of the Last Supper, such as that in the Carmelite missal.[302] These different perceptions of the nature of the economy of the holy were born in divergent but intersecting discourses. This lends special significance to the fact that soon after his death Wyclif's curate at Lutterworth, John Horne, was telling the tale that Wyclif had suffered his stroke on the feast of the Holy Innocents, 1384, at the very moment of the elevation.[303] Or to the story that, similarly, two Czech scholars who had come to copy Wycliffite writings *c.*1406 also visited Lutterworth and went away with chips of Wyclif's tomb . . .[304]

## USES AND ABUSES: THE ECONOMY OF THE EUCHARIST

As a sacrament the eucharist was 'a thing perceptible to the senses which possesses the power both of effecting and signifying sanctity and righteousness'.[305] The eucharist specifically created a link between the present and the moment in the past when power, and the access to it, was defined. The consecrated species were understood to effect a fundamental change in the nature of things: sickness into health, well-being into misfortune, the revelation of truth out of a mass of inconclusive facts in the working of ordeals. In all its uses, in the moment of the mass within the church, the host was associated with multifarious life practices. From the very nature of its sacramental status, it belonged in every area of life, mediating between sacred and profane, supernatural and natural.[306] The rituals within which it was enfolded offered ideas of further and analogous uses in other spheres of life.[307] The struggle over such extrapolating uses was a power struggle, a compe-

---

[302] See above, pp. 299–300, and figure 19.
[303] Crompton (1968–9), p. 17.
[304] Hudson (1986a), p. 77.
[305] Turner (1962), p. 171.
[306] On magic in the Middle Ages with particular attention to the position and activities of the clergy, see Kieckhefer (1989).
[307] *Ibid*, p. 173.

tition over supernatural power. The church attempted to protect the design of its central symbol; it was willing to adjust and absorb readings and usages which were not fundamentally threatening, but there were practices too ambiguous, which could not be tolerated, and which none the less did take place. This highlights the difficulty of the clergy's position: facing the constant confrontation with the variety of eucharistic uses and ideas at the parochial level, and yet sharing in a clerical discourse which was increasingly systematising, defining and prescribing magical lore and its many manifestations.[308] The story that unfolds from our eucharistic ethnography is one of testing and practice, of analogy and extrapolation of some sacramental tenets, in contexts for which it had never been designed. Or had it been? And where did its design stop? In universities? At synods? In a parish church? In a home?

When fields were protected against evil spirits through the presence of the eucharist held in a priest's hands, all was well.[309] But when in 1509–10 a group of priests and laymen in Bingley (Yorkshire) protected themselves with the consecrated bread against malevolent spirits, they were tried for heresy.[310] So those who attempted to handle the eucharist were condemned, while a priest was allowed to apply the same usage. Several such practices were elaborations within a sacramental economy in cases of need or crisis. As early as the eleventh century Burchard of Worms described in his *Corrector* of 1008×12 a custom of burying a dead baptised child with a host in one hand, and a chalice in the other,[311] and ten days of penance were enjoined for this practice. But did it not attempt to provide a *viaticum* for a child who was too young to have received communion? There were numerous cases in romances and chronicles describing knights before battle, in the absence of a priest, communicating with three blades of grass. This was makeshift communion. Thus, in the *Chanson de Raoul de Cambrai*, in the version which existed by the thirteenth century:

> De iij poux d'erbe, q'autre prestre n'i a
> S'arme et son cors a Jhesu commanda.[312]

---

[308] Peters (1972), pp. 37–8. For the early modern period see O'Neil (1984).
[309] Browe (1929b).
[310] *Reg. Bainbridge*, fols. 68–73ᵛ as in Dickens (1959), p. 16.
[311] 'Cum infans noviter natus est, et statim baptismatus, et sic mortuus fuerit, dum sepeliunt eum, in dexteram manum ponunt ei patenam ceream cum oblata, et in sinistram manum calicem cum vino similiter cereum ponunt ei', Burchard, 'Decretorum libri xx' col. 975; Vogel (1976), p. 757. Perhaps a similar practice of leaving bread at a dead child's head was denounced in *Handlyng synne (a)*, lines 9675–8, p. 241.
[312] Raoul of Cambrai, *Chanson de geste*, lines 2429–30, p. 83; the text was largely established around *c*. 1150, but extensions were made into the thirteenth century. Dr Sarah Kay who is preparing the definitive edition of the *Chanson* has kindly conveyed her views on the poem to me.

The *Brut* chronicle described the English at Agincourt in 1415: 'Then oure men knelit doune al attones, and made a cros on þe grounde, did kissit it, and put hem in þe mercy of God'.[313] Are these not *in extremis* circumstances, which in the case of baptism, marriage and extreme unction would have allowed a lay person to act sacramentally?

Another extension of the sacramental economy is gleaned from ordeals. It was believed that the mass could empower an oath or a pact. In 1326 Emperor Louis of Bavaria and Duke Ferdinand of Austria committed themselves to mutual fidelity and support; they sealed their pact by an oath taken over a host which was then divided and consumed by the two in communion.[314] Eucharistic ordeals reveal a further application. The participation of the clergy in ordeals was increasingly circumscribed from the eleventh century; but ordeals which used the host came to be used occasionally in judicial cases involving the clergy.[315] The logic was that God's body would refuse to remain within a perjurer's body and that this would be made visible. An oath formula of such an ordeal is recorded in the Hirsau (Württemburg) chronicle for the year 1224:

And if it is other than I have said and sworn, then this body of our Lord will not pass through my throat, but stick to my gullet, strangle me, suffocate me, and kill me on the spot.[316]

But this type of procedure was increasingly criticised and the use of ordeals declined sharply in the thirteenth century. Yet how different is the rationale operating here from that in tales which taught sacramental orthodoxy? There were stories about people who received the host in sin or with bad intent and found that it choked and killed them or simply escaped from their bodies. A sinful woman 'kept the Lord's body in her mouth' for use in magic and found that it had turned into flesh which stuck to her palate.[317] A licentious priest kept the host in his mouth in order to cast a spell on the woman he kissed, and grew so large that he stuck to the church roof.[318] A dying monk had not properly

---

[313] *Brut chronicle* II, p. 555.

[314] 'facto tamen sibi prius iuramento supra corpore Christi, de quo uterque hostia divisa in duas in eadem missa communicavit', William of Nangis, 'Chronique de St Denis', p. 642.

[315] Bartlett (1986), pp. 81–90, 95; for early medieval eucharistic ordeals, see pp. 17 n. 12, 72.

[316] 'Et si aliter est quam dixi et iuravi, tunc hoc domini nostri corpus non pertranseat guttur meum, sed haereat in faucibus meis, strangulet me, suffocet me, ac interficiat me statim in momento', quoted in Patetta (1890), p. 209.

[317] 'Corpus domini in ore reservasset', James of Vitry, *The exempla*, no. 270, p. 113; *Liber exemplorum*, no. 15, p. 8; or in another version where it jumped out of her cheek, in an early fourteenth-century collection BL Harley 2478, fol. 15ʳ.

[318] *DM* 9,6, pp. 112–13; the version of a fifteenth-century English collection had the earth swallowed him, BL Harley 1288, fol. 40ᵛ.

confessed and was unable to swallow the eucharist given him on his death-bed.[319] The same understanding of the eucharist's properties and its operation is exhibited in both types of story, the one prohibited, the other didactically useful.

In a similar way stories of subsistence on the eucharist alone appear in diametrically different contexts. Ida of Louvain was known to have lived on nothing but the eucharist for years,[320] and like many saintly beguines Alpais of Cudot (near Sens) was reputed to have eaten nothing but the eucharistic elements.[321] King Mordrain in the *Queste del seint graal* was said to have lived on nothing but the host: 'ne gousta de viande . . . fors de cele meismes que li prestre nos mostre ou sacrament de la messe'.[322] Another type of story tells of a woman who was served an unconsecrated wafer, and was tormented by bodily hunger until a priest gave her a consecrated host;[323] in 1433 Lidwina of Schieden vomited when an unconsecrated host was given to her.[324] Evidently, then, the eucharist was understood to be a superior type of food which satisfied a special hunger. This was a view addressed by Thomas Netter in the anti-Lollard work *Doctrinale fidei*: would the eucharist have sustained these women for so long had it been nothing but material bread?[325]

But the self-same practices could also be undertaken by heretics in an attempt to disprove claims of eucharistic power. Ronald Bandinelli recorded the case of a person who ate nothing but the host for fourteen days, to show that his body's excretions must have contained the digested material bread of the host, but who died on the fifteenth day. Roland explained that he had been consuming his own humours.[326] In other words, the eucharist was rich enough to sustain some human bodies for years, but not one sinful body for more than fourteen days. Its users willed it to have a stable economy; so too did its guardians who told tales which taught its rules. But the context in which it was encountered determined which economy was appropriate and which was not. In theological debates this had been discussed, and the question of digestion so often levelled against the eucharistic claim

[319] Jehan Mansel's late fifteenth century collection, *Examples moraux*, BL Royal 15 D 5, fol. 345[vb]. The same image was used in a story about Margaret of Oingt (d.1310), who consumed a mere crum of the host which swole so much in her mouth that it (almost) choked her, filling her and satiating her for a long time, Bynum (1987), p. 130.

[320] Roisin (1947), p. 113.

[321] Browe (1928b), pp. 20–1.

[322] Baumgartner (1981), p. 127. For another (male) example see Camporesi (1988), p. 40.

[323] *DM* 9,4, p. 111; *Alphabet*, no. 162, p. 113.

[324] Bynum (1985), p. 7.

[325] Thomas Netter, *Doctrinale fidei catholicae* II, col. 376–8; also cd. 380.

[326] Gietl (1891), pp. 232–3.

was resolved in the formulation that the substance remained only as long as the eucharistic form was maintained, and once the accidents were dissolved in the mouth the host was no longer Christ's body.[327]

The eucharist was thus closely observed in an on-going attempt to understand its properties by empirical observation, and its nature was assimilated into other types of knowledge. The consistency of the eucharistic claims was sometimes tested literally, like the story of a woman who was said to have taken the host home after communion and tried to bake it in her oven like any other bread.[328] Magical manipulation usually followed some ritual pattern which was inverted or incorporated into other procedures.[329] A charm said over three hosts was an English remedy for fevers,[330] and a similar procedure was recommended in a thirteenth-century Provençal recipe book, where three hosts were inscribed with quasi-liturgical Latin words, and one consumed daily by the patient with a *Pater noster*.[331] Here the Latin and the number three and the *Pater nosters* provided the ritual framework for manipulation. Holinshed's *Chronicle* described Lady Alice Kyteler's sorcery: a wafer found in her house in 1324 was stamped with the devil's name, as opposed to an orthodox wafer usually inscribed with the letters IHS.[332] The mass for the dead could be inverted and injure living enemies: waxen images were placed under the altar pall so that masses for the dead be said over them, and these images would harm those represented in them.[333] The council of Trier of 1227 prohibited the display of biers in churches and the celebration of masses for the living 'so that they die sooner'.[334] *Dives et pauper* describes a practice of dressing the altar with mourning clothes and singing a requiem for a living person in order to cause him or her suffering.[335]

---

[327] 'Id est quamdiu valent discerni species tamdiu est ibi Christus; tamen quidam aliter dixerunt sed eorum ratio non est probabilis', Albert the Great, IV *Sent.* d. 9 a. 5 *in fine*.

[328] In a mid-fifteenth-century collection of religious tales BL Harley 206, fol. 98ᵛ.

[329] On the structural similarity between medical and magical procedures, see Schmitt (1986), p. 144.

[330] Gray (1974), p. 59; BL Sloane 2457, fol. 29.

[331] Saye (1935), pp. 165–6. A Jewish version uses apples rather than hosts in the same procedure.

[332] 'In rifling the closet of the ladie, they found a wafer of sacramentall bread, having the divel's name stamped thereon in steed of Jesus Christ'; *Holinshed's chronicle of Ireland*, pp. 251–2; see the testimonies in the trial in *A contemporary narrative of the proceedings against Dame Alice Kyteler*.

[333] 'Iterum, quod flens dico, hoc tantum sacramentum quidam in artem magicam verterunt, celebrando, missas super imagines cereas ad imprecandum alicui', Gerald of Wales, *Gemma ecclesiastica* I, 49, p. 137.

[334] 'Ut citius moriantur', Mansi 23, 30, c. 6; Harmening (1977), p. 223. On saying masses in use of Anglo-Saxon magical charms, see Jolly (1985), pp. 286–9.

[335] *Dives et pauper* I, c. 34, pp. 158–9: 'And he þo þat for hate or wratthe . . . takyn awey þe cloþis of þe auter and cloþyn þe auter with dolful cloþyng or besettyn þe auter or þe cros aboutyn with þornys and withdrawyn lyht out of chirche or syngyn or don syngyn messe

Conversely, the beneficial effect of the mass was tapped, as recorded in the synodal statutes of Angers in 1270. Women of the diocese who wished to be purified after child-birth but who were not reconciled to the church, would sneak into the church after the beginning of mass, believing that this would have a purifying effect.[336]

The position of the parish clergy here was extremely complicated: within the economy of the eucharist they were brokers as well as monopolists. At the synodal level there were attempts to protect and control the species,[337] but at the same time the tools of orthodox teaching, the *exempla,* encouraged the appreciation of the eucharist's useful power. Such was the tale which originated in Caesarius of Heisterbach's collection about the distracted bishop who regained his sanity after receiving communion,[338] or the many tales about cures through the host, such as St Bernard's curing a man who had been bewitched by a woman by holding the *ciborium* over his head.[339] The host was so powerful that it could even cure by proxy; a woman was cured by an abbot who had touched the host earlier in the day; the cure was said to have been effected solely through contact with the host, not through any other meritorious act.[340]

All these practices implied some co-operation by the clergy which sometimes meant turning a blind eye to protruding wax figures under the altar cloths or allowing an empty bier to stand in the church during mass. Ecclesiastical legislation attempted to protect the host, and to punish those clergy who traded in it. Gerald of Wales admonished priests lest the hosts in their charge fall into the hands of magicians.[341] In 1306 the chapter of Fiesole excommunicated

---

of requeim for hem þat ben olyue in hope þat þey shuldyn faryn þe werse and þe sonere deye'. For such practice, see also Franz (1963), p. 100.

[336] 'Latenter seu clandestine ecclesias ingrediuntur, postquam sacerdotes missarum sollempnia inceperint, se facientes a dictis improvisis sacerdotibus purificari', *Statuts synodaux* III, p. 102.

[337] Browe (1930), pp. 146–7.

[338] *DM* 9,43, p. 147; 9,50, pp. 154–5.

[339] 'Ibique superposito capiti ejus vasculo Eucharistiam continente, in ipsius sacramenti virtute, a laesione Christiani jubet daemonem prohiberi', William of St Thierry, 'Vita Bernardi prima', col. 255.

[340] Caesarius of Heisterbach, VIII *libri miraculorum* I, c. 9, in Kaufmann (1862), pp. 179–80: 'Tam veraciter sicut hodie digitis istis corpus Christi tractavi, tam veraciter de infirmitate convalescat'. But some did not work; when a corporal was shaken by a priest in front of the face of a sick person, it had no effect, and cure was only achieved at the shrine of St John of Montmirail (d. 1217), an obvious power competition within the *Vita*, Platelle (1980), p. 402, n. 75.

[341] Gerald of Wales, *Gemma ecclesiastica*, D. 1, c. 9, p. 32. Cases reserved for episcopal audience in the diocese of Sisteron were listed in 1249, among them 'de sacrilegio, de sortilegiis, et maxime de abusu corporis Christi', *Statuts synodaux* II, c. 32, p. 198.

All priests and clerics and any lay person who give Christ's body, chrism or holy oil, to any man or woman, or receive them, except as a sacrament.[342]

The danger was considered in the *Book of vices and virtues* when discussing the sin of avarice; its fifth bough is 'whan any wyȝt doþ any þing wiþ goddes body oþer þan riȝt is, as don heretikes or wiches or euele prestes for to wynne . . .'[343] The sixth bough is simony, a clerical vice, buying and selling the sacrament.[344] In 1517 the council of Florence imposed heavy fines on members of clergy who provided witches with the eucharist or other sacramental materials.[345]

What made such condemnations so problematical was that the church did, in fact, offer similar applications of sacred materials in its *functiones sacrae* or *sacramentalia*.[346] These ranged from the use of holy water, lending of crosses for funerals, to the use of the eucharist in exorcism.[347] But these were practices that had no place in the pristine design of the sacraments:[348] they were an area of activity which was highly unregulated, but necessary, and given over to local custom and uses. Penitential books regularly enjoined penance on clerics who consecrated chrism and oil for use outside the church, but these were in reality routines on which parishioners could rely. Indeed, they came to understand it as their right. The parishioners of All Saints in the Walls, London, complained in 1493 that their priest did not follow the custom of sprinkling holy water on Sunday;[349] in the community of Denton (Kent), Archbishop Warham's visitation found in 1511 that the parish was not being properly served with either sacraments or sacramentals.[350] At Barfreston (Kent), the visitation heard the complaint that the rector Henry Tankard was malicious and denied in his anger both holy bread and holy water; he was removed by the archbishop.[351] The eucharist was another matter, its approved use as a sacramental is not

---

[342] 'Omnes sacerdotes et clericos et laycos quoscunque qui corpus Christi, chrisma, vel oleum sanctum alicui viro vel mulieri dederint, vel qui receperunt nisi in sacramento', *Florentine synodal law*, p. 189.

[343] *The book of vices and virtues*, p. 36.

[344] *Ibid*, p. 37.

[345] 'Contra cleicos qui sacramenta maleficiis impartiunt. Clericum quoque qui eucharistiam aut alia sacramenta maleficiis dederit . . . in ducatis quinquaginta condemnari voluit', Mansi 35, c. 7, p. 235.

[346] MacCulloch (1932), p. 164; Franz (1909), pp. 10–37; Scribner (1984), esp. pp. 53–66 and figures 1–3.

[347] Walker (1981), pp. 4–5.

[348] Netter claimed that Wyclif opposed them since they had no scriptural basis, Thomas Netter, *Doctrinale fidei* III, cols. 3–4.

[349] *Series of precedents*, no. 127, p. 34.

[350] *Warham's visitations*, no. 88, p. 140.

[351] *Ibid*, no. 39, p. 97.

much in evidence, but being the most powerful material the church possessed, people struggled to gain access to it.

Many tales described these attempts, such as the story told by Caesarius of Heisterbach and many others about the woman who stole the host and sprinkled it over her cabbage patch, and was struck by paralysis;[352] or one about the woman who took it away to sprinkle into her hive to fructify her bees.[353] The eucharist could be used as a cure for fever, when it was inscribed with Latin words and swallowed by the sick person on consecutive days.[354] It could be used as an amulet,[355] or to induce fertility, as in German towns where it was often exposed in weather and field blessing processions.[356] Wherever the eucharist was used, for better or for worse, it was no ordinary thing.[357] If its power undoubtedly belonged to the realm of the supernatural, its use and allocation, the access to it and control of it were open to struggle and competition.

The eucharist could also cause harm. It was used to induce miscarriages,[358] or to poison altogether. The chronicle of St Denis reported the Jewish plot to poison the wells in 1321 through the mediation of lepers who administered a poison. This poison was said to have contained herbs, human urine, blood and the eucharist.[359] The ointment used by witches to make them fly used consecrated hosts mixed with blood into a paste.[360] The formula of abjuration for those accused of sorcery provided by Bernard Gui in his manual for inquisitors *Practica officii inquisitionis heretice pravitatis* of 1323×4 included the clause: 'I abjure . . . Item, any sorcery or witchcraft done or made with the sacrament or with Christ's holy body'.[361]

Whether it induced benefit or harm, the people insisted on treating the eucharist as a relic; they wanted to possess it, to be close to it,

---

[352] *DM* 9,9, pp. 115–16.

[353] *DM* 9.8, pp. 114–15; *Alphabet of tales*, no. 695, p. 465.

[354] Saye (1935).

[355] Kieckhefer (1989), pp. 79–80.

[356] Browe (1929b), pp. 747–8. It lent protection and led Stephen's forces in the Battle of the Standard of 1138, Richard of Hexham, 'De gestis regis Stephani', p. 163: 'In summitate vero ipsius arboris quandam argenteam pixidem cum corpore Christi, et sanctorum Petri apostoli, et Johannis Beverlacensis et Wilfridi Ripensis confessorum ac pontificum, vexilla suspenderunt'.

[357] A similar point is made in the context of a very different type of argument by John Ven Enghen (1986), p. 550: 'To cast a host into a raging fire . . . was to deploy the power believed inherent in the body of Christ'.

[358] Browe (1930).

[359] 'Fiebant de sanguine humano et urina, de tribus herbis . . . etiam . . . corpore Christi', William of Nangis, 'Chronique de St Denis', p. 628; Trachtenberg (1943), p. 101.

[360] Lea (1922) III, p. 500.

[361] 'Abjuro . . . Item, quodcumque sortilegium seu maleficium factum aut fiendum cum sacramento aut de sacro corporis Christi', Bernard Gui, *Manuel de l'inquisiteur* II, p. 152.

believing it could generate health or injury through sympathetic transformation. As we have seen, attempts were made to counter this trend,
but in reality it was practised in a variety of ways. At an inquiry at
Wittlaer (Westphalia) in 1436 tales of miraculous healing at the eucharistic shrine were told: a crippled woman was healed, the lame restored,
terrible head-aches dispelled – the stuff of pilgrimage tales.[362] The mode
in which eucharistic power operated induced speculation and discussion of procedures for its containment and conservation. This economy
was present in the formulation of Christ's words to Gertrude of Helfta
in her vision: that eucharistic power did not 'rub off' on the officiating
priest in any significant way that was denied to a worthy lay recipient.[363] Conversely, in a 1273 sermon of Ranulph de la Houblonière a
story was told of St Thomas of Biville (d.1257) who used to stay in
church in the presence of the eucharist expecting benefits to accrue, just
as those who persisted in the entourage of a prelate were eventually
rewarded by their closeness to his power and patronage.[364]

### FANTASY

The system of symbols which can accommodate daily experience, fear
and hope, which provides a language of social relations, of hierarchy
and exchange, will ultimately be tested against the inchoate, the realm
of fantasy, hardly explorable, always enticing, inherently unstable. In
looking at the horizon of eucharistic receptions we can explore fantasies which surface in our sources in some rare cases. 'Mass-fantasies'[365]
are cases when the eucharistic symbol incited a highly unusual and
personal reading, where interpretation is inordinately distant from the
clusters of reading which have produced the series of meanings which
we have explored here. Some of the symbolic interpretations, the
exegetical exercises worked on eucharistic texts, are really fantasies, and
Reynolds deals with one such case of the ninth century, a discursive
invention of new attributes for the mass. We shall encounter here some
cases where the constraints were even more lax, where a language of
religion, and (since I dare not say private language) an individual
consciousness operated particularly creatively.

---

[362] Torsy (1972). When the host failed it may have been maltreated: the council of Florence of
1517 excommunicated those who harmed the eucharist, 'Quod si sanctissimum eucharistiae sacramentum simili accesserint injuria', Mansi 35, c. 4, col. 235.
[363] Bynum (1977), p. 207.
[364] '. . . ideo ego facio sibi libenter societatem in ecclesia sua, ubi ipse semper est sub specie
sacramenti et libentius facio petitiones meas ibi quam alibi', Bériou (1987) II, pp. 142–50,
p. 149.
[365] A pun struck by Reynolds (1988).

Let us look at an interesting fantasy which centred on the eucharist, that of a woman, Aude Fauré. She was the wife of prosperous peasant of Merveil, a rural parish near the northern border of the Sabarthès, near the famous Montaillou, and she was thus immortalised with her neighbours through the inquisitorial records of 1318×25. Aude had married young and was privileged, she was the mistress of a comfortable rural household, and had always found belief in the eucharist rather difficult. According to the transcript of her testimony she demanded from her aunt Emengard an explanation:

> Aunt, how can it be that I cannot believe that it is God even that Christ's body is elevated by the chaplain at the altar, nor can I pray to him, nor believe that it is Christ's body.[366]

She marvelled that others could believe. We meet her after child-birth, when she was feeling rather low, and when rumour arrived through one of her maids that a woman had given birth in the vicinity and out of doors, due to the hasty coming of delivery. Aude became obsessed with this story and could not get it out of her mind, nor ever contemplate the body of Christ without thinking of the 'defilement' which came out of the woman's body at birth.[367] She could no longer think of the elevated body of Christ, which had already vexed her before, without reference to the excretion of blood and tissue which had come out of her own body not too long before, after her own child-birth. The obsession here is with pollution. In the period after child-birth, the body had become so estranged, terrifying, painful – yet life-giving – that the physicality of another kind, that stark physicality taught about Christ in the eucharist, became mingled with it, each superimposed upon the other in her thoughts. Was Christ born in such 'defilement' (*turpitudo*)? The tensions of disbelief over a good many years,[368] and their exacerbation in her state of self-disgust, the constraining requirement to imagine Christ as physical as the placenta, were expressed in this act of transgression, of associating the holiest with the most polluted, the lining of the womb expelled from the mother's body. The eucharist coalesced as a centre of meaning for these intimate doubts and fears within.

---

[366] 'Tia, qualiter potest esse quod non possum credere Deum nec cum eciam elevatur corpus Christi per capellanum in altari possum rogare ipsum nec credere quod sit corpus Christi?', *Reg. Fournier* II, p. 87; for a slightly corrected version of the text, see Dronke (1984), p. 272.

[367] 'Nocte precedenti quaedam mulier quandam filiam [pepererat] in via intus castrum de Muro Veteri, ita quod non potuerat pervenisse ad hospicium, quo audito cogitavit turpitudinem quam emittunt mulieres pariendo, et cum videret elevari in altari corpus Domini, habuit cogitationem ex illa turpitudine quod esset infectum corpus Domini', *Reg. Fournier* II, p. 94; Le Roy Ladurie (1978), p. 323.

[368] She claimed that this had been going on for eight years! *Reg. Fournier* II, p. 94.

Similar narratives of encounter with a child in the host dominated the fantasies told by women, especially by those attached to the eucharist.[369] These could be violent and pathetic like Jane Mary of Maillé's (d.1414) vision of a wounded child elevated in the host.[370] It could also be deeply loving: Agnes of Montepulciano (d.1317) and Margaret of Faenza (d.1330) were each so intoxicated with the baby they saw that they refused to give it up, and Ida of Louvain played with the child revealed to her.[371] These are fantasies of the experience of motherhood; Lidwina of Schieden was sick and could eat nothing but her breasts were abundant with milk, and had to be sucked dry.[372] The image of the child in the host created this contact, and inspired the expression of a warmth which for some was the compensation for an unusual life pattern and the absence of family. It may even be echoed in another context, in the over-sweet and genteel fascination of Chaucer's Prioress with the story of little Hugh of Lincoln, the alleged child-victim of the Jews.[373] The eucharist was constructed to bear these meanings as a symbol which still retained an enormous space between signifier and signified to allow such a broad array of articulations. But it was becoming increasingly over-determined.

A strange and perhaps less comprehensible eucharistic fantasy was constructed by George Carter, a thresher in the service of Sawtry Abbey (Hunts.). He claimed that the host contained the body of Christ in all but its very outer rim, which is 'veraie white breade the thickness off a small twyne threde'.[374] The background for this claim was the notion that Christ's body and blood had to be 'contained' in some way, or they might 'spill out' and wet the lips of communicants. And George Carter was also visited by a vision which substantiated this claim. In the dream he saw a priest with thirteen maids and several men at the moment of consecration and in the host elevated:

ouer the priestes heade, a chylde holding forth his red heart . . . except thuttermost circle which was white as breade the thyckness off a small twyne threde & he thonketh yt was white breade.[375]

When the host was broken it dripped with blood, so this led him to

---

[369] Bynum (1984), p. 182.
[370] Kieckhefer (1984), p. 171.
[371] Bynum (1984), p. 189.
[372] Bynum (1985), p. 6.
[373] Hahn (1988).
[374] Peacock (1885), p. 252.
[375] *Ibid*, p. 253.

believe that 'the litle white circle goyng about the hoste is white breade
& holdeth in the blode'.[376]

George Carter's problem was that he believed only too well in the
eucharist as the very body and blood of Christ, and like flesh and blood
he knew that these were messy, they dripped and were liable to spill if
not contained in our skin. He was exploring the physics of surface, so
basic and yet so complex, like modern philosophers who are debating
just how much of an object is its surface and whether that surface can be
separated or differentiated from its substance in any way. George
Carter, and perforce those who took his visions to be heretical, were
asking the same questions. Need the designation as surface, as 'containing', differentiate that rim, which he insisted was so very thin, from its
contents? If so, this meant that not the whole of the host was transubstantiated, and this smacked too much of remanence to be tolerated.
George Carter's fantasy of the eucharist is instructive in its imagery
dense with eucharistic symbols, the elevation, the child in the host, the
blood, the heart. He absorbed this image into his fantasy of the
eucharistic Christ speaking to him, in the most vulnerable of states, as a
child offering its own heart, closely identified with Christ's sacrifice,
and thus closing the eucharistic circle. The eucharist to George Carter
was a focus for an exploration of the relation between the natural and its
rules, and the supernatural, erratic and inchoate.

## PARODY

How does one treat fun amongst the readings and uses of the eucharist?
How does one analyse parody without exaggerating its importance as a
critique? Latin parodies of the mass circulated in England and Germany, and fit into the underworld of clerical writing, the goliardic
literature of students who were as yet lower clergy. The parody
displays great familiarity with the mass, for the delight of *afficionados*,
those who could appreciate the humour of 'Potemus' instead of 'Ore-
mus', or of 'Dolus vobiscum et cum gemitu tuo' instead of 'Pax
vobiscum et cum spiritu tuo'.[377] The parody works by retaining the
formulae and inverting meaning, making Bacchus king and wine-
drinking his sacrament. Thus, the *Pater noster* becomes: 'Pater noster,
qui es in ciphis, sanctificetur vinum istud, adveniat Bachi potus'.[378] This
tells us more about the life-worlds of celibate clergy or monks than of a

---

[376] *Ibid.*
[377] Lehmann (1923), pp. 59–67.
[378] *Ibid.* In the manner of votive masses, a parody is presented as 'Missa de potatoribus',
*Reliquiae antiquae* II, pp. 208–10.

particular type of eucharistic reading. It is the professional's self-irony, the aspirant's mockery but never the undermining of the system to which he is being integrated. It is fun, but not as creative as some of the applications of the eucharist which we have seen.

More opaque and fascinating are 'throw-away' remarks on the margins of liturgical books, prayer-books and books of law, which have an antinomian relation to the general tenor of these books, and are potentially more disturbing.[379] Such is a small scene at the bottom of a folio in a late-thirteenth-century psalter, with a mitred ape elevating the host;[380] or in an English Book of Hours of *c.*1300 where a mitred ape wearing a chasuble elevates a sheep's head at a wash-stand.[381] The illuminator is not involved in an explicit political contest, but he is expressing some of the tensions over sacerdotal efficacy; dress an ape up as a bishop and teach him the words of the consecration . . . Here again the relation between appearance and substance arises as the central problem. It has been the driving force in the construction of images in readers and hearers and viewers of the eucharistic symbolic, through the process of *bricolage*.[382] As *bricoleurs* they were continually reconstructing meaning by the use of old materials to signify new perceptions and to express altered points of view. From the eucharistic symbolic 'odds and ends', reset and combined anew, almost endless combinations articulating a variety of notions were created.

[379] Randall (1966).
[380] Oxford Bodleian Douce 118, fol. 18ʳ.
[381] Cambridge Trinity B.11.22, fol. 4ʳ. Or consider the ape shown at an altar in the Tournai psalter of 1315 which belonged to Bishop Louis le Hutin (Tournai Cathedral treasury, fol. 166ᵛ); Randall (1966), p. 63.
[382] Lévi-Strauss (1972), pp. 16–33, 35–6.

# Conclusion

How does one conclude the study of a cult which became the central symbol of a culture – it is as difficult to explain an ending, as it is the point of departure in the interpretation of evolving and changing ideas and practices. Yet we do face at the end of the Middle Ages the two Reformations, whose programmes redesigned the symbolic order with the eucharist at its heart, in very different ways. The events of the sixteenth century can satisfactorily be explained only in terms of the dynamics of cultural change: they are inconceivable without the existence of deeply divergent attitudes towards virtue, authority and holiness, and differing symbolic constructions of these moods. A site where some (but not only) divergent concepts were articulated, the eucharist possessed enormous importance; its correct understanding bespoke a host of attitudes and endowed identities. The eucharist, thus, could never be simply reformed; attempts to do so in the fifteenth century failed to produce sharp and apt new formulations in the language of sacramental religion. If the eucharist were to change, it had to be a dramatic change; it could either be wholly espoused – Christ, miracle, well-being – or negated and rejected. And as the world of the sixteenth century came both to realise this necessity and to undertake the new design, the eucharist became identified as a controversial object, a militant emblem of a struggle unto death. There were no two ways about it, so when a crisis about its use and meaning emerged, Europe was thrown into turmoil for 150 years over it. The eucharist was fought over regionally and nationally, personally as well as communally, and became a touchstone of attitudes towards community, family, virtue – and politics.

The eucharist's sacramental claims were designed at the beginning of our period in discussions and debates which began in the eleventh century and matured in the twelfth, whose implications were widely disseminated by the thirteenth century, and were subject to wide-ranging creativity and application in the next two centuries. The eucharist, it is true, was an important symbol in early Christianity, but it was refigured in the eleventh and twelfth centuries to create a new structure of relations, thus modifying the symbolic order, and the social relations and political claims which could be attached to it. In this new order we witness the raising of a fragile, white, wheaten little disc to amazing prominence, and fallible, sometimes ill-lettered, men to the status of mediator between Christians and the supernatural. The eucharist emerged as a unifying symbol for a complex world, as a symbol unburdened by local voices and regional associations. Its language differed from that associated with pilgrimage sites and the cult of saints;[1] thus it was one which provided a framework for interaction and communication between disparate interests and identities. It linked together identities already locally bound in the emerging quasi-national units which were more closely in touch in the increasingly more cosmopolitan world which the eleventh and twelfth centuries heralded. Within the developing parochial net cast over Europe in these centuries the eucharist was reckoned to be equally efficacious in Vienna or Valladolid, viewed or received by woman or man, at cathedral altar or village chancel: it mediated grace and supernatural power in rituals independent of contingent boundaries of political variation. Thus, it possessed universal meaning.

Sacramental mediation was not the only metaphor for expressing the world, but it was one which highlighted a stage in the narrative of Christian medieval culture. Tensions inherent in the scriptural tales themselves, the versions of the synoptic gospels and in the Pauline epistles, were resolved in the eucharist in the creation of a symbol which bound the essential narratives of incarnation, crucifixion, and the legacy of redemption.[2] It was this-worldly in emphasising that channels of regeneration and salvation were available and attainable, renewable and never exhaustible. It possessed little of the eschatological pull which informed the cultural worlds of late antiquity, or of the early modern era, but was geared towards the present, was fulfilled here and now, offering powerful and tangible rewards to the living in the present, as well as to their relatives, the dead. The eucharist provided an axis around which worlds revolved; in it were bound order and hierarchy, inducements towards conformity and promises of reward in health, prosperity, tranquillity. Our task has been to trace and interpret the workings of this world of meaning, its construction and use by some and by others, its implications, threats and promises.

So in the orthodox teaching, in vernacular preaching, in story and

[1] Geary (1978), p. 28.
[2] I am grateful to Paula Frederickson for her illuminating comments on this point.

tale, in magic as in civic ceremonial, the eucharist was used and reused, determined and applied. Those who possessed power and authority could articulate the symbol through their own positions most forcefully.[3] They did so by inducing moods, designing rituals, commissioning works of art, in drama, by exerting authority and charisma, and thus influencing directions in eucharistic readings, creating hegemonic symbolic idioms around themselves. The power exercised in the networks of social relations is always realised through symbolic formations which tend to attach themselves to the holy.[4] A variety of local and universal, individual and collective, lay and sacerdotal claims came to reside in the eucharist; and they were sometimes fleeting and private and at other times public, sometimes bespeaking a single perception, and other times densely inscribed in ways which *overdetermined* the symbol. It thus became linked to partly compatible, but also varying and vying claims which militated against the smooth, lofty, universal, equally shared and accessible pristine nature which had made it so powerful at the outset. This gave it the power to encompass divergent notions about authority, the supernatural, virtue and legitimacy. In its use, however, it was interpreted through a process which entailed the filling up of gaps and spaces for evasion and ambiguity; we have here the aging of a symbol.

This overdetermination was again a subject of concern and attention for those who wished to claim a single articulatory position within the language of religion. We witness in the later Middle Ages attempts to recapture, redesign, reclaim its lost symbolic innocence. This is clear not only from the vehemence of anti-heretical activity, but more interestingly in the redrawing of boundaries of prescribed behaviour. Jean Gerson (1363–1429) criticised the irreverence shown by people to the eucharist in the very proliferation of its celebrations; he recommended the observance of fewer feasts and reiterated the view that celebration of the sacraments was the role of priests alone, not even of mendicant friars.[5] He significantly shifted one of the emphases which had been maintained in pastoral teaching over some 300 years when he underlined human unworthiness to receive the eucharist, even to prepare for its reception, and as he posited these as dependent on God's grace alone, grace which was manifest in the creation of the sacraments, and which merited hope since it alone could effect worthiness.[6] Simi-

---

[3] At the beginning of the period they seem to be reinforcing elements. For some thoughts on the tension between local and central ideas on history in Chinese culture, see Sangren (1987), pp. 215–25.

[4] On this issue, see the collected essays in *Rites of power*, esp. Ruiz (1985).

[5] Brown (1987), pp. 56, 78.

[6] *Ibid*, pp. 87, 70.

larly, the German councils of the 1450s decided to allow eucharistic processions only on Corpus Christi and its octave, and to draw the eucharist back into the interior of churches with only infrequent and necessary processional exhibition and transportation.[7] At the same time the area around the altar was being reclaimed, divided from the nave by ever thicker and more elaborate rood-screens.[8] These were no longer the open structures with thin arches, but now the more opaque wood or stone curtains which by the fifteenth century enclosed the area of consecration and elevation.[9]

These preoccupations with access to and understanding of the eucharist, the eucharist seen as the essence of stability of social order and of dominant ideology, possessed an urgency which arose from the very centrality of the symbol. Within the language of religion with the eucharist at its heart many objections, criticisms and attacks could be tolerated, as long as they were not aimed at that heart. Thus Wyclif's trenchant criticism of papal authority, the wealth of the church, the religious orders, images and pilgrimages were all tolerated early in his career, until he began to pronounce on the eucharist.[10] From 1381 on, with the publication of his *Confessio*, his views were subjected to ecclesiastical condemnation, the patronage of John of Gaunt was withdrawn, some of his followers were chased out of Oxford, and he retired to his parish of Lutterworth in Leicestershire.[11] Similarly, and some 250 years later, the formulations of Galileo's optics, as published in *The Assayer* in 1623, were condemned by the Congregation of the Doctrine of the Faith by 1625 because of their implications when applied to the edifice of eucharistic doctrine.[12] His corpuscular theory of physics threatened to change the way in which substance and accidents were related, and contradicted the Aristotelian foundations which were so necessary for the maintenance of the eucharist as a mystery of Christ's body with the appearance of bread. Galileo's atomistic theory meant that the colour, taste, smell and heat, the accidents, were contained in tiny particles of substance which must remain, in the case of bread and wine, even after the consecration to produce the accidents of bread and wine, and this was obviously anathema. It was this which probably

---

[7] Above, pp. 291–2.
[8] Bond (1908).
[9] Brooke (1967–8).
[10] Pope Gregory XI condemned nineteen opinions contained in Wyclif's Latin writings already in 1377, but this did not affect attitudes in England until 1380, Hudson (1984), pp. 250–1; Hudson (1988b), pp. 281–2.
[11] Keen (1986b); albeit some remained in Oxford for the next thirty years, Hudson (1986).
[12] Redondi (1987).

convinced the Holy Office that it was necessary to bring Galileo to trial for heresy.[13]

The desire to multiply prayers, relics and indulgences, which so characterised late medieval religious practice is also evident in late medieval eucharistic practice.[14] The claims about the eucharist stressed that whenever it was celebrated, wherever it was consecrated, however it was apprehended, it remained the very same historic suffering body of Christ. As such, it differed from other images of sanctity, since it was a source of power itself, one which could not be procured by the laity, nor dispersed in the manner of the cult of relics and holy images. The dominant eucharistic idiom was one of unity and exclusivity, and yet in the ways it was perceived there was a pressure towards fragmenting and apportioning it. The economy of the holy was none the less applied to the eucharist in the widespread understandings of it which developed in practices, in forms of containment and approach current in the cult of saints' relics. Attempts at its multiplication, desire to have tactile contact with it, the increase of frequency of exposition, all exerted pressures which contradicted the dominant trope – that of a powerful unique universal nature.

The eucharist also came to be associated with sectional interests and identities, with claims to power by groups and institutions. We have observed the competition which developed within towns over the processions and drama of the eucharist feast of Corpus Christi. The feast was also taken up as a theme for patrician virtue in English towns.[15] The hierarchies which the eucharist marked within the public sphere enabled, if not forced, an identification of order and a disposition of power, and in so doing it also suggested the critique of this order. Thus, the claims of Lollards and Hussites, as well as the assertions of heretics all over late medieval Europe, presented the eucharist, both in its orthodox formulations of the mass as in its processional and ritual manifestations, as a symbol of political and social privilege. When they articulated an alternative it was in terms of a different symbolic ordering of access to God, in refashioning the eucharist and the ritual attached to it. This is evident in Lollard claims against the sacerdotal efficacy and transubstantiation, and in the claims of Hussites for

---

[13] *Ibid*, see especially chapter 9, pp. 272–320. See the document which discusses these implications for eucharistic theology, and which led to the trial, *ibid*, pp. 333–46.

[14] On multiplication in the economy of the eucharist in the later Middle Ages, see Ball (1976), p. 263; Chiffoleau (1980), pp. 147, 323–7, 339–41; Schmitt (1986), p. 142.

[15] See above, pp. 240–2. And about universalism and particularism in elite organisation, see Cohen (1981), esp. chapter 9.

Utraquism, which broke down the barriers between priest and laity and expressed a more egalitarian and anti-authoritarian creed.[16]

The eucharist could never really be reformed; it could only be wholly accepted or negated outright. The more abstract and 'spiritual' interpretations of the practices of religion offered by such as Erasmus in the early sixteenth century were too evasive to provide a true alternative, a language of religion, useful and resonant.[17] Attacks on the eucharist were thus attacks on the heart of living faith, ritual practice, ideological bonding, institutional purpose. When the Council of Trent confronted all these issues, raised by both Catholic and Protestant reformers in the sixteenth century, it came up with formulations which none the less asserted Real Presence, sacerdotal efficacy, moderate frequency of communion, the cult and veneration of the eucharist, and a powerful affirmation of the feast of Corpus Christi.[18] As opposed to the Lutheran position which related the mass/sacrifice to its historic-mythical dimension and produced the living tension of justification which yearned towards it but could never quite claim to recreate it, the Council of Trent affirmed the sacramental routine which somewhat reenacted and completed the promise of the Last Supper. To Lutherans, the mass in vernacular was an occasion for teaching, for concerted remembrance and inspiration,[19] a bolster to faith, a source of hope. Christ had founded it:

in his memory, because the mass was instituted so that the faith of those who consume it will remember the benefits which they receive from Christ.[20]

Thus, the eucharistic experience was sufficiently lived through communion: no need for gazing, responding, kneeling. It should be received rather by 'using', internalising, commemorating that sacrifice which cannot be compared or repeated but only remembered through the presence of the materials of Christ's own Last Supper. With Zwingli and Calvin the mass evolved into a symbolic re-enactment – no more was it properly tangible, usable.[21] The new English prayer book of 1549

---

[16] Utraquism and the celebration of mass in the vernacular were the demands of many Reformers in the 1520s, like Andrew von Karlstadt, Eire (1986), p. 61, but such positions tended to develop into further and extensive refashioning of the eucharist.

[17] On Erasmus' views on the eucharist, see Eire (1986), pp. 51–2.

[18] Duval (1946), pp. 399–410.

[19] *Ibid*, p. 389.

[20] 'In sui memoriam, quare missa instituta est, ut fides in iis qui utuntur sacramento, recordetur quae beneficia accipiant per Christum', *Corpus reformatorum* 26, p. 30.

[21] John Calvin, *Institutes of the Christian religion* II (book 4, cs. 17–18), pp. 1359–448. On Zwingli's disputations in Geneva, see Eire (1986), p. 142.

designed a new eucharist – one didactic in tone, spoken in the vernacular, and given in communion in both kinds.[22]

The eucharist was the hinge on which the symbolic world turned. In the words of the bishop of Vienne to Pope Paul III in 1536, before convening the Council of Trent, 'there, indeed is the hinge around which things revolve'.[23] He, therefore, recommended that the pope pay special attention to eucharistic matters:

The heresies are many, and very grave, Yet Your Holiness must first and foremost consider those which concern the mass and the sacrament of the eucharist.[24]

If the eucharist was a mystery which summoned God into the workaday world at every altar over which the consecration was said, then God was all too available – and priests too powerful, and too little was required from those who came into contact with the eucharist, be it by sight, sound, smell and ultimately, touch and taste at communion. When ridiculing the 'popishe kingdome' the Protestant Naogeorgas marvelled:

That no ungodly man defiles, this holye blessed thing;
And that the wicked man as well, doth Christ from heaven bring.[25]

The procession with the host was the epitome of the sacramental system; it expressed and enacted the world view which saw in the ritual of the mass renewal of Christ's sacrifice, in proximity to the host, a real benefit, in the material, the most spiritual. This feeling was shared by Protestants and their sympathisers in European towns where the mass and Corpus Christi processions became occasions for violent confrontation, the most heated encounter between the opposing world views, the most inciting of ritual events.[26]

Even if moderate Catholic and Protestants could still agree on issues such as justification and frequent communion, they could never meet over the sacramental underpinning of liturgical practice. The Ratisbon Diet of 1541 was able to produce formulations which were accepted by both camps on a number of issues, but found no common ground on eucharistic questions.[27] Thus the Council of Trent could only reiterate

---

[22] Spufford (1974), p. 242.
[23] 'Pro sacrificio missa (ibi enim cardo rerum vertitur) . . . fortiter pugnandum erit', *Concilium Tridentinum* IV, p. 57.
[24] 'Et quamquam multae sunt gravissimae haereses, cum primis tamen Sua Sanctitas considerare debet ea, quae spectant ad officium missae ac sacramentum Eucharistiae', *ibid* IV, c. 43, p. 16.
[25] Thomas Naogeorgus, *The popish kingdome*, third book, p. 32.
[26] On iconoclasm, see Eire (1986), chapter 4, pp. 105–65.
[27] Duval (1946), p. 399.

and reinforce, not fundamentally refashion, cancel or discard. The cult of the eucharist was discussed at its first session, in October 1551, and emerged in the Council's canons recognised in its full medieval repertoire of practice and gesture: eucharistic exposition, the *viaticum* ceremony, Corpus Christi processions.[28] In the words of discussion of the eucharist a new language of contest, strife and victory was used:

And it is necessary that the victorious truth should triumph in this manner over lies and heresy, so that its enemies should lose courage and be broken by the sight of so great a splendour and such joy of the universal church, or rather, affected by shame and confused, let them come to their senses.[29]

The most concentrated, heated and violent attention was paid to the eucharist in the religious contests of the sixteenth century, as symbolic worlds clashed, as people strove to discredit and annihilate the worldview of their adversaries. When the Protestants of Geneva marched on the cathedral in 1535 the tabernacle with its contents of consecrated hosts was desecrated; the round white hosts, 'dieux blancs' as they were derisively called, were taken out and fed to animals.[30] The eucharist – in church, in procession – became the emblematic focus of the struggle.[31] The nature of the eucharist could be debated in 1538 in inns such as the Sign of the Bell in Northampton between a priest, an ex-friar and a butcher in complex detail,[32] but positions hardened all over Europe by mid-century: by the 1560s we find in the inventories of churchwardens in English parishes mentions of defaced canopies and mass vestments, and broken paxes.[33] A much more violent contest was experienced in France during the wars of religion. In clashes between Protestants and Catholics in France in the 1560s and 1570s the eucharist in the hands of the Catholic clergy was a source of pollution and disgust to the former, while Christ's flesh and blood were worthy of struggle and sacrifice to the latter.[34] Defiance against ordinances in Catholic towns centred on the eucharistic processional route, as Protestants refused to hang

[28] *COD*, PP. 693–8; Duval (1946), pp. 401–2.
[29] 'Ac sic quidem oportuit victricem veritatem de mendacio et haeresi triumphum agere, ut eius adversarii in conspectu tanti splendoris et in tanta universae Ecclesiae laetitia positi vel debilitati et fracti tabescant vel pudore affecti et confusi aliquando resipiscant', 'Decretum de sacramento', c. 5, *COD*, P. 696.
[30] Eire (1986), p. 146.
[31] On views of the eucharist at the Reformation, see Clark (1967).
[32] Bowker (1981), pp. 166–7; see another example of such debates in an alehouse, Spufford (1974), p. 245.
[33] Peacock (1966), pp. 45, 74, 106.
[34] For a seminal discussion of the violent clashes between these symbolic worlds, see Davis (1973). In Lyon in 1561 Catholics shouted: 'For the flesh of God, we must kill all the Huguenots', while a Protestant painter threw himself at the 'God of Paste' willing to destroy him in every parish of the world, *ibid*, p. 73.

clothes and decoration during the *processions générales*; Corpus Christi
became the occasion for assertion of religious identity, in its unambiguous ritual statements it elicited responses that were violent and
uncompromising.[35] Luther had after all expostulated that there was no
feast which he detested so much as Corpus Christi.

The eucharist was the organising principle of Catholic reform, and of
the struggle against Protestant heresies. It shielded Catholics against
evil; from the fleshly turpitude in which heretics were steeped it
purified them.[36] And this central symbol was dangerously at stake in
the sixteenth century; it thus became the subject of intense attention,
love, regulation, dedication, in its support, affirmation. These happened under the guidance of popes and bishops and through the efforts
of an army of militant Catholic layfolk, such as members of the newly
conceived fraternities of the Sacred Sacrament which flourished in
northern Italy and in France.[37] New devotions developed around the
eucharist in the post-Tridentine world: frequent communion, the
Forty Hours, new and vigorous sacramental fraternities.[38] In the efforts
to restate sacramental and sacerdotal claims the eucharist was vigorously represented in architecture and art of the Counter-Reformation.[39] Cardinal Borromeo (1538–84) limited the access of laity to the
chancel, and more attention was being drawn to the ways in which
altars were decorated.[40] Reservation of the eucharist was gradually
drawn away from side-chapels and altars, even from the specially
dedicated chapels of eucharistic fraternities, to be kept at the high altar,
safely, publicly and singularly.[41] Newly approved themes for decoration are evident in Tridentine altarpieces which had strong eucharistic
tones, where saints were depicted in the priestly office, in mass vestments or celebrating the mass.[42] When Clement VIII (1592–1605) had
the Lateran Church redecorated, he commissioned an altar of the
sacrament. His was the pope's tabernacle in his local church, the
episcopal see of Rome, with relics that had been brought from the Holy
Land by St Helena herself. The theme of the edifice was one of eucharist
and history, Constantine and the eucharistic tabernacle, eucharist not

[35] *Ibid*, pp. 52, 73, 86–7; Duval (1946), pp. 393–4. For a criticism of Corpus Christi among
    other Catholic practices see Thomas Becon, *The relics of Rome*, fols 174ᵛ–5ᵛ.
[36] McGinness (1988), *passim*.
[37] On the Venetian foundations, see Hills (1983), pp. 31–3 and n.7.
[38] McGinness (1988), pp. 102–8; Evennett (1968), p. 38.
[39] McGinness (1988), p. 101.
[40] On the development of eucharistic themes in pictures which flenked the altar, *laterali*, and
    which often elaborated eucharistic themes, see Hills (1983), pp. 33–4 and plates 23–4.
[41] Cope (1979) on the chapels of the sacrament in northern Italy.
[42] Mâle (1932), pp. 72–86.

only as founded by Christ, but as empowered within the establishment of the Roman church which was born in that Emperor's day.[43] The grand cycles and the heroic and monumental compositions of wall-paintings provided the proper setting for the eucharist of the Counter-Reform. Rubens' cycle of tapestries, the *Triumph of the eucharist*, was commissioned by the Infanta Isabella, Governer of the Spanish Netherlands, for her favourite religious house, the convent of the Descalzas Reales in Madrid.[44] Scenes from the Old and New Testaments were related in a series of twelve known scenes in which medieval biblical typologies were recast in the new agonistic idiom; every eucharistic epiphany was represented as a triumph, a revelation. The drama of the eucharist was the drama of struggle, proof, authentication and triumph, or defeat. The grandiose compositions reiterated what had become a living and unfolding truth: that the eucharist could either be accepted or rejected; there was no middle way.

In mid-seventeenth-century France a network of some fifty confraternities of the Holy Sacrament, religious charitable associations of clergy and lay enthusiasts, undertook the creation of new types of hospital foundation. Their first *hôpital général* was founded in Paris in 1656 and combined incarceration, relief and correction, in a model which was to be implemented throughout France.[45] These confraternities were hierarchical operations, and they interpreted their devotion to the eucharist as an occasion and focus for a world of correction, in campaigns against Protestants, prostitutes, gypsies, and the poor. This emphasis is stronger than it had ever been in the Middle Ages.[46] Here the host was removed from the altar, lights, bells, incense, adoring community; in its nature as offering, and as concentrated power and authority it was also constructed as a token of benevolent charity, and a licence for coercive virtue.

The eucharist continued to live with differing meanings within the sacramental symbolic order of the *ancien régime,* and imaginations redesigned it even in contexts where it was not visible. Later still Jules Michelet (1798–1874), who was a convert to Christianity, applied his newly acquired eucharistic symbolism to the issues which most troubled him. He pinned his hopes on Christ's sacrifice as an image of the lost spirit of the French Revolution which he wished to revive. His romantic yearnings in the post-Napoleonic era were not a longing for

---

[43] Freiberg (1988) I, chapter 5, pp. 195–248, esp. pp. 216–21. On the eucharistic theme in Roman basilicas of the period, see Scribner (1982), p. 34.
[44] *Ibid*, pp. 15–17.
[45] Jones (1985), pp. 144–6.
[46] On medieval Corpus Christi fraternities, see above, pp. 232–43 and Rubin (1986).

an old religion, but a call for a renewed transubstantiation, that which turned stones into bread, men into fighters and martyrs, through willed suffering and sacrifice for a cause, which alone can make history.[47] As symbol of a true act of sacrifice, the eucharist could reinspire the spirit of 1789, when spirit had emboldened and uplifted the carnal, in a heroic, violent act.[48] Michelet lectured to the young men at the Collège de France in the 1830s and 1840s on a religion of love and sacrifice – but not under an overbearing church. His was not an androgenous victimised Christ of grace, but a heroic man of action, in unison gained through sacrifice with other such men.[49] His spirit spoke not in univocal unanimity imposed by priests, but like a concert of disparate voices blended through a formative ritual of knowing sacrifice. To Michelet *this* was the language of the eucharist.

The eucharist unfolds in its after-medieval after-lives.[50] And a question which looms as we witness the array of eucharistic readings – not only those which coexisted in the medieval language, but those which developed over time – touches on the valence of the eucharist as symbol. In our interpretive venture we are not obliged to assign a causal necessity between symbol and its meanings, its referents. Artifacts do not possess inherent stable meanings since they are always constructed in the context of their use, their apprehension. Yet symbols have the power to suggest,[51] so what do we make of the wheaten bread, the wine, the eating, the body of the eucharist as they emerge packed with associations into new powerful symbolic configurations, as they become apt metaphors which reordered the sacred and the profane, the natural and the supernatural? Why did a ritual of mediation, the symbol of the supernatural upon earth, the source of virtue and salvation, come to reside in the bread and the wine? This can only be interpreted, contextualised – never explained. And it must be seen as a product of an on-going process of *bricolage,* that is, of the creative combinations of existing texts and symbols to produce new meanings leading to different types of action.[52] This is the essence of cultural formation.[53] The structure of relations between symbols creates their meaning and thus very old symbols can appear in different contexts with differing meanings. Culture is always old, and yet the possibilities of change within it

---

[47] Bowman (1974), pp. 830–1, 844.
[48] Haac (1985).
[49] Bowman (1974), p. 832.
[50] It even forced the resignation of a British cabinet minister as late as 1908, see Machin (1983), on the eucharistic controversy of that year.
[51] See Ricoeur (1972).
[52] Fernandez (1977), p. 119.
[53] Lévi-Strauss (1966); Fernandez (1977), pp. 119–25.

are infinite and fresh. The eucharist of the central and later Middle Ages was thus not invented, it was recreated.

The late medieval language of religion posited certain dispositions of power as both natural and necessary, and thus created, by association, an ideology which suggested that this was so. The church, royalty, urban elites, the gentry, used the language of religion in a variety of idioms hinged on central symbols. Conversely, the boldly stated symbolic order also generated change through processes of creative extrapolation, comparison, analogy and extension. Religion has manifested itself here as a mythopoeic field, as creative in the intense metaphorisation that it necessitates to effect the signification of the holy from the very mundane and material, of life and death, of the passing and the eternal.[54] And religion's universal claims do, none the less, leave space for personal dispositions and notions, for *action* in the use of language itself, in the formulation of a single utterance of it. The creative processes of acting through language bring together materials into structures of relations which recreate their very meaning.

We could not attempt to see culture thus operating had we not discarded the disengagement of the 'religious' from the 'social', as we did the establishment of hierarchies of determination which privilege one domain over the other: the social determining the political determining the cultural simply will not do.[55] The approach which sees language as the prime framework for the investigation of human activities, also suggests means of viewing these as contingent and discursively constructed through practices which seek to undermine any single authoritative entry into a text be it ritual, prayers, words, gesture, song. Further, the textual paradigm may not be able to accommodate states of mind and dispositions which have strong visual dimensions and which are not articulated in words.[56] In this exercise the stable factor of inquiry is the commitment to exploration of conditions of possibility within a culture, of the understandings, images and internal rules which make a speech-act possible, meaningful. This commitment entails a sibling interest – to reveal the unsaid, unpronounced, unutterable.[57] These problems of polysemy of any communicative token, which is the life blood of identity and of meaning, and of human creativity, were contemplated by Augustine, Abelard and Jean de Meung. The struc-

---

[54] See Ricoeur's definition of myth as 'a symbol developed into narrative form, articulated within a time and space that cannot be coordinated with critical history and geography', Ricoeur (1972), p. 316.

[55] This is the gist of the argument in Clark (1983).

[56] For some thoughts on this, see Luhrmann (1989), pp. 195–6, 354–5.

[57] On these problems in the consciousness of medieval intellectuals, see Shoaf (1989).

tural necessity of the creation of the *other* in every sentient act, in every word we utter, induces the eternal tension of form and content, of structure and change. And these are to be sought and explored, never resolved, in explorations of the gaps between symbol and the realities which they were meant to capture, explain and transcend. The very linguistic nature of our consciousness justifies and dictates this turn to our most vital and creative capacities, present or past, to exert our understandings of the unity of human interdependence through communicative acts, and in the rush of human experience seeking recognition through articulation.

It is, therefore, of special interest to attempt and understand the compelling power of a symbol related so closely to the image of the body,[58] because the body seems so natural, so inclusive and familiar to all, and yet at a closer glance, it is burdened with layers of expectation and interpretation in medieval culture. In early Christianity the mortified body was a site for glorious triumph over the world and human frailty; the body rose from it pulled by eschatological powers which made bearable and meaningful the sufferings of the flesh of Simon Stylites or Pachomius in the desert.[59] In medieval culture representations of the body sometimes powerfully assimilated it into moments of agonising sacrificial torment within the language of religion, occasions on which it was made most human, suffering, passing, feminine, tormented, vulnerable.[60] At such moments frailty and humanity were celebrated, and thus expressed a pact between the supernatural and the natural, earthly and heavenly, the godly and the human. It was a symbol of many reconciliations.[61]

The body is always a complex image, and eating the body is a particularly disturbing one especially that of eating a sacrificed body, sometimes in the form of a child's body. The juxtaposition of simplest natural act, of eating, with the holiest and most taboo-ridden of nourishments, the human body, associates acts and symbols which in any other contexts would be abhorrent and unutterable.[62] Cannibalism is never absent from any society, either in the form of threats, or in rumours and tales about such transgression in cases of extreme need

[58] On the body as symbol, see Firth (1973), pp. 226–30.
[59] On the theme of bodily renunciation in early Christianity, see Brown (1988a), *passim*; and esp. pp. 217, 333, 437.
[60] Bynum (1987).
[61] See such views in Gregory the Great's 'prematurely' medieval thoughts: to him the holy man played some of the roles which became routinised and sacramentalised in the High Middle Ages, Straw (1988), pp. 70–1, 74.
[62] This may be one of the reasons that the chalice was removed from the laity, as suggested to me by Peter Brown.

and hunger.[63] But in the eucharist God's body was said to be eaten, blood, flesh and all, as a matter of course. Heretics homed in on the horror of it,[64] just as Christians had once accused pagans of cannibalistic excesses, and as ritual murder accusations imputed the sacrifice and eating of a child to the Jews.[65] It is probably best to go no further into psychological speculation on the meaning of all this. We know too little about the inner workings of minds to be able to assess the impact of invocation of the taboo of eating human flesh, the fears and desires related to it. But what we can assert is that by combining the most holy with the most aberrant/abhorrent, the routine workings of sacramental power – an image of the fulness of life-giving, which dwells in the image of utmost transgression – a very powerful symbol was created, as awesome as it was promising.[66] In the elaboration of perfectly orthodox tales of eucharistic miracles in which flesh stuck in believers' throats, in which a child appeared in a host poised for the priest's consumption, transgression of taboo was sanctioned in limited areas. This area of the symbolic gave the occasion for playing with things dangerous, and going away from them unscathed.

There are, of course, issues which this book has not treated, such as a comparison between the Byzantine cultural world and that of Western Europe. The sacred was highly mystified in Byzantine ritual; it was not parcelled and pinpointed but rather unfolded in a *déroulement,* in a whole drama of liturgical interaction which never settled for a particular climax. The varieties of Byzantine eucharistic sentiment only partially overlapped with those that developed in the West from the twelfth century. Whereas in the East the mass remained a very solemn unfolding of sacerdotal mystery, part of which was not only hidden by the priest's body, as in the West, but took place behind a screen, in the West forms of parcelling and allocation, sharing and consumption of the holy were developing and the attendant procedures and routines

---

[63] See notions of cannibalism as organising the world-view of a fairly peaceful people in Overing (1986), esp. p. 90: 'The idiom of cannibalism is therefore all-pervasive in Piaroa thinking about social relationships – whether about the relationships between Gods, between Gods and humans, between humans and animals, and finally between humans', also pp. 100–1.

[64] Theologians and preachers reflected the difficulty of the image of eating a man's flesh in the eucharist in the explanation sometimes given to the fact that Christ does not reveal himself in flesh and blood in the eucharist, the reason given is that this would be abhorrent to the recipients of communion, and that it would earn the ridicule of heretics. See James of Vitry, 'De sacramentis', p. 209; and John of Peckham, 'De eucharistia', BL Add. 24660, fols. 22ᵛ–23ʳ.

[65] On the myth of the ritual murder particularly in late medieval and early modern Germany, see Hsia (1988).

[66] For a comparative cross-cultural study of cannibalism in myth and practice, see Sanday (1986), chapters 1–2, pp. 3–55.

spelt out. Nor have I attempted to map exhaustively the arrays of eucharistic practice; through a comparative mode English practices have been most closely explored. Although further work must examine the dynamics of cultural variation in the many European idioms, this can only be done after the nature of the language of religion has been considered, as in this book.

A narrative has organised the making of this book, a story of ongoing emergence and appropriation, of symbols which speak differently to different people. It is a story of the emptying and replenishing of meaning in symbols which were sometimes shared and sometimes divergent, and of the necessity of this being so. It may be sometimes exasperating in allowing for no strong causal drive – no narrative of the Rise of the Individual, no Secularisation, no Decline of the Church – in having refused to be persuaded by and to make use of the accepted narratives about this period of some five centuries. And yet a process is suggested by the material, not a story of causation and directed growth, but one of unfolding capabilities, a story about the filling unto density of a symbol through the testing of its possible meanings and uses. The eucharist was related to a compelling narrative, to a most powerful ritual, to most useful and familiar practices, and it became the receptacle of power as well as a way of challenging such power. Throughout the period which we have examined the eucharist became full of meanings and associations concocted from the private, the contingent, the questioning, against the background of the certain and the authoritative. I would like to suggest that within the routines imposed by the working of power on the symbolic in attempts to organise people's utmost feelings, thoughts and actions, there are still opportunities to objectify and subvert, to create and hope and reform. We must learn to do justice to these creative capacities, in order to be able to channel energies away from sometimes futile, frustrating and violent resistance, without due recognition of that which still remains to be confronted, the clouds in our very minds. Systems are inescapable inasmuch as we share life with others, but we must learn how to negotiate liberating meanings within them. It is the processes of repression, and of creation, which are most interesting and potent in our lives, in our work and in the lives of those we study in the past.

# Bibliography

## A. MANUSCRIPTS

*Aachen*
Diocesan Library
    Ms. 15
    Ms. 33
    Ms. 40

*Birmingham*
Public Library
    091/MED/6

*Box Hill (Victoria, Australia)*
St Paschal's College
    Missal

*Bristol*
Bristol Archive Office
    St John's Book

*Brussels*
Royal Library (Bibliothèque Royale)

*Cambridge*
Emmanuel College Library
    Ms. 27
Fitzwilliam Museum
    Ms. 12
    Ms. 34
    Ms. 48
    Ms. 262
    Ms. 369
    Ms. 3–1954
    Ms. 84–1972
    Ms. 1058–1975
    Ms. CFM 5
Gonville and Caius College
    Ms. 112
    Ms. 670*/647

Queens' College Library
    Ms. 17(H.29)
St John's College Library (SJC)
    Ms. 4(A4(4))
    Ms. 137**(E36)
    Ms. 139(F2)
    Ms. 151(F4)
    Ms. 215(H13)
    Ms. 262(K21)
Trinity College Library
    B.11.3
    B.11.4
    B.11.11
    B.11.20
    B.11.22
    B.11.23
    B.14.50
    B.15.20
    O.3.5.8
    R.3.20
University Library
    Add. 2792
    Dd.1.1
    Dd.12.16
    Dd.12.69
    Ee.1.12
    Ee.2.2
    Ee.3.59
    Ee.4.24
    Ff.1.18
    Ff.2.31
    Ff.2.38
    Ff.5.48
    Ff.6.31
    Ff.6.44
    Gg.3.21
    Gg.4.16
    Gg.5.31
    Hh.6.15
    Ii.3.8
    Ii.3.26
    Ii.4.20
    Ii.6.2
    Kk.2.6
    Ll.2.2
    Mm.4.15
    Le Bas Prize Essay 7

*Durham*
Hunter Library (Dean and Chapter)
    Ms. 98

*Glasgow*
University Library
    Euing 29
    Gen. 288

*Ipswich*
Ipswich and East Suffolk Record Office (IESRO)
    S. Ipswich 352
    C4/2

*Leeds*
University Library
    Brotherton Collection 502

*Liège*
State Archive (Archives de l'Etat)
    St Martin 79

*Lincoln*
Cathedral Library
    Ms. 1.5.5
City archives
    Misc. Don 169

*London*
British Library
    Add. 10826
    Add. 10925–6
    Add. 11872
    Add. 15216
    Add. 16697
    Add. 16975
    Add. 17388
    Add. 18144
    Add. 18364
    Add. 18719
    Add. 18929
    Add. 22029
    Add. 24660
    Add. 32320
    Add. 34193
    Add. 36683
    Add. 37787
    Add. 38116
    Add. 40672
    Add. 41506

Add. 43437
Add. 44892
Arundel 407
Arundel 506
Burney 335
Burney 361
Egerton 1070
Egerton 3245
Harley 206
Harley 331
Harley 565
Harley 1001
Harley 1288
Harley 2316
Harley 2478
Harley 2592
Harley 2851
Harley 2398
Harley 4196
Harley 4664
Harley 7026
Harley charter 43 A 14
Harley roll T 11
Nero A 3
Royal 2 B 7
Royal 7 C 1
Royal 10 D 7
Royal 10 E 4
Royal 15 D 5
Royal 17 A 16
Royal 17 A 27
Sloane 2457
Sloane 2593
Guildhall Library
  Ms. 3313
Lambeth Library
  Ms. 69
  Ms. 546
Public Record Office
  C47/37–C47/48
  E164/30
  E163/22/2/82
  Miniature no. 2
Society of Antiquaries
  Ms. 712

*Lucerne*
Central Library
  KBP Msc. 19

*Manchester*
Public Library
  f. 091. f. 9

*Norwich*
Cathedral Library (deposited in Norwich and Norfolk Record Office)
  Ms. 5
Norwich Record Office
  MC 16/8
St Peter Hungate Church
  Ms. 158.926.4e

*Oxford*
Bodleian Library
  Ashmole. 61
  Ashmole. 1525
  Auct D.4.4
  Bodley 110
  Bodley 270b
  Bodley 923
  Can. lit. 286
  Can. lit. 389
  Digby 102
  Douce 1
  Douce 5–6
  Douce 118
  e Musaeo 180
  Gough lit. 19
  Eng. Th. C57
  Lat. lit. e. 10
  Lat. lit. e. 39
  Lat. lit. f. 26
  Lat. misc. 2
  Laud. lat. 15
  Laud. misc. 3a
  Laud. misc. 200
  Rawlinson C241
  Rawlinson C670
  Rawlinson lit.d.1
  Rawlinson lit.e.1*
  Th.b.4
Corpus Christi College Library
  Ms. 70

Keble College Library
    Ms. 54
Magdalen College Library
    Lat. 100
New College Library
    Ms. 310
Oriel College Library
    Ms. 75
Trinity College Library
    Ms. 7
    Ms. 89


*Paris*
Arsenal Library
    Ms. 135
    Ms. 203
    Ms. 601
    Ms. 621
    Ms. 623
    Ms. 5218
Jacquemart-André Museum
    Ms. 2
Mazarine Library
    Ms. 406
Marmottan Museum
    Exhibit no. 139
National Library
    Fr. 13442
    Lat. 733
    Lat. 755
    Lat. 764
    Lat. 835
    Lat. 838
    Lat. 839
    Lat. 842
    Lat. 865a
    Lat. 875
    Lat. 880
    Lat. 884
    Lat. 885
    Lat. 957
    Lat. 1022
    Lat. 1052
    Lat. 1089
    Lat. 1105
    Lat. 1143
    Lat. 1332

Lat. 1366
Lat. 3112–13
Lat. 3555
Lat. 8886
Lat. 9441
Lat. 9444
Lat. 10483
Lat. 10484
Lat. 10502
Lat. 12061
Lat. 12065
Lat. 17311
Lat. 17323
Nouv.acq.fr. 4509–10
Nouv.acq.lat. 1171
Nouv.acq.lat. 1590
Nouv.acq.lat. 1689
Nouv.acq.lat. 1773


*Vatican*
Vatican Apostolic Library
    Archivio San Pietro A 25
    Archivio San Pietro B 63
    Archivio San Pietro B 76
    Archivio San Pietro E 6
    Archivio San Pietro E 9
    Barberini Lat. 400
    Burgh. 53
    Chigi A IV 74
    Chigi D V 71
    Lat. 2043
    Lat. 2492
    Lat. 2534
    Lat. 4756
    Ottoboni Lat. 140
    Pal. lat. 39
    Pal. lat. 500
    Rossiani 99
    Rossiani 178
    Santa Maria Maggiore 52
    Urb. lat. 110
    Vat. lat. 12992


*Vendôme*
Municipal Library (Bibliothèque municipale)
    Ms. 16

*Venice*
Marciana Library
 Lat. III (18) 2283–4
 Lat. III (46) 2099
 Lat. III (111) 2116
 Lat. III (120) 2116
 Lat. III (45) 2444
 Lat. III (120) 2478

*Wisbech*
Wisbech and Fenland Museum
 Wisbech Corporation Archives
 Accounts of the Holy Trinity Guild

*York*
Borthwick Institute
 Prob. Reg. 2
 Register Melton

## B. PRINTED SOURCES

*Aberdeen Extracts from the council register of the burgh of Aberdeen 1398–1570*, Spalding Club, Aberdeen, 1844

*Acta capitulorum generalium ordinis predicatorum*, ed. B. M. Reichert, 2 vols., MOPH 3, 4, Rome, 1898–9.

*Age of chivalry: art in Plantagenet England, 1200–1400*, ed. J. Alexander and P. Binski, London, 1987.

*AH Analecta hymnica medii aevi*, ed. G. M. Dreves and C. Blume, 55 vols., Leipzig, 1886–1922, repr. New York, 1961.

Alan of Lille, *Liber poenitentialis*, ed. J. Longère, Analecta mediaevalia Namuracensia 17, Louvain and Lille, 1965.

 'Summa de arte praedicatoria', *PL* 210, cols. 109–98.

Albert the Great, 'De sacramentis', ed. A. Ohlmeyer, in *Alberti magni ordinis fratrum praedicatorum opera omnia*, vol. 26, Aschendorff, 1958.

Alexander of Hales, *Glossa in quatuor libros sententiarum*, ed. PP. of the college of St Bonaventure, Bibliotheca franciscana scholastica medii aevi 12–15, 4 vols., Quaracchi, 1951–7.

Alexander Neckham, *De naturis rerum*, ed. T. Wright, RS 34, London, 1863.

Alger of Liège, 'De sacramentis corporis et sanguinis Dominici', *PL* 180, cols. 743–854.

*The alliterative Morte Arthure: a critical edition*, ed. V. Krishna, New York, 1976.

*An alphabet of tales*, ed. M. M. Banks, 2 vols., EETS 126–7, London, 1904–5.

Ambrose, 'De sacramentis', *PL* 16, cols. 427–82.

*The ancient Cornish drama*, ed. E. Norris, 2 vols., Oxford, 1859.

*Andover Archives of Andover* part 1, ed. C. Collier and R. H. Clutterbuck, Andover, n.d. [1885?].

*Anecdotes*   Stephen of Bourbon, *Anecdotes historiques, légendes et apologues tirés du recueil inédit d'Etienne de Bourbon, dominicain du XIII<sup>e</sup> siècle*, ed. A. Lecoy de la Marche, Paris, 1877.

'Annales monaterii de Waverleia', ed. H. R. Luard, in *Annales monastici* II, RS 36, London, 1865, pp. 127–411.

*Ashburton   Churchwardens' accounts of Ashburton, 1479–1580*, ed. A. Hanham, Devon and Cornwall Record Society new ser. 15, 1970.

Augustine, *Enarrationes in psalmos* LI–C, ed. E. Dekkers and I. Fraipont, CCSL 39, Turnholt, 1956.

*Die Ausgaben der apostolischen Kammer unter Johann XXII*, ed. K. H. Schäfer, Vatikanische Quellen zur Geschichte der päpstlichen Hof-und Finanzverwaltung 1316–78, II, Paderborn, 1911.

*Ayenbite of Inwyt*   Don Michel, *Ayenbite of Inwyt or remorse of conscience*, ed. R. Morris, EETS 23, London, 1868.

*Barking ordinal   The ordinale and customary of the Benedictine nuns of Barking Abbey*, ed. J. B. L. Tolhurst, 2 vols., HBS 65–6, London, 1927–8.

Bartolomew of Lucca, 'Historia ecclesiastica nova', in *RIS* XI, Milan, 1727, repr. 1977, cols. 753–1,306.

Berengar of Tours, *De scara coena adversus Lanfrancum*, ed. W. H. Beekenkamp, Kerkhistorische studien behoorende bij het nederlandsch Archief voor Kerkgeschiedenis 2, The Hague, 1941.

Bernard Gui, *Manuel de l'inquisiteur*, ed. G. Mollat, 2 vols., Paris, 1926–7.

Berthold of Regensburg, *Deutsche Predigten*, ed. D. Richter, Kleine deutsche Prosadenk-mäler oes Mittelalters 5, Munich, 1968.

*Beverley town documents*, ed. A. F. Leach, Selden Society 14, 1900.

*Biblia sacra cum glossa ordinaria*, 6 vols., Douai, 1617.

*Bishop Stortford   The records of S. Michael's Parish Church, Bishop Stortford*, ed. J. L. Glasscock, London, 1882, pp. 1–109.

Bonaventure, *Oprea omnia*, ed. P.P. of the college of St Bonaventure, 10 vols. in 9, Quarracchi, 1882–1902.

*The book of the knight of La Tour-Landry*, ed. T. Wright, EETS 33, London, 1906.

*The book of vices and virtues: a fourteenth century translation of the 'Somme le Roi' of Lorens d'Orléans*, ed. W. N. Francis, EETS 217, London, 1942.

*The Bridgettine breviary of Syon Abbey*, ed. A. J. Collins, HBS 96, London, 1969.

*Bridgewater   Bridgewater borough archives, 1200–1468*, 4 vols., ed. T. B. Dilks, Somerset Record Society 48,53, 58, 60. Bridgewater, 1933–48.

*Bristol, All Saints (a)*   E. G. C. F. Atchley ed., 'Some documents relating to the parish of All Saints, Bristol', *Archaeological Journal* new ser. 8 (1901), pp. 147–81.

*Bristol, All Saints (b)*   E. G. C. F. Atchley, 'On the parish records of the church of All Saints, Bristol', *Transactions of the Bristol and Gloucestershire Archaeological Society* 27 (1904), p. 221–74.

*Bristol, St Augustine   Two compotus rolls of St Augustine's Abbey, Bristol*, ed. G. Beachcroft and A. Sabin, Bristol Record Society publications 9, 1938.

*Bristol, St Ewen (a)*   J. Maclean, ed., *Transactions of the Bristol and Gloucestershire Archaeological Society* (1891), pp. 139–82, 254–96.

*Bristol, St Ewen (b)   The church book of St Ewen's, Bristol, 1454–1584*, ed. B. R.

Masters and E. Ralph, Bristol and Gloucestershire Archaeological Society Record Section, 6, 1967.

*The Bruce* John Barbour, *The Bruce, or the book of Robert de Broyss, king of Scots (1286–1332)*, ed. W. W. Skeat, 2 vols., EETS ES 11, 55, London, 1870–89.

*The Brut or the chronicles of England*, ed. F. W. D. Brie, EETS 131, 136, London, 1906–8.

Burchard of Worms, 'Decretorum libri viginti', *PL* 140, cols. 537–1,058.

*Bushmead cartulary  The cartulary of Bushmead Priory*, ed. G. H. Fowler and J. Godber, Publications of the Bedfordshire Historical Record Society 22, 1945.

*Cambrai, statuts synodaux*  Boeren, P. C., 'Les plus anciens statuts synodaux du diocèse de Cambrai', *Revue de droit canonique* 3 (1953), pp. 1–32, 131–72; 4 (1954), pp. 131–58.

*Cambridge gild records (1298–1389)*, ed. M. Bateson, Cambridge Antiquarian Society 39, Cambridge, 1903.

*Cartulaire de l'église St.-Lambert de Liège*, ed. S. Bormans, E. Schoolmeesters and E. Poncelet, 6 vols., Liège, 1893–1933.

*Catalogue of Romances in the department of manuscripts in the British Museum*, ed. H. L. D. Ward and J. A. Herbert, 3 vols., London, 1883–1910.

*Central European manuscripts in the Pierpoint Morgan library*, ed. M. Harrsen, New York, 1958.

*Le Cérémonial papal:* I – XIIIᵉ *siècle;* II – *De Rome en Avignon ou le cérémonial de Jacques Stefaneschi;* III – *Les textes avignonnais;* IV – *Le retour à Rome ou le cérémonial de patriarche Pierre Ameli*, ed. M. Dykmans, Bibliothèque de l'Institut historique belge de Rome, 24–7, Brussels and Rome, 1977–85.

*The changing plan of Hull, 1290–1650: a guide to documentary sources for the early topography of Hull*, ed. R. Horrox, Hull, 1978.

*Chapters of Augustinian canons*, ed. H. E. Salter, Oxford Historical Society 74, Oxford, 1920.

*Chartularium universitatis Parisiensis*, ed. H. Denifle with A. Chatelain, 4 vols., Paris, 1889–97.

*The chastising of God's children*, ed. J. Bazire and E. Colledge, Oxford, 1957.

*The Chester mystery cycle*, ed. R. M. Lumiansky and D. Mills, 2 vols., EETS.SS 3, 8, 1974–86.

*Chester processional  The processional of the nuns of Chester*, ed. J. W. Legg, HBS 18, London, 1899.

*Chronicon monasterii de Abingdon* (AD *201–1189*), ed. J. Stevenson, 2 vols., RS 2, London, 1858.

Clement Maydston, *The tracts of Clement Maydeston (1497) with the remains of Caxton's Ordinale (1477)*, ed. C. Wordsworth, HBS 7, London, 1894.

*Clementines CIC* II, cols. 1133—1200 [see also *Constituciones*].

*The collegiate church of Ottery St Mary being the ordinacio et statuta ecclesie sancte Marie de Ottery*, ed. J. N. Dalton, Cambridge, 1917.

*The commonplace book of Robert Reynes of Acle. An edition of Tanner ms. 407*, ed. C. Louis, Garland medieval texts 1, New York and London, 1980.

*Concilia Magnae Britanniae et Hiberniae* AD *446–1718*, ed. D. Wilkins, London, 1737.

*Conciliorum oecumenicorum decreta,* ed. G. Alberigo *et al.,* Bologna, third edn, 1973.

*Concilium Tridentinum: diariorum, actarum, epistolarum tractatuum nova collectio,* ed. Görres Society, 13 vols., Fribourg, 1901–38.

Conrad of Clairvaux, *Exordium magnum Cisterciense sive narratio de initio Cisterciensis ordinis auctore Conrado,* ed. B. Griesser, Series scriptorum s. ordinis Cisterciensis, Rome, 1961.

*Constituciones Clementis papae quinti cum apparatu Iohannis Andreae,* Nuremberg, 1486.

*A contemporary narrative of the proceedings against Dame Alice Kyteler,* ed. T. Wright, Camden Society 24, London, 1843.

*I corali del duomo di Siena,* ed. M. G. Ciardi Dupre, Siena, 1972.

*Corpus iuris canonici,* ed. E. Friedberg, 2 vols., Leipzig, 1879–81.

*The corpus of miniatures in the manuscripts of decretum Gratiani,* ed. A. Melinkas, Studia Gratiana 16–18, 3 vols., Rome, 1975.

*Councils and synods with other documents relating to the English church* I *(871–1204),* ed. D. Whitelock, M. Brett and C. N. L. Brooke, Oxford, 1982.

*Councils and synods with other documents relating to the English church,* II *(1205–1313),* ed. F. M. Powicke and C. R. Cheney, Oxford, 1964.

CPL   *Calendar of entries in the papal registers relating to Great Britain and Ireland: papal letters, 1198–1492,* 15 vols., ed. W. H. Bliss, C. Johnson, J. A. Twemlow and M. J. Haren, London and Dublin, 1893–1978.

*A critical and historical corpus of Florentine painting,* ed. R. Offner, section III, New York, 1931–67.

Croscombe   *Church-wardens accounts of Croscombe, Pilton, Patton, Tintinhull, Morebath and St Michael, Bath,* ed. E. Hobhouse, Somerset Record Society 4, 1890.

*Customary of the benedictine monasteries of Saint Augustine, Canterbury, and Saint Peter, Westminster,* ed. E. M. Thompson, 2 vols., HBS 23, 28, London, 1902–4.

Decretum   Gratian, *Concordantia discordantium canonum,* ed. E. Friedberg, in *Corpus iuris canonici* I, Leipzig, 1879.

Darby, All Saints   *The chronicles of the collegiate church or free chapel of All Saints, Derby,* ed. J. C. Cox and W. H. St John Hope, London, 1881.

*Dives and pauper,* ed. P. Barnum, vol. I in two parts, EETS 225, 280, London, 1976–80.

DM   Caesarius of Heisterbach, *The dialogue of miracles,* ed. C. C. S. Bland and H. von E. Scott, 2 vols., London, 1929.

*Documents relating to the university and colleges of Cambridge,* 3 vols., London, 1852.

Dunmow   L. A. Majendie, 'The Dunmow parish accounts', *Transactions of the Essex Archaeological Society* 2 (1863), pp. 229–37.

*The Early English carol,* ed. R. L. Greene, Oxford, 1935.

*Early English proverbs,* ed. W. W. Skeat, Oxford, 1910.

*Early Gothic manuscripts 1250–1285,* ed. N. Morgan, 2 vols., A survey of manuscripts illuminated in the British Isles 4, London, 1982–8.

Eckbert (abbot of Schönau), 'Sermones contra catharos', *PL* 195, cols. 11–98.

*Der Egerer Fronleichnamsspiel,* ed. G. Milchsack, Bibliothek des literarischen Vereins in Stuttgart 156, Tübingen, 1881.

*Ely chapter ordinances and visitation records 1241–1515,* ed. S. J. A. Evans, Camden miscellany 17, London, 1940.

*English fragments from Latin medieval service-books,* ed. H. Littlehales, EETS ES 90, London, 1903.

*English gilds,* ed. T. Smith and L. T. Smith with L. Brentano, EETS 40, London, 1870.

*English Wycliffite sermons:* I, ed. A. Hudson; II, ed. P. Grandon; III, ed. A. Hudson, Oxford, 1983–1990.

*Erzählungen des Mittelalters in deutscher Übersetzung und lateinische Urtext,* ed. J. Klapper, Breslau, 1914, repr. Hildesheim, 1978.

*Exempla aus Handschriften des Mittelalters,* ed. J. Klapper, Sammlung mittellateinischer Texte herausgegeben von Alfons Hilka 2, Heidelberg, 1911.

*Exeter ordinal Ordinale Exoniense,* ed. J. N. Dalton, 2 vols., HBS 37, 38, London, 1909.

*Fasciculi zizaniorum,* ed. W. W. Shirley, RS 5, London, 1858.

*Festial* John Mirk, *Mirk's Festial,* ed. T. Erbe, EETS 96, London, 1905.

*Fontes vitae s. Thomae Aquinatis,* ed. D. Prümmer, Toulouse, n.d.

Gabriel Biel, *Canonis misse expositio,* ed. H. A. Oberman and W. J. Courtenay, 5 vols., Veröffentlichungen des Instituts für Europäische Geschichte in Mainz 31–4, 79, Wiesbaden, 1963–76.

*Sermones de festivitatibus Christi,* Cologne, 1619.

Geoffrey Chaucer, *The Riverside Chaucer,* ed. L. D. Benson, third edn, Boston, 1987.

Gerald of Wales, *Giraldi Cambrensis Gemma ecclesiastica,* ed. J. S. Brewer, RS 21,2, London, 1862.

Gilbert Crispin, *The works of Gilbert Crispin, abbot of Westminster,* ed. A. S. Abulafia and G. R. Evans, Auctores Britannici medii aevi 8, London, 1986.

*The Gilbertine rite,* ed. R. M. Wooley, HBS 59–60, London, 1921–2.

*Glastonbury, St John* W. E. Daniel, 'Churchwardens' accounts of St John' Glastonbury', *Somerset and Dorset Notes and Queries* 4 (1894–5), pp. 89–96, 137–44, 185–92, 235–40, 329–36.

*The goodman of Paris,* ed. E. Power, London, 1928.

*Gothic manuscripts 1285–1385,* ed. L. F. Sandler, A survey of manuscripts in the British Isles 5, 2 vols., Oxford, 1986.

Gregory the Great, *Dialogues,* ed. A. de Vogüé, Sources chrétiennes 251, 260, 265, 3 vols., Paris, 1978–80.

Guibert of Nogent, 'De sanctis er eorum pignoribus', *PL* 156, cols. 611–80.

Guitmund of Aversa, 'De corporis et sanguinis Christi veritate in eucharistia', *PL* 149, cols. 1,427–94.

*Handlyng synne (a)* Robert Mannyng of Brunne, *Handling synne,* ed. I. Sullens, Medieval and Renaissance studies 14, Binghamton (NY), 1983.

*Handlyng synne (b)* Robert Mannyng of Brunne, *Handling synne, a.d. 1301,* ed. F. J. Furnivall, EETS 119, 123, London, 1901–3.

*Hemingsby's register,* ed. H. M. Chew, Wiltshire Record Society 18, 1963.

Henry Knighton, *Chronicon,* ed. J. R. Lumby, 2 vols., RS 92, London, 1889–95.

Henry Langenstein of Hesse, *Secreta sacerdotum que in missa teneri debent*, Augsburg (Auguste), 1503.

Herbert of Clairvaux, 'De miraculis libri tres', *PL* 185, cols. 1273–1384.

*The Hereford breviary*, ed. W. H. Frere and L. E. G. Brown, 3 vols., HBS 26, 40, 46, London, 1904–15.

*Heresy trials in the diocese of Norwich, 1428–1431*, ed. N. P. Tanner, Camden Society fourth ser. 20, London, 1977.

Hildegard of Bingen, *Scivias*, ed. A. Führkötter with A. Carlevaris, 2 vols., CCCM 43–43A, Turnholt, 1978.

*Historia Albigensium* Peter of Vaux Cernay (Vallium Cernaii), 'Historia Albigensium', *PL* 213, cols. 543–712.

*Historia et cartularium monasterii S. Petri Gloucestriae*, ed. W. H. Hart, 3 vols., RS London, 1863–7.

*Hoccleve's minor poems*: I, ed. F. J. Furnivall; II, ed. I. Gollancz; EETS ES 61, 73, London, 1892–1925.

*Holinshed's chronicle* *Holinshed's chronicles of England, Scotland and Ireland* VI, London, 1808.

*Horae beatae Mariae virginis or, Sarum and York primers*, ed. E. Hoskins, London, 1901.

Hugh of Langres, 'Tractatus de corpore et sanguine Christi', *PL* 142, cols. 1,325–34.

Hugh of Lincoln, *Life* *Magna vita sancti Hugonis: the life of St Hugh of Lincoln*, ed. and trans. D. L. Douie and H. Farmer, 2 vols., London, 1961–2.

Humbert of Romans, *Beati Umberti sermones*, Venice, 1603.

*Hyde breviary* *The monastic breviary of Hyde Abbey, Winchester*, ed. J. B. L. Tolhurst, 3 vols., HBS 69, 70, 71, London, 1932–4.

*Illuminated manuscripts in the Bodleian Library, Oxford*, ed. O. E. Pächt and J. J. G. Alexander, 3 vols., Oxford, 1966–73.

*Illustrations of the occasional offices of the church in the Middle Ages from contemporary sources*, ed. H. S. Kingford, Alcuin Club collections 24, London, 1921.

*Index* *The index of Middle English verse*, ed. C. F. Brown and R. H. Robbins, New York, 1943, with supplement Lexington (Ky.), 1965.

*Instructions (a)* John Mirk, *Instructions for parish priests by John Mirc*, ed. E. Peacock and rev. F. J. Furnivall, EETS 31, London, 1868, rev. edn, 1902.

*Instructions (b)* John Mirk's *Instructions for parish priests*, ed. G. Kristensson, Lund studies in English 49, Lund, 1974.

*IqD* *Calendarium rotulorum chartarum (1199–1438) et inquisitionum ad quod damnum (1307–1461)*, ed. J. Caley and R. Lemon, London, 1803.

*Italian manuscripts in the Pierpoint Morgan Library*, ed. M. Harrsen and G. K. Boyce, New York, 1953.

*Italian paintings: a catalogue of the collections of the Metropolitan Museum of Art, Florentine School*, ed. F. Zeri, New York, 1971.

*Jacob's well. An English treatise on the cleansing of man's conscience*, ed. A. Brandeis, EETS 115, London, 1900.

James of Vitry, *The exempla or illustrative stories from the 'sermones vulgares' of Jacques de Vitry*, ed. T. F. Crane, London, 1890.

*Die Exempla aus den sermones feriales et communes des Jakob von Vitry*, ed. J. Greven, Sammlungen mittellateinisher Texte 9, Heidelberg, 1914.

'De sacramentis', in *The 'Historia occidentalis' of Jacques de Vitry: a critical edition*, ed. J. F. Hinnebusch, Spicilegium Friburgense 17, Freiburg, 1972, pp. 192–246.

'Vita Beate Mariae Ogniacensis', in *AASS* Junii 4, Antwerp, 1707, pp. 636–66.

Jean Gerson, *Oeuvres complètes*, ed. P. Glorieux, 10 vols., Paris, 1966–73.

Jean Hérolt, *Sermones . . . de tempore et de sanctis cum duobus exemplorum promptoariis*, Lyon, 1514.

John XXII, *Extravagantes Johannis XXII*, ed. J. Tarrant, Monumenta iuris canonici series B: corpus collectionum 6, Vatican, 1983.

*Lettres communes analysées d'après les registres dits d'Avignon ou du Vatican*, ed. G. Mollat, 3 vols., Vatican, 1904–06,

*Lettres de Jean XXII (1316–1334)*, ed. A. Fayen, Analecta Vaticano-Belgica 2–3, Rome, Paris and Brussels, 1908–09.

John Amundesham, *Chronica monasterii S. Albani V: Annales monasterii S. Albani, 1421–40*, ed. H. T. Riley, RS 28, 2 vols., London, 1870.

John Audelay, *The poems of John Audelay*, ed. E. K. Whiting, EETS 184, London, 1931.

John Beleth, *Summa de ecclesiasticis officiis*, ed. H. Douteil, 2 vols., CCCM 41–41A, Turnholt, 1976.

John Bromyard, *Summa praedicantium*, Antwerp, 1614.

John Calvin, *Institutes of the Christian religion*, ed. J. T. McNeill and F. L. Battles, 2 vols., Library of Christian classics 20, Philadelphia (Pa), 1960.

Joinville's *Creed   Text and iconography for Joinville's 'Credo'*, ed. L. J. Friedman, Medieval Academy of America publications 68, Cambridge (Mass.), 1958.

Lanfranc, 'Liber de corpore et sanguine domini', *PL* 150, cols. 407–42.

Lanfranc, *Constitutions   The monastic constitutions of Lanfranc*, ed. D. Knowles, Nelson Medieval Texts, London, 1951.

*The lay folks' catechism or the English and Latin versions of Archbishop Thoresby's instruction for the people*, ed. T. F. Simmons and H. E. Nolloth, EETS 118, London, 1901.

*Legenda aurea   James of Voragine, The golden legend*, trans. P. Ryan and H. Ripperger, London and New York, 1941.

*Legend of the holy rood: symbols of the Passion and cross poems*, ed. R. Morris, EETS 46, London, 1871.

*Leicester records   The records of the borough of Leicester, 1103–1603*, ed. M. Bateson and rev. W. H. Stevenson and J. E. Stocks, 3 vols., Cambridge, 1899–1905.

*Leicester, St Martin   A chronicle of the church of St Martin in Leicester*, ed. T. North, London and Leicester, 1866.

'Liber de Vita Christi ac omnium pontificum (AD 1–1474)', *RIS* 3,1, ed. G. Carducci and V. Fiorini, new edn, Milan, 1932.

*Liber exemplorum ad usum praedicantium*, ed. A. G. Little, British Society of Franciscan Studies 1, Aberdeen, 1908.

*Der Liber Ordinarius der Essener Stiftkirche*, ed. F. Arens, Paderborn, 1908.

*Liber pontificalis of Edmund Lacy, bishop of Exeter*, ed. R. Barnes, Exeter, 1847.

*Libri rationum camerae Bonifatii papae VIII. Archivio Segreto Vaticano Collect 446 & Int. et exit. 5*, ed. T. Schmidt, Littera antiqua 2, Vatican, 1984.

*The Libro Cerimoniale of the Florentine republic*, ed. R. C. Trexler, Travaux d'humanisme et Renaissance 15, Geneva, 1978.

*Liège, St Jean  Inventaire analytique des chartes de la collégiale de Saint-Jean l'Evangeliste à Liège*, ed. L. Lahaye, 2 vols., Liège, 1921–31.

*Liège, St Lambert  Inventaire analytique et chronologique des chartes du chapitre Saint-Lambert à Liège*, ed. J.-G. Schoonbroodt, Liège, 1863.

*Liège, St Martin  Inventaire analytique et chronologique des chartes du chapitre de St Martin à Liège*, ed. J. G. Schoonbroodt, Liège, 1871.

*Lincoln diocese documents, 1450–1544*, ed. A. Clark, EETS 149, London, 1914.

*Liturgical manuscripts for the mass and the divine office: the Pierpoint Morgan Library*, ed. J. Plummer, New York, 1964.

*Livre des mestiers  Le Livre des mestiers de Bruges et ses dérivés*, ed. J. Gessler, 6 parts, Bruges, 1931.

*Livre des seintz medecines*  Henry of Lancaster, *Le Livre des seintz medecines*, ed. E. J. Arnold, Oxford, 1940.

*Lollard sermons*, ed. G. Cigman, EETS 294, London, 1989.

*London, All Hallows  The churchwardens' accounts of the parish of All Hallows, London Wall, in the city of London, 33 Henry VI to 27 Henry VIII (AD 1455–AD 1536)*, ed. C. Welch, London, 1912.

*London assize of nuisance 1301–1431: a calendar*, ed. H. M. Chew and W. Kellaway, London Record Society 10, 1973.

*London consistory court wills (1492–1547)*, ed. I. Darlington, London Record Society 3, 1967.

*London and Middlesex chantry certificates 1548*, ed. C. J. Kitching, London Record Society 16, 1980.

*London, St Andrew Hubbard*, J. C. Crosthwaite, 'Ancient churchwardens' accounts of a city parish', *British magazine* 31 (1847), pp. 241–50, 394–404, 526–37; 32 (1847), pp. 30–40, 144–57, 272–82, 390–9; 33 (1848), pp. 564–79, 664–77; 34 (1848), pp. 15–33, 171–87, 292–307, 395–409, 524–33; 35 (1848), pp. 50–7, 178–86, 273–84, 396–405, 520–9, 635–4.

*London, St Margaret Pattens*  'Churchwardens' accounts of the parish of St Margaret Pattens, London', *Sacristy* 1 (1871), pp. 258–62.

*London, St Mary Hill  The medieval records of a London city church (St Mary at Hill) AD 1420–1559*, ed. H. Littlehales, EETS 125, 128, London, 1904–5.

*London, St Michael's Cornhill  The accounts of the churchwardens of the parish of St Michael, Cornhill, in the city of London from 1456 to 1608*, ed. W. H. Overall, London, 1871.

*London, St Peter Cheap (a)*  W. Sparrow Simpson, 'Inventory of the vestments, plate and books, belonging to the church of St Peter Cheap in the city of London, in the year 1431', *Journal of the British Archaeological Association* 24 (1868), pp. 150–60.

*London, St Peter Cheap (b)*  W. Sparrow Simpson, 'On the parish of St Peter Cheap in the city of London', *Journal of the British Archaeological Association* 24 (1868), pp. 248–68.

Lothar of Segni, 'De sacro altaris mysterio libri sex', *PL* 211, cols. 763–920.

*Lydgate's minor poems* John Lydgate, *The minor poems of John Lydgate* 1, ed. H. N. MacCracken, EETS ES 107, London, 1909.

*The making of King's Lynn: a documentary survey,* ed. D. M. Owen, British Academy Records of Social and Economic History new ser. 9, London, 1984.

*Manipulus curatorum* Guido of Monte Rocherii, *Manipulus curatorum,* London, 1508.

Mansi *Sacorum conciliorum nova et amplissima collectio,* ed. J. D. Mansi, 53 vols., Florence, Venice and Paris, 1759–98, reiss. Paris, 1901–1927.

*Manuale ad usum Ecclesie Westmonasteriensis,* ed. J. W. Legg, 2 vols., HBS 1,5, London, 1891–3.

*Manuale et processionale ad usum insignis ecclesiae Eboracensis,* ed. W. G. Henderson, Surtees Society 63, Durham, 1875.

*Manuscrits enluminés d'origine italienne.* I: VI$^e$–XII$^e$ *siècles,* ed. F. Avril and Y. Zaluska, Paris, 1980; II: XIII$^e$ *siècle,* ed. F. Avril, Paris, 1984.

*Les Manuscrits liturgiques latins de la Bibliothèque Vaticane,* ed. P. Salmon, Studi e Testi 251, 253, 260, 267, 270, Vatican, 1968–72.

Margery Kempe, *The book of Margery Kempe,* ed. S. B. Meech and H. E. Allen, EETS 212, London, 1940.

Master Simon, *De sacramentis Maître Simon et son groupe. De sacramentis,* ed. H. Weisweiler, Louvain, 1937.

Matthew Paris, *Chronica maiora,* ed. H. R. Luard, 7 vols., RS 57, London, 1872–1883.

*Historia anglorum sive ut vulgo dicitur historia minor,* ed. F. Madden, 3 vols., RS 44, London, 1866–1869.

*Medieval English lyrics: a critical anthology,* ed. R. T Davies, London, 1963.

*Medieval manuscripts in British libraries,* ed. N. Ker, 3 vols., Oxford, 1969–1983.

*Medieval miniatures, from the Department of Manuscripts (formerly the 'Library of Burgundy') the Royal Library of Belgium,* ed. L. M. J. Delaissé, London, 1965.

*Medieval and Renaissance illustrated manuscripts in Australian collections,* ed. M. M. Manion and V. F. Vine, Melbourne, London and New York, 1984.

*The meditations on the life and passion of Christ,* ed. C. d'Evelyn, EETS 158, London, 1921.

*Meditations on the life of Christ: an illustrated manuscript of the fourteenth century,* ed. I. Ragusa and R. B. Green, trans. I. Ragusa, Princeton monographs in art and archaeology 35, Princeton (NJ), 1961.

*Memorials of London and London life,* ed. H. T. Riley, London, 1868.

*Die Messe Gregors des Grossen. Vision, Kunst, Realität. Katalog und Führer zu einer Ausstellung im Schnütgen-Museum der Stadt Köln,* ed. V. Westfeling, Cologne, 1982.

*The Middle English charters of Christ,* ed. M. C. Spalding, Bryn Mawr College monograph ser. 15, Bryn Mawr (Pa.), 1914.

*Middle English sermons,* ed. W. O. Ross, EETS 209, London, 1940.

*The minor poems of the Vernon ms.,* ed. C. Horstmann and F. J. Furnivall, 2 vols., EETS 98, 117, London, 1892–1901.

*Mirrour* Nicholas Love, *The mirrour of the blessed lyf of Jesu Christ,* ed. L. F. Powell, Oxford, 1908.

*Missale ad usum ecclesie Westmonasteriensis*, ed. J. W. Legg, HBS 1, 5, 12, London, 1891–7.

*Monumenta Vizelliacensia. Textes relatifs à l'histoire de l'abbaye de Vézelay*, ed. R. B. C. Huygens, CCCM 47, Turnholt, 1976.

*Motif-index of folk literature*, ed. S. Thompson, 5 vols., Folklore Fellows communications 106–09, 116, Helsinki, 1932–5.

*The N-town plays: a facsimile of British Library manuscript Cotton Vespasian D VIII*, with intr. by P. Meredith and S. J. Kahrl, Medieval drama facsimiles 4, Leeds, 1977.

Nicholas of Clamanges, *Opera omnia*, ed. I. M. Lydius, Lyons, 1613, repr. Farnborough, 1967.

*The non-cycle plays and fragments*, ed. N. Davis, EETS SS 1, London, 1970.

Norwich   *Records of the city of Norwich*, ed. W. Hudson and J. C. Tingey, 2 vols., Norwich, 1906–10.

*Norwich customary   The customary of the cathedral priory church of Norwich*, ed. J. B. L. Tolhurst, HBS 82, London, 1948.

*Norwich, St Peter Mancroft*   W. H. St John Hope, 'Inventories of the parish church of St Peter Mancroft, Norwich', *Norfolk Archaeology* 14 (1898–1900), pp. 153–240.

*Nottingham, St Peter's   The account books of the gilds of St George and St Mary in the church of St Peter Nottingham*, ed. R. F. B. Hodgkinson and intr. L. V. D. Owen, Thoroton Society record series, 7, 1939.

*Les Ordinaires des collégiales Saint-Pierre à Louvain et Sts Pierre-et-Paul à Anderlecht d'après des manuscrits du XIV* siècle, ed. P. F. Lefèvre, Bibliothèque de la *RHE* 36, Louvain, 1960.

*The ordinal of the papal court from Innocent III to Boniface VIII and related documents*, ed. S. P. J. Van Dijk and completed by J. H. Walker, Spicilegium Friburgense 22, Freiburg, 1975.

*Ordinale Sarum sive Directorium sacredotum*, ed. W. Cooke, 2 vols., HBS 20,22, London, 1901.

*Oxford, St Peter-in-the-East*, ed. R. S. Mylne, *Proceedings of the Society of Antiquaries of London*, second ser. (1884), pp. 25–8.

*Painting in Renaissance Siena 1420–1500*, ed. K. Christiansen, L. B. Kanter and C. B. Strehlke, New York, 1988.

*Parish fraternity register. Fraternity of the Holy Trinity and SS Fabian and Sebastian in the parish of St Botolph without Aldersgate*, ed. P. Basing, London Record Society 18, London, 1982.

Paschasius Radbert, *De corpore et sanguine domini*, ed. B. Paulus, CCCM 16, Turnholut, 1969 [or *PL* 120, cols. 1,267–350].

*The peasants' revolt of 1381*, ed. R. B. Dobson, London, 1970.

Peter the Chanter, *Summa de sacramentis et animae consiliis*, ed. J.-A. Dugauquier, 3 vols. in 5, Analecta mediaevalia Namuracensia 4, 7, 11, 16, 21, Lille, 1954–67.
'Verbum abbreviatum', in *PL* 205, cols. 23–370.

Peter Comestor, 'De sacramentis', ed. R. M. Martin, in appendix to *Maître Simon et son groupe*, ed. H. Weisweiler, Louvain, 1937.
'Sermones', *PL* 198, cols. 1721–1843.

Peter Damian, *Sermons*, ed. I. Lucchesi, CCCM 57, Turnholt, 1983.

Peter Lombard, 'Sententiarum libri IV', *PL* 192, cols. 519–1, 112.

Peter of Poitiers, 'Sententiae', *PL* 211, cols. 789–1,280.

Peter the Venerable, *Contra Petrobrusianos*, ed. J. Fearns, CCCM 16, Turnholt, 1968.

*De miraculis libri duo*, ed. D. Bouthillier, CCCM 83, Turnholt, 1988.

*Proverbia sententiaeque latinitatis medii aevi*, ed. H. Walther, 6 vols., Carmina medii aevi posterioris latinae II, 1–6, Göttingen, 1963–9.

*Provinciale* William Lyndwood, *Provinciale, seu constitutiones Angliae*, Oxford, 1679, 2 vols., repr. Farnborough, 1968.

Raoul of Cambrai, *Chanson de geste*, ed. P. Meyer and A. Longnon, Paris, 1882.

Ratramnus of Corbie, *De corpore et sanguine domini. Texte établi d'après les manuscrits et notice bibliographique*, ed. J. N. Bakhuizen van den Brink, Verhandlingen der koninklijke Nederlandse Akademie van Wetenschappen, Letterkunde 61 (1), Amsterdam, 1954.

*Reading, St Laurence* C. Kerry, *A history of the municipal church of St Laurence, Reading*, Reading and Derby, 1883.

*Les Recettes et les dépensées de la chambre apostolique pour la quatrième année du pontificat de Clement V (1308–1309)*, ed. B. Guillemain, Rome, 1978.

*REED: York*, ed. A. F. Johnston and M. Rogerson, 2 vols., Toronto, 1979.

*Regesta pontificum romanorum*, ed. A. Potthast, 2 vols., Berlin, 1874–5.

*Reg. Bainbridge* *Liber pontificalis Chr. Bainbridge archiepiscopi Eboracensis*, ed. W. G. Henderson, Surtees Society 61, Durham, 1875.

*Reg. Giffard (Worcester)* *Register of Bishop Godfrey Giffard*, ed. J. W. Willis Bund, Worcestershire Historical Society, Oxford, 1902.

*Reg. Giffard (York)* *The register of Walter Giffard, Lord Archbishop of York 1266–1279*, ed. W. Brown, Surtees Society 109, Durham, 1904.

*Reg. Grandisson* *The register of Bishop John de Grandisson*, ed. F. C. Hingeston-Randolph, 3 vols., London and Exeter, 1894–9.

*Reg. Gregory VII* *Das Register Gregors VII*, ed. E. Caspar, 2 vols., MGH Epistolae selectae II fasc. 1–2, Berlin, 1920–3.

*Reg. Hethe* *Registrum Hamonis Hethe, diocesis Roffensis*, AD *1319–52*, ed. C. Johnson, 2 vols., Kent Archaeological Society Records Branch. Kent Records 4, Oxford, 1915–48.

*Reg. Lacy* *The register of Edmund Lacy, bishop of Exeter, 1420–1455: registrum commune*, ed. G. R. Dunstan, Devon and Cornwall Record Society new ser. 7, 10, 13, 16, 18, Torquay, 1963–72.

*Reg. Polton* *Registrum Thome Poltone, episcopi Herefordiensis* AD *1420–1422*, ed. W. W. Capes, Cantilupe Society, 1916, and Canterbury and York Society 22, 1918.

*Reg. Repingdon* *The register of Bishop Philip Repingdon 1405–1419*, ed. M. Archer, 3 vols., Lincoln Record Society 57–8, 74, 1963–82.

*Reg. Stapledon* *The register of Walter Stapledon, bishop of Exeter* AD *1307–1326*, ed. F. C. Hingeston-Randolph, London and Exeter, 1892.

*Reg. Turotte* E. Scoolmeesters, 'Les Regestes de Robert de Thourotte, prince-évêque de Liège', *Bulletin de la société d'art et d'histoire du diocèse de Liège* 13 (1906), pp. 1–126, 449–54.

*Reg. Worc. vac.   The register of the diocese of Worcester during the vacancy of the see 1301–1345*, ed. J. W. Willis Bund, 3 vols., Worcestershire Historical Society, Oxford, 1893–5, 1897.

*The register of the gild of the Holy Cross, the Blessed Virgin Mary and St John the Baptist of Stratford-upon-Avon (1406–1535)*, ed. J. Harvey Bloom, London, 1907.

*The register of the guild of Corpus Christi in the city of York*, ed. R. H. Skaife, Surtees Society 57, 1872.

*Le Registre d'inquisition de Jacques Fournier évêque de Pamiers (1318–1325)*, ed. J. Duvernoy, 3 vols., Toulouse, 1965.

*Les Registres d'Urbain IV (1261–1264)*, ed. J. Guiraud, Bibliothèque des Ecoles françaises d'Athènes et de Rome, 4 vols., Paris, 1904–58.

*Registrum statutorum et consuetudinum ecclesiae cathedralis sancti Pauli Londoniensis*, ed. W. Sparrow Simpson, London, 1873.

*Religious lyrics of the fourteenth century*, ed. C. Brown, Oxford, 1924.

*Religious lyrics of the fifteenth century*, ed. C. Brown, Oxford, 1939.

*Reliquiae antiquae. Scraps from ancient manuscripts illustrating chiefly early English literature and the English language*, ed. T. Wright and J. O. Halliwell, 2 vols., London, 1841–3.

Richard of Hexham, 'Historia de gestis regis Stephani et de bello de standardo (1135–1139)', in *Chronicles of the reign of Stephen, Henry II, and Richard I* III, ed. R. Howlett, RS 82, London, 1886, pp. 137–78.

*Ripon acts   Acts of the chapter of the collegiate church of SS Peter and Wilfrid, Ripon, AD 1452 to AD 1506*, ed. J. T. Fowler, Surtees Society 64, Durham, 1875.

*The rites of Durham*, ed. J. T. Fowler, Surtees Society 107, 1902.

Robert Pullen, 'Sententiarum libri octo', *PL* 186, cols. 639–1,010.

*Le Roi Rene et son temps, 1382–1481*, Catalogue of an exhibition at the Granet Museum, April 1981, Aix-en-Provence, 1981.

Roland Bandinelli, 'Sententiae', in Gietl (1891), pp. 1–322.

*Rotherfield   Canon Goodwyn, 'An old churchwardens' account book of Rotherfield', Sussex archaeological collections* 41 (1896), pp. 25–48.

*Salisbury, St Edmund and St Thomas   Churchwardens' accounts of St Edmund and St Thomas, Sarum 1443–1702*, ed. H. J. F. Swayne, Wiltshire Record Society, Salisbury, 1896.

*The Sarum missal edited from three early manuscripts*, ed. J. W. Legg, Oxford, 1916, repr. 1969.

*Scarborough, St Mary*   W. H. St John Hope, 'Inventory of the parish church of St Mary Scarborough, 1434; and that of the white friars or Carmelites of Newcastle-on-Tyne', *Archaeologia* 51 (1888), pp. 61–72.

*School book   A fifteenth century school book from a manuscript in the British Museum (ms. Arundel 249)*, ed. W. Nelson, Oxford, 1956.

*Selected rentals and accounts of medieval Hull, 1293–1528*, ed. R. Horrox, Yorkshire Archaeological Society record series 141, 1983.

*A selection of English carols*, ed. R. L. Greene, Oxford, 1962.

*Selections from English Wycliffite writings*, ed. A. Hudson, Cambridge, 1978.

*A series of precedents and proceedings in criminal causes extending from the year 1475 to 1640*, ed. W. Hale Hale, London, 1847.

*Songs, carols and other miscellaneous poems,* ed. R. Dyboski, EETS ES 101, London, 1907.

*Southwell visitation* Visitations and memorials of Southwell minster, ed. A. F. Leach, Camden Society 48, London, 1891.

*Speculum christiani: a Middle English religious treatise of the fourteenth century,* ed. G. Holmstedt, EETS 182, London, 1933.

*Speculum laicorum,* ed. J. T. Welter, Paris, 1914.

*Speculum sacerdotale,* et. E. H. Weatherly, EETS 200, London, 1936.

*St Albans chronicle* Chronica monasterii S. Albani Johannis Amundhem; Annales monasterii S. Albani regnante Henrico sexto (AD 1421–1431), ed. H. T. Riley, 2 vols., RS 28, London, 1870–1.

*St Paul's churches* Visitation of the churches belonging to St Paul's Cathedral 1249–52, ed. W. Sparrow Simpson, Camden Society 53 and miscellany 9, London, 1895.

*ST* Thomas Aquinas, *Summa theologiae. Latin text and English translation,* ed. T. Gilbey, 61 vols., London, 1964–80.

*Statuta capitulorum generalium ordinis cisterciensis (1116–1789),* ed. J. M. Canivez, Bibliothèque du Revue d'Histoire Ecclésiastique, Louvain, 1933.

*Statutes of Lincoln Cathedral,* ed. H. Bradshaw and C. Wordsworth, 3 vols., Cambridge, 1892–7.

*Statuti e regesti dell'Opera di Santa Maria di Orvieto,* ed. L. Fumi, Rome, 1891.

*Les Statuts synodaux français du XIII^e siècle.* I: Les statuts de Paris et le Synodal de l'Ouest (XIII^e siècle), ed. O. Pontal, Collection de documents inédits sur l'histoire de France, Section d'histoire médiévale et de philologie 9, Paris, 1971.

*Les Statuts synodaux français du XIII^e siècle.* II: Les Statuts de 1230 à 1260, ed. O. Pontal, Collection de documents inédits sur l'histoire de France, Section d'histoire médiévale et de philologie 15, Paris, 1983.

*Les Statuts synodaux français du XIII^e siècle.* III: Les statuts synodaux angevins de la seconde moitié du XIII^e siècle, ed. J. Avril, Collection de documents inédits sur l'histoire de France, Section d'histoire médiévale et de philologie 19, Paris, 1988.

*Les Statuts synodaux de Jean de Flandre évêque de Liège 16/2/1288,* ed. E. Schoolmeesters, Liège, 1908.

*A survey of London* John Stow, *A survey of London,* ed. C. L. Kingsford, 2 vols., Oxford, 1908.

*Synodal law in Florence and Fiesole, 1306–1518,* ed. R. C. Trexler, Studi e testi 268, Vatican, 1971.

*La tabula exemplorum secundum ordinem alphabeti,* ed. J. T. Welter, Thesaurus exemplorum 3, Paris, 1926.

*Templum dei* Robert Grosseteste, *Templum dei,* ed. J. Goering and F. A. C. Mantello, Pontifical Institute of Mediaeval Studies. Toronto Medieval Latin texts 14, Toronto, 1984.

*Testamenta Eboracensia: a selection of wills from the registry of York (1300–1551),* ed. J. Raine Sr., J. Raine Jr. and J. W. Clay, 6 vols., Surtees Society 4, 30, 45, 53, 79, 106, Durham, 1836–1902.

*Thame* F. G. Lee, *A history, description and antiquities of the prebendal church of the Blessed Virgin Mary of Thame, in the county of Oxford,* London, 1883.

Thomas Aquinas, *Scriptum super sententiis magistri Petri Lombardi*, ed. M. F. Moos, Paris, 1947.

Thomas Becon, *The relics of Rome*, second edn, London, 1583.

Thomas Brinton, *The sermons of Thomas Brinton, bishop of Rochester (1373–1389)*, ed. M. A. Devlin, Camden third ser. 85–6, London, 1954.

Thomas of Cantimpré, *Bonum universale de apibus*, Douai, 1627.

Thomas of Eccleston, 'De adventu fratrum minorum in Angliam', in *Monumenta franciscana* 1, ed. J. S. Brewer, RS 4, London, 1858.

Thomas à Kempis, *Le Manuscrit autographe de Thomas à Kempis et 'l'Imitation de Jésus-Christ'*, ed. L. M. J. Delaissé, 2 vols., Publication de Scriptorium 2, Paris and Brussels, 1956.

Thomas Naogeorgus, *The popish Kingdome, or the reigne of Antichrist*, trans. B. Googe, London, 1570.

Thomas Netter, *Defensor fidei catholicae*, 3 vols., Venice, 1671 repr. Farnborough, 1967.

*Three Middle English sermons from Worcester chapter manuscript F.10*, ed. D. M. Grisdale, Leeds School of English language texts and monographs 5, Leeds, 1939.

*Tintinhull   Church-wardens accounts of Croscombe, Pilton, Patton, Tintinhull, Morebath and St Michael's, Bath*, ed. E. Hobhouse, Somerset Record Society 4, 1890.

*Les Très Riches Heures du Duc de Berry, Musee Conde, Chantilly*, London, 1969.

*The Wakefield pageants in the Towneley cycle*, ed. A. C. Cawley, Old and Middle English texts 1, Manchester, 1948.

*Tracts on the mass*, ed. J. W. Legg, HBS 27, London, 1904.

*Twenty-six political and other poems* part 1, ed. J. Kail, EETS 124, London, 1904.

*Urkunden der Stadt Hildesheim*, ed. R. Doebner, Hildesheim, 1881.

*The use of Sarum*, ed. W. H. Frere, 2 vols., Cambridge, 1898–1901.

*Vetus registrum Sariberiense alias dictum registrum S. Osmundi episcopi. The register of S. Osmund*, ed. W. H. Rich, 2 vols., RS 78, London, 1883–4.

*Visitation of churches belonging to St Paul's Cathedral 1249–52*, ed. W. Sparrow Simpson, Camden Society new ser. 53, London, 1895.

Walter Map, *De nugis curialium: courtier's trifles*, ed. and trans. M. R. James and rev. by C. N. L. Brooke and R. A. B. Mynors, Oxford, 1983.

*Warham visitations   Kentish visitations of Archbishop Warham and his deputies, 1511—1512*, ed. K. Wood-Legh, Kent records (1984).

William of Auvergne, 'De sacramento altaris', in *Opera omnia* I, Orleans, 1674.

William of Auxerre, *Summa aurea*, Paris, 1500, repr. Frankfurt, 1964.

William Durandus, *Rationale divinorum officiorum*, ed. V. d'Avino, Naples, 1859.
   *The symbolism of church and church ornaments: a translation of the first book of the Rationale divinorum officiorum*, ed. J. M. Neale and B. Webb, Leeds, 1943.

William Langland, *Piers the plowman: B Text (Preface and Passus* I – VIII), ed. J. A. W. Bennett, Oxford, 1972.
   *Piers plowman: the B version*, ed. G. Kane and E. T. Donaldson, London, 1975.
   *Piers plowman: an edition of the C-text*, ed. D. Pearsall, York medieval texts second ser., London, 1978.

William of Middleton, *Quaestiones de sacramentis*, ed. C. Piana and G. Gal, 2 vols., Bibliotheca franciscana scholastica medii aevi 22–3, Florence, 1961.

William of Nangis, 'Chronique de St Denis', *RHGF* 20, Paris, 1840.

William of Ockham, *Quaestiones et decisiones in IV libros sententiarum*, Lyon, 1495.

*De sacramento altaris*, ed. T. B. Birch, Burlington (Iowa), 1930.

William of St Thierry, 'De sacramento altaris', *PL* 180, cols. 341–66.

'Sancti Bernardi Vita Primi', *PL* 185, cols. 225–68.

William of Tocco, 'Historia beati Thomae de Aquino', in *S. Thomae Aquinatis vitae fontes praecipuae*, ed. A. Ferrua, Alba, 1968, pp. 29–132.

*Wymondham Abbey before the dissolution*, ed. S. Yaxley, Dereham, 1986.

*Yeovil* J. G. Nichols, 'Accounts of the proctors of the church of Yeovil county Somerset, 36 Henry VI 1457–8', *Collectanea topographica et geneologica* 3 (1836), p. 134–41.

*York art: a subject list of extant and lost art including items relevant to early drama*, ed. C. Davidson and D. E. O'Connor. Early drama, art and music reference series 1, Kalamazoo (Mich.), 1978.

*York breviary* *Breviarium ad usum insignis ecclesie Eboracensis*, ed. J. Raine, 2 vols., Surtees Society 71, 75, 1879–82.

*York civic records*, ed. A. Raine, 5 vols., Yorkshire Archaeological Society record ser. 98, 103, 106, 108, 110, 1939–46.

*York, municipal records* *Extracts from the municipal records of the city of York*, ed. R. Davies, repr. Gloucester, 1976.

*The York plays*, ed. R. Beadle, London, 1982.

*York, St Mary's* *The chronicle of St Mary's Abbey, York, from Bodley ms. 39*, ed. H. H. E. Craster and M. E. Thornton, Surtees Society 148, Durham, 1934.

*Zurich Cathedral statutes* *Die Statutenbücher des Propstei St Felix und Regula (Grossmünster) zu Zürich*, ed. D. W. H. Schwarz, Zurich, 1952.

## C. SECONDARY WORKS

Adam, P. (1964). *La Vie paroissale en France au xiv^e siècle*, Paris.

Agnew, J. C. (1986). *Worlds apart: market and theater in Anglo-American thought, 1550–1750*, Cambridge.

Allen, H. E. (1936). 'A fifteenth-century "associations of beasts, of birds, and of men": the earliest text with "language for carvers"', *PMLA* 51, pp. 602–6.

Almazan, V. (1967). 'L'Exemplum chez Vincent Ferrer', *Romanische Forschungen* 79, pp. 289–332.

Amelli, A. (1924). 'Una probabile fonte del "Laude Sion"', *Scuola cattolica*, pp. 188–9.

Anciaux, E. H. P. (1949). *La Théologie du sacrement de pénitence au XII^e siècle*, Louvain.

Anderson, M. D. (1955). *The imagery of British churches*, London.

(1963). *Drama and imagery in English medieval churches*, Cambridge.

(1971). *History and imagery in British churches*, London.

Andrieu, M. (1950). 'Aux origines du culte du saint-sacrement. Reliquaires et monstrances eucharistiques', *Analecta Bollandiana*, 68, pp. 397–418.

Ansiaux, P. (1937). 'Les Prieurs des frères prêcheurs en la cité de Liège des origines

. . . à 1417', *Bulletin de la société d'art et d'histoire du diocèse de Liège* 28, pp. 93–158.

Arasse, D. (1981). 'Entre dévotion et culture: fonctions de l'image religieuse au xv<sup>e</sup> siècle', in *Faire croire. Modalités de la diffusion et de la réception des messages religieux du xii<sup>e</sup> au xv<sup>e</sup> siècle,* Collections de l'Ecole française de Rome 51, Rome, pp. 131–46.

Arduini, M. L. (1987). *Ropert von Deutz (1076–1129) und der 'Status Christianitatis' seiner Zeit: symbolisch-prophetische Deutung der Geschichte,* Beihefte zum Archiv für Kulturgeschichte 25, Vienna.

Armstrong, C. A. J. (1942). 'The piety of Cicely, Duchess of York: a study in late medieval culture', in *For Hilaire Belloc,* ed. D. Woodruff, London, pp. 73–94.

Arnold-Forster, F. (1899). *Studies in church dedications,* 3 vols., London.

Arnould, E. J. (1940). *Le Manuel des péchés dans la littérature religieuse de l'Angleterre,* Paris.

Assion, P. (1968). 'Die mittelalterliche Mirakel-Literatur als Forschungsgegenstand', *Archiv für Kulturgeschichte* 50, pp. 172–80.

Aston, M. (1977). 'Lollardy and literacy', *History* 62, pp. 347–71.
(1988). *England's iconoclasts.* 1: *Laws against images,* Oxford.

Atkinson, C. W. (1983) *Mystic and pilgrim. The 'Book' and the world of Margery Kempe,* Ithaca (NY).

d'Avray, D. L. (1985) *The preaching of the friars. Sermons diffused from Paris before 1300,* Oxford.

Avril, J. (1983). 'La Pastorale des malades et des mourants aux xii<sup>e</sup> et xiii<sup>e</sup> siècles', in *Death in the Middle Ages,* ed. H. Braet and W. Verbeke, Subsidia mediaevalia ser. 1 studia 9, Louvain, pp. 88–106.

Axters, S. (1948). *La Spiritualité des Pays-Bas,* Bibliotheca Michlinensis 2 ser 1, Louvain [*The spirituality of the old Low Countries,* trans. D. Attwater, London, 1954].

Axton, R. (1974). *European drama of the early Middle Ages,* London.

Backhouse, J. (1985). *Books of hours,* London.

Baethgen, F. (1928–9). 'Quellen und Untersuchungen zur Geschichte der päpstlichen Hof- und Finanzverwaltung unter Bonifaz VIII', *Quellen und Forschungen aus italienischer Archiven und Bibliotheken* 20, pp. 114–37.

Bailey, T. (1971). *The processions of Sarum and the Western church,* Pontifical Institute of Mediaeval Studies. Studies and Texts 21, Toronto.

Baix, F. (1947). 'La Première célébration de la Fête-Dieu à Fosses en 1246', *Annales de la société archéologique de Namur* 44, pp. 157–80.

Baix, F. and Lambot, C. (1946). *La Dévotion à l'eucharistie et la vii<sup>e</sup> centenaire de la Fête-Dieu,* Gembloux and Namur.

Baker, G. (1822–41). *The history and antiquities of the county of Northampton,* 2 vols., London.

Balau, S. (1903). *Le Sources de l'histoire de Liège au moyen-âge,* Mémoires couronnés publiés par l'Académie royale de Belgique 61, Brussels.

Balau, S. and Fairon, E. (1913–31). *Chroniques liégoises,* 2 vols., Liège.

Baldwin, C. S. (1959). *Medieval rhetoric and poetic (to 1400),* Gloucester (Mass.).

Baldwin, J. W. (1970). *Masters, princes and merchants. The social views of Peter the Chanter and his circle,* 2 vols., Princeton (NJ).

Ball, R. M. (1976). 'The education of the English parish clergy in the later Middle Ages with particular reference to the manuals of instruction', PhD thesis, Cambridge University.

Barb, A. A. (1956). '*Mensa sacra*. The round table and the holy grail', *JWCI* 19, pp. 40–67.

Barbiero, G. (1944). *Le confraternità del santissimo sacramento primo del 1539. Saggio storico*, Treviso.

Baring-Gould, S. (1892). 'The Workleigh tabernacle', *Transactions of the Exeter diocesan architectural society* new ser. 5, pp. 126–30.

Barron, C. (1985). 'The parish fraternities of medieval London', in *The church in Pre-Reformation society: essays in honour of F. R. H. Du Boulay*, ed. C. Barron and C. Harper-Bill, Woodbridge, pp. 13–37.

Bartlett, R. (1982). *Gerald of Wales 1146–1223*, Oxford.

Bataillon, L.-J. (1974). 'Un Sermon de S. Thomas d'Aquin sur la parabole du festin', *RSPT* 58, pp. 451–6.

(1980). 'Approaches to the study of medieval sermons', *Leeds studies in English* new ser. 11, pp. 19–35.

(1983). 'Le Sermon inédit de S. Thomas *Homo quidam fecit coenam magnam*. Introduction et édition', *RSPT* 67, pp. 353–69.

(1985). '*Similitudines* et *exempla* dans les sermons du XIIIᵉ siècle', in *The bible in the medieval world: essays in memory of Beryl Smalley*, ed. K. Walsh and D. Wood, SCH Subsidia 4, Oxford, pp. 191–205.

Bauerreiss, P. (1931). *Pie Jesu. Das Schmerzensmann-Bild und sein Einfluss auf die mittelalterliche Frömmigkeit*, Munich.

Baumgartner, F. (1981). *L'Arbre et le pain: essai sur La Queste del Saint Graal*, Paris.

Beadle, H. R. L. (1977). The medieval drama of East Anglia: studies in dialect, documentary records and stagecraft', 2 vols., PhD thesis, York University.

Becker, M. B. (1981). *Medieval Italy. Contrasts and continuity*, Bloomington (Ind.).

Beckwith, S. (1986). 'A very material mysticism: the medieval mysticism of Margery Kempe', in *Medieval literature. Criticism, ideology and history*, ed. D. Aers, Brighton, pp. 34–57.

Bell, R. M. (1985). *Holy anorexia*, Chicago and London.

Bennett, H. S. (1952). *English books and readers, 1475 to 1557*, Cambridge.

Bercé, Y. M. (1976). *Fête et revolte: des mentalités populaires du XVIᵉ au XVIIIᵉ siècles: essai*, Paris.

Bériou, N. (1987). 'La Prédication au béguinage de Paris pendant l'année liturgique 1272–1273', *Recherches augustiniennes* 13, pp. 105–229.

(1987). *La Prédication de Ranulphe de la Houblonnière. Sermons aux clercs et aux simple gens à Paris au XIIIᵉ siècle*, 2 vols., Paris.

Berlière, D. (1919). *Les Evêques auxiliaires de Liège*, Bruges.

Berliner, R. (1955). 'Arma christi', *Münchner Jahrbuch der bildenden Kunst* 6, pp. 35–152.

Berlioz, J. (1980). 'Le Récit efficace: l'*exemplum* au service de la prédication (XIIIᵉ–XVᵉ siècle', *Mélanges de l'Ecole français de Rome. Moyen-âge – temps modernes* 92, pp. 113–46.

(1981). '"Quand dire c'est faire dire". *Exempla* et confession chez Etienne de Bourbon', in *Faire croire. Modalités de la diffusion et de la réception des messages religieux du XII⁰ au XV⁰ siècles*, Collections de l'Ecole française de Rome 51, Rome, pp. 299–335.

Berlioz, J. and David, J. M. (1980). 'Introduction bibliographique', *Mélanges de l'Ecole français de Rome* 92, pp. 15–31.

Bernstein, D. (1982). 'The blinding of Harold and the meaning of the Bayeux tapestry', *Anglo-Norman studies* 5, pp. 40–64.

Berry, W. (1815). *The history of the island of Guernsey part of the ancient duchy of Normandy*, London.

Bertamini, T. (1968). 'La bolla "Transiturus" di papa Urbano IV e l'ufficio del "Corpus domini" secondo il codice di S. Lorenzo di Bognanco', *Aevum* 42, pp. 29–58.

Bettey, J. H. (1979). *Church and community: the parish church in English life*, Bradford-upon-Avon.

Binz, L. (1973). *Vie religieuse dans le diocèse de Genève pendant le Grand Schisme et le crise conciliaire (1378–1450)*, Geneva.

Bishop, E. (1918). *Liturgica historica: papers on the liturgy and religious life of the western church*, Oxford.

Blair, L. (1940). 'A note on the relation of the Corpus Christi procession to the Corpus Christi play in England', *MLN* 55, pp. 83–95.

Blomefield, F. and Parkin, C. (1805–10). *An essay towards a topographical history of the county of Norfolk*, 11 vols., edn. of London.

Boeren, P. (1978). 'Un traité eucharistique inédit du XII⁰ siècle. *Convenientibus vobis in unum* (I Cor. 11.20)', *Archives d'histoire doctrinale et littéraire du moyen âge* 45, pp. 181–214.

Boitani, P. (1982). *English medieval narrative in the thirteenth and fourteenth centuries*, trans. J. K. Hall, Cambridge.

Bolton, B. (1973). '*Mulieres sanctae*', *SCH* 10, pp. 77–95.

(1978). '*Vitae matrum*: a further aspect of the *Frauenfrage*', in *Medieval women: dedicated and presented to Professor Rosalind M. T. Hill on the occasion of her seventieth birthday*, ed. D. Baker, SCH Subsidia I, Oxford, pp. 253–73.

Bond, F. (1908). *Screens and galleries in English churches*, London.

(1910). *Wood carvings in English churches: stalls and tabernacle work*, London.

(1916). *The chancel of English churches*, London.

Bonniwell, W. R. (1944). *A history of the Dominican liturgy 1215–1945*, New York.

de Boom, G. (1946). 'La Culte de l'eucharistie d'après la miniature du moyen-âge', *Studia eucharistica*, pp. 326–32.

Bossy, J. (1973). 'Blood and baptism: kinship, community and Christianity in Western Europe from the fourteenth to the seventeenth centuries', *SCH* 19, pp. 129–43.

(1983). 'The mass as a social institution, 1200–1700', *PP* 100, pp. 29–61.

(1985). *Christianity in the West, 1400–1700*, Oxford.

Boureau, A. (1984). *La Légende dorée. Le système narratif de Jacques de Voragine 1298*, Paris.

Boutémy, A. (1946). 'Giraud de Berri et Pierre le Chantre: une source de la *Gemma ecclesiastica*', *Revue du moyen-âge latin* 2, pp. 45–62.

Bouthellier, D. (1975). 'L'Univers religieux de Pierre le Vénérable d'après le 'De miraculis' à la lumière des autres oeuvres de l'auteur et de la tradition bénédictine et cistercienne', 2 vols., PhD thesis, Montreal University.

Bowker, M. (1968). *The secular clergy in the diocese of Lincoln 1495–1520*, Cambridge.

(1981). *The Henrician Reformation: the diocese of Lincoln under John Longland, 1521–1547*, Cambridge.

Bowman, F. P. (1974). 'Michelet et les métamorphoses de Christ', *Revue d'histoire littéraire de la France* 74, pp. 824–51.

Boyle, L. E. (1955). 'The *Oculus sacerdotis* and some other works of William of Pagula', *TRHS* fifth ser. 5, pp. 81–110.

(1956). 'A study of the works attributed to William of Pagula with special reference to the *Oculus sacerdotis* and *Summa summarum*', DPhil thesis, Oxford University.

(1974). 'The *quodlibets* of St Thomas and pastoral care', *The thomist* 38, pp. 232–56.

(1979). 'Robert Grosseteste and the pastoral care', *Mediaeval and Renaissance Studies* 8, pp. 3–51.

(1986). 'The inter-conciliar period 1179–1215 and the beginnings of pastoral manuals', *Miscellanea Rolando Bandinelli papa Alessandro III*, ed. F. Liotta, Siena, pp. 184–93.

Bradley, R. (1984). 'Julian of Norwich: writer and mystic', in *An introduction to the medieval mystics of England*, ed. P. E. Szarmach, Albany (NY), pp. 195–216.

Brady, M. T. (1954). 'The *Pore Caitif*: an introductory study', *Traditio* 10, pp. 529–48.

Braet, H. (1975). *Le Songe dans la chanson de geste au XIIe siècle*, Ghent.

Brand, J. and Rev. H. Ellis (1905). *Observations on popular antiquities chiefly illustrating the origin of our vulgar customs, ceremonies and superstitions*, 2 vols., London.

Braun, J. (1924). *Der christlichen Altar in seiner geschichtlichen Entwicklung*, 2 vols., Munich.

Bremond, C., Le Goff, J. and Schmitt, J.-C. (1982). *L' 'Exemplum'*, Typologie des sources du moyen-âge occidentale 40, Turnhout.

Breuer, W. (1970). *Die lateinische Eucharistiedichtung des Mittelalters von ihren Anfänge bis zum Ende des 13. Jahrhunderts*, Beihefte zum *Mittelalterliche Jahrbuch* 2, Wuppertal.

Brieger, P. (1957). *English art 1216–1307*, Oxford.

Brigden, S. (1984). 'Religion and social obligation in early sixteenth century London, *PP* 103, pp. 67–102.

Brigué, L. (1936). *Alger de Liège, un théologien de l'eucharistie au début du XIIe siècle*, Paris.

Brittain, F. (1953). *The medieval Latin and Romance lyric to AD 1300*, Cambridge.

Brooke, C. N. L. (1961). *From Alfred to Henry III, 871–1272*, Edinburgh.

(1971). 'Religious sentiment and church design in the later Middle Ages', in *Medieval church and society: collected essays*, London, pp. 162–82 [originally published in *Bulletin of the John Rylands library* 50 (1967–8), pp. 13–33].

(1974). *Monasteries of the world: the rise and development of the monastic tradition*, New York.

(1989). *The medieval idea of marriage*, Oxford.

Brooke, C. and Highfield, R. (1988). *Oxford and Cambridge*, Cambridge.

Brooks, N. C. (1933). 'Processional drama and dramatic procession in Germany in the High Middle Ages', *JEGP* 32, pp. 141–71.

(1936). 'An Ingolstadt Corpus Christi procession and the *Biblia pauperum*', *JEGP* 35, pp. 1–16.

Brooks, N. P. and Walker, H. E. (1978). 'The authority and interpretation of the Bayeux tapestry', *Anglo-Norman studies* 1, pp. 1–34.

Brouette, E. (1960). 'Un manuscrit de la vie de Ste Julienne de Cornillon écrit à Valduc', *Leodium* 47, pp. 5–13.

Browe, P. (1928a). 'Die Ausbreitung des Fronleichnamsfestes', *Jahrbuch für Liturgiewissenschaft* 8, pp. 107–43.

(1928b). 'Die eucharistische Speisewunder des Mittelalters', *Theologie und Glaube* 20, pp. 18–26.

(1929a). 'Die Elevation in der Messe', *Jahrbuch für Liturgiewissenschaft* 9, pp. 20–66.

(1929b). 'Die eucharistische Flurprozessionen und Wettersegen', *Theologie und Glaube* 21, pp. 742–55.

(1929c). 'Die eucharistische Verwandlungswunder des Mittelalters', *Römische Quartalschrift* 37, pp. 137–64.

(1929d). 'Die scholastische Theorie der eucharistischen Verwandlungswunder', *Theologische Quartalschrift* 110, pp. 305–32.

(1930). 'Die Eucharistie als Zaubermittel im Mittelalter', *Archiv für Kirchengeschichte* 20, pp. 134–54.

(1932). 'Die Kommunionvorbereitung im Mittelalter', *Zeitschrift für katholische Theologie* 56, pp. 375–415.

(1933). *Die Verehrung der Eucharistie im Mittelalter*, Munich, repr. Freiburg, 1967.

(1934). 'Die Kommunionersatz im Mittelalter', *EL* 48, pp. 534–48.

(1938a). *Die häufige Kommunion im Mittelalter*, Münster.

(1938b). *Die eucharistischen Wunder des Mittelalters*, Breslauer Studien zur historischen Theologie new ser. 4, Breslau.

(1940). *Die Pflichtkommunion im Mittelalter*, Münster and Regensburg, 1940.

(1950). 'Zur Geschichte des Dreifaltigkeitsfestes', *Archiv für Liturgiewissenschaft* 1, pp. 65–81.

Brown, C. (1934). 'Sermons and miracle plays', *MLN* 49, pp. 394–6.

Brown, D. C. (1987). *Pastor and laity in the theology of Jean Gerson*, Cambridge.

Brown, P. (1981). *The cult of the saints: its rise and function in Latin Christianity*, London.

(1988a). *The body and society: men, women, and sexual renunciation in early Christianity*, New York.

Brown, P. F. (1988b). *Venetian narrative painting in the age of Carpaccio*, New Haven (Conn.).

Brückner, W. (1958). *Die Verehrung des Heiligen Blutes in Walldürn*, Veröffentlichungen des Geistliches- und Kunstvereins Aschaffenburg 3, Aschaffenburg.

Bühler, C. F. (1964). 'Prayers and charms in certain Middle English scrolls', *Speculum* 39, pp. 270–78.

Bueschner, G. N. (1950). *The eucharistic theology of William Ockham*, Washington (DC).

Burns, T. and McLaughlin Jr., C. D. (1979). 'Ritual and social power', in *The structure of ritual: a biogenetic structural analysis*, ed. E. G. d'Aquili, C. D. McLaughlin Jr. and J. McManus, New York, pp. 249–79.

Burr, D. (1972). 'Scotus and transubstantiation', *MS* 34, pp. 336–50.

(1984). *Eucharistic presence and conversion in late fifteenth-century Franciscan thought*, Transactions of the American Philosophical Society 74,3, Philadelphia (PA).

Bynum, C. W. (1982a). 'Jesus as mother and abbot as mother: some themes in twelfth-century Cistercian writing', in *Jesus as mother. Studies in the spirituality of the High Middle Ages*, Berkeley (Ca.), pp. 110–69.

(1982b). 'Women mystics in the thirteenth century: the case of the nuns of Helfta', in *Jesus as mother. Studies in the spirituality of the High Middle Ages*, Berkeley (Ca.), pp. 170–262.

(1984). 'Women mystics and eucharistic devotion in the thirteenth century', *Women's studies* 11, pp. 179–214.

(1985). 'Fast, feast and flesh: the religious significance of food to medieval women', *Representations* 11, pp. 1–25.

(1986a). 'The body of Christ in the later Middle Ages: a reply to Leo Steinberg', *Renaissance quarterly* 39, pp. 394–439.

(1986b). 'Introduction: the complexity of symbols', in *Gender and religion: on the complexity of symbols*, ed. C. W. Bynum, S. Harrell, P. Richman, Boston (Mass.), pp. 1–20.

(1987). *Holy feast and holy fast: the religious significance of food to medieval women*, Berkeley (Ca.).

Cabrol, F. (1931). 'Le Culte de la Trinité dans la liturgie et l'institution de la fête de la Trinité', *EL* 45, pp. 270–8.

Calhoun, C. J. (1980). 'Community: towards a variable conceptualization for comparative research', *Social history* 5, pp. 105–29.

Calkins, R. G. (1983). *Illustrated books of the Middle Ages*, London.

Callaey, F. (1948). 'Documentazione eucharistica liegese, del vescovo de Liegi Roberto di Torote al pap Urbano IV (1240–1264)', in *Miscellanea Pio Paschini. Studia di storia ecclesiastica*, Lateranum new ser. 4, Rome, pp. 215–35 [repr. in *Eucaristia*, ed. A. Piolanti, Rome, 1957, pp. 907–33].

(1957). 'Origine e sviluppo della festa del "Corpus Domini" ', *Euntes docete* 10, pp. 3–33.

Callebaut, A. (1926). 'Autour de la rencontre à Florence de S. François et du Cardinal Huggolin (en été 1217)', *AFH* 19, pp. 530–58.

Cambiaso, D. (1917). *L'Anno ecclesiastico e le feste dei santi in Genova e loro svolgimento storico*, Genoa.

Camille, M. (1985). 'Seeing and reading: some visual implications of medieval literacy and illiteracy', *Art history* 8, pp. 26–49.

Camporesi, P. (1988). *The incorruptible flesh: bodily mutation and mortification in religion and folklore*, Cambridge.

(1989). 'The consecrated host: a wondrous excess', in *Fragments for a history of the human body*, ed. M. Feher, R. Nadaff and N. Tazi, 3 vols., New York, pp. 220–37.

Carmichael, A. G. (1989). 'Past fasts: medieval saints with the will to starve', *Journal of interdisciplinary history* 19, pp. 635–44.

Caspari, H. (1969). *Das Sakramentstabernakel in Italien bis zum Konzil von Trient, gestalt, Ikonographie und Symbolik, kultische Funktion*, Munich.

Cassee, E. (1980). *The missal of Cardinal Bertrand de Deax. A study in fourteenth-century Bolognese miniature painting*, Publicazioni dell'Istituto universitario olandese di storia dell'arte a Firenze 11, Florence.

Catto, J. (1985). 'John Wyclif and the cult of the eucharist', in *The bible in the medieval world: essays in memory of Beryl Smalley*, ed. K. Walsh and D. Wood, SCH Subsidia 4, Oxford, pp. 269–86.

Catto, J. I. 'Ideas and experience in the political thought of Aquinas', *PP* 71, pp. 3–21.

Cawley, A. C. (1955). 'The "grotesque" feast in the *Prima pastorum*', *Speculum* 30, pp. 213–17.

(1975). 'Medieval English metrical versions of the decalogue with reference to the English Corpus Christi cycles', *Leeds studies in English* new ser. 8, pp. 129–45.

Chadwick, H. (1989). '*Ego Berengarius*', *Journal of theological studies* new ser. 40, pp. 414–45.

Chaineux, M.-C. (1981). *Culture de la vigne et commerce du vin dans la région de Liège au moyen-âge*, Centre belge d'histoire rurale 65, Liège and Liguge.

Chambers, E. K. (1903). *The medieval stage*, 2. vols., Oxford.

Champion, B. A. (1980). 'The gilds of medieval Beverley', in *The medieval town in Britain*, ed. P. Riden, Cardiff papers in local history 1, Cardiff, pp. 51–66.

Chartier, R. (1984). 'Culture as appropriation: popular cultural uses in early modern France', in *Understanding popular culture: Europe from the Middle Ages to the nineteenth century*, ed. S. L. Kaplan, New Babylon. Studies in the Social Sciences 40, Berlin, pp. 229–53.

(1985). 'Text, symbols, and Frenchness', *Journal of modern history* 57, pp. 682–95.

(1987). 'Ritual and print, disruption and invention: the fête in France from the Middle Ages to the Revolution', in *The cultural uses of print in early modern France*, trans. L. G. Cochrane, Princeton (NJ), pp. 13–31.

(1988). *Cultural history: between practices and representations*, trans. L. G. Cochrane, Cambridge.

Cheetham, F. (1984). *English medieval alabasters with a catalogue of the collection in the Victoria and Albert Museum*, Oxford.

Cheney, C. R. (1972–73). 'Law and letters in fourteenth-century Durham: a study of Corpus Christi, Corpus Christi College, Cambridge, ms. 450', *Bulletin of the John Rylands Library* 55, pp. 60–85.

(1984). 'The gilds of the Blessed Virgin Mary and of Corpus Christi', *Corpus Association letter*, pp. 24–35.

Chenu, M. D. (1968). *Nature, man, and society in the twelfth century: essays on new theological perspectives in the Latin west*, ed. and trans. J. Taylor and L. K. Little, Chicago.

Chiffoleau, J. (1980). *La Comptabilité de l'au delà: les hommes, la mort et la religion dans la région d'Avignon à la fin du moyen-âge,* Publications de la Sorbonne, Histoire ancienne et médiévale 14, Rome.

(1984). *Les Justices du pape: délinquance et criminalité dans la région d'Avignon au quatorzième siècle,* Publications de la Sorbonne. Série histoire ancienne et médiévale 14, Paris.

Clapham, A. and Major, K. (1946). 'Lincolnshire priories, abbeys and parish churches', *Archaeological journal* 103, pp. 168–88.

Clark, A. (1980). 'The functions of the offertory rite in the mass', *EL* 64, pp. 309–44.

Clark, F. (1967). *Eucharistic sacrifice and the Reformation,* second edn, Oxford.

Clark, S. (1983). 'French historians and early modern culture', *PP* 100, pp. 62–99.

(1985). 'The *Annales* historians', in *The return of grand theory in the human sciences,* ed. Q. Skinner, Cambridge, pp. 177–98.

Clifford, J. (1983). 'On ethnographic authority', *Representations* 1, pp. 118–46.

Cohen, A. (1981). *The politics of elite culture: explorations in the dramaturgy of power in modern African society,* Berkeley (Ca.).

Colish, M. L. (1983). *The mirror of language. A study in the medieval theory of knowledge,* Lincoln (Nebraska), revised edn.

Collins Jr., F. (1932). 'Music in the craft cycles', *PMLA* 47, pp. 613–21.

(1972). *The production of medieval church music-drama,* Charlottesville (Va.).

Collon-Gevaert, S. (1951). *Histoire des arts du métal en Belgique,* Académie royale de Belgique, Classe des beaux-arts, Mémoires second ser. 7, Brussels.

Constable, G. (1971). 'Twelfth-century spirituality and the late Middle Ages', in *Renaissance studies in honor of Hans Baron,* ed. J. A. Tedeschi, Florence, pp. 3–28.

Conde, A. L. (1986). 'La liturgia de la misa en el sínodo del obispo de Segovia Pedro de Cuéllar, 1325', *Anuario de estudios medievales* 16, pp. 127–45.

Contreras Villar, A. (1987). 'La corte del Condestable Iranzo: la ciudad y la fiesta', in *La ciudad hispanica durante los siglos* XIII *al* XVI III, Madrid, pp. 305–22.

Cook, W. R. (1973). 'John Wyclif and Hussite theology 1415–1436', *Church history* 42, pp. 335–49.

Cope, M. (1979). *The Venetian chapel of the sacrament in the sixteenth century,* New York.

Cottiaux, J. (1963). 'L'Office liégeois de la Fête-Dieu, sa valeur et son destin', *RHE* 58, pp. 405–59.

Coulet, N. (1982). 'Processions, espace urbain, communauté civique', *Cahiers de Fanjeaux* 17, pp. 381–97.

Courtenay, W. J. (1978). *Adam Wodeham: an introduction to his life and writings,* Studies in medieval and reformation thought 21, Leiden.

Cowdrey, H. E. J. (1987). 'Towards an interpretation of the Bayeux tapestry', *Anglo-Norman studies* 10, pp. 49–65.

Cowling, D. (1976). 'The liturgical celebration of Corpus Christi in medieval York', *REED newsletter,* no. 2, pp. 5–9.

Cox, J. C. (1913). *Churchwardens' accounts from the thirteenth century to the close of the seventeenth century,* The Antiquary's books, London.

(1923). *English church fittings, furniture and accessories,* London.

Craddock, L. G. (1950). 'Franciscan influences on early English drama', *Franciscan studies* 10, pp. 383–417.

Craig, H. (1914). 'The Corpus Christi procession and the Corpus Christi play', *JEGP* 13, pp. 589–602.

(1955). *English religious drama of the Middle Ages*, Oxford.

Cristiani, M. (1968). 'La Controversia eucaristica nella cultura del secolo xi', *Studi medievali* 3rd ser. 9, pp. 167–233.

Crompton, J. (1968–9). 'Leicester Lollards', *Transactions of the Leicestershire archaeological and historical society* 44, pp. 11–44.

Cross, C. (1975). 'Popular piety and the records of the unestablished churches, 1460–1660', *SCH* 11, pp. 269–92.

(1978). '"Great reasoners in scripture": the activities of women Lollards', in *Medieval women*, ed. D. Baker, SCH Subsidia 1, Oxford, pp. 359–80.

Crowley, J. M. and Bloxham, R. N. (1967). 'Church wafer ovens', *The amateur historian* 7, pp. 161–5.

Cutts, E. L. (1914). *Parish priests and the people in the Middle Ages*, London.

Dale, W. S. A. (1984). '"Latens deitas": the holy sacrament altarpiece of Dieric Bouts', *Revue d'art canadienne/Canadian art review* 11, pp. 110–16.

Daris, J. (1891). *Histoire du diocèse et de la principauté de Liège pendant le xiii*ᵉ *et le xiv*ᵉ *siècles*, Liège.

Darnton, R. (1984). *The great cat massacre and other episodes in French cultural history*, New York.

Darsonville, Abbé (1902). 'Urbain IV et la Fête-Dieu à Laon', *Bulletin de la société d'art et d'histoire du diocèse de Liège* 13, pp. 297–402.

David, P. (1936). *Un Légendier roman du temps d'Innocent IV et d'Urbain IV*, Collectanea theologica 17, Lwow.

Davidson, C. (1977). *Drama and art*, Kalamazoo (Mich.).

Davies, W. (1983). 'Priests and rural communities in East Brittany in the ninth century', *Etudes celtiques* 20, pp. 177–97.

Davis, N. Z. (1973). 'The rites of violence: religious riots in sixteenth-century France', *PP* 59, pp. 51–91.

(1982). 'From popular religion to religious cultures', in *Reformation Europe: a guide to research*, ed. S. Ozment, St Louis (Mo.), pp. 321–42.

(1987). *Fiction in the archives. Pardon tales and their tellers in sixteenth century France*, Stanford (Ca.).

Delaissé, L. M. J. (1949). 'Le Remaniement d'un légendier témoin de l'évolution de la liturgie romane au xiii*ᵉ siècle (Paris lat. 755)', *Scriptorium* 3, pp. 26–44.

(1950). 'A la recherche des origines de l'office du Corpus Christi dans les manuscrits liturgiques', *Scriptorium* 4, pp. 220–39.

(1974). 'The importance of Books of Hours for the history of the medieval book', *Gatherings in honor of Dorothy E. Miner*, ed. U. E. McCracken, L. M. C. Randall and R. H. Randall Jr., Baltimore (Md.), pp. 203–35.

Delcorno, C. (1976). 'L' "Exemplum" nella predicazione di Bernardino da Siena', in *Bernardino predicatore nella società del suo tempo*, Convegni del Centro di studi sulla spiritualità medievale 16, Todi, pp. 71–107.

Delehaye, H. (1926–7). 'Les Lettres d'indulgence collectives', *Analecta bollandiana*

44 (1926), pp. 342–79, 45 (1927), pp. 97–123, 323–44; 46 (1928), pp. 149–57, 287–343.

Demay, G. (1880). *Le Costume au moyen-âge d'après les sceaux*, Paris.

Demus, O. (1968). (Completed by M. Hirmer). *Romanische Wandmalerei*, Munich.

Dendy, D. R. (1959). *The use of lights in Christian Worship*, Alcuin Club collections 41, London.

Denis, E. (1927). *Sainte Julienne et Cornillon*, Liège.

(1935). *La Vraie histoire de Sainte Julienne de Liège et de l'institution de la Fête-Dieu*, Paris and Tournai.

Dereine, C. (1951). 'L'Ecole canonique liégeoise et la reforme grégorienne', *Miscellanea tornacensia: mélanges d'archéologie et d'histoire. Annales du 33e congrès de la Fédération archéologique et historique de Belgique. Tournai 1949* II, Brussels, pp. 79–94.

Despy, G. (1953). 'Note sur les offices de la curie d'Avignon: les fonctions du *magister-capellae*', *Bulletin de l'institut historique belge de Rome* 28, pp. 21–30.

Destrée, J. (1930). 'Partie supérieure d'un tabernacle ou armoire du saint-sacrement', *Bulletin des musées royaux d'art et d'histoire* 2, pp. 119–23.

Devlin, D. (1975). 'Corpus Christi: a study in medieval eucharistic theory, development and practice', PhD thesis, University of Chicago.

Dickens, A. G. (1959). *Lollards and protestants in the diocese of York, 1509–1558*, Oxford.

Dolan, D. (1975). *Le Drame liturgique de Pâques en Normandie et en Angleterre au moyen-âge*, Publications de l'Université de Poitiers, lettres et sciences humaines 16, Paris.

Dolan, G. (1897). 'Devotion to the Sacred Heart in mediaeval England', *Dublin review* 120, pp. 373–85.

Dondaine, A. (1947). 'Le Manuel de l'inquisiteur (1230–1330)', *AFP* 17, pp. 85–194.

(1961). 'Les "opuscula fratris Thomae" chez Ptolémée de Lucques', *AFP* 31, pp. 142–203.

Dorrell, M. (1971). 'The mayor of York and the Coronation pageant', *Leeds studies in English* new ser. 5, pp. 35–45.

Dossat, Y. (1968). 'Les Cathars d'après des documents de l'inquisition', *Cahiers de Fanjeaux* 3, pp. 71–104.

(1976). 'Les Confréries de Corpus Christi dans le monde rural pendant la première moitié du XIVe siècle', *Cahiers de Fanjeaux* 11, pp. 365–85.

Douglas, M. D. (1970). *Natural symbols: explorations in cosmology*, London.

Douteil, H. (1969). *Studien zu Durantis 'Rationale divinorum officiorum' als kirchenmusikalische Quelle*, Kölner Beiträge zur Musikforschung 52, Regensburg.

Doyle, A. I. (1948). 'A prayer attributed to St Thomas Aquinas', *Dominican studies* 1, pp. 229–38.

Dronke, P. (1978). *The medieval lyric*, London, second edn.

(1984). *Women writers of the Middle Ages*, Cambridge.

Dugmore, C. W. (1958). *The mass and the English reformers*, London.

Dumoutet, E. (1925). 'Les Origins de la fête et de la procession du Saint-Sacrement', *La Vie et les arts liturgiques* 11, pp. 343–8.

(1925–6). 'L'Introït du premier Dimanche de l'Avent dans les missels à peintures du moyen-âge, *La Vie et les arts liturgiques* 12, pp. 34–6.

(1926). *Le Désir de voir l'hoste et les origines de la dévotion au saint-sacrement*, Paris.

(1928). 'Autour d'une dévotion médiévale', *Revue apologetique* 46, pp. 182–95.

(1931). 'Aux origines des saluts du saint-sacrament', *Revue apologetique* 52, pp. 409–31, 529–42.

(1932). *Le Christ selon la chaire et la vie liturgique au moyen-âge*, Paris.

(1942). *Corpus domini. Aux sources de la piété eucharistique médiévale*, Paris.

(1943–5). 'La Théologie de l'eucharistie à la fin du xiie siècle: le témoignage de Pierre le Chantre d'après la "Summa de sacramentis"', *Archives d'histoire doctrinale et littéraire du moyen-âge* 18–20, pp. 181–262.

Dunn, E. C. (1960). 'The medieval "cycle" as history play', *Studies in the Renaissance* 7, pp. 76–89.

(1973). 'Popular devotion in the vernacular drama of medieval England', *Mediaevalia et humanistica* 4, pp. 55–68.

Durkheim, E. (1915). *The elementary forms of the religious life*, trans. J. W. Swain, London.

Dutka, J. (1978). 'Mystery plays at Norwich: their formation and development', *Leeds studies in English* 10, pp. 107–20.

Duvernoy, J. (1976). 'L'Acception: "Haereticus" (Irelge) "parfait cathare" en Languedoc au xiiie siècle', in *The concept of heresy*, ed. W. Lourdaux and D. Verhelst, Mediaevalia lovaniensia ser. I studia 4, Louvain, pp. 198–210.

Dyer, C. (1983). 'English diet in the later Middle Ages', *Social relations and ideas. Essays in honour of R. H. Hilton*, ed. T. H. Aston, P. R. Coss and J. Thirsk, Cambridge, pp. 191–216.

Dykmans, M. (1972a). 'Le Missel de Clément V (1305–1314)', *EL* 86, pp. 449–73.

(1972b). 'Le Cérémonial de Grégoire X (vers 1273)', *Gregorianum* 53, pp. 535–65.

(1985). *Le Pontifical roman révisé du xve siècle*, Studi e testi 311, Vatican.

Ehrle, F. (1886–7). 'Zur Vorgeschichte des Concils von Vienne', *ALK* 2, (1886), pp. 353–416, 3 (1887), pp. 1–195.

(1888). 'Ein Bruchstück der Acten des Concils von Vienne', *ALK* 4, pp. 361–470.

Eisler, C. (1969). 'The golden Christ of Cortona and the Man of Sorrows in Italy', *Art bulletin* 51, pp. 107–18, 233–46.

Eleen, L. (1982). *The illustration of the Pauline epistles in French and English bibles of the twelfth and thirteenth centuries*, Oxford.

Endres, J.-A. (1917). 'Die Darstellung der Gregoriusmesse im Mittelalter', *Zeitschrift für christliche Kunst* 30, pp. 146–56.

Epiney-Burgard, G. (1984). 'L'Influence des beguines sur Ruusbroec', in *Jan Van Ruusbroec. The sources, content and sequels of his mysticism*, ed. P. Mommaers and N. de Paepe, Mediaevalia lovaniensia ser. I studia 12, Louvain, pp. 68–85.

Erb, P. C. (1971). 'Vernacular material for preaching in ms. Cambridge University Library Ii.3.8', *MS* 33, pp. 63–84.

Erikson, C. (1976). *The medieval vision: essays in history and perception*, Oxford.

Evennett, H. O. (1968). *The spirit of the Counter-Reformation*, Cambridge.

Farthing, J. L. (1988). *Thomas Aquinas and Gabriel Biel: interpretations of St Thomas Aquinas in German nominalism on the eve of the Reformation*, Duke monographs in medieval and Renaissance studies 9, Duke (NC).

Fehr, B. (1902). 'Die Lieder der Hs. Sloane 2593', *Archiv für das Studium der neueren Sprachen* 109, pp. 33–72.

Ferguson, G. (1954). *Signs and symbols in Christian art*, New York.

Fernandez, J. W. (1971). 'Persuasions and performances: of the beast in everybody and the metaphors of everyman', in *Myth, symbol, and culture*, ed. C. Geertz, New York, pp. 39–60.

(1974). 'The mission of the metaphor in expressive culture', *Current anthropology* 15, pp. 119–33.

(1977). 'The performance of ritual metaphors', in *The social use of metaphor: essays on the anthropology of rhetoric*, ed. J. D. Sapir and J. C. Crocker, Philadelphia (Pa), pp. 100–31.

(1982a). *Bwiti. An ethnography of the religious imagination in Africa*, Princeton (NJ).

(1982b). 'The dark at the bottom of the stairs: the inchoate in symbolic inquiry and some strategies for coping with it', in *On symbols in anthropology: essays in honor of Harry Hoijer*, ed. J. Maquet, Malibu (Ca.), pp. 13–43.

(1988). 'Historians tell tales: of Cartesian cats and Gallic cockfights', *Journal of modern history* 60, pp. 113–27.

Ferruolo, S. (1985). *The origins of the university: the schools of Paris and their critics, 1100–1215*, Stanford (Ca.).

Firth, R. (1973). *Symbols public and private*, London.

Fletcher, A. J. (1980). 'Unnoticed sermons from John Mirk's *Festial*', *Speculum* 55, pp. 514–22.

Forni, A. (1981). 'La "Nouvelle prédication" des disciples de Foulques de Neuilly: intentions, techniques et réactions', *Faire croire. Modalités de la diffusion et de la réception des messages religieux du XII<sup>e</sup> au XV<sup>e</sup> siècle*, Collections de l'Ecole française de Rome 51, Rome, pp. 19–37.

Forsyth, W. H. (1970). *The entombment of Christ: French sculptures in the fifteenth and sixteenth centuries*, Cambridge (Mass.).

Forsyth, I. H. (1972). *The throne of wisdom: wood sculptures of the Madonna in Romanesque France*, Princeton (NJ).

Fowler, J. T. (1912). 'On painted glass at St Anthony's Chapel, Cartmel Fell', *Transactions of the Cumbria and Westmorland antiquarian society* new ser. 12, pp. 297–311.

Franceschini, E. (1965). 'Origine e stile della bolla "Transiturus"', *Aevum* 39, pp. 218–43.

Franz, A. (1909). *Die kirchlichen Benediktionen im Mittelalter*, 2 vols., Frieburg.

(1963). *Die Messe im deutschen Mittelalter: Beiträge zur Geschichte der Litrugie und des religiösen Volkslebens*, Freiburg, 1902, repr. Darmstadt.

Freed, J. B. (1972). 'Urban development and the "cura monialium" in thirteenth-century Germany', *Viator* 3, pp. 311–27.

(1977). *The friars and German society in the thirteenth century*, Cambridge (Mass.).

Freiberg, J. (1988). *The Lateran and Clement VIII*, 2 vols., PhD thesis, New York University.

Friedländer, M. J. (1956). *Early Netherlandish painting from Van Eyck to Bruegel*, London.

Fries, M. (1984). 'Margery Kempe', in *An introduction to the medieval mystics of Europe*, ed. P. E. Szarmach, Albany (NY), pp. 217–35.

Fry, T. (1967). 'The antiquity of the tradition of triads in the English cycle plays', *American benedictine review* 18, pp. 465–81.

Fryer, A. C. (1902). 'On fonts with representations of the seven sacraments', *Archaeological journal* 59, pp. 17–66.

Fulton, R. (1987). 'The crowned bride: aspects of the cult of the Blessed Virgin Mary, with special reference to the Commentary of the Song of Songs by William of Newburgh', Diploma dissertation, Cambridge University.

Fumi, L. (1891). *Il duomo di Orvieto e i suoi restauri. Monografie storiche condotte sopra i documenti*, Rome.

Funkenstein, A. (1986). *Theology and the scientific imagination from the Middle Ages to the seventeenth century*, Princeton (NJ).

Fürstenberg, P. (1917). 'Zur Geschichte der Fronleichnamsfeier in der alten Diözese Paderborn', *Theologie und Glaube* 9, pp. 314–25.

Gabriel, A. L. (1955). *Student life in Ave Maria College, mediaeval Paris: history and chartulary of the college*, University of Notre Dame publications in mediaeval studies 14, Notre Dame (Ind.).

Galizzi, G. P. (1963). 'Le Scuole del Corpo di Cristo in uno statuto del quattrocento', *Bergamum* 37, pp. 23–38.

Gallet, R. M. (1946). 'Bibliographie bij het Festum Corporis Christi', in *Studia eucharistica*, pp. 428–50.

Galpern, A. N. (1975). *The religions of the people in sixteenth century Champagne*, Harvard historical studies 92, Cambridge (Mass.).

Gardiner, H. C. (1946). *Mysteries' end: an investigation of the last days of the medieval stage*, New Haven (Conn.), repr. 1967.

Gatzweiler, O. (1924). 'Die liturgischen Handschriften des Aachner Münsterstifts', *Zeitschrift der Aachner Geschichtsvereins* 46, pp. 1–222.

Gaudemet, J. (1973). 'La Paroisse au moyen-âge', *Revue d'histoire de l'Eglise de France* 59, pp. 5–21.

Geary, P. (1978). *Furta sacra: thefts of relics in the central Middle Ages*, Princeton (NJ)

Geertz, C. (1960). *The religion of Java*, Glencoe (Ill.).

(1971). *Islam observed: religious development in Morocco and Indonesia*, Chicago.

(1973a). 'Thick description: towards an interpretive theory of culture', in *The interpretation of cultures: selected essays*, New York, p. 3–30.

(1973b). 'Religion as a cultural system', in *The interpretation of cultures: selected essays*, New York, pp. 87–125.

(1979–80). 'Blurred genres', in *American scholar*, pp. 165–79.

(1980). *Negara: the theater state in nineteenth-century Bali*, Princeton (NJ).

(1983a). 'Common sense as a cultural system', in *Local knowledge: further essays in interpretive anthropology*, New York, pp. 73–93.

(1983b). 'Local knowledge: fact and law in comparative perspective', in *Local knowledge: further essays in interpretive anthropology*, New York, pp. 167–234.

(1985). 'Centers, kings and charisma: reflections on the symbolics of power', in *Rites of power: symbolism, ritual, and politics since the Middle Ages*, ed. S. Wilentz, Philadelphia (Pa.), pp. 13–38.

Geiselmann, J. R. (1926). *Die Eucharistielehre der Vorscholastik*, Paderborn.

Gellrich, J. M. (1985). *The idea of the book in the Middle Ages: language, theory, mythology and fiction*, Ithaca (NY).

Génicot, L. (1968). 'Haut clergé et noblesse dans le diocèse de Liège du XIᵉ au XVᵉ siècles', in *Adel und Kirche. Gerd Tellenbach zum 65. Geburtstag dargebracht von Freunden und Schülern*, Freiburg, pp. 237–58.

Georges, E. (1866). *Histoire du pape Urbain IV et son temps 1185–1264*, Arcis-sur-Aube.

Geremek, B. (1980). 'L'*Exemplum* et la circulation de la culture au moyen-âge', *Mélanges de l'Ecole français de Rome. Moyen-âge – temps modernes* 92, pp. 153–79.

Gerulaitis, L. V. (1967). 'The canonization of Saint Thomas Aquinas', *Vivarium* 5, pp. 25–46.

Gibson, G. M. (1981). 'Bury St Edmunds, Lydgate, a and the *N-town cycle*', *Speculum* 56, pp. 56–90.

Gibson, M. (1978). *Lanfranc of Bec*, Oxford.

Gietl, A. M. (1891). *Die Sentenzen Rolands nachmals Papstes Alexander III*, Freiburg.

Gilbert, C. E. (1974). 'Last Suppers and their refectories' in *The pursuit of holiness in late medieval and Renaissance religion*, ed. C. Trinkaus and H. A. Oberman, Leiden, pp. 371–402.

Gillespie, V. (1980). '*Doctrina* and *predicacio*: the design and function of some pastoral manuals', *Leeds studies in English* new ser. 11, pp. 36–50.

Ginzburg, C. (1980). *The cheese and the worms, the cosmos of a sixteenth-century miller*, trans. J. Tedeschi and A. Tedeschi, Baltimore (MD).

Gneuss, H. (1968). *Hymnar und Hymnen im englischen Mittelalter*, Buchreihe der Anglia Festschrift 12, Tübingen.

Godding, R. (1981). 'Une Oeuvre inédite de Thomas de Cantimpré', *RHE* 76, pp. 241–316.

Godwin, F. G. (1951). 'An illustration to the *De sacramentis* of St Thomas Aquinas', *Speculum* 26, pp. 609–14.

Goering, J. (1982). 'The changing face of the village parish. II. The thirteenth century', in *Pathways to medieval peasants*, ed. J. A. Raftis, PIMS Papers in mediaeval studies 2, Toronto, pp. 323–33.

Goffen, R. (1986). *Piety and patronage in Renaissance Venice: Bellini, Titian and the Franciscans*, New Haven (Conn.).

Goodgal, D. R. (1981). 'The iconography of the Ghent altarpiece', PhD thesis, University of Pennsylvania.

Goodich, M. (1981). 'The contours of female piety in later medieval hagiography', *Church history* 50, pp. 20–32.

Goody, J. (1983). *The development of family and marriage in Europe*, Cambridge.

Gougaud, L. (1923–4). 'Avant le coeur eucharistique de Jésus la plaie du coté et l'eucharistie', *La vie et les arts liturgiques* 10, pp. 160–9.

(1925). *Dévotions et pratiques ascétiques du moyen-âge*, Collection Pax 21, Paris.

(1927). *Devotional and ascetic practices in the Middle Ages*, trans. G. C. Bateman, London.

Grant, G. G. (1940). 'The elevation of the host: a reaction to the twelfth century heresy', *Theological studies* 1, pp. 228–50.

Gray, D. (1963). 'The five wounds of Our Lord', *Notes and queries* 208, pp. 50–1, 82–9, 127–34, 163–8.

(1972). *Themes and images in the medieval English religious lyric*, London.

(1974). 'Notes on Middle English charms', in *Chaucer and Middle English studies in honour of Russell Hope Robbins*, ed. B. Rowland, London, pp. 56–71.

Greene, R. L. (1960). 'The meaning of the Corpus Christi carol', *Medium aevum* 29, pp. 10–21.

Gregg, J. Y. (1977). 'The exempla of "Jacob's well": study in the transmission of medieval sermon stories', *Traditio* 33, pp. 359–80.

Grendi, E. (1965). 'Le Compagnie del SS. Sacramento a Genova', *Annali della Facoltà di giurisprudenza dell'Università degli studi di Genova* 4, pp. 454–80.

Grimberg, M. (1974). 'Carnaval et société urbaine xiv⁰–xvi⁰ siècles: le royaume dans la ville', *Ethnologie française* 4, pp. 215–44.

Grundmann, H. (1935). *Religiöse Bewegungen im Mittelalter. Untersuchungen über die geschichtlichen Zusammenhänge zwischen der Ketzerei, den Bettelorden und der religiösen Frauenbewegung im 12. und 13. Jahrhundert und über die geschichtlichen Grundlagen der deutschen Mystik*, Historische Studien 267, Berlin.

Guenée, B. and Lehoux, F. (1968). *Les Entrées royales françaises de 1328 à 1515*, Sources d'histoire médiévale 5, Paris.

Gueusquin-Barbichon, M.-F. (1977). 'Organisation sociale de trois trajets rituels (les Rogations, la Fête-Dieu et la St Roch) à Bazoches, Morvan', *Ethnologie française* 7, pp. 29–44.

Guillemain, B. (1962). *La Cour pontificale d'Avignon (1309–1376): étude d'une société*, Paris.

Guillereau, L. (1911–13). 'Chapitres généraux et statuts de Guillaume de Sabran abbé de Saint-Victor de Marseille (1294–1312)', *Revue Mabillon* ser 5 (1911–12), pp. 224–43, (1912–13), pp. 381–400.

Guillotin de Carson. (1879). 'Les Usages de l'église de Rennes au moyen-âge', *Revue de Bretagne et de Vendée* fifth ser. 5, pp. 5–16.

Gurevich, A. I. (1985). *Categories of medieval culture*, trans. G. L. Campbell, London.

(1988). *Medieval popular culture: problems of belief and perception*, trans. J. M. Bak and P. A. Hollingsworth, Cambridge.

Gwynn, A. (1937–8). 'The sermon diary of Richard FitzRalph, archbishop of Armagh', *Proceedings of the Royal Irish Academy* 46, pp. 1–57.

Gy, P.-M. (1960). 'Collectaire, rituel, processionel', *RSPT* 44, pp. 441–69.

(1980a). 'L'Office du Corpus Christi et S. Thomas d'Aquin: état d'une recherche', *RSPT* 64, pp. 491–507.

(1980b). 'Les Paroles de la consécration et l'unité de la prière eucharistique selon les théologiens de Pierre Lombard à S. Thomas d'Aquin', in *Lex orandi, lex credendi: miscellanea in onore di p. Cipriano Vagaggini*, ed. G. J. Bekes and G. Farnedi, Rome, pp. 221–33.

(1982). 'L'Office du Corpus Christi et la théologie des accidents eucharistiques', *RSPT* 66, pp. 81–6.

(1983). 'La Relation au Christ dans l'eucharistie selon S. Bonaventure et S. Thomas d'Aquin', in *Sacrements de Jesus-Christ*, ed. J. Doré, Jesus et Jesus-Christ 12, Paris, pp. 69–106.

(1984). 'La Bible dans la liturgie au moyen-âge', in *Le Moyen-âge et la bible*, ed. P. Riché and G. Lobrichon, Bibliothèque de tous les temps 4, Paris, pp. 537–52.

(1985). 'Bulletin de liturgie', *RSPT* 69, pp. 310–19.

Haas, A. M. (1983). 'Themen und Aspekten der Mystik Mechtilds', in *Temi e problemi della mystica feminile trecentesca*, Convegno del Centro di studi sulla spiritualità medievale 20, Todi, pp. 47–83.

Hackett, M. B. (1970). *The original statutes of Cambridge University: the text and its history*, Cambridge.

Häring, N. (1948). 'Berengar's definitions of *sacramentum* and their influence on medieval theology', *MS* 10, pp. 109–46.

(1958). 'A study in the sacramentology of Alger of Liège', *MS* 20, pp. 41–78.

(1976). 'The interaction between canon law and sacramental theology in the twelfth century', in *Proceedings of the fourth international congress of medieval canon law*, ed. S. Kuttner, Monumenta iuris canonici ser. C, subdidia 5, Vatican, pp. 483–93.

Hahn, T. (1988). 'Female voice, male authority, and Chaucer's Prioress', unpublished paper.

Haimerl, T. X. (1937). *Die Prozessionswesen des Bistum Bamberg im Mittelalter*, Münchner Studien zur historischen Theologie 14, Munich.

Hall, M. B. (1974). 'The *tramezzo* in Santa Croce, Florence, reconstructed', *Art bulletin* 56, pp. 325–41.

Hamilton, W. E. M. C. (1942). 'L'Interpretation mystique de *La Queste del Saint Graal*', *Neophilologus* 27, pp. 94–110.

Harding, C. (1988). 'Pictorial narrative and religious experience in fourteenth-century Italy', unpublished paper.

Hardison, O. B. (1965). *Christian rite and Christian drama in the Middle Ages*, Baltimore (Md.).

Harmening, D. (1977). *Superstitio. Uberlieferungs- und theoriegeschichtliche Untersuchungen zur kirchlich-theologischen Aberglaubensliteratur des Mittelalters*, Berlin.

Harty, K. J. (1981). 'The Norwich Grocers' play and its three cyclic counterparts: four English mystery plays on the fall of man', *Studia neophilologica* 53, pp. 77–89.

Hatfield, R. (1970). 'The Compagnia de'magi', *JWCI* 33, pp. 107–61.

Häussling, A. A. (1986). 'Literaturbericht zum Fronleichnamsfest', *Jahrbuch für Volkskunde* new ser. 9, pp. 228–40.

Heath, P. (1984). 'Urban piety in the later Middle Ages: the evidence of Hull wills', in *The church, politics and patronage in the fifteenth century*, ed. B. Dobson, Gloucester, pp. 209–34.

Heers, J. (1973). 'Les Métiers et les fêtes "médiévales" en France du Nord et en Angleterre', *Revue du Nord* 55, pp. 193–206.

(1985). *Espaces publiques et espaces privés dans la ville: le Liber Terminorum de Bologne (1294)*, Cultures et civilisations médiévales 3, Paris.

Hefele, C. J. and Leclercq, H. (1912–15). *Histoire des conciles* v–vi, Paris.

Heffernan, T. J. (1984). 'Sermon literature', in *Middle English prose: a critical guide to major authors and genres*, ed. A. S. G. Edwards, Rutgers (NJ), pp. 177–207.

Heilig, K. J. (1935–6). 'Die Einführung des Fronleichnamsfestes in der Konstanzer Diözese nach einer vergessenen Urkunde Bischof Heinrichs III. von Brandis', *Zeitschrift für die Geschichte des Oberrheins* 49, pp. 1–16.

Heimpl, H. (1972). 'Characteristics of the late Middle Ages in Germany', in *Pre-Reformation Germany*, ed. G. Strauss, London, pp. 43–72.

Heitz, C. (1974). 'Architecture et liturgie processionelle à l'époque préromane', *Revue de l'art* 24, pp. 30–47.

Hendrix, G. (1978). 'Primitive versions of Thomas of Cantimpré's *Vita Liutgardis*', *Cîteaux* 29, pp. 153–206.

Herrmann-Mascard, N. (1975). *Les Reliques des saints. Formation coutumière d'un droit*, Société d'histoire du droit. Collection d'histoire institutionelle et sociale 6, Paris.

Hills, P. (1983). 'Piety and patronage in cinquecento Venice: Tintoretto and the *scuole del sacramento*', *Art history* 6, pp. 30–43.

Hindringer, R. (1932). *Weiheross und Rossweihe*, Munich.

Hirn, Y. (1958). *The sacred shrine*, London.

Hissette, R. (1977). *Enquête sur les 291 articles condamnées à Paris le 7 Mars 1277*, Louvain and Paris.

Hodgson, P. (1948). '*Ignorancia sacerdotum:* a fifteenth-century discourse on the Lambeth constitutions', *Review of English studies* 24, pp. 1–11.

Hödl, L. (1962). 'Die Confessio Berengarii von 1059', *Scholastik* 37, pp. 370–94.

Holdsworth, C. J. (1963). 'Visions and visionaries in the Middle Ages', *History* 48, pp. 141–53.

Hontoir, C. (1946a). 'La Dévotion au saint sacrement chez les premiers cisterciens (XIIᵉ–XIIIᵉ siècles)', *Studia eucharistica*, pp. 132–56.

(1946b). 'Ste-Julienne et les cisterciens', *Collectanea ordinis Cisterciensium reformatorum* 8, pp. 109–16.

Horrox, R. (1989). 'Medieval Beverley', *A history of Yorkshire. East Riding* VI, VCH, London, pp. 2–62.

Hoy, J. F. (1973–4). 'On the relationship of the Corpus Christi plays to the Corpus Christi procession at York', *Modern philology* 71, pp. 166–8.

Hsia, R. P.-C. (1988). *The myth of ritual murder: Jews and magic in Reformation Germany*, New Haven (Conn.) and London.

Hudson, A. (1973). 'The examination of Lollards', *Bulletin of the Institute of Historical Research* 46, pp. 145–59.

(1978). 'A neglected Wycliffite text', *JEH* 29, pp. 257–79.

(1984). 'Wycliffite prose', in *Middle English prose: a critical guide to major authors and genres*, ed. A. S. G. Edwards, Rutgers (NJ), pp. 249–70.

(1985). 'A new look at the *Lay folks' catechism*', *Viator* 16, pp. 243–58.

(1986). 'Wycliffism in Oxford 1381–1411', in *Wyclif in his times*, ed. A. Kenny, Oxford, pp. 67–84.

(1988a) 'The *Lay folks' catechism:* a postscript', *Viator* 19, pp. 307–9.

(1988b). *The premature reformation*, Oxford.

(1988c). 'The mouse in the pyx: popular heresy and the eucharist', unpublished paper.

Hughes, A. (1982). *Medieval manuscripts for mass and office: a guide to their organization and terminology*, Toronto.

Hughes, P. (1986). *Worcester streets: Blackfriars*, Worcester.

Hughes, M. E. J. (1983). ' "The feffement that Fals hath ymaked": a study of the image of the document in Middle English literature', CUL Le Bas Prize Essay 7.

Hughes, J. (1988). *Pastors and visionaries: religion and secular life in late medieval Yorkshire*, Woodbridge.

Iser, W. (1974). 'The reading process: a phenomenological approach;, in *New directions in literary history*, ed. R. Cohen, Baltimore (Md.).

Iserloh, E. (1961). 'Der Wert der Messe in der Diskussion der Theologen vom Mittelalter bis zum 16. Jahrhundert', *Zeitschrift für katholische Theologie* 83, pp. 44–79.

James, E. O. (1961). *Seasonal feasts and festivals*, London.

James, M. (1983). 'Ritual, drama and social body in the late medieval town', *PP* 98, pp. 3–29.

Jodogne, O. (1972). 'Le Théâtre français du moyen-âge: recherches sur l'aspect dramatique des textes', in *The medieval drama*, ed. S. Sticca, Albany (NY), pp. 1–21.

Jörres, P. (1902). 'Beiträge zur Geschichte der Einführung des Fronleichnamsfestes im Nordwesten des alten deutschen Reiches', *Römische Quartalschrift* 16, pp. 170–80.

Johnston, A. F. (1973–4). 'The procession and play of Corpus Christi in York after 1426', *Leeds studies in English* new ser. 7, pp. 55–62.

(1975). 'The plays of the religious guilds of York: the Creed play and the Pater Noster play', *Speculum* 50, pp. 55–90.

(1976). 'The guild of Corpus Christi and the procession of Corpus Christi in York', *MS* 38, pp. 372–84.

Johnston, A. F. and Dotrell, M. (1971). 'The Doomsday pageant of the York mercers, 1433', *Leeds studies in English* new ser. 5, pp. 29–34.

(1972). 'The York mercers and their pageant of Doomsday, 1433–1526', *Leeds studies in English* new ser. 6, pp. 10–35.

Jolly, K. L. (1985). 'Anglo-Saxon charms in the context of a Christian world view', *Journal of medieval history* 11, pp. 279–93.

Jones, C. (1985). 'Hospitals in seventeenth-century France', *Seventeenth-century French studies* 7, pp. 139–52.

Jones, W. R. (1973). 'Lollards and images: the defense of religious art in later medieval England', *Journal of the history of ideas* 34, pp. 27–50.

Jordan, W. C. (1979). *Louis IX and the challenge of the crusade: a study in rulership*, Princeton (NJ).

Jorissen, H. (1965). *Die Entfaltung der Transsubstantiationslehre bis zum Beginn der Hochscholastick*, Münsterische Beiträge zur Theologie 28 (1), Münster.

Jungmann, J. (1951–5). *The mass of the Roman rite*, New York.

(1962). *Missarum sollemnia: eine genetische Erklärung der römischen Messe*, fifth rev. edn, Vienna, Friedburg and Basel.

Kahrl, S. J. (1973). 'The civic religious drama of medieval England: a review of recent scholarship', *Renaissance drama* new ser. 6, pp. 237–48.

(1985). 'Secular life and popular piety in medieval England', in *The popular literature of medieval England*, ed. T. J. Heffernan, Tennessee studies in literature 28, Knoxville, pp. 85–107.

Kaminsky, H. (1967). *A history of the Hussite revolution*, Berkeley (Ca.).

Kaufmann, A. (1862). *Caesarius von Heisterbach. Ein Beitrag zur Kulturgeschichte des zwölften Jahrhunderts*, Cologne.

Keeler, W. (1987). *Javanese shadow plays, Javanese selves*, Princeton (NJ).

Keen, M. (1986a). 'The influence of Wyclif', in *Wyclif in his times*, ed. A. Kenny, Oxford, pp. 127–45.

(1986b) 'Wyclif, the Bible, and transubstantiation', in *Wyclif in his times*, ed. A. Kenny, Oxford, pp. 1–16.

Kellner, K. A. H. (1908). *Heortology: a history of the Christian festivals from their origin to the present day*, International Catholic library 14, London.

Kelly, H. A. (1985). *The devil at baptism: ritual, theology, and drama*, Ithaca (NY).

Kemmler, F. (1984). *'Exempla' in context: a historical and critical study of Robert Manyng of Brunne's 'Handlyng synne'*, Tübingen.

Kempf, F. (1973). 'Chiesa territoriale e chiesa romana nel secolo VIII', in I *problemi dell'occidente nel secolo* VIII, Settimana di studi, Spoleto, pp. 293–317.

Kennedy, V. L. (1940). 'The Franciscan *Ordo missae* in the thirteenth century', *MS* 2, pp. 204–22.

(1943). 'A handbook of Master Peter Chancellor of Chartres', *MS* 5, pp. 1–38.

(1944). 'The moment of consecration and the elevation of the host', *MS* 6, pp. 121–50.

(1946). 'The date of the Parisian decree on the elevation of the host', *MS* 8, pp. 87–96.

Kern, A. (1954). 'Das Offizium "De corpore christi" in österreichischen Bibliotheken', *RB* 64, pp. 46–67.

Khare, R. S. (1977). 'Prestations and prayers: two homologous systems in northern India', in *Language and thought: anthropological perspectives*, ed. W. C. MacCormack and S. Wurm, The Hague, p. 295–307.

Kieckhefer, R. (1984). *Unquiet souls: fourteenth-century saints and their religious milieu*, Chicago and London.

(1989). *Magic in the Middle Ages*, Cambridge.

Kightly, C. (1975). 'The early Lollards. A survey of popular Lollard activity in England, 1382–1428', PhD thesis, University of York.

King, A. A. (1957). *The liturgy of the Roman church*, London and New York.

(1965). *Eucharistic reservation in the western church*, London.

Kinn, J. W. (1960). *The pre-eminence of the eucharist among the sacraments according to Alexander of Hales, St Albert the Great, St Bonaventure and St*

*Thomas Aquinas,* Pontifica facultas theologica seminarii Sanctae Mariae ad Lacum, Dissertationes ad lauream 31, Mundelein (Ill.).

Klein, T. H. (1962). *Die Prozessionsgwsänge der Mainzer Kirche aus dem 14. bis 18. Jahrhundert,* Quellen und Abhandlungen zur mittelalterlichen Kirchengeschichte 7, Speyer.

Kolve, V. A. (1966). *The play called Corpus Christi,* London.

Kreider, A. (1979). *English chantries: the road to dissolution,* Cambridge (Mass.).

Kretzmann, P. E. (1916). *The liturgical element in the earliest forms of medieval drama, with special reference to England and German plays,* Studies in language and literature 4, Minneapolis (Mn.).

Kully, R. M. (1979). 'Le Drame religieux en Allemagne: une fête populaire', in *La Culture populaire au moyen-âge,* ed. P. Boglioni, Montreal, pp. 203–30.

Kupper, J.-L. (1981). *Liège et l'église impériale, xi^e–xii^e siècles,* Bibliothèque de la Faculté de philosophie et lettres de l'Université de Liège 228, Paris.

Kurth, G. (1909). *La Cité de Liège au moyen-âge* I, Brussels and Liège.

Kuttner, S. (1964). 'The date of the constitution "Saepe", the Vatican manuscripts and the Roman edition of the Clementines', in *Mélanges Eugène Tisserant* IV, Studi e testi 234, Vatican, pp. 427–52.

(1965). 'The *Apostillae* of Johannes Andreae on the Clementines', in *Etudes d'histoire du droit canonique dediées à Gabriel Le Bras* I, Paris, pp. 195–201.

La Capra, D. (1988). 'Chartier, Darnton, and the great symbol massacre', *Journal of modern history* 60, pp. 95–112.

Lacroix, B. and Landry, A.-M. (1979). 'Quelques thèmes de la religion populaire chez le théologien Thomas d'Aquin', in *La Culture populaire au moyen-âge,* ed. P. Boglioni, Montreal, pp. 163–81.

Ladner, G. B. (1961). 'The gestures of prayer in papal iconography of the thirteenth and early fourteenth centuries', in *Didascaliae: studies in honor of Anslem M. Albareda,* ed. S. Prete, New York, pp. 245–75.

Lambert, M. D. (1977). *Medieval heresy: popular movements from Bogomil to Hus,* London.

Lambot, C. (1942). 'L'Office de la Fête-Dieu; aperçus nouveaux sur ses origines', *RB* 54, pp. 61–123.

(1946a). 'Eve de St. Martin et les premiers historiens liégeois de la Fête-Dieu', *Studia eucharistica,* pp. 10–36.

(1946b). 'La Fête-Dieu à Fosses à 1246', *Revue diocésain de Namur* 1, pp. 156–65. [repr *RB* 79 (1969), pp 215–22].

(1946c). 'Un précieux manuscrit de la vie de Sainte Julienne du Mont-Cornillon', *Miscellanea historica in honorem Alberti de Meyer,* Recueil des travaux d'histoire et de philologie ser. 3 fasc. 22, Louvain, I, pp. 603–12.

(1947). 'Les Anciennes Peintures de l'église de Cornillon représentant l'histoire de Ste. Julienne', *Bulletin de la Société royale Le Vieux Liège* 71 (1947), pp. 173–6 [repr. *RB* 79 (1969), pp. 255–60].

(1948). 'La Bulle d'Urbain IV à Eve de St Martin sur l'institution de la Fête-Dieu', *Scriptorium* 2 (1948), pp. 69–77 [repr. *RB* 79 (1969), pp. 261–70].

(1969). 'Une oeuvre liégeoise inédite de Jacques de Troyes le futur pape Urbain IV', *RB* 79, pp. 305–15.

Lambot, C. and Fransen, I. (1946). *L'Office de la Fête-Dieu primitive,* Maredsous.

Lane, G. B. (1970). 'The development of medieval devotional gestures', PhD thesis, University of Pennsylvania.

(1984). *The altar and the altarpiece: sacramental themes in early Netherlandish painting*, New York.

Laurentin, R. (1952–3). *Maria, ecclesia, sacerdotium*, 2 vols., Paris.

Lauwers, M. 1987). '"Religion populaire", culture folklorique, mentalité. Notes pour une anthropologie culturelle du moyen âge', *RHE* 28, pp. 221–58.

Lavin, M. A. (1967). 'The altar of Corpus Domini in Urbino: Paolo Uccello, Joos Van Ghent, Piero della Francesca', *Art bulletin* 49, pp. 1–24.

(1977). 'The mystic winepress in the Mérode altarpiece', in *Studies in late medieval and Renaissance painting in honor of Millard Meiss*, ed. I. Lavin and J. Plummer, New York, I, pp. 297–301, II, pp. 103–5.

Lawn, B. (1963). *The Salernitan questions, an introduction to the history of medieval and Renaissance problem literature*, Oxford.

Lazzarini, A. (1952a). 'La mancata effetuazione della bolla "Transiturus" (1264)', *Archivio storico italiano* 110, pp. 205–15.

(1952b). *Il miracolo di Bolsena. Testimonianze e documenti dei secoli* XIII *e* XIV, Rome.

Lea, H. C. (1888). *A history of the inquisition of the Middle Ages*, 3 vols., New York, repr. 1922.

Leach, A. F. (1893–5). (no title) *Proceedings of the Society of Antiquaries of London* second ser. 15, pp. 103–18.

Lears, T. J. J. (1985). 'The concept of cultural hegemony: problems and possibilities', *AHR* 90, pp. 567–93.

Le Bras, G. (1940–1). 'Les Confréries chrétiennes: problèmes et propositions', *Revue historique de droit français et étranger* 19–20, pp. 310–63.

Lecler, J. (1964). *Vienne*, Histoire des conciles oecuméniques 8, Paris.

Lefèvre, P. (1947). 'Un problème de chronologie liégeoise au XIII⁰ siècle. La date primitive de la Fête-Dieu', *RHE* 42, pp. 417–22.

(1957). *La liturgie de Premontré: histoire, formulaire, chant et ceremonial*, Bibliotheca analectorum praemonstratensium 1, Louvain.

Legg, J. W. (1890). 'On an inventory in the vestry in Westminster Abbey, taken in 1388', *Archaeologia* 52, pp. 195–286.

Le Goff, J. (1984). *The birth of purgatory*, trans. A. Goldhammer, Chicago.

Leguay, J.-P. (1975). 'La Confrérie des merciers de Rennes au XV⁰ siècle. Contribution à l'histoire économique et sociale de la ville de Rennes', *Francia* 3, pp. 147–220.

Lejeune, J. (1948). *Liège et son pays: naissance d'une patrie* (XIII⁰–XIV⁰*siècles*), Liège.

Lerner, R. (1972). *The heresy of the Free Spirit in the later Middle Ages*, Los Angeles (Ca.).

(1985). 'Poverty, preaching, and eschatology in the revelation commentaries of 'Hugh of St Cher', in *The bible in the medieval world: essays in memory of Beryl Smalley*, ed. K. Walsh and D. Wood, SCH Subsidia 4, Oxford, pp. 157–89.

Le Roy Ladurie, E. (1978). *Montaillou: cathars and catholics in a French village*, trans. B. Bray, London.

(1980). *Carnival in Romans: a people's uprising at Romans, 1579–1580*, trans. M. Feeney, London.

Lestrade, J. (1937). 'Fondation de la confrérie du Saint-Sacrement à Buzet-sur-Tarn en 1344', *Revue historique de Toulouse* 24, pp. 231–8.

Lévi-Strauss, C. (1972). *The savage mind*, second edn., London.

Lewry, O. (1981). 'Boethian logic in the medieval west', in *Boethius: his life, thought and influence*, ed. M. Gibson, Oxford, pp. 90–134.

Light, L. (1987). 'The new thirteenth-century bible and the challenge of heresy', *Viator* 18, pp. 257–88.

Little, A. G. and Easterling, R. C. (1927). *The Franciscans and Dominicans of Exeter*, Exeter.

Longère, J. (1975). *Oeuvres oratoires des maîtres parisiens au XII$^e$ siècle: étude historique et doctrinale*, 2 vols., Paris.

Loomis, R. S. (1963). *The grail: from Celtic myth to Christian symbolism*, Cardiff.

Loomis, R. S. with Loomis, L. H. (1938). *Arthurian legends in medieval art*, New York.

Lovatt, R. (1982). 'Henry Suso and the medieval mystical tradition', in *The medieval mystical tradition in England. Papers read at Dartington Hall, July 1982*, ed. M. Glasscoe, Exeter, pp. 47–62.

de Lubac, H. (1949). *Corpus mysticum: l'eucharistie et l'église au moyen-âge. Etude historique*, Théologie: études publiées sous la direction de la Faculté de Théologie S. J. de Lyon-Fouvière 3, second rev. edn, Paris.

Luhrmann, T. M. (1989). *Persuasions of the witch's craft*, Oxford.

Lukes, S. (1977). 'Political ritual and social integration', in *Essays in social theory*, London, pp. 52–73, 205–10.

MacCulloch, J. A. (1932). *Medieval faith and fable*, London.

MacDonald, A. J. (1930). *Berengar and the reform of sacramental doctrine*, London.

McDonnell, E. W. (1954). *Beguines and beghards in medieval culture*, New Brunswick (NJ).

MacGarry, L. (1936). *The holy eucharist in Middle English homiletic and devotional verse: a dissertation*, Washington (DC).

McGinniss, F. J. (1988). '*Roma sancta* and the saint: eucharist, chastity, and the logic of Catholic reform', *Historical reflections* 15, pp. 99–116.

McGuire, B. P. (1981). 'The Cistercians and the transformation of friendship', *Analecta Cisterciensia* 37, pp. 3–65.

(1985). 'Monastic friendship and toleration in twelfth-century Cistercian life', *SCH* 22, pp. 147–60.

McHardy, A. K. (1972). 'Bishop Buckingham and the Lollards of Lincoln diocese', *SCH*, pp. 131–45.

Machin, G. I. T. (1983). 'The liberal government and the eucharistic procession of 1908', *JEH* 34, pp. 559–83.

Mackerell, B. (1738). *The history and antiquities of the flourishing corporation of King's Lynn in the county of Norfolk*, London.

MacKinnon, H. (1969). 'William de Montibus: a medieval teacher', in *Essays in medieval history presented to Bertie Wilkinson*, ed. T. A. Sandquist and M. R. Powicke, Toronto, pp. 32–45.

McNeir, W. F. (1951). 'The Corpus Christi Passion plays as dramatic art', *Studia philologica* 48, pp. 601–28.

Macy, G. (1973). 'The theological fate of Berengar's oath of 1059: interpreting a blunder become tradition', in *Interpreting tradition. The art of theological reflection* 29, pp. 27–38.

(1984). *The theologies of the eucharist in the early scholastic period*, Oxford.

(1988) 'Berengar's legacy as heresiarch', unpublished paper.

(1989). 'Reception of the eucharist according to the theologians: a case of theological diversity in the thirteenth and fourteenth centuries', unpublished paper.

Mâle, E. (1928). *L'Art religieux de la fin du moyen-âge en France: Etude sur l'iconographie du moyen-âge et sur ses sources d'inspiration*, third edn, Paris.

(1932) *L'Art religieux de la fin du XVI$^e$ siècle, du XVII$^e$ et du XVIII$^e$ siècle*, Paris.

(1940). *L'Art religieux du XII$^e$ siècle en France*, fourth edn, Paris.

Mandrou, R. (1975). *De la culture populaire aux XVII$^e$ et XVIII$^e$ siècles: la Bibliothèque bleue de Troyes*, Paris.

Mann, J. (1979). 'Eating and drinking in "Piers Plowman" ', *Essays and studies* new ser. 32, pp. 26–43.

Marrow, J. H. (1979). *Passion iconography in northern European art of the late Middle Ages and the early Renaissance*, Ars neerlandica 1, Kortrijk.

Marsicano, V. (1982). 'Adaptations of the pseudo-Augustine *Sermon against the Jews* in the *Benediktbeuern Christmas play* and the *Frankfurt Passion play*', *Colloquia germanica* 15, pp. 59–65.

Martin, J. H. (1975). 'The eucharistic treatise of John Quidort of Paris', *Viator* 6, pp. 195–240.

Mason, E. (1976). 'The role of the English parishioner, 1100–1500', *JEH* 27, pp. 17–29.

Masters, R. (1831). *History of the College of Corpus Christi and the Blessed Virgin Mary in the University of Cambridge*, ed. J. Lamb, London.

Matarasso, P. (1979). *The redemption of chivalry: a study of the Quest del Graal*, Geneva.

Matern, G. (1962). *Zur Vorgeschichte und Geschichte de Fronleichnamsfeier besonders in Spanien*, Sprache Forschungen des Görresgesellschaft 2, Münster.

Mayer, A. L. (1938). 'Die heilbringende Schau in Sitte und Kult', in *Heilige Uberlieferung. Festschrift für Ildefons Herwegen*, ed. O. Casel, Münster, pp. 234–62.

Meersseman, G. G. (1948). 'Les Frères prêcheurs et le mouvement dévot en Flandre au XIII$^e$ siècle', *AFP* 19, pp. 69–130.

Megivern, J. J. (1963). *Concomitance and communion. A study in eucharistic doctrine and practice*, Studia Friburgiensia new ser. 33, Freiburg.

Meiss, M. (1968). *French painting in the time of Jean de Berry. The Boucicaut master*, London.

Meredith, P. (1981). 'The York cycle and the beginning of vernacular religious drama in England', in *Le laudi drammatiche umbre delle origini. Atti del V convegno di studio, Viterbo 1980*, Viterbo, pp. 311–33.

Mérimée, H. (1913). *L'Art dramatique à Valencia*, Toulouse.

Merlo, G. G. (1977). *Eretici e inquisitori nella società piemontese del trecento,* Turin.

(1981). 'Coercion et orthodoxie: modalités de communication et d'imposition d'un message religieux hégémonique', in *Faire croire. Modalités de la diffusion et de la réception des messages religieux du XIIᵉ au XVᵉ siècles,* Collections de l'Ecole française de Rome 51, Rome, pp 101–18.

Mertes, R. G. K. A. (1987). 'The household as a religious community', in *People, politics and community in the later Middle Ages,* ed. J. Rosenthal and C. Richmond, Gloucester, pp. 123–39.

Messenger, R. E. (1953). *The medieval Latin hymn,* Washington (DC).

Michael, W. (1972). 'Tradition and originality in the medieval drama in Germany', in *The medieval drama,* ed. S. Sticca, Albany, (NY), pp. 23–37.

Michaud-Quantin, P. (1962). *Sommes de casuistique et manuels de confessions au moyen-âge (XIIᵉ–XVIᵉ siècles),* Paris.

(1970a). *Universitas: expressions du mouvement communautaire dans le moyen-âge latin,* Paris.

(1970b). 'Les Méthodes de la pastorale du XIIIᵉ au XVᵉ siècle', in *Methoden in Wissenschaft und Kunst des Mittelalters,* ed. A. Zimmermann, Miscellanea mediaevalia 7, Berlin, pp. 76–91.

Mill, A. J. (1950). 'The York plays of the Dying, Assumption and Coronation of Our Lady', *PMLA* 65, pp. 866–76.

Mitterwieser, A. (1930). *Geschichte der Fronleichnamsprozession in Bayern,* Munich.

Mollat, G. (1965). *Les papes d'Avignon,* fourth edn, Paris.

de Montclos, J. (1971). *Lanfranc et Bérengar: la controverse eucharistique du XIᵉ siècle,* Spicilegium sacrum Lovaniense. Etudes et documents 37, Louvain.

Monter, E. W. (1983). *Ritual, myth and magic in early modern Europe,* Brighton.

Moran, J. A. H. (1985). *The growth of English schooling: learning, literacy, laicization in pre-Reformation York diocese,* Princeton (NJ).

Morin, D. G. (1910). 'L'Office cistercien pour la Fête-Dieu comparé avec celui de saint Thomas d'Aquin', *RB* 27, pp. 236–46.

Morris, R. H. (1893). *Chester in the Plantagenet and Tudor periods,* Chester.

Morrison, K. F. (1982). *The mimetic tradition of reform in the West,* Princeton (NJ).

Müller, E. (1934). *Das Konzil von Vienne 1311–1312: seine Quelle und seine Geschichte,* Vorreformationsgeschichtliche Forschungen 12, Münster.

Muir, E. (1981). *Civic ritual in Renaissance Venice,* Princeton (NJ).

Murphy, G. R. (1979). 'A ceremonial ritual: the mass', in *The structure of ritual: a biogenetic structural analysis,* ed. E. G. d'Aquili, C. D. McLaughlin Jr. and J. McManus, New York, pp. 249–79.

Murray, A. (1981). 'Confession as a historical source in the thirteenth century', *The writing of history in the Middle Ages. Essays presented to Richard William Southern,* ed. R. H. C. Davis and J. M. Wallace-Hadrill, Oxford, pp. 275–322.

Neel, C. (1989). 'The origins of beguines', *Signs* 14, pp. 321–41.

Nelson, A. H. (1970–1). 'The Wakefield Corpus Christi play: pageant, procession and dramatic cycle', *Records of Renaissance drama* 13–14, pp. 221–33.

(1974). *The medieval English stage: Corpus Christi pageants and plays,* Chicago.

Newman, B. (1987). *Sister of wisdom. St Hildegard's theology of the feminine,* Berkeley.

Nicholls, J. F. and Taylor, J. (1881–2). *Bristol, past and present,* 3 vols., Bristol.

Niedermeyer, H. (1974–5). 'Uber die Sakramentsprozession im Mittelalter. Ein Beitrag zur Geschichte der kirchlichen Umgänge', *Sacris erudiri* 22, pp. 401–36.

Nitecki, A. K. (1981). 'The dramatic impact of the didactic voice in the York cycle of mystery plays', *Annuale medievale* new ser. 21, pp. 61–76.

Oliver, J. H. (1988). *Gothic manuscript illumination in the diocese of Liège (c.1250– c.1330),* 2 vols., Louvain.

O'Neil, M. R. (1974). '*Sacerdote ovvero strione*: ecclesiastical superstitious reme-dies in sixteenth-century Italy', in *Understanding popular culture: Europe from the Middle Ages to the nineteenth century,* ed. S. L. Kaplan, Babylon studies in the social sciences 40, Berlin, pp. 53–83.

Ong, W. J. (1947). 'Wit and mystery: a revaluation in medieval Latin hymnody', *Speculum* 22, pp. 310–41.

Oppel, H. D. (1972). 'Zur neueren Exempla-Forschung', *Deutsches Archiv für Erforschung des Mittelalters* 28, pp. 240–3.

  (1976). 'Exemplum und Mirakel. Versuch seiner Begriffsbestimmung', *Archiv für Kulturgeschichte* 58, pp. 96–114.

Ortner, S. B. (1975). 'God's bodies, God's food: a symbolic analysis of a Sherpa ritual', in ed. J. J. Fox, pp. 133–69.

Ott, S. (1980), 'Blessed bread, "First neighbours" and asymmetric exchange in the Basque country', *Archives européens de sociologie* 21, pp. 40–58.

Overing, J. (1986). 'Images of cannibalism, death and domination in a 'non-violent' society', in *The anthropology of violence,* ed. D. Riches, Oxford, pp. 86–102.

Owst, G. R. (1926). *Preaching in medieval England: an introduction to the sermon manuscripts of the period c.1350–1450,* Cambridge.

  (1933). *Literature and pulpit in medieval England,* Cambridge.

Ozment, S. E. (1980). *The age of reform 1250–1500. An intellectual and religious history of late medieval and Reformation Europe,* New Haven (Conn.).

Panofsky, E. (1946). *Abbot Suger on the abbey church of Saint-Denis,* Princeton (NJ).

  (1953). *Early Netherlandish art: its origins and character,* 2 vols., Cambridge (Mass.).

Pantin, W. A. (1955). *The English church in the fourteenth century,* Cambridge.

Paravicini Bagliani, A. (1969). 'Gregorio da Napoli, biografo di Urbano IV', *Römische historische Mitteilungen* 11, pp. 59–78.

  (1972). *Cardinali di curia e 'familiae' cardinalizie dal 1227 al 1254,* 2 vols., Italia sacra 18–19, Padua.

Parker, A. A. (1943). *The allegorical drama of Calderon: an introduction to the autos sacramentales,* Oxford and London.

Patchovsky, A. (1975). *Die Anfänge einer ständigen Inquisition in Böhmen. Ein Prager Inquisitoren-Handbuch aus der ersten Hälfte des 14. Jahrhunderts,* Beiträge zur Geschichte und Quellenkunde des Mittelalters 3, Berlin.

Patetta, F. (1890). *Le ordalie: studio di storia del diritto e scienze del diritto comparato*, R. Università di Torino, Istituto di esercitazioni nelle scienze giuridico-politiche 8, Turin.

Patterson, F. A. (1927). 'Hymnal from ms. Additional 34193, British Museum', in *Medieval studies in memory of Gertrude Schoepperle Loomis*, Paris and New York, pp. 443–88.

Payen, J. C. (1977). 'La Pénitence dans le contexte culturel des XII$^e$ et XIII$^e$ siècles', *Revue des sciences philosophiques et théologiques* 61, pp. 399–428.

Peacock, E. (1866). *English church furniture, ornaments and decorations at the period of the Reformation*, London.

(1885). 'Extracts from Lincoln episcopal visitations in the fifteenth, sixteenth and seventeenth centuries', *Archaeologia* 48, pp. 249–69.

(1889). 'Kirton-in-Lindsey: churchwardens' accounts etc.', *Antiquary* 19, pp. 18–22.

Pearsall, D. (1970). *John Lydgate*, London.

(1977). *Old and Middle English poetry*, London.

Peck, F. (1727). *Academia tertia Anglicana, or the antiquarians annals of Stamford*, London.

(1785). Rev. W. Harrod, *The antiquities of Stamford and St Martin's*, Stamford.

Peck, R. A. (1975). 'Public dreams and private myths: perspective in Middle English literature', *PMLA* 90, pp. 461–8.

Peckham, J. L. (1934). *Archbishop Peckham as a religious educator*, New Haven (Conn.).

Pelzer, A. (1922). 'Les 51 articles de Guillaume Occam censurés en Avignon, en 1326', *RHE* 18, pp. 240–70.

Peters, E. (1978). *The magician, the witch and the law*, Hassocks.

Pfaff, R. W. (1970). *New liturgical feasts in later medieval England*, Oxford.

Pfander, H. G. (1936). 'Some medieval manuals of religious instruction in England and observations on Chaucer's Parsons's Tale', *JEGP* 35, pp. 243–58.

(1937). *The popular sermon of the medieval friar*, New York.

Pfleger, L. (1933). 'Besondere eucharistische Devotionsformen des späteren Mittelalters', *Archiv für elsassische Kirchengeschichte* 8, pp. 457–61.

Phythian-Adams, C. (1972). 'Ceremony and the citizen: the communal year at Coventry 1450–1550', in *Crisis and order in English towns, 1500–1700*, ed. P. Clark and P. Slack, London, pp. 57–85.

(1977). *Desolation of a city: Coventry and the urban crisis of the late Middle Ages*, Cambridge.

Pierson, M. (1915). 'The relation of the Corpus Christi procession to the Corpus Christi play in England', *Transactions of the Wisconsin Academy of Sciences, Arts and Letters* 18, pp. 110–65.

Pikulik, J. (1974). 'Oficjum o bożym ciele w świetle historyczno-krytycznym [The Corpus Christi office from the historical point of view']', *Collectanea theologica* 44, pp. 27–40.

Pincus, D. (1984). 'Christian relics and the body politic: a thirteenth-century relief plaque in the church of San Marco', in *Interpretazioni veneziane: studi di storia dell'arte in onore di Michelangelo Muraro*, ed. D. Rosand, Venice, pp. 39–57.

Pixton, P. B. (1985). 'Watchmen on the tower: the German episcopacy and the implementation of the decrees of the fourth Lateran council, 1216–1274', in *Proceedings of the sixth international congress of medieval canon law*, ed. S. Kuttner and K. Pennington, Monumenta iuris canonici ser. C subsidia 7, Vatican, pp. 579–93.

Platelle, H. (1970). 'La Vie religieuse à Lille', in *Histoire de Lille* 1, ed. L. Trenard, Lille, pp. 309–417.

(1979). 'Le Recueil des miracles de Thomas de Cantimpré et la vie religieuse dans les Pays-Bas et le Nord de la France au XIII^e siècle', in *Actes du 97e congrès des sociétés savantes, Nantes 1972, section de philologie et d'histoire jusqu'à 1610*, Paris, pp. 469–98.

(1985). 'Le Miracle au moyen-âge d'après un ouvrage nouveau', *Mélanges des sciences religieuses* 42, pp. 177–84.

Plumb, D. (1987). 'John Foxe and the later Lollards of the Thames valley', PhD thesis, Cambridge University.

Polain, E. (1933). 'La Formation territoriale de la cité de Liège, *Revue du Nord* 18, pp. 161–80.

Pope-Hennessy, J. (1939). *Sassetta*, London.

Post, R. R. (1968). *The modern devotion: confrontation with Reformation and Humanism*, Leiden.

Pouchelle, M.-C. (1987). 'Mots, fluides et vertiges: les fêtes orales de la mystique chez Gautier de Coinci', *Annales* 42, pp. 1,209–30.

Powers, J. (1967). *Eucharistic theology*, New York.

Prado, G. (1932). 'Les "danzantes" de Séville et les "mudanzes" de Silos', *Revue du chant grégorien* 36, pp. 8–13.

*Prêcher d'exemples: récits de prédicateurs du moyen-âge*, ed. J.-C. Schmitt, Paris, 1985.

Pritchard, V. (1967). *English medieval grafitti*, Cambridge.

Prosser, E. (1961). *Drama and religion in the English mystery plays: a reevaluation*, Stanford studies in language and culture 23, Stanford (Ca.).

Raby, F. J. E. (1927). *A history of Christian-Latin poetry from the beginnings to the close of the Middle Ages*, Oxford.

Radding, C. (1985). *A world made by men*, Chapel Hill (NC).

Randall, L. M. C. (1966). *Images in the margins of Gothic manuscripts*, California studies in the history of art 4, Berkeley (Ca.).

Rando, D. (1983). ' "Laicus religiosus" tra strutture civili ed ecclesiastiche: l'ospedale di Ognissanti in Treviso (sec. XIII)', *Studi medievali* 24, pp. 617–56.

Raynaud, F. (1974). 'Contribution à l'étude des danseurs et des musiciens des fêtes du Corpus Christi et de l'Assomption à Tolède aux XVI^e et XVII^e siècles', *Mélanges de la Casa Velázquez* 10, pp. 133–68.

Réau, L. (1955–9). *Iconographie de l'art chrétien*, 3 vols., Paris.

Redondi, P. (1987). *Galileo: heretic*, trans. R. Rosenthal, Princeton (NJ).

Reinburg, V. (1985). 'Popular prayers in late medieval and Reformation France', PhD thesis, Princeton University.

Remnant, G. L. and Anderson, M. D. (1969). *A catalogue of misericords in Great Britain*, Oxford.

Renardy, C. (1979). *Le Monde des maîtres universitaires du diocèse de Liège: 1140–1350*, Paris.

(1981). *Les Maîtres universitaires de Liège: répertoire biographique*, Paris.

Renouard, Y. (1937). 'Comment les papes d'Avignon expédiaient leur courrier', *Revue historique* 180, pp. 1–29.

Reynolds, R. E. (1983). 'Image and text: a Carolingian illustration of modifications in the early Roman eucharistic *ordines*', *Viator* 14, pp. 59–75.

(1988) 'An early medieval mass fantasy. The correspondence of pope Damasus and St Jerome on a Nicene canon', *Proceedings of the 7th international congress of medieval canon law, 1984*, Monumenta iuris canonici ser. C subsidia 8, ed., Vatican, pp. 73–89.

Reynolds, S. (1984). *Kingdoms and communities in Western Europe, 900–1300*, Oxford.

Rhees, R. (1969). *Without answers*, New York.

Rice Jr., E. F. (1985). *St Jerome in the Renaissance*, Baltimore (Md.) and London.

Richmond, C. (1984). 'Religion and the fifteenth-century gentleman', in *The church, politics and patronage in the fifteenth century*, ed. B. Dobson, Gloucester, pp. 193–208.

Rickert, M. (1941). 'The reconstruction of an English Carmelite missal', *Speculum* 16, pp. 92–102.

Ricoeur, P. (1971). 'The model of the text: meaningful action considered as text', *Social research* 30, pp. 529–62.

(1972). 'The symbol gives rise to thought', in *Ways of understanding religion*, ed. W. H. Capps, New York, pp. 309–17.

Riehle, W. (1980). 'English mysticism and the morality play: wisdom who is Christ', in *The medieval mystical tradition in England: papers read at the Exeter symposium, July 1980*, ed. M. Glasscoe, Exeter, pp. 202–15.

(1981). *The Middle English mystics*, trans. B. Standring, London.

Righetti, M. (1956). *Manuale di storia liturgica*, 4 vols., Milan.

Ringbom, S. (1969). 'Devotional images and imaginative devotions. Notes on the place of art in late medieval private piety', *Gazette des beaux-arts* ser. 6, 73, pp. 159–70.

Ritchie, B. M. (1974). 'Preaching and pastoral care in John Tauler', in *Contemporary reflections on medieval Christian tradition. Essays in honor of Ray C. Petry*, ed. G. H. Shriver, Durham (N.C.), pp. 3–18.

Robbins, R. H. (1939a). 'Popular prayers in Middle English verse', *Modern philology* 39, pp. 337–50.

(1939b). 'The Gurney series of religious lyrics', *PMLA* 54, pp. 369–90.

(1939c). 'The *anima christi* rolls', *MLN* 34, pp. 415–21.

(1942–3). 'Levation prayers in Middle English verse', *Modern philology* 40, pp. 131–46.

Roberts, M. E. (1986). 'The relic of the holy blood and the iconography of the thirteenth century north transept portal of Westminster Abbey', in *England in the thirteenth century. Proceedings of the 1984 Harlaxton symposium*, ed. W. M. Ormrod, Woodbridge, pp. 129–42.

Robertson Jr., D. W. (1945). 'The *Manuel des péchés* and an English episcopal decree', *MLN* 60, pp. 439–47.

(1947). 'The cultural tradition of *Handlyng synne*', *Speculum* 22, pp. 162–85.

(1980). 'The question of typology and the Wakefield *Mactacio Abel'*, in *Essays in medieval culture*, Princeton (NJ), pp. 219–32.

Rode, R. (1957). 'Studien zu den mittelalterlichen Kind-Jesu-Visionen', PhD thesis, J. W. Goethe University of Frankfurt.

Roisin, S. (1943). 'L'Efflorescence cistercienne et le courant féminin de piété au xiiie siècle', *RHE* 39, pp. 342–78.

(1947). *L'Hagiographie cistercienne dans le diocèse de Liège au xiiie siècle*, recueil de travaux d'histoire et de philologie ser. 3 fasc. 27, Louvain and Brussels.

Ronzani, M. (1980). 'L'Organizzazione della cura d'anime nella città di Pisa (secoli xii–xiii), in *Istituzioni ecclesiastiche della Toscana medievale*, Galatia, pp. 35–85.

Rosaldo, R. (1986). 'From the door of his tent: the fieldworker and the inquisitor', in *Writing culture: the poetics and politics of ethnography*, ed. J. Clifford and G. E. Marcus, Berkeley, pp. 77–97.

Rosser, A. G. (1984). 'The essence of medieval urban communities: the vill of Westminster', *TRHS* fifth ser. 34, pp. 91–112.

(1987). 'The town and guild of Lichfield in the late Middle Ages', *Transactions of the South Staffordshire Archaeological and Historical Society* 27, pp. 39–47.

(1988). 'Communities of parish and guild in the late Middle Ages', in *Parish, church and people: local studies in lay religion 1350–1750*, ed. S. J. Wright, London, pp. 29–55.

Rowland, B. (1978). *Birds with human souls: a guide to bird symbolism*, Knoxville (Tenn.).

Rubin, M. (1986). 'Corpus Christi fraternities and late medieval lay piety', *SCH* 23, pp. 97–109.

(1987). *Charity and community in medieval Cambridge*, Cambridge studies in medieval life and thought fourth ser. 4, Cambridge.

(1991a). 'Fraternities and lay piety in the later Middle Ages', *Städteforschungen*.

(1991b). 'Small groups: identity and solidarity in the late Middle Ages', in *Enterprise and individualism in the fifteenth century*, ed. J. Kermode, Gloucester.

Rücklin-Teuscher, G. (1933). *Religiöses Volksleben des ausgehendes Mittelalters in den Reichsstädten Hall und Heilbronn*, Historische Studien 226, Berlin.

Ruiz, T. F. (1985). 'Unsacred monarchy: the kings of Castile in the late Middle Ages', in *Rites of power: symbolism, ritual, and politics since the Middle Ages*, ed. S. Wilentz, Philadelphia (Pa.), pp. 109–44.

Russell, G. H. (1962). 'Vernacular instruction of the laity in the later Middle Ages in England: some texts and notes', *Journal of religious studies* 2, pp. 98–119.

Russell, J. B. (1965). *Dissent and reform in the early Middle Ages*, Publications of the Center for medieval and Renaissance studies 1, Berkeley and Los Angeles.

Rye-Clausen, H. (1981). *Die Hostienmühlenbilder*, Stein Christiana.

Salter, F. M. (1935). *The Trial and the Flagellation with other studies in the Chester cycle*, Malone Society studies, Oxford.

(1955). *Medieval drama in Chester*, Toronto.

Sanday, P. R. (1986). *Divine hunger: cannibalism as a cultural system*, Cambridge.

Sangren, P. S. (1988). 'Rhetoric and the authority of ethnography. "Postmodernism" and the social reproduction of texts', *Current anthropology* 79, pp. 403–35.

Saxer, V. (1966). 'Les Calendriers liturgiques de St Victor et le sanctoral médiéval de l'abbaye', *Provence historique* 16, pp. 463–519.

(1971). 'Un Bréviaire d'Apt du xiv$^e$ siècle retrouvé à Toulon', *Provence historique* 21, pp. 109–27.

Saxl, F. (1942). 'A spiritual encyclopaedia of the later Middle Ages', *JWCI* 5, pp. 107–17.

Saye, H. (1935). 'Holy wafers in medicine', *Bulletin of the history of medicine* 3, pp. 165–7.

Scarisbrick, J. J. (1984). *The Reformation and the English people*, Oxford.

Scattergood, V. J. (1971). *Politics and poetry in the fifteenth century*, London.

Scheeben, H. C. (1931). 'Die *Tabulae* Ludwigs von Valliadolid im Chor der Predigerbrüder von St Jakob in Paris', *AFP* 1, pp. 223–63.

Schieffer, T. (1960). 'La chiesa nazionale di osservanza romana', in *Le chiese nei regni dell'Europa occidentale e i loro rapporti con Roma fino all'800*, Settimana di studi, Spoleto, pp. 73–94.

Schillebeeckx, E., *The eucharist*, London.

Schiller, E. (1912). *Bürgerschaft und Geistlichkeit in Goslar (1290–1365)*, Kirchenrechtliche Abhandlungen 77, Stuttgart.

Schimmelpfennig, B. (1971). 'Die Organisation der päpstlichen kapelle in Avignon', *Quellen und Forschungen aus italienischer Archiven und Bibliotheken* 50, pp. 80–111.

(1973). *Die Zeremonienbücher der römischen Kurie im Mittelalter*, Bibliothek des deutschen historischen Instituts in Rom 40, Tübingen, 1973.

Schlette, H. R. (1959). *Die Lehre von der geistlichen Kommunion bei Bonaventura, Albert dem Grossen, und Thomas von Aquin*, Munich.

Schmitt, J.-C. (1977). 'Recueils franciscains d'*exempla* et perfectionnement des techniques intellectuelles du xiii$^e$ au xv$^e$ siècle', *Bibliothèque de l'Ecole des chartes* 135, pp. 5–22.

(1979). 'La parola addomesticata: San Domenico, il gatto e le donne di Fanjeaux', *Quaderni storici* 41 (1979), pp. 416–39.

(1981). 'Du bon usage du "credo"', in *Faire croire. Modalités de la diffusion et de la réception des messages religieux du xii$^e$ au xv$^e$ siècle*, Collections de l'Ecole française de Rome 51, Rome, pp. 337–61.

(1983). *The holy greyhound: Guinefort, healer of children since the thirteenth century*, Cambridge studies in oral and literate culture 6, Cambridge.

(1985). 'Introduction', in *Prêcher d'exemples: récits de prédicateurs du moyenâge*, ed. J.-C. Schmitt, Paris, pp. 9–24.

(1986). 'Religion et guérison dans l'occident médiéval', in *Historiens et sociologues aujourd'hui. Journées d'études annuelles de la Société française de sociologie. Lille, 1984*, Paris, pp. 135–50.

Schnitzler, T. (1973). 'Die erste Fronleichnamsprozession. Datum und Character', *Münchner theologische Zeitschrift* 24, pp. 352–62.

Schoolmeesters, E. (1907). 'Les Actes du cardinal-legat Hugues de St-Cher en Belgique durant les années de sa légation, 1251–1253', *Leodium* 6, pp. 72–6, 150–66.

Scott, J. W. (1988). *Gender and the politics of history*, New York.

Scribner, C. (1982). *The Triumph of the Eucharist tapestries designed by Peter Paul Rubens*, Ann Arbor (Mich.).

Scribner, R. W. (1984). 'Ritual and popular religion in catholic Germany at the time of the Reformation', *JEH* 35, pp. 47–77.

(1986). 'The incombustible Luther: the image of the reformer in early modern Germany', *PP* 110, pp. 38–68.

(1987). 'Ritual and Reformation', in *Popular culture and popular movements in Reformation Germany*, London, pp. 103–22.

(1989). 'Is the history of popular culture possible?', *History of European ideas* 10, pp. 175–91.

Sekules, V. (1986). 'The tomb of Christ at Lincoln and the development of the sacrament shrine: Easter sepulchres reconsidered', in *Medieval art and architecture at Lincoln Cathedral*, British Archaeological Association conference transactions 8, pp. 118–31.

Sengpiel, O. (1932). *Die Bedeutung der Prozession für das geistliche Spiel des Mittelalters im Deutschland*, Germanistische Abhandlungen 66, Breslau.

Shahar, S. (1990). *Childhood in the Middle Ages*, London.

Sharp, T. (1825). *A dissertation on the pageants or dramatic mysteries anciently performed at Coventry*, Coventry, 1825, repr. with intro. by A. C. Cawley, East Ardsley, 1973.

Sheedy, C. E. (1947). *The eucharistic controversy of the eleventh century against the background of pre-scholastic theology*, Catholic University of America studies in sacred theology second ser. 4, Washington (DC).

Sheingorn, P. (1982). 'The moments of resurrection in the Corpus Christi plays', *Mediaevalia et humanistica* new ser. 11, pp. 111–29.

Shoaf, R. A. (1989). 'Medieval studies after Derrida, after Heidegger', in *Sign, sentence, discourse: language in medieval thought and literature*, ed. J. N. Wasserman and L. Roney, Syracuse (NY), pp. 9–30.

Shrader, C. R. (1973). 'The false attribution of an eucharistic tract to Gerbert of Aurillac', *MS* 35, pp. 178–204.

Shull, V. (1937). 'Clerical drama in Lincoln Cathedral, 1318 to 1561', *PMLA* 52, pp. 946–66.

Sievert, W. (1896). 'Das Vorleben des Papstes Urban IV', *Römische Quartalschrift* 10, pp. 451–505, 12 (1898), p. 127–61.

Sigal, P.-A. (1985). *L'Homme et le miracle dans la France médiévale*, xi^e–xii^e siècle, Paris.

Silvestre, H. (1951). 'Renier de Saint-Laurent et le declin des écoles liégeoises au xii^e siècle', *Miscellanea tornacensia. Annales du 33e congrès de la Féderation archéologique et historique de Belgique. Tournai 1949* II, Tournai, pp. 112–23.

Simenon, G. (1921–2). 'Les Origines de la Fête-Dieu', *Revue ecclésiastique de Liège* 13, pp. 345–58.

(1934–5). 'Urbain IV à Liège', *Revue ecclésiastique de Liège* 26, pp. 84–94.

(1946). 'Les Origines liégeoises de la Fête-Dieu', *Studia eucharistica*, pp. 1–19.

Smalley, P. (1952). *The study of the bible in the Middle Ages*, Oxford.

Somerville, R. (1972). 'The case against Berengar of Tours – a new text', *Studi gregoriani* 9, pp. 55–75.

Southern, R. W. (1948). 'Lanfranc of Bec and Berengar of Tours', in *Studies in medieval history presented to F. M. Powicke*, ed. R. W. Hunt, W. A. Pantin and R. W. Southern, Oxford, pp. 27–48.

(1958). 'The English origins of the "Miracles of the Virgin"', *Mediaeval and Renaissance studies* 4, pp. 176–216.

(1986). *Robert Grosseteste. The growth of an English mind in medieval Europe*, Oxford.

Spagnolo, A. (1901). *La processione del Corpus Domini in Verona ne'secoli* xv–xviii, Verona.

Sperber, D. (1975). *Rethinking symbolism*, trans. A. L. Morton, Cambridge studies in social anthropology 11, Cambridge.

de Spiegeler, P. (1979). 'La Draperie de la cité de Liège des origines à 1468', *Moyen-âge* 85, pp. 45–86.

Spufford, M. (1974). *Contrasting communities: English villagers in the sixteenth and seventeenth centuries*, Cambridge.

Steckman, L. L. (1937). 'A late fifteenth century revision of Mirk's "Festial"', *Studies in philology* 34, pp. 36–48.

Stein, F. M. (1977). 'The religious women of Cologne: 1120–1320', PhD thesis, Yale University.

Steinberg, L. (1973). 'Leonardo's *Last supper*', *Art bulletin* 36, pp. 297–410.

Stemmler, T. (1970). *Liturgische Feiern und geistliche Spiele: Studien zu Erscheinungsformen des Dramatischen im Mittelalter*, Buchreihe der Anglia Festschrift 15, Tübingen.

Stevens, J. (1973). *Medieval romance: themes and approaches*, London.

Stevens, M. (1972). 'The York cycle: from procession to play', *Leeds studies in English* new ser. 6, pp. 37–61.

Sticca, S. (1970). *The Latin Passion play: its origins and development*, Albany (NY).

(1973). 'Drama and spirituality in the Middle Ages', *Mediaevalia et humanistica* new ser. 4, pp. 69–87.

Stock, B. (1983). *The implications of literacy. Written language and models of interpretation in the eleventh and twelfth centuries*, Princeton (NJ).

Stone, L. (1955). *Sculpture in Britain. The Middle Ages*, Harmondsworth.

Straw, C. (1988). *Gregory the great: perfection in imperfection*, Berkeley (Ca.).

Sylla, E. (1975). 'Autonomous and handmaiden science: St Thomas Aquinas and William of Ockham on the physics of the eucharist', in *The cultural context of medieval learning*, ed. J. E. Murdoch and E. D. Sylla, Boston studies in the philosophy of science 26, Dordrecht and Boston (Mass.), pp. 349–91.

Sylvester, W. (1897). 'The communing with three blades of grass, of the knights-errant', *Dublin review* 121, pp. 80–98.

Szöffervy, J. (1964). *Die Annalen der lateinischen Hymnendichtung*, 2 vols., Berlin.

Tamborini, A. (1935). *Il Corpus Domini a Milano*, Rome.

Tarrant, J. (1974). 'The Clementine decrees on the beguines: conciliar and papal versions', *AHP* 12, pp. 300–7.

(1984–5). 'The manuscripts of the *Constitutiones Clementinae*', *Zeitschrift der Savigny Stiftung für Rechtsgeschichte. Kanonistische Abteilung* 70 (1984), pp. 67–133, 71 (1985), pp. 76–146.

Tavis, A. (1986). 'Fairy tales from a semiotic perspective', in *Fairy tales and society:*

*illusion, allusion, and paradigm,* ed. R. B. Bottigheimer, Philadelphia (Pa.), pp. 195–202.

Taylor, J. (1972). 'The dramatic structure of the Middle English Corpus Christi, or cycle, plays', in *Medieval English drama: essays critical and contextual,* ed. J. Taylor and A. H. Nelson, Chicago, pp. 148–56.

Teetaert, A. (1930). 'Un Compendium de théologie pastorale du XIII$^c$–XIV$^c$ siècles', *RHE* 22, pp. 66–102.

Tellenbach, G. (1959). *Church, state and Christian society at the time of the investiture contest,* trans. R. F. Bennett, Oxford.

Tentler, T. N. (1977). *Sin and confession on the eve of the Reformation,* Princeton (NJ).

De Tervarent, G. (1933). 'Les Tapisseries du Ronceray et leurs sources d'inspiration', *Gazette des beaux-arts* 10, pp. 79–99.

Thomas, K. V. (1971). *Religion and the decline of magic,* London.

Thompson, S. (1978). 'The problem of the Cistercian nuns in the twelfth and early thirteenth centuries', in *Medieval women: dedicated and presented to Professor Rosalind M. T. Hill on the occasion of her seventieth birthday,* ed. D. Baker, SCH Subsidia I, Oxford, pp. 227–52.

Thurston, H. (1907). 'The elevation. Seeing the host', *Tablet,* pp. 684–6.

(1928). 'The case of blessed Christina of Stommeln', *The month* 156, pp. 289–301, 425–37.

Torrell, J.-P. and Bouthillier, D. (1986). *Pierre le vénérable et sa vision du monde: sa vie, son oeuvre, l'homme et le démon,* Spicilegium sacrum lovaniense 42, Louvain.

Torsy, J. (1972). 'Zur Verehrung der Eucharistie im Spätmittelalter: eine Fronleichnamsprozession in Wittlaer im Jahre 1436', in *Von Konstanz nach Trient,* ed. T. Bäumer, Munich, pp. 335–42.

Trachtenberg, J. (1943). *The devil and the Jews,* New Haven (Conn.)

Travis, P. W. (1985). 'The social body of the dramatic Christ in medieval England', *Early English Drama. Acta* 13, pp. 17–36.

Trexler, R. C. (1964). 'Economic, political and religious effects of the papal interdict on Florence 1376–1378', PhD thesis, J. W. Goethe University, Frankfurt.

(1974). 'Ritual in Florence: adolescence and salvation in the Renaissance', in *The pursuit of holiness in late medieval and Renaissance religion,* ed. H. Oberman and C. Trinkaus, Leiden, pp. 200–64.

de Troeyer, B. (1980). 'Béguines er tertiaires en Belgique et aux Pays-Bas aux XIII$^c$– XV$^c$ siècles', in *I frati penitenti di San Francesco nella società del due e trecento,* ed. M. d'Altari, Atti del 2° convegno di studi francescani, Rome, pp. 133–8.

Tuck, J. A. (1969). 'The Cambridge parliament, 1388', *EHR* 84, pp. 225–43.

Tudor-Craig, P. (1986). 'Richard III's triumphant entry into York, August 29th, 1483', in *Richard III and the north,* ed. R. Horrox, University of Hull Centre for Regional and Local History, Studies in regional and local history 6, pp. 108–16.

Turner, V. W. (1962). 'Three symbols of *passage* in Ndembu circumcision ritual: an interpretation', in *Essays on the ritual of social relations,* ed. M. Gluckman, Manchester, pp. 124–73.

(1969). *The ritual process: structure and anti-structure*, London.

(1974). 'Social drama and ritual metaphors', in *Dramas, fields, and metaphors: symbolic action in human society*, Ithaca (NY), pp. 23–59.

Tutini, C. (1641). *Dell'origine e fundatione de'seggi di Napoli*, Naples.

Underdown, D. (1985). *Revel, riot and rebellion: popular politics and popular culture in England, 1603–1660*, Oxford.

Unwin, G. (1963). *The guilds and companies of London*, London, fourth edn.

Uyttebrouck, A. (1978). 'L'Enseignement et les bourgeois', *Revue de l'Université de Bruxelles*, pp. 451–66.

Uzielli, G. (1901). 'L'Orazione della misure di Cristo', *Archivio storico italiano* 27, pp. 334–45.

Uzureau, I. (1933). 'Le Sacre d'Angers', *Anjou historique* 33, pp. 129–35.

Vale, M. G. A. (1976). *Piety, charity and literacy among the Yorkshire gentry, 1370–1480*, Borthwick papers 50, York.

Van der Lof, L.-J. (1964). 'Eucharistie et présence réelle selon Saint Augustin (à propos d'un commentaire sur *De civitate dei* x,vi)', *Revue des études augustiniennes* 10, pp. 295–304.

Van Dijk, S. J. P. (1939). 'De fontibus "Opusculi super missam" f. Guillelmi de Melitona ord. min.', *EL* 53, pp. 291–349.

(1963). *Sources of the modern Roman liturgy. The ordinals by Haymo of Faversham and related documents*, Studia et documenta franciscana 1–2, Leiden, 1963.

Van Dijk, S. J. P. and Walker, J. H. (1960). *The origins of the modern Roman liturgy: the liturgy of the papal court and the Franciscan order in the thirteenth century*, Westminster (Md.).

Van Engen, J. (1986). 'The Christian Middle Ages as a historiographical problem', *AHR* 91, pp. 519–52.

Van Moos, P. (1984). 'The use of *exempla* in the *Policraticus* of John of Salisbury', in *The world of John of Salisbury*, ed. M. Wilks, SCH Subsidia 3, Oxford, pp. 207–61.

Vauchez, A. (1981). *La Sainteté en occident aux derniers siècles du moyen-âge d'après les procès de canonisation et les documents hagiographiques*, Biblithèque de l'Ecole française de Rome 141, Rome.

Vaughan, R. (1958). *Matthew Paris*, Cambridge.

Vaultier, R. (1965). *Le Folklore pendant le Guerre de Cent Ans d'après les lettres de rémission du Trésor des Chartes*, Paris.

Vercauteren, F. (1945). *Luttes sociales à Liège. XIII^e et XIV^e siècles*, Brussels.

Verdeyen, P. (1987). 'Parole et sacrement chez Guillaume de Saint-Thierry', *Collectanea cisterciensia* 49, pp. 218–28.

Very, F. G. (1962). *The Spanish Corpus Christi procession: a literary and folkloric study*, Valencia.

Violante, C. (1982). 'Le strutture organizzative della cura d'anime nelle campagne dell'Italia centro-sententrionale (secoli v–x)', in *Cristianizzazione ed organizzazione ecclesiastica delle campagne nell'alto medioevo: espansione e resistenze* ii, Settimane di studio del Centro Italiano di Studi sull'alto medioevo 28, Spoleto, pp. 963–1,158.

Vloberg, M. (1946). *L'Eucharistie dans l'art*, 2 vols., Grenoble and Paris.

Vogel, F. G. (1976). 'Pratiques superstitieuses au début du XI^e siècle d'après le *Corrector sive medicus* de Burchard, évêque de Worms', in *Etudes de civilisation médiévale (IX^e–XII^e siècles). Mélanges offerts à E.-R. Labande*, Poitiers, pp. 751–61.

de Vogüé, A. (1986). 'Eucharistie et vie monastique', *Collectanea cisterciensia* 48, pp. 120–30.

Von Nolcken, C. (1981). 'Some alphabetical appendices and how preachers used them in fourteenth-century England', *Viator* 12, pp. 271–88.

(1984). 'Julian of Norwich', in *Middle English prose: a critical guide to major authors and genres*, ed. A. S. G. Edwards, Rutgers (NJ), pp. 97–108.

(1985–6). 'An unremarked group of Wycliffite sermons in Latin', *Modern philology* 83, pp. 233–49.

Wakefield, W. L. (1973). 'Some unorthodox popular ideas of the thirteenth century', *Mediaevalia et humanistica* new ser. 4, pp. 25–35.

Walker, D. P. (1981). *Unclean spirits: possession and exorcism in France and England in the late sixteenth and seventeenth centuries*, London.

Walz, A. (1966). 'La presenza di San Tommaso a Orvieto e l'ufficiatura del Corpus Domini', *Studi eucaristici*, pp. 321–55.

Ward, B. (1982). *Miracles and the medieval mind*, London.

Weckwerth, A. (1972). 'Der Name "Biblia pauperum"', *Zeitschrift für Kirchengeschichte* 83, pp. 1–33.

Weisheipl, J. A. (1974). *Friar Thomas d'Aquino. His life, thought and works*, Oxford.

Welter, J. T. (1930). 'Un Nouveau recueil franciscain d'*exempla* à la fin du XIII^e siècle', *Etudes franciscaines* 42, pp. 432–76, 594–629.

Wensky, M. (1982). 'Women's guilds in Cologne in the later Middle Ages', *Journal of European economic history* 11, pp. 631–50.

Wenzel, S. (1978). *Verses in sermons*, Mediaeval Academy of America publication 87, Cambridge (Mass.).

Westlake, H. F. (1919). *The parish guilds of medieval England*, London.

Weston, J. L. (1923). 'Notes on the Grail romances. Caput Johannis–Corpus Christi', *Romania* 49, pp. 273–8.

White, E. N. (1984). 'People and places: the social and topographical context of drama in York 1554–1609', PhD thesis, University of Leeds.

White, H. V. (1987). *The content of the form: narrative discourse and historical representation*, Baltimore (Md.).

White, J. F. (1974). 'Durnadus and the interpretation of Christian worship', in *Contemporary reflections on medieval Christian tradition. Essays in honor of Ray C. Petry*, ed. G. H. Shiver, Durham (NC), pp. 41–52.

Whiting, R. (1989). *The blind devotion of the people: popular religion and the English Reformation*, Cambridge.

Wickham, G. W. G. (1959–81). *Early English stages 1330–1660*, 3 vols. in 4 parts, London.

Willemaers, Y. (1975). 'Franciscains à Liège au 13^e siècle', *Franciscana* 30, pp. 100–30.

Wilmart, A. (1932). *Auteurs spirituels et textes dévots du moyen-âge latin: études d'histoire littéraire*, Paris.

(1940). 'Les Mélanges de Mathieu préchantre de Rievaulx au début du xiii<sup>e</sup> siècle', *RB* 52, pp. 15–84.

Wilson, A. (1970). *Culture and personality*, second edn, New York.

Wilson, F. B. (1969). *The English drama 1485–1585*, ed. G. K. Hunter, Oxford.

Wimsatt, J. I. (1970). *Allegory and mirror, tradition and structure in Middle English literature*, New York.

Woolf, R. (1972). *The English mystery plays*, London.

Wormald, F. (1966–8). 'Some pictures of the mass in an English xivth century manuscript', *Walpole society* 41, pp. 39–45.

Wright, D. F. (1977). 'A medieval commentary on the mass: *Particulae* 2–3 and 5–6 of the *De missarum mysterium* (c. 1195) of Cardinal Lothar of Segni (Innocent III)', PhD thesis, University of Notre Dame (Ind.).

*Writing culture: the poetics and politics of ethnography*, ed. J. Clifford and G. E. Marcus, Berkeley (Ca.), 1986.

Young, A. A. (1985). 'Plays and players: the Latin terms for performance (part II)', *REED newsletter* 10, pp. 9–16.

Young, K. (1933). *The drama of the medieval church*, 2 vols., Oxford.

Zafarama, Z. (1983). 'La predicazione ai laici dal secolo xiii al xv', *Studi medievali* 24, pp. 265–75.

Zawilla, R. J. (1985). 'The biblical sources of the *Historia Corporis Christi* attributed to Thomas Aquinas: a theological study to determine their authenticity', PhD thesis, University of Toronto.

Zeeman, E. (1957–8). 'Two Middle English versions of prayer to the sacrament', *Archiv für das Studium der neueren Sprachen* 194, pp. 113–21.

Ziegler, J. (1988). 'The *curtis* beguinages in the southern Low Countries and art patronage: interpretation and historiography', *Bulletin de l'Institut historique belge de Rome* 58, pp. 31–70.

Zika, C. (1988). 'Hosts, processions and pilgrimages in fifteenth-century Germany', *PP* 118, pp. 25–64.

Zinsmaier, P. (1953). 'Die Einführung des Fronleichnamsfestes in Stadt und diözese Konstanz', *Zeitschrift für die Geschichte des Oberrheins* 10, pp. 265–8.

# INDEX

eu. – eucharist        CC – Corpus Christi